CW00402412

CHAMBERS
SCHOOL DICTIONARY

Compiled by

A. B. ANDERSON, M.A.

and

J. E. ARKIESON, M.A.

Edited by

T. C. COLLOCOTT, M.A.

W. & R. CHAMBERS, LTD.
EDINBURGH and LONDON

FOREWORD

THE aim of the compilers of this dictionary has been to include all words which are likely to be met with in the course of ordinary reading. Accordingly, the work comprises some 20,000 words which are fully defined, and nearly 10,000 more the meanings of which follow readily from the definitions given in the main headings. It has not been judged necessary, in view of space limitations, to give adverbial and other derivatives which present no difficulty.

The definitions have been made as simple as accuracy allows. In a great many instances common usage is indicated by illustrative examples; in addition, many idiomatic phrases have been given; these are to be found under the heading where they are most likely to be sought.

Most of the words have their pronunciation indicated by respelling in accordance with the system detailed on page iv. In the case of many words respelling would be superfluous to anyone acquainted with the elements of English pronunciation; such words, however, have their accentuation marked, frequently with an indication of vowel-length.

The Appendix at the end of the volume gives (a) a table of the principal parts of over 200 verbs which, by reason of irregularity in conjugation or complexity of spelling, often give trouble in writing; (b) the more common prefixes, suffixes, and roots (with meanings and examples), abbreviations and contractions, foreign phrases, etc.

Latest Reprint . 1972

Printed in Great Britain
by T. and A. CONSTABLE LTD., Hopetoun Street
Printers to the University of Edinburgh

ADDITIONAL LIST OF WORDS

apartheid, a-part´hāt, *n.* keeping apart of people of different races living in the same country.

aqualung, ak´wah-lung, *n.* a face-mask, breathing tube, and container with oxygen, used by divers.

articulated vehicle, ar-tik´ū-lāt-ed vē´i-kl, one easier to move in a tight place because the (detachable) front part can turn while the back is standing still.

astronaut, as´trō-nawt, *n.* one who travels in space by space ship.

atomic power, power for making electricity or other purposes got by breaking up atoms.—**atomic submarine,** etc., one driven by atomic power.

boutique, boo-tēk´, *n.* a small independent esp. clothes shop.

break´through, *n.* a sudden solution or success after effort.

cine-camera, sin´i-kam´er-a, *n.* a camera for taking moving pictures.

closed shop, a business or other organisation in which no-one has any chance of being employed unless he belongs to a trade union, or to one particular trade union, or to some other special group.

cloverleaf, *n.* a place where one road crosses above another and short roads connecting the two make the pattern of a four-leaved clover.

cold front, the surface of a moving mass of cold air where it meets a mass of warmer air.

combine (harvester), a machine that both cuts and threshes grain.

compère, kom´per, *n.* a person who introduces the items of an entertainment.—Also *v.*

commuter, ko-mūt´er, *n.* a person who travels daily between home and work.—*v.* **commute´.**

computer, kom´-pūt´er, *n.* a large electronic machine which makes long and difficult calculations with great speed.

cosmonaut, koz´mō-naut, *n.* a Russian astronaut.

depression, *n.* an area where the pressure of the atmosphere is low.

electron´ic, *adj.* having to do with electrons or with electronics, the art of making devices such as the cathode ray tube.

fall´-out, *n.* dangerous dust scattered by an atomic or hydrogen bomb, or as the result of an accident near a nuclear reactor.

frogman, *n.* a diver equipped to swim and work under water.

gimmick, gim´ik, *n.* a trick: a gadget: something to catch attention.

hi-fi, or **high-fidelity,** *adj.* giving very clear sound.

hov´ercraft, *n.* a vehicle kept just above the surface of water or land by a cushion of air.

monitor, *v.* to listen to broadcast sound, or look at a television picture, by special means, usually in order to make sure it is good.

motorway, *n.* a road for the use of fast motor traffic only.

open-cast, *adj.* of a mine, open overhead, not underground.

plank´ton, *n.* very small plants and animals that drift in water.

pressure cooker, a strong container, from which little steam escapes, in which food becomes very hot and cooks quickly.

scramble, *v.* to jumble (a message) so that any person not meant to receive it will not understand it.

snor´kel, snort, *ns.* a tube for bringing air to a submarine or to an underwater swimmer.

stereophonic, ster-, or stēr-e-o-fon´ik, *adj.* giving the effect of sound coming from different directions.

3-D, *adj.* of a picture, seeming to have three dimensions—height, breadth, and depth.

tranquilliser, trank´wil-īz-er, *n.* a soothing drug.

transistor, tran-sist´or, *n.* a tiny device, very much smaller than a valve, for increasing sound in a wireless set.

warm front, the surface of a moving mass of warm air where it meets a mass of colder air.

iii

PRONUNCIATION

Pronunciation is indicated according to the following system :

Sound		Example	Pronunciation
ā	as in date	reign	rān
a	as in cat	naphtha	naf'tha
ah	as in ah!	calm	kahm
aw	as in saw	halter	hawlt'er
ē	as in even	chief	chēf
e	as in met	meadow	med'ō
ī	as in mine	isle	īl
i	as in pit	liquid	lik'wid
ō	as in go	ochre	ō'ker
o	as in pot	knock	nok
oi	as in boil	coign	koin
oo	as in foot, or in boot	pull, rule	pool, rool
ow	as in cow	tousled	towz'ld
ū	as in tube	beauty	bū'ti
u	as in but	dozen	duzn
ȳ	as in fly	hȳ'dra	—
y	as in merry	will'y-nill'y	—
ch	as in much	treachery	trech'er-i
g	as in get	guitar	gi-tar'
j	as in jump	gentle	jen'tl

In the case of words containing the following easy sounds pronunciation has often been omitted as being unnecessary :

ai	as in wait	-ge	as in cage
ay	as in may	-le	as in table, uncle, paddle, etc.
au	as in haul	oa	as in road
ce-	as in certain	ou	as in out
-ce	as in dance	-ous	as in jealous
ci-	as in cinder	oy	as in boy
ea	as in sea	qu-	as in queen
ee	as in meet	-sion	as in mission
-ey	as in donkey	-tion	as in station
-ful	as in cheerful		

The syllable bearing the main stress is marked ', e.g. but'ter.

ABBREVIATIONS USED

adj., adjs.	=adjective(s)	i.e.	=that means
adv., advs.	=adverb(s)	masc.	=masculine
conj., conjs.	=conjunction(s)	n., ns.	=noun(s)
esp.	=especially	oppos.	=opposite
e.g.	=for example	prep., preps.	=preposition(s)
etc.	=and other things,	pron., prons.	=pronoun(s)
	and so on	v., vs.	=verb(s)
fem.	=feminine		

iv

aback', *adv.* backwards. — **taken aback**, taken by surprise.

ab'acus, *n.* a counting-frame.

abaft', *adv.* and *prep.* on the aft or back part of a ship : behind.

aban'don, *v.* to give up : to forsake. —*adj.* **aban'doned**, forsaken : very wicked.

abase', *v.* to cast down : to humble. —*n.* **abase'ment**.

abash', *v.* to make ashamed.

abate', *v.* to lessen : to grow less. —*n.* **abate'ment**, lessening : an amount taken off (e.g. The landlord made an *abatement* of £10 in the rent).

abattoir, a-bat-war', *n.* a public slaughter-house.

abbé, ab'ā, *n.* a French name for a priest or clergyman.

abb'ess, *n.* the female head of an abbey or a convent.

abbey, ab'e, *n.* a monastery or convent ruled by an abbot or an abbess : the home of monks or nuns :—*pl.* **abb'eys**.

abb'ot, *n.* the head of an abbey :— *fem.* **abb'ess**.

abbreviate, ab-brē'vi-āt, *v.* to shorten.—*n.* **abbrevia'tion**.

ab'dicate, *v.* to give up an office (e.g. The king was forced to *abdicate*).—*n.* **abdica'tion**.

abdōmen, *n.* the belly : the part of the body below the chest.— *adj.* **abdom'inal**.

abduct', *v.* to take away by force or fraud.—*n.* **abduc'tion**.

abed', *adv.* in bed.

abet', *v.* to help or to encourage (generally to do wrong).—*n.* **abet'tor**.

abeyance, a-bā'ans, *n.* used in phrase *in abeyance*, e.g. The matter was left *in abeyance*=left undecided ; The office of king was *in abeyance* =left unfilled for the time being.

abhor', *v.* to shrink from with horror : to loathe.—*n.* **abhor'rence**, very great hatred.—*adj.* **abhor'rent**, hateful.

abide', *v.* to wait for : to endure : to stay : to dwell.—*adj.* **abīd'ing**, lasting.

ability, a-bil'i-ti, *n.* power to do a thing : skill : cleverness.—*n.pl.* **abil'ities**, the powers of the mind.

ab'ject, *adj.* worthless : miserable (e.g. He is an *abject* coward).

abjure, ab-joor', *v.* to swear to give up : to swear to leave for ever.

able, ā'bl, *adj.* having power to do a thing : skilful.—*adv.* **ā'bly**.

ablution, ab-loo'shun, *n.* washing of the body.

ab'negate, *v.* to deny.—*n.* **abnega'tion**, denial.

abnor'mal, *adj.* unusual : irregular. —*n.* **abnormal'ity**, something unusual.

aboard', *adv.* and *prep.* on board (a ship, train, aeroplane, etc.).

abode', *n.* a dwelling-place.

abol'ish, *v.* to put an end to : to do away with.—*ns.* **aboli'tion**, the doing away with ; **aboli'tionist**, one who seeks to do away with anything, esp. slavery.

abom'inate, *v.* to hate very much : to loathe. — *adj.* **abom'inable**, hateful : disgusting.—*n.* **abomina'tion**, great hatred : anything disgusting.

aborigines, ab-o-rij'in-ēz, *n.pl.* the original or native inhabitants of a country.—*adj.* **aborig'inal**.

abortive, ab-ort'iv, *adj.* coming to nothing, useless (e.g. He made an *abortive* attempt).

abound', *v.* to be very plentiful : to have great quantity (of).

above, a-buv', *prep.* and *adv.*, over : higher (than).—*adj.* **above-board**, frank : honourable.

abrade', *v.* to scrape or rub off : to wear away by rubbing. — *ns.* **abra'sion**, the act of rubbing off : a grazed or skinned place (e.g. of one's body) ; **abra'sive**, something used for rubbing or polishing (e.g. emery-paper).

1

abreast, a-brest′, *adv.* with fronts in a line : side by side.—**abreast of the times**, up to date in one's knowledge, dress.

abridge, a-brij′, *v.* to shorten.—*n.* **abridg′ment** or **abridge′ment**.

abroad, a-brawd′, *adv.* out of doors : in another country.

ab′rogate, *v.* to set aside, to do away with (e.g. a law).—*n.* **abroga′tion**.

abrupt′, *adj.* broken off quickly : sudden : steep : rude in manner.

abscess, ab′ses, *n.* a collection of diseased matter in some part of the body : a boil.

abscond′, *v.* to run away secretly.

abs′ent, *adj.* being away : not present : paying no attention.—*v.* (abs-ent′) to keep one's self away.—*ns.* **abs′ence**, the state of being away : inattention ; **absentee′**, one who is absent.—*adj.* **abs′ent-mind′ed**, forgetful.

ab′solute, *adj.* unbounded : complete : not limited by rules or laws (e.g. an *absolute* monarch).—*n.* **absolu′tion**, setting free from punishment : forgiveness.

absolve, ab-zolv′, *v.* to set free : to pardon.

absorb′, *v.* to suck in : to take up the whole attention.—*adjs.* **absorbed** (ab-sorbd′), entirely taken up with ; **absorb′ent**, drinking in.—*n.* that which drinks in.—*n.* **absorp′tion**, the act of absorbing : entire occupation of mind.

abstain′, *v.* to hold one's self back from.—*ns.* **abstain′er**, one who holds back from something, esp. from strong drink ; **absten′tion**, a holding back.

abstemious, abs-tēm′i-us, *adj.* sparing in food, drink, or enjoyments.

abs′tinent, *adj.* holding back from (e.g. from strong drink, pleasure).—*n.* **abs′tinence**.

abstract′, *v.* to draw or take away.—*adj.* **abstract′ed**, taken away : absent in mind.—*n.* **abstrac′tion**, absence of mind.

abs′tract, *adj.* existing only in the mind : difficult to understand.—*n.* a summary.

abstruse, abs-troos′, *adj.* hidden : difficult to understand.

absurd′, *adj.* clearly wrong : ridiculous.—*n.* **absurd′ity**.

abund′ance, *n.* great plenty.—*adj.* **abund′ant**, plentiful.

abuse, ab-ūz′, *v.* to use wrongly : to ill-use : to scold violently.—*n.* **abuse** (ab-ūs′), ill use : rude language.—*adj.* **abūs′ive**.

abut′, *v.* to border (on).

abyss, a-bis′, *n.* a bottomless depth.—*adj.* **abys′mal**, bottomless.

acacia, a-kā′shi-a, *n.* a family of thorny plants.

acad′emy, *n.* a higher school : a society for encouraging science or art.—*adjs.* **academ′ic**, learned : not practical ; **academ′ical**, belonging to an academy or college.

accede, ak-sēd′, *v.* to agree (to).

accelerate, ak-sel′er-āt, *v.* to increase speed.—*ns.* **accelera′tion** ; **accel′erātor**, that which increases speed : a lever (e.g. in a motor-car) by which the speed is increased.

accent, ak′sent, *n.* stress on a syllable or word : a mark used to show this stress : a tone of voice (e.g. He speaks with a Scottish *accent*).—*v.* **accent′**, to lay stress on a syllable or word.—*v.* **accent′-uāte**, to lay stress on.

accept, ak-sept′, *v.* to take something offered : to agree to.—*adj.* **accept′able** (ak-sept′a-bl or ak′sept-a-bl), satisfactory : pleasing.—*ns.* **accept′ance**, the act of accepting ; **accepta′tion**, the meaning of a word as generally understood.

access, ak′ses, *n.* right or means of approach : increase.—*n.* **accessibil′ity**.—*adj.* **access′ible**, easily approached.—*ns.* **access′ion**, a coming to (e.g. the *accession* of a king to his throne) : an increase ; **access′ary**, a helper (esp. in wrong-doing) ; **access′ory**, a tool (e.g. for a motor-car).

accident, ak′sid-ent, *n.* that which happens : an unexpected event : a mishap.—*adj.* **accident′al**, happening by chance.

acclaim′, *v.* to welcome with a glad shout.—*n.* **acclama′tion**, a shout of applause.

accli′matise, *v.* to accustom to another climate.—*n.* **acclimatisā′tion**.

accliv′ity, *n.* a slope upwards.

accom′modate, *v.* to find room for : to make suitable : to supply (with). — *adj.* **accom'modāting**, finding room for: obliging.—*n.* **accommodā'tion**, space: lodgings.

accompany, ak-kum'pan-i, *v.* to go with: to play an instrument (e.g. piano) while someone sings or plays.—*ns.* **accom'paniment**, that which goes along with: the music played to help a singer; **accom'panist**, one who plays while another sings.

accomplice, ak-kom'plis, *n.* one who takes part, esp. in wrong-doing.

accom'plish, *v.* to complete: to bring about.—*adj.* **accom'plished**, well trained or educated.— *n.* **accom'plishment**, completion: something one is good at (e.g. Dancing was an *accomplishment* of hers).

accord', *v.* to agree: to give.—*n.* agreement.—*n.* **accord'ance**, agreement.—*adv.* **accord'ingly**, therefore.—**according to**, as told by (e.g. The Gospel *according to* St John).—**of one's own accord**, of one's own free will; **with one accord**, with one will, nobody being against.

accor'dion, *n.* a small musical wind-instrument with keys.

accost', *v.* to go up to and speak to.

account', *v.* to reckon: to value: (with *for*) to give a reason.—*n.* a bill: a reckoning up of money: a story.— *adj.* **account'able**, answerable: responsible. — *n.* **account'ant**, one whose duty it is to look after accounts.—**on account of**, because of.

accoutre, ak-koo'ter, *v.* to dress or fit out (esp. a warrior).—*n.pl.* **accou'trements**, a soldier's dress and arms.

accred'ited, *adj.* having power to act: trusted.

accrue, ak-kroo', *v.* to come by growth.—*adj.* **accrued'**.

accumulate, ak-kūm'ūl-āt, *v.* to heap up: to gather: to increase. —*ns.* **accumulā'tion**, a heaping up: a mass or pile; **accum'-ulator**, a box, fitted with plates, for storing electricity.

accurate, ak'kūr-āt, *adj.* correct: exact.—*n.* **ac'curacy**.

accursed, ak-kurs'ed, *adj.* lying under a curse: doomed.

accuse, ak-kūz', *v.* to bring a charge against: to blame.—*ns.* **accusā'tion**, a charge brought against any one; **accused'**, one charged with wrong-doing; **accus'er**.

accustom, ak-kus'tum, *v.* to make well-known by use.—*adj.* **accus'tomed**, usual: (with *to*) used to (e.g. I am *accustomed to* the heat).

ace, ās, *n.* the one at dice, cards, dominoes, etc.: a first-class airman: a very good player of a game.

acerbity, as-er'bi-ti, *n.* bitterness: harshness.

acetylene, a-set'i-lēn, *n.* a kind of gas used for giving light and heat.

ache, āk, *n.* a continued pain.—*v.* to be in continued pain.

achieve, a-chēv', *v.* to do: to accomplish: to win.—*n.* **achieve'ment**, something done: a great deed.

acid, as'id, *adj.* sour: sharp.—*n.* a sour substance.—*v.* **acid'ify**, to make sour.—*n.* **acid'ity**, sourness.

acknowledge, ak-nol'ej, *v.* to confess: to say one has received something.—*n.* **acknow'ledgment** or **acknow'ledgement**.

acme, ak'mē, *n.* the highest point: perfection.

ā'corn, *n.* the seed of the oak.

acoustic, a-koost'ik or a-kowst'ik, *adj.* having to do with hearing or sound.—*n.* **acoust'ics**, the science which deals with sound.

acquaint, ak-kwānt', *v.* to let one know: to inform.—*n.* **acquaint'-ance**, knowledge: a person whom one knows.

acquiesce, ak-kwi-es', *v.* to agree to. —*n.* **acquies'cence**.

acquire, ak-kwīr', *v.* to gain: to get. —*ns.* **acquire'ment**, something learned or got; **acquisition** (ak-kwi-zish'un), the act of getting: something got.—*adj.* **acquis'itive**, eager to get.

acquit, ak-kwit', *v.* to free from blame: to behave or conduct (one's self).—*n.* **acquit'tal**, a setting free.

acre, ā'ker, *n.* a land measure containing 4840 square yards.—*n.* **a'creage**, the number of acres in a piece of land.

acrid, ak'rid, *adj.* harsh: bitter.

acrimony, ak'ri-mun-i, *n.* bitterness of feeling or speech.—*adj.* **acrimō'nious**, sharp, bitter.

ac'robat, *n.* one who does body-twisting and balancing tricks (e.g. a rope-dancer).—*adj.* **acrobat'ic.**

acrop'olis, *n.* a fortress in an old-time Greek city.

acrost'ic, *n.* a poem in which the first or last letters of each line, taken in order, spell a word or words.

act, *v.* to do : to conduct one's self : to pretend : to play a part (e.g. in a play).—*n.* something done : a law : a part of a play.—*ns.* **act'or,** *fem.* **act'ress,** one who acts or plays a part, esp. in a play ; **action,** a deed : a battle : a law-case.—*adj.* **ac'tionable,** likely to cause a law-case (e.g. an *actionable* statement).—*adj.* **act'ive,** busy : nimble : lively.—*n.* **activ'ity.**

actual, akt'ū-al, *adj.* real.—*n.* **actual'ity.**—*adv.* **act'ually.**

actuary, akt'ū-ar-i, *n.* one who makes the calculations in an insurance office.—*adj.* **actuā'rial.**

actuate, akt'ū-āt, *v.* to put into action : to drive or urge on.

acū'men, *n.* sharpness : quickness of understanding.

acute', *adj.* sharp-pointed : quick at understanding : (of a disease) severe but not lasting very long. —*n.* **acute'ness.**

ad'age, *n.* an old saying : a proverb.

ad'amant, *n.* a very hard stone : the diamond.—*adj.* hard, like adamant: unwilling to give way.

adapt', *v.* to make suitable : to alter so as to fit.—*adj.* **adapt'able,** easily put to a different use.

add, *v.* to put one thing to another : to sum up.—*n.* **addi'tion,** the act of adding : the thing added.—*adj.* **addi'tional.**

adden'dum, *n.* something added : —*pl.* **adden'da.**

ad'der, *n.* the common name of the viper : a poisonous serpent.

addict', *v.* to give (one's self) up to (generally to an evil habit).—*n.* **ad'dict,** one who is given up to some evil habit.

ad'dle, *v.* to make rotten : to muddle.—*adj.* **ad'dled.**

address', *v.* to speak or write to : to direct a letter.—*n.* the name of the house, street, and town where a person stays : the name,

etc. on the envelope of a letter : a speech : manners : cleverness.

adduce', *v.* to bring forward : to quote as an example.

ad'enoids, *n.* growths at the back of the nose which hinder breathing.

adept, ad-ept' or ad'ept, *adj.* very skilful.—*n.* one very skilful at a thing.

adequate, ad'e-kwāt, *adj.* sufficient. —*n.* **ad'equacy.**

adhere, ad-hēr', *v.* to stick to.— *n.* **adher'ence.**—*adj.* **adher'ent,** sticking to.—*n.* a follower, one who sticks to a cause.

adhesion, ad-hē'zhun, *n.* the act of sticking to.—*adj.* **adhēs'ive,** sticky, gummed.—*n.* a gummy substance.

adieu, a-dū', good-bye : farewell. —*n.* a farewell :—*pl.* **adieus** or **adieux** (a-dūz').

adipose, ad'i-pōz, *adj.* fatty.

ad'it, *n.* an opening or passage, esp. into a mine.

adjacent, ad-jās'ent, *adj.* lying near to.

adjective, ad'jek-tiv, *n.* a word which tells something about a noun (e.g. the *black* dog ; a *high* hill ; the work is *hard*).—*adj.* **adjectīv'al.**

adjoin', *v.* to lie next to.—*adj.* **adjoin'ing.**

adjourn, ad-jurn', *v.* to put off to another day : to leave off.—*n.* **adjourn'ment.**

adjudge, ad-juj', *v.* to decide : to settle.

adjudicate, ad-joo'di-kāt, *v.* to settle, as a judge does : to give a decision.—*ns.* **adjudicā'tion,** a decision or judgment ; **adju'dicātor,** one who gives a decision.

ad'junct, *n.* something joined or added.

adjure, ad-joor', *v.* to charge on oath.

adjust', *v.* to prepare : to settle.— *adj.* **adjust'able.**—*n.* **adjust'ment.**

adjutant, ad'joot-ant, *n.* an officer who assists a commanding officer : a large stork-like bird found in India.

admin'ister, *v.* to manage : to carry out : to give (e.g. help, medicine, etc.) to.—*n.* **administrā'tion,** management : the body that carries on the government of a country.—*adj.* admin'istrative. —*n.* administra'tor, one who manages: a governor.

ad'miral, *n.* the commander of a navy.—*n.* ad'miralty, the government office which formerly managed naval affairs.

admire', *v.* to think very highly of.—*adj.* ad'mirable, worthy of being admired.—*adv.* ad'mirably. —*ns.* admira'tion; admir'er.

admit', *v.* to let in : to own the truth of : (with *of*) to make possible.— *ns.* admis'sion, a letting in : money paid to allow one to enter a meeting, concert, etc. : a confession ; admit'tance, the right or leave to enter.—*adj.* admiss'ible, allowable. — *adv.* admit'tedly, without a doubt.

admix', *v.* to mix.—*n.* admix'ture.

admon'ish, *v.* to warn : to reprove. —*n.* admoni'tion, a warning.— *adj.* admon'itory.

ado, a-doo', *n.* trouble : fuss.

adolescent, ad-o-les'ent, *adj.* growing to manhood or womanhood. —*n.* a growing person of either sex.—*n.* adoles'cence, the period of youth.

adopt', *v.* to choose : to take as one's own.—*n.* adop'tion.

adore, ad-ōr', *v.* to worship : to love very much.—*adj.* ador'able, worthy of being loved.—*adv.* ador'ably.—*ns.* adora'tion, worship : great regard.

adorn', *v.* to make beautiful. — *n.* adorn'ment, ornament.

adrift', *adv.* floating hither and thither.

adroit, a-droit', *adj.* clever : skilful.

adulation, ad-ū-lā'shun, *n.* praise : flattery.—*adj.* ad'ulatory.

adult, ad-ult', *adj.* grown up.—*n.* (ad'ult) a grown-up person.

adulterate, ad-ult'er-āt, *v.* to make impure (e.g. by mixing water with milk).—*n.* adultera'tion.

adult'ery, *n.* a breaking of the marriage promise : unfaithfulness to one's wife or husband.— *n.* adult'erer (*fem.* adult'eress).

advance, ad-vans', *v.* to put forward : to go forward : to rise : to lend (money).—*adj.* advanced', far on (e.g. in age, school career, etc.).—*ns.* advance', a going forward : progress : improvement : a loan (of money); advance-guard, a part of an army sent on in front ; advance'ment, progress. —in advance, beforehand.

advantage, ad-vant'āj, *n.* a gain or benefit.—*v.* to help.—*adj.* advantā'geous, profitable : helpful.

ad'vent, *n.* a coming.—Advent, the period of about a month before Christmas.

adventitious, ad-vent-ish'us, *adj.* happening by chance.

adventure, ad-vent'ūr, *n.* a risk : a bold or risky undertaking.—*v.* to dare : to risk.—*n.* advent'urer, one who does bold deeds or takes risks.

ad'verb, *n.* a word which gives a more definite meaning to a verb, adjective, or other adverb (e.g. he writes *neatly*; the sky is *beautifully* clear ; he works *very* slowly).—*adj.* adverb'ial, belonging to an adverb.

adversary, ad'vers-ar-i, *n.* an enemy.

adverse, ad'vers, *adj.* acting against : harmful.—*n.* advers'ity, misfortune.

advert', *v.* to turn one's attention to.

advertise, ad-vert-īz', *v.* to make known to the public.—*ns.* advert'isement, a public announcement ; advertis'er.

advice, ad-vīs', *n.* something said as a help : counsel.—*v.* advise (ad-vīz'), to give advice to : to recommend.—*adj.* advis'able, wise : suitable.—*ns.* advisabil'ity; advis'er.—*adj.* advis'ory, advicegiving.—*adv.* advis'edly, purposely.

advocate, ad'vo-kāt, *n.* a defender : one who pleads for another : in Scotland, a court lawyer.—*v.* to plead for : to recommend.

adze, adz, adz, *n.* a kind of axe used by a carpenter.

æon, eon, ē'on, *n.* a very long period of time : an age.

aerate, ā'er-āt, *v.* to put air (or some other gas) into.

aerial, ā-ēr'i-al or ār'i-al, *adj.* belonging to the air : placed high up or overhead (e.g. an *aerial* railway) : having to do with aeroplanes and airships.

aerial, ār'i-al, *n.* a wire or rod (or a set of these) by means of which wireless or television signals are received or sent.

aerie or **aery,** ā'ri or ē'ri or ī'ri, *n.* an older spelling of **eyry.**

aerobatics, ār'o-bat'iks, *n.* stunting by an aircraft in the air.

aerodrome, ār'o-drōm, *n.* an aeroplane or airship station.

aeronaut, ār'o-nawt, *n.* an airman.

aeroplane, ār'ō-plān, *n.* a flying-machine heavier than air.

aesthetic, ēs-thet'ik, *adj.* having to do with beauty.

affable, af'fa-bl, *adj.* pleasant: easy to speak to.—*n.* **affabil'ity.**

affair, af-fār', *n.* something to be done: business: a matter.

affect, af-fekt', *v.* to act upon: to move the feelings: to pretend.—*adjs.* **affect'ed,** moved in the feelings: not natural, sham; **affect'ing,** moving the feelings.—*n.* **affecta'tion,** a striving after something not natural: pretence.

affection, af-fek'shun, *n.* kindness or love.—*adj.* **affec'tionate,** loving.—*adv.* **affec'tionately.**

affianced, af-fī'anced, *adj.* engaged to be married.

affidavit, af-fi-dā'vit, *n.* a written statement made on oath.

affinity, af-fin'i-ti, *n.* nearness of kin: likeness: close agreement.

affirm, *v.* to state firmly.—*n.* **affirmā'tion,** a firm statement: a statement made but not on oath.—*adj.* **affirm'ative,** saying ' yes.'—*n.* a statement which means yes. —to answer **in the affirmative,** to reply ' yes.'

affix, *v.* to fix to: to add.—*n.* **af'fix,** an addition to a word either before or after it.

afflict, af-flikt', *v.* to give continued pain.—*adj.* **afflict'ed,** suffering.—*n.* **afflic'tion,** great suffering: misery: grief.

affluent, af'floo-ent, *adj.* wealthy.—*n.* a stream flowing towards a river or lake.—*n.* **af'fluence,** abundance: wealth.

afford', *v.* to yield: to be able to pay for.

affor'est, *v.* to turn land into forest. —*n.* **afforestā'tion.**

affray, af-frā', *n.* a fight causing alarm : a brawl.

affright, af-frīt', *v.* to frighten.—*n.* great fear.—*adj.* **affright'ed.**

affront, af-frunt', *v.* to insult.—*n.* an insult.

afire, a-fīr', *adv.* on fire.

aflame, a-flām', *adj.* and *adv.* flaming: blazing.

afloat, a-flōt', *adv.* and *adj.* floating.

afoot', *adv.* on foot: happening, or about to happen.

aforesaid, a-fōr'sed, *adj.* said or named before.

aforetime, a-fōr'tim, *adv.* in past times.

afraid, a-frād', *adj.* struck with fear.

afresh', *adv.* again, anew.

Afrikan'er. *n.* a white person born in South Africa, esp. one of Dutch descent.—**Afrikaans',** the South African Dutch language.

aft'er, *prep.* and *adv.* behind: later : done in the same way as (e.g. The picture was *after* Landseer).

aft'ermath, *n.* a second mowing of grass in the same season : the bad effects of something, esp. of a war (e.g. Poverty is the *aftermath* of war).

aft'ernoon', *n.* the time between noon and evening.

afterthought, aft'er-thawt, *n.* a later thought.

aft'erward, aft'erwards, *adv.* later.

against', *prep.* opposite to.

agape, a-gāp', *adj.* or *adv.* gaping : with open mouth.

agate, ag'āt, *n.* a kind of precious stone.

age, āj, *n.* a long period of time: the time a person or thing has lived or existed.—*v.* to grow old : to make old.—*adj.* **aged** (āj'ed), old : (ājd) of the age of.—*n.pl.* (āj'ed) old people.—*adjs.* **age'less,** never growing old ; **age'long,** lasting for a great length of time.

agenda, aj-end'a, *n.* things to be done : a note of matters to be brought before a meeting.

agent, āj'ent, *n.* a person or thing that acts: one who acts for another.—*n.* **ag'ency,** the office or business of an agent : action or power (e.g. Many seeds are scattered by the *agency* of wind).

agglomerate, ag-glom′er-āt, v. to gather together.—n. **agglomerā′tion,** a heap.

aggrandise, ag′grand-īz, v. to make greater.—n. **aggrandisement** (ag-grand′iz-ment).

aggravate, ag′grav-āt, v. to make worse: to annoy.—adj. **ag′-gravating.**—n. **aggravā′tion.**

aggregate, ag′greg-āt, v. to add together.—n. a total.—n. **aggregā′tion,** a collection.

aggress′, v. to attack first.—adj. **aggress′ive,** ready to attack first: quarrelsome. — ns. **aggress′iveness; aggress′ion; aggress′or.**

aggrieve, ag-grēv′, v. to pain or injure.

aghast, a-gast′, adj. struck with horror.

agile, aj′il, adj. active: nimble.—n. **agil′ity.**

agitate, aj′i-tāt, v. to stir up: to disturb. — ns. **agitā′tion; ag′i-tator.**

aglow, a-glō′, adj. and adv. very warm: red-hot.

agog′, adj. and adv. eager: astir.

agony, ag′on-i, n. great pain.—v. **ag′onise,** to cause great pain.—adj. **ag′onising.**

agrarian, ag-rā′ri-an, adj. having to do with land and farming.

agree, a-grē′, v. to be alike (in thinking, in appearance, etc.): to consent.—adj. **agree′able,** suitable: pleasant: ready to agree.—adv. **agree′ably.**—n. **agree′-ment,** likeness (e.g. of opinions, appearance): a written statement making a bargain.

agriculture, ag′ri-kult-ūr, n. the tilling of the land: farming.—adj. **agricult′ural.**—n. **agricult′urist,** a farmer.

ague, ā′gū, n. a fever.

ahead, a-hed′, adv. in front.

aid, v. to help, assist.—n. help.

aide-de-camp, ād′-de-kong, n. an officer who carries messages to and from a general on the field: —pl. **aides′-de-camp.**

ail, v. to be ill: to trouble.—n. **ail′ment,** a trouble, disease.

aim, v. to point at (e.g. with a gun): to try to do.—n. the act of pointing at: plan or intention.—adj. **aim′less,** without aim.

air, ār, n. the mixture of gases which we breathe: a light breeze: a tune or the leading part of a tune: the look or manner (of a person).—v. to expose to the air: to dry: to make known.—n. **air′ing,** the act of exposing to the air: a short walk or drive in the open air.—adjs. **air′y; air′less.**—adv. **air′ily,** in a lively fashion.—ns. **air′craft,** flying-machines: **air′gun,** a gun from which the bullet is driven by the force of air; **air′-liner,** an aeroplane for carrying passengers and mails; **air′man,** one who pilots an aircraft; **air′-pump,** a pump for sucking out air; **air′-raid,** an attack by aeroplanes; **air-raid precautions,** see **A.R.P.; air-raid warden,** one who, during an air-raid, is expected to see to the safety of the public; **air-raid warning,** a signal or sound which gives warning of a coming air-raid; **air′ship,** a great balloon which can be steered and driven.—adjs. **air-borne,** in, or carried by, the air; **air′-tight,** made so that air cannot pass in or out.

aisle, īl, n. the side part of a church: a passage between the seats.

ajar′, adv. partly open.

akim′bo, adv. with hand on hip and elbow bent outward.

akin′, adj. related by blood: similar.

alabas′ter, n. a marble-like substance.

alack′! a cry showing sorrow.

alacrity, a-lak′ri-ti, n. briskness: cheerful readiness.

alarm′, n. sudden fear: something which rouses to action or gives warning of danger (e.g. an *alarm-clock,* a *fire-alarm*).—v. to frighten.—adj. **alarm′ing.**—adv. **alarm′-ingly.**—n. **alarm′ist,** one who frightens others needlessly.

alas′! a cry showing grief.

al′batross, n. a large sea-bird.

albe′it, although it be: even if.

al′bert, n. a short watch-chain.

albino, al-bē′no, n. a person or animal with white skin and hair and pink eye-pupils :—pl. **albi′nos.**

al′bum, n. a book with blank pages for holding photographs, stamps, signatures, etc.

albumen, al-bū'men, *n.* the white of eggs: a substance like it found in animals and vegetables.

alchemy, al'ke-mi, *n.* the changing of other metals into gold: a complete change.—*n.* **al'chemist**, one who tries to change metals to gold.

alcohol, al'kŏ-hol, *n.* pure spirit which forms the strong part of strong drinks.—*adj.* **alcohol'ic**.

al'cove, *n.* a small room off a larger room: a summer-house in a garden.

alder, awl'der, *n.* a tree often found growing beside ponds and rivers.

alderman, awl'der-man, *n.* a member of a town council next in rank to the mayor.

ale, *n.* a drink made from malt.—*n.* **ale'-house**, a house in which ale is sold.

alert', *n.* signal to be ready for action.—Also *v.*—*adj.* watchful: brisk.—**on the alert**, on the watch.

al'fa or **hal'fa**, *n.* esparto grass.

alfal'fa, *n.* a kind of grass.

alfresco, al-fresk'o, *adj.* and *adv.* in the open air.

algebra, al'je-bra, *n.* a method of counting, using letters and signs.

alias, ā'li-as, *adv.* otherwise.—*n.* a false name :—*pl.* **a'liases**.

alibi, al'i-bī, *n.* the plea that a person charged with a crime was elsewhere when the deed was done.

alien, āl'yen, *adj.* foreign: different in kind.—*n.* a foreigner.—*v.* **ā'lienate**, to take away: to make strange or unfriendly.

alight, a-līt', *v.* to come down: to settle upon.

alight, a-līt', *adj.* on fire.

align, a-līn', *v.* to set in line.—*n.* **align'ment**, arrangement in a line.

al'iment, *n.* food.—*adj.* **aliment'ary**, having to do with food.

alkali, al'ka-li, or **-li**, *n.* a substance such as soda or potash, the opposite of an acid.—*adj.* **al'kaline**.

all, *adj.* and *pron.* every one: the whole.—*n.* **all-clear**, the signal that an air-raid is over.—**all right**, quite good or suitable.

Allah, al'la, *n.* the Arab name for God.

allay', *v.* to calm.

allege, al-lej', *v.* to give as one's opinion.—*n.* **allega'tion**.

allegiance, al-lēj'i-ans, *n.* obedience: the duty of a subject to his king: loyalty.

allegory, al'le-gor-i, *n.* a story or fable describing one thing under the image of another: a parable.—*adj.* **allegor'ical**.

alleviate, al-lēv'i-āt, *v.* to make light: to lessen.—*n.* **alleviā'tion**.

alley, al'li, *n.* garden walk: a narrow passage :—*pl.* **all'eys**.

All-fools'-day, *n.* April first.

alliance, al-li'ans, *n.* union, esp. by marriage or treaty.

al'ligator, *n.* a kind of crocodile.

alliteration, al-lit-er-ā'shun, *n.* the repetition of the same sound at the beginning of two or more words close together, e.g. ' Sing a Song of Sixpence.'

allocate, al'lo-kāt, *v.* to place : to give to each his share.—*n.* **allo-cā'tion**.

allot', *v.* to give to each his share: to distribute : to parcel out.—*n.* **allot'ment**, the act of giving out : a small plot of ground for growing vegetables, etc.

allow', *v.* to grant: to permit.—*adj.* **allow'able**.—*n.* **allow'ance**, a fixed sum or amount : an excuse (e.g. The judge made *allowance* for the age of the prisoner, and set him free).

al'loy, *n.* a mixture of two or more metals.

allude, al-lood', *v.* to mention in passing: to refer to.—*n.* **allu'sion**.—*adj.* **allus'ive**.

allure, al-lūr', *v.* to entice.—*n.* **allure'ment**.—*adj.* **allur'ing**.

alluvium, al-lū'vi-um, *n.* earth brought down and left by rivers in flood.—*adj.* **allū'vial**.

ally, al-li', *v.* to join one's self to (by treaty, etc.).—*adj.* **allied'**.—*n.* **ally** (al'lī), a helper : friend.

almanac, a(w)l'ma-nak, *n.* a calendar : a yearly list of days, weeks, and months.

almighty, awl-mīt'i, *adj.* all-powerful.—**The Almighty**, God.

almond, ah'mund, *n.* the fruit or nut of the almond-tree.

almoner, al'mun-er, *n.* one who gives out gifts.—**hospital almoner**, one of the hospital staff who helps patients in difficulty.

alms, ahmz, *n.* gifts to the poor.— *n.* **alms'house,** a house for the poor.

aloe, al'ō, *n.* a plant used in medicines.—*n.* **al'oes,** a bitter drug got from aloes.

aloft', *adv.* on high.

alone, al-ōn', *adj.* standing by itself. —*adv.* singly, by itself.

alongside, al-ong-sīd', *adv.* beside : side by side : close to a ship's side.

aloof', *adv.* at a distance.—*n.* **aloof'-ness,** lack of interest : coldness of manner.

aloud', *adv.* so as to be heard.

alp, *n.* a high mountain : a cattle-meadow on a mountain.—*adj.* **alp'ine,** belonging to the Alps or other high mountains.

alpaca, al-pak'a, *n.* a kind of sheep, with long silky wool, found in Peru : cloth made of this wool.

alpenstock, alp'n-stok, *n.* a long staff used in climbing mountains.

alpha, al'fa, *n.* the first letter of the Greek alphabet : the beginning.

alphabet, al'fa-bet, *n.* the letters of a language given in order.—*adjs.* **alphabet'ic, -al,** in the order of the alphabet.

already, awl-red'i, *adv.* beforehand : even now.

alsatian, al-sā'shi-an, *n.* a large, wolf-like dog.

altar, awlt'er, *n.* a raised place where sacrifices are offered : in Christian churches, the communion table.

alter, awl'ter, *v.* to change.—*n.* **altera'tion.**

altercate, awl'ter-kāt, *v.* to dispute or quarrel.—*n.* **alterca'tion.**

alternate, awl'ter-nāt, *v.* to cause to follow by turns : to happen by turns.—*adj.* **alter'nate,** happening or coming time about or in turns.—*adv.* **alter'nately.** —*n.* **alterna'tion.**—*adj.* **alter'native,** offering a choice of two things.— *n.* a choice between two things.

although, awl-thō', *conj.* though.

alt'itude, *n.* height above sea-level.

alt'o, *n.* the male voice of the highest pitch : the female voice of lowest pitch (really *contralto*).

altogether, awl-too-geth'er, *adv.* all gathered in one place : wholly.

altruism, al'troo-ism, *n.* something done for the good of others.— *adj.* **altruist'ic.**

al'um, *n.* a mineral salt having a sharp taste.

aluminium, a-lum-in'i-um, *n.* a very light metal, looking rather like silver.

always, awl'wāz, *adv.* for ever.

amain, a-mān', *adv.* with full force or speed.

amal'gam, *n.* a mixture of mercury with another metal.—*v.* **amal'-gamāte,** to unite.—*n.* **amalgamā'-tion.**

amanuensis, a-man-ū-en'sis, *n.* one who writes to dictation : a secretary :—*pl.* **amanuen'sēs.**

amass', *v.* to gather in large quantity.

amateur, am'at-ūr or am-at-er', *n.* one who takes part in a thing for the love of it, not for gain.— Also *adj.*—*adj.* **amateur'ish,** imperfect : not the best.

amatory, am'at-or-i, *adj.* having to do with love : affectionate.

amaze, a-māz', *v.* to astonish : to surprise greatly.—*adv.* **amāz'edly.** —*n.* **amāze'ment.**

am'azons, *n.pl.* in old tales, a nation of warrior women who fought under their queen.

ambass'ador, *n.* a minister of the highest rank sent to look after the affairs of one country in another country.

am'ber, *n.* a yellowish substance, like resin, used for ornaments, beads, etc.—*adj.* made of amber : amber-coloured.

ambergris, am'ber-grēs, *n.* a sweet-smelling substance of an ash-grey colour, found floating on warm seas (it comes from a kind of whale).

ambidextrous, am-bi-decks'trus, **am-bidex'ter,** *adjs.* able to use both hands with equal skill.—*n.* **ambi'-dexter'ity.**

ambiguous, am-big'ū-us, *adj.* having two meanings : not clear.—*n.* **ambigū'ity.**

ambition, am-bish'n, *n.* the desire to rise : a wish for power or fame. —*adj.* **ambi'tious,** hoping to do great things.

amble, am´bl, v. to move like a horse (i.e. by lifting together both legs on one side and then those on the other): to move at an easy pace. —n. a pace of a horse—between a trot and a walk.

ambrosia, am-brō´z(h)i-a, n. in old stories, the food of the gods, which gave eternal youth and beauty to those who ate it : something very sweet and pleasing.

ambulance, am´būl-ans, n. a van (usually motor) for carrying the sick or injured.—Also adj. (e.g. *ambulance* train, ship).

ambush, am´boosh, am´buscade, ns. a hidden body of troops, waiting to attack by surprise.—v. to lie in wait for an enemy and attack him by surprise.

ameliorate, a-mēl´yor-āt, v. to make better : to improve : to grow better.—n. **ameliorā´tion**.

āmen, or ah-men, so let it be !

amē´nable, adj. easily led : ready to take advice.

amend´, v. to correct : to improve. —n. **amend´ment**, a change (e.g. in a law).—v. **to make amends**, to make up for having done wrong.

amenity, am-en´i-ti, n. pleasantness of situation and surroundings.

amethyst, a´meth-ist, n. a precious stone of a bluish-violet colour.

amiable, ām´i-a-bl, adj. lovable : of a sweet nature.—n. **amiabil´ity**.

amicable, am´ik-a-bl, adj. friendly.

amid´, amidst´, preps. in the middle : among. — adv. **amid´ships**, halfway between the stem and stern of a ship.

amiss´, adj. wrong.—adv. in a faulty manner.—adj. **amiss´ing**, lost : wanting.

amity, am´i-ti, n. friendship : goodwill.

ammō´nia, n. a strong-smelling gas given off by smelling-salts, burning feathers, etc. : a mixture of this gas in water.—adj. **ammōn´-iated**, containing ammonia.

ammunition, am-mūn-ish´un, n. powder, bullets, shells, bombs.

amnesty, am´nest-i, n. a general pardon of wrong-doers.

amok´. See **amuck**.

among, amongst, a-mung(st)´, prep. in the midst of : along with.

amorous, am´or-us, adj. loving: ready to love.

amount, a-mownt´, v. to come or rise to (e.g. His savings *amounted* to ten pounds).—n. the sum.

ampère, am´per, n. the unit used in measuring an electric current.

amphibian, am-fib´i-an, n. an animal that can live on land and in water (pl. **amphib´ia, amphib´-ians**) : a vehicle for use on land and water.—adj. **amphib´ious**.

amphitheatre, am-fi-thē´a-ter, n. in the time of the Romans, a round building having rows of seats one above another, around an open space, called the arena, in which public shows were given.

am´ple, adj. plenty : large enough.

amplify, am´pli-fī, v. to increase : to make bigger.—ns. **amplificā´-tion**; **am´plifier**, (in wireless) a part of the set for increasing sound.

amplitude, am´pli-tūd, n. largeness : size.

amputate, am´pūt-āt, v. to cut off (e.g. a limb).—n. **amputā´tion**.

amuck´ or **amok´**, adv. madly—hardly ever used save in the phrase ' to run *amuck* ' (i.e. to run mad and do damage).

amulet, am´ū-let, n. something worn as a charm against evil.

amuse, a-mūz´, v. to give pleasure to : to entertain.—n. **amuse´ment**. —adj. **amus´ing**, giving pleasure: funny.

anachronism, an-a´kron-izm, n. the mistake of mentioning something which did not exist at the time spoken about (e.g. in Shakespeare's play *Julius Cæsar*, which refers to the year 44 B.C., the mention of a striking clock is an *anachronism* ; mechanical clocks were not invented till the 10th century A.D.).

anaconda, an-a-kon´da, n. a large South American water-snake.

anæmia, an-ēm´i-a, n. poorness of blood in the body. — adj. **anæ´mic**, bloodless : pale or ill-looking.

anæsthetic, an-ēs-thet´ik, n. a substance (e.g. chloroform) that takes away feeling for a time. —ns. **anæsthē´sia, anæsthē´sis** ;

anæsthet'ist, *n.* one who gives anæsthetics.

an'agram, *n.* a word or sentence formed by rewriting (in a different order) the letters of another word or sentence (e.g. 'live '= ' evil,' ' Florence Nightingale '= ' Flit on, cheering angel ').

analogy, an-al'o-ji, *n.* a likeness.— *adj.* anal'ogous.

analysis, an-al'is-is, *n.* a breaking up of a thing into its parts :—*pl.* anal'yses.—*v.* an'alyse.—*n.* an'alyst, a person who analyses : a chemist.

anarchy, an'ark-i, *n.* a state of lawlessness in a country due to there being no government : disorder or confusion.—*n.* an'archist, one who wishes to do away with law and government.

anath'ema, *n.* a solemn curse by the Church : anything hateful or cursed.

anatomy, an-a'tom-i, *n.* the part of a doctor's training which has to do with the cutting up of the body and the study of its different parts : the body.—*n.* anat'omist.

ancestor, an'ses-tur, *n.* a forefather : —*fem.* an'cestress.—*adj.* ances'-tral.—*n.* an'cestry, the list of one's forefathers.

anchor, ang'kor, *n.* a heavy piece of iron, with hooked ends, for holding a ship fast to the bed of the sea or river.—*v.* to fix by anchor : to throw out the anchor. —*n.* anch'orage, a place where a ship can anchor.—to cast anchor, to let down the anchor ; to weigh anchor, to take up the anchor so as to be able to sail away.

anchorite, ang'kor-īt, anchoret, ang'-kor-et, *n.* a hermit.

anchovy, an-chō'vi, *n.* a small fish of the herring family.

ancient, ān'shent, *adj.* old.—*n.pl.* an'cients, those who lived long ago.

andante, an-dan'te, *n.* a piece of music moving evenly and somewhat slowly.

anecdote, an'ek-dōt, *n.* a short story.

anemometer, a-ne-mom'et-er, *n.* an instrument for measuring the speed or pressure of the wind.

anemone, a-nem'o-ne, *n.* a plant of the crowfoot family.

anent', *prep.* concerning.

an'eroid, *n.* a barometer in which the pressure of the air is measured without the use of mercury.

anew, a-nū', *adv.* afresh : again.

angel, ān'jel, *n.* a messenger sent by God : a person bringing help or good news.—*adj.* angel'ic.

angelica, an-jel'i-ka, *n.* a plant, found in woods and meadows, with an umbrella-like flower.

angelus, an'je-lus, *n.* the ' Hail Mary,' or prayer to the Virgin : the bell rung in Roman Catholic countries at morning, noon, and sunset.

anger, ang'ger, *n.* a bitter feeling against one who we think has done wrong.—*v.* to make angry. —*adj.* an'gry.—*adv.* an'grily.

angle, ang'gl, *n.* a corner : the point where two lines meet : the space between these lines.—*adj.* ang'-ūlar.—*n.* angūlar'ity.

angle, ang'gl, *v.* to fish with a rod, etc. : to entice.—*n.* angl'er.

Anglican, ang'glik-an, *adj.* belonging to the Church of England.

anglicise, ang'gli-sīz, *v.* to turn into English.

Anglo, ang'glo, *prefix* English.—*n.* and *adj.* Ang'lo-Sax'on, a name for the people of England and their language before the Norman Conquest. (The *Angles* and *Saxons* were two of the peoples who came from northwest Europe to settle in England in the 5th and 6th centuries.)

angora, ang-gō'ra, *n.* a goat with long silky hair.

angry. See anger.

anguish, ang'gwish, *n.* very great pain of body or mind : agony.

aniline, an'il-in, *n.* a product of coal-tar much used in dyeing.

animadvert, an-im-ad-vert', *v.* to draw attention to : to blame.— *n.* animadver'sion.

an'imal, *n.* a living being which can feel and move of its own accord. —*adj.* having to do with animals : high-spirited.

animalcule, an-im-al'kūl, *n.* a very tiny animal.

animate, an'im-āt, v. to give life to : to stir up.—*adj.* living.—*adj.* **an'imated,** lively.—*n.* anima'tion, liveliness.

animosity, an-im-os'i ti, *n.* bitter hatred : enmity.

an'imus, *n.* feeling against.

an'iseed, *n.* a seed with flavour like that of liquorice.

ankle, angk'l, *n.* the joint connecting the foot and leg.—*n.* **ank'let,** ornament for the ankle.

annals, an'alz, *n.pl.* history told year by year : story (e.g. The *annals* of our club are interesting).—*n.* **ann'alist,** a writer of annals.

anneal, an-ēl', v. usually, to heat strongly then cool slowly (glass or metal), in order to soften it for some purpose : also used to mean 'to toughen'.

annex', v. to add to the end : to take possession of.—*ns.* **annexe** (an'nex), a building added ; **annexā'tion.**

annihilate, an-nī'hil-āt, v. to destroy so completely that nothing is left.—*n.* **annihilā'tion.**

anniver'sary, *n.* a birthday : the day of each year when some event is remembered (e.g. November 11 is the *anniversary* of the end of the First World War).

annotate, an'not-āt, v. to make notes upon.—*n.* **annotā'tion.**

announce an-nowns', v. to make known.—*ns.* **announce'ment ; announc'er,** in broadcasting, one who makes known the items of a wireless programme.

annoy', v. to vex : to tease.—*n.* **annoy'ance,** that which annoys.

annual, an'nū-al, *adj.* yearly.—*n.* a plant that lives only one year : a book published yearly.—*adv.* **an'nually.**

annuity, an-nū'i-ti, *n.* a yearly payment made for a certain time or for life.—*n.* **annū'itant,** one who receives an annuity.

annul', v. to do away with : to abolish.—*n.* **annul'ment.**

annular, an'nūl-ar, *adj.* ring-shaped.

annunciate, an-nun'si-āt, v. to announce.—*ns.* **annun'ciation ; An-nunciation Day,** a church festival, held on 25th of March (Lady Day).

anodyne, an'o-dīn, *n.* a medicine that soothes pain.

anoint', v. to smear with ointment or oil : to make holy by pouring on oil.—*n.* **anoint'ing.**

anomaly, an-om'al-i, *n.* something not according to rule.—*adj.* **anom'alous.**

anon', *adv.* at once: some time soon.

anonymous, an-on'im-us, *adj.* without a name.—*n.* **anonym'ity.**

answer, an'ser, v. to reply to, esp. to a question : to find the result (e.g. of a sum or problem) : to be suitable : to be to blame for : to suffer for.—*n.* a reply : a solution.—*adj.* **an'swerable,** able to be answered : suitable for : to be blamed for.

ant, *n.* a small, hard-working insect.

antag'onist, *n.* an enemy : one's opponent in a game.—*n.* **antag'onism,** enmity.—*v.* **antag'onise,** to make an enemy of someone.—*adj.* **antagonis'tic,** opposed to.

Antarctic, ant-ark'tik, *adj.* opposite the Arctic : having to do with the South Pole.—**Antarctic Circle,** a circle drawn on the map round the South Polar regions.

antecedent, an-te-sēd'ent, *adj.* going before in time.—*n.* that which goes before in time : one who lived at an earlier time : an ancestor.

antechamber, an'te-chām-ber, *n.* a small room leading to a larger room.

an'tedate, v. to date before the true time.

antediluvian, an-te-di-lū'vi-an, *adj.* existing or happening before the Flood : very old-fashioned.

antelope, an'te-lōp *n.* a graceful, swift-running, deer-like animal.

antenna, an-ten'a, *n.* feeler of an insect : an aerial.

anterior, an-tē'ri-or, *adj.* before (in time or place) : in front.

an'teroom, *n.* a room leading into a large room.

an'them, *n.* a piece of sacred music sung in parts : any song of praise.

an'ther, *n.* (in a flower) the top of the stamen holding the pollen.

anthology, an-thol'oj-i, *n.* a collection of specially chosen poems, stories, etc.

anthracite, an'thras-ĭt, *n.* a kind of coal that burns nearly without flame, smell, or smoke.

an'thrax, *n.* a disease common among sheep and cattle, and sometimes attacking men.

anthropoid, an'throp-oid, *adj.* like a human being in shape or look.— **anthropoid apes**, monkeys which, in many ways, are like human beings (gorillas, chimpanzees).

an'ti, *prefix*, against.—**anti-aircraft gun**, a gun for firing at aeroplanes.

antics, *n.pl.* tricks: capers.

anticipate, an-tis'ĭp-āt, *v.* to foresee: to expect.—*n.* anticipā'tion.

anticli'max, *n.* the arranging of ideas so that they become less important towards the end.

anticyclone, an-ti-sī'klōn, *n.* a system of winds blowing round and out from an area of high pressure.

antidote, an'ti-dōt, *n.* that which is given to act against the effect of poison: a cure.

antimacassar, an-ti-mak-as'ar, *n.* a covering for sofas, cushions, etc.

antimony, an'ti-mun-i, *n.* a bluish-white metal.

antipathy, an-tip'ath-i, *n.* dislike.

antipodes, an-tip'od-ēz, *n.pl.* places on the earth's surface exactly opposite each other, such as Britain and New Zealand.

antiquary, an'ti-kwar-i, *n.* one who is interested in the past: a collector of relics.—*adj.* antiquāri'an, having to do with ancient times, customs, etc.—*n.* one who studies these.

antique, an-tēk', *adj.* old, but to be admired.—*n.* anything very old: an ancient relic.—*n.* antiquity (an-tik'wi-ti), ancient times, esp. those of the Greeks and Romans: great age.—*adj.* an'tiquated, grown old, or out of fashion.

antiseptic, an-ti-sept'ik, *adj.* germ-destroying.—*n.* something which destroys germs and so prevents disease.

antithesis, an-tith'e-sis, *n.* thoughts or words set in opposition: the opposite.

antitox'in, *n.* a substance in the blood able to fight against certain poisons.

ant'lers, *n.pl.* the horns of a deer.

an'vil, *n.* an iron block on which smiths hammer metal into shape.

anxious, angk'shus, *adj.* worried about what may happen.—*n.* anxiety (ang-zī'i-ti), state of being anxious.

aorta, ā-or'ta, *n.* a great blood-vessel leading from the heart.

apace, a-pās', *adv.* at a quick pace: fast.

apart'ment, *n.* a separate room in a house: rooms in a house set aside for the use of people other than those living there always: lodging.

apathy, ap'ath-i, *n.* want of feeling or interest.—*adj.* apathet'ic.

ape, āp, *n.* a monkey, especially gorilla, chimpanzee, orang-utan, or gibbon: a person who imitates another foolishly.—*v.* to imitate.

aperient, a-pē'ri-ent, *n.* any laxative or opening medicine.

aperture, a'pert-ūr, *n.* an opening: a hole.

apex, ā'peks, *n.* the top or summit: the highest point of anything.

aphorism, af'or-izm, *n.* a short, wise saying: an adage.

apiary, āp'i-ar-i, *n.* a place where bees are kept.—*ns.* ap'iarist, one who keeps an apiary: one who studies the habits of bees: api-culture (ā'pi-cult-ūr), bee-keeping.

apiece, a-pēs', *adv.* for each piece, thing, or person.

aplomb, a-plom', *n.* self-confidence: presence of mind.

Apocalypse, a-pok'al-ips, *n.* the name of the last book of the New Testament.

Apocrypha, a-pok'rif-a, *n.pl.* certain books of the Old Testament not printed in our Bibles: hidden or secret things of which the truth is not certain.—*adj.* apoc'ryphal, doubtful: untrue.

apologetic, -al, a-pol-oj-et'ik, -al, *adj.* making excuses: saying one is sorry.

apology, a-pol'oj-i, *n.* an open confession that a wrong has been done.—*v.* apol'ogise, to make excuse: to express regret for a fault.

apoplexy, ap'o-pleks-i, *n.* a kind of fit, caused by too much blood in the brain.—*adj.* **apoplec'tic.**

apostasy, *n.* breaking away from one's religion, faith, or promises. —*n.* **apost'ate,** one who breaks his vows.

apostle, a-pos'l, *n.* one sent to preach the gospel: one of the twelve disciples of Christ.

apostrophe, a-pos'trof-e, *n.* a sudden turning away from the ordinary course of a speech to address some person or object: a mark (') to show the possessive case (e.g. the boy's knife), or that a letter has been missed out (e.g. one o'clock). —*v.* **apos'trophise,** to speak to by apostrophe.

apothecary, a-poth'ek-ar-i, *n.* a druggist: one who makes up or sells drugs for medicine.

appal, ap-pawl', *v.* to make afraid: to terrify.—*adj.* **appal'ling,** shocking.

apparatus, ap-par-ā'tus, *n.* set of instruments: tools: material to do a piece of work.

apparel, *n.* clothing: dress.

apparent, ap-pār'ent or ap-par'ent, *adj.* easily seen: evident.

apparition, ap-par-ish'un, *n.* something which appears suddenly: a ghost.

appeal, ap-pēl', *v.* to ask earnestly: (in law) to take one's case to a higher court: to be pleasing (to). —Also *n.*—*adj.* **appeal'ing,** imploring, asking earnestly.

appear, ap-pēr', *v.* to come into view: to seem.—*n.* **appear'ance.**

appease, ap-pēz', *v.* to quieten by giving what was asked for: to make peaceful.

appellant, *n.* one who appeals in a court of law.—*n.* **appellā'tion,** a name: title.

append, *v.* to hang one thing to another: to add.—*ns.* **appen'dage,** something appended; **appen'dix,** a part added at the end of a book: a small worm-like part of the bowels which, when diseased, causes a painful illness called **appendici'tis.**

appertain', *v.* to belong to.

appetite, ap'pet-īt, *n.* hunger: desire for food.—*adj.* **appetis'ing,** tempting to the appetite.—*n.*

appetis'er, something which makes one feel hungry.

applaud, ap-plawd', *v.* to praise by clapping the hands: to praise loudly.—*n.* **applause'.**

ap'ple, *n.* a well-known fruit, usually red or green.

apply, ap-plī', *v.* to lay on (e.g. an ointment): to make a request: to fix the mind on: to be suitable.—*ns.* **appli'ance,** a tool or instrument; **ap'plicant,** one who applies or asks; **applicā'tion,** the act of applying: hard work, diligence: a request.—*adj.* **ap'plicable,** able to be applied: suitable.

appoint', *v.* to fix: to place in a job (e.g. He was *appointed* manager). —*n.* **appoint'ment,** a job or situation: an arrangement to meet someone.

apportion, ap-pōr'shun, *v.* to divide in fair shares.

apposite, ap'poz-ĭt, *adj.* suitable.

appraise, ap-prāz', *v.* to set a price on: to value.—*n.* **apprais'er,** one whose work it is to value property.

appreciate, ap-prē'shi-āt, *v.* to be aware of the good points in: to value highly: to understand: to rise in value.—*n.* **apprēciā'tion,** a good opinion of: gratitude.— *adj.* **apprēc'iable,** able to be noticed: of some amount.

apprehend, ap-pre-hend', *v.* to lay hold of: to seize: to understand. —*n.* **apprehen'sion,** the act of seizing: power to understand: fear.—*adj.* **apprehens'ive,** afraid of something to come.

apprentice, ap-prent'is, *n.* one who is learning a trade: a beginner. —*v.* to take on as an apprentice. —*n.* **apprent'iceship,** the time during which one is an apprentice.

approach, ap-prōch', *v.* to come near: to be like.—*n.* a coming near to: a path or road leading to a place.—*adj.* **approach'able,** able to be reached: (of persons) pleasant to speak to.

approbation, ap-prob-ā'shun, *n.* a good opinion of.

appropriate, ap-prō'pri-āt, *adj.* suitable.—*v.* to take to one's self as one's own.—*n.* **apprōpriā'tion.**

approve, a-proov', v. to think well of, to be pleased with.—n. **approv'al,** good opinion : permission (e.g. I shall do it with your *approval*).—**on approval,** on trial, to test worth (e.g. The shoes were sent to him *on approval*).

approximate, ap-proks'im-āt, adj. nearly correct.—v. to come near. —n. **approxima'tion,** answer to a sum, not exactly correct but correct enough for the purpose.

appur'tenance, n. something which belongs to a person or thing.

apricot, ā'pri-kot, n. an orange-coloured fruit of the plum kind.

April, ā'pril, n. the fourth month of the year.—n. **A'pril-fool,** one sent upon a useless errand on the 1st of April.

apron, ā'prun, n. cloth or a piece of leather worn before one to protect the dress.

apropos, a-pro-pō', adv. to the purpose : at the right moment : (with *to* or *of*) in connection with.

apse, aps, n. the rounded end at the east end of a church.

apt, adj. liable : quick : alert : clever. —ns. **apt'ness,** fitness ; **apt'itude,** readiness : cleverness.

aquarium, a-kwā'ri-um, n. a tank or set of tanks for keeping fish or water animals :—pl. **aquā'ria.**

aquatic, a-kwăt'ik, adj. having to do with water : living or growing in water.

aqueduct, ak'we-dukt, n. a channel by which water is led from one place to another : a bridge for taking water, such as a canal, across a valley.

aqueous, ā'kwe-us, adj. watery : (of rocks) laid down by water.

aquiline, ak'wil-īn, adj. like an eagle : curved or hooked, like an eagle's beak.

arable, ar'a-bl, adj. fit for ploughing.

ar'biter, n. someone chosen to settle a quarrel by giving a decision : a judge.—v. **ar'bitrate,** to act as a judge : to decide.—ns. **arbitra'tion,** the act of deciding : a decision ; **ar'bitrātor,** a judge.

arbitrary, ar'bi-trar-i, adj. not fixed by rules : uncertain.

arboreal, ar-bō're-al, adj. like a tree : living in trees.—ns. **arborē'tum,** a

park or garden in which different kinds of trees are grown ; **ar'boricul'ture,** tree-growing.

arbour, ar'bur, n. a seat in a garden shaded by tree-branches, bushes, or creepers : a bower.

arc, ark, n. a curve.

arcade, ark-ād', n. a row of arches supported by pillars : a passage or road under a row of arches, often with shops along the side.

arch, n. the curved part above one's head in a gateway or between pillars.—v. to cover with an arch : to shape like an arch.—adj. **arched.**—n. **arch'way,** a passage or road beneath an arch, such as that leading into a castle.

arch, adj. cunning.

archæology, ark-ē-ol'oj-i, n. the study of the people of long-past times from what remains of their buildings, etc.—adj. **archæolog'ical.**—n. **archæol'ogist,** one who studies archæology.

archaic, ark-ā'ik, adj. ancient : out of date : (of words) no longer used (e.g. *eftsoons*=soon afterwards).—n. **ar'chāism,** a word now out of use.

archangel, ark-ān'jel, n. a chief among angels.

archbish'op, n. a chief bishop, having other bishops under his rule.— n. **archbish'opric,** the rank of an archbishop : the district under an archbishop.

archdeacon, arch-dē'kn, n. the chief of the assistants of a bishop.

archduke, arch-dūk', n. the title of certain princes who are higher than dukes :—fem. **archduch'ess.** —adj. **archdū'cal,** belonging to an archduke.—n. **archduch'y,** the land owned by an archduke.

arch-enemy, n. the chief enemy : Satan.

arch'er, n. one who shoots with a bow and arrows.—n. **arch'ery,** the art of shooting with the bow.

archipelago, ark-i-pel'a-gō, n. a sea having many small islands : a group of small islands.

architect, ark'i-tekt, n. one who plans buildings.—n. **architect'ure,** the style or fashion in which a building has been made : the study of building.

archives, ark′īvz, *n.* the place in which government papers are kept: government papers.

arctic, ark′tik, *adj.* belonging to the district round the North Pole: very cold.—**Arctic Circle,** a circle drawn on the map round the North Polar regions.

ardent, *adj.* fiery: eager. — *n.* **ardour,** eagerness.

arduous, ard′ū-us, *adj.* difficult.— *n.* **arduousness.**

area, ā′rē-a, *n.* the amount of surface in anything, usually given in acres, square miles, square yards, etc.: a shut-in space, such as that round the bottom of a building.

arena, *n.* the sanded space where gladiators fought: any place where a big fight or show is held.

argosy, ar′go-si, *n.* a large trading-ship with a valuable cargo.

argue, arg′ū, *v.* to try to prove by giving reasons: to talk excitedly: to quarrel in words.— *n.* **argument,** a collection of one's reasons given as proof: a heated talk: the summary of a book.—*adj.* **argumentative,** fond of arguing.

arid, *adj.* dry.—*ns.* **aridity, aridness.**

arise, a-rīz′, *v.* to rise up: to come into view or hearing.

aristocracy, ar-is-tok′ras-i, *n.* the government of a country by the nobles or persons of rank: nobles and persons of rank.—*n.* **aristocrat** (ar′is-to-krat or ar-is′-), a nobleman: a haughty person. —*adj.* **aristocratic.**

arithmetic, ar-ith′met-ik, *n.* that part of learning dealing with numbers and counting. — *adj.* **arithmetical.**— *n.* **arithmetician,** one good at arithmetic.

ark, *n.* a chest or box (e.g. that in which the Israelites kept the Tables of the Law): the boat in which Noah and his family lived during the Flood.

arm, *n.* the part of the body between the shoulder and the hand: anything jutting out (e.g. an inlet of the sea, a rail at the side of a chair).—*ns.* **arm′chair,** a chair with arms or rests at each side; **arm′let,** a band round the arm; **arm′-pit,** the hollow under the shoulder.

arm, *n.* a weapon:—*pl.* **arms,** weapons for fighting: a crest or badge belonging to noble families. —*v.* to fit or supply with weapons.—*adj.* **armed,** fitted or supplied with weapons.

armada, ar-mä′da or ar-ma′da, *n.* a fleet of warships or warplanes (e.g. the fleet of warships sent by Spain against England in 1588).

armadillo, *n.* a small American animal whose body is protected by broad bands of bone.

armament, *n.* the guns of a warship, tank, or aeroplane.

armistice, arm′ist-is, *n.* in war, a rest from fighting for the time being (e.g. to bury the dead, or to arrange for the making of peace).

armorial, *adj.* having to do with a coat-of-arms or family crest.

armour, arm′ur, *n.* a steel suit worn by knights in olden times: an army's tank forces.—*n.s.* **arm′our-bearer,** one who carried a knight's armour; **arm′ourer,** one who makes, mends, or looks after arms; **arm′oury,** an arms store. —*adj.* **arm′our-plat′ed,** protected by plates of steel.

army, arm′i, *n.* a large number of men armed for war: a number of men gathered together for some special reason.

aroma, *n.* sweet smell. — *adj.* **aromatic,** sweet-smelling.

around, a-rownd′, *prep.* on all sides of.—*adv.* on every side.

arouse, *v.* to awaken: to stir up.

A.R.P., short for *Air Raid Precautions,* i.e. the steps taken to protect people against bombs from aeroplanes.

arquebus, ar′kwi-bus, *n.* an old-fashioned musket—also **har′quebus.**—*n.* **arquebusier′,** a soldier armed with an arquebus.

arraign, ar-rān′, *v.* to accuse.—*n.* **arraign′ment,** a trial in court.

arrange, ar-rānj′, *v.* to set in a rank or row: to put in order: to plan. —*n.* **arrange′ment,** act of setting in order: a plan to do something.

arrant, *adj.* very bad.

arras, ar′ras, *n.* a screen of tapestry.

array', *n.* order : dress.—*v.* to put in order : to dress.

arrear, ar-rēr', *n.* that which is in the rear or behind : that which remains unpaid or undone (used mostly in *pl.*).

arrest', *v.* to seize, esp. by power of the law : to stop : to catch (the attention).— *n.* capture by the police : stoppage.

arrive, ar-rīv', *v.* to reach any place.—*n.* **arriv'al**, the act of arriving : persons or things that arrive.

ar'rogant, *adj.* taking too much power or importance for one's self : proud and haughty.—*n.* **ar'rogance**.

arrow, ar'rō, *n.* a straight, pointed weapon, made to be shot from a bow.

arrowroot, ar'rō-root, *n.* a starchy food.

ar'senal, *n.* a factory or store for the weapons, ammunition, etc. of a navy or army.

arsenic, ar'sen-ik, *n.* a poisonous chemical.

ar'son, *n.* the crime of setting fire to anything to get money from insurance : fire-raising.

art, *n.* cleverness, skill : drawing, painting, sculpture, etc. :—*pl.* learning, as in the phrase *Master of Arts*.—*adjs.* **art'ful**, wily : cunning ; **art'less**, simple.

artery, ar'ter-i, *n.* a tube which carries blood from the heart to pass through the body.—*adj.* **artēr'ial**, belonging to an artery : like an artery.—**artēr'ial road**, the main traffic road among narrower roads.

artesian, ar-tē'zhan, an adjective used to describe wells made by boring until water is reached.

artichoke, ar'ti-chōk, *n.* a thistle-like plant, part of whose flower-head is eaten.—**Jerusalem artichoke**, a plant whose tubers are used as food.

article, art'i-kl, *n.* a thing, object : a composition in a newspaper, journal, etc. : each separate part of a treaty or an agreement : (*pl.*) an agreement or set of rules.

articulate, ar-tik'ūl-āt, *adj.* distinct : clear.—*v.* to join together : to speak distinctly.—*n.* **articulā'-**

tion, a putting or joining together, esp. of sounds in speaking : way of speaking.

artifice, art'i-fis, *n.* a cunning trick.—*n.* **artif'icer**, a worker.—*adj.* **artific'ial**, not natural, made by man : not real.—*n.* **artificial'ity**.

artillery, ar-til'er-i, *n.* cannon : the part of the army that manages the cannon.

artisan, art-i-zan', *n.* one good at an art or trade : a workman.

art'ist, *n.* one who is good at painting, sculpture, etc.—*adj.* **artis'tic**, having to do with art : beautiful : loving beautiful things.—*n.* **art'istry**, skill as an artist.

artiste, ar-tēst', *n.* one clever or tasteful in any art, as a cook, a hairdresser, etc. : someone who performs in public (e.g. a film star, concert singer).

asbes'tos, *n.* a fibrous or thread-like mineral which resists heat.

ascend, as-send', *v.* to climb : to rise or slope upwards.—*ns.* **ascend'ency**, **ascend'ancy**, power over others : mastery ; **ascent'**, a going up : a slope upwards ; **ascen'sion**, a going up.—**Ascension Day**, the day on which the Church remembers Christ's ascent to Heaven (i.e. Holy Thursday).

ascertain, as-ser-tān', *v.* to find out : to make certain.—*adj.* **ascertain'able**.

ascetic, as-set'ik, *n.* one who, in his manner of living, keeps away from all kinds of pleasure: a strict hermit.—*n.* **ascet'icism**.

ascribe, a-skrīb', *v.* to give praise or blame to somebody for something (e.g. The general *ascribed* the victory to the bravery of his soldiers).—*n.* **ascrip'tion**.

ash, *n.* a hard-wood tree.

ash or **ash'es**, *n.*what is left after anything is burnt.—*adj.* **ash'en**, pale, like the colour of ashes.—**Ash-Wednesday**, the first day of Lent.

ashamed, a-shāmd', *adj.* feeling shame.

ash'lar, *n.* building-stone cut and shaped ready for use.

ashore, a-shōr', *adv.* on shore.

Asiatic, ā-zhi-at'ik, **Asian**, āzh'yan, *adj.* belonging to Asia.

aside, a-sīd′, *adv.* on or to one side : apart.—*n.* words spoken in a low voice, so as not to be heard by others present.

asinine, as′in-īn, *adj.* of or like an ass : stupid.

askance, a-skans′, *adv.* sideways : with a side glance.— **to look askance at**, to look at with distrust.

askew, a-skū′, *adv.* off the straight : to one side.

asp, *n.* a small poisonous snake.

asparagus, *n.* a plant whose young shoots are eaten as a vegetable.

aspect, *n.* look : view : outlook.

aspen, asp′en, *n.* a kind of poplar tree.

asperity, asper′ity, *n.* roughness : harshness of temper : crabbedness.

aspersion, as-per′shun, *n.* an untrue or spiteful statement about a person.

asphalt, as′falt, *n.* a tarry substance used to make pavements, paths, etc. : pitch.—*v.* as′phalt, to lay or cover with asphalt.

asphyxia, as-fik′si-a, *n.* a stoppage in breathing : suffocation (by smoke or other fumes).—*v.* asphyx′iate, to suffocate.—*n.* asphyxia′tion.

aspidistra, as-pid-ist′ra, *n.* a pot-plant with large leaves.

aspire, as-pīr′, *v.* to aim at high things (e.g. prizes, jobs) : to be ambitious.—*ns.* aspirant (as-pīr′ant or as′pir-ant), one who tries hard (e.g. for a prize, a job) : a candidate : aspira′tion, eager desire or longing.

aspirin, n. a soothing drug.

ass, *n.* a donkey : a stupid person.

assagai, assegai, as′sa-gī, *n.* a thin wooden spear, with an iron tip.

assail, as-sāl′, *v.* to attack : to leap out upon.—*n.* assail′ant, one who attacks.

assassin, *n.* one who, usually for money, kills by surprise.—*v.* assas′sinate, to murder by sudden and secret attack.—*n.* assassina′tion.

assault, as-sawlt′, *n.* an attack with blows or weapons.—*v.* to make an assault or attack upon.

assay, *v.* to find the amount of pure metal in a lump of raw metal, or in a mixture containing metal.

assemble, *v.* to bring or put together : to meet together.—*n.* **assembly**, a meeting of persons, esp. one to talk over church or government affairs.

assent′, *v.* to agree.—*n.* permission : a statement, in words or writing, that one agrees (e.g. All our laws must have the queen's *assent*).

assert′, *v.* to say firmly.—*n.* asser′tion, a strong claim or statement.—*adj.* asser′tive, not shy.—**to assert one's self**, to push one's self forward, to make one's self noticed.

assess′, *v.* to fix an amount to be paid, esp. of a tax.—*ns.* assess′ment, the amount fixed ; assess′or.

assets, *n.pl.* the money with which one may pay one's debts.—**a great asset**, a great help.

asseverate, as-sev′er-āt, *v.* to declare solemnly.—*n.* assevera′tion.

assiduity, as-sid-ū′i-ti, *n.* eager attention to what one is doing : diligence.—*adj.* assid′uous, persevering : hard-working.

assign, as-sīn′, *v.* to give to someone as his share : to fix (e.g. The judge *assigned* a day for the trial).—*n.* assign′ment, a fixed amount of work or study to be done.

assimilate, *v.* to digest (food).—*n.* assimila′tion.

assist′, *v.* to help : to be present at.—*ns.* assist′ance, help : aid ; assist′ant, a helper.

assizes, as-sīz′es, *n.pl.* the name of certain law courts in England.

associate, as-sō′shi-āt, *v.* to join with, as a friend or partner.—*adj.* assō′ciate, joined or connected with.—*ns.* assō′ciate, a friend, partner, companion ; associa′tion, a number of persons gathered together for a purpose.—**Association football**, the game played under the rules of the Football Association, with eleven players a side (not fifteen as in *Rugby*).

assort′, *v.* to divide into kinds : to arrange : to match, well or ill (e.g. an *ill-assorted* pair).—*adj.* assort′ed, arranged in sorts : mixed.—*n.* assort′ment, a collection of different sorts of a thing : a mixture of kinds.

assuage 19 attainder

assuage, as-swāj′, *v.* to soothe (e.g. pain, hunger, thirst).

assume, as-sūm′, *v.* to take upon one's self: to take for granted: to pretend to possess.—*adj.* **assumed,** taken to one's self: pretended.—*adj.* **assum′ing,** haughty: proud.—*n.* **assumption** (as-sum′-shun), act of assuming: something taken as being true, without proof.

assure, a-shoor′, *v.* to make sure: to give confidence.—*n.* **assur′ance,** sureness: a promise.—*adj.* **assured** (a-shoord′), certain.

as′terisk, *n.* a star (*) used in printing to point to a note at the bottom or at the side of the page.

astern′, *adv.* in the back part of a ship: backwards.

asthma, as(th)′ma, *n.* an illness with great shortness of breath.—*adj.* **asthmat′ic,** suffering from asthma: panting: short-winded.

astir′, *adv.* on the move: out of bed.

aston′ish, *v.* to strike with sudden surprise or wonder: to amaze.—*n.* **aston′ishment,** amazement: wonder.

astound, as-townd′, *v.* to amaze: to strike dumb with wonder.—*adj.* **astound′ing.**

astrakhan, as-tra-kan′, *n.* lamb-skin with a curled wool.

as′tral, *adj.* belonging to the stars.

astray′, *adv.* out of the right way.

astride, a-strīd′, *adv.* sitting with the legs apart, like a rider on horse-back.

astringent, as-trin′jent, *n.* something which draws together (e.g. certain medicines, ointments, etc. used to draw together the cut parts of a wound).

astrology, as-trol′o-ji, *n.* the study of the stars in order to tell the future.—*n.* **astrol′oger,** one who foretells good or bad fortune from the stars.

astron′omy, *n.* the study of the stars and their movements.—*n.* **astron′omer.**

astute′, *adj.* cunning: careful about one's own affairs.

asun′der, *adv.* apart: into parts.

asylum, a-sīl′um, *n.* a place of refuge or safety: a home for the blind or the mentally ill.

atheism, ā′the-izm, *n.* belief that there is no God.—*n.* **a′theist,** one who does not believe in a God.—*adj.* **atheist′ic.**

atheling, ath′el-ing, *n.* in old-time England, a prince of the royal family (e.g. Edgar, the *Atheling*).

athirst′, *adj.* thirsty: eager for.

athlete, ath′lēt, *n.* one of strong body: one good at sports (running, leaping, etc.).—*adj.* **athlet′ic,** having to do with games: strong, vigorous.—*n.pl.* **athlet′ics,** running, games, etc.

athwart′, *prep.* across.—*adv.* sidewise: wrongly.

at′las, *n.* a book of maps.

atmosphere, at′mo-sfēr, *n.* the air round the earth: the air in a room: feeling (e.g. There is a friendly atmosphere in this class).—*adj.* **atmospher′ic.**—*n.pl.* **atmospher′ics,** in wireless, air disturbances causing crackling noises.

atoll, a-tol′ or at′ol, *n.* a coral island or reef.

at′om, *n.* the tiniest possible part of any substance: anything very small.—**atomic energy,** very great force got by breaking up the atoms of some substances; it is used in the *atomic bomb.*

atone′, *v.* to make up for wrongdoing.—*n.* **atone′ment.**

atrocious, a-trō′shus, *adj.* cruel or wicked: very bad.—*n.* **atrocity** (a-tros′i-ti), a cruel deed.

atrophy, at′rof-i, *n.* a wasting away (esp. of the body or part of it).

attach′, *v.* to tie to: to connect.—*adj.* **attached′,** fastened, fixed: fond of.—*n.* **attach′ment,** something fastened: liking for.

attaché, at-tash′ā, *n.* a junior ambassador.—*n.* **attaché-case,** a small case for papers, etc.

attack′, *v.* to fall upon suddenly or violently: to begin a fight: (of a disease) to begin to affect.—Also *n.*

attain′, *v.* to reach.—*adj.* **attain′able,** able to be reached.—*n.* **attain′ment,** act of reaching: the thing reached.—*pl.* **attain′ments,** knowledge: learning.

attainder, at-tān′der, *n.* a punishment by which a person loses his rights as a citizen.—*v.* **attaint′.**

at′tar, *n.* a sweet-smelling oil got from rose petals: a scent.

attempt, at-temt′, *v.* to try.—*n.* a trial or effort: an attack (on a person with the purpose of killing him).

attend′, *v.* to wait on, or go along with: to be present at: to give attention.—*n.* **attend′ance,** act of waiting on or of being present: the persons present.—*adj.* **attend′ant,** going along with.—*n.* one who attends or goes with: a servant.—*n.* **atten′tion,** heed: politeness: care.—*adj.* **attent′ive,** full of attention: polite: mindful.

attenuate, at-ten′ū-āt, *v.* to make or become thin: to grow less.

attest′, *v.* to bear witness to (e.g. by signing one's name).—*n.* **attestā′-tion.**

at′tic, *n.* a room in the roof of a house.

attire′, *v.* to dress.—*n.* dress.

attitude, at′ti-tūd, *n.* position of the body: manner of behaving.

attorney, at-tur′ni, *n.* one who has power to act for another: a lawyer who prepares cases for a court of law.—*n.* **attor′ney-gen′eral,** the chief lawyer in the government.

attract′, *v.* to draw to: to entice.—*n.* **attrac′tion,** act of drawing to: the force which draws bodies to each other: that which attracts.—*adj.* **attract′ive,** able to attract: pleasing.

attribute, at-trib′ūt, *v.* to put along with or think of as belonging to.—*adj.* **attrib′utable.**—*n.* **at′tribute,** a point in a person's character (e.g. Thrift is an *attribute* of a Scotsman).

attune′, *v.* to put in tune: to make to agree.

auburn, aw′burn, *adj.* golden or reddish-brown in colour.

auction, awk′shun, *n.* a public sale in which the price is increased step by step, and the article to be sold goes to him who offers the most.—*v.* to sell by auction.—*n.* **auctioneer′,** one who sells by auction.

audacious, aw-dā′shus, *adj.* daring: bold: impudent.—*n.* **audacity** (aw-das′i-ti), boldness: daring.

audible, awd′i-bl, *adj.* able to be heard.—*n.* **audibil′ity.**

audience, awd′i-ens, *n.* the persons gathered within hearing, esp. at a concert or meeting: a hearing (e.g. The minister had an *audience* with the king).

audit, awd′it, *v.* to look into an account to see if it is correct.—Also *n.*—*n.* **aud′itor,** one who is trained to the work of auditing.

auditory, awd′it-or-i, *adj.* having to do with the sense of hearing.—*ns.* **audi′tion,** a test given to a singer or other performer; **audito′rium,** the part of a hall where the hearers (or audience) sit.

auger, aw′ger, *n.* a carpenter's tool used for boring holes in wood.

aught, awt, *n.* anything: a part.

augment′, *v.* to increase in size or number: to grow larger.—*n.* **augmentā′tion.**

augur, aw′gur, *n.* among the Romans, one who foretold events from watching how birds behaved: a prophet.—*v.* to foretell from signs.—*n.* **au′gury,** a sign for the future.

august, aw-gust′, *adj.* stately.

auk, awk, *n.* a short-winged seabird, found in northern seas.

aunt, ant, *n.* a father's or a mother's sister—also the wife of one's uncle.

aureate, awr′i-āt, *adj.* golden or gold-coloured.—*n.* **aureole** (awr′i-ōl), in old paintings, a gold circle round the heads of sacred persons.

auriferous, awr-if′er-us, *adj.* bearing or yielding gold.

aurora, aw-rō′ra, *n.* the dawn: a glow in the sky, probably caused by electricity—the *Aurora Borealis* (bō-rē-ā′lis), or *Northern Lights,* is seen in regions about the North Pole; the *Aurora Australis* (aw-strāl′is), or *Southern Lights,* around the South Pole.

auspice, aw′spis, *n.* a sign got from watching birds.—*adj.* **auspi′cious,** promising success: favourable: lucky.—**under the auspices of,** under the control of (e.g. The sports were *under the auspices of* the School Sports Association).

austere, aws-tēr′, *adj.* harsh : severe : stern.—*ns.* **austere′ness, auster′ity.**

austral, aws′tral, *adj.* southern.

authentic, aw-thent′ik, *adj.* true : reliable : to be believed.—*v.* **authent′icate**, to prove to be true. —*n.* **authenticity** (aw-then-tis′- i-ti), state of being true : truth.

auth′or, *n.* the writer of a book, poem, play, etc. : the beginner of anything :—*fem.* **auth′oress.**

authorise, awth-or-īz, *v.* to give a person power to do something.

authority, awth-or′it-i, *n.* power or right : permission : a person whose opinion is of importance, an expert : a number of persons who, acting together, look after something (e.g. the Port of London *Authority*):—*pl.* **author′ities,** persons in power : the government.—*adj.* **author′itātive,** said by someone whose opinion is important.

autobiography, aw-to-bī-og′raf-i, *n.* a person's life written by himself.

autocrat, aw′to-krat, *n.* a ruler who has full power.—*adj.* **autocrat′ic.**

autograph, aw′to-graf, *n.* one's own handwriting or signature.—*v.* to write one's name.—**autograph album**, book in which one collects signatures of famous people, etc.

automaton, aw-tom′a-ton, *n.* machine that appears to move of itself : person who acts like a machine :—*pl.* **autom′atons** or **autom′ata.**—*adj.* **automat′ic,** self-moving.—*n.* **automation** (aw-to-mā′shun), use in factories, etc., of machines for calculating and for controlling other machines.

automobile, aw-to-mō-bēl′, *n.* a motor-car.

autonomy, aw-ton′om-i, *n.* the power or right of a country to govern itself.—*adj.* **auton′omous.**

autumn, aw′tum, *n.* the third season of the year.—*adj.* **autumn′al,** belonging to autumn.

auxiliary, awg-zil′yar-i, *adj.* helping : additional.—*n.* a helper.

avail, a-vāl′, *v.* to be of use or value.—*n.* benefit : use : service. —*adj.* **avail′able,** able to be made use of.—*n.* **availabil′ity.**

avalanche, av′al-ansh, *n.* a mass of snow and ice sliding down from a mountain.

avarice, av′ar-is, *n.* eager desire for getting and storing up of wealth. —*adj.* **avari′cious,** very greedy.

avenge, a-venj′, *v.* to punish someone for the wrong he has done : to take vengeance for.—*n.* **aven′ger.**

avenue, av′en-ū, *n.* a wide and handsome street : the main road to a mansion-house, usually bordered by trees : a double row of trees.

aver′, *v.* to declare to be true : to state as a fact.—*n.* **aver′ment.**

average, av′er-āj, *n.* the result got by adding several amounts and dividing the total by the number of amounts (e.g. The *average* of 3, 7, 9, 13 is 8 $(32 \div 4)$).—*adj.* ordinary : of medium size : not very good.—*v.* to find the average.

averse′, *adj.* not fond of (e.g. I am *averse* to picture-shows).—*n.* **aver′sion,** dislike : something that is hated.

avert′, *v.* to turn aside : to prevent.

aviary, ā′vi-ar-i, *n.* a place for keeping birds.

aviation, ā-vi-ā′shun, *n.* the science of flying (in aeroplanes, airships). —*n.* **a′viātor,** an airman.

avidity, *n.* eagerness : greediness.— *adj.* **av′id,** greedy : eager.

avocation, a-vo-kā′shun, *n.* a sideline from one's regular work : a hobby.

avoid′, *v.* to try to escape from : to shun : to leave alone.—*adj.* **avoid′able.**—*n.* **avoid′ance,** the act of avoiding.

avoirdupois, av-or-dū-poiz′, *adj.* and *n.* the system of measuring weights in pounds and ounces (1 lb. = 16 oz.).

avouch, a-vowch′, *v.* to say firmly.

avow′, *v.* to declare openly : to admit.—*adj.* **avowed′.**—*n.* **avow′al,** an open statement or confession.

await′, *v.* to wait or look for : to be in store for.

awake′, *v.* to rouse from sleep : to stop sleeping.—*adj.* **awake′,** not asleep : watchful.—*v.* **awak′en,** to rouse from sleep : to open the eyes after sleep.—*ns.* **awak′ing, awak′ening,** the moment of stirring after sleep.

award′, v. to give something to someone, after judging.—n. judgment: what is awarded (e.g. payment, prize, or punishment).

aware, a-wār′, adj. on one's guard: knowing of.

awe, aw, n. wonder mixed with fear: dread.—v. to strike with fear.—adjs. **aw′ful,** causing fear and wonder: (slang) ugly; **awe′some,** causing fear; **awe′struck,** full of fear and wonder.—adv. **aw′fully,** (slang) very.—n. **aw′fulness,** dreadfulness.

awhile, a-whīl′, adv. for some time: for a short time.

awk′ward, adj. clumsy: not graceful: difficult to deal with.—n. **awk′wardness.**

awl, n. a pointed tool for boring small holes in leather.

awn′ing, n. a covering (e.g. of canvas) to give shelter from the sun's rays.

awry, a-rī′, adj. twisted to one side: crooked.—adv. unevenly.

axe, n. a tool for hewing or chopping:—pl. **ax′es.**

axiom, aks′yum, n. a statement usually taken to be true and needing no proof.—adj. **axiomat′ic,** easily seen to be true.

ax′is, n. the line, real or imaginary, on which a thing turns, e.g. the axis of the earth, i.e. the line (joining the North Pole and South Pole) around which the earth turns:—pl. **axes** (aks′ēz).

axle, aks′l, **axle-tree,** n. the pin or rod on which a wheel turns.

ay, aye, ī, adv. yes: indeed.

ayah, ī′ya, n. a native Indian waiting-maid or nurse-maid.

aye, ay, ā, adv. ever: always: for ever.—**for aye,** for ever.

azure, āzh′ūr, adj. sky-blue.—n. the clear blue sky: sky.

B

bab′ble, v. to speak like a baby: to tell secrets.—ns. **bab′ble, bab′bling,** silly talk: murmuring (as of a stream flowing over stones); **bab′bler.**

bā′bel, n. a jumble of sounds.

baboo, babu, ba′boo, n. an Indian who has learned English but does not write it quite correctly.

baboon′, n. a kind of large monkey.

baby, bā′bi, n. a very young child: an infant.—n. **babyhood** (bā′bi-hood), the time when one is a baby.

bach′elor, n. an unmarried man: one who has passed certain examinations at a university (e.g. Bachelor of Arts, usually written B.A.): a young knight. —n. **bach′elor's-but′ton,** a name for many kinds of flowering plants having button-like flowers (e.g. certain kinds of buttercups).

bacillus, ba-sil′us, n. a rod-shaped kind of germ:—pl. **bacil′li.**

back, n. the hinder part of anything: one who plays in front of the goal in some team-games (e.g. football, hockey).—adj. belonging to or placed in the hinderpart. —adj. **back′ward,** moving towards the back: shy: not very clever.—adv. **back′ward, back′wards,** towards the hinder part— opposite of forward, forwards.—n. **back′wardness.**—v. **back,** to move backwards: to help or support. —ns. **back′er,** one who helps or supports; **back′ing,** help or support.—v. **back′bite,** to speak evil of anyone behind his back or in his absence.—ns. **back′bone,** the bone of the back: the main support of anything: firmness; **back′-door,** a door in the back part of a building; **back′-end,** the late autumn; **back-fire′** (in motors), a loud noise in the exhaust-pipe; **back′ground,** the space behind the principal figures of a picture; **back′-hand,** handwriting with the letters sloped backwards (to the left); **back′-number,** an old copy of a newspaper or magazine: something out of date; **back′slider,** one who turns from good to bad behaviour; **back′-wash,** a backward current, such as that of a wave going out; **back′water,** water held back by a dam: a quiet part of a river: the swell of the sea formed by the passing of a steamship; (pl.) **back'woods,** the part of a country not yet cleared of forests.

backgam'mon, n. a game something like draughts, played with dice.

back'ward, back'wards, adv. See back.

bā'con, n. pig's flesh salted and dried.

bacterium, bak-tē'ri-um, n. a kind of germ found in the air, water, earth, in living and dead bodies, and usually in things going bad: —pl. bactē'ria.—adj. bactē'rial.— ns. bacteriol'ogy, the study of bacteria; bacteriol'ogist.

badge, n. a mark or sign or brooch-like ornament by which a person is known.

badger, baj'er, n. a burrowing animal about the size of a fox. —v. to pester or annoy.

badinage, bad'in-äzh, n. playful talk.

bad'minton, n. a game something like tennis, played with shuttle-cocks.

bad'-tempered, adj. cross.

baffle, baf'l, v. to check or make useless: to be too difficult or too clever for (e.g. This sum baffles me; the thief baffled the detective).

bag, n. a sack, pouch: the quantity of fish or game caught.—v. to bulge: to seize or steal.

bagatelle, bag-a-tel', n. a board-game, in which balls are struck into numbered holes: a trifle.

bag'gage, n. the tents and stores of an army: luggage.

bag'pipe, n. a musical instrument made up of a bag and several pipes. (It is played by the bands of Highland regiments.)

bail, n. one who gets an untried prisoner out of prison for the time being by promising that the prisoner will come back for trial when sent for: money put down for the prisoner's release.

bail, n. in cricket, one of the cross pieces on the top of the wickets.

bail, v. to clear (a boat) of water with shallow buckets.

bail'ey, n. the outer court of an old castle.

bail'ie, n. in Scotland, a member of a town council, above a councillor.

bail'iff, n. one who acts for a sheriff: an estate or farm manager.

bait, n. food put on a hook to make fish bite: anything tempting.— v. to put bait on a hook or trap: to set dogs on to worry another animal (e.g. a bear): to worry, annoy.

baize, n. a coarse woollen cloth.

bake, v. to cook by the heat of the sun or of fire: to make bread or other food in an oven: to work as a baker.—ns. bake'house, bā'kery, a place used for baking in; bā'ker, a person who bakes or sells bread.

balalaika, ba-la-lī'ka, n. a Russian musical instrument, like a guitar.

bal'ance, n. a weighing-machine: the money needed to make the two sides of an account equal.— v. to be the same in weight: to make both sides of an account the same: to keep from falling.

balcony, balk'on-i, n. a platform built out from the wall of a building: an upper floor or gallery in theatres, cinemas, etc.

bald, bawld, adj. without hair: bare.

bald'erdash, n. nonsense.

baldric, bawld'rik, n. a cross-belt from shoulder to waist, for carrying sword, bugle, etc.

bale, n. a bundle of goods.

bale, n. evil: woe.—adj. bale'ful.

balk, baulk, bawk, n. a line of turf between ploughed land : a wooden beam for building.—v. to avoid: to cheat or dodge.

ball, n. anything round: the round object used in playing many games: a bullet.

ball, n. dancing.—n. ball'room.

bal'lad, n. a simple story-poem usually in verses of four lines: a short song.—n. bal'ladist, writer or singer of ballads.

bal'last, n. sand, gravel, etc., put into a ship or truck, to steady it.

ballet, bal'lā, n. dancing to music on the stage of a theatre.

balloon', n. an air-tight ball of thin rubber, silk, etc., which floats in the air when filled with light gas. —n. balloon'ist, one who goes up in the air in a balloon.— balloon barrage, a network of wires supported by balloons, used as a defence against aeroplanes.

bal′lot, *n.* a way of voting in secret by putting a ball or ticket or paper into a box.—*v.* to vote by ballot: to choose by secret voting.—*n.* **ball′ot-box**, the box used for voting by ballot.

balm, bahm, *n.* a sweet-smelling healing ointment: a scent.—*adj.* **balmy** (bah′mi), sweet-smelling: mild.—*n.* **balm′iness**.

balmor′al, *n.* a kind of Scottish cap.

balsam, bawl′sam, *n.* a kind of plant: an oily substance with sweet smell and healing powers.

bal′uster, *n.* a post holding up the rail of a staircase, etc.—*n.* **bal′ustrade**, a row of balusters joined by a rail.

bamboo′, *n.* the hard stem of a very tall Indian grass, used for canes, rods, etc.

bamboo′zle, *v.* to trick: to puzzle.

ban, *n.* an order forbidding something: disapproval that stops or prevents.—*v.* to forbid, prevent.

bana′na, *n.* the yellow fruit of a tropical tree.

band, *n.* that by which loose things are held together: a strip of cloth to bind round anything, as a hat-band, waist-band, etc.—*ns.* **band′age**, a strip of cloth for protecting a hurt or sore; **band′box**, a light kind of box for holding bands, caps, etc.

band, *n.* a number of persons gathered together for any purpose: a number of musicians playing together.—*v.* to join together.

bandan′a, *n.* a spotted silk or cotton handkerchief, gaily coloured.

bandeau, ban′dō, *n.* a narrow band worn by women to keep the hair in position (esp. at games).

ban′dicoot, *n.* an Australian animal, like a very large mouse: in India and Ceylon, a large kind of rat.

ban′dit, *n.* an outlaw: a robber.

bandolier′, bandoleer′, *n.* a belt across the body for carrying cartridges.

ban′dy, *v.* to toss from one to another.—**to bandy words**, to exchange angry words: to argue.—*adj.* **ban′dy-legged**, having bent or bow legs.

ban′dy, *n.* in India, a kind of carriage or bullock-cart.

bane, *n.* ruin: great harm: poison.—*adj.* **bane′ful**, deadly: harmful.

bangle, bang′gl, *n.* a ring worn on arms or legs.

ban′ian, ban′yan, *n.* an Indian fig-tree.

ban′ish, *v.* to order to leave a country: to drive away.—*n.* **ban′ishment**.

ban′ister, *n.* the posts and rail along the edge of a staircase.

ban′jo, *n.* a musical instrument like a guitar, having a long neck and a round body.—*n.* **banjō′ist**.

bank, *n.* a mound of earth: the edge of a river, etc.: a seat for rowers: a place where money is put for safety.—*v.* to put earth round: to cover up a fire with coal, so that it will not burn away quickly: to put money in a bank: to tilt an aeroplane for a turn.

bank′rupt, *n.* one who is unable to pay what he owes.—Also *adj.*—*n.* **bank′ruptcy**.

ban′ner, *n.* an army flag: a flag carried in processions.

ban′nock, *n.* a flat home-made cake of oatmeal, barley, or pease-meal.

banns, *n.pl.* a public notice saying that a marriage is to take place.

banquet, bangk′wet, *n.* a feast.

ban′shee, *n.* a wailing Irish ghost.

ban′tam, *n.* a small kind of fowl.

ban′ter, *v.* to tease in fun: to joke or jest at.—Also *n.*

baobab, bā′o-bab, *n.* a splendid tree of Western Africa.

baptise′, *v.* to christen, give a name to.—*n.* **bapt′ism**, dipping in, or sprinkling with water as a sign of being taken into the Christian Church.—*adj.* **baptis′mal**.

bar, *n.* a rod of anything solid: something standing in the way, a hindrance (e.g. a bank of sand, gravel, etc. lying at the mouth of a river): the counter across which drinks are served in a public-house: the wooden rail at which prisoners stand for trial: the lawyers in a court: a division in music: a band across a shield.—*prep.* except.—*v.* to fasten with a bar: to hinder or shut out.

barb, *n.* the backward prong or spike on an arrow, fish-hook, or wire.—*adj.* **barbed** (barbd), having a barb or barbs (e.g. **barbed-wire**).

bar'barous, *adj.* savage: brutal.—*ns.* **bar'barism, barbar'ity,** a rough, lawless way of living: cruelty; **barbā'rian,** a rough ill-mannered fellow.

barbecue, barb'ekū, *n.* a frame on which to dry and smoke meat above a fire: an animal roasted whole.

bar'bican, *n.* a tower jutting out over the gate of a castle.

barcarole, bar'ka-rōl, *n.* a song of the boat-men of Venice.

bard, *n.* in olden times, one who sang war-songs, etc.: a poet.

bare, *adj.* uncovered: naked: open to view.—*adv.* **bare'ly,** hardly, scarcely.—*v.* to strip or uncover.—*adj.* **bare'faced,** impudent.

bar'gain, *n.* an agreement about buying or selling something: something bought cheaply.—*v.* to make an agreement: to argue about a price: to expect (e.g. I did not *bargain* for such wet weather).—**into the bargain,** over and above; **to strike a bargain,** to agree about a price.

barge, *n.* flat-bottomed boat for carrying goods, used on rivers and canals.—*v.* to move clumsily or roughly.—*n.* **bar'gee,** one who owns or works on a barge.

bar'itone, *n.* in singing, a man's voice between high (tenor) and low (bass).

bark, *n.* the cry made by a dog, wolf, etc.—*v.* to yelp like a dog.

bark or **barque,** bark, *n.* a three-masted sailing vessel: a boat.

bark, *n.* the rind or covering of the trunk and branches of a tree.—*v.* to strip or peel the bark from: to rub off (skin).

bar'ley, *n.* a grain used for food, and for making beer and whisky.

barn, *n.* a building in which grain, hay, etc. are stored.

barnacle, bar'na-kl, *n.* a shellfish which sticks to rocks and the bottoms of ships.

barom'eter, *n.* an instrument which measures the weight or pressure of the air and shows changes of weather.—*adj.* **baromet'ric.**

bar'on, *n.* a nobleman's title.—*ns.* **bar'oness,** a baron's wife; **bar'ony,** the land of a baron.—*adj.* **barō'nial.**

bar'onet, *n.* a title (' Sir ').—*n.* **bar'onetcy,** the rank of baronet.

barque. Same as **bark.**

bar'rack, *n.* (usually in *pl.*) a place for housing soldiers.—*v.* to shout insults at.

barrage, bar'āj, *n.* a bar across a river to make the water deeper: machine-gun or artillery fire barring the approach to a place.

bar'rel, *n.* a wooden cask or vessel with curved sides: the metal tube of a gun through which the shot is fired.

bar'ren, *adj.* unfruitful: not giving a profit.—*n.* **bar'renness.**

barricade, bar'ik-ād, *n.* a barrier to keep back an enemy.—*v.* to put up a barrier: to make strong for defence.

bar'rier, *n.* something standing in the way (e.g. a strong fence to keep back a crowd).

bar'rister, *n.* a lawyer who defends people in court.

bar'row, *n.* a small hand-cart.

bar'row, *n.* a mound raised over graves in former times.

bar'ter, *v.* to give one thing in exchange for another.—*n.* trading by exchange of goods, instead of buying and selling.

bart'isan, bart'izan, *n.* a small overhanging turret.

basalt, bas-awlt', *n.* a hard, dark-coloured rock thrown up as lava from volcanoes.—*adj.* **basalt'ic.**

base, *n.* that on which a thing rests: a starting-place or stopping-place in games: place from which supplies and extra men are sent to a fighting army.—*v.* to use as a foundation (e.g. I *base* my opinion on what I have heard).—*adj.* **base'less,** without a foundation: untrue.—*n.* **base'ment,** the lowest storey of a building, esp. the storey below ground-level.

base, *adj.* low: mean: worthless.

base'-ball, *n.* a ball game, something like rounders, played in America.

bash, *v.* to beat or smash in.—Also *n.*

bash'ful, *adj.* shy.

basilisk, baz′il-isk, *n.* in fables, a beast whose look or breath killed : a kind of dragon.

basin, bās′n, *n.* a shallow dish : any large hollow holding water (e.g. a dock) : the land drained by a river and its tributaries.

basis, bās′is, *n.* that on which a thing rests : the foundation or beginning : — *pl.* **bās′es.** — *adj.* **bās′ic.**

bask, *v.* to lie in warmth.

bas′ket, *n.* a vessel made of plaited twigs or rushes.

bas-relief, ba-re-lēf′, *n.* in sculpture and carving, figures which stand out a little from the ground on which they are formed.

bass, bās, *n.* the low part in music : a male singer with a deep voice. — *adj.* low or deep in tone.

bass, basse, bas, *n.* a fish like the perch.

bassoon′, *n.* a musical instrument with low notes, played by blowing.

baste, bāst, *v.* to beat with a stick : to drop fat or butter over meat while roasting to keep it from burning : to sew loosely together with big stitches : to tack.

bastinado, bast-in-ād′o, *v.* to beat the soles of the feet with a stick.

bastion, bast′yun, *n.* a kind of tower at a bend in the wall of a fort.

bat, *n.* a shaped piece of wood for striking a ball in some games. — *v.* to use the bat in cricket. — *ns.* **bats′man,** one who wields the bat at cricket, etc.

bat, *n.* a flying animal with a mouse-like body.

batch, *n.* the quantity of bread baked at one time : a set, group, or bundle.

bā′ted, *adj.* lowered (e.g. *bated* breath).

bath, *n.* a vessel or other place containing water in which the body is washed. — *v.* to wash the body in a bath.

bāthe, *v.* to plunge in deep water (e.g. river, lake, sea) : to wash water gently over (a hurt). — *n.* **bāth′er.**

bat′man, *n.* an army officer's servant.

bat′on, *n.* a small wooden club carried by policemen : a light stick used by a band conductor.

battalion, bat-al′yun, *n.* a part of a regiment of foot-soldiers.

bat′ten, *v.* to grow fat.

bat′ten, *n.* a piece of board : in ships, a strip of wood used to fasten down the hatches.

bat′ter, *v.* to beat heavily. — *n.* a beaten-up mixture (such as flour and water) for cooking. — *n.* **bat′tering-ram,** in olden times, a war weapon for battering down walls ; it consisted of a large beam with an iron head like that of a ram.

bat′tery, *n.* a number of cannon : a number of connected cells for storing electricity.

battle, bat′l, *n.* a fight, esp. between armies. — Also *v.* — *ns.* **battle-axe ; battle-cry ; battlefield ; battleship.**

battledore, bat′l-dōr, *n.* a light bat for striking a ball or shuttlecock.

battlement, bat′l-ment, *n.* a wall on the top of a building, with openings or notches for firing from.

bauble, baw′bl, *n.* a child's plaything : a jester's stick, having a head and ass's ears on the end.

bawl, *v.* to shout or cry out loudly. — Also *n.*

bay, *adj.* reddish-brown. — *n.* a bay-coloured horse.

bay, *n.* an opening of the sea : an inward bend of the shore.

bay, *n.* the laurel-tree : a wreath of bay given as a prize.

bay, *n.* the sound of barking : the deep cry of hunting dogs. — Also *v.* — **to hold** (or **keep**) **at bay,** to keep an enemy at his distance ; **to stand** (or **be**) **at bay,** to turn and face an enemy near at hand.

bay′onet, *n.* a steel dagger that can be fixed to the muzzle of a rifle. — *v.* to stab with a bayonet.

bay′-win′dow, *n.* a window which juts out.

bazaar′, bazar′, *n.* in the East, a street of shops or a market-place : a shop : a sale of work.

beach, *n.* the shore of the sea or of a lake, esp. when sandy or pebbly. — *v.* to haul a boat up on the beach.

bea′con, *n.* a fire on a hill used as a sign of danger : anything that warns of danger (e.g. a light or other sign to mark rocks, street crossings, etc.).

bead, *n.* a small ball of glass, amber, etc. strung along with others to form a necklace.

beadle, bēd´l, *n.* a servant in a church, college, etc.: in Scotland, the church-officer.

beagle, bē´gl, *n.* a small hound used in hunting hares.

beak, *n.* the bill of a bird.

beak´er, *n.* a large drinking-bowl or cup: a chemist's measuring-glass.

beam, *n.* a large and straight piece of timber or iron: a ray of light: the greatest breadth of a ship.

bean, *n.* the name of several kinds of pod-bearing plants and their seeds.

bear, bār, *v.* to carry: to endure: to bring forth.—*adj.* **bear´able,** able to be borne or endured.—*ns.* **bear´er,** a carrier or messenger; **bear´ing,** behaviour: direction.

bear, bār, *n.* a heavy four-footed animal with long shaggy hair and hooked claws.—*ns.* **bear´-bait´ing.** See **bait;** **bear´skin,** the high fur cap worn by the Guards in the British Army.

beard, bērd, *n.* the hair that grows on the chin and cheeks.—*v.* to take by the beard: to face up to.

beast, *n.* a four-footed animal: a brutal person.—*adj.* **beast´ly,** like a beast in actions or behaviour: coarse.—*n.* **beast´liness.**

beat, *v.* to strike again and again: to overcome or defeat: to throb: to rouse birds by hitting the bushes, heather, etc. with sticks. —*n.* a stroke: a round or course (e.g. a policeman's *beat*).—*adj.* **beat´en,** made smooth or hard by beating: worn by use: defeated.

beatify, bē-at´i-fī, *v.* to make blessed or happy.—*adj.* **beatif´ic,** very happy.

Beatitudes, bē-at´i-tūdz, *n.pl.* the sayings of Christ (Matt. v.) as to who are the happiest people.

beat´nik, *n.* one who likes untidy dress and unconventional ways.

beauty, bū´ti, *n.* pleasing appearance (e.g. of a person or thing), or pleasing sound (e.g. of music, poetry, voices, etc.): anything graceful or very good: a fine-looking woman.—*adjs.* **beau´tiful, beau´teous.**—*v.* **beau´tify,** to make beautiful.

beav´er, *n.* a large gnawing animal, which lives both on land and in water: a hat or glove made of beaver fur.

becalm, be-kahm´, *v.* to make calm, still, or quiet.—*adj.* **becalmed,** (of a sailing-ship) unable to move for want of wind.

because, bē-kawz´, *conj.* by reason of the fact that.

beck´on, *v.* to make a sign to.—**at a person's beck and call,** always willing to act the slave to a person.

become, be-kum´, *v.* to pass from one state to another: to come to be: to suit.—*adj.* **becom´ing,** suitable: graceful.

bed, *n.* a place on which to rest or sleep: a plot in a garden: the bottom of a river.—*ns.* **bed´ding,** mattress, bed-clothes, etc.: straw, etc. for cattle to lie on; **bed´-rock,** the solid rock farthest from the surface of the ground; **bed´room,** a room for sleeping; **bed´stead,** a frame for supporting a bed.—*adj.* **bed´ridden,** kept in bed by sickness or illness.

bedaub, *v.* to smear (with paint, etc.).

bedeck´, *v.* to adorn.

bediz´en, *v.* to dress in gay colours.

bed´lam, *n.* an asylum for mad persons: a noisy place.

Bedouin, bed´oo-in, *n.* a desert Arab who leads a roaming life.

bedraggle, be-drag´l, *v.* to soil by dragging in the wet or dirt.—*adj.* **bedrag´gled,** untidy.

bee, *n.* a four-winged insect that makes honey.—*ns.* **bee´hive,** a case or box in which bees are kept; **bee´-line,** the shortest road from one place to another; **bees´wax,** the wax made by bees, and used by them in forming their cells.

beech, *n.* a common forest tree whose wood is hard and useful.

beef, *n.* the flesh of an ox or cow:— *pl.* **beeves, oxen.**—*ns.* **beef´-eat´ers,** certain men, wearing old-time dress, who act as guards for the Queen and the Tower of London; **beef´steak** (-stāk), a thick slice of beef for cooking; **beef´tea,** food for the sick and ill, made from the strained juice of beef.—*adj.* **beefy,** fleshy: stout and strong.

beer, *n.* a drink made from barley flavoured with hops.

beet, *n.* a carrot-shaped plant whose root (**beetroot**) is eaten. Sugar is got from *white beet.*

beetle, bē'tl, *n.* an insect with four wings, the front pair forming hard covers for those behind.

bee'tle, *n.* a heavy wooden hammer used for beating down paving-stones, etc. : a wooden masher.

bee'tle, *v.* to jut, to hang over.—*adj.* **beetle-browed,** frowning.

befall', *v.* to happen.

befit', *v.* to fit, to be suitable for.—*adj.* **befit'ting,** suitable.

befogged, be-fogd', *adj.* wrapped in fog : confused.

before, be-fōr', *prep.* and *adv.* in front of : earlier or sooner (than).—*adv.* **before'hand,** before the time.

befriend, be-frend', *v.* to act as a friend to.

beg, *v.* to ask money from : to ask earnestly : to pray.—*n.* **beg'gar,** one who begs : a mean fellow : a poor fellow.—*v.* to make poor : to go beyond (e.g. The scene *beggared* description).—*adj.* **beg'garly,** poor : mean : worthless.

beget', *v.* to bring into life : to bring forth : to cause.

begin', *v.* to take rise : to enter on something new : to commence.

begird', *v.* to put a girdle or belt round : to surround.—*adj.* **begirt',** surrounded : shut in.

begone, be-gon', be off !

begrime, *v.* to make dirty.

begrudge, be-gruj', *v.* to grudge : to envy someone because of something he has.

beguile, be-gīl', *v.* to cheat : to pass (time) pleasantly.

behalf, be-haf', used in the phrase **on (or in) behalf of,** instead of : in aid of : on the side of.

behave, be-hāv', *v.* to conduct one's self, esp. to conduct one's self well : to act.—*n.* **behaviour** (be-hāv'yur), conduct : good conduct.

behead, -hed', *v.* to cut off the head.

behest', *n.* command.

behind, be-hind', *prep.* and *adv.* at or towards the back (of).—*adv.* **behind'hand,** late.—**behind the times,** not up-to-date.

behold, be-hōld', *v.* to look at or on :

to see.—*adj.* **behold'en,** forced to feel grateful because of a good turn done.—**Behold!** Look! See!

behove, behoove, be-hoov', *v.* to be right or necessary for—now only used with *it* (e.g. It *behoves* us to be careful, i.e. we must be careful).

belabour, be-lā'bur, *v.* to beat or thrash soundly.

belated, be-lā'ted, *adj.* arriving late.

belay', *v.* (used by sailors) to wind a rope round a wooden peg (*belaying-pin*) so that it cannot slip.

belch, *v.* to cast up or throw off.

beldam, beldame, bel'dam, *n.* an ugly old woman : a witch.

beleaguer, be-lēg'er, *v.* to surround a city to make it give in.

bel'fry, *n.* the part of a steeple or tower in which the bells are hung.

belie, be-lī', *v.* to be false to : to show something to be wrong.

believe, be-lēv', *v.* to think of as true : to trust (in) : to think or suppose.—*n.* **belief,** what we think to be true : faith.—*adjs.* **believ'able ; believ'ing,** trustful.—**to make believe,** to pretend.

belit'tle, *v.* to make small : to scoff at.

bell, *n.* a hollow vessel of metal which gives forth a ringing sound when struck by the tongue or clapper inside.—*ns.* **bell'-tent,** a bell-shaped tent ; **bell'-tow'er,** a tower built to contain bells.

belle, bel, *n.* a good-looking woman.

bellicose, bel'ik-ōs, *adj.* quarrelsome : warlike.

belligerent, bel-ij'er-ent, *adj.* carrying on war.—*n.* a nation or person carrying on a war or fight.

bellow, bel'lō, *v.* to roar like a bull : to shout aloud.—Also *n.*

bellows, bel'lōz, *n.pl.* an instrument for making a blast of air.

bel'ly, *n.* the part of the body between the chest and the thighs, containing the bowels.—*v.* to swell or bulge out.

belong, *v.* to be one's property : to be born in, or have a home in (e.g. He *belongs* to London).—*n.pl.* **belong'ings,** what one possesses : what is one's own.

beloved, be-luvd' or be-luv'ed, *adj.* much loved, very dear.—Also *n.*

belt, *n.* a girdle or band : a strong leather band connecting moving wheels in machinery : a broad strip of anything which holds or keeps in.—*v.* to put a belt round : to thrash with a belt.—*adj.* **belt'ed,** wearing a belt.

bemoan', *v.* to weep about.

ben, *n.* a mountain peak (in Scotland).

bench, bensh, *n.* a long seat : a work-table : the judges of a court.

bend, *v.* to curve : to turn : to strain one's self to.—*n.* a turn (e.g. in a road).

benediction, ben-e-dik'shun, *n.* a prayer asking for God's blessing : a blessing.

benefaction, ben-e-fak'shun, *n.* the act of doing good : a good deed.—*n.* **benefac'tor,** one who does good to another.

beneficence, be-nef'i-sens, *n.* goodness : kindness.—*adj.* **benef'icent,** kindly.

beneficial, ben-e-fish'al, *adj.* useful : bringing gain.—*n.* **benefic'iary,** a person who has money left to him by will.

ben'efit, *n.* profit : a favour : money received under an insurance plan (e.g. unemployment *benefit*, sickness *benefit*).—*v.* to do good to : to gain advantage.

benev'olence, *n.* will to do good : a kind act.—*adj.* **benev'olent,** kindly.

benighted, be-nīt'ed, *adj.* overtaken by night : having no learning.

benign, ben-īn', *adj.* gentle : gracious : kindly.—*adj.* **benig'nant,** kind : gracious.—*n.* **benig'nity,** goodness of nature : kindness.

ben'ison, *n.* a blessing.

bent, *n.* a natural liking.

bent, *n.* a stiff or wiry grass.

benumb, be-num', *v.* to deaden (e.g. with cold) : to make powerless.

benzene, ben'zēn, *n.* a clear liquid, easily taking fire, obtained when gas is made from coal.—*n.* **benzine** (ben'zēn), a kind of petrol.

bequeath, be-kwēth', *v.* to leave by will.—*n.* **bequest** (be-kwest'), the money, etc. left by a will.

berate', *v.* to scold.

bereave', *v.* to rob a person of anything valued.—*adjs.* **bereaved',**

s.d.—2

robbed by death of some dear relative or friend ; **bereft',** robbed of.—*n.* **bereave'ment.**

beret, ber'ā, *n.* a flat, round cap.

ber'ry, *n.* **a juicy fruit enclosing the seeds.**

berth, *n.* a room or sleeping-place in a ship, sleeping-carriage, etc. : a situation, job, or place of work : the place where a ship is tied up in a dock.—*v.* to moor a ship : to give a berth to.—**to give a wide berth to,** to keep well away from.

beryl, ber'il, *n.* a precious stone like an emerald.

beseech', *v.* to ask or pray earnestly.

beset', *v.* to set upon from all sides : to surround.

beshrew, be-shroo', *v.* to call down evil upon : to curse.

beside', *prep.* and *adv.* by the side of, near : over and above : apart from.—**to be beside one's self,** to be out of one's senses.

besides', *prep.* and *adv.* in addition to : over and above.

besiege, be-sēj', *v.* to set an army around or before (a fortress or town) in the hope of capturing it : to crowd round.—*n.* **besie'ger.**

besmirch', *v.* to make dirty : to stain (e.g. a person's name).

besom, bē'zum, *n.* a broom.

besot'ted, *adj.* dull, stupid, foolish.

bespat'ter, *v.* to sprinkle with dirt.

bespeak, be-spēk', *v.* to speak for : to order beforehand.

best, *adj.,* good in the highest degree.—*v.* to defeat.—**best man,** see under groom.

best'ial, *adj.* like a beast : beastly.

bestir', *v.* to waken up, make lively.

bestow, be-stō', *v.* to give.—*n.* **bestow'al.**

bestride', *v.* to stand or sit over with a leg on each side.

bet, *n.* money put down to support one's opinion (e.g. as to which horse will win a race, etc.).—Also *v.*

betake', *v.* (with *one's self*) to go.

bethink', *v.* to try to remember.

betide', *v.* to happen to.

betimes', *adv.* in good time : early : at the right time.

betoken, be-tō'kn, *v.* to show by a sign : to show beforehand.

betray', v. to give up (e.g. secrets, one's friends, etc.) to an enemy shamefully: to show.—n. **betray'al.**

betrŏth, v. to promise in marriage.—n. **betrŏthal**, promise of marriage.

bet'ter, adj. good in a higher degree.—v. to improve.—**to get the better of**, to defeat, to overcome.

between', prep. and adv., in the middle of two persons, places, or times.—Also **betwixt'.**

bev'el, n. a slanting edge (e.g. of a toothed wheel, mirror, etc.).

beverage, bev'er-āj, n. a drink, esp a pleasant or strengthening one.

bev'y, n. a flock, esp. of birds.

bewail', v. to mourn loudly over.

beware', v. to be on one's guard: to be watchful for danger.

bewil'der, v. to puzzle: to confuse.—n. **bewil'derment**, confusion.

bewitch', v. to put under a spell: to charm.—adj. **bewitch'ing**, charming: very beautiful.

beyond', prep. farther than: too far gone for (e.g. broken beyond repair, lost beyond recall).—Also adv.

bi'as, n. a weight on one side of a bowl (in the game of bowls), making it lean or turn to one side: a leaning to one side (esp. in a person's opinions).—v. to make to lean to one side.

Bible, bī'bl, n. the holy book of the Christian Church.—adj. **Bib'lical.**

bibliography, bib-li-og'raf-i, n. the knowledge of books, their authors, subjects, etc.: a list of books about a subject.—n. **bibliog'rapher.**

bibliophile, bib'li-ō-fīl, n. a lover of books, esp. of rare books.

bibulous, bib'ū-lus, adj. fond of drinking: thirsty.

bĭcentē'nary, n. the two hundredth year after an event.

biceps, bī'seps, n. the muscle in front of the upper part of the arm.

bick'er, v. to quarrel over small matters: to move quickly, as running water.—Also n.

bicycle, bī'si-kl, n. a cycle with two wheels.

bid, v. to offer: to invite: to command: to offer to pay at a sale.—n. an offer of a price: a bold try.

biennial, bī-en'yal, adj. lasting two years: happening once in two years.—n. a plant that flowers only in its second year, then dies.

bier, bēr, n. a carriage or frame of wood for carrying a dead body.

big'amy, n. the crime of having two wives or two husbands at once.—n. **big'amist.**—adj. **big'amous.**

bight, bīt, n. a small bay.

big'ot, n. one who too strongly believes or supports anything (e.g. an opinion about religion).—n. **big'otry.**

bil'berry, n. a plant with a dark-blue berry, called also whortleberry and, in Scotland, blaeberry.

bile, n. a fluid coming from the liver: bad humour.—adj. **bil'ious**, ill with bile: sick: greenish-yellow in colour.—n. **bil'iousness.**

bilge, bilj, n. the bulging part of a cask: the broadest part of a ship's bottom.—n. **bilge-water** or **bilge**, water which lies in the ship's bottom: anything evil-smelling.

bilingual, bī-ling'gwal, adj. speaking two languages.

bilk, v. to dodge: to cheat.

bill, n. a battle-axe: a hatchet with a long blade: the beak of a bird: an account for money: a law before it has been talked over and declared: a printed sheet or advertisement.

bil'let, n. a short note or letter: a small log for the fire: a lodging, esp. for soldiers.—v. to lodge (soldiers) in private houses.

billiards, bil'yardz, n. a game played with a stick (cue) and balls on a table which has six pockets.

billion, bil'yun, n. as used in Britain, France, etc., a million millions (1,000,000,000,000); in U.S.A., a thousand millions (1,000,000,000).

billow, bil'ō, n. a great wave.—adj. **bill'owy.**

bin, n. a place for storing corn, wine, etc., or for holding dust and ashes.

bind, bīnd, v. to tie with a band: to fasten together: to make to promise: to hold firmly.—n. **bind'ing**, the act of binding: anything that binds: the covering of a book.

bing, n. a heap or pile.

binnacle, bin'a-kl, n. (on ships) the box in which the compass is kept.

binoculars, bin-ok'ū-lars, *n.pl.* a telescope having two eye-pieces.

biography, bī-og'raf-i, *n.* a written account of the life of a person.— *n.* biog'rapher, one who writes biography.—*adj.* biograph'ical.

biology, bī-ol'oj-i, *n.* the science that deals with living things.— *adj.* biolog'ical.—*n.* biol'ogist.

bi'ped, *n.* an animal with two feet.

birch, *n.* a hard-wood tree : a switch of birch twigs, used for flogging.—*v.* to flog.

bird, *n.* a feathered, egg-laying creature.—bird of prey. See prey ; bird's-eye view, a wide view, as would be seen from above.

birth'day, *n.* the day on which one is born : the day of the same date each year.—*n.* birth'right, the right which one may claim because of one's birth.

biscuit, bis'kit, *n.* bread baked hard in small cakes, and usually sweetened or flavoured.—*adj.* pale brown in colour.

bisect', *v.* to cut in two equal parts.

bish'op, *n.* a clergyman of high rank (next to an archbishop) in the Church of England and Roman Catholic Church.—*n.* bish'opric, the district ruled by a bishop.

bison, bī'son, *n.* a large wild animal like a bull : an American buffalo.

bit, *n.* a small piece : a small tool for boring : the part of the bridle which the horse holds in its mouth.

bite, *v.* to seize or tear with the teeth.—*n.* a grasp by the teeth : the amount torn away : (in fishing) a nibble at the bait.

bit'ter, *adj.* sharp, esp. to the taste : unpleasant : painful.

bit'tern, *n.* a bird like a heron.

bivouac, biv'oo-ak, *n.* a rest for the night in the open air.—*v.* to pass the night in the open air.

bi-weekly, *adj.* happening twice a week or once every two weeks.

bizarre, bi-zar', *adj.* odd : strange.

blab, *v.* to talk much : to let out a secret.

black, *adj.* — *ns.* black'amoor, a black man, negro ; black'berry, the berry of the bramble ; black'-cock, a kind of grouse ; black-guard (blag'ard), a wicked person, rogue, sneak ; black'lead, a black

mineral (not lead) used in making pencils, etc. ; black'leg, one who works when his comrades are on strike ; blackmailer, a person who says he will let out a secret unless paid money (called black-mail) to keep quiet ; black market, illegal or dishonest buying and selling ; black-out, darkness caused by the putting out of all lights ; black'smith, a man who makes articles of iron.

blad'der, *n.* a thin bag of skin or rubber.

blade, *n.* the leaf of grass or corn : the cutting part of a knife, sword, etc. : the flat part of an oar.

blaeberry, blā'ber-i. See bilberry.

blame, *v.* to find fault with.—*n.* fault. —*adjs.* blam'able ; blame'less ; blame'worthy.

blanc-mange, bla-mawngzh', *n.* a jelly-pudding made with milk.

bland, *adj.* smooth : gentle : mild.

bland'ish, *v.* to flatter and coax.— *n.* bland'ishment.

blank, *adj.* without writing or marks (e.g. *blank* paper) : empty.— *n.* an empty space.—*ns.* blank'-cart'ridge, a cartridge without a bullet ; blank-verse, poetry without rhyme.

blank'et, *n.* a woollen bed-covering.

blare, *v.* to sound loudly.—Also *n.*

blar'ney, *n.* flattery or coaxing talk. —*v.* to cheat with such talk.

blaspheme, blas-fēm', *v.* to speak lightly or wickedly of God : to curse and swear. — *ns.* blas-phem'er ; blas'phemy.—*adj.* blas'-phemous.

blast, *n.* a blowing or gust of wind : a loud note on a trumpet : an explosion.—*v.* to blow with great force : to break (stones, a bridge, etc.) by explosion : to curse.—*n.* blast'-fur'nace, a furnace (e.g. one used in iron-smelting) into which hot air is blown.

blātant, *adj.* noisy : loud : showy.

blaze, *n.* a rush of light or of flame : a mark made on a tree by cutting off a strip of bark.—*v.* to burn with a flame : to throw out light : to mark trees in passing in order to show which way one has gone. —*n.* blaz'er, a sports jacket of bright colour.

blazon, blā′zn, v. to make known:
to show off.—n. blaz′onry, the art
of drawing coats of arms.

bleach′, v. to whiten.—ns. bleach′-
field, bleach′ing-green, a place
for bleaching cloth.

bleak, adj. dull and cheerless: cold,
unsheltered.—n. bleak′ness.

blear, adj. sore or inflamed (e.g.
blear-eyed).

bleat, v. to cry as a sheep.—Also n.

bleb, n. a blister.

bleed, v. to lose blood: to draw
blood from.—n. bleed′ing, a flow
of blood.

blem′ish, n. a stain: a fault or flaw.
—v. to stain.

blench, blensh, v. to start back.

blend, v. to mix together.—Also n.

bless, v. to make happy: to wish
happiness to: to praise.—adj.
bless′ed, happy: prosperous.—n.
bless′ing, a wish or prayer for
happiness or success: any means
or cause of happiness.

blight, blīt, n. a disease in plants
which withers them: anything
that destroys.—v. to destroy.

blind, adj. without sight: unable
to look ahead.—n. a window-
screen: a shade: something
which leads astray.—v. to make
blind: to dazzle.—n. blind′ness.
—adj. blind′fold, having the eyes
bandaged, so as not to see.—n.
blind′-alley, a street open only at
one end: a job that leads nowhere.

blink, v. to wink: to see with
the eyes half-closed: to shine
unsteadily.—n. a glimpse, glance,
or wink: a gleam of light.—n.pl.
blink′ers, pieces of leather over a
horse's eyes to prevent it seeing
in any direction except in front.

bliss, n. very great happiness:
heaven.—adj. bliss′ful.

blis′ter, n. a thin bubble on the skin
full of watery matter.—v. to raise
a blister.

blithe, blīth, adj. happy: gay: lively.
—adj. blithe′some, joyous.

bliz′zard, n. a blinding storm of
wind and snow.

bloat, v. to swell or puff out.—adj.
bloat′ed, puffed and swollen in
appearance.

bloat′er, n. a smoked herring.

blob, n. a drop of liquid.

block, n. a lump of wood, stone,
etc.: the wood on which persons
are beheaded: a group of houses:
large pulley.—v. to bar the way.
—n. block′head, a stupid fellow.

blockade, blok-ād′, v. to surround a
fort or country so that food and
supplies cannot reach it.—Also n.

blonde, n. a woman of fair skin and
light-coloured hair.

blood, blud, n. the red liquid in the
veins of men and animals: one's
descent or parentage (e.g. He
is of royal blood).—adjs. blood′y;
blood′less; blood′-thirsty, cruel,
eager to kill; blood′-shot, marked
with blood.—ns. blood′-horse, a
pure-bred horse; blood′-hound,
a large dog, with a keen scent,
used for tracking; blood′shed,
the spilling of blood: slaughter;
blood′-vessel, a vein (of the body)
in which the blood travels.

bloom, v. to put forth blossoms: to
flower.—n. a blossom or flower:
rosy colour.

blos′som, n. a flower-bud: the
flowers on a fruit-tree.—v. to put
forth blossoms or flowers.

blot, n. a spot or stain.—v. to spot
or stain: to dry writing with
blotting-paper.

blotch, n. a dark spot on the skin.—
v. to mark with blotches.—adjs.
blotched, blotch′y.

blouse, blowz, n. a loose outer garment, tucked in at the waist.

blow, blō, n. a stroke or knock: a
sudden piece of bad luck.

blow, blō, v. to bloom or blossom.

blow, blō, v. (of air or wind) to
move: to drive air upon or
into: to breathe hard or with
difficulty: to boast.—adj. blow′y,
windy.—to blow up, to destroy
by explosion.

blub′ber, n. the fat of whales and
other sea animals.—v. to weep.

bludgeon, bluj′n, n. a short stick
with a heavy end.

blue, bloo, n. the colour of the sky
when clear: a person who is one
of the best players of a game at
a university.—ns. blue′bell, the
wild hyacinth: the harebell;
blue′-bottle, a large fly often seen
in houses; blue′-jacket, a sailor
in the navy; blue′-pē′ter, a blue

flag with white centre, hoisted when a ship is about to sail; **blue'-print,** a sketch plan of work to be done; **blue'-stocking,** a learned lady.

bluff, *adj.* rough and jolly in manners : outspoken : steep.—*n.* a high steep bank overlooking the sea or a river : boasting.—*v.* to deceive.

blun'der, *v.* to make a bad mistake. —Also *n.*

blun'derbuss, *n.* a short hand-gun with a wide mouth.

blunt, *adj.* having an edge or point that is not sharp : rough in manner.—*v.* to dull the edge or point : to weaken.

blur, *n.* a blot, stain, or spot.— Also *v.*

blurt, *v.* to speak without thinking.

blush, *n.* a red glow on the face caused by shame, etc. : any reddish colour.—*v.* to show shame or confusion by growing red in the face : to grow red.

blus'ter, *v.* to make a noise like a blast of wind : to boast : to bully. —*n.* a blast or roaring as of the wind : boasting language.

boa, bō'a, *n.* a certain kind of serpent (such as the **boa-constric'tor),** which kills its prey by winding itself round it and crushing it : a long scarf of fur or feathers.

boar, bōr, *n.* the male pig.

board, bōrd, *n.* a broad and thin strip of timber : a table to put food on : food : the persons who are appointed to look after a business, public service, etc. (e.g. *Board* of Trade, Governors) : the deck of a ship : stiff paper used in the binding of books.—*v.* to cover with boards : to supply with food at fixed terms : to enter a ship : to attack.—*ns.* **board'er,** one who receives board (food) ; **board'ing-house,** a house where boarders are kept ; **board'ing-school,** a school in which board (food) is given as well as lessons.

boast, *v.* to brag, to speak proudly, esp. of one's self.—*n.* something said in a bragging or boasting manner : a person who brags or boasts.—*adj.* **boast'ful,** fond of bragging.

boat, *n.* a vessel for sailing, a ship : a boat-shaped dish (e.g. a *sauce-boat).*—*v.* to sail about in a boat.

boatswain, bō'sn, *n.* an officer who looks after a ship's boats, rigging, flags, etc.—often shortened to **bō'sun.**

bob'bin, *n.* a small piece of wood on which thread is wound.

bode, *v.* to foretell : to be a sign of.

bodice, bod'is, *n.* a woman's garment.

bod'kin, *n.* a small dagger : a large blunt needle.

bod'y, *n.* the main part of a man or animal : the main part of anything : a person : a number of persons gathered together.—*adj.* and *adv.* **bod'ily,** having to do with the body (not with the mind).—*n.* **bod'yguard,** a guard to protect a person (such as a king) from attack.

bog, *n.* soft ground : a marsh.

bogey, bōg'i, *n.* a goblin : something greatly feared.

bog'gle, *v.* to be shy at starting something : to jump with fright.—*n.* **bogg'ler,** one who is in doubt : one who makes a bad job of something.

bogie, bogey, bōg'i, *n.* a low truck : an under-carriage, as in a railway engine.

bogle, bōg'l, *n.* a ghost or goblin : a scarecrow.

bō'gus, *adj.* false.

boil, *v.* to bubble up owing to heat : to heat until boiling takes place : to be excited.

boil, *n.* a reddened and swollen sore.

boisterous, bois'ter-us, *adj.* wild : noisy : stormy.

bōld, *adj.* daring, full of courage : cheeky.—*adj.* **bold'-faced,** cheeky.

bole, *n.* the trunk of a tree.

bōl'ster, *n.* a long round pillow or cushion.—*v.* to support.

bōlt, *n.* an iron screw used to fasten a door, etc. : an arrow : a thunderbolt.—*v.* to fasten with a bolt : to swallow hurriedly : to rush away.—*adv.* **bolt'-up'-right,** upright and straight as an arrow.

bomb, bom, *n.* a case containing material that explodes or causes fires or does other damage.—*v.* **bombard',** to attack with shells or bombs.—*ns.* **bombardier, -dēr',** the bomb-aimer in a bombing-aeroplane: an artillery-man next in rank above a gunner; **bombard'ment; bomb'er,** an aeroplane fitted for dropping bombs; **bomb'-shell,** a bomb: a startling piece of news.

bom'bast, *n.* high-sounding language.—*adj.* **bombas'tic,** high-sounding but not meaning much.

bonbon, bong'bong, *n.* a sweet.

bond, *n.* that which binds: a written promise to pay or do something: a building or ware-house where spirits, tobacco, etc. are kept until the taxes are paid for them.—*v.* to put into such a warehouse. — *ns.* **bond'maid, bond'man,** a servant; **bond'age,** slavery.

bone, *n.* a hard material forming the skeleton of animals.—*v.* to take the bones out of meat.—*adj.* **bon'y,** full of bones: made of bone.—*n.* **bone'-set'ter,** one who puts together broken legs, arms, etc., so that they may heal.

bon'fire, *n.* a large fire in the open air.

bon'net, *n.* a woman's hat of the old-style: a soft cap: the cover-ing over a motor-car engine.

bon'ny, *adj.* good-looking.

bonspiel, bon'spēl, *n.* curling match.

bō'nus, *n.* an extra payment (e.g. of wages) given as a gift.

boo'by, *n.* a silly or stupid fellow.— **booby prize,** a prize for the person who is last in a competition; **booby trap,** something placed above a door, so that it falls when a person enters.

book, *n.* printed pages bound to-gether for reading: the Bible. —*v.* to order beforehand (e.g. *Book* two seats for the circus next Monday).—*n.* **book'worm,** a per-son who reads many books.

boom, *n.* a pole by which a sail is stretched: a barrier across a harbour or river-mouth.

boom, *v.* to make a hollow sound or roar: to become rich or success-ful all of a sudden: to push something into people's notice.— *n.* a loud, hollow sound: a rush or increase of trade.

boom'erang, *n.* a curved wooden stick used by natives of Australia in hunting game (if missing the mark when thrown, it returns to the thrower).

boon, *n.* something very much asked for: a gift: favour.

boon, *adj.* gay, merry: kind.

boor, *n.* a countryman, a peasant: a coarse or awkward person.— *adj.* **boor'ish.**

boot, *n.* a covering for the foot and lower part of the leg, generally made of leather: an instrument of torture, in which the legs were forced into a strong case and crushed.—*v.* to kick.—*ns.* **boot'-jack,** an instrument for taking off boots; **boots,** a servant at a hotel who cleans the boots, runs errands, etc.

boot, *v.* to bring profit to: to be of use to.—*adj.* **boot'less,** without profit: useless.

booth, *n.* a hut: a covered stall at a fair or market.

boot'y, *n.* plunder taken in war or by force.

bor'der, *n.* the edge or margin of anything: the boundary of a country, esp. that between Eng-land and Scotland: a flower-bed in a garden.—*v.* to be near to: to put an edging round.

bore, *v.* to make a hole by piercing: to weary or annoy.—*n.* a hole made by boring: the size across the tube of a gun: a person or thing that wearies.—*n.* **bore'-dom,** weariness.

bore, *n.* a flood or wave which at high tide rushes with great force up the mouths of certain rivers.

boreas, bō're-as, *n.* the north wind.

borough, bur'ō, *n.* a town which has a mayor and town council: a town which sends a member or members to the House of Com-mons (*parliamentary borough*).

borrow, bor'ō, *v.* to get from another on loan.—*adj.* **borr'owed,** taken on loan: pretended, false.

bor'zoi, *n.* a dog like the grey-hound but with a long-haired coat.

bosh, *n.* nonsense : foolish talk.

bosom, booz'um, *n.* the breast.—*adj.* close (e.g. a *bosom* friend).

boss, *n.* a knob or stud.

boss, *n.* a leader or master.—*v.* to manage, order about.

bosun. See **boatswain.**

bot'any, *n.* the branch of knowledge connected with plants.—*adjs.* **botan'ic, botan'ical.**—*n.* **bot'anist,** one who studies botany.—**botanic garden,** a large public garden where plants and trees of different countries are grown for show.

botch, *n.* work badly done.—*v.* to mend clumsily : to do badly.

both'er, *v.* to be a nuisance to : to trouble.—*n.* **bother,** trouble.

both'y, both'ie, *n.* a hut : a sleeping-place for navvies, workers, etc.

bottle, bot'l, *n.* a hollow vessel (with a narrow opening) for holding liquids.—*v.* to put in a bottle : to shut up in a narrow space.

bot'tom, *n.* the lowest part of anything.—*adj.* **bott'omless.**

boudoir, bood'war, *n.* a lady's private room.

bough, bow, *n.* a branch of a tree.

boulder, bōld'er, *n.* a large stone, esp. one made round by water.

boulevard, bool'e-var, *n.* a broad walk or avenue, bordered with trees.

bounce, bowns, *v.* to jump or spring suddenly : to boast.—Also *n.*— *adj.* **bounc'ing,** large and heavy : strong.

bound, bownd, *n.* an edge or border (often used in *pl.*).—*v.* to mark a limit (e.g. The sea *bounds* Britain). —*adj.* **bound'less.**—*n.* **bound'ary,** something marking the edge or border (e.g. of a playing-field).

bound, bownd, *v.* to spring or leap. —Also *n.*

bound, bownd, *adj.* ready to go, going (e.g. He is *bound* for London) : forced to : sure to.

bounty, bown'ti, *n.* a gift : kindness : money given as a help.— *adjs.* **boun'teous, boun'tiful,** giving plentifully.

bouquet, book'ā, *n.* a bunch of flowers.

bourgeois, boorzh'wa, *n.* a citizen : one of the middle class : a merchant or shopkeeper.—*n.* **bour-** **geoisie** (boorzh'waw-zē), the middle class of citizens.

bout, bowt, *n.* a fight or trial of strength (e.g. boxing, fencing, illness, etc.).

bovine, bō'vīn, *adj.* having to do with cattle : like cattle : stupid.

bow, *v.* to bend in greeting a person : to give in : to crush.—*n.* a bending of the head or body as a sign of respect or welcome.

bow, bō, *n.* a weapon for shooting arrows, made of a stick of springy wood bent by a string : looped knot : the stick by which the strings of a violin are played.— *adj.* **bow'-legged,** having legs bent like a bow.—*ns.* **bow'shot,** the distance to which an arrow can be shot from a bow ; **bow-win-dow,** a window built in a curve.

bow, *n.* the front part of a ship (often used in *pl.*).

bow'els, *n.pl.* the inmost parts of the body.

bow'er, *n.* a shady spot in a garden : an inner room.

bowl, bōl, *n.* a basin for kitchen use.

bowls, bōls, *n.pl.* a game played on a green, heavy balls (*bowls*) being rolled towards a smaller white ball, called a *jack*.—*v.* **to bowl,** to play at bowls : to move speedily like a bowl : (in cricket) to send the ball at the wicket : to put out a batsman by knocking his wicket with the ball.—*n.* **bowl'er,** one who bowls : a black hat with a rounded top.—**to bowl over,** to knock down.

bowsprit, bō'sprit, *n.* a strong spar jutting out over the bows of a sailing-ship.

box, *n.* a hard-wood tree : a case for holding anything : in a theatre, private closed-in seats : the driver's seat on a carriage.— *n.* **Box'ing-day,** the day after Christmas Day.—**to box the compass,** to name the 32 points of the compass in order.

box, *v.* to strike with the hand or fist.—*n.* **box'ing,** a sport consisting of fighting with the fists, padded gloves being worn.

boy, *n.* a male child : a native servant.

boy'cott, *v.* to refuse to deal with (e.g. a merchant), usually in revenge for unfriendly act.—Also *n.*

brace, *n.* anything that draws together and holds tightly : a pair or couple : a carpenter's tool used in boring : (*pl.*) straps for holding up the trousers : ropes for the masts of a ship.—*v.* to tighten or strengthen, to give firmness to.—*adj.* **brac'ing,** giving strength.

bracelet, brās'let, *n.* an ornament for the wrist.

brack'en, *n.* a coarse kind of fern.

brack'et, *n.* a support for something fastened to a wall : (*pl.*) marks used in printing—( ), [ ].

brack'ish, *adj.* (of water) rather salt.

brad, *n.* a small nail.—*n.* **brad'awl,** a tool to pierce holes.

brae, brā, *n.* (in Scotland) a hill-slope.

brag, *v.* to boast.—*adj.* **brag'gart,** boastful.—*n.* a vain boaster.

braggadocio, brag-a-dō'shi-o, *n.* one who boasts much : empty boasting.

Brah'man, Brah'min, *n.* among the Hindus of India, a member of the highest or priestly class.

braid, *v.* to plait or twine together. —*n.* cord made by plaiting.

braille, brāl, *n.* raised marks on paper which blind people can read by feeling.

brain, *n.* the part of the body inside the skull, the centre of feeling and thinking.—*v.* to dash out the brains.—*adjs.* **brainy,** clever. —*n.* **brain'washing,** gradually forcing a person to change his views.

braise, brāz, *v.* to stew meat in little liquid.

brake, *n.* a thicket.

brake, *n.* a part of a bicycle, motorcar, train, etc., used for slowing down the speed.

bram'ble, *n.* the blackberry bush and its fruit.

bran, *n.* the outer skin of grain.

branch, bransh, *n.* a shoot or arm-like limb of a tree : a small shop, bank, library, etc. belonging to a bigger one.—*v.* to divide into branches : to spread out like a branch.

brand, *n.* a burning piece of wood : a mark burned into anything with a hot iron : a make of goods having a special brand or mark : a sword : a mark of disgrace.—*v.* to burn or mark with a hot iron : to fix a mark of disgrace upon. —*adj.* **brand'-new,** quite new.

brand'ish, *v.* to wave.

brand'y, *n.* a strong drink.

brass, *n.* metal made by mixing copper and zinc.

brat, *n.* a scornful name for a child.

brava'do, *n.* a show of bravery : a boastful threat.

brave, *adj.* daring : noble : finely dressed : handsome.—*v.* to meet boldly : to defy.—*n.* a Red Indian warrior.—*n.* **brā'very.**

Brav'o! Well done ! Excellent !

brawl, *n.* a noisy quarrel.—Also *v.*

brawn, *n.* muscle : strength : a mixture of meat made from pig's head and ox-feet.—*adj.* **brawn'y,** big and strong.

bray, *n.* a cry like that of the ass : the sound of a trumpet.—Also *v.*

braze, *v.* to patch with melted brass. —*adj.* **brā'zen** or of like brass : impudent.—*v.* **brā'zen,** to behave cheekily.—*ns.* **brā'zen-face,** one having an impudent face ; **brā'-zier, brā'sier,** a pan for holding burning coals : one who works in brass.

breach, *n.* a break or opening (e.g. in the walls of a fort) : a breaking of a law, of a promise, etc. : a quarrel.—*v.* to make a break or opening in a wall.

bread, bred, *n.* food made of flour or meal baked : food : means of living.—*n.* **bread'-winner,** one who earns a living for a family.

breadth, bredth, *n.* distance from side to side : width.

break, brāk, *v.* to dash in pieces : to tame (a horse).—*ns.* **break'age,** the act of breaking : the thing broken ; **break'-down,** an illness, such as that caused by working too hard : the stopping of a machine or motor, etc. (e.g. owing to engine trouble) ; **break'er,** a wave broken on rocks or the shore ; **break'water,** a barrier or bank (of stones and cement) to break the force of the waves.—**break'neck**

speed, great and reckless speed which is likely to end up with a broken neck.

breakfast, brek′fast, n. the first meal of the day.—Also v.

bream, n. a small fish.

breast, brest, n. the front part of one's chest.—v. to struggle against.—ns. **breast′plate**, a plate or piece of armour for the breast; **breast′work**, a hastily built rampart for defence.

breath, breth, n. the air drawn into and then sent out from the lungs: a very slight breeze.—adj. **breath′less**, out of breath.

breathe, brēth, v. to draw in and send out air from the lungs.

breech, n. the back part of a gun:—pl. **breeches** (brich′ez), trousers (esp. those coming just below the knee and fastening there).—n. **breech′load′er**, a gun loaded at the breech instead of at the mouth.

breed, v. to bring forth: to train or bring up: to cause (e.g. Dirt *breeds* disease).—n. that which is bred: kind (e.g. a *breed* of dogs). —n. **breed′ing**, act of producing: good manners.

breeze, n. a wind: a quarrel.—adj. **breez′y**, fanned by breezes: bright, lively.

brer, n. brother.

breth′ren, n.pl. brothers.

breve, brēv, n. the longest note used in music, ‖◡‖.

breviary, brēv′i-ar-i, n. book containing the daily service of the Roman Catholic Church.

brev′ity, n. shortness.

brew, broo, v. to make beer: to make tea: to be gathering (e.g. Trouble is *brewing*).—n. **brew′ery**, a place for making beer.

briar, brier, brī′er, n. the wild rose: a heather-plant whose wood is used in the making of tobacco-pipes.

bribe, n. a gift (usually money) given secretly and dishonestly to persuade a person to do something.—v. to win over with a bribe.—n. **brib′ery**.

bric-à-brac, brik′a-brak, n. small odds and ends (often articles of value).

brick, n. an oblong piece of burned clay.

bri′dal, n. a marriage feast: a wedding.—adj. having to do with a bride or with a wedding.

bride, n. a woman about to be married, or newly married. — ns. **bride′groom**, a man about to be married, or newly married; **bride's′-maid**, an unmarried woman who attends the bride at a wedding.

bridge, brij, n. a track or road built across a river, etc.: the captain's platform on a ship: a thin piece of wood holding up the strings of a violin: a card-game.—v. to build a bridge over: to get over (a difficulty).—n. **bridge′-head**, a fortification at the end of a bridge.

bridle, brī′dl, n. the straps and bit on a horse's head, by which it is guided.—v. to put on a bridle: to hold back.—n. **bri′dle-path, -road**, a path or way for horsemen.

brief, brēf, n. a short statement of any kind (esp. that of a lawyer about a law case).—adj. short, said in few words.—**in brief**, in few words.

brier, brī′er, n. See briar.

brig, n. a sailing vessel with two masts and square-cut sails.

brigade′, n. a body of soldiers.—ns. **brigadier′, brigadier′-gen′eral**, an officer who commands a brigade.

brig′and, n. a robber.—n. **brig′and-age**, plundering: robbery.

brigantine, brig′an-tēn, n. a two-masted ship like a brig.

bright, brīt, adj. shining: full of light: clever.—v. **bright′en**, to make or grow bright.

brilliant, bril′yant, adj. sparkling: very clever.—n. a fine diamond. —ns. **brill′iancy, brill′iance**.

brim, n. the rim (e.g. of a cup).—v. to be full.—adj. **brim′ful**.

brim′stone, n. sulphur.

brindled, brin′dld, adj. grey or brown and marked with streaks.

brine, n. salt water.—n. the **brin′y**, the sea.

bring, v. to fetch: to carry.—**to bring about**, to cause; **to bring to**, to revive; **to bring up**, to rear: to feed and educate.

brink, n. the edge (e.g. of a cliff).

briquette, bri-ket', *n.* a brick-shaped block of coal made from coal-dust.

brisk, *adj.* full of life : going at a quick pace.—*n.* **brisk'ness.**

bristle, bris'l, *n.* a short, stiff hair (e.g. of a pig).—*v.* to stand on end : to show anger.—*adj.* **brist'ly,** having bristles : rough.

bristol-board, bris'tul-bōrd, *n.* a smooth cardboard.

brit'tle, *adj.* easily broken.

broach, brōch, *v.* to open up : to begin to talk about (e.g. He *broached* the subject of the money).

broad, brawd, *adj.* wide : large : also used to describe a way of speaking that is different from the ordinary (e.g. He speaks *broad* Scots ; his accent is *broad*).—*vs.* **broad'cast,** to scatter freely : to send out by wireless ; **broad'en,** to make or grow broad or broader.—*ns.* **broad'ness ; broad'side,** the side of a ship : all the guns on one side of a ship of war firing at the same time : a sheet of paper printed on one side ; **broad'sword,** a sword with a broad blade.

brocade, brok-ād', *n.* a silk cloth on which fine patterns are sewn.

broc'coli, *n.* a kind of cauliflower.

brochure, bro-shoor', *n.* a small book.

brock, *n.* a badger.

brogue, brōg, *n.* a strong shoe : a broad way of saying words.

broil, *v.* to cook over hot coals : to grill.—*n.* a noisy quarrel.

bro'ker, *n.* one who buys and sells for others : a second-hand dealer.

bronchitis, bron-kī'tis, *n.* an illness (affecting the windpipe) in which breathing is difficult.—*adj.* **bron-chial** (bron'ki-al), having to do with the windpipe.

broncho, bronco, brong'ko, *n.* a half-tamed horse.

bronze, *n.* a mixture of copper and tin.—Also *adj.*

brooch, brōch, *n.* a fancy safety-pin, esp. one set with jewels.

brood, *v.* to sit as a hen on eggs : to think anxiously for some time.—*n.* children or family : the number (e.g. of chickens) hatched at once.

brook, *n.* a small stream.

brook, *v.* to bear or endure.

broom, *n.* a well-known plant, with yellow flowers : a brush for sweeping.—*n.* **broom'stick,** the handle of a broom.

brose, *n.* a food made by pouring boiling water or milk on oatmeal, with salt and butter added.

broth, *n.* soup made with vegetables.

brother, bruth'er, *n.* a male born of the same parents as one's self :—*pl.* **broth'ers,** sometimes **breth'ren.** —*adj.* **broth'erly,** like a brother : kind : affectionate.—*n.* **broth'er-in-law,** the brother of a husband or wife : a sister's husband.

brow, *n.* the forehead : the edge of a hill.—*v.* **brow'beat,** to frighten with stern looks or speech : to bully.

brown, *adj.* of a dark colour (something between red and yellow) : sunburnt.—Also *n.*

brown'ie, *n.* a helpful fairy or goblin : a member of the junior Girl Guides, having a brown uniform.

browse, *v.* to feed on the shoots or leaves of plants : to read.

bruin, broo'in, *n.* a name for a bear.

bruise, brooz, *v.* to crush by beating : to beat into small pieces.—*n.* a wound, with skin crushed and darkened in colour, made by a blow or a fall.

brunette, broon-et', *n.* a woman with brown or dark hair.

brunt, *n.* the force of a blow.

brush, *n.* an instrument for removing dust : a slight fight, a skirmish or encounter : the tail of a fox. —*v.* to remove dust, etc. by sweeping : to touch lightly in passing.—*n.* **brush'wood,** rough close bushes : a thicket.

brusque, broosk or brusk, *adj.* sharp and short in manner, rude.—*n.* **brusque'ness.**

brus'sels, *n.* a kind of carpet.—*n.pl.* **bruss'els-sprouts,** a kind of cabbage with sprouts like small cabbages on the stem.

brute, broot, *n.* an animal : a cruel person.—*adj.* **brut'al,** like a brute, cruel.—*n.* **brutal'ity.**— **brute strength,** great strength.

bub'ble, *n.* a bladder of water blown out with air : a cheating scheme. —*v.* to rise in bubbles.

buccaneer', *n*. an old-time pirate.—*n*. buccaneer'ing.

buck, *n*. the male of the deer, goat, hare, and rabbit.—*n*. buck'skin, a soft leather made of deerskin or sheepskin.

buck'et, *n*. a container for water, etc.

buck'le, *n*. a clip (of metal, etc.) for fastening straps or bands.—*v*. to fasten with a buckle.—*n*. buck'ler, a small shield.

buck'ram, *n*. coarse cotton or linen.

bud, *n*. the first shoot of a tree or plant.—*v*. to put forth buds.—*adj*. bud'ding, showing signs of becoming (e.g. a *budding* author).

budge, *buj*, *v*. to move or stir.

budgerigar', *n*. a kind of small parrot. Often shortened to budgie.

budget, *buj'et*, *n*. a sheaf of papers or heap of letters : the sum of money set aside each year by Parliament to pay for the country's army, navy, schools, etc.

buff, *n*. a kind of soft leather : a military coat : a light yellow colour.

buf'falo, *n*. a kind of ox.

buf'fer, *n*. something which lessens the force of a blow or collision (e.g. the springs at ends of a railway carriage).

buf'fet, *n*. a slap or a blow.—*v*. to strike with the fist, to slap : to struggle against.

buffet, *boo'fā*, *n*. a counter where food and drink may be got : a kind of sideboard.

buffoon', *n*. a clown : a fool.—*n*. buffoon'ery, silly behaviour, clowning.

bug, *n*. a name for any small nasty insect.—*n*. bugbear (bug'bār), a thing that frightens or annoys : the thing one hates most (e.g. Spelling was his *bugbear*).

bug'gy, *n*. a kind of light horse-carriage, a gig.

bugle, *bū'gl*, *n*. a hunting-horn : a small trumpet.—*ns*. bū'gler, one who plays upon the bugle ; bugle-call, in the army, a short tune played on the bugle as a signal.

build, *bild*, *v*. to put together the parts of anything (e.g. a house, bridge, aeroplane).—*n*. build'-ing.—build'ing soci'ety, a kind of bank which lends people money for building houses.

bulb, *n*. the ball-shaped part of plants like the hyacinth, tulip, onion, etc., containing a store of food for the young plant which is inside : an electric-light lamp.—*adj*. bul'bous, ball-shaped.

bulge, *bulj*, *n*. a swelling.—*v*. to swell out.—*adj*. bul'gy.

bulk, *n*. size : the greater part.—*v*. to be of importance.—*adj*. bulk'y, taking up much room.

bulk'head, *n*. a wall in the inside of a ship, meant to keep out water in a collision.

bull, *bool*, *n*. the male of the ox family, also of the whale, walrus, elephant, moose, etc.—*ns*. bull'-dog, a kind of dog, strong in body and fierce-looking, once used for worrying bulls ; bull'-terr'ier, a dog something like a bulldog ; bull's-eye, the mark in the middle of a target : a striped sweet.

bull, *bool*, *n*. a command or order from the Pope, written in Latin.

bulldozer, *n*. a machine for levelling land and clearing away obstacles.

bullet, *bool'et*, *n*. the ball of lead or other metal fired from a pistol or rifle.—*adj*. bull'et-proof, not able to be pierced by bullets.

bulletin, *bool'e-tin*, *n*. a short news report : a report telling how a sick person is getting on.

bullion, *bool'yun*, *n*. gold and silver in bars before being made into coins.

bully, *bool'i*, *n*. one who uses his size and strength to hurt or frighten those who are weaker.—Also *v*.

bulrush, *bool'rush*, *n*. a large strong reed which grows on wet land or in water.

bulwark, *bool'wark*, *n*. the part of a ship's side above the deck : anything strong for defence.

bum'ble-bee, *n*. a large kind of bee that makes a humming noise.

bump, *v*. to make a heavy noise : to strike with a dull sound.—Also *n*.—*n*. bump'er, a cup or glass filled to the brim.—*adj*. full up.

bump'kin, *n*. a clumsy country fellow.

bumptious, *bump'shus*, *adj*. self-important : meddling, fussy.

bun, *n*. a kind of cake : a rounded mass of hair.

bunch, bunsh, *n.* a number of things tied together or growing together. —*v.* to crowd together.

bun'dle, *n.* a number of things loosely bound together.—*v.* to tie in a bundle : to push roughly.

bung, *n.* the stopper of the hole in a barrel : a large cork.—*v.* to stop up with a bung.—*n.* **bung'-hole**, a hole in a cask through which it is filled, closed by a bung.

bungalow, bung'ga-lō, *n.* a house of one storey, usually standing by itself.

bungle, bung'gl, *v.* to do a thing badly or clumsily.—Also *n.*

bunion, bun'yun, *n.* a lump or swelling on the foot.

bunk, *n.* a sleeping-place, esp. in a ship's cabin.—*ns.* **bunk'er**, large box for keeping e.g. coal : a sand-pit on a golf-course ; **bunk'ering**, putting coal or oil, etc., into a ship, aircraft, etc.

bunk'um, *n.* foolish talk, nonsense.

bun'ny, *n.* a pet name for a rabbit.

bunt'ing, *n.* a thin cloth used for making flags.

bunt'ing, *n.* a bird of the finch family.

buoy, boi, *n.* a floating mark which acts (by its shape, colour, light, sound, etc.) as a guide or as a warning for ships : something which acts as a float (e.g. a *life-buoy*).—*v.* to keep afloat, bear up : to cheer up.—*n.* **buoy'ancy**, lightness (making floating easy).— *adj.* **buoy'ant**, light, cheerful.

bur, boi, burr, *n.* the prickly seed-case or head of certain plants.

bur'den, *n.* a load : cargo : something difficult to bear (e.g. blame, sin, sorrow) : the chorus or refrain of a song.—*adj.* **bur'den-some**, heavy.

bureau, bū-rō', *n.* a writing-table : a room or office where such a table is used : an office :—*pl.* **bureaux**, **bureaus** (bū-rōz').

burette, bū-ret', *n.* a glass tube for measuring liquids.

burgh, bur'a, *n.* a Scottish word meaning the same as the English **borough**.—*ns.* **burgher** (burg'er), a dweller in a borough ; **burgess** (bur'jes), one who has certain rights in a borough.

burg'lar, *n.* one who breaks into a house by night to steal.—*n.* **burg'lary**.

burial, ber'i-al, *n.* See **bury**.

burlesque, bur-lesk', *n.* a piece of writing, acting, or drawing, making fun of somebody.

bur'ly, *adj.* broad and strong.—*n.* **bur'liness**.

burn, *n.* a small stream or brook.

burn, *v.* to waste by fire : to be on fire : to feel very angry.—*n.* a hurt or mark caused by fire.—*ns.* **burn'er**, the part of a lamp or gas-jet from which the flame rises ; **burnt'-off'ering**, something burned upon an altar as a sacrifice.

burn'ish, *v.* to polish.—Also *n.*— *n.* **burn'isher**, an instrument for polishing metal.

burrow, bur'ō, *n.* a hole in the ground dug by certain animals (e.g. rabbits, moles, foxes).—*v.* to make holes in the ground.

bur'sar, *n.* in English schools and colleges, the one who collects fees and pays bills, the treasurer : in Scotland, one who (usually by examination) wins a money prize to pay for his schooling or other studies.—*n.* **burs'ary**, in Scotland, the money paid to a bursar.

burst, *v.* to break into pieces : to break open suddenly.—Also *n.*

bury, ber'i, *v.* to hide in the ground : to place a dead body in the ground.—*n.* **bur'ial**.

bus, *n.* short for **omnibus**.

busby, buz'bi, *n.* a fur hat worn by mounted soldiers.

bush, boosh, *n.* a plant thick with branches : forest : wild, desert country.—*adj.* **bush'y**, full of bushes : like a bush.—*n.* **bush'-ranger**, in Australia, an outlaw living in the wilds.

bushel, boosh'el, *n.* a measure (8 gallons) for measuring grain, fruit, etc.

business, biz'nes, *n.* one's work or job : trade (e.g. *Business* is good just now) : something that concerns a person (e.g. This is my *business*).

bus'kin, *n.* a kind of boot reaching to below the knee.

bust, *n.* a statue, painting, or photograph, showing the head and shoulders of a person : the part of the human body above the waist.

bus′tard, *n.* a kind of bird something like the crane.

bustle, bus′l, *v.* to busy one's self noisily.—Also *n.*

bustle, bus′l, *n.* a stuffed pad once worn by ladies under the skirt of their dress.

busy, biz′i, *adj.* working hard : active.—*adv.* bus′ily.—*ns.* bus′iness ; bus′ybody, one busy about others' affairs, a meddling person.

butcher, booch′er, *n.* one whose work is to kill animals for food : one who delights in killing and slaughtering.—*v.* to kill cruelly.—*n.* butch′ery, great or cruel slaughter.

but′ler, *n.* a man-servant who looks after the wines, etc., and who serves them.

butt, *v.* to strike with the head.

butt, *n.* a large cask : a target for archers : the mound of earth behind rifle-targets to catch wide shots : one of whom others make fun : the thick heavy end of a stick, rifle, etc.

but′ter, *n.* a fatty food made by churning cream.—*v.* to spread over with butter.—*ns.* but′termilk, the milk that is left after butter has been made ; but′tercup, a plant with a cup-like flower of a golden yellow ; but′terfly, a winged insect with large and beautiful wings : a gay, light-hearted person ; but′ter-scotch, a kind of toffee made with butter.

but′tery, *n.* a storeroom in a house for wines, ale, etc.—*n.* but′tery-bar, the ledge for holding drinking-vessels in the buttery.

but′ton, *n.* a knob of metal, bone, etc., used to fasten the dress : the knob of an electric bell, etc. : (*pl.*) a young boy servant in uniform, a page-boy.—*v.* to fasten by means of buttons.

but′tress, *n.* a support (e.g. on the outside of a wall).—*v.* to support, as by a buttress.

bux′om, *adj.* gay, lively, jolly.

buy, bī, *v.* to get something by giving money for it.—*n.* buy′er.

buzz, *v.* to make a humming noise like bees.—Also *n.*

buz′zard, *n.* a bird of prey like a falcon.

by, bī, *prep.* and *adv.*—*adv.* by′-and-by, soon, presently.—*ns.* by′-election, an election for parliament or town-council to appoint a member in place of one who has died or has given up his place ; by′-law, a law made by a town or club ; by′name, a nickname ; by′path, by′road, by′way, a side road ; by′-pro′duct, something useful obtained during the manufacture of something else (e.g. Coke is a *by-product* obtained when gas is made from coal) ; by′stander, a looker-on ; by′word, a common saying : something mocked at.—*adj.* by′-gone, past. —*n.pl.* by′-gones, happenings that are over and done with.

bye, bī, *n.* in cricket, a ball sent past the wicket : a run made from such a ball.

byre, bīr, *n.* a cow-house.

C

cab, *n.* a hired carriage, horse-drawn or motor-driven (*taxi-cab*).

caballero, ka-bal-yā′rō, *n.* a Spanish gentleman.

cabaret, kab′a-rā, *n.* a restaurant, with dancing, singing, etc.

cabbage, kab′āj, *n.* a well-known vegetable.

cab′in, *n.* a hut or cottage : a small room, esp. in a ship, for officers or passengers.—*n.* cab′in-boy, a boy who looks after the cabins of a ship.

ca′binet, *n.* a small room : a fancy wooden case with drawers : a cupboard with shelves and doors (e.g. china *cabinet*): a number of statesmen who advise the king and who really govern the country.

cable, kā′bl, *n.* a strong rope or chain : a line of covered telegraph wires laid under the sea : a message or telegram sent by such a line : an underground wire (e.g. electric *cable*).—*v.* to telegraph by cable.—*n.* ca′blegram, a telegram sent by cable.

cabriolet, kab'ri-ō-lā, *n.* a light carriage.

cacao, ka-ka'o or ka-kā'o, *n.* a tree from whose seeds cocoa and chocolate are made.

cachalot, kash'a-lot, *n.* a kind of whale.

cache, kash, *n.* a hiding-place for treasure, stores, ammunition, etc.: the stores hidden.

cachet, kash'ā, *n.* a seal (e.g. for a letter).

cachinnation, kak-in-ā'shun, *n.* loud laughter.

cack'le, *n.* the sound made by a hen or goose.—Also *v.*

cacophony, ka-kof'ō-ni, *n.* an unpleasant sound.

cac'tus, *n.* a prickly plant.

cad, *n.* a low, mean fellow: a sneak.

cadaverous, ka-dav'er-us, *adj.* looking like a dead body: sickly-looking.

caddie, kad'i, *n.* one who attends a golfer at play, carrying the clubs.

cad'dy, *n.* a small box for holding tea.

cadence, kā'dens, *n.* the fall of the voice at the end of a sentence: pleasant rise and fall of sound.

cadet', *n.* the younger or youngest son: a member of the younger branch of a family: a youth studying to be an officer in the army or navy: a schoolboy who takes military training.

cadge, kaj, *v.* to beg, or go about begging.—*n.* cadg'er.

café, kaf'ā, *n.* a tea-shop, a restaurant.

caffeine, kaf-ē'in, *n.* a drug.

cage, kāj, *n.* a box made of wire and wood for holding birds or animals: in a mine, a lift used by the miners.—*v.* to close up in a cage.

cairn, kārn, *n.* a heap of stones, esp. one raised over a grave, or as a mark on a mountain-top.

caisson, kās'on, *n.* an ammunition wagon: a strong case for keeping out the water while the foundations of a bridge are being built.

caitiff, kā'tif, *n.* a mean fellow.

cajole, ka-jōl', *v.* to coax: to cheat by flattery.—*n.* cajol'ery.

cake, *n.* a small loaf of fine bread: sweetened, fancy bread: anything pressed flat (e.g. a *cake* of soap).

cal'abash, *n.* a tree with a melon-like

fruit: the shell of this fruit, often used for carrying water, etc.

calam'ity, *n.* a great misfortune.—*adj.* calam'itous.

calcareous, kal-kā're-us, *adj.* having to do with chalk or lime.

calcium, kal'si-um, *n.* a substance which forms the chief part of lime.

calculate, kal'kū-lāt, *v.* to count or reckon: to think out.—*adjs.* cal'culating, thinking selfishly; cal'culable, able to be counted or measured. — *n.* calculā'tion, a reckoning, a sum.

caldron. See cauldron.

cal'endar, *n.* a table or list showing the year divided into months, weeks, days, etc.

cal'ender, *n.* in a laundry or paper-mill, a machine for giving a polished finish: a cloth-presser.

calf, kahf, *n.* the young of the cow, elephant, and whale: calf-skin leather: the back of the lower part of one's leg:—*pl.* calves (kahvz).

calibre, kal'i-ber, *n.* the measurement across the opening of a tube or gun: power.

cal'ico, *n.* a cotton cloth.—Also *adj.*

calif, caliph, khalif, kā'lif or kal'if, *n.* a Turkish ruler (the name taken by those who ruled after Mohammed).—*n.* cal'ifate, cal'iphate, the rank or government of a calif.

caligraphy. See calligraphy.

cal'ipers, *n.pl.* an instrument like compasses, used for measuring thicknesses of tubes, etc.

caliph, caliphate. See calif.

calk, *v.* See caulk.

calk, kawk, *n.* a pointed piece of iron on a horse-shoe to prevent slipping.

call, kawl, *v.* to cry aloud: to make a short visit: to name: to summon.—Also *n.*—*n.* call'ing, one's trade or job.—a close call, a narrow escape.

cal'ler, *adj.* fresh.

calligraphy, caligraphy, kal-lig'ra-fi, *n.* handwriting, esp. beautiful handwriting.

callous, kal'us, *adj.* unkind: hard-hearted. — *ns.* call'ousness; callos'ity, a hard swelling on the skin.

callow, kal'ō, *adj.* not covered with feathers: not having much experience: simple.

calm, kahm, *adj.* still or quiet.—*n.* absence of wind : quietness: peacefulness.—*v.* to make peaceful.—*n.* **calm'ness.**

calorie, kal'or-i, *n.* a measure of heat.—*n.* **calorim'eter,** an instrument for measuring heat.

calumet, kal'ū-met, *n.* the ' peace pipe ' of the North American Indians.

calumny, kal'um-ni, *n.* an untruth which hurts a person's good name. —*v.* **calum'niate,** to say untrue things about a person.—*ns.* **calum'niātion; calum'niātor.**—*adj.* **calum'nious.**

Cal'vary, *n.* the name of the place where Jesus was crucified.

calve, kahv, *v.* bring forth a calf.

calypso, ka-lip'sō, *n.* a West Indian folk-song made up as the singer goes along.

calyx, calix, kal'iks or kā'liks, *n.* the outer covering or cup of a flower.

cam'ber, *n.* a slight curve or bulge on a road, etc., making the middle higher than the sides.

cambric, kām'brik, *n.* a kind of fine white linen.

cam'el, *n.* an animal of Asia and Africa with a humped back, used as a beast of burden and for riding. — **camel's hair,** the hair of the camel : the hair of the squirrel's tail used for paintbrushes.

cam'elopard, *n.* the giraffe.

cameo, kam'ē-ō, *n.* a gem or precious stone on which a carved figure or design stands out :— *pl.* **cam'eos.**

cam'era, *n.* an instrument for taking photographs. — **in camera,** in private.

cam'isole, *n.* a woman's underbodice.

cam'omile, *n.* a plant, or its dried flowers, used in medicine.

camouflage, kam'oo-flazh, *n.* a trick to deceive an enemy (e.g. the painting of a ship in odd colours so that it cannot be seen easily at a distance).—Also *v.*

camp, *n.* the ground on which an army pitch their tents : the tents of an army : a fixed military station, as at Aldershot : any sleeping-place or stopping-place for explorers, hikers, etc.—*v.* to encamp or pitch tents.

campaign, kam-pān', *n.* a war or part of a war : a number of meetings, speeches, etc. for a special purpose.—*n.* **campaign'er,** one who has served in campaigns : a tried soldier.

campanile, kam-pan-ē'lā, *n.* a tower with pealing bells.

campanula, kam-pan'ū-la, *n.* a family of bell-like flowers, the best-known kinds being the harebell or Scottish bluebell and the Canterbury bell.

camphor, kam'for, *n.* a solid oil, got from the camphor laurel tree of India, China, and Japan; it has a strong smell.—*adj.* **cam'phorāted,** containing camphor.

can, *pres.* tense of *v.* *to be able.* **I can**=*I am able to.*

can, *n.* a tin case for holding liquids. —*v.* to put (food) into a closed tin to keep it from going bad.—*n.* **can'nery,** a place where food is canned.

canal', *n.* a waterway (for ships or barges) made by man.—*v.* **can'alise,** to build up the banks of a river and deepen it, so that boats may use it easily.

canard, ka-nar', *n.* a false rumour.

canary, ka-nā'ri, *n.* a light sweet wine from the *Canary* Islands : a song-bird (finch) found in the Canary Islands.—*adj.* canary-coloured, bright yellow.

cancel, kan'sel, *v.* to stroke out by crossing with lines : to put off (e.g. The picnic was *cancelled* owing to bad weather).

cancer, kan'ser, *n.* a disease which eats away the body.—*n.* **Cancer,** a group of stars.

candelabrum, kan-de-lā'brum, *n.* a branched and ornamented candlestick :—*pl.* **candelā'bra.**

can'did, *adj.* saying just what one thinks, frank.—*n.* **candour.**

can'didate, *n.* one who tries for a situation or a position, or who enters for an examination, etc.—*n.* **can'didature.**

can'died. See candy.

can'dle, *n.* wax stalk, containing a wick, used for giving light.—*ns.* **can'dle-light; can'dle-pow'er,** the amount of light given by one candle; **can'dle-stick,** a holder for a candle.

Can'dlemas, *n.* the beginning of February: a day (2nd February) on which special services are held in Roman Catholic churches.

candour, kan'dur, *n.* See candid.

can'dy, *n.* a sweet made of sugar: anything preserved in sugar.—*v.* to preserve or cover with sugar. —*adj.* **can'died.**

cane, *n.* the stem of certain plants (e.g. bamboo and sugar-cane): a walking-stick.—*v.* to beat with a cane.—*ns.* **cane'-su'gar,** sugar got from the sugar-cane; **can'ing,** a thrashing with a cane.

canine, ka-nīn' or kā'nīn, *adj.* having to do with dogs.—**canine teeth,** the four sharp-pointed teeth, one on each side of the upper and lower jaw.

can'ister, *n.* a box or case, usually of tin, for holding tea, etc.

can'ker, *n.* a spreading sore: a disease in trees, plants, etc.

can'nel, *n.* a kind of coal.

can'nibal, *n.* a savage who eats human flesh.—*n.* **cann'ibalism,** the habit of eating human flesh.

can'non, *n.* a great gun used in war: a stroke in billiards.—*v.* to make a cannon at billiards: to collide. —*ns.* **cannonade',** an attack with cannon; **cann'on-ball,** a ball to be shot from a cannon.

can'ny, *adj.* knowing: wise: careful with money.—*n.* **cann'iness.**

canoe, ka-noo', *n.* a boat made of the hollowed trunk of a tree, or of bark or skins: a light boat driven by paddling.—**to paddle one's own canoe,** to do things for one's self.

cañon, kan'yon, *n.* a deep hollow between high and steep banks.

can'on, *n.* a law or rule: a standard to judge by: a clergyman of the English or Roman Catholic Church whose duties are connected with the cathedral: a list of saints.—*v.* **can'onise,** to put someone on the list of saints.

can'opy, *n.* a covering over a throne, bed, pulpit, etc.

cant, *n.* words understood by a particular class only (e.g thieves' *cant*): talk which is not sincere.

cant, *n.* a slope.—*v.* to tilt something from a level position.

cantaloup, kan'ta-loop, *n.* a kind of melon.

cantankerous, kan-tang'ker-us, *adj.* cross: quarrelsome.

canta'ta, *n.* a story (usually from the Bible) which is set to music and sung.

canteen', *n.* a place where soldiers, sailors, or workmen can obtain food and drink: a box containing a set of knives, forks, and spoons.

can'ter, *n.* an easy gallop.—*v.* to move at an easy gallop.

canticle, kan'ti-kl, *n.* a short song or hymn.

cantilever, kan'ti-lēv-er, *n.* a large bracket used in building for holding up heavy parts like balconies and stairs. (The same plan has been used in bridge-building—the Forth Bridge is made up of three pairs of giant *cantilevers* fixed back to back.

can'to, *n.* a part of a long poem.

can'ton, *n.* a part of a country, something like our shire (Switzerland is divided into twenty-two *cantons*).—*n.* **canton'ment;** a camping-place for soldiers: (in India) a town for soldiers.

cant'rip, *n.* a tricky joke: a witch's spell.

can'vas, *n.* a coarse cloth used for sails, tents, etc., and for painting on: the sails of a ship.

can'vass, *v.* to go round asking for votes, money, etc.: to talk about. —*n.* **can'vasser,** one who, during an election, asks the promise of votes: one who seeks orders for goods, books, newspapers, etc.

canyon. Same as cañon.

caoutchouc, kowt'shook, *n.* india-rubber.

cap, *n.* a soft head-dress without brim (e.g. that of a schoolboy): a cover: a person who has won a cap for his skill in football, cricket, etc.—*v.* to put on a cap: to give a university degree to: to choose a player for an important match.

capable, kāp'a-bl, *adj.* able: fitted or suitable for.—*n.* **capabil'ity.**

capacity, kap-as′i-ti, *n.* power of understanding or being able to do a thing: the amount that a barrel, tank, hall, etc. can hold.—*adj.* capā′cious, roomy: wide.

cap-à-pie, kap-a-pē′, *adv.* (of a knight's armour) from head to foot.

cape, *n.* a covering for the shoulders.

cape, *n.* a point of land running into the sea.

caper, kā′per, *n.* the flower-bud of a bush that grows in Italy (used to make caper-sauce).

caper, kā′per, *v.* to leap: to dance about.—*n.* a leap: a prank.

capercailzie, kā-per-kāl′yi, *n.* a kind of grouse, almost as large as a turkey.

capil′lary, *adj.* very fine, like a hair·—*n.* a very fine tube.

cap′ital, *adj.* having to do with the head: chief: excellent.—*n.* the top part of a column or pillar: the chief city: a large letter: goods or money for carrying on business.—*n.* cap′italism, a system in which the country's wealth is owned by individuals (cap′italists), not by the State, as it is under socialism.—capital pun′ishment, punishment by death: capital ship, a large warship.

Cap′itol, *n.* a lofty temple in old-time Rome: in America, the house where parliament meets.

capitulate, kap-it′ūl-āt, *v.* to give in, after making a treaty.—*n.* capitulā′tion.

cā′pon, *n.* a young fattened cock.

caprice, ka-prēs′, *n.* a sudden change of mind: a sudden fancy.—*adj.* capricious (kaprish′us), changing often: taking sudden fancies.

Cap′ricorn, *n.* a group of stars.

capsize′, *v.* to upset: to overturn.

cap′stan, *n.* on a ship or quay, a machine turned by spokes or by a steam-engine, used for winding or hauling.

cap′sule, *n.* the seed-case of a plant: gelatine case for dose of medicine: metal or other container.

cap′tain, *n.* the commander of a troop of horse, a company of infantry, or a ship: the leader of a team or club: the head-boy of a school.—*v.* to lead.—*n.* cap′taincy, the rank of a captain.

caption, kap′shun, *n.* a heading (in newspapers, etc.).—*adj.* captious (kap′shus), ready to find fault.

cap′tivate, *v.* to charm.

captive, kap′tiv, *n.* a prisoner, esp. a prisoner of war.—*adj.* taken or kept prisoner: not free.—*ns.* captiv′ity, the state of being a prisoner; cap′tor, one who takes a prisoner; cap′ture, the act of taking: the thing taken: an arrest.—*v.* to take by force.

car, *n.* a carriage on wheels, esp. a motor-car.

carabine. See carbine.

carafe, ka-raf′, *n.* a water-bottle for the table.

car′amel, *n.* brown sugar melted: a kind of sweet, made of chocolate, sugar, and butter.

car′at, *n.* a measure of the purity of gold—12 carat, 18 carat, etc., up to 24 carat (pure gold): a measure of weight used in weighing gems.

car′avan, *n.* a number of merchants, travellers, etc. crossing the desert together for safety against attack from robbers: a house on wheels.—*n.* caravan′sary or -serai, an inn where caravans stop.

car′away, *n.* a plant whose seeds are used to flavour cakes, etc.

car′bine, *n.* a short light musket—also car′abine. —*n.* carbineer′, carabineer′, a soldier armed with a carbine.

carbol′ic a′cid, *n.* an acid used to kill germs.

car′bon, *n.* a substance of which charcoal is an example.—*adjs.* carbonā′ceous, carbon′ic, made of carbon; carbonif′erous, producing or containing coal.—*v.* car′bonise, to make into carbon.

car′buncle, *n.* a fiery-red precious stone: a painful boil.

carburet′ter or **carburet′tor,** *n.* the part of a motor-car engine which changes the petrol into vapour.

carcass, carcase, kar′kas, *n.* the dead body of an animal.

card, *n.* a piece of pasteboard (e.g. one used for playing the game of *cards*; or one with a person's address upon it).—*n.* cards, a table game played with a pack of cards (usually 52 in number).

card, *n.* a tool for combing wool or flax.—*v.* to comb wool, etc.

car'diac, *adj.* having to do with the heart.

car'digan, *n.* a knitted woollen jacket.

car'dinal, *adj.* principal, important. —*n.* a person of very high rank in the Roman Catholic Church. —**cardinal numbers,** numbers telling how many (1, 2, 3, etc.; 1st, 2nd, 3rd, etc., are *ordinals*); **cardinal points,** the four chief points of the compass — north, south, east, and west.

care, *n.* heed: close attention: worry.—*v.* to look after: to be worried or vexed.—*adjs.* **care'ful,** attentive; **care'less,** paying little attention: not neat; **care'-free,** having no worries; **care'-worn,** looking very worried.—*ns.* **care'-fulness; care'lessness; care'-taker,** one who looks after a building.—**care of** (c/o), at the house of; **I don't care for,** I'm not very fond of.

careen', *v.* to lay a ship on her side to repair her bottom and keel: (of a ship) to lean to one side.

career', *n.* one's life's work, trade, profession (e.g. He had a success-ful *career* as an engineer): head-long rush.—*v.* to gallop: to move or run rapidly.

caress', *v.* to throw the arms round lovingly: to fondle.—Also *n.*

car'et, *n.* a mark, ∧, to show where to put in something that has been left out.

car'go, *n.* a ship's load:—*pl.* **car'-goes.**

caribou, kar-i-boo', *n.* the American reindeer.

caricature', *n.* a likeness of anything so drawn as to appear funny.—*v.* to draw a caricature.—*n.* **caricatur'ist.**

caries, kā'ri-ēz, *n.* rottenness, esp. of the teeth.

carillon, ka-ril'yon, *n.* a number of musical bells for playing tunes: the tune played on these.

cark, *n.* worry.—*adj.* **cark'ing,** caus-ing worry.

carl, *n.* a rough country fellow: a stupid fellow.—*n.* **car'line,** an old woman: a witch.

car'mine, *n.* a bright red colour.

carnage, kar'nāj, *n.* slaughter.

car'nal, *adj.* having to do with the body: sinful.

carnation, kar-nā'shun, *n.* a sweet-smelling garden flower.

carnelian, kar-nē'li-an, *n.* a fine red stone.—Also **cornē'lian.**

car'nival, *n.* a time of merriment or feasting.

carniv'ora, *n.pl.* flesh-eating animals. —*adj.* **carniv'orous,** flesh-eating.

car'ol, *n.* a song of joy or praise.— *v.* to sing a carol.

carot'id, *adj.* having to do with the two great blood-vessels of the neck.

carouse, kar-owz', **carous'al,** *n.* a drinking-bout: a noisy drunken feast.—*v.* to hold a drinking-bout.

carp, *v.* to pick out small faults or errors.

carp, *n.* a fresh-water fish common in ponds.

car'penter, *n.* one who does the wood-work in the building of a house, etc.—*n.* **car'pentry,** the trade of a carpenter.

car'pet, *n.* the woven covering of floors, stairs, etc.

carriage, kar'ij, *n.* the act or cost of carrying: a vehicle for carrying people: way of walking.

car'rion, *n.* rotting animal flesh.

carronade', *n.* a short cannon with large mouth.

car'rot, *n.* a vegetable whose long reddish-yellow root is eaten.

car'ry, *v.* to lift and take to another place: to take by force.—*ns.* **carr'ier,** one who carries goods: an instrument for carrying; **carr'ier-pig'eon,** a homing pigeon which carries letters.—**to carry on,** to continue doing: to behave wildly; **to carry out** (or **through**), to bring to a successful finish; **to be carried away,** to be overcome by one's feelings.

carse, *n.* fertile land beside a river.

cart, *n.* a vehicle (drawn by a horse) used on farms.—*v.* to carry in a cart.—*ns.* **cart'er; cart-horse; cart-load; cartwright** (kart'rit), a car-penter who makes carts.

car'tilage, *n.* gristle.

cartography, kar-tog'ra-fi, *n.* the art of map-making.—*n.* **carto'grapher.**

car'ton, n. a thin pasteboard box.

cartoon', n. a large drawing, esp. a comic drawing.—n. cartoon'ist.

cartridge, kar'trij, n. a case holding the powder and bullet fired by a gun.

carve, v. to make or shape by cutting : to cut up (meat) into slices.

cascade', n. a waterfall.

casca'ra, n. the bark of a tree, used in a medicine.

case, n. a covering or box.

case, n. that which happens (e.g. a *case* of measles) : an event : a trial in a law-court.

case'ment, n. a window-frame : a window that swings on hinges.

cash, n. money, esp. coins and notes.—v. to turn into, or change for, money.—n. cashier', a cash-keeper : one who sees to the receiving and paying of money.

cashier, kash-ēr', v. to dismiss (e.g. from the army or navy) in disgrace.

cashmere, kash'mēr, n. a shawl made from fine soft goats' hair : a fine woollen cloth.

casino, kas-ē'nō, n. a building with public dance halls, gambling-tables, etc.

cask, n. a little barrel.

cask'et, n. a small case for holding jewels, etc.

casque, kask, cask, n. a cover for the head : a helmet.

cassa'va, n. the manioc plant, from which tapioca is got.

cass'erole, n. a stew-pan.

cas'sock, n. a long robe worn by priests.

cassowary, kas'ō-war-i, n. a big, running bird like the ostrich, found in Australia and New Guinea.

cast, v. to throw or fling : to throw off, drop (e.g. clothes, a dog's hair, etc.) : to shape in a mould. —n. the distance anything is thrown : a squint (in the eye) : something shaped in a mould : the actors in a play : the small heap of earth thrown up by a worm. —ns. cast'away, a deserted or shipwrecked person ; cast'-iron, -steel, iron or steel that has been melted, cast into lumps, and rolled out into bars.—adj. cast'-

off, no longer used (e.g. *cast-off* clothes).

cas'tanets, n.pl. hollow shells of ivory or hard wood, which make a cracking sound when struck together.

caste, kast, n. a class or rank of people, esp. in India.

castellan, castellated. See castle.

cas'tigate, v. to punish : to thrash : to scold.—n. castigā'tion.

castle, kahs'l, n. a fortified house, a fortress : the house of a prince or nobleman : a large country house.—n. cas'tellan, captain of a castle.—adj. cas'tellated, having walls and towers like those of a castle.

cas'tor, n. a small wheel on the legs of furniture : a sugar, pepper, or salt dish, with sprinkler top— also cast'er.—castor sugar, caster sugar, white powdered sugar.

cas'tor-oil, n. an oil (from a kind of palm) used as medicine.

casual, kazh'ū-al or kaz'ū-al, adj. happening by chance : not in a regular job (e.g. a *casual* labourer) : not caring much.— n. cas'ualty, that which happens by accident : a person who is killed or wounded (e.g. in a war).

cat, n. a well-known household animal : a spiteful woman : (short for cat-o'-nine-tails) a whip with nine tails or lashes, with three or four knots on each.—ns. cat'gut, cord made from the stomachs of sheep, and used as strings for violins, and as thread for stitching up wounds ; cat'kin, a crowded spike or tuft of small flowers as seen on the willow, hazel, etc. ; cat's-paw, a person who is used by someone else to do something dangerous or unpleasant.

cataclysm, kat'a-klizm, n. a great flood of water : great change.

catacomb, kat'a-kōm, n. an underground burial-place.

catafalque, kat-a-falk', n. a wooden monument in which the coffin of a famous person is placed before the funeral.

catalogue, kat'a-log, n. a list of names, books, etc. set out in order.—v. to put in a catalogue : to make a list.

catamaran, kat′a-mar-an′, *n.* a kind of raft, an Indian surf-boat.

cat′apult, *n.* in olden times, a weapon for hurling heavy stones in warfare : a small forked stick having an elastic string fixed to the two prongs, used for firing small stones.

cat′aract, *n.* a waterfall : a disease of the eye.

catarrh, kat-ar′, *n.* a watery running, esp. of the nose, caused by cold in the head : the cold itself.

catastrophe, kat-as′trō-fe, *n.* a sudden accident, with terrible results. —*adj.* **catastroph′ic.**

catch, *v.* to take hold of : to take (a disease) : to be entangled in anything.—*n.* a haul of fish : something worth having : a trick, esp. a play on words.—**to catch a train,** to be in time for it and travel by it ; **to catch up (on),** to overtake.

catechise, kat′e-kīz, *v.* to ask many questions.—*n.* **cat′echism** (-kizm), a book which teaches by asking questions and giving the answers.

cat′egory, *n.* a class or kind.—*adj.* **categor′ical,** full, absolute.

cā′ter, *v.* to provide food.— *n.* **cā′terer.**

cat′erpillar, *n.* a grub that lives upon the leaves of plants.—*adj.* moving on endless metal belt.

cat′erwaul, *v.* to howl or yell like a cat : to shriek.—Also *n.*

catgut. See **cat.**

cathedral, kath-ēd′ral, *n.* the church of a bishop, the chief church in the district ruled by the bishop.

cath′erine-wheel, *n.* a firework which in burning turns like a wheel.

cathode ray tube, *n.* a device in which a narrow beam of electrons strikes against a screen, as in a television set.

cath′olic, *adj.* being everywhere, general : taking in all, shutting out none.—*n.* **Cath′olic** (short for *Roman Catholic*), a member of the Roman Catholic Church.

catkin. See **cat.**

cat′tle, *n.pl.* beasts that eat grass, esp. oxen, bulls, and cows.

caul′dron, cal′dron, *n.* a large kettle.

caul′iflower, *n.* a kind of cabbage, of which one eats the flower-head.

caulk, calk, kawk, *v.* to fill or pack the seams of a ship to make it watertight.

cause, *n.* the fact owing to which anything happens : reason : something in which one is interested (e.g. He fights for the *cause* of peace).—*v.* to make to happen.

causerie, kōz′er-ē, *n.* a talk or gossip in a newspaper or magazine.

causeway, kawz′wā, *n.* a pathway paved with stone : a paved street.

caus′tic, *adj.* burning : bitter, severe. —*n.* a substance that eats into the flesh.—*v.* **caut′erise,** to burn away flesh with caustic or a hot iron in order to make a sore heal cleanly.

caution, kaw′shun, *n.* warning : heed : care.—*v.* to warn.—*adj.* **cau′tious,** careful : watchful.

cavalcade, kav-al-kād′, *n.* a procession of persons on horseback.

cavalier, kav-al-ēr′, *n.* a knight : a supporter of the king in the Civil War of the 17th century : a swaggering fellow. — *adj.* like a cavalier : gay : warlike : haughty, free-and-easy.

cav′alry, *n.* horse-soldiers.

cave, *n.* a hollow place in the earth : a den.—*ns.pl.* **cave′-dwell′ers, cave′-men,** people who, in very far-off times, lived in caves.

caveat, kā′ve-at, *n.* a notice of warning.

cav′ern, *n.* a deep hollow place in the earth.—*adj.* **cav′ernous,** hollow : full of caverns.

caviare, caviar, kav-i-ar′, *n.* a kind of food made from the eggs of fish such as the sturgeon : something whose flavour is too fine for most people's taste.

cav′il, *v.* to grumble over trifles.

cav′ity, *n.* a hollow place, a hole.

cavy, kāv′i, *n.* an animal of the guinea-pig kind.

caw, *v.* to call like a crow.—Also *n.*

cayenne, kā-en′, **cayenne-pepper,** *n.* a very hot red pepper.

cay′man, *n.* a name for various kinds of alligator, esp. those found in S. America.

cease, sēs, *v.* to stop : to put an end to.—*adj.* **cease′less,** without stop.

cedar, sē′dar, *n.* a large evergreen tree with hard sweet-smelling wood.

cede, sēd, v. to yield or give up to another.—n. cession (sesh'un).

ceiling, sē'ling, n. the roof of a room.

cel'andine, n. (*Lesser Celandine* or *Pilewort*) a small yellow wild flower: (*Greater Celandine*) a wild plant of the poppy family, with yellow flowers.

cel'ebrate, v. to hold a special church service in memory of some event: to feast and make merry in honour of a marriage, birthday, or other happy event.—adj. cel'ebrated, famous.—ns. celebra'tion; celeb'rity, fame: a famous person.

celer'ity, n. quickness: speed.

cel'ery, n. a vegetable grown for its long white juicy stalks.

celestial, sel-est'yal, adj. having to do with the sky: dwelling in heaven.

celibacy, sel'i-bas-i, n. the state of not being married—that is, single.—adj. cel'ibate, living single.

cell, n. a small room in a prison, monastery, etc.: a cave: a very small part of living matter (i.e. of plants or animals): a part of an electric battery.—adj. cell'ular, made of, or having cells: shaped like a cell.—ns. cell'uloid, an ivory-like stuff that is used for making knife-handles, piano-keys, combs, dolls, etc.; cell'ulose, a substance (got from wood-pulp and cotton) which, treated with chemicals, is used in the making of artificial silk, paper, films, etc.

cel'lar, n. an underground room, esp. one for storing coal, wine, etc.

cello, chel'ō. Short for violoncello.

Celts, kelts or selts, n. a race of people which includes the Welsh, Irish, Scottish Highlanders.—adj. Cel'tic.—n. Cel'tic, the native language of Celtic people (e.g. Gaelic).

cement', n. anything that makes two things stick together: the plaster put between the bricks or stones in house-building.—v. to put together with cement: to join firmly.

cem'etery, n. a burying-ground.

cenotaph, sen'ō-taf, n. a monument to a person or persons buried elsewhere.

cen'ser, n. a pan in which incense is burned.

cen'sor, n. one who examines written or printed matter to see if it contains anything objectionable, e.g. morally.—adj. censō'rious, fault-finding.

censure, sen'shūr, n. a scolding, blame.—v. to blame.

cen'sus, n. a counting of the people in a country.

cent, n. a coin which is the hundredth part of a larger coin (e.g. of a dollar).

cent'aur, n. in fables, a monster, half-man half-horse.

centenary, sen-tēn'ar-i, n. a hundredth birthday: the hundredth year since an event took place (e.g. The *centenary* of Sir Walter Scott's death was in 1932).—n. centenār'ian, a person a hundred years old.—adj. centen'nial, happening once in a hundred years.

cent'igrade, adj. having a hundred degrees. (On the *centigrade* thermometer water freezes at 0 degrees and boils at 100 degrees.)

centime, song-tēm', n. a small French coin, the hundredth part of a franc.

centipede, sen'ti-pēd, n. a crawling creature with many legs.

centre, sen'ter, n. the middle point or part: the point toward which all things move or are drawn.—adj. cen'tral, belonging to the centre, principal.—v. cen'tralise, to draw to a centre.

centrifugal, sen-trif'ū-gal, adj. flying or moving away from the centre.—adj. centrip'etal, moving towards the centre.

century, sen'tū-ri, n. a hundred: a hundred years: a hundred in number (e.g. runs in cricket).

ceram'ic, ker-am'ik, adj. having to do with pottery.

cereal, sē'ri-al, n. food made from grain (e.g. porridge). — n.pl. cereals, grain used as food.

ceremony, ser'e-mon-i, n. the solemn show or display that goes with an important event (e.g. the coronation *ceremony*).—master of ceremonies (M.C.), one who sees that a programme is carried through in an orderly way; to stand on ceremony, to demand respect: to insist upon one's rights—n. cere-

mō′nial, outward show : the display that takes place at a ceremony (e.g. A coronation is a time for much *ceremonial*).—*adj.*
ceremō′nious, full of ceremony : paying attention to ceremony : very polite : fussy.

cerise, ser-ēz′, *n.* cherry-colour.

cer′tain, *adj.* sure : not to be doubted : fixed : regular.—*adv.* **cer′tainly.**—*n.* **cer′tainty.**

cer′tes, *adv.* certainly.

certifi′cate, *n.* a written (or printed) statement that something has happened or been done (e.g. birth *certificate* : marriage *certificate* : school *certificate*—written proof of examinations passed).—*v.* **cer′-tify**, to set a matter down in writing so that it can be used as proof.

cessation, ses-ā′shun, *n.* a ceasing or stopping : a rest : a pause.

cession. See cede.

cess′pool, *n.* a pool or hollow in which filthy water collects, esp. in drainage.

chāfe, *v.* to make hot or sore by rubbing : to wear by rubbing : to rage.

chā′fer, *n.* a kind of beetle, the cockchafer.

chaff, *n.* the husks of corn after threshing : anything left over of no great value : teasing, good-natured talk.—*v.* to tease jokingly.

chaf′fer, *v.* to bargain : to argue about a price.

chaf′finch, *n.* a little song-bird.

chagrin, sha-grēn′, *n.* that which worries the mind : annoyance.

chain, *n.* a number of links or rings (esp. of metal) passing through one another : a number of things coming after each other : a range of hills or mountains : a measure of distance (=22 yards).—*v.* to fasten with a chain.

chair, *n.* a movable seat for one, with a back to it : a seat of office (e.g. of the person in charge of a meeting or of a university professor) : an iron support for a rail on a railway, held by wooden wedges, and fastened to a wooden sleeper. —*v.* to carry in triumph.—*n.* **chair′man**, one who takes the chair, or presides at a meeting.

chaise, shāz, *n.* a light open carriage.

chalcedony, kal-sed′ō-ni, *n.* a beautiful white or bluish-white stone.

chalet, shal′ā, *n.* a summer hut used by Swiss herdsmen in the Alps : a wooden house.

chalice, chal′is, *n.* a cup or bowl : a cup used in church services.

chalk, chawk, *n.* a well-known white substance much used for writing, drawing.—*v.* to mark with chalk. —*adj.* **chalk′y.**

chal′lenge, *v.* to ask another person to settle a matter by fighting or by playing a match : to question another's right to do a thing : to accuse : to object to.—*n.* a call to a contest of any kind, but esp. to a duel : the call ('Who goes there?') of a sentry.—*n.* **chal′lenger.**

chamber, chām′ber, *n.* a room : the place where a meeting is held : the people meeting there (e.g. *Chamber of Commerce*): the part of a gun that holds the cartridges (e.g. a *six-chambered* revolver).

chamberlain, chām′ber-lin, *n.* one appointed by a king, town-council, or nobleman, to carry out certain duties (e.g. *Lord Chamberlain, Town Chamberlain,* etc.).

chameleon, ka-mēl′yun, *n.* a small lizard able to change its colour.

cham′fer, *n.* a slope made by shaving off the edge of a piece of wood or stone work.—Also *v.*

chamois, sham′waw, *n.* a goat-like deer living among the Alps and other high mountains of southern and central Europe : (sham′i), a soft kind of leather made from its skin.

champ, *v.* to make a snapping noise with the jaws in chewing.

champagne, sham-pān′, *n.* a white sparkling wine.

cham′pion, *n.* one who is best, or has beaten all others (e.g. in games) : a leader in a good cause (right, freedom, etc.).—*adj.* very good.—*n.* **cham′pionship.**

chance, *n.* a risk : something unexpected : a turn : the right time at which to act.—*v.* to risk : to happen.—*adj.* happening by luck. —**by chance**, not arranged, unexpectedly; **to chance upon**, to meet unexpectedly.

chan'cel, *n.* the eastern part of a church.

chan'cellor, *n.* a high government minister (e.g., in Britain, *Chancellor of the Exchequer*), who looks after the money required to govern the country: the chief judge of England (*Lord Chancellor*): the head of a university.

chan'cery, *n.* a high English law-court.

chandelier, shan-de-lēr', *n.* a frame with branches for holding lights.

chand'ler, *n.* a merchant selling candles, oil, ships' stores, etc.

chānge, *v.* to make or become different: to give up or leave one thing for another (e.g. one's job, house; also of money—pounds for dollars, etc., shillings for pounds, pennies for shillings, etc.): to put on different clothes. —*n.* the act of making or turning to something different: another set of clothing: loose money: money given back by a shopkeeper when a buyer gives more than the price of an article: a holiday in another place.— *adjs.* **change'able, change'ful.**— *n.* **change'ling,** a child taken or left by the fairies in place of another.

chan'nel, *n.* the bed of a stream: a passage for ships: a narrow sea: a path for radio or TV signals.

chanson, shong'song, *n.* a song.

chant, *v.* to sing: to recite in a singing manner.—*n.* song: a kind of sacred music.—*n.* **chanty** (shant'i), a sailor's song.

chant'icleer, *n.* a cock.

chaos, kā'os, *n.* shapeless mass: disorder.—*adj.* **chaot'ic.**

chap, *v.* to crack: to knock at a door.—*n.* a crack in the skin, caused by frost, wet, etc.: a knock.—*adj.* **chapped,** (of the skin) cracked.

chap-book. See **chapman.**

chapeau, shap-ō, *n.* a hat.

chap'el, *n.* a church, for Roman Catholics, Methodists, etc.: a little church, or a private church (e.g. in a palace, school, prison).

chaperon, shap'e-rōn, *n.* an older lady, who attends a younger one when she goes out in public, as to a dance, a party, etc.—*v.* **chap'eron.**

chap'lain, *n.* a clergyman with the army, navy, or air force.

chap'let, *n.* a garland or wreath for the head: a string of beads used in counting prayers.

chap'man, *n.* one who buys or sells at the door: a pedlar.—*n.* **chap'-book,** a book of rhymes or stories once sold by chapmen.

chap'ter, *n.* a division of a book: a meeting of the clergy of a cathedral: a branch of a society such as Freemasons.—**chapter of accidents,** accident after accident.

char, *v.* to burn until black.

char or **chare,** *v.* to do odd jobs of housework.—*n.* **char'woman,** a woman hired by the day to do housework for other people.

char, *n.* a kind of trout.

charabanc, shar'-a-bang, *n.* a long open motor-car with rows of seats.

character, kar'ak-ter, *n.* a letter of the alphabet: the ways and manners which make people or nations different from each other: the good points (honour, truthfulness, etc.) of a person: a written account of a person's good points in work: a person noted for odd or strange ways: a person in a play, story, film, etc.—*n.* **characteris'tic,** a point which is easily noticed about a person or a people.—Also *adj.*— *v.* **char'acterise,** to describe.

charade, shar-ad', *n.* a word-guessing game.

char'coal, *n.* wood burnt black.

charge, *v.* to load: to fill: to lay a task upon a person: to accuse: to ask a price for: to attack: *n.* an attack: the gunpowder in a shell or bullet: price: blame (for wrong-doing): someone looked after by another person: duty as minister of a church.—**to take charge of,** to take command of; **to take in charge,** to arrest.

charg'er, *n.* war-horse: large plate.

char'iot, *n.* carriage used for fighting. —*n.* **charioteer',** chariot-driver.

char'ity, *n.* love for all people: kindness to poor people.—*adj.* **char'itable,** giving to the poor: kindly.

charlatan, shar´la-tan, *n.* one who pretends to have wonderful cures, a quack-doctor.

char´lock, *n.* a plant with yellow flowers, that grows as a weed in cornfields.

charlotte, shar´lot, *n.* a kind of fruit-tart.

charm, *n.* something (e.g. a locket) having the power of magic: a spell: beauty in appearance or manners.—*v.* to please: to put under a spell. — *adj.* **charmed,** pleased: under a magic charm.

char´nel-house, *n.* a place where the bones of the dead are put.

chart, *n.* a map, esp. one of seas or lakes, showing rocks, islands, currents, depth, etc.: a rough map.

char´ter, *n.* a written paper granting rights, favours, lands, etc., esp. one given by a king or a government to a town, university, bank, etc., or to the people (e.g. *Magna Carta,* signed by King John in 1215).—*v.* to take on hire (e.g. a boat, aeroplane).

charwoman. See **char.**

châ´ry, *adj.* doubtful.

chase, *v.* to run after: to hunt: to drive away.—*n.* a hunt.

chasm, kazm, *n.* a big empty space between high rocks.

chassis, shas´ē, *n.* the frame, wheels, and machinery of a motor-car: an aeroplane's landing-carriage.

chaste, chāst, *adj.* pure-minded.— *n.* **chas´tity.**

chasten, chās´n, *v.* to make humble: to punish, usually by scolding.— *adj.* **chas´tened.**

chastise´, *v.* to punish, usually by whipping or beating.—*n.* **chastisement** (chas´tis-ment).

chat, *v.* to talk about things that are not important.—Also *n.*

chat, *n.* a small bird.

château, sha´tō, *n.* a French castle.

chat´tels, *n.pl.* things that a person owns and can move from place to place.

chat´ter, *v.* to talk idly or rapidly: to sound the teeth when one shivers.—Also *n.*—*n.* **chat´terbox,** one who chatters a great deal.

chauffeur, shō-fer´, *n.* a motor-car driver.

cheap, chēp, *adj.* low in price.—*v.* **cheap´en,** to make cheap.

cheat, chēt, *v.* to deceive.—*n.* a fraud: one who cheats.

check, *v.* to bring to a stop: to hinder or hold back: to scold: to see if something (e.g. a sum) is correct: to mark into squares.—*n.* a sudden stop or set-back: a square (e.g. on a draught-board): cloth with a pattern marked in squares.

check´ers, *n.pl.* the game of draughts.

ched´dar, *n.* a kind of cheese.

cheek, *n.* the side of the face below the eye: impudence.—*adj.* **cheek´y,** impudent.

cheep, *v.* to make a faint sound.

cheer, *n.* a shout of joy or welcome: kind treatment: food. — *v.* to comfort: to shout joyfully.—*adjs.* **cheer´ful, cheer´y,** jolly; **cheer´less,** sad, gloomy. — **What cheer?** What news?

cheese, *n.* a food made from milk.— *adj.* **cheese´-pār´ing,** mean, greedy.

chee´tah, *n.* an animal like the leopard.

chef, shef, *n.* a head cook (a man).

chef d'œuvre, shā-derv´r, *n.* the best piece of work of a painter, sculptor, etc.

chemistry, kem´is-tri, *n.* the science which finds what substances are made of, and how one substance will work with another.—*adj.* **chem´ical,** having to do with chemistry.—*n.* a substance with which a chemist works.—*n.* **chem´ist,** one who studies chemistry: one who makes up and sells medicines.

cheque, chek, **check,** *n.* a written order by one having money in a bank, to pay out a certain amount.

chequer, chek´er, *n.* a chess-board: a coloured square, as on a chess-board: (*pl.*) draughts, chess-men. —*v.* to mark in squares of different colours. — *adj.* **cheq´uered, check´ered,** marked like a chessboard: partly good, partly bad (e.g. *a chequered life,* a life with good and bad times in it).

cher´ish, *v.* to protect and treat with kindness: to keep in the mind.

cheroot, sher-oot´, *n.* a small cigar.

cher′ry, *n.* a small bright-red stone-fruit : the tree that bears it.

cher′ub, *n.* an angel having wings and the plump face and body of a child : a beautiful child :—*pl.* cher′ubs, cher′ubim.

chess, *n.* a game for two persons, played with 'pieces,' which are moved on a chequered board.

chest, *n.* a large strong box : the part of the body between the neck and the waist.

chest′nut, ches′nut, *n.* a large tree producing reddish-brown nuts.—*adj.* reddish-brown.—*n.* a reddish-brown horse : an old joke.

chevalier, shev-a-lēr′, *n.* a knight.

chevron, shev′ron, *n.* the V-shaped band of braid or gold lace worn on the sleeve of a corporal's or sergeant's coat.

chev′y, chiv′y, *n.* a cry, shout : a hunt.—*v.* to chase.

chew, choo, *v.* to break up (food) with the teeth before swallowing.

chicane, shi-kān′, *n.* a trick.—*n.* chica′nery, dishonest smartness.

chick, chick′en, *ns.* the young of fowls, esp. of the hen : a pet name for a child.—*adj.* chick′en-heart′ed, cowardly.—*n.* chick′en-pox, a kind of fever ; chick′weed, a garden weed, often given to cage-birds.

chic′ory, *n.* a plant whose root is ground to mix with coffee.

chide, *v.* to scold by words.

chief, chēf, *adj.* head : principal, highest, first.—*n.* a head or principal person : a leader.—*n.* chief′tain, the head of a clan : a leader.

chiffon, shif′ong, *n.* a thin flimsy stuff used as a trimming.—*n.* chiffonier (shif-on-eer′), a piece of furniture like a cupboard.

chil′blain, *n.* a painful swelling which occurs in cold weather on hands and feet.

child, chīld, *n.* an infant or very young person : (in old ballads) a youth of noble birth :—*pl.* chil′dren.—*n.* child′hood, the time when one is a child.—*adjs.* child′ish, of or like a child : silly ; child′-like, innocent.

chill, *n.* coldness : a cold that causes shivering.—*v.* to make cold : to freeze meat (to make it keep).—*adj.* shivering with cold : slightly cold.—*adj.* chilly, rather cold.

chime, *n.* the sweet sound of bells : (*pl.*) a set of bells.—*v.* to sound sweetly : to strike (e.g. 'Big Ben' *chimes* the quarter-hours).

chimerical, kim-er′i-kl, *adj.* fanciful.

chim′ney, *n.* an opening or hole for the escape of smoke or heated air from a fire :—*pl.* chim′neys.—*ns.* chim′ney-can, or -pot, a pipe of earthenware, iron, etc. placed at the top of a chimney to increase the draught ; chim′ney-stack, a number of chimneys built up together ; chim′ney-stalk, a very tall chimney ; chim′ney-sweep, chim′ney-sweep′er, one who sweeps or cleans chimneys.

chimpanzee′, *n.* an African ape, the most man-like of the apes.

china, chīn′a, *n.* fine kind of earthenware, first made in *China* : porcelain.—*adj.* Chinese (chī-neez′), having to do with China, with the people of China, or with the language of China.—*n.* a person who belongs to China : the language of the people of China.—*n.* Chi′naman, a Chinese person : a Chinese ship.

chinchil′la, *n.* a small animal of South America, valued for its soft grey fur.

chine, *n.* the spine or backbone : a piece of the backbone for cooking (e.g. a *chine* of bacon) : a ridge : a small valley.

chink, *n.* a narrow opening.

chink, *n.* a ringing sound, as of coins.—Also *v.*

chintz, *n.* a cotton cloth with brightly coloured patterns.

chip, *v.* to chop or cut into small pieces.—*n.* a small fragment of wood, etc.

chip′munk, *n.* a kind of squirrel, common in North America.

chiropodist, kir-op′o-dist, *n.* one who removes corns, etc.

chirp, chir′rup, *n.* the sharp, shrill sound of some birds and insects.—Also *v.*—*adj.* chir′py, merry.

chis′el, *n.* an iron or steel tool to cut or hollow out wood, stone, etc.—*v.* to cut with a chisel.

chit, *n.* a note : an order or pass.

chivalry, shiv'al-ri, *n.* the ways of knights of olden times, who made vows to do brave deeds : bravery and kindness, esp in aiding the weak.—*adj.* **chiv'alrous.**

chlorine, klō'rēn, *n.* a yellowish-green poisonous gas.—*v.* **chlo'rinate,** to add chlorine, or substance containing it, to (water).—**chlo'ride of lime,** a bleaching powder.

chloroform, klō'ro-form, *n.* a drug which, when breathed in, causes deep sleep and deadens the senses.

chock, *n.* a wedge, to keep casks, etc. from rolling.—*adj.* **chock'-full, choke'full,** quite full.

choc'olate, *n.* a paste got from the seeds of the cacao-tree, used in sweet-making : a drink made from it.—*adj.* dark brown in colour, like chocolate.

choice, *n.* act or power of choosing : the thing chosen.—*adj.* worthy of being chosen.

choir, kwīr, *n.* a chorus or band of singers, esp. in a church : the part of a church where the choir sits.—*adj.* **choral** (kō'ral), having to do with a choir.

choke, *v.* to seize by the throat and stop the breathing : to feel as if breathing were going to stop : to stop up (e.g. The drain is *choked*).

choler, kol'er, *n.* anger.—*adj.* **chol'eric.**

cholera, kol'er-a, *n.* a deadly disease common in hot countries.

choose, *v.* to take one thing rather than another : to select.—*n.* **choice.**

chop, *v.* to cut with a sudden blow : to cut into small pieces : (of the wind) to shift suddenly.—*n.* a blow : a slice of mutton or pork, containing a rib.—*n.* **chop'per,** a knife or axe for chopping.—*adj.* **chop'py,** (of the sea) having many waves.

chops, *n.pl.* the jaws.—*adj.* **chop'fall'en,** sad.

chop'-sticks, *n.pl.* two small sticks of wood, ivory, etc., used by the Chinese instead of knife and fork.

choral, chorale. See **choir.**

chord, kord, *n.* a musical sound made by the blending of several notes played together : the straight line joining the ends of a curve.

chorus, kō'rus, *n.* a band of singers and dancers : the refrain of a song.—*v.* to sing or say together.—*n.* **chor'ister,** a member of a choir.

chough, chuf, *n.* a kind of crow.

Christ, krīst, *n.* a name given to Jesus.—*n.* **Christ'ian,** a follower of Christ.—Also *adj.*—*ns.* **Christian'ity,** the religion having Christ as its centre ; **Chris'tendom,** Christians as a whole : that part of the world inhabited by Christian peoples.—*v.* **christen** (kris'n), to baptise in the name of Christ : to give a name to.—*n.* **chris'tening.**—**Chris'tian name(s),** one's first name (or names), given usually when christened (e.g. John William are the *Christian names* of John William Smith) ; **Chris'tian ē'ra,** the years counted from the birth of Christ : the period of time since Christ's birth.

Christmas, kris'mas, *n.* a yearly holiday or festival, in memory of the birth of Christ, held on the 25th of December.—*ns.* **Christ'-mas-box,** a Christmas gift; **Christ'-mas-eve,** evening of December 24.

chromatic, krō-mat'ik, *adj.* having to do with colours : coloured.

chromium, krō'mi-um, *n.* a bright metal which does not rust.

chronic, kron'ik, *adj.* lasting a long time, esp. of a disease.

chronicle, kron'i-kl, *n.* a record of events in order of time : a history.—*v.* to write down events in order.—*n.* **chron'icler,** a historian.

chronological, kron-o-loj'ik-al, *adj.* having to do with time : arranged in the order of happening (*chronological order*).

chronometer, kron-om'e-ter, *n.* an instrument for measuring time : a watch.

chrysalis, kris'a-lis, *n.* an insect, such as a butterfly, at an early part of its life, when it is without wings, and is shut up in a shell or soft covering.

chrysanthemum, kris-an'the-mum, *n.* a garden flower.

chub, *n.* a small fat river-fish.—*adj.* **chub'by,** plump.

chuck, *n.* a gentle blow (e.g. under the chin).—*v.* to pat gently (under the chin): to throw.

chuck'le, *n.* a kind of laugh.—*v.* to laugh in a quiet manner, showing pleasure.

chum, *n.* a friend.

chunk, *n.* a thick piece.

church, *n.* a building used for Christian worship: any people of the same beliefs who meet together: the clergy as a whole. —*ns.* **churchwar'den**, one who looks after the affairs of a parish or church: a long clay-pipe; **church'yard**, the burial-ground round a church.

churl, *n.* a country labourer: a rough-mannered fellow.—*adj.* **churl'ish**, rude, ill-bred.

churn, *n.* a machine used for making butter.—*v.* to whirl cream so as to obtain butter.

chute, **shoot**, *n.* a waterfall: a channel for sending down logs, parcels, etc.

chut'ney, *n.* a hot sauce.

cicatrix, sik'a-triks, *n.* the scar over a wound after it is healed—also **cic'atrice**.

cider, sī'der, *n.* a drink made from the juice of apples.

cigar', *n.* a roll of tobacco-leaves for smoking.—*n.* **cigarette'**, a roll of fine tobacco enclosed in thin paper.

cinchona, sin-kō'na, *n.* the tree from whose bark quinine is got.

cincture, singk'tūr, *n.* a belt.

cin'der, *n.* burnt-out coal.

cinema, sin'e-ma, *n.* a picture-house (short for **cinemat'ograph** or **kinemat'ograph**—the machine that shows moving-pictures).

cin'erary, *adj.* holding ashes.

cinnamon, sin'a-mon, *n.* a spice got from the bark of a Ceylon tree: a light yellowish-brown colour.

cipher, sī'fer, *n.* a nought (0): any of the figures 1-9: anything of little value: secret writing, code.

cir'cle, *n.* a figure of this shape— ○ : any society or group of people (e.g. He moves in court *circles*, i.e. he is friendly with people at court).—*v.* to move round.

circuit, ser'kit, *n.* the act of moving round: a round made by judges for holding the courts of law: the judges making the round: (in wireless, electricity, etc.) a wired-up part through which a current may pass.—*adj.* **circū'itous**, round about.

circular, ser'kū-lar, *adj.* round.—*n.* a copy of a letter sent round to a number of persons.—*v.* **cir'cūlate**, to make to go round in a circle: to spread: to move round.—*n.* **circūlā'tion**, the act of circulating: the movement of the blood: the sale of a newspaper, magazine, etc.

circumcision, ser-kum-sish'un, *n.* among Jews, a religious ceremony at which infant boys (eight days old) receive their names.—*v.* **cir'cumcise'**.

circum'ference, *n.* the outside line of a circle.

circumlocū'tion, *n.* a roundabout way of saying something.

circumnav'igate, *v.* to sail round (e.g. the world).—*n.* **circumnav'igātor**.

circumscribe', *v.* to draw a line round: to shut in within certain bounds.—*n.* **circumscrip'tion**.

circumspect', *adj.* looking round on all sides watchfully: careful.—*n.* **circumspec'tion**, watchfulness.

cir'cumstance, *n.* something that happens, an event: (*pl.*) the state of one's affairs (*in good circumstances*, well off).—*adj.* **circumstan'tial**, made up of a number of small things or details.—*v.* **circumstan'tiate**, to prove by giving details.

circumvent', *v.* to get the better of a person by trickery: to get round a difficulty.—*n.* **circumven'tion**.

cir'cus, *n.* a round building where displays of games, horse-riding, etc. are given: a group of houses arranged in the form of a circle.

cir'rus, *n.* a fleecy kind of cloud, floating high in the sky.

cist, *n.* a stone coffin.

cis'tern, *n.* a tank for holding water.

cit'adel, *n.* a fortress in a city.

cite, *v.* to summon a person to appear in court: to quote: to name as proof.—*n.* **citā'tion**, a summons to appear in court.

cith'ara, *n.* a musical instrument of olden times, very like a guitar.— *n.* **cith'er**, **cith'ern**, a metal-stringed musical instrument.

cit'izen, *n.* one who lives in a city or state : a townsman.—*n.* cit'izenship, the rights of a citizen.

cit'ron, *n.* a fruit like a lemon.

cit'y, *n.* a large town : a town with a cathedral : the business centre or oldest part of a large town.—*adj.* civ'ic, having to do with a city or a citizen.—*n.pl.* civ'ics, the study of one's duties as a good citizen.

civ'et, *n.* perfume got from the civ'et-cat (small animal of Africa, Asia).

civ'il, *adj.* having to do with the ordinary people of a country, not with its armed forces : polite.—*ns.* civil'ian, one who is not in the armed forces ; civil'ity, politeness, good manners.—civil defence, in Britain, the name for all those public services which aim at protecting ordinary citizens against enemy bombs, fires, gas, etc. ; civil engineer, one who plans railways, docks, etc. ; civil service, the paid servants of the country who are not in the armed forces ; civil war, war between citizens of a country.

civ'ilised, *adj.* (people) living under a regular system of laws, government, and education : not savage.—*v.* civ'ilise, to bring (a people) under such a system.—*n.* civilisā'tion, life under such a system : the civilised nations as a whole.

claim, *v.* to call for : to demand as a right.—Also *n.*—*n.* claim'ant, one who makes a claim.

clairvoyance, klār-voi'ans, *n.* the supposed power to see into the future or into the world of spirits. —*n.* clairvoy'ant.

clam'my, *adj.* moist and sticky.

clam'ant, *adj.* calling aloud or earnestly.

clam'ber, *v.* to climb, grasping with the hands and feet.

clam'our, *n.* a loud, lasting cry : any loud noise.—*v.* to cry aloud for something.—*adj.* clam'orous, noisy.

clamp, *n.* a piece of timber, iron, etc., used to fasten things together.—*v.* to bind with clamps.

clan, *n.* a tribe, or a number of families, under a chief.—*adj.* clan'nish, loyal to one another like the members of a clan.— *n.* clans'man, a member of a clan.

clandes'tine, *adj.* hidden secret.

clang, *v.* to make a sharp, ringing sound.—Also *n.*—*n.* clang'our, a sharp, shrill, harsh sound.

clank, *n.* a sharp sound, like that made by a chain.

clap, *n.* the noise made by the sudden striking together of two things (e.g. the hands) : a burst of sound, esp. thunder : a slap.— *v.* to strike noisily together (esp. the hands, to show pleasure) : to pat with the hand : to imprison (e.g. to *clap* a person in prison).— *ns.* clap'per, the tongue of a bell ; clap'trap, meaningless words, nonsense.

cla'ret, *n.* a red wine.

clar'ify, *v.* to make clear.

clar'inet, clar'ionet, *n.* a wind-instrument, usually of wood.

clar'ion, *n.* a kind of trumpet : the sound of a trumpet.

clarity, klar'i-ti, *n.* clearness.

clash, *n.* a loud noise, such as is caused by the striking together of weapons : a coming together in a fight.—*v.* to dash noisily together : to disagree : (of events) to take place at the same time.

clasp, *n.* a hook for fastening : an embrace.—Also *v.*

class, *n.* a rank or order of persons or things : high rank : a number of scholars or students who are taught together : a division or arrangement : the position in order of merit of scholars after an examination.—*v.* to make into a class : to arrange in some order : to give a certain rank to.—*v.* class'ify, to make into classes : to arrange.—*n.* classificā'tion.

class'ic, *n.* any great writer or book : (*pl.*) Greek, Roman, and modern writers who are looked upon as of the highest rank—also their books.—*adj.* class'ical, of the highest rank or class : having to do with the best Greek and Roman writers.

clat'ter, *n.* a repeated rattling noise.

clause, *n.* a sentence or part of a sentence : a part of a will, act of parliament, etc.

claw, *n.* the hooked nail of a beast or bird : a foot with hooked nails. —*v.* to scratch or tear : to scrape.

clay, *n.* soft, sticky earth, different kinds of which are used in making china, drain-pipes, bricks, tiles, etc.—*adj.* clay´ey.

claymore´, *n.* a large sword once used by the Highlanders.

clean, *adj.* free from dirt: pure: neat: complete.—*adv.* quite (e.g. He was *clean* bowled).—*v.* to make clean, or free from dirt.—*adv.* clean´ly.—*n.* clean´ness.—*adj.* cleanly (klen´li), clean in habits.—*n.* cleanliness (klen´li-ness).

cleanse, klenz, *v.* to make clean.

clear, *adj.* pure: undimmed: free from difficulty or hindrance: easy to see or hear: without a stain: not guilty: plain: distinct.—*v.* to make clear: to empty: to free from guilt: to leap over: to make profit: (of the sky, weather) to become bright.—*ns.* clear´ness; clear´ance, act of clearing; clear´-ing, land cleared of wood.

cleave, *v.* to divide, to split: to crack.—*n.* cleav´age.

cleave, *v.* to stick to: to join together.—*n.pl.* clea´vers, a plant (*goose-grass*) which clings to one's clothes.

clef, *n.* a musical sign fixing the pitch of the notes.

cleft, *n.* an opening made by splitting: a crack.

cleg, *n.* the gadfly, horse-fly.

clem´atis, *n.* a creeping plant.

clem´ent, *adj.* mild: gentle: merciful.—*n.* clem´ency, readiness to forgive.

clench. See clinch.

cler´gy, *n.* the ministers of the Christian religion.—*adj.* cler´ical, having to do with the clergy.—*ns.* cler´gyman, cler´ic, clerk (klark), one of the clergy, a regular minister.

clerk, klark, *n.* one who works in an office, writing letters, keeping accounts, etc.—*v.* to act as clerk.—*adj.* cler´ical, having to do with office-work (e.g. *clerical* error).

clev´er, *adj.* quick in understanding: quick in moving: skilful.—*n.* clev´erness.

clew, kloo, *n.* a ball of thread: the corner of a sail.—*v.* to tie up sails to the yards.

click, *n.* a short, sharp sound.—Also *v.*

cli´ent, *n.* a customer: one who goes to a lawyer for advice or to get him to act for him.—*n.* clientele (klī´en-tel), the customers of a lawyer, shopkeeper, etc.

cliff, *n.* a high steep rock: the steep side of a mountain.

cli´mate, *n.* the weather conditions (heat, cold, rain, wind, etc.) of a place or country.—*adj.* climat´ic.

cli´max, *n.* the arranging of details or events so that they rise in importance to the last: an exciting finish.

climb, klīm, *v.* to go up by clutching with the hands and feet: to mount.—*n.* climber (klīm´er), one who climbs: a plant which climbs up other plants, walls, etc.

clime, *n.* a country and the climate it enjoys: climate.

clinch, klinsh, clench, klensh, *v.* to fasten or rivet a nail: to grasp tightly: to set firmly (e.g. the teeth): to settle (an argument, a bargain).—*n.* in boxing, a position in which the boxers hold each other with their arms.

cling, *v.* to stick close to.

clin´ic, *n.* teaching by gathering students round a sick person's bed: a hospital where such teaching is given.—*adj.* clin´ical.

clink, klingk, *n.* a ringing sound.

clink´ers, *n.pl.* the waste stuff when iron is smelted: a kind of brick: flakes or scales off red-hot iron.

clip, *v.* to cut off: to go quickly.—*n.* the thing clipped off (e.g. wool shorn off sheep): a smart blow.—*n.* clip´per, a fast-sailing vessel.

clip, *n.* a small fastener (e.g. for paper).—*v.* to fasten with a clip.

clique, klēk, *n.* a small band of persons who have joined together, usually for some mean purpose: a gang.

cloak, *n.* a loose outer garment: something which hides.—*v.* to cover as with a cloak: to hide.

clock, *n.* a machine for measuring time: an ornament sewn on the side of stockings or socks.—*n.* clock´work, machinery such as that of a clock.—*adj.* smooth-working.—*adj.* clock´wise, turning in the same direction as the hands of a clock.

clod, *n.* a thick lump, esp. of turf: a stupid fellow.—*n.* **clod′hopper,** a stupid clumsy person.

clog, *n.* a shoe with a wooden sole. —*v.* to hinder or choke (e.g. This pipe is *clogged* with rubbish).— *n.* **clog′-dance,** a dance in which the dancer wears clogs.

clois′ter, *n.* a covered-in walk in a monastery or nunnery.

close, *klōs, adj.* shut up, with no opening: without fresh air, stuffy: narrow: mean: near in time or place: hidden: beloved, very dear (e.g. a *close* friend).— *n.* any shut-in place: a narrow passage off a street: the gardens, walks, etc. near a cathedral.

close, *klōz, v.* to shut: to draw together and join: to finish: to come to grips (with).—*ns.* the end; **clos′ure,** the end: the stopping of a debate in Parliament; **closet** (kloz′et), a small private room.

clot, *n.* a lump or thickening that forms in some liquids (e.g. blood, cream) when heated or exposed to air.—*v.* to form into clots.

cloth, *n.* woven material of cotton, wool, linen, silk, etc.—*ns.* **clothes** (klōthz), **clō′thing,** garments.— *v.* **clōthe,** to put garments on.— *n.* **clō′thier,** one who makes or sells clothes.

cloud, *n.* a bank of mist floating in the sky: water-vapour: a great number of anything (e.g. a *cloud* of locusts): anything dark or gloomy.—*v.* to blot out or become dark, as with a cloud.—*adjs.* **cloud′y; cloud′ed; cloud′less.**—*n.* **cloud′-burst,** a sudden heavy fall of rain in one place.

clout, *n.* a rag: a mark shot at by archers: a shot, a blow.—*v.* to deal a blow to.

clove, *n.* a flower-bud of the clove-tree, used as a spice, and also for giving ' oil of cloves.'

clov′en, *adj.* split.—*adjs.* **clov′en-foot′ed, clov′en-hoofed,** having the hoof divided, as the ox, sheep.

clō′ver, *n.* a well-known field plant, common in pastures.

clown, *n.* a country-fellow: an ill-bred fellow: a fool.—*n.* **clown′-ing,** silly behaviour.—*adj.* **clown′-ish,** like a clown: awkward.

cloy, *v.* to fill until dislike comes: to sicken.

club, *n.* a heavy stick: a bat or stick used in certain games: a number of persons meeting for study, games, etc.: the place where these people meet.—*v.* to beat with a club: to join together for some purpose.

cluck, *n.* the call as of a hen to her chickens.—Also *v.*

clue, kloo, *n.* any sign or piece of evidence that helps to clear up a mystery.

clump, *n.* a cluster of trees or shrubs.

clum′sy, *adj.* shapeless: awkward. —*n.* **clum′siness.**

clus′ter, *n.* a bunch: a crowd.—*v.* to grow in clusters.

clutch, *v.* to hold firmly: to seize or grasp.—*n.* a grasp: part of a motor-car used in changing gear.

clut′ter, *n.* stir: noise.—*v.* to crowd together.

coach, *n.* a large, closed, four-wheeled horse or motor carriage: a railway carriage: a private teacher: one who trains footballers, rowers, boxers, etc.—*v.* to prepare others for an examination, rowing contest, boxing match, etc.—*n.* **coach′man,** the driver of a coach.

coagulate, ko-ag′ū-lāt, *v.* to go hard or lumpy (as when milk goes sour).

coal, *n.* a black substance (the wood of very ancient trees) dug out of the earth and used for burning.—*v.* to load with coal.—*ns.* **coal′field; coal′-mine; coal′-pit; coal′-scut′tle,** a fireside box for holding coal; **coal-tar,** a thick black liquid got from coal.

coalesce, kō-al-es′, *v.* to grow together or unite.

coalition, kō-al-ish′un, *n.* a joining together of different parts or parties.—Also *adj.* (e.g. *a coalition government,* one made up of different parties).

coarse, *adj.* rough: rude: harsh.— *v.* **coars′en,** to make coarse.—*n.* **coarse′ness.**

coast, *n.* side or border of land next the sea.—*v.* to sail along or near a coast.—*ns.* **coast′al.**—*ns.* **coast′-guard,** one who acts as a guard along the coast to prevent smuggling; **coast'-line,** the line or boundary of a coast: shore-line.

coat, *n.* a kind of outer garment with sleeves: an overcoat: the hair or wool of a beast: any covering (e.g. paint).—*v.* to cover with a coat or layer.—*n.* **coat'ing,** a covering: cloth for coats.—**coat of arms,** the family badge or crest; **coat of mail,** a piece of armour for the upper part of the body, made of metal rings linked one with another.

coax, *v.* to get someone to do what is wanted by petting or praising.

cob, *n.* a short-legged strong horse: a head of corn, wheat, etc.

cobalt, kō'bawlt, *n.* a metal and a blue colouring got from it.

cob'ble, cobble-stone, *ns.* a rounded stone used in paving.

cob'ble, *v.* to mend shoes coarsely.—*n.* **cobb'ler,** one who mends shoes.

cō'ble, cōb'ble, *n.* a small flat-bottomed boat.

cō'bra, *n.* a poisonous snake, found in India and Africa.

cob'web, *n.* the spider's web or net.

cocaine, ko-kān', *n.* a drug used to deaden pain.

cochin, koch'in, *n.* a large hen with feathered legs.

cochineal, koch'i-nēl, *n.* a scarlet dye made from the dried bodies of certain insects gathered from the cactus plant in Mexico, the West Indies, etc.

cock, *n.* the male of birds: a tap: a hammer-like part of a gun which, when the trigger is pulled, fires the shot.—*v.* to draw back the cock of a gun: to set upright (e.g. one's ears): to turn or tilt knowingly (e.g. one's head, hat). —*ns.* **cockade',** a knot of ribbons or something similar worn on the hat as a badge; **cock'chafer,** a brownish beetle; **cock'er,** a small spaniel; **cock'erel,** a young cock; **cock'-horse,** a rocking-horse; **cock'pit,** a closed-in space where game-cocks fight: a place where war is always raging: part of a warship used for the wounded: the space for the pilot in an aeroplane; **cock'roach** the black-beetle; **cocks'comb,** the

comb or crest on a cock's head: a fop; **cock'tail,** a mixed strong drink.—*adj.* **cock'sure,** quite sure, often without cause.

cock, *n.* a small pile of hay.

cockatoo', *n.* a kind of parrot.

cock'atrice, *n.* (in fables) a monster like a serpent.

cock'-boat, *n.* a small boat.

cock'le, *n.* a weed among corn, with a purple flower.

cock'le, *n.* a shellfish.—*n.* **cock'le-shell,** the shell of a cockle: a weakly built boat.

Cock'ney, *n.* one born in London: a Londoner's way of talking.

cō'cō, *n.* a palm-tree growing in hot countries—its fruit is the **coco-nut.**

cocoa, kō'kō, *n.* a drink made from the finely ground seeds of the cacao tree.

cocoon', *n.* a sheath or case of silk spun by the larva (grub) of some insects (e.g. silk-moth), where it rests till hatched out.

cod, cod'fish, *n.* a fish much used as food, found in the northern seas. —*n.* **cod'ling,** a small cod.

cod, *n.* a shell containing seeds.

cod'dle, *v.* to pamper, to pet.

code, *n.* a way of signalling or sending secret messages, using words, letters, etc. agreed on beforehand: a book or collection of laws, rules, etc. (e.g. the *Highway Code,* the rules of the road).—*v.* **cod'ify,** to arrange in an orderly way (e.g. Napoleon *codified* the laws of France).

codicil, kod'i-sil, *n.* a note added to a will or treaty.

cod'ling, cod'lin, *n.* a kind of apple. See also **cod.**

coequal, ko-ē'kwal, *adj.* of the same rank.—Also *n.*

coerce, kō-ers', *v.* to make to do, to compel.— *n.* **coercion** (kō-er'shun), force: government by force.—*adj.* **coer'cive,** using force.

coeval, kō-ē'val, *adj.* of the same age or time.

co-exist', *v.* to exist at the same time.—*n.* **co-exist'ence.**—*adj.* **co-exist'ent.**

coff'ee, *n.* a drink made from the ground beans or seeds of the coffee-tree.

coff'er, *n.* a chest for holding money or treasure.—*n.* **coffer-dam**, a water-tight dam placed in a river so that the foundations of a bridge may be built inside it.

cof'fin, *n.* box for a dead body.

cog, *n.* a tooth on a wheel.—*n.* **cog'-wheel**, a toothed wheel.

cog, *n.* a small boat.

cō'gent, *adj.* (of speaking or writing) having the power to make people believe (e.g. a *cogent* argument). —*n.* **cō'gency**.

cogitate, koj'i-tāt, *v.* to turn a thing over in one's mind: to ponder.—*n.* **cogitā'tion**, deep thought.

cognac, kon'yak, *n.* a French brandy.

cog'nate, *adj.* of the same family, kind, or nature : related to.

cog'nisance, *n.* knowledge or notice. —*adj.* **cog'nisant**, aware of.

cognō'men, *n.* a surname : a nickname.

cohere, kō-hēr', *v.* to stick together.—*n.* **cohēr'ence**, connection (between thoughts, ideas, etc.).—*adj.* **cohēr'ent**, sticking together: clear in thought or speech. —*n.* **cohē'sion**, the act of sticking together.—*adj.* **cohē'sive**.

cō'hort, *n.* among the Romans, a body of soldiers from 300 to 600 in number, forming a tenth part of a legion : a band of armed men.

coif, *n.* a covering for the head.—*ns.* **coiffeur** (kwof-er'), a hairdresser ; **coiffure** (kwof-eer'), style of hairdressing : a head-dress.

coign, koin, *n.* a corner.—**coign of vantage**, a position of advantage, either for seeing or doing.

coil, *v.* to wind in rings : to twist.— *n.* a rope or wire which has been gathered into rings.

coin, *n.* a piece of metal used as money.—*v.* to make metal into money : to stamp : to make a new word.—*n.* **coin'age**, the act of coining : the coins (halfcrowns, shillings, etc.) in use : a newly made word.

coincide, kō-in-sīd', *v.* to be like or the same as : to happen at the same time as.—*n.* **coincidence** (kō-in'-sid-ens), the happening of one thing at the same time as another, by chance or without planning.

coir, *n.* outside fibre of the coco-nut.

coke, *n.* fuel made by heating coal till the gas is driven out.

col'ander, *n.* a vegetable strainer.

cōld, *adj.* the opposite of hot : shivering : unfriendly. — *n.* the state of being cold : a disease, due to germs, causing shivering, running nose and eyes.—*n.* **cold'ness**. —*adjs.* **cold'ish**; **cold'-blooded**, having cold blood, as fishes: cruel. —**to give the cold shoulder to**, to refuse to have anything to do with : to scorn.

colic, *n.* a severe stomach-pain.

coliseum. See **colosseum**.

collab'orātor, *n.* one who works along with another (e.g. in writing a play, doing scientific work, etc.).—*n.* **collaborā'tion**.

collapse', *n.* a falling away or breaking down.—*v.* to fall or break down.—*adj.* **collaps'ible**, able to be folded up (e.g. a *collapsible* chair, boat, etc.).

col'lar, *n.* something worn round the neck.—*v.* to capture.

collate', *v.* to examine and compare (e.g. books and old writings) : to place the sheets of a book in order for binding.—*n.* **collā'tion**, a light meal.

collat'eral, *adj.* side by side.

colleague, kol'ēg, *n.* a person who is engaged upon the same work as one's self : a fellow-worker (e.g. The teacher who was going away received a gift from his *colleagues*), i.e. from the other teachers).

collect', *v.* to bring together : to gather.—*n.* **col'lect**, a short prayer.—*adj.* **collect'ed**, gathered together : cool : firm.—*ns.* **collec'tion**, act of collecting : money gathered at a meeting : a number of anything : a number of things which collects (tickets, money, etc.).— *adj.* **collect'ive**, acting together : thought of as one, not many.

col'leen, *n.* (in Ireland) a girl.

col'lege, kol'ej, *n.* a number of persons joined together for the purpose of learning (e.g. a *college* of a university—the universities of Oxford and Cambridge are made up of a number of colleges): a high school.—*adj.* **collē'giate**.

collide', *v.* to come together with great force : to dash together.— *n.* **collision** (kol-izh'un).

col'lie, *n.* a shepherd's dog.

collier, kol'yer, *n.* one who works in a coal-mine : a ship that carries coal.—*n.* **coll'iery**, a coal-mine.

col'lop, *n.* a slice of meat.

colloquy, kol'o-kwi, *n.* a speaking together : a conversation.—*adj.* **collō'quial**, used in everyday talk but not in correct writing or speaking (e.g. An 'awfully sweet' hat is a *colloquial* expression or **collō'quialism**).

collu'sion, *n.* a secret agreement (usually for some evil purpose).

cō'lon, *n.* the mark (:) used to show a break in a sentence : a part of the bowel.

colonel, kur'nel, *n.* an officer who has command of a regiment.

colonnade', *n.* a row of columns or pillars forming arches : a row of trees.

col'ony, *n.* a number of persons of a nation who settle in another country : the settlement they make.—*adj.* **colōn'ial.**—*n.* **col'onist**, one who lives in a colony.— *v.* **col'onise**, to make into a colony : to send settlers to live in a foreign country.

colossus, kol-os'us, *n.* a huge statue or person.—*adj.* **colos'sal**, very big, giant-size.—*n.* **colossē'um**, **colisē'um**, in olden days, a large open-air theatre in Rome, now in ruins : any large theatre.

colour, kul'ur, *n.* the appearance of an object to one's eye—red, green, blue, white, black, grey, etc.: shade, tint, hue : paint : (*pl.*) a flag or standard : paints.—*v.* to put colour or paint on : to blush. —*adj.* **col'oured**, not white-skinned.—*n.* **col'ouring**, anything used to give colour.—*adj.* **col'our-blind**, unable to tell one colour from another.—*n.* **col'our-ser'geant**, the sergeant who carries a regiment's flag.

colporteur, kol-pōr-ter', *n.* a traveller selling church leaflets.

cōlt, *n.* a young horse : a clumsy or awkward young person.

colter, kōl'ter, **coulter**, *n.* the metal cutting-part at the front of the blade of a plough.

col'umbine, *n.* a blue wild-flower.

column, kol'um, *n.* a stone or wooden pillar standing upright : soldiers arranged in narrow ranks one behind the other : figures, one below the other, to be added up : divisions of a page of a book, newspaper, etc. (e.g. This page has two *columns*).—*adj.* **colum'nar**, having columns.

cō'ma, *n.* deep sleep.—*adj.* **cōm'a-tose**, drowsy.

comb, kōm, *n.* a toothed instrument for separating and cleaning hair, wool, flax, etc.: the crest of a cock : cells for honey.—*v.* to arrange or clean with a comb.

combat, kum'bat or kom'bat, *v.* to fight, to struggle against.—*n.* a fight or struggle.—*n.* **com'batant**, one who is fighting.— *adj.* **com'bative**, quarrelsome.

comber, kōm'er, *n.* a foaming wave.

combine', *v.* to join together.— *n.* (kom'bīn), a number of traders who join together.—*n.* **combinā'tion**, a union of things or people : the series of letters or figures dialled to open a safe.

combust'ible, *adj.* liable to take fire and burn.—*n.* anything that will take fire.—*n.* **combus'tion**, burning.

come, kum, *v.* to move towards this place (the opposite of *go*) : to draw near : to happen.—*n.* **com'ing.**

com'edy, *n.* a play which is clever or funny, and not on a serious subject : any funny happening. —*n.* **comē'dian**, one who acts in a comedy : a funny person.

comely, kum'li, *adj.* pleasing : graceful.—*adv.* in a comely manner.— *n.* **come'liness.**

com'et, *n.* a kind of star, usually giving off a bright light, and having a tail of light following.

comfit, kum'fit, *n.* a sweetmeat.

comfort, kum'fort, *v.* to ease from trouble : to soothe : to cheer up. —*n.* ease : quiet enjoyment : anything that makes us happier or stronger to bear bad luck.—*adj.* **com'fortable**, giving or enjoying comfort.—*n.* **com'forter**, one who comforts : a long woollen scarf.

com'ic, *adj.* having to do with comedy: causing laughter.—*adj.* **com'ical**, funny, amusing.

com'ma, *n.* in punctuation, the mark (,).

command', *v.* to order: to be at the head of, or in charge of: to look over or down upon (e.g. This hill *commands* a fine view of the city).—*n.* an order.—*adj.* **command'ing**, showing mastery, powerful.—*ns.* **commandant'**, an officer who has command of a place or of troops; **command'er**, one who commands: in the navy, an officer next in rank below captain: **command'ment**, an order or command, esp. one of the *Ten Commandments* (see Exodus xx.).

commandeer', *v.* to seize (food, lodgings, etc.) for an army.

comman'do, *n.* (in British army) a soldier trained for hard tasks.

commem'orate, *v.* to bring to memory by some act, as a church service.—*n.* **commemora'tion**.

commence', *v.* to begin.—*n.* **commence'ment**, the beginning.

commend', *v.* to give into the care of: to praise.—*n.* **commenda'tion**.—*adjs.* **commend'able**, worthy of praise; **commend'atory**, praising.

commen'surate, *adj.* equal in measure or size (e.g. His marks were not *commensurate* with the amount of study he had done).

com'ment, *n.* a note making more clear something already written: a remark.—*v.* (kom'ent or koment'), to make remarks about: to add notes so as to make more clear.—*n.* **com'mentary**, a remark or number of remarks.—**a running commentary**, a description of an event by someone who is looking on.

com'merce, *n.* buying and selling of goods between people or nations: trade, business.—*adj.* **commer'cial**, having to do with commerce.—**commercial traveller**, a person who travels about to show goods and take orders for them.

commingle, kom-ing'gl, *v.* to mix with.

commis'erate, *v.* to pity: to be sad along with another.—*n.* **commisera'tion**, pity.

com'missary, *n.* one who is in command (e.g. *police commissary*): an officer who sees to an army's provisions, etc.—*n.* **commissa'riat**, that part of an army that looks after the food supply.

commission, kom-ish'un, *n.* the act of committing: the thing committed: a job, situation: an order to start work on a job: a letter (the *King's Commission*) appointing an officer for the army, navy, or air force: the rank of officer: a number of people ordered to find out about, or look into, important matters (e.g. *Civil Service Commission, Royal Commission on Historical Monuments*): payment for work done.—*v.* to appoint or give power to.—*ns.* **commissionaire'**, a uniformed man, messenger, or attendant (at picture-houses, hotels, etc.); **commis'sioner**, one who is ordered or commissioned to do a piece of business.

commit', *v.* to give into the trust or charge of another: to do.—*ns.* **commit'ment**, an order for sending to prison: a promise: something undertaken; **commit'tee**, a number of people chosen to see that something is done, or to find out the best way of doing it.

commo'dious, *adj.* roomy: comfortable.—*n.* **commod'ity**, convenience: an article of trade: (*pl.*) goods, produce.

com'modore, *n.* an officer of high rank in the navy and air force.

common, kom'un, *adj.* shared by many: happening often: easy to be got: of little value: vulgar: of low rank.—*n.* land belonging to the people of a town, parish, etc.: (*pl.*) the people of the land: those who stand for them in the House of Commons: allowance of food (e.g. *short commons*, a small allowance of food).—*ns.* **comm'oner**, one who is not a noble: a member of the House of Commons; **comm'onsense**, good sense, wisdom; **com'mon-place**, a common subject of talk: something which everybody knows.—Also *adj.*

commonweal, kom'un-wēl, **commonwealth**, kom'un-welth, *n.* government in which the people have the power.

commotion, kom-ō'shun, *n.* an excited movement, esp. of people : a riot.

commūne', *v.* to share with others : to talk together : to receive Holy Communion. — *adj.* **communal** (kom-ū'nal or kom'), shared by many.

communicate, kom-ū'ni-kāt, *v.* to give a share of : to give : to send word to.—*adj.* **commū'nicable**, that may be communicated.—*n.* **communicā'tion**, a message : a way of passing from place to place.—*adjs.* **commū'nicable**, able to be passed on to others ; **commū'nicative**, willing or ready to give news : telling much.

communiqué, kom-ū'ni-kā, *n.* an announcement by a government.

Commū'nion, Holy Communion, *n.* the Lord's Supper.

com'munism, *n.* the kind of socialism developed in Russia or China.—*n.* **com'mūnist**, one who believes in communism and thinks other countries should copy Russia or China.—*adj.* **commūnist'ic.**

commū'nity, *n.* a sharing of something by many : the people who share : citizens.

commūte', *v.* to change a punishment for one less severe.—*n.* **commutā'tion.**

compact', *adj.* fastened or packed together.—*n.* **compact'ness.**

com'pact, *n.* a bargain or agreement : a treaty.

companion, kom-pan'yun, *n.* a friend. — *adj.* **compan'ionable**, friendly.—*n.* **compan'ionship.**

compan'ion, *n.* (on ships) the window-frame through which light passes to a lower deck or cabin.—*ns.* **compan'ion-ladd'er, compan'ion-way**, a staircase from deck to cabin.

company, kum'pa-ni, *n.* a gathering of persons : a number of persons who have joined together to form a business firm : part of a regiment : a ship's crew.

compare', *v.* to set things together to see how far they are, or are not, alike : to say one thing is like another.—*adjs.* **com'parable; compar'ative,** judged against something else.—*n.* **compar'ison,** the act of comparing.—**beyond compare,** beyond all rivals.

compart'ment, *n.* a separate part or division (e.g. of a railway carriage).

compass, kum'pas, *n.* an instrument for showing direction (used in ships, aeroplanes, etc.) : distance round, or up and down (e.g. of the voice, or of a musical instrument) : (*pl.*) an instrument (made up of a fixed leg and a movable leg) for drawing circles. —*v.* to go round, surround : to succeed in doing : to lay plans to do something evil.

compassion, kom-pash'un, *n.* sorrow for another : pity.—*adj.* **compas'sionate**, pitying: merciful.

compat'ible, *adj.* in agreement with : able to agree.—*n.* **compatibil'ity.**

compatriot, kom-pā'tri-ot, *adj.* of the same country.—Also *n.*

compeer', *n.* one who is equal to another : a companion.

compel', *v.* to drive on by force : to make to do.

compen'dium, *n.* a shortening : a book which contains a great deal of information.—*adj.* **compen'dious.**

com'pensate, *v.* to reward : to make up for wrong or damage done.— *n.* **compensā'tion**, something (usually money) given to make up for wrong done or injuries received.

compēte', *v.* to strive along with others (e.g. for a prize).—*ns.* **competi'tion; compet'itor**, one who competes : a rival.—*adj.* **compet'itive.**

com'petent, *adj.* fit : able to do : skilled in doing : lawful.—*ns.* **com'petence, com'petency,** fitness : an amount which is just enough for comfort (e.g. He retired on a modest *competence*).

compile', *v.* to write (e.g. a book) by collecting the facts from other books : to collect.—*ns.* **compilā'tion; compi'ler.**

complā'cent, *adj.* pleased with one's own cleverness : calm.—*ns.* **complā'cence, complā'cency.**

complain', v. to grumble: to say one has been badly treated.—n. **complaint'**, a statement of one's sorrow, trouble, etc.: an illness.

com'plement, n. that which completes or fills up: full number or quantity (e.g. *ship's complement*, the full number of men required to work it).—adj. **complement'ary**, completing: together making up a whole.

complete', adj. lacking in no way: perfect: finished: whole.—v. to finish: to make perfect.—ns. **complete'ness; comple'tion**.

com'plex, adj. made up of many parts: not simple.—n. **com-plex'ity**.

complexion, kom-plek'shun, n. colour (e.g. of the skin of the face): appearance.

compli'ance. See comply.

com'plicate, v. to make difficult.—n. **complica'tion**, a new difficulty added to others: a fresh disease coming on the top of one which a person already has.—adj. **com'plicated**, containing a great many parts or details: difficult to understand.

complicity, kom-plis'i-ti, n. a share in a crime (e.g. He was accused of *complicity* in the robbery).

com'pliment, n. praise: flattery: good wishes.—v. **compliment'**, to praise: to say one is pleased at another's success.—adj. **compliment'ary**, flattering: praising: given free as a mark of respect (e.g. *complimentary* ticket).

comply', v. to yield: to say 'yes' to (e.g. He *complied* with my request).—n. **compli'ance**.—adj. **compli'ant**, agreeing to: yielding.

compo'nent, adj. making up one whole thing, along with other parts.—n. a part (e.g. of a wireless set).

comport', v. to behave.—n. **comport'ment**, behaviour.

compose', v. to make something by putting parts together: to arrange parts, as a musician does in writing music, or a printer in arranging types: to set at rest, to soothe.—adjs. **composed'**, quiet, calm; **com'posite**, made up of parts.—ns. **composi'tion**, the act of putting together in order: the thing put together or made up (e.g. a piece of music, a short piece of writing): a mixture of substances; **compos'itor**, a person who puts together the types for printing; **com'post**, a gardener's mixture of manures; **compo'sure**, calmness.

compound, kom-pownd', v. to mix together: to settle by an agreement, to come to terms.—adj. **com'pound**, made up of a number of different parts: not simple.—n. a mixture made up of a number of parts: a mixed medicine.

com'pound, n. a railed-off space round a house.

comprehend', v. to understand: to include.—adjs. **comprehen'sible**, able to be understood; **comprehen'sive**, taking in or including much.—n. **comprehen'sion**, power to understand.

compress', v. to press together: to force into a narrower space.—n. **compres'sion**.

comprise', v. to include: to contain.

com'promise, n. a settlement of a quarrel by both sides giving up some part of what is claimed.—v. to settle by agreement: to bring under suspicion: to put in a difficult position.

compul'sion, n. force driving a person to do a thing.—adj. **compul'sory**, requiring to be done: forced upon one.

compunction, kom-pungk'shun, n. regret: pity.

compute', v. to count or reckon.—n. **computa'tion**.

com'rade, n. a true companion or friend.

con, v. to learn thoroughly or by heart.

concatena'tion, n. a number of things joined together like the links in a chain: a number of events following each other.

con'cave, adj. hollow or curved inwards (e.g. the inner side of a spoon).—n. **concav'ity**, a hollow.

conceal', v. to hide: to keep secret.—n. **conceal'ment**, act of hiding: secrecy: hiding-place.

concede', v. to give up or yield: to admit (e.g. that something is true).

conceit, kon-sēt', *n.* a too high opinion of one's self or of one's good points: an odd way of thinking or writing.—*adj.* **conceit'ed,** having a high idea of one's self, vain.—*n.* **conceit'edness.**

conceive, kon-sēv', *v.* to form in the mind : to imagine.—*adj.* **conceiv'able,** able to be imagined.

con'centrate, *v.* to bring to the centre or to one place : to bring wandering thoughts back to what should be thought about : to pack close together : to make stronger (e.g. *concentrated* acid).—*n.* **concentra'tion.**

concen'tric, *adj.* having the same point for centre.

con'cept, *n.* a general idea about something.—*n.* **concep'tion,** the act of beginning or forming (in the mind) : an idea : a plan.

concern', *v.* to have to do with : to make uneasy.—*n.* that which has to do with one : that which interests one : worry, uneasiness : a business, or those in it.—*prep.* **concern'ing,** about.

con'cert, *n.* the doing of things together or after planning (e.g. The thieves acted in *concert*) : a musical entertainment or show.—*v.* **concert',** to plan together.—*adj.* **concert'ed,** planned or practised together.

concertina, kon-ser-tē'na, *n.* a musical wind-instrument, with bellows and keys.

concerto, kon-cher'to, *n.* a long piece of music for violin or piano, with an accompaniment from an orchestra.

concession, kon-sesh'un, *n.* a giving up of something : what is given up.

conch, kongk, *n.* a sea-shell.—*n.* **conchol'ogy,** the study of shells.

concil'iate, *v.* to win over as a friend : to make friends.—*n.* **concilia'tion,** a peace-making : the bringing together of those who have quarrelled.—*adj.* **concil'iatory.**

concise', *adj.* cut short : brief.—*n.* **concise'ness.**

con'clave, *n.* a secret and important meeting.

conclude, kon-klood', *v.* to end : to make a decision or a judgment.—*adj.* **conclud'ing,** closing : nearing the end.—*n.* **conclu'sion,** end, close, last part : what is thought or settled in the mind.—*adj.* **conclu'sive,** settling, deciding (e.g. *conclusive* proof).—**to try conclusions (with),** to fight with : to compete against.

concoct', *v.* to mix together : to make up (e.g. a story) in order to deceive.—*n.* **concoc'tion,** food or drink made ready for use.

concom'itant, *adj.* going along with.

con'cord, *n.* agreement.—*n.* **cord'ance,** agreement : a dictionary telling the best known parts of a book (e.g. a Bible *Concordance*).

concourse, kon'kōrs, *n.* a crowd.

con'crete, *adj.* solid : made of concrete.—*n.* a mixture of sand, cement, etc. used in building.

concur', *v.* to agree.—*n.* **concur'rence,** a meeting (e.g. of lines) : agreement to do something.—*adj.* **concur'rent.**

concussion, kon-kush'on, *n.* a great shock or shaking, as when two things knock together : harm done to the brain when one receives a knock on the head : the force of an explosion.

condemn, kon-dem', *v.* to say that one is guilty or at fault : to blame.—*n.* **condemna'tion.**—*adj.* **condem'natory,** blaming.

condense', *v.* to make to go into smaller space : to change to a stronger or denser kind (e.g. steam or vapour to water, or fresh milk to *condensed* milk).—*ns.* **condensa'tion ; condens'er,** a machine for changing vapour to liquid : something for collecting electricity (e.g. a *condenser* in a wireless set).

condescend, kon-de-send', *v.* to act or speak as if one is doing a favour to someone : to make one's self humble.—*adj.* **condescend'ing,** acting as if one was lowering one's self.—*n.* **condescen'sion.**

condign, kon-dīn', *adj.* well-deserved (e.g. *condign* punishment).

con'diment, *n.* a sauce.

condition. kon-dish´un, n. state in which anything is (e.g. in a bad *condition* of health ; a car in good *condition*) : rank : something that must happen before some other thing happens (e.g. He was allowed to stay on *condition* that he kept quiet) : a term of a bargain, treaty, etc.—*adj.* **condi´tional,** depending on certain things happening.

condole´, v. to share another's sorrow.—n. **condol´ence.**

condone´, v. to forgive : to allow (an offence) to pass unchecked.

con´dor, n. large vulture (S. America).

conduc´ive, adj. helping towards (e.g. Such conduct is not *conducive* to good health).

conduct´, v. to lead or guide : to direct : to behave.—ns. **con´duct,** act or method of leading or managing : behaviour ; **conduct´or,** something that *conducts* (i.e. leads away ; e.g. a *lightning conductor* catches electricity and conducts it to the earth) : a manager : a director of an orchestra : one in charge of a bus, etc. :—*fem.* **conduct´ress.**

conduit, kun´dit, n. a channel or pipe to carry water, etc.

cone, n. a shape, round at the bottom, and coming to a point : anything like a cone (e.g. a fir-cone).—*adj.* **con´ical,** cone-shaped.

coney. See cony.

confec´tion, n. a sweetmeat.—ns. **confec´tioner,** one who makes or sells sweets ; **confec´tionery,** sweets in general : the shop or business of a confectioner.

confed´erate, adj. joined together by a treaty.—n. a person who has agreed to act with others (often for an evil purpose).—ns. **confedera´tion,** a group of people interested in the same things ; **confed´eracy,** persons united for some evil purpose.

confer´, v. to give : to talk together. —n. **con´ference,** a meeting to talk over matters.

confess´, v. to own up (e.g. that one has done wrong ; that something is true, etc.) : (of a priest) to hear a person admit his sins.—ns. **confes´sion,** owning up to

wrong : an open statement of what one believes ; **confes´sional,** the seat from which a priest hears confession of sins.—*adj.* **confessed** (kon-fest´), not secret : outspoken.

confet´ti, n. small pieces of coloured paper thrown at a newly married couple.

confide´, v. to trust fully or have faith (with *in*) : to hand over to someone's care.—ns. **confidant´,** one trusted with a secret :—*fem.* **confidante´** ; **con´fidence,** firm trust or belief : faith : boldness. —*adjs.* **con´fident,** trusting firmly : very sure ; **confiden´tial,** to be kept as a secret ; **confid´ing,** trusting.

configura´tion, n. shape : outline.

confine´, n. border, boundary.—v. **confine´,** to shut up in a small place : to imprison.—n. **confine´ment.**

confirm´, v. to make firm, to strengthen : to make sure : to take into the Church.—n. **confirma´tion,** a making sure : proof : the church ceremony in which a person is made a full member.—*adjs.* **confirm´atory,** confirming, making sure ; **confirmed** (kon-firmd´), settled in habits (usually bad—e.g. a *confirmed* drunkard).

con´fiscate, v. to take away, as a punishment.—n. **confisca´tion.**

conflagra´tion, n. a big fire.

con´flict, n. a struggle or contest : a battle.—v. **conflict´,** to fight : to be in opposition.—*adj.* **conflict´ing,** not in agreement, contradicting each other.

confluence, kon´floo-ens, n. a meeting-place (e.g. of rivers).—*adj.* **con´fluent,** flowing into one.

conform´, v. to obey : to agree with : to follow the religion fixed by law.—*adj.* **conform´able,** like : agreeing with.—ns. **conforma´tion,** shape or build ; **conform´ity,** likeness : obedience to the religion fixed by law.

confound, kon-fownd´, v. to surprise, to puzzle : to defeat.—*adj.* **confound´ed,** astonished, puzzled.

confront, kon-frunt´, v. to stand up to : to bring face to face.

confuse´, v. to mix so that the parts cannot be made out : to puzzle :

to mistake.—*n.* **confū′sion**, lack of order: untidiness: shame.

confute′, *v.* to prove to be false.—*n.* **confutā′tion**.

congeal, kon-jēl′, *v.* to become hard: to freeze.

congenial, kon-jē′ni-al, *adj.* of the same nature as one's self (e.g. a *congenial* friend): pleasant.

congen′ital, *adj.* born in a person (e.g. *congenital* lameness).

conger, kong′ger, *n.* a sea-eel.

congest′, *v.* to crowd together: to fill too full.—*n.* **congest′ion**, over-fullness: illness caused by having too much blood in any part (e.g. *congestion* of the lungs): state of being too crowded.

conglom′erate, *adj.* brought together in a shapeless lump.—*n.* a rock made up of stones stuck together.—*n.* **conglomerā′tion**, a heap or collection.

congrat′ulate, *v.* to wish joy to a person on any success: to think (one's self) lucky.—*n.* **congratulā′tion**.—*adj.* **congrat′ulatory**.

con′gregate, *v.* to come together in a crowd.—*n.* **congregā′tion**, a gathering: the people in a church.

cong′ress, *n.* a meeting of persons (e.g. statesmen, doctors, or teachers, etc.) from different parts, to talk over matters that interest them. — **Congress**, the name for the parliament of the United States of America.

congruent, kon′groo-ent, *adj.* agreeing, fit, suitable.—*n.* **congru′ity**.—*adj.* **con′gruous**, fit, suitable.

conif′erous, *adj.* (of trees) bearing cones in which the seeds are held (e.g. the pine).—*n.* **con′ifer**, a cone-bearing tree.

conjec′tūre, *n.* a guess.—*v.* to guess at.—*adj.* **conject′ural**, done by guesswork: doubtful.

conjoin′, *v.* to join together.—*adjs.* **conjoined′**, **conjoint′**, joined together.

con′jugal, *adj.* having to do with marriage.

con′jugate, *v.* to give the main parts of a verb.—*n.* **conjugā′tion**.

conjunct′, *adj.* joined together: happening at the same time.—*n.* **conjunc′tion**, a joining word (e.g. *and*).

conjure, kun′jer, *v.* to work magic: to do tricks by quickness of hand.—*n.* **con′juror**, one who does conjuring tricks.

conjure, kon-joor′, *v.* to beg or ask earnestly, as if calling up spirits to help: to ask solemnly.—*n.* **conjurā′tion**.

connect′, *v.* to join: to fasten together.—*n.* **connec′tion**, something that joins.—**in connection with**, concerning: **well connected**, of good birth: knowing important people.

conn′ing-tower, *n.* the place on a war-ship or submarine from which orders for steering are given.

connive′, *v.* to be aware of something (usually a fault) but to pretend not to see.—*n.* **conniv′ance**.

connoisseur, kon-es-ser′, *n.* one who knows all about a thing (e.g. a *connoisseur* of wines): a person of good taste (in music, painting, etc.).

connū′bial, *adj.* having to do with marriage.

conquer, kong′ker, *v.* to gain by force: to defeat completely: to be the winner.—*ns.* **con′queror**, one who conquers; **conquest** (kon′kwest), something won by force.

consanguinity, kon-sang-gwin′it-i, *n.* relationship by blood.

conscience, kon′shens, *n.* one's sense of right and wrong, an inward feeling by which we know right from wrong.—*adj.* **conscientious** (kon-shi-en′shus), careful and earnest in one's work.—*n.* **conscien′tiousness**.

conscious, kon′shus, *adj.* able to hear, see, think, etc.—*n.* **con′sciousness**.

con′script, *n.* a person who is obliged by law to serve as a soldier or sailor or to work at war work.—*n.* **conscrip′tion**, forced service in army or navy or on war work.

con′secrate, *v.* to make holy.—*n.* **consecrā′tion**.

consecutive, kon-sek-ū-tiv, *adj.* coming in order, one after the other.

consen′sus, *n.* an agreement (of opinion).

consent, v. to think the same as: to say 'yes' to, to agree.—n. agreement.

consequence, kon'se-kwens, n. that which comes after: result: importance (e.g. people of *consequence*).—*adjs*. con'sequent, coming as a result; consequen'tial, thinking one's self important.

conserve', v. to keep from being wasted: to keep back for later use.—n. conservā'tion.—*adj*. conserv'ative, not liking sudden changes.—*ns*. conservatoire (konser-va-twar'), conservatō'rium, a school for musicians; conser'vator, a keeper of a museum, public garden, etc.; conserv'atory, a glass-house for plants.

consid'er, v. to think carefully or seriously about: to allow for.—*adjs*. consid'erable, more than a little: important; consid'erate, thoughtful about others, kind.—n. considerā'tion, serious thinking: importance: a reason: a reward: a small payment.—*prep*.consid'ering, making allowance for.

consign, kon-sīn', v. to send: to give into the care of.—n. consign'ment, a load (e.g. of goods).

consist', v. to be made of.—n. consist'ency, thickness or firmness (e.g. Mix to the *consistency* of paste): the quality of always being the same.—*adj*. consist'ent, fixed: not changing.

console', v. to comfort, cheer up.—n. consolā'tion, something that makes trouble more easy to bear: comfort.

consol'idate, v. to make solid or strong: to unite: to grow stronger.—n. consolidā'tion.

con'sonant, n. a letter of the alphabet that is not a vowel.

con'sort, n. a partner: a husband or wife.—v. consort', to keep company: to agree.

conspicuous, kon-spik'ū-us, *adj*. clearly seen.

conspire', v. to plan together, often for something evil.—*ns*. conspir'acy, a coming together for an evil purpose: a plot; conspir'ator, one who takes part in the working of an evil plan.

constable, kun'sta-bl, n. a police-

man: (in olden times) a King's servant of high rank (e.g. *High Constable of Scotland*): (in olden times) the keeper of a castle.—n. constab'ulary, the police force of a town or county.

con'stant, *adj*. fixed: never changing: faithful.—n. con'stancy.

constellā'tion, n. a group of stars.

consternation, kon'ster-nā'shun, n. terror: dismay.

constipā'tion, n. too slow working of the bowels.

con'stitute, v. to set up: to form or make up.—n. constit'uency, the voters in a district who send a member to parliament.—*adj*. constit'uent, making or forming.—n. a necessary part: a person staying in a voting district.—n. constitū'tion, the way the body or mind is formed (e.g. *a good constitution*, a strong and healthy body): a set of rules, laws, etc. by which a country or body of people is governed.—*adj*. constitū'tional, having to do with the laws of a country.—n. a short walk for the sake of one's health.

constrain', v. to force a person to act in a certain way.—n. constraint'.

constrict', v. to press together.—n. constrict'or, a large snake, the boa-constrictor, which crushes its prey.

construct', v. to build.—n. construc'tion, anything built: the arrangement of words in a sentence: meaning.

construe', v. to put into another language: to explain.

con'sul, n. a person who looks after his country's affairs in a foreign country: in old-time Rome, a chief ruler.—*adj*. con'sular, having to do with a consul.

consult', v. to ask for advice.—n. consultā'tion.

consume', v. to eat up: to use.—n. consū'mer, one who eats or uses.

con'summate, v. to raise to the highest point: to finish off.—*adj*. (kon-sum'āt) complete: perfect.

consumption, kon-sum'shun, n. the act of using up—the opposite of *production*: a lung disease in which the sufferer wastes away.—*adj*. consump'tive, wasting away: having the disease consumption.

con'tact, *n.* touch.—**to make contact with, to come in contact with, to meet**: to touch

contagious, kon-tā'jus, *adj.* (of disease) able to be passed on to anyone who comes near.

contain', *v.* to hold: to hold back.—*n.* contain'er, a box, tin, jar, bottle, etc. for holding anything.

contam'inate, *v.* to make dirty: to make bad.—*n.* contaminā'tion.

contemn, kon-tem', *v.* to look down on, to despise.

con'template, *v.* to look at seriously: to think seriously about: to mean to do.—*n.* contempla'tion.

contem'porary, *adj.* living at, or belonging to, the same time.—*n.* a person living at the same time (e.g. Napoleon was a *contemporary* of the Duke of Wellington).—*adj.* contemporā'neous, living or happening at the same time.

contempt', *n.* a low opinion of a person or thing: scorn.—*adjs.* contempt'ible, deserving scorn: of little worth; contempt'uous, haughty, showing scorn.

contend', *v.* to fight against: to hold to a belief.—*n.* conten'tion, an opinion strongly held.—*adj.* conten'tious, quarrelsome.

con'tent, *n.* that which is inside anything:—often used in *pl.*, e.g. the *contents* of a pail, of a book.

content', content'ed, *adjs.* pleased: having enough to please.—*ns.* content'; content'ment.—*v.* content', to please: to make quiet.

contest', *v.* to fight over something.—*n.* con'test, a fight.—*n.* contest'ant, one who contests.

con'text, *n.* the place in a book to which a certain part belongs.

contig'uous, *adj.* placed so near as to touch.—*n.* contigū'ity.

con'tinent, *n.* one of the five great divisions of the earth's landsurface (Europe, Asia, Africa, Australia, America).—*adj.* continent'al, like, or having to do with, a continent: European.

con'tinent, *adj.* holding one's self back (e.g. from doing wrong).—*n.* con'tinence.

contin'gent, *adj.* depending on something else: happening by chance.—*n.* a body of soldiers sent by one country to help another in a war (e.g. The South African *contingent*).—*n.* contin'gency, something that may possibly happen.

contin'ue, *v.* to keep on doing or making: to stay the same.—*adjs.* contin'ual, going on without stop; contin'uous, coming one after the other without a gap or break until the end (e.g. three *continuous* performances).—*ns.* contin'uance, the state of going on without stopping or dying (e.g. The *continuance* of peace is of great importance); continuā'tion, the act of carrying something farther or extending: the part extended (e.g. I am busy with the *continuation* of the story); continū'ity, the state of having no gaps or breaks.

contort', *v.* to twist or turn violently.—*ns.* contor'tion, a violent twisting; contor'tionist, one who can twist his body violently.

contour, kon'toor, *n.* outline, shape.—**contour line,** a line drawn on a map through points all at the same height above sea-level.

con'traband, *n.* goods not allowed to enter a country: goods which a neutral country may not supply to a country at war.

contract', *v.* to become or make less: to bargain for: to promise in writing.—*ns.* con'tract, an agreement between two persons or sides; contrac'tion, a shortening (e.g. of a word—*gym.* for *gymnasium*); contract'or, one who promises to do work, or supply goods, at an arranged price (e.g. a *contractor* for school-books).

contradict', *v.* to say the opposite of: to deny.—*n.* contradic'tion.—*adj.* contradict'ory.

contral'tō, *n.* the deepest or lowest singing voice in women.

con'trary, *adj.* doing or saying the opposite: opposite.—*n.* the opposite.—*n.* con'trariness (or -trā').

contrast', *v.* to set one thing alongside another to show how much they are different.—*n.* con'trast, difference between two things.

contravēne', *v.* to break (e.g. a law).—*n.* contraven'tion.

contretemps, kong'tr-tong, *n.* a slight mishap at an awkward moment : a hitch.

contrib'ute, *v.* to give along with others : to pay a share : to write for magazine, newspaper, etc.—*ns.* **contribu'tion** ; **contrib'utor**.

con'trite, *adj.* very sorry for having done wrong.—*n.* **contrition** (kon-trish'un), deep sorrow for sin.

contrive', *v.* to plan : to invent : to bring about.—*n.* **contriv'ance**, act of contriving : invention.

control', *n.* power to guide, govern, or hold in check (e.g. *control* over a car, *control* over one's temper) : means by which a driver keeps a machine under his power (e.g. steering-wheel, switch, brake).—*v.* to keep in check : to have power over.—**out of** control, not able to be held back.

con'troversy, *n.* an argument : a quarrel.—*adj.* **controver'sial.**—*v.* **controvert'**, to deny.

contumacious, kon-tū-mā'shus, *adj.* stubborn : rebelling.—*ns.* **contumā'ciousness**, **con'tumacy.**

con'tumely, *n.* rudeness with impudence.—*adj.* **contumē'lious.**

conun'drum, *n.* a riddle.

convalesce', kon-val-es', *v.* to get back health.—*n.* **convales'cence**, gradual return to health and strength.—*adj.* and *n.* **convales'cent.**

convene', *v.* to call people to a meeting : to meet.—*n.* **convēn'er**, one who calls a meeting.

convēn'ient, *adj.* suitable : handy.—*n.* **convēn'ience.**

con'vent, *n.* a dwelling for nuns or monks.—*adj.* **convent'ūal.**

conventicle, kon-vent'i-kl, *n.* a secret meeting for worship, held usually in the fields or mountains.

conven'tion, *n.* a way of acting that has become usual (e.g. Shaking hands when we meet is a *convention*) : a meeting specially called : a treaty or agreement.—*adj.* **conven'tional**, done by habit.

converge', *v.* to come together, to meet at a point.—*adj.* **conver'gent.**—*n.* **conver'gence.**

converse', *v.* to talk.—*ns.* **conversā'tion**, **con'verse**, talk. — *adjs.* **con'versant**, able to talk about something, because one has studied the matter ; **conversā'tional**, having to do with talk : talking freely.

con'verse, *adj.* turned round : opposite.—*n.* something which is the opposite of another thing.

convert', *v.* to change from one thing to another : to turn from one religion to another, or from an evil to a religious life.—*ns.* **conver'sion** ; **con'vert**, one who has changed his opinions, esp. his religion : one who has become religious after a wicked life.—*adj.* **convert'ible**, able to be changed from one thing to another.

con'vex, *adj.* curved on the outside like the back of a spoon.—*n.* **convex'ity.**

convey, kon-vā', *v.* to carry : to send : to hand over to.—*n.* **convey'ance**, something which carries (e.g. a cart, motor-bus).

convict', *v.* to say that a person is guilty.—*ns.* **con'vict**, one who has been sent to prison for a number of years ; **convic'tion** (in a law-court) the passing of a sentence upon a guilty person.

convince', *v.* to make someone believe that something is true : to persuade by showing.—*adj.* **convinc'ing**, forcing one to believe : clearly proved.—*n.* **convic'tion**, strong belief.

conviv'ial, *adj.* merry : fond of feasting.—*n.* **convivial'ity.**

convoke', *v.* to call together.—*n.* **convocā'tion**, a meeting, esp. of bishops, or heads of a university.

convol'vulus, *n.* a kind of twining or trailing plant—*bindweed.*

convoy', *v.* to go along with and protect.—*n.* **con'voy**, a protecting guard : merchant ships protected by warships : a string of army lorries with armed guard.

convulse', *v.* to shake violently (e.g. He was *convulsed* with laughter) : to have spasms, or fits (e.g. of pain).—*n.* **convul'sion**, a kind of fit : a great shaking.

cō'ny, **cō'ney**, *n.* a rabbit.

coo, *v.* to make a sound like that of a dove.—Also *n.*

cook, *v.* to make food ready for eating.—*n.* one who sees to making food ready for table.—*n.* **cook′ery**, the art of cooking.

cool, *adj.* slightly cold : calm, not excited : rather cheeky.—*v.* to make or grow cool : to calm.—*adv.* **cool′ly**.—*n.* **cool′ness**.

cool′ie, *n.* an Indian or Chinese worker.

coomb, comb, koom, *n.* a deep little wooded valley : a hollow in a hill-side.

coon, *n.* a negro : a silly fellow.

coop, *n.* a tub, a barrel : a box or cage for fowls or small animals.—*v.* to shut up as in a coop.—*ns.* **coop′er**, one who makes barrels ; **coop′erage**, the workshop of a cooper.

cō-op′erate, *v.* to work together.—*n.* **cō-operā′tion**, a working together.—**co-op′erative society**, a shop or store owned by the people who buy from it. They divide the profits between themselves.

co-ordinate, kō-or′di-nāt, *adj.* of the same rank or kind.—*v.* to make the same.—*n.* **co-ordinā′tion**.

coot, *n.* a short-tailed water-fowl.

cō′pal, *n.* a clear varnish.

cō-part′ner, *n.* a workman who has a share in the profits of his work.

cope, *n.* a covering : a cap or hood : a sleeveless, hooded garment worn by clergymen.

cope, *v.* to be a match for : to struggle with.

cō′ping, *n.* the top layer of stone in a wall.—*n.* **coping-stone**, the top stone of a wall.

copious, kō′pi-us, *adj.* plentiful.

cop′per, *n.* a hardish red metal: money made from copper : a large vessel made of copper, usually to boil water in.—*n.* **cop′per-plate**, very fine and regular handwriting.

coppice, kop′is, **copse**, kops, *n.* a wood of low-growing trees.

cop′ra, *n.* the dried kernel of the coco-nut, yielding coco-nut oil.

copse. See coppice.

cop′y, *n.* an imitation.—*v.* to paint, write, etc. in imitation.—*n.* **cop′y-right**, the right of one person or body to publish a book, perform a play, print music, etc.—*adj.* protected by the law of copyright. (A book, play, etc. which is *copyright* can be printed, acted, etc. only by the person who *owns the copyright*, or by those who have his permission.)

coquet, coquette, ko-ket′, *v.* to trifle with.—*n.* **coquette**, a flirting woman.—*adj.* **coquet′tish**, playful.

cor′acle, *n.* a kind of rowing boat, used by early Britons, made from skins stretched over basket-work.

cor′al, *n.* a hard substance, found in the sea in warm countries, made up of the skeletons of tiny sea-insects (coral-insects).—**coral reef**, a rock-like mass of coral in the sea.

cor′bie, *n.* a crow.

cord, *n.* a thin rope : a thick kind of string.—*v.* to bind with a cord.—*n.* **cord′age**, a quantity of cords or ropes : the rigging of a ship.

cordial, kor′di-al, *adj.* cheery, as if coming from a merry heart.—*n.* anything that cheers up : a refreshing drink.—*n.* **cordial′ity**, cheeriness of nature : friendliness.

cord′ite, *n.* a kind of gunpowder.

cor′don, *n.* a line of guards, police, etc. to keep people back.

corduroy′, *n.* imitation corded-velvet cloth, usually made from cotton.

core, *n.* the heart : the inner part of anything, esp. of fruit.—*v.* to take out the core of fruit.

cork, *n.* the outer bark of the cork-tree (an oak found in S. Europe, N. Africa, etc.) : a stopper made of cork.—*adj.* made of cork.—*v.* to stop with a cork.—*n.* **cork′-screw**, a screw for taking out corks.—*adj.* shaped like a cork-screw.

cor′morant, *n.* a big sea-bird.

corn, *n.* a grain, such as wheat, rye, etc. : a grain or seed of any kind.—*v.* to sprinkle with salt in grains (e.g. *corned beef*).—*ns.* **corn′crake**, a bird which lives in corn-fields and has a harsh croaking cry ; **corn′-flour**, finely ground maize ; **corn′-flower**, a plant, found in corn-fields, with a blue flower.

corn, *n.* painful hard skin on a toe or foot, caused by rubbing or by tightness of shoes.

corne′lian, *n.* a precious stone.

cor′ner, *n.* the point where two lines meet : a secret place : a buying-up of all supplies of a thing in order to sell later at a high price for big profit.—*v.* to drive into a place from which there is no escape, to catch at last.—*n.* **cor′ner-stone**, the stone at the corner of the foundation of a building : something upon which much depends.

cor′net, *n.* a musical instrument played by blowing—a kind of trumpet : in old-time armies, a cavalry officer.

cornice, kor′nis, *n.* a row of plaster figures and ornaments round the top of the walls of a room.

corol′la, *n.* the petals of a flower.

corol′lary, *n.* something which may be taken for granted when some-thing else has been proved : a natural result.

corona′tion, *n.* the crowning of a king or queen.

cor′oner, *n.* in England, one who holds a court to look into causes of sudden death (from accidents, etc.).

cor′onet, *n.* a nobleman's (e.g. a duke's) crown : a small crown.

cor′poral, *n.* in the British army, the rank next below sergeant.

cor′poral, *adj.* having to do with the body (e.g. *corporal* punishment). —*adj.* **cor′porate**, working to-gether as one : making up one body (e.g. The many clubs—foot-ball, cricket, etc.—are parts of the *corporate* life of a school).—*n.* **corpora′tion**, a number of people acting as one (e.g. the mayor (or provost) and councillors of a town).

corps, kōr, *n.* a division of an army.

corpse, korps, *n.* the dead body of a human being.

cor′pulence, *n.* fatness of body.— *adj.* **cor′pulent**, fat.

corpuscle, korp′sl, *n.* a very small part (e.g. of blood), only to be seen through a strong magnifying-glass.

corral′, *n.* a fenced space for animals.

correct′, *v.* to set right : to take away faults and errors : to punish.—*adj.* having no errors :

true.—*n.* **correc′tion**, the putting right of a mistake : punishment.

cor′relate, *v.* to link (facts) together for consideration.

correspond′, *v.* to send letters to, to write to : to suit, to be the same as. —*ns.* **correspond′ence**, letters : like-ness to ; **correspond′ent**, one who writes letters, etc.—*adj.* corre-spond′ing, like (e.g. Britain has a Parliament ; the *corresponding* body in America is Congress).

cor′ridor, *n.* a passage-way.

corrigen′dum, *n.* a mistake (e.g. in a book) which must be corrected : —*pl.* **corrigen′da.**

corrob′orate, *v.* to give evidence which strengthens evidence al-ready given.—*n.* **corrobora′tion.** —*adj.* **corrob′orative.**

corrode′, *v.* to rust : to eat away, as acid eats into metal.—*n.* **corro′-sion.**—*adj.* **corros′ive.**

cor′rugate, *v.* to put wrinkles or folds in.—**cor′rugated iron**, iron rolled into sheets and marked with ridges and furrows.

corrupt′, *v.* to make evil or rotten : to persuade someone (usually by a money-offer) to turn dishonest.— *adj.* not honest : taking bribes.— *adj.* **corrupt′ible**, able to be bribed. —*n.* **corrup′tion**, evil, sin : bribery.

cor′sair, *n.* a pirate : a pirate-ship.

cor′set, *n.* a tight-fitting under-garment to support the body.

cortège, kor-tezh′, *n.* a procession, esp. a funeral procession.

corvette, kor-vet′, *n.* a small swift warship, used against submarines.

cosmet′ics, *n.pl.* face powder, cream, lip-stick, etc.

cosmopol′itan, *adj.* belonging to all the world : made up of people of many races (e.g. New York is a *cosmopolitan* city).

cost, *v.* to be priced at : to require something to be spent or given as payment (e.g. His folly *cost* him his life).—*n.* what must be spent or suffered in order to get something.—*adj.* **cost′ly**, high-priced, dear : valuable.—*n.* **cost′-liness.**

cos′ter, **cos′termonger**, *ns.* a street-seller of apples and other fruit.

cos′tume, *n.* way of dressing : a woman's coat and skirt.

cō′sy, *adj.* snug : comfortable.—*n.* a covering used for a teapot.

cot, *n.* a small dwelling : a small bed for children.

cote, *n.* a place for birds or animals (e.g. *dove-cote*, *sheep-cote*).

cō′terie, *n.* a number of persons interested in the same things.

cotillion, ko-til′yun, **cotillon**, ko-tē′yong, *n.* a lively dance.

cot′tage, *n.* a small dwelling-house. —*ns.* **cott′ager**, one who dwells in a cottage ; **cot′tar** or **cot′ter**, a farm-worker who, as part of his pay, has the right to live in a cottage.

cot′ton, *n.* a soft fluffy substance got from the pods of the cotton plant : cloth made of cotton.— Also *adj.*—*n.* **cott′on-wool**, cotton in a fluffy and woolly state before it is spun into thread.

cotylē′don, *n.* the seed-leaf of a plant.

couch, kowch, *v.* to put into words (e.g. The letter was *couched* in good English) : to lie flat for sleep or hiding.—*n.* a resting- or sleeping-place : a bed.—*adj.* **couch′ant**, lying down (e.g. A *lion couchant*, on flags, crests, etc., is the figure of a lion lying down with head up).

cougar, koo′gar, *n.* the puma.

cough, kof, *n.* a noisy effort of the lungs to throw out harmful matter coming from the throat. —*v.* to make this effort.

coulter. See **colter.**

council, kown′sil, *n.* a meeting to talk over and decide matters : the people in such a meeting.— *n.* **coun′cillor**, a member of a council.

counsel, kown′sel, *n.* advice : plan : one who advises in matters of law, a lawyer.—*v.* to give advice : to warn.—*n.* **coun′sellor**, one who advises.

count, kownt, *n.* a foreign noble : —*fem.* **count′ess.**

count, kownt, *v.* to number : to add up : to think (e.g. *Count* yourself lucky to get off so lightly). —*n.* numbering : the number counted, a sum : a charge brought against a prisoner in a court.—*n.* **count′er**, one who

counts : something which shows number or value (e.g. pieces of metal or cardboard) : a table on which money is counted or goods are laid for show.—*adj.* **count′less**, too many to be counted : very many.—*n.* **count′ing-house**, a room where counting is done : an office.

countenance, kown′ten-ans, *n.* the face : the look on a person's face. —*v.* to allow.

counter, kown′ter, *adv.* against : in the opposite direction.—Used to give the opposite of many words, e.g. *v.* **counteract′**, to act in the opposite direction, i.e. to check or hinder.—*ns.* **coun′terattack**, an attack made by the defenders upon an attacking enemy ; **coun′terattrac′tion**, something which draws away the attention.—*v.* **counterbal′ance**, to act against with equal weight.—*n.* **coun′terblast**, something done or said in reply to another thing.—*v.* **coun′terfeit** (-fēt), to make a copy, to imitate.—*adj.* not true : made in imitation (e.g. *counterfeit* coins ; *counterfeit(ed)* joy).—*n.* **coun′terfoil**, a part of a cheque, postal-order, etc. kept by the sender.— *vs.* **countermand′**, to give an order which goes against one already given ; **coun′termarch**, to turn and march the other way.— *ns.* **coun′terpane**, a cover for a bed, esp. one made up of squares ; **coun′terpart**, something which is just like something else : a part which goes along with another part ; **coun′terpoise**, a weight which balances another weight.

country, kun′tri, *n.* a district which is not in a town : a stretch of land : a nation : the land in which one was born, or in which one lives.— *adj.* belonging to the country : simple or rough in one's manners. —*n.* **coun′try-side**, the fields, woods, hills, etc. which one sees in the country.

county, kown′ti, *n.* a division of a country : a shire.

coup, koo, *n.* a blow, stroke : a successful hit.—**coup de grâce** (koo-de-gras), a knock-out blow.

couple, kupˈl, *n.* a pair, two of a kind together: husband and wife.—*v.* to join together.—*ns.* coupˈlet, two lines of rhyming verse; coupˈling, a kind of link for joining together parts of machinery, railway carriages, etc.

coupon, kooˈpon, *n.* a ticket or slip of paper for which money or goods will be given in exchange: an entry form.

courage, kurˈāj, *n.* bravery: lack of fear.—*adj.* courāˈgeous.

courier, kooˈri-er, *n.* a messenger.

course, kōrs, *n.* the road or ground on which one runs, travels, plays games, etc.: direction (e.g. The ship went off its *course*): a division of a meal: a number of things following each other (e.g. a *course* of twelve lectures): one of the rows of bricks in a wall.—*v.* to chase or run after (e.g. Greyhounds *course* hares): to move quickly.—*n.* coursˈer, a swift horse: a hunter.

court, kōrt, *n.* a shut-in space (e.g. one surrounded by houses): the persons who attend a king at his palace: attention, politeness (e.g. to pay *court* to a lady): the judges, etc., who decide law cases: the place where they meet.—*v.* to pay attention to, to woo: to seek (e.g. He *courted* the praise of the onlookers).—*adjs.* courtˈeous (kurtˈyus), polite: obliging; courtˈly, having manners like those of the people at a palace: stately.—*ns.* courtˈier, one who goes to the king's palace: a flatterer; courtˈmartial (marˈshal), a court held by navy or army officers to try those who break navy or army laws:—*pl.* courtsˈ-martial; courtˈship, time of wooing; courtˈyard, a court or enclosed space about a house.

courtesy, kurtˈe-si, *n.* politeness.

cousin, kuzˈn, *n.* the son or daughter of an uncle or aunt: a relation.

cove, *n.* a small inlet of the sea: a bay: a small seaside cave among rocks (e.g. the smugglers' *cove*).

covenant, kuvˈe-nant, *n.* an important agreement (e.g. the Scottish National *Covenant* (1638); the Solemn League and Covenant (1643).—*v.* to promise to do: to undertake.—*n.* Covenantˈer, one who held to the Scottish National Covenant and fought for his beliefs.

cover, kuvˈer, *v.* to hide: to clothe: to stretch over (e.g. The thefts *covered* a year): to be enough for (e.g. £15 should *cover* a week's holiday): to point a weapon at: to put on one's hat.—*ns.* coverˈing, something which covers; coverlet (kuvˈer-let), a bed-cover.—*adj.* covˈert, secret: not said openly.—*n.* a hiding-place, for animals, birds, etc., when hunted.

covet, kuvˈet, *v.* to desire or wish for eagerly: to wish for something belonging to another person.—*adj.* covˈetous.—*n.* covˈetousness.

covey, kuvˈi, *n.* a flock of birds, esp. partridges.

cow, *n.* the female animal of the ox kind: the female of certain other animals (e.g. elephant, whale).—*ns.* cowˈboy, a man who has the charge of cattle on a ranch; cowˈherd, one who looks after cows.

cow, *v.* to frighten.—*adj.* cowed.

coward, *n.* a faint-hearted person: one without courage.—*adj.* cowˈardly, afraid of danger: mean.—*n.* cowˈardice, want of courage.

cower, *v.* to sink down, or shrink back, through fear, etc.

cowl, *n.* a cap or hood, esp. that of a monk: a cover for a chimney.

cowrie, cowry, *n.* a kind of shell used for money in some countries.

cowslip, *n.* a beautiful kind of primrose, common in English meadows.

coxcomb, koksˈkōm, *n.* a strip of red cloth notched like a cock's comb, which jesters used to wear: a fool: a fop.

coxswain, cockswain, kokˈswān or kokˈsn, *n.* one who steers a boat: an officer in charge of a boat and crew (often shortened to cox).

coy, *adj.* shy: modest.

coyote, ko-yōtˈe or kīˈōt, *n.* a small wolf of North America.

cozen, kuzˈn, *v.* to cheat.

crab, *n.* a shellfish with a pair of large claws and four pairs of legs : a wild bitter apple : a sour-tempered person.—*adj.* **crab'bed,** bad-tempered : (of handwriting) hard to read.

crack, *v.* to give out a sharp sudden sound : to chat.—Also *n.*—*adj.* excellent (e.g. a *crack* horseman).—*adj.* **cracked,** split : crazy.—*ns.* **crack'er,** a small paper firework : a thin crisp biscuit ; **cracks'man,** a burglar.

crack'le, *v.* to make a cracking noise.—*ns.* **crack'ling,** the rind, or outer skin, of roast pork ; **crack'nel,** a light, easily broken biscuit.

crād'le, *n.* a bed in which a child is rocked : anything cradle-shaped (e.g. a frame to rest a broken limb, a frame on which a ship is built).

craft, *n.* cleverness : slyness : a trade : a small ship.—*n.* **crafts'man,** one who works at a trade.—*adj.* **craft'y,** having skill : deceitful.

crag, *n.* a rough steep rock.

cram, *v.* to press close : to eat greedily : to learn up enough of a subject to pass an examination.

cramp, *n.* a painful stiffening of the muscles (often after too much exercise).—*v.* to hinder : to put where there is not enough space.

cran, *n.* a herring measure (4 baskets—about 1,000 herrings).

cran'berry, *n.* a red, sour berry.

crane, *n.* a large wading bird, with long legs, neck, and bill : a machine for raising heavy weights.—*v.* to stretch out the neck.

crā'nium, *n.* the skull : the bones round the brain.

crank, *n.* a handle : (in machines) a lever or arm which turns movement to and fro into movement round and round : a person with queer ideas.—*adj.* **crank'y,** crabbed, queer.

cranny, kran'i, *n.* a split, a small crack : a secret place.

crape, *n.* a thin silk cloth, usually dyed black, used at funerals.

crash, *n.* a noise as of things breaking : the shock of two things meet-ing : the failure of a business.—Also *v.*

crash, *n.* a coarse strong linen.

crass, *adj.* thick : stupid.

crate, *n.* a box or packing-case, made from nailed spars.

crā'ter, *n.* the bowl-shaped mouth of a volcano,

cravat', *n.* a scarf.

crave, *v.* to beg earnestly : to long for.

crā'ven, *n.* a coward.—*adj.* cowardly.

crawfish. See crayfish.

crawl, *v.* to move slowly along the ground : to move on hands and knees : to creep.—*n.* the act of crawling : a swimming stroke. —*n.* **crawl'er,** something which crawls : a baby's overall.

cray'fish or craw'fish, *n.* an eatable shellfish, something like a small lobster.

cray'on, *n.* a coloured pencil used for drawing.

craze, *n.* a fashion or fad : a mad liking for something.—*adj.* **crāz'y,** mad.

creak, *v.* to make a sharp, grating sound.—*adj.* **creak'y.**

cream, *n.* the fatty substance which forms on milk and gives butter when churned : the best part of anything : anything like cream (e.g. *cold cream, ice cream,* etc.).—*v.* to take off the cream.— *n.* **cream'ery,** a place where butter and cheese are made.—*adj.* **cream'y,** full of, or like cream.

crease, krēs, *n.* a mark made by folding or doubling anything : (in cricket) a line showing the position of a batsman and bowler. —*v.* to make creases.

create, krē-āt', *v.* to make out of nothing : to bring into being : to make.—*ns.* **creā'tion,** the act of creating (e.g. the *creation* of the world by God as told in *Genesis*) : that which is created ; **creā'tor,** one who creates : God (*The Creator*) ; **creature** (krē'tūr), something which has been created (esp. things with life, e.g. animals, men).—*adj.* **creā'tive,** able to create.

crèche, kresh, *n.* a nursery for children while their mothers are at work.

cre'dence, *n.* belief : trust.—*n.pl.*
credentials (kre-den'shalz), letters
which a person carries to show
strangers so that they may trust
him.

cred'ible, *adj.* able to be believed.—
n. **credibil'ity.**

cred'it, *n.* belief : good character :
goods sold but not paid for
at the time : money lying in a
bank for a person's use (e.g. He
had £10 to his *credit* in the
Savings Bank).—*v.* to believe :
to sell or lend on trust : to put
to the credit of.—*adj.* **cred'itable,**
bringing honour or good name to
one.—*n.* **cred'itor,** one to whom
money is due.

cred'ulous, *adj.* believing too easily :
simple-minded.—*n.* **credu'lity.**

creed, *n.* what is believed, esp. in
matters of religion.

creek, *n.* a small inlet or bay of the
sea : a small river.

creel, *n.* a fish basket.

creep, *v.* to move along the ground :
to go on hands and knees : to
shiver with fear or disgust.—*n.
pl.* great fear ; **creep'er,** a plant
growing along the ground, or up
a wall ; **creep'ie,** a low stool.

cremate', *v.* to burn a dead body.—
ns. **crema'tion ; cremato'rium,** a
place where bodies are burnt.

crenellat'ed, *adj.* having battlements.

cre'osote, *n.* an oily kind of tar
used to keep wood from rotting.

crescendo, kresh-en'dō, *adv.* (in
music) getting gradually louder.
—*n.* music marked or played
this way.

crescent, kres'ent, *adj.* growing
bigger : sickle-shaped, like the
'growing' moon, ☽.—*n.* the moon
as it grows towards half-moon
(opposite of *waning*): anything
shaped in a curve (e.g. a *crescent*
of houses).

cress, *n.* a plant with leaves of a
slightly bitter taste, used for
making salads.

cres'set, *n.* an iron basket or open
lamp filled with burning stuff,
placed on a beacon, lighthouse,
wharf, etc. : a torch.

crest, *n.* the comb or tuft on the
head of a cock : the top of a hill,

wave, etc. : a plume of feathers
on the top of a helmet : a badge.
—*adj.* **crest'fallen,** down-hearted.

cretonne, kret-on', *n.* a strong
printed cotton cloth used for
curtains, etc.

crevasse, krev-as', *n.* a crack or
split in deep snow or ice.

crevice, krev'is, *n.* a crack or narrow
opening.

crew, kroo, *n.* the sailors on a ship :
a gang.

crib, *n.* a manger : a stall for oxen :
a child's bed : a small cottage.—
v. to steal the work of another.

crib'bage, *n.* a card game.

crick, *n.* a sharp pain in the neck.

crick'et, *n.* an insect like a grasshopper.

cricket, krik'et, *n.* an outdoor game
played with bats, a ball, and
wickets, between two sides of
11 each.—*ns.* **crick'eter ; crick'et-
match.**

cri'er, *n.* a town officer who has to
read out public notices.

crime, *n.* a breaking of the law : a
sin.—*adj.* **crim'inal,** forbidden by
law : very wrong.—*n.* one guilty
of crime.

crimp, *v.* to wrinkle : to seize
sailors or soldiers for service.

crim'son, *n.* a deep red colour.

cringe, krinj, *v.* to bow or bend the
body humbly before a person.

crink'le, *v.* to twist, wrinkle.—*adj.*
crink'ly.

crinoline, krin'o-lin, *n.* a petticoat
or skirt made to stick out all
round by means of hoops.

crip'ple, *n.* a lame person.—*adj.*
lame.—*v.* to make lame : to
throw out of action.

cri'sis, *n.* the deciding moment or
turning-point : a serious happening :—*pl.* **crises** (krī'sēz).

crisp, *adj.* having a wavy surface :
so dry as to be crumbled easily :
fresh or interesting (e.g. *crisp* air,
crisp talk, etc.).—*n.* **crisp'ness.**

crite'rion, *n.* a means or rule by
which something can be judged :
a test :—*pl.* **crite'ria.**

crit'ic, *n.* one who picks out the
good and bad points in a thing
(e.g. a picture, play, book, etc.):
one who finds bad points only,
a fault-finder.—*adj.* **crit'ical,** find-

ing good and bad : fault-finding : serious.—*v.* **crit´icise**, to give one's opinions on something.— *n.* **crit´icism**, a judgment on a thing, esp. one showing up faults.

croak, *v.* to make a low, hoarse sound, as a frog or raven : to grumble.—Also *n.*—*adj.* **croak´y**.

crochet, krō´shā, *n.* fancy-work done with a hooked needle.

crock, *n.* a pot or jar.—*n.* **crock´ery**, china and earthenware dishes.

croc´odile, *n.* a large land-and-water beast : a two-by-two procession. —**crocodile tears**, sham tears shed while doing evil.

crō´cus, *n.* a bulb plant with yellow, purple, or white flowers.

croft, *n.* a small farm with a dwelling-house.—*n.* **croft´er**.

cromlech, krom´lek, *n.* a group of standing stones, a stone circle.

crone, *n.* an old woman.

crō´ny, *n.* an old and close friend.

crook, *n.* a bend : anything bent (e.g. a staff bent at the end, as a shepherd's or bishop's) : a sly, wicked fellow.—*v.* to bend or form into a hook.—*adj.* **crook´ed**, bent like a crook : not straight : not honest.—*n.* **crook´edness**.

croon, *v.* to utter a low sound like a baby : to sing or hum in a low voice.—*ns.* **croon´er ; croon´ing**.

crop, *n.* that which is gathered from fields, trees, or bushes (e.g. wheat *crop*, apple *crop*, etc.) : a part of a bird's stomach : a riding-whip with a loop instead of a lash : hair (of the head) cut short.—*v.* to cut short : to mow, reap, or gather.

crop´per, *n.* a fall : failure.

croquet, krō´kā, *n.* a game in which the players, using long-handled wooden hammers, try to drive wooden balls through a number of arches set in the ground.

crō´sier, crō´zier, *n.* the staff or crook of a bishop or abbot : an archbishop's cross.

cross, *n.* in olden times, a frame on which those who were condemned were nailed : anything shaped thus : + or × (e.g. a medal (*Victoria Cross*), or a *market cross*) : a place where roads meet : a trouble or grief that one must bear.—*v.* to **mark with a cross** : to go to the far side of : to meddle with, disturb, or annoy.—*adj.* lying across : ill-tempered, sulky.—*ns.* **cross´ing**, a place where a street, river, etc. may be crossed ; **cross´ness**, bad temper, sulkiness.—**cross** is used with many words as a prefix, e.g. *ns.* **cross´-bones**. See **skull**; **cross´-bow**, a weapon for shooting arrows, made by placing a bow crossways on a stock or stand ; **crosscut-saw**, a large saw with a handle at each end ; **cross´-ref´erence**, in a book such as a dictionary, a statement that what is wanted will be found in another place (e.g. above, **cross-bones**. See **skull**); **cross´-roads**, a meeting place of roads ; **cross´-word**, a form of word-puzzle.—*vs.* **cross´-exam´ine, cross´-question**, to test the truth of what someone has said by asking him questions about it.

crotchet, kroch´et, *n.* a hook : a note in music : a queer notion or fancy.—*adj.* **crotch´ety**, having queer ideas.

crouch, *v.* to bend close to the ground.

croup, kroop, *n.* a children's throat-disease, causing a hard cough.

croup, kroop, *n.* the place on a horse behind the saddle.

croupier, kroo´pi-er, *n.* one who sits at the lower end of the table at a public dinner : a person who collects the money at gambling.

crow, krō, *n.* a large bird, generally black : the cry of a cock.—*v.* to cry like a cock : to boast.—*ns.* **crow´-bar**, a large iron bar used as a lever ; **crow's´-nest**, a sheltered and enclosed platform near the mast-head of a ship for the lookout-man.—**as the crow flies**, in a straight line.

crowd, *n.* a number of persons or things together, without order.— *v.* to gather into a lump or crowd.

crown, *n.* the jewelled cap worn by kings or queens on great occasions : highest honour or reward : highest part or top of anything (e.g. of the road, the head) : a five-shilling piece.—*v.* to set a crown on.

crozier. See crosier.

crucial, kroo'shi-al, *adj.* testing, deciding—usually in the phrase *the crucial moment*, the moment when an important step has to be taken.

crucible, kroo'si-bl, *n.* a melting-pot for metals, etc.

crucify, kroo'si-fī, *v.* to put to death by fixing the hands and feet to a cross: to torture.—*ns.* cru'cifix, a figure or picture of Christ fixed to the cross; crucifix'ion, death on the cross, esp. that of Christ.

crude, krood, *adj.* raw, not purified (e.g. *crude oil*): roughly made or done (e.g. a *crude* piece of work).—*ns.* crude'ness, crud'ity.

cruel, kroo'el, *adj.* causing pain: not heeding the suffering of others.—*n.* cru'elty.

cruet, kroo'et, *n.* a small jar for sauces, salt, pepper, etc.

cruise, krooz, *v.* to sail to and fro.—Also *n.*—*n.* cruis'er, a middle-sized warship.

crumb, krum, *n.* a small bit of bread: a small bit of anything.—*v.* crum'ble, to break into crumbs or small pieces: to decay.—*adj.* crumb'ly.

crum'ple, *v.* to crush out of shape.

crunch, *v.* to chew anything hard, and so make a noise.

crup'per, *n.* a strap of leather fastened to the saddle and passing under the horse's tail to keep the saddle in its place: the hind part of a horse.

crusade, kroo-sād', *n.* an expedition of Christians to win back the Holy Land from the Turks: any movement undertaken for some noble cause.—*n.* crusād'er, one who goes on a crusade.

cruse, krooz, *n.* an earthen pot.

crush, *v.* to squeeze together: to beat down or overcome: to ruin.—*n.* a violent squeezing: a vast crowd of persons or things: a drink made by squeezing fruit.

crust, *n.* the hard outside coating of anything (bread, pie, the earth, etc.).—*adj.* crust'y, having a crust: (of people) cross.

crutch, *n.* a supporting stick for lame people.

crux, *n.* the difficult part of a problem.

cry, *v.* to make a shrill loud sound, as in pain or sorrow: to weep: to call noisily.—Also *n.*—*adj.* cry'ing, calling loudly: calling for notice (e.g. a *crying* shame).—to cry over spilt milk, to be vexed over a misfortune that is past and cannot be helped.

crypt, kript, *n.* underground cell or chapel, esp. one used for burial.—*adj.* cryp'tic, full of mystery.

crystal, kris'tal, *n.* clear sparkling glass: the regular shape taken by each small part of certain substances (e.g. salt, suga., ice crystals).—*adj.* crys'talline, made up of (or like) crystals.—*v.* crys'tallise, to form into the shape of a crystal: to take a form or shape, become clear.—*n.* cryst'allīsā'tion, the act of crystallising.

cub, *n.* the young of certain animals (e.g. foxes): a junior Scout.

cube, *n.* a solid body having six equal square faces, a solid square: the answer of such sums as, $2 \times 2 \times 2$, $4 \times 4 \times 4$; 8 is the *cube* of 2, 64 is the *cube* of 4; 2 is the *cube root* of 8, and 4 the *cube root* of 64.—*adj.* cū'bic, having to do with cubes: having the shape of a cube. (A *cubic foot* has its length, breadth, and depth each one foot.)

cū'bicle, *n.* a small bedroom inside a large one.

cubit, kū'bit, *n.* an ancient measure of length (18–22 inches—the distance from elbow to middle-finger tip).

cuckoo, kook'koo, *n.* a bird which visits Britain in summer; it is well known from its cry—'Cuckoo.'

cū'cumber, *n.* a creeping-plant with a long green fruit (used in salads and pickles).

cud, *n.* food brought back from the stomach and chewed a second time by certain animals (e.g. the sheep, cow, etc.).

cud'dle, *v.* to hug.—Also *n.*

cudgel, kuj'el, *n.* a heavy staff: a club.—*v.* to beat with a cudgel.—*n.* cud'gelling.

cue, kū, *n.* a hint (e.g. telling a person what to say next): the striking-stick in billiards.

cuff 79 current

cuff, *n.* a blow with the open hand. —Also *v.*

cuff, *n.* the end of the sleeve near the wrist.

cuirass, kwi-ras′ or kū-, *n.* a piece of armour made up of a breast-and-back plate.—*n.* **cuirassier′**, a horse-soldier armed with such.

cuisine, kwe-zēn′, *n.* a kitchen: cookery.

cul′inary, *adj.* having to do with the kitchen or cookery.

cull, *v.* to pick out.

cul′minate, *v.* to reach the highest point: to end in.—*n.* **culminā′tion.**

cul′pable, *adj.* guilty.

cul′prit, *n.* a wrong-doer: a person who is to blame.

cult, *n.* worship or religious belief.

cul′tivate, *v.* to work the soil by digging or ploughing: to try hard to get (e.g. He *cultivated* his neighbour's friendship).—*n.* **cultivā′tion**, ploughing: good manners.

culture, kul′tūr, *n.* a good upbringing: learning.—*adj.* **cul′tured**, well-educated: refined in manners, etc.

cul′verin, *n.* an old-time cannon.

cul′vert, *n.* an arched drain for carrying water beneath a road, railway, etc.

cum′ber, *v.* to trouble or hinder with something useless.—*adjs.* **cum′bersome**, heavy; **cum′brous**, hindering: clumsy.

cum′merbund, *n.* a sash.

cū′mulate, to heap up.—*adj.* **cūm′ūlātive**, with all previous parts added on.—*n.* **cū′mūlus**, a kind of cloud common in summer, consisting of rounded heaps.

cunn′ing, *adj.* knowing: skilful: sly, deceitful.—*n.* knowledge: skill: slyness.

cup, *n.* a hollow vessel to hold liquid, usually for drinking: that which we must receive or suffer (troubles or blessings).—*ns.* **cup′-bear′er**, one who stands by at a feast to hand out the wine; **cupboard** (kub′urd), a place for keeping dishes, etc.; **cup′ful**, as much as fills a cup:—*pl.* **cup′fuls.**

cūpid′ity, *n.* greed.—*n.* **Cū′pid**, the god of love.

cū′pola, *n.* a curved ceiling on the top of a building: a dome.

cur, *n.* a dog of poor breed: a mean, cowardly person.

cū′rate, *n.* a Church of England clergyman assisting a rector or a vicar.—*n.* **cūr′acy**, the district under a curate.

cūrā′tor, *n.* one who has charge of a museum, art-gallery, etc.

curb, *v.* to hold back, check.—*n.* a check or hindrance: a chain or strap for keeping back the horse.

curds, *n.pl.* thickened milk. — *v.* **curd′le**, to thicken.

cūre, *n.* act of healing: that which heals: the district or charge of a clergyman.—*v.* to heal: to preserve, as by drying, salting, etc.—*adjs.* **cūr′able**; **cūr′ative**, likely to cure.

cur′few, *n.* the ringing of an evening bell, as a signal to put out all fires and lights.

cū′rio, *n.* an article which is valued by a collector because of its oddness or rareness.

cū′rious, *adj.* anxious to find out: showing great care: skilfully made.—*n.* **curios′ity**, strong desire to find out: anything rare or unusual.

curl, *v.* to twist into ringlets: to be wavy: to play at the game of curling.—*n.* a ringlet, e.g. of hair. —*n.* **curl′ing**, a game, common in Scotland, played by hurling heavy smooth stones along a sheet of ice.—*adj.* **curl′y**, having curls.

cur′lew, *n.* a wading-bird with very long slender bill and legs, and a short tail.

curmudgeon, kur-muj′un, *n.* a greedy, ill-natured person.

cur′rant, *n.* a small kind of black raisin: any such fruit (e.g. *black-*, *red-currant*).

cur′rent, *adj.* running or flowing: passing from person to person: belonging to the present time (e.g. the *current* month).—*n.* a stream of water or air moving in a certain direction.—*n.* **curr′ency**, the money (notes and coins) of a country: state of being well-known (e.g. The story gained *currency*).

curric´ulum, *n.* the course of study at a university, school, etc.

cur´ry, *n.* a hot seasoning.

cur´ry, *v.* to dress leather : to rub down a horse.—**to curry favour,** to seek eagerly for favour.

curse, *v.* to swear : to call down evil upon.—*n.* an oath : a wish for evil : an evil.—*adj.* **curs´ed,** under a curse : hateful.

cur´sory, *adj.* hurried : careless.

curt, *adj.* short : rudely short.—*n.* **curt´ness.**

curtail, *v.* to cut short.—*n.* **curtail´ment.**

curtain, kur´tin, *n.* a hanging before a window, etc.—**iron curtain,** a barrier of secrecy which prevents outsiders from knowing what is happening in a country.

curt´sy, curt´sey, *n.* deep bow, made by bending the knees.

curve, *n.* anything bent : a bend as in a road or railway.—*v.* to bend : to form into a curve.—*n.* **cur´vature,** a bending, as of the spine.

cushion, koosh´un, *n.* a case filled with some soft stuff, for resting on : any soft pad.

cus´tard, *n.* milk, eggs, etc., flavoured, and cooked together.

cus´tody, *n.* a watching or guarding : care : imprisonment.—*n.* **custo´dian,** a keeper : a care-taker (e.g. of a museum, monument, etc.).

cus´tom, *n.* what one is in the habit of doing : regular buying of goods at the same place : (*pl.*) taxes on goods coming into a country.—*adj.* **cus´tomary,** usual.—*ns.* **cus´tomer,** one who buys regularly from the same shop ; **cus´toms-house,** the place where customs taxes on goods are collected.

cut, *v.* to make a slit or opening : to divide with knife, scissors, etc. : to shorten : to pass by a person without greeting him : to run away.—*n.* a slit or opening : a wound : a stroke or blow : a thrust with a sword : style or fashion (e.g. the latest *cut*).—*ns.* **cut´ter,** in a tailor's shop, the one who measures and cuts out the cloth : a small ship ; **cut´-throat,** a wicked, dangerous fellow ; **cut´-ting,** a piece cut from a newspaper : a passage for a road or railway, cut out of the rock : a twig or shoot for planting out.

cūte, *adj.* smart, clever.

cū´ticle, *n.* the top, thin skin, which can be broken without hurt.

cut´lass, *n.* a short, broad sword.

cut´ler, *n.* one who makes or sells knives.—*n.* **cut´lery,** knives, forks, spoons, etc.

cut´let, *n.* a slice of meat (generally the rib) cut off for cooking.

cut´tle-fish, *n.* a sea-creature which gives out black, inky liquid when attacked : an octopus.

cut´ty, *n.* a short clay pipe.

cycle, sī´kl, *n.* a number or round of events coming one after the other, over and over again (e.g. the *cycle* of the seasons—spring, summer, autumn, winter, spring, . . . etc.): a number of poems, songs, stories, written about one main person or event (e.g. the *Idylls of the King*—verse stories about King Arthur and his Knights): a bicycle.—*v.* to ride a bicycle.—*n.* **cy´clist,** one who rides a bicycle.

cyclone, sī´klōn, *n.* a whirling windstorm.—*adj.* **cyclon´ic.**

Cyclops, sī´klops, *n.* in old-time fables, a one-eyed giant who lived in Sicily:—*pl.* **Cyclō´pes.**

cyder. Same as cider.

cygnet, sig´net, *n.* a young swan.

cylinder, sil´in-der, *n.* a roller-shaped solid : in mechanics, the hollow tube in which a piston works.—*adj.* **cylin´drical.**

cymbals, sim´bals, *n.pl.* hollow brass, basin-like, musical instruments, beaten together in pairs.

cynic, -al, sin´ik, -al, *adj.* surly : snarling : sneering at what most people like or do.—*ns.* **cyn´ic,** a sneering person ; **cynicism** (sin´i-sizm), crossness, sneering discontent.

cynosure, sin´o-shoor or sī´, *n.* anything that draws attention.

cypress, sī´pres, *n.* an evergreen tree—a sign of mourning.

cyst, sist, *n.* a kind of boil or blister.

czar, czarina. See tsar.

D

dab, v. to strike gently with something soft or moist.—n. a gentle blow: a small lump or patch of anything soft or moist: a small kind of flounder.

dab′ble, v. to play in water with hands or feet: to do anything in a trifling way.—n. **dabb′ler.**

dace, n. a small river-fish.

dachshund, daks′hoont, n. a dog with short legs and a long body.

dacoit′, dakoit′, n. an Indian robber.

dā′do, n. the wooden or wall-paper border on the lower part of walls.

daf′fodil, daf′fodowndil′ly, ns. a yellow flower, which grows from a bulb.

daft, adj. silly.

dag′ger, n. a short sword for stabbing: a printer's mark (†—the ′ double dagger ′ is ‡).

dā′go, n. a name for a dark-skinned person (e.g. a Spaniard or Italian).

dahlia, dāl′i-a, n. a garden plant with large flowers.

dai′ly, adj. and adv. every day.—n. a daily paper.

dain′ty, adj. pleasant-tasting: neat.—n. anything pleasant (e.g. tasty food).—n. **dain′tiness.**

dai′ry, n. the place in a farm-house where milk is kept, and butter and cheese are made: a shop which sells milk.—ns. **dai′ry-farm; dai′rymaid; dai′ryman.**

dā′is, n. a raised floor at the upper end of a hall: a platform.

dai′sy, n. a common wild-flower.

dale, n. the low ground between hills.

dal′ly, v. to lose time by idleness or trifling: to play.—n. **dall′iance.**

Dalmatian, dal-mā′shun, n. a large spotted dog.

dam, n. a bank or wall of earth, concrete, etc., to keep back water: the water thus kept in (e.g. a mill-dam).—v. to keep back any rush (e.g. a rush of water).

dam, n. a mother, esp. of prize animals.

dam′age, n. hurt, injury, loss: the value of what is lost: (pl.) money paid, by order of a law-court, by one person to another **to make up**

for hurts, carelessness, insults, etc.—v. to harm.

dam′ask, n. silk, linen, or cotton cloth, with figures and designs.

dame, n. the mistress of a house: a noble lady.—n. **dame′-school,** a private school kept by a woman.

damn, dam, v. to condemn as wrong: to sentence to unending punishment.—n. an oath: a curse.—adj. **dam′nable,** deserving to be condemned: hateful.—n. **damnā′tion,** condemnation: unending punishment.

damp, n. mist: moist air.—v. to wet slightly: to check: to make dull.—adj. moist, foggy.—n. **damp′ness.**—v. **damp′en,** to make or become damp or moist.—n. **damp′er,** that which checks: a movable plate of metal in a chimney to make a bigger or smaller draught.

dam′sel, n. an unmarried girl.

dam′son, n. a small plum.

dance, v. to move in time to music: to spring.—Also n.

dandeli′on, n. a common plant with a yellow flower.

dan′dle, v. to fondle or toss (e.g. a baby) in the arms.

dand′riff, dand′ruff, n. a scaly scurf which forms on the skin under the hair.

dan′dy, n. a man who pays great attention to his dress and looks.—v. **dan′dify,** to dress up.

danger, dān′jer, n. risk, peril.—adj. **dān′gerous,** unsafe, full of risks.

dangle, dang′gl, v. to hang loosely.

dank, adj. moist, wet.

dap′per, adj. little and active: neat.

dap′ple, dap′pled, adjs. marked with spots or splashes of colour.

dare, v. to be bold enough: to venture: to defy, challenge.—n. **dare′-dev′il,** a rash fellow, fond of taking risks.—adj. **dar′ing,** bold, fearless.—n. boldness.

darg, n. a day's work.

dark, adj. without light: black, or somewhat black: without learning.—ns. **dark, dark′ness.**—v. **dark′en,** to make or grow dark or darker.

dar′ling, n. a little dear: a favourite.

darn, *v.* to mend (e.g. a hole in a stocking).—*n.* the place so mended.

dart, *n.* a pointed, arrow-like weapon for throwing with the hand.—*v.* to move quickly.—*n.* **darts,** a game in which small darts are thrown by hand at a board marked off in circles and numbered sections.

dash, *v.* to throw with force: to break by knocking: to rush with speed or violence.—*n.* a striking or rushing: in writing, a mark (—) to show a break.—*adj.* **dash'ing,** hasty: making much show.

das'tard, *n.* a cowardly fellow.—*adj.* **das'tardly,** cowardly.

dā'ta, *n.pl.* facts which, when studied, give certain information.

date, *n.* the time of any event: a fixed day.—*v.* to give a date to: to belong to a certain time (e.g. This castle *dates* from the 12th century).—**out of date,** old-fashioned, no longer used; **up to date,** in fashion.

date, *n.* the fruit of the date-palm.

daub, *v.* to smear: to paint coarsely.

daughter, daw'ter, *n.* a female child. —*n.* **daugh'ter-in-law,** a son's wife.

daunt, *v.* to frighten.—*adj.* **daunt'-less,** unable to be frightened.

dauphin, daw'fin, *n.* the eldest son of the king of France.

dav'its, *n.* on a big ship, supports holding ropes to lower or raise small boats.

Dā'vy Jones, *n.* a sailor's name for the spirit of the sea, the devil.— **Davy Jones's locker,** the sea, as the grave of men drowned at sea.

dā'vy-lamp, *n.* a safety-lamp for coal-miners.

daw, *n.* a bird of the crow kind.

daw'dle, *v.* to waste time by trifling: to move slowly.—*n.* **daw'dler.**

dawn, *v.* to become day: to begin to appear.—*n.* **daybreak:** beginning.—*n.* **dawn'ing,** dawn.

day, *n.* the time of light, from sunrise to sunset: twenty-four hours, from one midnight to the next.—*ns.* **day'-dream,** a dreaming while awake; **day'-school,** a school which is not a boarding-school: a school whose classes meet during the day (i.e. not an *evening school*); **day-spring,** dawn.

daze, *v.* to knock the senses out: to stun.

daz'zle, *v.* to daze or confuse with a strong light.

dea'con, *n.* the lowest rank of clergyman (in the English Church): a church official (in other churches): —*fem.* **dea'coness.**

dead, ded, *adj.* without life: at rest: cold and cheerless: truly aimed, certain.—*n.* the time of greatest stillness, as 'the dead of night.'—*adj.* **dead'ly,** likely to cause death: fatal.—*ns.* **dead'ness; dead'liness.**—*v.* **dead'en,** to make dead: to lessen (e.g. pain). —*ns.* **dead'-heat,** a race in which two or more runners are equal; **dead'lock,** a complete failure to agree (e.g. in any talk to settle a difficulty).—*adjs.* **dead'-and-alive',** dull, having little life; **dead'-beat,** having no strength left.

deaf, def, *adj.* unable to hear.—*v.* **deaf'en,** to make deaf.—*ns.* **deaf'-ness; deaf'-mute,** one who is both deaf and dumb.

deal, *n.* a share: an amount or quantity: the dividing out of cards in a game: a fir or pine board: timber.—*v.* to divide, give out: to trade.—*n.* **deal'er,** one who deals: a trader.

dean, *n.* the chief clergyman in a cathedral church: an important officer of a university.

dear, *adj.* high in price: highly valued: much loved.—*n.* one who is loved.—*adv.* at a high price.—*adv.* **dear'ly.**—*n.* **dear'-ness.**

dearth, derth, *n.* scarcity: shortage.

death, deth, *n.* state of being dead. —*adj.* and *adv.* **death'ly,** like death.—*ns.* **death'-blow,** a blow that causes death; **death'-dū'ties,** taxes paid out of what a dead person leaves; **death'-roll,** a list of the dead.

debacle, de-bak'l, *n.* a miserable failure or defeat.

debar', *v.* to keep from: to prevent.

debase', *v.* to make lower in value. —*adj.* **debased',** made low: wicked. —*n.* **debase'ment.**

debate', *n.* an argument, a word-battle.—*v.* to argue: to think long about.—*adj.* **debāt'able**, able to be argued about : doubtful.

debauch', to make bad or wicked : to drink heavily.—*n.* a drinking bout.—*n.* **debauch'ery**, great drunkenness.

debil'itate, *v.* to make weak.—*n.* **debil'ity**, weakness.

deb'it, *n.* a debt.—*v.* to mark something down as a debt.

debonair', *adj.* of good appearance and manners : gay.

debouch, de-boosh', *v.* (of soldiers' ranks) to open out : to come out from a narrow place to open ground : to flow out.

débris, dā-brē, **debris**, deb'rē, *n.* ruins : rubbish.

debt, det, *n.* what one owes : a duty. —*n.* **debtor** (det'or), one who owes anything.

début, dā-boo, *n.* a beginning or first public appearance (e.g. of an actor).—*n.* **débutante** (dā-bootont'), a lady who makes her first appearance at a royal court.

dec'ade, *n.* a space of ten years.

dec'adence, *n.* decay : a decrease in importance.—*adj.* **dec'adent**.

Decalogue, dek'a-log, *n.* the Ten Commandments.

decamp', *v.* to run away.

decant', *v.* to pour wine from a bottle into glasses.—*n.* **decan'ter**, a fancy bottle with glass stopper.

decap'itate, *v.* to cut the head from. —*n.* **decapitā'tion**.

dēcay', *v.* to become bad or rotten : to waste away.—Also *n.*

dēcease', *n.* death.—*adj.* **deceased** (dē-sēst'), dead.—Also *n.*

deceit, de-sēt', *n.* anything meant to cheat : falseness.—*adj.* **deceit'ful**.

deceive, de-sēv', *v.* to tell untruths in order to lead someone astray : to cheat.—*n.* **deceiv'er**.

Decem'ber, *n.* the twelfth month.

decen'nial, *adj.* happening every ten years.

dē'cent, *adj.* proper : well-behaved : of fair size or amount.—*n.* **dē'cency**.

deception, de-sep'shun, *n.* act of deceiving, cheating.—*adj.* **decep'tive**, different from what it looks.

decide', *v.* to settle : to make up one's mind.—*adj.* **decīd'ed**, clear : with one's mind made up.

decid'ūous, *adj.* (of trees) having leaves that fall in autumn.

decimal, des'i-mal, *adj.* a name for fractions in the form ·3, ·03, etc.—*v.* **dec'imalise**, to change to decimals.

decimate, des'i-māt, *v.* to kill one out of every ten : to make much smaller in numbers (e.g. The army was *decimated* in this battle).

decipher, de-sī'fer, *v.* to read writing that is difficult to make out.

decision, de-sizh'un, *n.* the act of settling or deciding : the power to make up one's mind to do something.—*adj.* **decī'sive**, clear, final (e.g. a *decisive* defeat).

deck, *v.* to put ornaments on, to adorn.—*n.* a floor on a ship.

declaim', *v.* to make a speech in fine language.—*n.* **declamā'tion**. —*adj.* **declam'atory**, (of a speech) noisy or exciting.

declare', *v.* to make known : to announce, to say firmly : (in cricket) to give up an innings because the captain thinks that his side has scored enough runs. —*n.* **declarā'tion**.

decline', *v.* to refuse : to begin to fail, to get worse : to bend down. —*n.* a down-slope.

decliv'ity, *n.* a down-slope.

dēcompōse', *v.* to rot.—*n.* **decomposi'tion**.

dēcontam'inate, *v.* to free from harmful matter (e.g. to clear away poison gas from the streets).

dec'orate, *v.* to dress up : to ornament : to pin a badge or medal on (e.g. The king *decorated* the gallant airman).—*n.* **decorā'tion**. —*adj.* **dec'orātive**.

decorous, de-kō'rus or dek'o-rus, *adj.* behaving in a proper way : quiet in conduct.—*n.* **decō'rum**, good conduct.

decoy', *v.* to lead into a trap or into evil.—*n.* anything to lead another into a trap (e.g. a *decoy-duck*, a wild-duck trained to draw other wild ducks to a trap).

decrease', *v.* to make or become less. —*n.* (dē'krēs) a growing less : loss.

decree', *n.* an order : a judge's decision.—*v.* to make a decree.

decrep'it, *adj.* worn out : broken-down by age.—*n.* **decrep'itūde**.

decry′, *v.* to make out to be worthless (e.g. He *decried* everything that I said).

ded′icate, *v.* to set apart as holy: to give completely to some good cause (e.g. He *dedicated* his life to the poor): to name a person in the front page of a book (e.g. I *dedicate* this book to my father). —*n.* dedicā′tion.

deduce′, *v.* to find out something new by putting together all that is known.—*n.* deduc′tion.

deduct′, *v.* to subtract.—*n.* deduc′tion, a taking away from: subtraction (e.g. A *deduction* of ten marks may be made for bad handwriting).

deed, *n.* something done, an act: an exploit: (in law) a signed statement or bargain.

deem, *v.* to think.

deep, *adj.* reaching far down: hard to understand: cunning: heartfelt.—*n.* that which is deep: the sea.—*v.* deep′en, to make deep.

deer, *n.* a four-footed animal, such as the stag, reindeer, etc.—*n.* deer′-for′est, land (not always woodland) for keeping deer.

deface′, *v.* to spoil the fresh look of anything.—*n.* deface′ment.

defal′cate, *v.* to take for one's self money held on trust.—*n.* defalcā′tion.

defame′, *v.* to speak evil of.—*n.* defamā′tion.—*adj.* defam′atory, harmful to a person's good name.

default′, *n.* a failing in duty, such as not paying a debt when it is due.—*n.* default′er, one who defaults: a law-breaker.

defeat′, *v.* to beat in a fight.—*n.* defeat′.

defect′, *n.* a want: a flaw.—*n.* defec′tion, failure in duty: a revolt. —*adj.* defect′ive, faulty.

defence′, *n.* a stand or guard against attack: means of protection: a person's answer to a charge made against him, esp. in a law-court.— *adj.* defence′less, without defence.

defend′, *v.* to guard or protect: to stand against attack.—*n.* defend′ant, one who resists attack: the accused person in a law-case.—*adjs.* defens′ible, able to be defended; defens′ive, on guard, guarding: in a position to defend.—*n.* defen′sive, the state of defending (e.g. The army was on the *defensive*, i.e. had to defend itself).

defer′, *v.* to put off to another time.

defer′, *v.* to give way to the wishes of another.—*n.* def′erence.—*adj.* deferen′tial, giving way to get favour with another.

defi′ance, *n.* a challenge to a fight: impudent boldness.—*adj.* defi′ant, bold and impudent: resisting to the end.

deficient, de-fish′ent, *adj.* being short of what one should have. —*ns.* defic′iency; deficit (def′is-it), a shortage, esp. of money.

defile′, *v.* to march one behind another (i.e. in file).—*n.* dē′file, a narrow pass where people can walk only in file.

defile′, *v.* to make dirty: to soil.— *n.* defile′ment.

define′, *v.* to fix the bounds or limits of: to fix the meaning of. —*adjs.* def′inite, having clear limits: exact; defin′itive, quite fixed, final.—*ns.* def′initeness; defini′tion, an explanation of the exact meaning of a word or phrase.

deflect′, *v.* to turn aside or knock out of line.—*n.* deflec′tion.

deform′, *v.* to change to an ugly shape.—*adj.* deformed′, badly formed.—*n.* deform′ity.

defraud′, *v.* to cheat: (with *of*) to take by fraud.

defray′, *v.* to pay for (the expenses of anything).—*n.* defray′al.

deft, *adj.* handy, clever.—*n.* deft′ness.

defunct′, *adj.* dead: no longer active (e.g. The School Dramatic Club has been *defunct* for 3 years).

defy′, *v.* to dare someone to do something: to challenge: to resist boldly.

degen′erate, *adj.* having become low or mean.—*v.* to become or grow bad.—*n.* degenerā′tion.

degrāde′, *v.* to lower in grade or rank: to disgrace.—*n.* degradā′tion.—*adj.* degrad′ing.

degree′, *n.* grade or rank (e.g. A man of high *degree*): a small part or division (e.g. *degrees* on a thermometer): an honour granted by a university.

deify, dē'i-fī, v. to worship as if a god : to make god-like.

deign, dān, v. to do as a favour (e.g. She *deigned* to answer us).

deity, dē'i-ti, n. a god or goddess. —The Deity, God.

deject'ed, adj. gloomy.—n. dejec'tion.

delay', v. to put off to a later time : to keep back, hinder.—Also n.

delect'able, adj. delightful : pleasing.—n. delecta'tion, delight.

del'egate, v. to send a person to speak or act for others : to hand over something to be done by another.—n. someone acting for another person.—n. delega'tion, a group of delegates.

delete', v. to rub out (e.g. writing) : to destroy.—n. dele'tion.

delete'rious, adj. hurtful : poisonous.

delf, n. short for deift'ware, a kind of pottery first made at *Delft*, Holland.

delib'erate, v. to think carefully or seriously (about).—adj. carefully thought over : intentional, not by accident : slow in making a decision.—n. delibera'tion, careful thought : coolness.

del'icate, adj. not strong, frail : dainty, done by fine work : pleasing to the senses, esp. the taste : gentle, polite. — n. delicacy (del'i-kas-i).

delicious, de-lish'us, adj. giving pleasure : pleasant to taste.— n. deli'ciousness.

delight, de-līt', v. to please highly : to be greatly pleased.—n. delight'. —adjs. delight'ed ; delight'ful.

delinquent, de-ling'kwent, adj. failing in duty.—n. one who fails in, or leaves his duty : a wrong-doer : a criminal.—n. delin'quency, failure in duty : crime.

delir'ious, adj. wandering in mind : mad. — n. delir'ium, state of being delirious : wild excitement.

deliv'er, v. to set free : to rescue : to hand over : to give out (e.g. a speech, blow).—ns. deliv'erance, a freeing : a judgment given ; deliv'ery, a giving up or handing over (e.g. letters, parcels, etc.): way of speaking.

dell, n. a hollow between hills.

delph. Same as delf.

del'ta, n. the △-shaped stretch of land at the mouth of rivers which reach the sea in two or more branches (e.g. the Nile, Ganges). —*Delta* (△) is the Greek letter D.

delude', v. to cheat.—n. delu'sion, a false belief : wrong way of thinking.—adj. delu'sive, deceiving.

del'uge, n. a great flow of water : a great amount of anything (e.g. work, requests) : the Flood.—v. to flood (with water, work, etc.).

delve, v. to dig.

demand', v. to call sharply for : to ask a question.—Also n.

demean', v. to behave one's self. —n. demean'our, behaviour, conduct.

demean', v. to lower, to make mean.

dement', v. to madden.—adj. dement'ed, out of one's mind.

demer'it, n. a short-coming : a fault.

demesne, de-mēn', n. a country house and its private grounds.

dem'igod, n. a person so much thought of as to be nearly a god.

demise', n. death.

demit', v. to give up, resign.

dēmob'ilise, v. to break up an army after a war is over.—n. demobilisa'tion.

democracy, de-mok'ra-si, n. government of the people by the people : government by a parliament which is made up of members sent by the people themselves.— n. dem'ocrat, one who believes in this kind of government.—adj. democrat'ic.

demol'ish, v. to destroy, lay in ruins.—n. demoli'tion.

dē'mon, n. an evil spirit : a devil.

dem'onstrate, v. to show clearly : to prove.—n. demonstra'tion, a show : a display : a noisy show of feeling. — adj. demon'strative, pointing out : showy, fussy.—n. dem'onstrator, one who shows (e.g. the working of a machine): a member of a noisy crowd.

demor'alise, v. to throw into confusion : to make evil.—n. demoralisa'tion.

demur', v. to say 'no' to. — Also n.

demūre′, *adj.* shy: quiet-looking. —*n.* **demure′ness.**

den, *n.* lair of wild beast: cave.

den′ier, *n.* a unit of weight of nylon, silk, rayon yarn.

denial. See **deny.**

den′izen, *n.* a dweller: an inhabitant (e.g. The birds are *denizens* of the trees).

denom′inate, *v.* to give a name to: to call.—*n.* **denominā′tion,** name or title: a number of people of the same religious beliefs (e.g. Anglicans, Baptists, etc.).—*adj.* **denominā′tional.**—*n.* **denom′inator,** that which names (e.g. the lower number in a vulgar fraction, which *names* the number of parts into which the whole number is divided).

denōte′, *v.* to mean: to show as a sign (e.g. John knew that cough —it *denoted* trouble).

dénouement, dā-noo′mong, *n.* the ‘point ’ or most important part of a story (e.g. the part where a mystery is solved).

denounce′, *v.* to say something against.—*n.* **denunciā′tion.**

dense, *adj.* close-packed: thick: very stupid.—*ns.* **dense′ness; dens′ity.**

dent, *n.* a hollow made by a blow or pressure.—*v.* to make a dent.

den′tal, *adj.* having to do with the teeth.

den′tifrice, *n.* paste or powder used for the cleaning of the teeth.

den′tist, *n.* one who cures tooth-troubles (by filling, drawing, etc). —*n.* **den′tistry,** the work of a dentist.

denūde′, *v.* to make naked: to lay bare.—*n.* **denudā′tion,** the wearing away of soil and rocks by rain, snow, etc.

denunciā′tion. See **denounce.**

denÿ′, *v.* to say that something is not true: to refuse or forbid (e.g. He *denied* me the right of entering): to go without (e.g. The hermit *denies* himself food). —*n.* **deni′al.**

deō′dorise, *v.* to take the smell from.—*ns.* **deodorisā′tion; deō′doriser,** a substance that does away with unpleasant smells.

depart′, *v.* to go away: to leave: to die.—*n.* **depart′ūre.**

depart′ment, *n.* a separate part or division (e.g. *Education Department, Electricity Department, Hardware Department,* etc.).

depend′, *v.* to rely on: to be held up or supported by: to be connected with.—*adjs.* **depend′able,** to be trusted: sure; **depend′ent,** relying on.—*ns.* **depend′ent,** one who is kept by another: **depend′ence,** the state of being supported by something or somebody else.

depict′, *v.* to describe.

deplēte′, *v.* to empty: to make smaller, in amount, number, etc.—*n.* **deplē′tion.**

deplōre′, *v.* to feel or show deep grief for.—*adj.* **deplōr′able,** very bad: sad.

deploy′, *v.* to unfold: (of troops) to open out from column into line.

depop′ūlate, *v.* to take away people from.—*adj.* **depopū′lated,** empty of people.

deport′, *v.* to send a person out of a country (for wrong-doing).— *n.* **dēportā′tion.**—*n.* **deport′ment,** way of bearing one’s self: behaviour.

depōse′, *v.* to remove from a high office (e.g. a king from his throne). *n.* **deposi′tion,** the act of deposing.

depos′it, *v.* to put or set down: to place: to store up (e.g. money in a bank).—*n.* that which is put down: something given into another’s care, esp. money put in a bank.—*ns.* **depos′itor;** **depos′itory,** a place where anything is deposited; **deposi′tion,** a written piece of evidence.

depot, dep′ō, *n.* a storehouse: a military station where stores are kept: the place where trams or buses are kept and repaired.

deprāve′, *v.* to make bad.—*adj.* **deprāved′,** of low mind: evil living. —*n.* **deprav′ity,** great wickedness: lowness of thought or act.

dep′recate, *v.* to speak against: to try to prevent by showing displeasure (e.g. I *deprecate* any attempt to force them to play).— *n.* **depreca′tion.**

depreciate, de-prē′shi-āt, *v.* to lower the worth of: to fall in value.—*n.* **depreciā′tion.**

depredā′tion, *n.* a plundering.

depress′, *v.* to press down : to make dull or of low spirits.—*n.* **depres′sion**, a hollow : sadness.

deprive′, *v.* to take something away from (e.g. He *deprived* me of butter).—*n.* **deprivā′tion**, hardship.

depth, *n.* deepness, a deep place : the sea : middle (e.g. *depth* of winter).—*n.* **depth-charge**, a heavy bomb which explodes under water.

depute′, *v.* to send another person to take one's place : to appoint.—*ns.* **deputā′tion**, persons chosen to speak or act for others (e.g. The manager received a *deputation* from the workers); **dep′uty**, one acting in place of another, a substitute.—*v.* **dep′utise**, to take another's place for a time, to act as substitute.

derail′, *v.* to cause to leave the rails.

derange′, *v.* to put out of place or order.—*adj.* **deranged′**, out of order : out of one's mind.—*n.* **derange′ment**.

der′elict, *adj.* forsaken : cast-off.—*n.* anything forsaken, given up as useless (e.g. a ship).—*n.* **derelic′tion**, the neglecting of what should be attended to (e.g. *dereliction* of duty).

deride′, *v.* to laugh at : to mock.—*n.* derision (de-rizh′un), act of deriding : mockery.—*adj.* **deri′sive**, jeering, mocking.

derive′, *v.* to trace the beginning of something (e.g. words) : to be descended from.—*ns.* **derivā′tion**, the manner in which a word has been formed ; **deriv′ative**, a word made from another word (e.g. *derivative* from *derive*).

derog′atory, *adj.* harmful to one's good name.

der′rick, *n.* a kind of crane for lifting weights.

der′ring-do, -doo, *n.* daring action.

derringer, der′in-jer, *n.* a short pistol.

der′vish, *n.* a Mohammedan monk.

descend, dē-send′, *v.* to climb down : to rush down on, to attack : to go from father to son : to have as one's forefathers.—*n.* **descend′ant**, one who has a certain person as a forefather (e.g. He is a *descendant* of Nelson).—*n.* **descent′**, a going down : a steep hill : an attack : the list of one's ancestors or forefathers.

describe′, *v.* to tell fully about : to trace out.—*adj.* **describ′able**.—*n.* **descrip′tion**, a picture in words : a written or spoken account : sort, kind (e.g. people of all *descriptions*).—*adj.* **descrip′tive**.

descry′, *v.* to espy.

des′ecrate, *v.* to make bad use of something sacred.—*n.* **desecrā′tion**.

desert′, *n.* what is deserved, either good or bad—often in *pl.* (e.g. He got his *deserts*).

desert′, *v.* to run away from : to leave.—*ns.* **deser′tion**, the act of forsaking ; **deser′ter**, a soldier who leaves his post or his regiment.

des′ert, *adj.* lonely : having no people : not having soil worth cultivating.—*n.* a stretch of barren country, usually hot, dry, and sandy.—**desert island**, a bare, lonely island without inhabitants.

deserve′, *v.* to be worthy of reward : to earn by well-doing.—*adj.* **deser′ving**.—*adv.* **deser′vedly**, justly.

des′iccate, *v.* to dry up.

design, de-zīn′, *v.* to make a plan or a sketch of : to plan.—*n.* a drawing or sketch : a plot : a thing taking shape in the mind, an intention.—*adv.* **design′edly**, intentionally.—*adj.* **design′ing**, making evil plans.

designate, des′ig-nāt, *v.* to name : to appoint : to point out.—*adj.* appointed to a post but not yet occupying it.—*ns.* **designā′tion**, a name, title.

desire′, *v.* to wish for greatly : to ask politely.—*n.* a longing for : a request.—*adj.* **desir′able**, pleasing : agreeable.—*n.* **desirabil′ity**.—*adj.* **desir′ous**, wishing : eager to get.

desist′, *v.* to stop from doing.

desk, *n.* a sloping table for writing, reading, etc.

des′olate, *v.* to make lonely : to lay waste.—*adjs.* **des′olate**, left lonely : empty of people ; **des′olated**, overcome by grief.—*n.* **desolā′tion**, loneliness : deep sorrow.

despair, de-spār', v. to be without hope : to give up hope.—n. want of hope : that which causes despair.—adj. despair'ing, having no hope.

despatch', dispatch', v. to send away : to finish off : to kill : to do quickly.—ns. despatch', act of sending away : a report (e.g. to a newspaper) : skill and speed in doing something : death, killing : the sending off of the mails : (pl.) important papers (e.g. orders) to troops ; despatch-rider, one who carries such messages.

desperä'do, n. one who commits cruel deeds (e.g. an outlaw, gangster).

des'perate, adj. having lost all hope : having no fear of danger.—n. despera'tion.

des'picable, adj. sneaking, mean.

despise', v. to look down upon with contempt : to scorn.

despite', prep. in spite of.

despoil', v. to rob : to spoil completely.—n. despoliä'tion.

despon'dent, adj. downhearted, gloomy : without hope of success.—n. despon'dency.—v. despond', to lose hope, to be downhearted.

des'pot, n. one (usually king or ruler of a country) whose power is not checked by any council or parliament.—adj. despot'ic.—n. des'potism.

dessert', n. fruits, sweets, etc. served at the end of a meal.

des'tine, v. to fix : to mark out, as if by fate (e.g. He was destined to succeed).—ns. destinä'tion, the place to which one is going : a journey's end ; des'tiny, what is settled as if by fate.

destitute, des'ti-tūt, adj. left alone : in want, needy.—n. destitü'tion.

destroy', v. to pull down, knock to pieces : to ruin : to kill.—n. destroy'er, one who destroys : see also torpedo.

destruc'tion, n. act of destroying : death.—adjs. destruc'tible, able to be destroyed ; destruc'tive, causing destruction : doing great damage (e.g. a destructive fire).—n. destruc'tor, a furnace for burning rubbish.

des'ultory, adj. jumping from one thing to another : without a fixed plan.

detach', v. to unfasten, to unhook : to separate.—adjs. detach'able, able to be loosed or taken off ; detached', standing apart : separated : calm.—n. detach'ment, something detached, esp. a body of troops : calmness of mind.

detail', v. to tell about something, leaving nothing out, however small : to set to a special job or task (e.g. The airman was detailed for night-flying).—n. detail' or de'tail, a small part.—adj. detailed', with nothing left out.

detain', v. to hold back : to keep late : to keep under guard.—n. deten'tion, imprisonment.

detect', v. to find out : to discover.—ns. detec'tion ; detect'ive, one who tracks criminals.

detention. See detain.

deter', v. to frighten from : to hinder or prevent.—adj. deter'rent, keeping back, hindering.—n. something which keeps back.

detë'riorate, v. to grow worse.—n. detëriora'tion.

deter'mine, v. to make up one's mind : to fix or settle.—adj. deter'mined, having one's mind made up : stubborn.—n. determinä'tion, the state of having one's mind fixed on doing something difficult : courage : stubbornness.

deterrent. See deter.

detest', v. to hate greatly.—adj. detest'able, very hateful.—n. detestä'tion, great hatred.

dethrōne', v. to remove from a throne.—n. dethrōne'ment.

det'onate, v. to explode.—ns. detonä'tion, an explosion with loud noise ; det'onätor, a cap that sets off an explosive : a cartridge.

detour, de-toor', n. a roundabout way : a turning aside.

detract', v. (with from) to take away from : to lessen (the good name of a person).

det'riment, n. damage : loss.—adj. detriment'al, causing damage.

deuce, dūs, n. a card with two spots : in tennis scoring, forty each : the devil.

dev'astate, v. to lay waste : to plunder.—n. devastä'tion.

devel'op, v. to grow bigger : to make to grow bigger : to unfold gradually : to use chemicals (called **de-vel′oper**) to make a photograph appear. — *n.* **devel′opment.** — to **await developments,** to wait and see what happens.

dē′viate, *v.* to turn aside : to take a roundabout way : to err. — *n.* **deviā′tion.**

device′, *n.* something made for a purpose : an invention : a crest on a shield, coat-of-arms : a trick.

dev′il, *n.* the spirit of evil, Satan : any evil spirit : a printer's message-boy. — *adj.* **dev′ilish,** like a devil : very wicked. — *ns.* **dev′ilment, dev′ilry,** behaviour like that of a mischievous spirit. — *adj.* **devil-may-care,** heedless, not caring what happens.

dē′vious, *adj.* out of the way : roundabout : erring.

devise′, *v.* to make up, to put quickly together : to plan or plot.

devoid′, *adj.* empty of : free from.

devolve′, *v.* to come to, to fall to one's lot (e.g. The task of replying *devolved* on the senior prefect).

devōte′, *v.* to give up wholly : to set aside for : to vow. — *adj.* **devō′ted,** loving greatly (e.g. a *devoted* son) : given up, as by a vow (e.g. a life *devoted* to healing). — *ns.* **devotee′,** one who follows a religion, game, etc. with very great eagerness ; **devō′tion,** prayer : great love. — *adj.* **devō′tional,** having to do with prayer.

devour′, *v.* to eat greedily : to destroy : to gaze on.

devout′, *adj.* holy : given up to religious thought and work : earnest. — *n.* **devout′ness.**

dew, *n.* tiny drops of water coming from the air as it cools at night : early freshness. — *adj.* **dew′y.** — *n.* **dew′-pond,** a hollow that fills with water from dew or mist (used for cattle when rain-water is scarce).

dew′lap, *n.* the loose-hanging skin under the throat of oxen, dogs, fowls, etc.

dexter′ity, *n.* cleverness, esp. in hand-movements. — *adj.* **dex′terous or dex′trous.**

dhow, dow, *n.* a native vessel of the eastern African and western Indian coasts : an Arab slave-vessel.

diabē′tes, *n.* a disease often causing great thirst and hunger. — *adj.* **diabet′ic.**

diabolic, -al, dī-a-bol′ik, -al, *adj.* devilish : very wicked.

dī′adem, *n.* a kind of crown.

diæresis, dī-ēr e-sis, *n.* a mark (··) placed over one of two vowels to show that each is to be pronounced separately, as *naïve* (na-eev′).

dī′agnose, *v.* to say, after examining a sick person, what disease he is suffering from (e.g. The doctor *diagnosed* scarlet fever). — *n.* **diagnō′sis.**

diag′onal, *adj.* going from corner to corner. — *n.* a line drawn from corner to corner (e.g. of a square).

dī′agram, *n.* a drawing to explain something.

dī′al, *n.* a round sheet of metal, cardboard, etc., with movable indicator (e.g. the face of a clock, watch, etc.) : the turning number-plate of a telephone. — *v.* to work or turn a dial : to find a number on an automatic telephone.

dī′alect, *n.* a way of speaking or writing found only in a certain district (e.g. the Lancashire *dialect*).

dī′alogue, *n.* a talk between two or more people.

diam′eter, *n.* the line drawn across a circle, passing through its centre. — **diametrically opposed,** the very opposite.

dī′amond, *n.* a very hard, precious stone, the most valuable of all gems : a shape like a diamond (as on playing-cards). — **dī′amond-jubilee, -wedding,** the sixtieth year of one's work, one's wedding.

dī′aper, *n.* unbleached linen or other cloth : a napkin.

diaphragm, dī′a-fram, *n.* a thin layer that divides parts (e.g. the thin metal disc in an ear-phone) : the part of the body that separates the chest and lower part.

diarrhœa, dī-a-rē′a, *n.* looseness of the bowels.

dī′ary, *n.* a book in which day-to-day happenings are written. — *n.* **dī′arist,** one who writes a diary.

dī′atribe, *n.* a long or angry attack in words or writing.

dib'ble, *n.* a pointed tool used for making holes for seed or plants.

dice. See die.

dick'ey, dick'y, *n.* a back, outside seat of a motor-car: a short, starched shirt-front.

dicotyledon, dī-kot-i-lē'don, *n.* a plant having two seed-leaves.

dictāte', *v.* to read out so that another may write down: to order about rudely.—*ns.* **dictā'tion;** **dictāt'or,** an all-powerful ruler.—*adj.* **dictatō'rial,** like a dictator: giving commands roughly.

dic'tion, *n.* manner of speaking: choice of words.

dic'tionary, *n.* a book having the words of a language in order, along with their meanings.

dic'tum, *n.* a wise, thoughtful saying (*pl.* **dic'ta**).

didac'tic, *adj.* meant to teach or instruct.

did'dle, *v.* to cheat.

die, dī, *v.* to lose life: to wither.

die, dī, *n.* a small cube, usually with numbered sides or faces, used in games of chance (*pl.* **dice**): a stamp or punch for making raised designs on money, etc. (*pl.* **dies**).

diesel (dēz'l) **engine,** *n.* an internal combustion engine in which heavy oil is ignited by heat generated by compression.

dī'et, *n.* food: kind of food (e.g. milk *diet,* rich *diet*).—*v.* to eat certain kinds of food only.—*n.* **dī'etary,** a course of diet: an allowance of food.—*adj.* **dietet'ic,** having to do with diet.

dī'et, *n.* a meeting of a court, parliament, church congregation, etc.

dif'fer, *v.* to be unlike: to disagree: to quarrel.—*n.* **dif'ference,** a point in which things are unlike: the amount by which one number is greater than another: a quarrel.—*adj.* **dif'ferent,** unlike.—*v.* **differen'tiate,** to make a difference between.

dif'ficult, *adj.* not easy: hard to please.—*n.* **dif'ficulty.**

dif'fident, *adj.* shy, bashful.—*n.* **diff'idence.**

diffūse', *v.* to send out in all directions: to scatter.—*adjs.* **diffūsed';** **diffū'sive,** spreading widely.—*n.* **diffū'sion.**—*adj.* **diffuse** (dif-ūs'),

widely spread: containing too many words.

dig, *v.* to turn up earth or soil (e.g. with a spade): to poke or push into (e.g. spurs into a horse).—*n.* a poke or thrust.—*n.pl.* **dig'gings,** gold or diamond mines.

digest, di-jest', *v.* to break up food (in the stomach) and turn it into a form in which the body can make use of it: to think over.—*adjs.* **digest'ive,** making digestion easy; **digest'ible,** easily digested.—*n.* **diges'tion,** power of digesting.

digest, dī'jest, *n.* a body of laws collected and arranged: a magazine.

dight, dīt, *adj.* adorned.

digit, dij'it, *n.* a finger: a finger's breadth: any of the numbers 1–9.—*adj.* **di'gital,** having to do with the fingers.—*n.* **digita'lis,** a family of plants, including the fox-glove.

dignify, *v.* to make high, noble, worthy.—*adj.* **dig'nified,** looking as if of high worth or rank: noble: haughty.—*ns.* **dig'nity,** nobility, high worth or rank; **dig'nitary,** a person of high rank.

dīgress', *v.* to wander from the point in speaking or writing.—*n.* **dīgres'sion.**

dīke, dȳke, *n.* a wall or earth-bank: a ditch.

dilap'idated, *adj.* (of buildings, walls, etc.) falling to pieces, needing repair.

dilāte', *v.* to swell: to make or grow bigger: to talk at great length.—*ns.* **dilatā'tion; dilā'tion.**

dil'atory, *adj.* lazy and slow: wasting time.

dilem'ma, *n.* a choice of two things, neither of which is pleasant: a difficulty.

diligent, dil'i-jent, *adj.* hard-working: working steadily without slacking.—*n.* **dil'igence,** steadiness in working: a stage-coach.

dil'ly-dal'ly, *v.* to loiter, trifle.

dilūte', *v.* to lessen the strength of a liquid by adding water, etc.—*adj.* weakened (e.g. *dilute* sulphuric acid).—*n.* **dilū'tion.**

dim, *adj.* not bright or distinct: somewhat dark: not seeing clearly.—*v.* to make dark: to become darkened.—*n.* **dim'ness.**

dime, *n.* the tenth part of an American dollar, about 5d.

dimen′sion, *n.* size : measurement.

dimin′ish, *v.* to make or grow less. —*n.* diminū′tion, a lessening.— *adj.* dimin′ūtive, small in size : undersized.

dim′ple, *n.* a small hollow, esp. on the cheek or chin.—*v.* to mark with dimples.

din, *n.* a loud, lasting noise.—*v.* to say over and over again.

dine, *v.* to take dinner.

ding, *v.* to ring : to keep sounding. —*n.* ding′-dong, the sound of bells ringing.

dinghy, dingy, dingey, ding′gi, *n.* a small rowing-boat, esp. one carried on board a bigger boat.

dingle, ding′gl, *n.* a little hollow or narrow valley.

dingy, din′ji, *adj.* not bright in colour : dirty-looking.—*n.* din′giness.

din′ner, *n.* the chief meal of the day : a feast.

di′nosaur, *n.* a giant lizard of very far-off times.

dint, *n.* a blow or stroke.—**by dint of**, as a result of.

diocese, dī′ō-sēs, *n.* a bishop's district.—*adj.* diocesan (dī-os′es-an).

dip, *v.* to dive or plunge into any liquid for a little : to lower (e.g. a flag) and raise again : to slope down.—*n.* a down-slope : a short bathe : a candle made by dipping a wick in tallow.

diphtheria, dif-thē′ri-a, *n.* a dangerous throat disease.

diphthong, dif′thong, *n.* two vowel-sounds pronounced as one syllable (as in *out*).

diplō′ma, *n.* a written statement that one has passed a certain examination.

diplō′macy, *n.* the business of making agreements, treaties, etc. between countries : cleverness in making people agree, tact.—*adj.* diplomat′ic, having to do with diplomacy : clever in arranging matters between people.—*n.* dip′lomat.

dire, *adj.* dreadful.

direct′, *adj.* straight : showing no doubt, clear : outspoken.—*v.* to point or aim at : to show the correct way : to order : to put a name and address on (a letter).— *adv.* direct′ly, soon, immediately : on one's own, without any other person taking part : in outspoken, straightforward way.—*ns.* direc′tion, the act of directing : a place to which one moves, looks, etc. (e.g. He went in a northerly *direction*) : an order or command : (usually *pl.*) notes how to do or make something ; direct′ness, straightness, esp. in a person's manner of speaking ; direct′or, one who guides or manages (e.g. a business) ; direct′ory, a book of names and addresses, etc.

dirge, *n.* a lament : a funeral hymn.

dirigible, dir′i-ji-bl, *adj.* able to be steered or guided.—*n.* an airship which can be steered.

dirk, *n.* a dagger.

dirt, *n.* any unclean substance, such as mud, loose earth.—*adjs.* dir′ty ; dirt-cheap, very cheap.

disa′ble, *v.* to take the power or strength away from : to put out of action.—*ns.* disa′blement ; disabil′ity, want of power : a hindrance.

disabūse′, *v.* to set right a wrong belief.

disadvan′tage, *n.* a drawback : a hindrance.—*adj.* disadvantā′geous.

disaffect′ed, *adj.* discontented : rebellious. — *n.* disaffec′tion, ill-feeling : a feeling of rebellion.

disagree′, *v.* to quarrel : to think differently from another : (of food) to be unsuitable and cause pain.—*adj.* disagree′able, unpleasant.—*n.* disagree′ment.

disallow′, *v.* not to allow : to refuse permission to.

disappear′, *v.* to go out of sight.— *n.* disappear′ance.

disappoint′, *v.* to make sad by not giving what was expected.—*adj.* disappoin′ted.—*n.* disappoint′ment.

disapprove, dis-a-proov′, *v.* (with *of*) to think of something or somebody as bad or worthless.—*n.* disapprov′al.

disarm′, *v.* to take weapons away from : to make powerless.—*n.* disarm′ament, the act of doing away with war weapons (warships, submarines, etc.).

disarrānge′, *v.* to throw out of order: to make untidy.—*n.* **disarrānge′-ment**.

disas′ter, *n.* an unfortunate happening, esp. one that causes great damage, loss, etc.—*adj.* **disas′trous**.

disavow′, *v.* to say one knows nothing about a thing or person.—*n.* **disavow′al**.

disband′, *v.* to break up and send home a band of soldiers, etc.—*n.* **disband′ment**.

disbelieve, dis-be-lēv′, *v.* to refuse to look upon something as true.—*ns.* **disbelief′**; **disbeliev′er**.

disburse′, *v.* to pay out.—*n.* **disburse′ment**, a paying out.

disc, disk, *n.* a flat, round shape.

discard′, *v.* to throw away as useless.

discern, diz-ern′, *v.* to see.—*adjs.* **discern′ing**, sharp at seeing or finding out; **discern′ible**, able to be seen.—*n.* **discern′ment**, power to look wisely at a matter.

discharge′, *v.* to free from a load or charge: to unload a cargo: to set free: to fire a gun: to perform (duties): to pay (an account).—*n.* act of discharging: unloading: setting free: dismissal: a flow (e.g. of matter from an ear): payment.

disciple, dis-ī′pl, *n.* one who learns from another: a follower (e.g. a *disciple* of Christ).

discipline, dis′i-plin, *n.* order, orderliness: training to obey orders.—*v.* to bring to order.—*n.* **disciplinā′rian**, one who is strict in seeing that orders are obeyed.

disclaim′, *v.* to give up all claim to: to refuse to have anything to do with.—*n.* **disclaim′er**, a denial.

disclōse′, *v.* to lay open: to tell openly.—*n.* **disclō′sure**, a surprising matter which has up till now been a secret.

discolour, dis-kul′ur, *v.* to take colour out of.—*n.* **discolorā′tion**.

discomfit, dis-kum′fit, *v.* to beat completely: to make uneasy.—*n.* **discom′fiture**.

discomfort, dis-kum′furt, *n.* want of comfort: uneasiness: pain.

disconcert′, *v.* to fluster.

disconnect′, *v.* to separate (with *from*).—*adj.* **disconnect′ed**, (of talking and writing) not well joined together, rambling.

discon′solate, *adj.* sad: disappointed.

discontent′, discontent′ed, *adjs.* not content: cross, ill-humoured.—*ns.* **discontent′**, **discontent′ment**, **discontent′edness**.

discontin′ue, *v.* to stop, to leave off.

dis′cord, *n.* unpleasant sound (e.g. from a musical instrument): a quarrel, bad feeling.

dis′count, *n.* a small sum taken off an account (e.g. if paid soon).—*v.* **discount′**, to allow something off: not to believe part of a story (e.g. You can *discount* half of his story of the accident).

discoun′tenance, *v.* to refuse support to: to discourage.

discourage, dis-kur′āj, *v.* to take away the courage of: to seek to check by showing disfavour to.—*n.* **discour′agement**.—*adj.* **discour′aging**, giving little hope or encouragement.

discourse, dis′kōrs, *n.* a speech, a sermon: a long piece of writing on something important.—*v.* **discourse′**, to talk learnedly.

discourteous, dis-kurt′yus, *adj.* not having good manners, rude.—*n.* **discourt′esy**.

discover, dis-kuv′er, *v.* to find out: to see.—*ns.* **discov′erer**; **discov′ery**, the act of finding out: the thing discovered.

discred′it, *n.* lack of good-name: disgrace.—*v.* to refuse to believe: to take away good-name or reputation.—*adj.* **discred′itable**, disgraceful: bringing shame to.

discreet′, *adj.* wise and careful: knowing.—*n.* **discretion** (dis-kresh′un).

discrepancy, dis-krep′an-si, *n.* a mistake: a shortage, a difference between what is got and what is expected.

discretion. See discreet.

discrim′inate, *v.* to pick out differences: to choose out.—*adj.* **discrim′inating**, showing good sense in judging things.—*n.* **discrim′ination**.

discur′sive, *adj.* (in speaking, writing) not keeping to the point.

discuss′, *v.* to talk about something or somebody, weighing up good and bad points.—*n.* **discus′sion**.

disdain′, v. to look down on, to despise.—n. a feeling of scorn.—adj. **disdain′ful.**

disease′, n. an illness.—adj. **diseased′,** having a disease.

disembark′, v. to come ashore : to land.—n. **disembarkā′tion.**

disembar′rass, v. to free from difficulty.—n. **disembarr′assment.**

disembod′y, v. to free (troops) from army service : to set free from the body (e.g. a *disembodied* spirit).

disengaged, dis-en-gājd′, adj. not in a job : not being used.

disentangle, dis-en-tang′gl, v. to free from knots.

disfā′vour, n. want of favour : dislike.—v. to show dislike to.

disfig′ure, v. to change to a worse form : to spoil the beauty of.—n. **disfig′urement.**

disfran′chise, v. to take away the right to vote.

disgorge′, v. to give up what has been greedily taken.

disgrace′, n. the state of being out of favour : shame.—v. to bring shame upon.—adj. **disgrace′ful.**

disgruntled, dis-grun′tld, adj. sulky.

disguise, dis-gīz′, v. to change one's appearance or look, e.g. by a change of dress : to hide.—n. a dress or costume which makes the wearer seem other than what he is : a false look or appearance.

disgust′, n. strong dislike.—v. to displease : to stir up dislike to.—adj. **disgust′ing,** sickening.

dish, n. a plate or basin for food : the food so held.—v. to put into a dish from a pot.

dishearten, dis-hart′n, v. to take away heart, courage, or spirits.—adjs. **disheart′ened ; disheart′ening.**

dishevel, di-shev′el, v. to make untidy, to ruffle (e.g. the hair). —adj. **dishev′elled.**

dishonest, dis-on′est, adj. not honest. —n. **dishon′esty.**

dishonour, dis-on′ur, n. want of honour : disgrace : shame.—v. to take away honour : to cause shame to : to refuse the payment of a cheque.—adj. **dishon′ourable,** having no sense of honour : disgraceful.

disillū′sion, v. to take away a wrong view or opinion.—n. **disillū′sionment.**

disinclinā′tion, n. unwillingness : dislike. — adj. **disinclined′,** unwilling.

disinfect′, v. to free from infection.—n. **disinfect′ant,** something which kills hurtful germs.

disinher′it, v. to take away the rights of an heir.

disin′tegrate, v. to go to pieces : to break up into parts.—n. **disintegrā′tion.**

disin′terested, adj. unselfish : not seeking any reward for one's self.

disjoin′ted, adj. not well connected together (esp. of a speech or writing).

disk. Same as disc.

dislike′, v. not to be pleased with : to disapprove of.—Also n.

dis′locate, v. to put out of joint : to upset, to put out of order.—n. **dislocā′tion.**

dislodge, dis-loj′, v. to drive from a hiding-place or defence.

disloy′al, adj. not loyal : false to one's king.—n. **disloy′alty.**

dis′mal, adj. gloomy : sorrowful.

disman′tle, v. to strip off : to take down fittings, furniture, etc.

dismay′, v. to terrify : to destroy one's courage.—Also n.

dismem′ber, v. to tear to pieces : to cut the limbs from a body.—n. **dismem′berment.**

dismiss′, v. to send away : to send a person from his job : to cast aside.—n. **dismis′sal.**

dismount′, v. to come down from, or off (e.g. a horse) : to take down (e.g. guns from carriages).

disobey, dis-o-bā′, v. to be unwilling or refuse to do what is commanded.—adj. **disobē′dient.**—n. **disobē′dience.**

disoblige′, v. to be unwilling to do what a person asks.—adj. **disoblig′ing,** not willing to carry out the wishes of others.

disor′der, n. want of order : confusion : disturbance : disease.—v. to throw out of order.—adj. **disor′derly,** out of order : behaving in a lawless manner. — n. **disor′derliness.**

B.D.—4

disor'ganise, v. to put out of order. —n. disorganisā'tion.

disown, diz-ōn', v. to refuse to have anything to do with.

dispar'age, v. to speak of a person or action as being of little worth or value : to speak hurtfully about. —n. dispar'agement.

dispar'ity, n. great difference : inequality.

dispas'sionate, adj. favouring no one : judging calmly.

dispatch. Same as despatch.

dispel', v. to drive away : to make to disappear.

dispense', v. to give or deal out (e.g. medicines).—to dispense with, to do without.—adj. dispen'sable, able to be done without.—ns. dispens'ary, a place where medicines and advice are given out; dispensā'tion, special leave (e.g. from a priest) to break a rule.

disperse', v. to scatter in all directions.—ns. disper'sal, disper'sion, a scattering.

dispir'ited, adj. sad, having lost heart.

displace', v. to put out of place : to disarrange.—n. displāce'ment, a movement out of place : the distance so moved : the quantity of water equal in weight to a floating body, such as a ship (e.g. a battleship of 20,000 tons displacement).

display', v. to set out for show.—n. show.

displease', v. to offend : to make a little angry.—n. displeasure (displezh'ur), the feeling of one who is offended.

disport', v. to play about in enjoyment, fun.—n. disport'ment.

dispōse', v. to arrange, to settle : to get rid of (e.g. He disposed of his motor-car) : to make inclined (e.g. Your excuse disposes me to forgive you).—n. dispō'sal, the act of disposing.—at my (your, his, etc.) disposal, for my (your, his, etc.) use (e.g. The general had a large army at his disposal).

disposition, dis-po-zish'un, n. arrangement : temper, frame of mind : (in law) a giving over of something to another (e.g. disposition of property).

dispossess', v. to take away from.

dispropor'tionate, adj. too big or too little : not fairly shared.

disprove, dis-proov', v. to prove to be false.

dispūte', v. to argue about.—n. a quarrel.—adj. dis'pūtable, not certain : able to be argued about. —n. disputā'tion, an argument.

disqualify, dis-kwol'i-fī, v. to put out of a competition, race, etc. for breaking rules.—n. disqualificā'tion.

disquiet, dis-kwī'et, n. uneasiness, restlessness.—v. to make anxious. —n. disquī'etūde.

disquisition, dis-kwi-zish'un, n. a written account or a speech telling about a careful search into any matter.

disregard', v. to pay no attention to. —n. want of attention : neglect. —adj. disregard'ful.

disrepair', n. the state of being out of repair.

disrepute', n. bad name or reputation.—adj. disrep'ūtable, having a bad reputation : disgraceful.

disrespect', n. rudeness: lack of politeness to parents, relatives, important people.—adj. disrespect'ful.

disrobe', v. to undress.

disrupt', v. to break up.—n. disrup'tion, a sudden break-up or bursting : the breaking away of some of the members of a Church.—adj. disrup'tive, causing disruption.

dissat'isfy, v. not to satisfy : to displease.—adj. dissat'isfied.—n. dissatisfac'tion.

dissect', v. to cut neatly into parts. —n. dissec'tion.

dissem'ble, v. to hide one's true feelings : to be false.—n. dissem'bler.

dissem'inate, v. to sow or scatter about.—n. disseminā'tion.

dissent', v. to say ' no' to : to have a different opinion.—n. a saying ' no.'—ns. dissen'sion, ill-feeling when people are not of the same opinion; dissent'er, an English Protestant who refuses to join the English Church; dissen'tient, one who objects or refuses to do as others do.—Also adj.

dissertā'tion, n. a long, learned piece of writing.

disser'vice, *n.* injury: an ill turn.

dissev'er, *v.* to separate, cut in two.

dissim'ilar, *adj.* not the same.

dissim'ulate, *v.* to pretend: to hide one's true feelings: to be false.

dis'sipate, *v.* to scatter: to waste.— *adj.* **dis'sipated,** having wasted one's strength, good looks, etc. by evil conduct.—*n.* **dissipā'tion,** wild manner of living.

dissociate, dis-sō'shi-āt, *v.* to take no part in: to separate.

dissolve', *v.* to melt (e.g. to *dissolve* salt in water): to put an end to (e.g. Charles I. *dissolved* Parliament).—*n.* **dissolū'tion,** melting: finish or break-up (e.g. of Parliament): death.—*adj.* **diss'olūte,** of bad habits: wicked.

dissuade, dis-swād', *v.* to advise someone not to do something.— *n.* **dissuā'sion.**—*adj.* **dissuā'sive.**

dis'taff, *n.* the stick which holds the bunch of flax or wool in spinning.

dis'tance, *n.* space between things: state of being far off: haughtiness or coldness of manner.—*adj.* **dis'tant,** placed far off: cold in manner.

distāste', *n.* dislike: disgust.—*adj.* **distāste'ful,** bad to taste: unpleasant.

distem'per, *n.* a kind of paint used chiefly for walls.—*v.* to paint with distemper.

distem'per, *n.* a disease of dogs.

distend', *v.* to swell: to stretch.— *n.* **disten'sion.**

distil', *v.* to get something in a pure state by heating to a steam or vapour and cooling: to fall in drops.—*ns.* **distillā'tion,** act of distilling; **distil'lery,** a place where distilling (of whisky, brandy, etc.) is done.

distinct', *adj.* clear: different: easily seen or made out.—*adj.* **distinc'tive,** different from others (e.g. There is something *distinctive* in her way of dressing).—*ns.* **distinc'tiveness;** **distinc'tion,** a difference: something which makes a thing or person stand out (e.g. a high mark in an examination: a medal for bravery).

distinguish, dis-ting'gwish, *v.* to make different (e.g. The white tail-feathers *distinguished* her from the other blackbirds): (with *-self*) to win fame (e.g. He *distinguished* himself in the hundred yards race): to see.—*adj.* **disting'uished,** famous.

distort', *v.* to twist out of shape: to turn from the true meaning. —*n.* **distor'tion,** the twisting of something out of shape: harsh unnatural speaking, singing, etc. over the wireless.

distract', *v.* to draw aside the attention.—*adj.* **distract'ed,** having the attention turned aside: mad (e.g. with pain, grief).—*n.* **distrac'tion,** something which draws away attention: madness.

distrain', *v.* to seize goods for debt. —*n.* **distraint'.**

distraught, dis-trawt', *adj.* very worried.

distress', *n.* pain, trouble: misfortune: anything that causes suffering.—*v.* to make uneasy: to cause pain.—*adjs.* **distress'ing;** **distressed'.**

distrib'ute, *v.* to divide among several: to deal out.—*n.* **distribū'tion,** a dealing or sharing out.

dis'trict, *n.* a part of a country.

distrust', *n.* want of trust or confidence: doubt.—*v.* to have no trust in.—*adj.* **distrust'ful.**

disturb', *v.* to throw into confusion: to worry (e.g. by noise, bad news): to interrupt.—*n.* **disturb'ance,** a breaking of quietness: a noisy fight: an interruption.

disūse', *n.* the state of being no longer used.—*v.* (dis-ūz') to cease to use.—*adj.* **disūsed',** not used.

ditch, *n.* a trench dug in the ground, esp. one for water.—*v.* to make a ditch.

dit'to, often shortened to **do.,** *adv.* the same as already written or said (used in columns of figures, etc. to save rewriting the same thing many times).

dit'ty, *n.* a little poem to be sung.

diur'nal, *adj.* daily: done in a day.

divan', *n.* a soft, long, low couch: a Turkish council.

dīve, *v.* to dip or plunge into.—*n.* a plunge.—*n.* **dī'ver,** one who dives: one who works under water in a special suit (a *diving-suit*): a diving bird.

diverge', *v.* to go different ways (e.g. At the inn the roads *diverge*). —*n.* diverg'ence.—*adj.* diver'gent.

di'vers, *adj.* an old word for *several*.

diverse', *adj.* different : unlike.—*v.* **divers'ify**, to make different : to give a pleasant change to something (e.g. The fair was *diversified* by a pageant).

diver'sion, *n.* a turning aside : a piece of fun : amusement.

diver'sity, *n.* difference.

divert', *v.* to turn aside : to change the direction of : to amuse.—*adj.* **divert'ing**, amusing : pleasant.

divest', *v.* to strip off (e.g. clothes) : to take away.

divide', *v.* to share among : to deal : to go into separate groups.—*n.* **divi'der**, a kind of compasses.

div'idend, *n.* that which is to be divided (see **divisor**) : share of profit (e.g. of a business).

divine', *adj.* belonging to God : holy. —*n.* a preacher of the gospel, a clergyman.—*v.* to foretell : to guess.—*ns.* **divina'tion**, art of foretelling ; **Divin'ity**, God ; **divin'ity**, any god : the study of the Bible ; **divin'ing-rod**, a rod, usually of hazel, used by certain people to discover water or metals under ground.

division, di-vizh'un, *n.* act of dividing : a barrier : a part or section (e.g. an *army division*) : a quarrel. —*adjs.* **divi'sional**, having to do with a division ; **divis'ible**, able to be divided.—*ns.* **divisibil'ity** ; **divi'sor**, the number by which another number is divided (e.g. in the sum 24÷6, 24 is the *dividend*, 6 the *divisor*).

divorce', *n.* an order (from a lawcourt) for the break-up of a marriage.—*v.* to put away : to separate.

div'ot, *n.* a piece of turf.

divulge', *v.* to let out, make known (e.g. news, a secret).

diz'zy, *adj.* giddy : confused : causing giddiness.—*n.* **dizz'iness**.

djinn. See **jinn**.

do, doo, *v.* to perform any action : to cheat, swindle : to get on (in health—e.g. ' How do you *do* ? ').

docile, dō'sīl, *adj.* easily managed : ready to learn.—*n.* docil'ity.

dock, *n.* a weed with large leaves and a long root.

dock, *v.* to clip : to cut to a stump.

dock, *n.* part of a harbour where ships go for loading, unloading, repair, etc. : the box in a lawcourt where the accused person stands. —*v.* to place in a dock : to reach a dock.—*ns.* **dock'yard**, a naval harbour with docks, stores, etc. : **dry'-dock**, **grav'ing-dock**, a dock that can be cleared of water so that a ship's hull may be repaired : **float'ing-(dry-)dock**, one that is sunk to allow a ship to enter it, and then raised again by taking out the water.

dock'et, *n.* a label stuck on goods : a short written statement.

doc'tor, *n.* one who is highly skilled in healing, law, music, etc. (usually the title is got from a university).—*v.* to treat, as a doctor does a patient : to tamper with, add something harmful to.

doc'trine, *n.* a belief that is taught.

doc'ument, *n.* a written statement, giving proof, evidence, information, etc. — *adj.* **documen'tary**, having to do with documents.

dod'der, *v.* to shake, tremble.

dodge, doj, *v.* to start aside or shift about : to use mean tricks.—*n.* a trick.

dō'dō, *n.* a large bird now extinct (i.e. no longer living).

doe, dō, *n.* female of certain animals (e.g. deer, rabbit, hare).

doer, doo'er, *n.* one who does anything.

doff, *v.* to take off (e.g. one's hat, gloves).

dog, *n.* a four-footed animal (esp. the male) : a mean fellow : a fire-iron.—*v.* to follow and watch constantly.—*ns.* **dog'cart**, a two-wheeled carriage with seats back to back ; **dog'-coll'ar**, a collar for dogs : a clergyman's collar ; **dog'-days**, the period from July 3 to August 11, named from the rising of the dog-star (*Sirius*), and having really nothing to do with dogs ; **dog'-fan'cier**, one who deals in dogs ; **dog'fish**, a small shark, common on British and American coasts; **dog'-rose**, the wild rose; **dog's'-ear**, the corner of the leaf of a book turned down like a dog's ear; **dog'-watch**, on a ship, the period of look-out from 4 to 6 a.m. or 6 to 8 p.m.— —*adj.* **dog'-tired**, tired as a dog, completely worn out.

doge, dōj or dō'je, *n.* the chief magistrate in old-time Venice and Genoa.

dog'ged, *adj.* refusing to give in.— *n.* **dog'gedness**.

dog'gerel, *n.* bad poetry.

dog'ma, *n.* what is usually believed about something (e.g. Christian *dogma*): opinion that is not to be contradicted.—*adj.* **dogmat'ic**, forcing one's opinions on others. —*v.* **dog'matise**, to state one's opinions as if they could not be wrong.

doi'ly, *n.* a fancy napkin (e.g. on plates in a cake-stand).

doings, doo'ingz, *n.pl.* things done: events.

dol'drums, *n.pl.* those parts of the ocean about the equator where calms are common: low spirits.

dole, *v.* to deal out small pieces.— *n.* a share: a sum of money.

dole, *n.* pain: grief, sadness.—*adj.* **dōle'ful**.—*n.* **dōle'fulness**.

doll, dol'ly, *n.* a toy-baby for a child.

dol'lar, *n.* an American coin ($), usually worth about 7s.

dol'men, *n.* a stone table.

dō'lorous, *adj.* full of complaints: sad.

dolphin, dol'fin, *n.* an animal like a porpoise.

dōlt, *n.* a stupid person.

domain', *n.* a kingdom: land in the country, an estate.

dome, *n.* roof-top or tower-top shaped like a half-ball: anything so shaped.—*adj.* **dōmed**.

domes'tic, *adj.* belonging to the house: tame (e.g. The *domestic* cat is a good pet, the *wild* cat is very fierce): not foreign.—*n.* a servant in the house.—*v.* **domes'-ticate**, to make accustomed to live in a house: to tame.—*ns.* **domestica'tion**; **domestic'ity**, fondness for home.

dom'icile, *n.* a house: country or place to which a person belongs.

dom'inant, *adj.* masterful: most outstanding: chief.—*n.* **dom'inance**.

dom'inate, *v.* to be lord over: to be the chief or most strong: to look over.—*n.* **domina'tion**.

domineer', *v.* to master or subdue by bullying.

dom'inie, *n.* a schoolmaster.

domin'ion, *n.* lordship: a territory with one ruler, owner, or government: the name for certain large parts of the British Empire (e.g. Canada, Australia, New Zealand, Union of South Africa).

dom'inō, *n.* a hooded or masked cape.—*n.* **dom'inoes**, a game played with wooden or ivory pieces marked with dots.

don, *n.* a Spanish title, like the English *Sir*: a learned member of a college.

don, *v.* to put on (e.g. coat, hat).

dona'tion, *n.* a gift of money or goods.—*v.* **donate'**, to present (a gift).—*n.* **dō'nor**, the giver of a generous gift.

donk'ey, *n.* an ass.—*n.* **don'key-en'gine**, a small engine used for light jobs (e.g. pumping water into the boilers, etc.).

dōnor. See donation.

doom, *n.* judgment: ruin: fate.— *v.* to sentence: to condemn.— *adj.* **doomed**, under sentence: as good as dead.—*n.* **Dooms'day**, the Day of Judgment.

door, dōr, *n.* the entrance into a house or room.—*n.* **door'way**, the space usually filled by a door.— **at death's door**, very nearly dead; **dead as a door-nail**, quite dead or out of use.

dope, *v.* to drug.—*n.* a drug.

dor'ic, *n.* a broad way of speaking (e.g. Scottish *doric*).

dor'mant, *adj.* sleeping: not active (e.g. a *dormant* volcano).

dor'mitory, *n.* a large sleeping-room (esp. in boarding-schools) with many beds.

dor'mouse, *n.* a mouse-like animal, which sleeps all winter (*pl.* **dor'-mice**).

dor'sal, *adj.* having to do with the back (e.g. *dorsal* fin).

dō'ry, *n.* a fish.

dose, *n.* the quantity of medicine to be taken at one time : any unpleasant thing that must be taken. —*v.* to give in doses.

dot, *n.* a small mark.—Also *v.*

dote, *v.* to be foolishly fond of.—*ns.* **dot´age,** foolishness of old age ; **dot´ard** a foolish old man.

double, dub´l, *v.* to multiply by two : to fold : to pass round or by : to run : to turn sharply back on one's course in running.—*n.* twice as much : a quick pace (short for *double-quick*) : a person so like another as to be able to take his place.—*adj.* containing twice as much : made up of two of the same sort together : deceitful. — *adv.* doub´ly.—*n.* **double-dealer,** a deceitful person.

doublet, dub´let, *n.* a close-fitting jacket, once worn by men.

doubloon, dub-loon´, *n.* an old Spanish gold coin.

doubt, dowt, *v.* not to be sure about : not to trust.—*n.* a feeling of not being sure : fear : a thing doubted. — *adj.* doubt´ful. — *adv.* doubt´less.

douche, doosh, *n.* a stream of water thrown on the body.—Also *v.*

dove, duv, *n.* a pigeon.—*n.* dove´-cote, a pigeon-house.

down, *n.* light feathers.

down-and-out, *adj.* having neither money nor work.—*adj.* downcast, sad at heart.

downs, *n.pl.* low, grassy hills.

dowry, *n.* money given to a woman at her marriage, usually by her parents.

doxol´ogy, *n.* a hymn of praise.

doyley. Same as doily.

doze, *v.* to sleep lightly.—Also *n.*

dozen, duz´n, *adj.* and *n.* twelve.

drab, *adj.* of dull colour : dingy.

draft, *n.* anything drawn or written (e.g. an order for payment of money, a rough sketch or plan) : anything drawn or taken from among others (e.g. a *draft* of soldiers).—*v.* to make a rough plan : to choose out (e.g. soldiers) and send for some special purpose.—*n.* drafts´man (or draughtsman), one who draws plans.

drag, *v.* to pull roughly or by force : to move slowly : to search in

deep water, by means of a net or hook (e.g. The boatmen *dragged* the lake for the lost treasure).— *n.* an open horse-carriage ; anything which keeps back (e.g. a brake under wheels).

drag´gle, *v.* to make wet and dirty by dragging on the ground.

drag´oman, *n.* a guide in Eastern countries :—*pl.* drag´omans.

drag´on, *n.* (in fables) a winged serpent : a fierce person.—*n.* drag´on-fly, a winged insect, with a long body and brilliant colours.

dragoon´, *n.* a heavy-armed horse-soldier.—*v.* to bully a person into doing something.

drain, *v.* to clear (land) of water by trenches or pipes : to drink dry : to use up money or strength. —*n.* anything (e.g. a ditch, water-pipe, trench) in which liquids may flow away.—*n.* drain´-age, the drawing-off of water by rivers, pipes, etc.

drake, *n.* the male of the duck.

drama, drah´ma, *n.* a play for acting on the stage : an exciting happening.—*adj.* dramat´ic, having to do with plays : exciting, thrilling.— *v.* dram´atise, to turn a story into a play for acting.—*ns.* dramatisa´-tion ; dram´atist, a writer of plays. —dram´atis personae (per-sō´nē), a list of the people who act in a play.

dra´per, *n.* a dealer in cloth and cloth goods.—*v.* drape, to arrange cloth-coverings to hang gracefully.—*n.* drap´ery, cloth goods : a draper's shop.

dras´tic, *adj.* stern : severe : thorough.

draught, drahft, *n.* a drawing (in pen, pencil, etc.) : something drawn out (e.g. a *draught* of fishes, *draught* of wine) : a current or rush of air : depth to which a ship sinks in water.— *n.pl.* draughts, a game for two, played by moving pieces on a squared board.—*adj.* draught´y, full of air-currents.—*ns.* draught´-horse, a horse for pulling heavy loads ; draughts´man. See drafts-man.

draw, *v.* to pull after or along : to make a picture : to attract (a crowd, attention) : to receive money (e.g. to *draw* a pension, a cheque): to require depth for floating (e.g. This ship *draws* 20 feet): to come near (e.g. Night *drew* on): to stop (e.g. The car *drew* up at the shop): to be equal with (in games—e.g. Surrey *drew* with Notts).—*n.* something which attracts: an undecided game (e.g. 1—1 in football, hockey).—*ns.* **draw'bridge,** a bridge (at the entrance to a castle) which could be drawn up or let down; **draw'ing,** a picture made by pen or pencil: (*pl.*) **draw'ings,** the money taken at a concert, fête, etc.; **draw'ingroom,** a room to which people withdraw after dinner.—**drawn and quartered,** having the body cut in pieces.

drawl, *v.* to speak in a slow, sleepy manner.—Also *n.*

dray, *n.* a low strong cart for heavy goods.

dread, dred, *n.* great fear.—*adj.* making afraid, terrifying.—*v.* to be greatly afraid of.—*adj.* **dread'ful,** terrible.—*n.* **dread'nought,** a battleship.

dream, *n.* thoughts, fancies, that come during sleep: something imagined, not real.—*v.* to see visions in sleep: to think of nothing.—*adj.* **dream'y,** looking as if not quite awake: slow, dull.

drear, drear'y, *adjs.* gloomy: cheerless.

dredge, drej, *v.* to drag a net or bucket along the bed of a river or of the sea in order to bring up fish, mud, etc.—*n.* an instrument with which dredging is done.—*n.* **dred'ger,** a ship which deepens a channel or harbour by lifting mud from the bottom in buckets on an endless chain.

dredge, *v.* to sprinkle with.—*n.* **dred'ger,** a box or jar with sprinkler-top (e.g. a sugar *dredger*).

dregs, *n.pl.* dirt that falls to the bottom (e.g. *dregs* of wine): the useless part of anything.

drench, drensh, *v.* to soak: to force medicine on.—*n.* a quantity (of animal medicine) to be drunk.

dress, *v.* to put on clothes or a covering: to arrange, put in order, set right: to line up.—*n.* covering for the body: a lady's gown, frock, etc.: style of clothing.—*n.* **dress'ing,** something put on—e.g. *top-dressing* of lime, *salad-dressing, dressing* (i.e. bandages, etc.) for a cut or hurt.—*adj.* **dress'y,** fond of stylish clothes.—*ns.* **dress'er,** a kitchen-sideboard; **dress'-coat,** a fine black tail-coat.

drib'ble, *v.* to fall in small drops (esp. of spittle): (in football) to kick the ball on, little by little.—*n.* **drib'let,** a small quantity.

drift, *n.* something driven by wind (e.g. ice, snow, sand, a current of water in sea or lake): meaning.—*v.* to go with the tide or current: (of snow) to be driven into heaps.—*n.* **drifter,** a fishing-boat which uses **drift-nets,** i.e. nets which remain near the surface of the water.

drill, *v.* to make holes in: to exercise soldiers, pupils, etc.: to sow seeds in rows.—*n.* a tool for boring: exercise, practice: a row of seeds: a strong cloth.

drink, *v.* to swallow a liquid.—*n.* something to be drunk: liquid which makes a person giddy and stupid (often called **strong drink**).

drip, *v.* to fall in drops.—*n.* a drop: a continual dropping (e.g. of water).—*n.* **drip'ping,** fat from meat in roasting.

drive, *v.* to force along: to hurry on: to hit hard (e.g. a ball, nail): to guide (e.g. a car, an aeroplane).—*n.* a pleasure run: an avenue or road: a hard stroke with a club or bat (in golf, cricket, tennis, etc.): a hunt.—*n.* **dri'ver,** one who drives: a wooden-headed golf-club.

driv'el, *v.* to talk nonsense.

driz'zle, *n.* a shower of fine rain.—*adj.* **drizz'ly.**

droll, drōl, *adj.* odd: funny.—*n.* a jester, clown.—*n.* **droll'ery.**

drom'edary, *n.* a one-humped Arabian camel.

drone, *v.* to make a low humming sound.—*n.* a low humming sound: the low-sounding pipe of a bagpipe: the male of the honey-bee: a lazy, idle fellow.

droop, *v.* to hang down: to grow weak or faint.

drop, *n.* a small quantity of liquid (e.g. *rain-drop*): a fall from a height (e.g. a *drop* of six feet): a small sweet.—*v.* to fall in small amounts (as rain in drops): to fall suddenly: to let go suddenly: to set down from a train, bus, etc.

drop'sy, *n.* an illness, causing swelling of limbs or body.—*adj.* **drop'-sical.**

dross, *n.* the scum which metals throw off when melting: waste matter: small or waste coal, slack.

drought, drowt, *n.* dryness: want of rain or of water: thirst.

drove, *n.* a number of driven cattle, or other animals.—*n.* **drov'er,** one who drives cattle.

drown, *v.* to sink in water and so cause death: to flood.

drowse, *v.* to be heavy as with sleep.—*n.* a half-sleeping state.—*adj.* **drows'y,** sleepy.

drub, *v.* to beat or thrash.—*n.* **drub'-bing,** a thrashing.

drudge, druj, *v.* to work hard: to do very humble work.—*n.* one who works hard: a slave.—*n.* **drudg'-ery,** hard, uninteresting work.

drug, *n.* any substance used in making up medicines: a dangerous medicine used to dull the senses: an article that cannot be sold through being too plentiful.—*v.* to take away feeling by putting something in one's food or drink: to take medicine too often.—*n.* **drug'gist,** one who deals in drugs: a chemist.

Druid, droo'id, *n.* a priest of the ancient Britons.

drum, *n.* an instrument of skin stretched on a frame of wood or metal, and beaten with sticks: anything shaped like a drum: an inner part of the ear.—*v.* to beat a drum: to tap with the fingers.—*ns.* **drum'mer; drum'stick.**

drunk'ard, *n.* one who drinks too much.—*adjs.* **drunk, drunk'en,** giddy or stupid through drinking too much strong drink.—*n.* **drunk'enness.**

dry, *adj.* not moist or wet: thirsty: uninteresting: (of manner) not hearty: (of wine) not sweet.—*v.* to make or become dry.—*adv.* **dry'ly, dri'ly.**—*ns.* **dry'-rot,** a rot-

ting of wood, in which it becomes dry and crumbly; **dry'salter,** a dealer in gums, dyes, etc.—*adjs.* **dry'-shod,** without wetting the shoes or feet; **dry'-stone,** (of walls) built of stone without cement.

dry'ad, *n.* a nymph of the woods.

du'al, *adj.* double: made up of two.—*n.* **dual'ity,** doubleness.

dub, *v.* to give a new name or nickname to: to make a man a knight by touching him on the shoulder with a sword: to soften leather.—*n.* **dub'bin, dub'bing,** a grease for softening leather.

du'bious, *adj.* doubtful: uncertain.—*n.* **dubi'ety.**

du'cal, *adj.* having to do with a duke.

duc'at, *n.* an old gold coin worth about 9s. 4d., once common in Europe.

duch'y, *n.* the land owned, or ruled over, by a duke.—*n.* **duch'ess,** the wife, or widow, of a duke.

duck, *n.* a coarse cloth for sails, sacking, etc.: (*pl.*) clothes made of duck.

duck, *v.* to dip for a moment in water: to lower the head quickly.—*n.* **duck'ing,** a wetting.

duck, *n.* a web-footed bird, with long bill.—*n.* **duck'ling,** a baby duck.

duck, *n.* (in cricket) a score of 0.

duct, *n.* (in the human body, plants, etc.) a tube for carrying liquid.

dude, dood, *n.* a fop or dandy.

dudgeon, duj'un, *n.* ill-temper: annoyance.

due, dū, *adj.* owed: that ought to be paid or done to another: expected to be ready, or to arrive.—*adv.* exactly: directly (e.g. *due* south).—*n.* that which is owed: what one has a right to.

du'el, *n.* a fight (with pistols or swords) between two people.—*n.* **du'ellist,** one who fights in a duel.

duet', a musical piece for two singers or players.—*n.* **duet'tist.**

duf'fer, *n.* a dull person.

dug'out, *n.* a boat made by hollowing out the trunk of a tree: a rough shelter *dug out* of a slope or bank or in a trench.

duke, *n.* a nobleman next in rank below a *prince*.—*n.* **duke'dom,** the title, rank, or lands of a duke.

dulcet, duls'et, *adj.* sweet to the taste, or to the ear: melodious.

dul'cimer, *n.* a musical instrument consisting of stretched wires which are struck with small hammers.

dull, *adj.* slow of hearing, learning, or understanding: not lively: sad or downcast: cloudy, not bright or clear: blunt.—*adv.* dull'y.—*ns.* dull'ard, a dunce: a stupid person; dull'ness, the state of being dull.

dulse, *n.* an eatable seaweed.

duly, dū'li, *adv.* properly: at the proper time: as expected.

dumb, dum, *adj.* without the power of speech: silent.—*adv.* dumb'ly, in silence.—*ns.* dumb'ness; dumb'-show, acting without words; dum'my, one who is dumb: a sham (e.g. an empty package for shop-window display): a person acting or appearing for another.—*v.* dumbfound', to strike with great surprise.

dump, *v.* to throw down: to sell at a low price.—*n.* a thud: a place for throwing out rubbish.

dump'ling, *n.* a kind of thick pudding or paste.

dumps, *n.pl.* dullness of mind, ill-humour.

dumpy, *adj.* short and thick.

dun, *adj.* of a dark colour, partly brown and black: dark.

dunce, *n.* one slow at learning: a stupid person.

dune, doon, *n.* a low sand-hill.

dung, *n.* the waste matter passed out of an animal's body.—*n.* dung'-hill, a heap of dung in a farmyard.

dun'garees, *n.pl.* a suit of overalls.

dungeon, dun'jun, *n.* a close, dark prison: a cell under ground.

dūpe, *n.* one easily cheated.—*v.* to deceive: to trick.

duplicate, doo'pli-kăt, *adj.* double.—*n.* another of the same kind, an exact copy.—*v.* to make a copy.—*ns.* duplicā'tion; du'plicator, a machine for turning out copies (e.g. of letters).

duplicity, doo-plis'i-ti, *n.* deceit, double-dealing.

dū'rable, *adj.* lasting: wearing well: hardy.—*ns.* durabil'ity; du'rance, imprisonment; durā'tion, time a thing lasts.

dur'bar, *n.* a great gathering of Indian princes.

dur'ra, dhur'ra, *n.* millet (a kind of corn).

dusk, *n.* twilight.—*adj.* dusk'y, dark-coloured: sad: gloomy. — *n.* dusk'iness.

dust, *n.* fine grains or specks of earth or sand: anything in the form of powder (e.g. coal-*dust*, brick-*dust*).—*v.* to free from dust: to sprinkle lightly with powder.—*n.* dust'er, a cloth for taking off dust.—*adj.* dust'y, covered with dust.

du'ty, *n.* something one ought to do: a spell of work (e.g. the man *on duty*, *off duty*): a tax.—*adjs.* du'tiful, obedient: careful to do what one should; du'tiable, on which tax is to be paid.

dux, *n.* a leader: the top boy or girl in a school or class.

dwarf, *n.* an under-sized person or animal.—*v.* to make to appear small (e.g. A seven-foot man *dwarfs* one of ordinary height).—*adj.* not growing to full height.

dwell, *v.* to stay, or have one's house, home, in a place: to pause: to speak for a time on a certain point.

dwin'dle, *v.* to grow less: to waste away.

dye, dī, *v.* to give a colour to something.—*n.* a liquid for colouring, or changing the colour.—*ns.* dye'ing, the putting of colour into cloth; dy'er, one whose trade is to dye cloth, etc.

dyke. Same as dike.

dynam'ic, *adj.* having to do with force: very strong, powerful (e.g. He was a man of *dynamic* character).—*n.* dynam'ics, the branch of knowledge which has to do with speed and force.

dy'namite, *n.* a powerful explosive.—*v.* to blow up with dynamite.

dy'namo, *n.* a machine for making electricity :—*pl.* dy'namos.

dynasty, din'as-ti, *n.* a succession of kings of the same family.—*n.* dy'nast, a ruler.—*adj.* dynas'tic.

dysentery, dis'en-ter-i, *n.* a disease causing fever, pain, and diarrhœa.

dyspepsia, dis-pep'si-a, *n.* indigestion.—*n.* dyspep'tic, a person who suffers from indigestion.

E

ea′ger, *adj.* keen, anxious to do or get.—*n.* ea′gerness.

ea′gle, *n.* a large bird of prey.—*n.* ea′glet, a young or small eagle.

eagre, ē′ger, *n.* rise of the tide in a river.

ear, ēr, *n.* the part of the body through which hearing is done: the power of knowing different sounds: attention.—*ns.* ear′ache, a pain in the ear; ear′drop, an ornament hanging from the ear; ear′drum, the middle part of the ear; ear′mark, an owner's mark, (e.g. that on the ears of sheep); ear′shot, the distance at which a sound can be heard; ear′wig, an insect.

ear, *n.* a husk of corn.

earl, erl, *n.* an English nobleman ranking between a marquis and a viscount:—*fem.* count′ess.—*n.* earl′dom, the lands or title of an earl.

early, er′li, *adj.* in good time: at or near the beginning: coming at the beginning: happening in the near future.—Also *adv.*—*n.* ear′liness.—early bird, an early riser.

earn, ern, *v.* to get (money, etc.) by work: to deserve.—*n.pl.* earn′ings, pay for work done.

earnest, er′nest, *adj.* serious: anxious.—*n.* earn′estness.—in earnest, meaning what one says or does.

earnest, er′nest, *n.* money given to make sure that a bargain will be completed later.

earth, erth, *n.* the globe on which we live: soil: dry land: a fox's hole: the end of a wireless set connected with the ground.—*v.* to burrow: to connect a wireless set with the ground.—*adjs.* earth′en, made of earth or clay; earth′ly, belonging to the earth: having no high thoughts (also earth′ly-mind′ed); earth′y, like soil: not heavenly.—*ns.* earth′enware, pottery, dishes made of clay; earth′quake, a shaking of the earth: a heaving of the ground; earth′-trem′or, a slight earthquake; earth′work, a fortification made of earth; earth′worm, the common worm.

ease, *n.* freedom from pain, difficulty, worry: rest from work: quiet.—*adj.* eas′y: not hard to do: not in pain: quiet: not strict.—*n.* eas′iness.—*adv.* eas′ily.

eas′el, *n.* a stand for an artist's picture, blackboard, etc.

east, *n.* one of the four chief directions: that part of the heavens where the sun rises.—Also *adj.*—*adjs.* east′erly, coming from or facing the east; east′ern; east′ernmost; eastward (also *adv.*).—the East, lands lying to the east of Europe, i.e. Turkey, India, China, etc.

East′er, *n.* the Sunday after Good Friday, when the Christian churches keep in memory Christ's rising from the dead.

eat, *v.* to chew and swallow (food): to waste away (e.g. Rust had *eaten* the bridge away).—*adj.* eat′able, fit to be eaten.

eaves, ēvz, *n.pl.* the overhanging edge of a roof over the walls.—*v.* eaves′drop, to listen for secrets.—*n.* eaves′dropper.

ebb, *n.* the flowing away of the tide after high-tide: lessening (e.g. His luck is *on the ebb*, i.e. growing less).—*v.* to flow away.

eb′ony, *n.* a black, hard wood.—Also *adj.*—*n.* eb′onite, a hard black substance made of rubber (used for wireless panels, insulators, etc.).

ebulli′tion, *n.* a noisy outburst (e.g. of bad temper).

eccentric, ek-sen′trik, *adj.* odd, acting strangely: not having the same centre.— *n.* eccentricity, (ek-sen-tris′i-ti), oddness of manner or conduct.

ecclesiastic, e-klē-zi-as′tik, *n.* a priest: a clergyman.—*adj.* ecclesias′tical, having to do with the Church.

echo, ek′ō, *n.* the repeating of a sound caused by its striking a surface and coming back: an imitation:—*pl.* echoes (ek′ōz).—*v.* to send back sound: to repeat a thing said: to imitate.

eclipse, e-klips′, *n.* a darkening of the face of the sun or moon. (An eclipse of the sun is caused by the moon coming between it and the earth; an eclipse of the moon by the falling of the earth's shadow on it): any great failure or defeat. —v. to throw into the shade: to blot out a person's glory by doing better than he.

eclogue, ek'log, n. a short poem of country life.

econ'omy, n. thrifty, careful management (e.g. of a country's money affairs, of a household or shop): wise spending of money.— adj. econom'ical, careful in spending; not wasteful.—ns. econom'ics, the study of the manner in which men and nations make and spend money, and make, buy, and sell goods; econ'omist, one who studies economics.—v. econ'omise, to be careful in spending.

ec'stasy, n. great excitement, almost as if out of one's mind: mad delight.—adj. ecstat'ic, madly delighted.

ec'zema, n. a skin disease.

ed'dy, n. a back-current of water or air: a whirlpool, whirlwind.— Also v.

edelweiss, ā'del-vīs, n. a plant with pretty white flowers, found in the Alps.

edge, ej, n. the border or brink of anything: the cutting side of an instrument: sharpness of appetite: keenness.—v. to put an edge or border on: to move little by little.—advs. edge'ways, edge'wise, sideways.—n. edg'ing, border or fringe.

ed'ible, adj. fit to be eaten.—n. something for food.

ē'dict, n. an order, command.

edifice, ed'if-is, n. a large and stately building.

ed'ify, v. to improve the mind.— adj. ed'ifying, healthy to the mind.—n. edifica'tion, progress in knowledge: pleasure of mind.

ed'it, v. to revise, prepare matter for printing, broadcasting, etc.— ns. edi'tion, number of copies of a book or newspaper printed at one time; ed'itor, one who edits: one who chooses what is to go into a book or newspaper.—adj. edito'rial, of an

editor.—n. the part of a newspaper written by the editor.

ed'ucate, v. to teach persons in a school, college, etc.— ns. educā'tion; educā'tionist, one who studies the different ways of educating. — adjs. educā'tional, having to do with education; ed'ucative, helping to educate (e.g. an educative book, lecture).

edūce', v. to draw out (e.g. an answer from a person).

eel, n. a long, ribbon-shaped fish.

e'er, ār, short for ever.

ee'rie, ee'ry, adj. causing fear of unknown, strange things (e.g. A ruin is an eerie place).

efface', v. to rub out: to keep (one's self) from being taken notice of.

effect', n. the result of an action (e.g. What is the effect of taking this drug?): strength, power (e.g. This drug has lost its effect): (pl.) goods, property: means of lighting and of making various noises which help to make a play more real.—v. to succeed in doing something: to bring about. —adjs. effec'tive, causing something wished for to happen: powerful; effec'tual, able to do what is required.

effem'inate, adj. womanish: unmanly.

effervesce, ef-fer-ves', v. to boil up: to froth up.—n. efferves'cence.— adj. efferves'cent.

effete, ef-fēt', adj. played out: having lost all strength or force.

efficacious, ef-fi-kā'shus, adj. able to bring about the result intended (e.g. an efficacious remedy). —n. efficacy (ef'i-ka-si).

efficient, ef-fish'ent, adj. able to do things well: fit, capable.—n. efficiency (ef-fish'en-si), fitness to do a job well.

effigy, ef'fi-ji, n. a dummy figure of a person.

ef'fort, n. a try with all one's strength: an attempt.—adj. ef'fortless, done as if without trying.

effrontery, ef-frunt'er-i, n. impudence: shameless boldness of conduct.

efful'gence, n. great brightness: a flood of light.—adj. efful'gent.

effuse', *v.* to pour forth or out.—*n.* effu'sion, a pouring out (e.g. *effusion* of blood, words, etc.).—*adj.* effu'sive, pouring forth words, and pretending to be sincere.

egg, *n.* an oval object, laid by birds, insects, etc.; from it their young are produced.

egg, *v.* to urge to do.

eg'lantine, *n.* the sweet-brier.

egoism, eg'ō-izm, *n.* selfishness: the belief that the best way of living is to think of ourselves.— eg'oist, one who holds this belief. —*adj.* egoist'ic.—*ns.* eg'otism, the habit of speaking much of one's self; eg'otist.

egregious, e-grē'ji-us, *adj.* standing out from the rest, usually because of badness (e.g. an *egregious* blunder).

ē'gress, *n.* act of going out: the way out.

egret, ē'gret, *n.* a young eagle.

eider, ī'der, *n.* the eider-duck, a northern sea-duck, valued for its fine down (ei'der-down).

Eisteddfod, ī-steth'vod, *n.* a gathering of the Welsh, for song, music, and poetry, held yearly.

ejac'ūlate, *v.* to shout out, exclaim. —*n.* ejacula'tion.—*adj.* ejac'ulatory.

eject', *v.* to throw out.—*n.* ejec'tion, a throwing-out: the putting of a person out of his house (e.g. for not paying rent).

eke, ēk, *v.* to add to, to make bigger (usually used with *out*.—e.g. He *eked out* his wages by writing stories).

eke, ēk, *adv.* in addition to: likewise.

elab'orate, *v.* to put extra work on a thing, to make it better: to explain fully.—*adj.* done with fullness and exactness: having much ornament or decoration.— *n.* elabora'tion.

élan, ā-long', *n.* keenness, dash.

ē'land, *n.* a kind of South African deer.

elapse', *v.* to slip away: to pass.

elas'tic, *adj.* able to stretch and spring back again: springy.— *n.* a piece of silk, cotton, etc. made springy by having rubber woven in it.—*n.* elastic'ity (el-as-tis'i-ti), springiness.

elate', *v.* to make glad or proud.— *adj.* elā'ted, in high spirits, joyful.—*n.* elā'tion.

elbow, el'bō, *n.* the joint where the arm bends: any sharp bend (e.g. on a road).—*v.* to push with the elbow, to jostle.—*ns.* el'bow-grease, hard rubbing; el'bow-room, plenty of room in which to move.

el'der, *n.* a tree from whose purple-black berries elderberry wine is made.

el'der, *adj.* older: having lived a longer time.—*n.* one who is older: an ancestor: an office-bearer in the Presbyterian Church.—*adjs.* eld'erly, oldish: nearing old age; eld'est, oldest.

El Dorado, el dō-ra'dō, the land (S. America) where gold was thought to be had for the lifting: any place where wealth is easily got.

elect', *v.* to choose: to select.—*adj.* and *n.* chosen.—*n.* elec'tion, the choosing (usually by voting) of people to sit in a town council, parliament, etc.—*v.* electioneer', to help to get votes in an election. —*ns.* elec'tor, one who has the right of electing; elec'torate, all the electors.

electricity, el-ek-tris'i-ty, *n.* an unseen force used to give light, heat, and power.—*adj.* elec'tric, having to do with electricity: very lively. — *n.* electrician (el-ek-trish'-an), one skilled in working with electricity.—*vs.* elec'trify, to supply with electricity: to surprise greatly; elec'trocūte, to kill by an electric current.

electron, el-ek'tron, *n.* an electrically charged particle existing within the atom.

el'egant, *adj.* graceful, neat.—*n.* el'egance.

elegy, el'e-ji, *n.* a poem about sad things (e.g. death of a friend).

el'ement, *n.* a necessary part: any one of about 100 pure substances of which all known things are made; e.g. carbon, oxygen, gold: surroundings necessary for life (e.g. Water is a fish's *element*): (*pl.*) first steps in learning: the powers of nature, the weather: bread and wine used at Communion.—*adjs.* element'al, having to do with the elements: as in the beginning; element'ary, at the first step or stage: simple (oppos. of *advanced*).

elephant, el'e-fant, *n.* the largest four-footed animal, having a very thick skin, a trunk, and two ivory tusks.—*adj.* elephan'tine, like an elephant: big and clumsy.—a white elephant, a fine-looking gift that turns out to be costly to keep up and of little use.

el'evate, *v.* to raise to a higher position: to make cheerful: to improve (the mind).—*ns.* eleva'tion, the act of raising up: rising ground: height: a drawing of a building as seen from a side: an angle measuring height (e.g. the sun's *elevation*, a gun's *elevation*); el'evator, a lift in a building: a high store-house for grain.

elf, *n.* a mischief-working fairy or sprite: a dwarf:—*pl.* elves.—*adjs.* elf'in, elf'ish, elv'ish, elv'an, elf-like.

elicit, e-lis'it, *v.* to draw out (e.g. news, information).

elide', *v.* to cut off (e.g. a sound not to be pronounced—*we're* for *we are*).—*n.* eli'sion.

eligible, el'i-ji-bl, *adj.* fit or worthy to be chosen.—*n.* eligibil'ity.

elim'inate, *v.* to get rid of: to strike out.—*n.* elimina'tion.

elision. See elide.

élite, ā-lēt', *n.* the best people (e.g. The wedding was attended by the *élite* of London).

elix'ir or **elixir of life**, *n.* a magic drink which, as people once thought, gave lasting life: any pleasant or refreshing drink.

elk, *n.* the largest kind of deer, found in North of Europe and in North America.

ell, *n.* a measure of length, the span of the outstretched arms (roughly a yard).

ellipse', *n.* an oval shape:—*pl.* ellip'ses.—*adjs.* ellip'tic, ellip'tical, oval: having part of the words or meaning left out.

elm, *n.* a well-known tree.

elocu'tion, *n.* the art of correct speech: recitation in public.—*n.* elocu'tionist, one who recites.

ē'longate, *v.* to stretch out lengthwise.—*n.* elonga'tion.

elope', *v.* to run away from home with one's lover.—*n.* elope'ment.

eloquent, el'o-kwent, *adj.* having plenty to say: good at speaking in public.—*n.* el'oquence.

elucidate, e-lū'si-dāt, *v.* to make something easy to understand.—*n.* elucida'tion.

elūde', *v.* to escape by a trick: to dodge.—*adj.* elū'sive, hard to catch.

elvan, elves, elvish. See elf.

el'ver, *n.* a young eel.

emaciated, e-mā'shi-āt-ed, *adj.* very thin, like a skeleton.—*n.* emacia'tion.

em'anate, *v.* to flow out from.—*n.* emana'tion, a flowing out (e.g. an *emanation* of deadly gas).

emancipate, e-man'si-pāt, *v.* to set free, release.—*n.* emancipa'tion.

embalm, em-bahm', *v.* to preserve a dead body from decay by treating it with drugs: to perfume.

embank'ment, *n.* earth piled up to keep water back: the down-slope beside a road, railway, etc.

embar'go, *n.* a government's order, to stop ships carrying certain cargoes: any order for the stoppage of trade:—*pl.* embar'goes.

embark', *v.* to put or go on board ship: to start on anything (e.g. He *embarked* on a career of crime).—*n.* embarka'tion.

embarrass, em-ba'ras, *v.* to put difficulties in the way: to put in an awkward position.—*n.* embar'rassment.

em'bassy, *n.* the persons sent to arrange important matters between countries: the offices, etc. of an ambassador in a foreign country.

embattled, em-bat'ld, *adj.* having battlements.

embel'lish, *v.* to make beautiful: to decorate.—*n.* embel'lishment.

em'ber, *n.* a cinder.

embez'zle, *v.* to use for one's self money given to one to look after.—*n.* embez'zlement.

embit'ter, *v.* to make bitter: to cause ill-feeling.

emblā'zon, *v.* to set out in blazing colours.—*n.* emblā'zonry, design on a shield.

em'blem, *n.* a badge: a sign (e.g. The dove is the *emblem* of peace).

embod'y, *v.* to form into a body or band: to include as part, along with other things.—*n.* **embod'iment**, a living example (e.g. He was the *embodiment* of evil).

embolden, em-bōld'n, *v.* to make bold or courageous.

emboss', *v.* to make a pattern stand out from flat surface (of leather, metal, etc.).—*adj.* **embossed'**, having a raised pattern.

embrace', *v.* to throw the arms round in affection: to hug.—Also *n.*

embrasure, em-brā'zhŭr, *n.* a door or window with the sides slanting outwards: an opening in a wall for cannon.

embroca'tion, *n.* an ointment for rubbing on the body (for stiffness, etc.).

embroid'er, *v.* to ornament with designs in needlework.—*n.* **embroid'ery**, the sewing of ornamental patterns on cloth, etc.

embroil', *v.* to get a person into a quarrel, or into mischief.

embryo, em'bri-ō, *n.* the young of an animal in its earliest stages: the part of a seed which forms the future plant: the beginning of anything:—*pl.* **em'bryos**.—*adj.* **embryon'ic**, having to do with anything at its early stages.

emend', *v.* to remove faults: to correct or improve.—*n.* **emenda'tion**, a correction.

em'erald, *n.* a beautiful green gem.— *adj.* green.—**Emerald Isle**, Ireland.

emerge, e-merj', *v.* to rise out of: to result.—*ns.* **emer'gence**; **emer'gency**, an unexpected happening: a sudden mishap.—**emergency exit**, a way out if anything goes wrong.

emer'itus, *adj.* retired (of a professor, clergyman).

em'ery, *n.* a very hard mineral, used as powder for polishing, etc.—*n.* **em'ery-cloth**, -**paper**, polishing cloth, paper covered with emery-powder.

emet'ic, *adj.* causing vomiting.—*n.* a medicine that causes vomiting.

em'igrate, *v.* to leave one's country to settle in another.—*ns.* **emi-**

gra'tion; **em'igrant**, one who emigrates; **émigré** (ā-mē-grā'), a royalist who fled from France during the Revolution.

em'inent, *adj.* rising above others: famous.—*n.* **em'inence**, a high place: a hill: a title (e.g. *His Eminence*).

emir, em-ēr', *n.* (in E. and N. Africa) a native chieftain.

emit', *v.* to send or give out (e.g. Chimneys *emit* smoke): to utter (e.g. a cry).—*ns.* **em'issary**, one sent on private business: a spy; **emis'sion**, the act of emitting.

emollient, e-mol'yent, *n.* a softener: a skin-softening substance.

emol'ument, *n.* wages, salary.

emo'tion, *n.* any feeling that disturbs or excites the mind (fear, hatred, etc.).—*adj.* **emo'tional**, moving the feelings: (of persons) having feelings that are easily excited.

empan'el, *v.* to write (names) on a list (e.g. The jury was *empanelled*).

em'peror, *n.* the head of an *Empire*: a powerful king:—*fem.* **em'press**.

emphasis, em'fa-sis, *n.* a raising of the voice on certain words or syllables to make the meaning clear.—*v.* **em'phasise**, to put weight or stress on (e.g. He *emphasised* the importance of silence).—*adj.* **emphat'ic**, spoken strongly.

em'pire, *n.* a large and powerful nation (usually ruled by an *Emperor*).

employ', *v.* to use: to give work to.—*ns.* **employ'**, employment; **employ'ee**, one who works for a master; **employ'er**, one who pays people to do work; **employ'ment**, work, trade, occupation.

empō'rium, *n.* a market: a shop, esp. a big shop selling many kinds of goods:—*pl.* **empo'ria** or **empo'riums**.

empow'er, *v.* to give power (to a person to do something).

empress. See emperor.

emp'ty, *adj.* having nothing in it: of no real use: foolish.—*v.* to make empty: to flow out: to spill.—*n.* an empty bottle, box, etc.:—*pl.* **emp'ties**.—*n.* **emp'tiness**.

ē′mū, *n.* an Australian bird, like the ostrich.

em′ūlate, *v.* to try to do as well as, or better than.—*n.* **emulā′tion,** an attempt to equal or do better than others : rivalry.

emulsion, e-mul′shun, *n.* a milky liquid made by mixing oil and water.

enā′ble, *v.* to make able.

enact′, *v.* to perform : to make a law.—*n.* **enact′ment,** a law.

enam′el, *n.* any thin, glossy coating (e.g. paint on metal ; the smooth white coating of the teeth).—*v.* to coat or paint with enamel.—*n.* **enam′elling.**

enamour, en-am′ur, *v.* to charm : to fill with love.

encamp′, *v.* to pitch tents and make camp : to halt on a march.—*n.* **encamp′ment,** a camp.

encase′, *v.* to cover in a case.

enchain′, *v.* to put in chains.

enchant′, *v.* to put a charm or spell on : to delight, please greatly.— *ns.* **enchant′er,** a magician (*fem.* **enchant′ress**) ; **enchant′ment,** a spell : wonder.

encircle, en-serk′l, *v.* to close round with a circle.

enclose′, *v.* to close or shut in.—*n.* **enclōs′ure,** something enclosed (e.g. land within a fence ; letters within an envelope).

encō′mium, *n.* very high praise.

encompass, en-kum′pas, *v.* to surround.

encore, ong-kōr′, *n.* a call from an audience to a performer to sing, dance, etc. again.—Also *v.*

encoun′ter, *v.* to meet : to come up against : to meet a rival in a competition.—*n.* a meeting : a fight.

encourage, en-kur′āj, *v.* to put courage in : to urge to do.—*n.* **encour′agement.**

encroach, en-krōch′, *v.* to go beyond one's rights or land and interfere with some other person's : to trespass.—*n.* **encroach′ment.**

encrust′, *v.* to cover with a crust or hard layer.

encum′ber, *v.* to hamper, hinder : to burden, load.—*n.* **encum′brance,** something which hinders.

encyclopædia, encyclopedia, cyclo-

pædia, (en)sī-klo-pē′di-a, *n.* a book containing much information, either on many subjects (e.g. an encyclopædia of general knowledge) or upon one subject (e.g. an encyclopædia of dogs).—*adj.* **encyclopæ′dic,** giving complete information.

end, *n.* the last point or part : death : purpose or object aimed at : a small piece.—*v.* to bring to an end : to destroy.—*n.* **end′ing,** the last part of anything.—*adjs.* **end′less** ; **end′wise,** going end first.

endanger, en-dān′jer, *v.* to place in danger.

endear′, *v.* to make dear or more dear.—*n.* **endear′ment.**

endeavour, en-dev′ur, *v.* to strive to do : to try.—*n.* a good attempt.

endorse′, *v.* to give one's support to something said or written : to write on the back (e.g. on a cheque, as a sign that money has been received for it ; on a motor-licence, as a sign that the owner has broken the law).—*n.* **endorse′ment.**

endow′, *v.* to leave money for the buying and upkeep of something (e.g. to *endow* a bed in a hospital) : to give a gift (e.g. Nature had *endowed* her with a good brain).— *n.* **endow′ment.**

endue, en-dū′, *v.* to supply with.

endūre′, *v.* to bear without giving way : to last.—*adj.* **endur′able,** bearable.—*n.* **endur′ance,** the power of bearing pain, hardship, etc. without giving in.

en′emy, *n.* one who hates or dislikes : a foe.—*n.* **en′mity.**

energy, en′er-ji, *n.* power of doing work : vigour : strength.—*adj.* **energetic** (en-er-jet′ik), active, lively.

en′ervate, *v.* to take strength out of.

enfee′ble, *v.* to weaken.

enfilade, en-fi-lād′, *n.* anything open or exposed from end to end : end-to-end firing (e.g. of machine-guns).

enfōld′, *v.* to wrap up.

enforce′, *v.* to do by force : to put (e.g. a law) in force.—*adj.* **enforce′able.**—*n.* **enforce′ment.**

enfranchise, en-fran′chiz, v. to set free : to give voting rights to.—n. enfran′chisement.

engage, en-gāj′, v. to promise or bind by a promise : to win over by charm : to start on : to be busy with.—adj. engaged′, bound by a promise, esp. of marriage : busy on something.—n. engage′ment, a promise of marriage : a fight (e.g. a naval engagement).—adj. engag′ing, pleasant, charming (e.g. an engaging manner).

engender, en-jen′der, v. to cause (e.g. Quarrels engender hatred).

engine, en′jin, n. any powerful self-working machine : a railway locomotive.—n. engineer′, one who makes, works, or looks after the working of, any kind of engine.—v. to arrange by planning.

English, ing′glish, adj. belonging to England or its people.—n. the language of the people of England.—v. to turn into English.

engrain′, v. to fix deeply in : to dye a lasting colour.

engrave′, v. to write or draw with a special tool on wood, steel, etc. : to make a deep mark on.—n. engrāv′ing, a cut-out drawing, etc., in metal or wood : a print made from the cut-out pattern.

engross, en-grōs′, v. to take up the whole interest or attention : to write out (a legal paper) in correct form for signature.—n. engross′ment.

engulf′, v. to swallow up wholly, as in a gulf.

enhance′, v. to make to appear greater (e.g. He has by his hard work enhanced his chances of winning).

enig′ma, n. a riddle, a puzzle : anything difficult to find meaning in.—adj. enigmat′ic, puzzling, mysterious.

enjoin′, v. to order.

enjoy′, v. to find pleasure in : to use with delight.—adj. enjoy′able.—n. enjoy′ment.

enlarge′, en-larj′, v. to make larger : to say more about something.—n. enlarge′ment, an increase in the size of anything (e.g. a larger photograph made from a smaller).

enlighten, en-līt′n, v. to throw light on : to make clear to the mind : to teach.—n. enlight′enment.

enlist′, v. to join as a soldier, etc. : to win over (support).—n. enlist′ment.

enli′ven, v. to put life into : to make active or cheerful.

enmity, en′mi-ti, n. ill-will : unfriendliness.

ennō′ble, v. to make noble : to raise to rank of lord or lady.—n. ennō′blement.

ennui, on′wē, n. a feeling of weariness or disgust.

enormous, e-nor′mus, adj. great in size or amount, immense.—n. enor′mity, hugeness : a great crime, great wickedness.

enough, e-nuf′, adj. satisfying want : sufficient.—Also adv. and n.—Sometimes written enow.

enquire. See inquire.

enrage, en-rāj′, v. to make angry.

enrap′ture, v. to please greatly.

enrich′, v. to make rich.—n. enrich′ment.

enrol, enroll, en-rōl′, v. to write (a name or names) in a register or roll.—n. enrol′ment.

ensam′ple. See example.

ensconce, en-skons′, v. to hide (one's self).

ensemble, ong-song′bl, n. all the parts of a thing taken together.

enshrine′, v. to close in as in a shrine : to keep as a treasure.

ensign, en′sīn, n. the sign or flag by which a nation or a regiment is known (e.g. White Ensign of the Royal Navy) : in olden days, a young officer who carried the flag.

enslave′, v. to make a slave of.

ensnare′, v. to catch in a trap.

ensue, en-sū′, v. to follow, to come after : to result.

ensure, en-shoor′, v. to make sure.

entail′, v. to leave land so that the heir cannot sell any part of it : to bring as a result (e.g. The manager's death entailed extra work for the staff).

entangle, en-tang′gl, v. to twist into a tangle, so as not to be easily separated.—n. entang′lement.

en′ter, v. to go or come in : to put (a name) into a list.

enter'ic. Another name for typhoid fever.

en'terprise, n. anything new taken on to be done: a spirit of boldness in trying new things: an adventure.—adj. **en'terprising,** adventurous.

entertain', v. to amuse: to give a party: to turn over in the mind, think about.—adj. **entertain'ing,** amusing.—ns. **entertain'er,** a person who gives amusement at a performance (e.g. *entertainer* at the piano); **entertain'ment,** any kind of light pleasure (e.g. a party, a concert, etc.).

enthral, en-thrawl', v. to give great delight, please greatly.

enthrone', v. to place on a throne.— n. **enthrone'ment.**

enthusiasm, en-thū'zi-azm, n. great interest: keenness.—n. **enthu'siast,** one who is very keen about something.—adj. **enthusias'tic,** acting with all one's powers: greatly interested in.

entice', v. to tempt: to draw on by promises, rewards, etc.—n. **entice'ment,** a bribe, promise of reward.—adj. **enti'cing.**

entire', adj. whole: complete.—n. **entire'ty,** wholeness.

entitle, en-tī'tl, v. to give a name to: to give a claim to.

en'tity, n. being: existence.

entomb, en-toom', v. to place in a tomb: to bury.—n. **entomb'ment,** burial.

entomology, en-to-mol'o-ji, n. insect-study.—n. **entomol'ogist,** one who studies insects and their ways.

entr'acte, ong-trakt', n. music played between acts: the tune between the acts of a play.

en'trails, n.pl. the inner parts of an animal's body, the bowels.

entrain', v. to put or get into a railway train.

en'trance, n. place for entering (e.g. a door): the act of coming in.— n. **en'trant,** one who comes in: one who goes in for a race, competition, etc.

entrance', v. to put into a trance: to fill with great delight.—n. **entrance'ment,** state of trance or of great joy.—adj. **entranc'ing,** charming.

entreat', v. to ask earnestly.—n. **entreat'y,** an earnest request: a prayer.

entrée, ong'trā, n. a dish served at dinner.

entrench', intrench', v. to put a trench round: to fortify with a trench.—n. **entrench'ment,** an earthwork or ditch for protection.

entrepôt, ong'tr'pō, n. a storehouse: a seaport through which exports and imports pass.

entrust', intrust', v. to trust something to the care of someone else.

en'try, n. act of entering: a door: a narrow passage-way (e.g. to a stairway): something written in a book (e.g. a name, a note, etc.).

entwine', v. to twine, twist round.

enū'merate, v. to count the number of: to name over.—n. **enumera'tion.**

enunciate, e-nun'si-āt, v. to pronounce distinctly: to utter.—n. **enuncia'tion,** way of speaking or pronouncing: a clear statement.

envel'op, v. to cover by wrapping: to surround entirely.—ns. **en'velope,** a wrapping or cover, esp. for a letter.

en'viable, en'vious. See envy.

envi'ronment, n. surroundings.— n.pl. **envi'rons,** outskirts (of a city): places round about.

envisage, en-viz'āj, v. to face: to consider.

en'voy, n. a messenger, esp. one sent to deal with the government of a foreign country.

en'voy, en'voi, n. the parting message at end of a poem or book.

en'vy, v. to look greedily at someone and wish that one had what he has.—Also n.—adjs. **en'viable,** worth envying, worth having; **en'vious,** wishing that one had what someone else has.

epaulet, epaulette, ep'ol-et, n. a shoulder-strap on a uniform.

ephemeral, ef-em'er-al, adj. short-lived.

ep'ic, adj. lofty: grand.—n. a poem on a great subject (e.g. Milton's *Paradise Lost*), written in a lofty style, and at great length: any heroic adventure.

ep'icure, *n.* one fond of eating good things : one who lives to 'eat, drink, and be merry.'

epidem'ic, *n.* an outbreak (e.g. of disease, crime) which affects many people.

epider'mis, *n.* the top covering of the skin.

ep'igram, *n.* any short, smart saying in prose or verse.—*adj.* **epigrammat'ic.**

epilep'sy, *n.* an illness, usually causing fits.—*n.* **epilep'tic**, one who takes these fits.

epilogue, ep'i-log, *n.* a speech, short poem, or other suitable ending to a play or book : a short service at the end of a wireless programme.

epis'copal, *adj.* (of churches) ruled by bishops : having to do with bishops.—*adj.* **episcopā'lian**, believing in **epis'copacy**, i.e. the ruling of the Church by bishops.

ep'isode, *n.* an interesting event or happening : an odd, unconnected event.

epistle, e-pis'l, *n.* a letter sent to a person.

epitaph, ep'i-taf, *n.* a statement on a grave-stone, telling about the dead person.

ep'ithet, *n.* an adjective or describing word (usually for persons and their actions).

epitome, e-pit'o-me, *n.* a summary (e.g. of a book, story).—*v.* **epit'omise**, to give the main points of a story in a short form.

epoch, ē'pok, *n.* a time famous for important events.—*adj.* **ep'ochmak'ing**, marking an important point in history (e.g. The steam-engine was an *epoch-making* discovery).

equable, ek'wa-bl, *adj.* of calm temper : (of climate) neither very hot nor very cold.

equal, ē'kwal, *adj.* of the same value : divided in fair measure : evenly balanced : fit.—*n.* something of the same value : a person of the same rank, cleverness, etc. as another.—*v.* to be equal with : to be the same as.—*v.* **e'qualise**, to make equal.—*ns.* **equality** (ē-kwol'-i-ti), the state of being equal ; **equā'tion**, a statement in which two things are looked on as equal.

equanimity, ē-kwa-nim'i-ti, *n.* calmness of temper.

equator, ek-wā'tor, *n.* an imaginary line round the earth, half-way between the North Pole and South Pole (in maps marked Latitude 0°).—*adj.* **equatōr'ial**, having to do with the equator : situated around the equator.

equerry, ek'we-ri, *n.* a person who goes with a king or prince.

equestrian, e-kwes'tri-an, *adj.* having to do with horses or horse-riding : (of statues) on horseback. —*n.* a horseman.

equi-, ē'kwi, a prefix meaning equal.—*adjs.* **equian'gular**, having equal angles ; **equidis'tant**, equally distant ; **equilat'eral**, having all sides equal.—*n.* **equilib'rium**, equal balance : level position.

equine, ē-kwīn, *adj.* having to do with horses, horse-like.

equinox, ē'kwi-noks, *n.* a time (about 21st March and 23rd September) in each year when day and night are of equal length.— *adj.* **equinoc'tial.**

equip, e-kwip', *v.* to fit out, to supply with everything needed for a task.—*ns.* **e'quipage**, attendants, carriages, etc. needed for a rich or important person ; **equip'ment**, outfit.

equity, ek'wi-ti, *n.* fairness : just-dealing.—*adj.* **e'quitable**, acting fairly or justly.

equivalent, e-kwiv'a-lent, *adj.* equal in value, meaning, etc.—Also *n.* —*n.* **equiv'alence.**

equivocal, e-kwiv'ō-kal, *adj.* having two meanings, usually to mislead or cheat.—*v.* **equiv'ocate**, to use words with two meanings in order to mislead : to tell lies cleverly.

ē'ra, *n.* a number of years counting from an important point in history (e.g. the Christian *era*, i.e. the years counted from the birth of Christ).

erad'icate, *v.* to root out : to get rid of completely.—*n.* **eradica'tion.**

erase, *v.* to rub or scrape out.—*ns.* **erā'ser**, that which erases, a rubber ; **erā'sure**, a rubbing-out : what has been rubbed out.

ere, ār, *prep.* and *conj.* before.

erect', v. to set up (e.g. a building, a monument). — adj. standing straight up.—n. erec'tion, act of erecting: anything erected.

er'mine, n. a stoat: its white fur.

erode', v. to wear away.—n. erō'sion.

err, v. to wander from the right way: to make a mistake: to sin.—adj. errat'ic, wandering: zig-zagging: not steady in behaviour.—n. errā'tum, an error in a book :—pl. errā'ta.

er'rand, n. a message.—a fool's errand, a useless undertaking.

er'rant, adj. wandering: roving.

er'ror, n. a mistake: a blunder.—adj. errō'neous, wrong.

erudite, er'oo-dīt, adj. having studied much.—n. erudi'tion, knowledge gained by study: learning.

erupt', v. to break out or through, as a volcano.—n. erup'tion, a breaking or bursting forth, as of a volcano, bad temper, a rash on the body.

erysipelas, er-i-sip'e-las, n. a disease, generally in the face, causing a bright redness of the skin.

es'calātor, n. a lift: a moving stairway.

escape', to get safe or free: to run away from: (of gas, water) to leak.—n. the act of escaping.—n. escapade', a mischievous adventure.

escarp'ment, n. the steep, cliff-like side of a hill.

eschew, es-choo', v. to shun: to avoid.

es'cort, n. a bodyguard: a guide: an attendant.—v. escort', to go with as a guide or guard.

escutcheon, es-kuch'un, n. a shield on which a coat of arms is shown. —a blot on the escutcheon, a stain on one's good name.

Es'kimo, n. a native of the Arctic regions (Greenland, Far North of Canada, Alaska).

espalier, es-pal'yer, n. a frame of wood against which fruit-trees are grown.

espar'to, n. a strong kind of grass (grown in Spain, N. Africa) used for making paper, baskets, ropes.

especial, es-pesh'al, adj. special: particular.—adv. espec'ially.

espionage, es'pi-on-āj, n. spy-work, spying.

es'planade, n. a level roadway along a sea-front.

espouse', v. to take as a wife: to work for, to do all to help (e.g. He espoused the cause of peace).

esprit, es-prē, n. liveliness.—esprit de corps (es-prē di kor), loyalty to one's companions.

espȳ', v. to catch sight of.

Esquimau, es'ki-mō (pl. Esquimaux, es'ki-mōz). Same as Eskimo.

Esquire, es-kwīr', n. (usually shortened to Esq.) a title of politeness put after a man's name (e.g. John Brown, Esquire).

es'say, n. a try, an attempt: a composition.—v. to try.—n. es'sayist, a writer of essays.

es'sence, n. the strong, pure part (e.g. coffee-essence, essence of rennet): the important part, with trifles left out (e.g. The essence of the matter is . . .).—adj. essen'tial, necessary: not to be done without.—Also n.

estab'lish, v. to settle or fix: to found, set up (e.g. The shop was established in 1850).—adj. estab'lished, firmly set: settled by law (e.g. The Established Church).—n. estab'lishment, anything set up to last (e.g. a large shop): the number of men making up an army or navy.

estate', n. a large piece of land owned by a person or a companys property, goods, wealth: rank.

esteem', v. to think highly of, to value.—Also n.—adjs. esteemed', respected: es'timable, able to be valued: worthy of our good opinion.—v. es'timate, to judge of the worth of a thing: to make a rough guess.—Also n.—n. estimā'tion, our opinion of other people.

estrange, es-trānj', v. to make unfriendly.—adj. estrānged', unfriendly.—n. estrānge'ment, a quarrel, causing unfriendliness.

estuary, es'tū-ar-i, n. the wide, lower part of a river, up which the tide travels.

et cetera, et set'er-a (usually written etc. or &c.), a phrase meaning ' and so on,' ' and other things of the same sort.'

etch, *v.* to make drawings on metal, glass, etc. by eating out the lines with acid.—*n.* etch′ing, the picture from the etched plate.

eter′nal, *adj.* lasting for ever: without stop: unchangeable.—*n.* eter′nity, time without end: the state or time after death.

ether, *n.* the clear, upper air: a liquid used by scientists, surgeons, etc. for deadening the senses, and other purposes.—*adj.* ethē′real, heavenly: fairy-like.

eth′ical, *adj.* having to do with right behaviour, justice, duty.—*n.* eth′ics, the study of right and wrong.

ethnology, eth-nol′o-ji, *n.* the study of the different races of mankind.

etiquette, et′i-ket, *n.* politeness, correct behaviour (e.g. table-*etiquette*, golf-*etiquette*).

etymology, et-i-mol′o-ji, *n.* the study of the history of words.—*adj.* etymolog′ical.—*n.* etymol′ogist, one who studies word-history.

eucalyptus, ū-kal-ip′tus, *n.* an Australian gum-tree: its oil.

Eucharist, ū′ka-rist, *n.* the Lord's Supper.

eulogise, ū′lo-jīz, *v.* to speak well of: to praise.—*adj.* eulogist′ic, full of praise.—*n.* eulogy (ū′lo-ji), praise, written or spoken.

eunuch, ū′nuk, *n.* in Eastern palaces, an attendant or minister of high rank who looks after the women's rooms.

euphemism, ū′fem-izm, *n.* a pleasant name for something unpleasant (e.g. 'Happy' is a *euphemism* for 'slightly drunk,' 'fell asleep' for 'died,' etc.).

euphony, ū′fo-ni, *n.* a pleasing sound.—*adj.* eupho′nious, pleasant in sound.—*n.* euphō′nium, a brass musical instrument with a low tone.

eurhythmics, ū-rith′micks, *n.* the art of graceful movement of the body.

European, ū′ro-pē′an, *adj.* belonging to Europe.—*n.* a native of Europe: a white person (e.g. in Africa) whose forefathers came from Europe.

evacuate, e-vak′ū-āt, *v.* to leave, withdraw from (e.g. The regiment *evacuated* the trench at dusk): to remove people from a dangerous to a safe place: to empty out.—*n.* evacūa′tion.

evade′, *v.* to escape by a trick: to trick.—*n.* evā′sion, a clever escape: an excuse.—*adj.* evā′sive, not straightforward (e.g. an *evasive* answer).

eval′ūate, *v.* to find the value of.

evanes′cent, *adj.* not lasting.

evangelical, e-van-jel′i-kal, *adj.* spreading Christ's teaching.—*n.* evan′gelist, one who goes preaching from place to place, trying to save sinners.

evap′orate, *v.* to turn into vapour (e.g. Heat *evaporates* water): to vanish.—*n.* evaporā′tion.

evasion. See evade.

eve, ēv, *n.* evening: night: the time just before any great or important happening (e.g. *eve* of the battle).

ē′ven, *adj.* flat: level: smooth: not odd, able to be divided by 2 without a remainder.—*v.* to make even or smooth.—*n.* e′venness.

evening, ēv′ning, *n.* the close of the daytime: end of anything, esp. of life (e.g. the *evening* of her days): an evening party.—*ns.* E′vensong, a prayer in the Church of England, said or sung at evening; e′ventide, evening.

event, *n.* that which happens: an item in a sports programme, etc. —*adjs.* event′ful, exciting; event′-ūal, happening as a result.—*n.* eventūal′ity, the result of certain events: an unexpected happening.—*adv.* event′ually, at last: finally.

ev′er, *adv.* always: at any time.— *adjs.* ev′ergreen, always green (e.g. an *evergreen* plant); ever-lasting, lasting for ever.—*adv.* evermore′, for ever.

ev′ery, *adj.* each one of a number: all taken separately.—*prons.* ev′erybody, ev′eryone, every person; ev′erything, all things.— *adj.* ev′eryday, of or belonging to every day, daily: common, usual: having to do with week-days, not Sunday.

evict′, *v.* to put people out of house and home by force of law.—*n.* evic′tion.

ev′ident, *adj.* easily seen or understood : clear to the mind.—*n.*
ev′idence, a clear sign : a trace : an account of what was seen, given by a witness in a law-court. —**to turn Queen's Evidence,** when accused of a crime, to give evidence against one's partners in order to receive freedom.

e′vil, *adj.* wicked : unpleasant : unlucky.—*n.* wickedness.

evince′, *v.* to show (e.g. The prisoner *evinced* surprise when he heard the evidence).

evoke′, *v.* to draw out or bring forth (e.g. His acting *evoked* great applause).

evolū′tion, *n.* a gradual growing from one form or state to another : the belief that all living things have come from simpler forms by very gradual change : (*pl.*) orderly movements, as of troops, warships, aeroplanes.

evolve′, *v.* to come as a result : to work out (e.g. The general *evolved* a plan of battle).

ewe, ū, *n.* a female sheep.

ewer, ū′er, *n.* a large jug with a wide spout.

exacerbate, eks-as′er-bāt, *v.* to make (e.g. a quarrel) more bitter : to make (e.g. a disease) more severe.

exact′, *v.* to force or wring from : to compel to pay.—*adj.* careful : accurate : punctual.—*adj.* **exact′-ing,** asking too much : tiring, wearing (e.g. an *exacting* job).— *ns.* **exac′tion,** a heavy tax ; **exact′-itūde, exact′ness,** accuracy, correctness.

exaggerate, eg-zaj′er-āt, *v.* to make things seem worse or better than they are : to overstate.—*ns.* **exaggerā′tion ; exagg′erator.**

exalt, eg-zawlt′, *v.* to raise in rank : to make joyful.—*n.* **exalta′tion,** highness of rank or position : great joy.

exam′ine, *v.* to put questions to : to put to a test or trial.—*ns.* **examinā′tion ; exam′iner.**

exam′ple, *n.* one case given to make other cases clear (e.g. a sum worked out to show how the others should be done) : a warning (e.g. ' Let this be an *example* to you ').

exas′perate, *v.* to make very angry. —*n.* **exasperā′tion.**

ex′cavate, *v.* to dig, to scoop out.—*ns.* **excavā′tion,** the act of digging out : a hollow made by digging ; **ex′cavator,** a machine used for excavating.

exceed, ek-sēd′, *v.* to go beyond what is allowed.—*adv.* **exceed′ingly,** greatly : very.

excel, ek-sel′, *v.* to be better than : to do well.—*ns.* **ex′cellence,** great merit, cleverness ; **Ex′cellency,** a title of high honour (e.g. His *Excellency* the French Ambassador).—*adj.* **ex′cellent,** of the very best kind : perfect.

except, ek-sept′, *v.* to leave out, not to count.—*preps.* **except ; except′-ing,** leaving out, not counting.— *n.* **excep′tion,** something left out : something that is unlike the rest (e.g. an *exception* to the rule) : objection, dislike (e.g. He took *exception* to the plan).—*adj.* **excep′tional,** standing out from the rest.—*adv.* **excep′tionally,** strangely : very.

excerpt, ek′serpt, *n.* a passage or part chosen from a whole work (e.g. an *excerpt* from a play or speech).

excess, ek-ses′, *n.* a going beyond what is usual or proper : the amount by which one thing is greater than another : very bad behaviour.—*adj.* beyond the amount allowed (e.g. *excess* luggage).—*adj.* **exces′sive,** beyond what is right and proper.

exchange, eks-chānj′, *v.* to give one thing and get another in return. —*n.* the act of exchanging : a place where business shares are bought and sold : the balance between the money systems of two countries.

exchequer, eks-chek′er, *n.* one of the courts of law : the part of government that has to do with money affairs : a person's money matters.

excise, ek-sīz′, *n.* a tax on certain articles made in a country : the government officers (**excisemen**) who collect this tax.—*adj.* **excīs′-able,** likely to be charged with this tax.

excise, ek-sīz', *v.* to cut off or out.—*n.* excision (ek-sish'un).

excite, ek-sīt', *v.* to stir, to move to action: to rouse.—*adj.* excit'able, easily roused.—*n.* excite'ment.

exclaim', *v.* to cry or shout out.—*n.* exclamā'tion, a sudden shout: an outcry: a mark (!) in punctuation to show surprise.—*adj.* exclamat'ory.

exclude, eks-klood', *v.* to shut out: to hinder from sharing.—*n.* exclus'ion.—*adj.* exclus'ive, shutting unwanted persons out (e.g. an *exclusive* club, school): not counting in (e.g. Dinner 6s., *exclusive* of wine).

excommunicate, eks-kom-ūn'i-kāt, *v.* to put out of the Church.—*n.* excommunicā'tion.

excrement. See excrete.

excrescence, eks-kres'ens, *n.* something unwanted which grows outwards (e.g. a wart, a tree fungus).

excrete, eks-krēt', *v.* (of animals) to cast out unwanted matter from the body.—*n.* ex'crement, the matter cast out, dung.

excruciating, ex-kroo'shi-āt-ing, *adj.* (of pain, torture) very severe, unbearably sore.

exculpate, *v.* to free from blame.

excursion, eks-kur'shun, *n.* an outing, usually for pleasure (e.g. a picnic).—*n.* excur'sionist, one who goes on a pleasure-trip.

excuse, ex-kūz', *v.* to overlook a fault: to set free from a duty or task (e.g. The teacher *excused* her from writing an essay): to pardon (e.g. ' *Excuse* me . . .').—*n.* excuse (ex-kūs'), one's reason for having done something wrong.—*adj.* excūs'able (-kūz'-), pardonable.

ex'ecrate, *v.* to curse.—*adj.* ex'ecrable, so bad as to call forth cursing.—*n.* execrā'tion, a cursing.

ex'ecute, *v.* to perform (e.g. *execute* a step-dance): carry into effect (e.g. *execute* commands): to put to death by order of the law.—*ns.* exec'utant, a skilled performer (e.g. on piano or violin): execū'tion, a doing or performing: the putting of words into deeds: death by order of the law; execū'tioner, one whose duty it is to put condemned persons to death; exec'utor (*fem.* exec'ūtrix), a person who sees to the carrying out of what is stated in a will.—*adj.* exec'ūtive, having power to act, carry out laws.—*n.* the part of a government (or society) having such power.

exem'plary, *adj.* worth following as an example (e.g. *exemplary* conduct): acting as a warning (e.g. *exemplary* punishment).

exem'plify, *v.* to show or prove by showing something of the same kind.

exempt', *v.* to set free from some duty, task, payment, etc.—Also *adj.*—*n.* exem'ption.

ex'ercise, *n.* a task for practice: training for body, mind, etc.—*v.* to train: to use (e.g. *Exercise* great care).

exert', *v.* to use actively: to make active.—*n.* exer'tion, effort: hard work.

exhale', *v.* to breathe out.—*n.* exhalā'tion.

exhaust, egz-awst', *v.* to use the whole strength of: to tell all about (a matter).—*n.* the wayout for steam, gas, etc. after it has done its work in an engine.—*n.* exhaust'ion, great tiredness, weariness.—*adjs.* exhaust'ed, tired out: emptied; exhaust'ive, telling completely about a subject (e.g. an *exhaustive* lecture).

exhibit, egz-ib'it, *v.* to show in public.—*n.* anything shown (e.g. a picture in a picture-gallery).—*ns.* exhibi'tion, a public show, an open display: a money-prize at a university; exhib'itor.

exhilarate, egz-il'a-rāt, *v.* to cheer up.—*adj.* exhil'arāting, causing a glad feeling: healthy.

exhort, egz-ort', *v.* to urge to good deeds.—*n.* exhortā'tion.

exhūme', *v.* to dig out of a grave.—*n.* exhumā'tion.

exigent, eks'i-jent, *adj.* demanding immediate attention: urgent.—*n.* ex'igency, a demand: a state of affairs needing quick action.

exiguous, eks-ig'ū-ous, *adj.* very slight.

exile, egz'īl, *n.* a person who is forced to stay outside his own country: his stay in a foreign land.—*v.* to

115

expose

drive a person away from his native country, to banish.

exist', v. to live: to be.—n. **exist'ence**.—adj. **exist'ent**.

ex'it, n. a way out: a going out.

ex'odus, n. a going away of many people (e.g. of the Israelites from the land of Egypt, as told in Exodus, the second book of the Old Testament).

exon'erate, v. to free from blame.—n. **exonera'tion**.

exor'bitant, adj. going beyond the usual limits: too dear.—n. **exor'bitance**.

exorcise, eks'or-sīz, v. to drive away an evil spirit or spell.—n. **ex'orcism**, the act of driving away evil spirits or spells.

exot'ic, adj. coming from a foreign country(e.g. *exotic* plants, flowers).

expand', v. to spread out: to open out.—ns. **expanse'**, a wide stretch; **expan'sion**, an increase: a growing, stretching, or spreading.—adj. **expan'sive**, spreading out.

expatiate, eks-pā'shi-āt, v. to talk a great deal about something.

expatriate, eks-pā'tri-āt, v. to send a person out of his native country: to banish or exile.

expect', v. to wait for: to look forward to: to hope.—adj. **expec'tant**, looking forward to. — ns. **expect'ancy**, state of expecting: hope; **expecta'tion**, what is expected.

expec'torate, v. to spit.

expe'dient, adj. advisable: suited to the time and to the occasion. —n. something done to get past an awkward position.—ns. **expa'dience**, **expe'diency**, fitness.

ex'pedite, v. to hasten, hurry on.— n. **expedi'tion**, speed, quickness: a journey with a purpose (e.g. Polar *expedition*).—adj. **expeditious** (ex-ped-ish'us), swift, speedy.

expel', v. to drive or force out: to send away in disgrace.—n. **expul'sion**.

expend', v. to spend.—ns. **expend'iture**, money spent: **expense'**, cost.—adj. **expens'ive**, costing much, dear.

expe'rience, n. any happening or event: wisdom, knowledge, gained by such a happening.—v.

to go through, undergo.—adj. **expe'rienced**, skilled.

exper'iment, n. something done for the purpose of discovery: a trial: a practical careless lesson.—v. to test or try out (e.g. a new method).—adj. **experiment'al**.

expert', adj. highly skilful.—n. **ex'pert**, one who is highly skilled.

expiate, eks'pi-āt, v. to make up for a wrong (e.g. by taking full punishment for it).—n. **expia'tion**.

expire', v. to die: to breathe out: to come to an end.—ns. **expira'tion**, the end or finish: act of breathing out; **expi'ry**, the end or finish.

explain', v. to make clear: to give reasons for.—n. **explana'tion**, a statement which makes clear matters that are hard to understand: reason (e.g. for conduct).—adj. **explan'atory**, meant to make clear.

expletive, ex'plet-iv, n. a swearword: (ex-plēt'iv) a word used merely to fill up a line.

explicable, eks'pli-kabl, adj. able to be explained.

explicit, eks-plis'it, adj. plainly stated: outspoken.—n. **explic'itness**.

explode', v. to blow up with loud noise: to prove a belief wrong. —n. **explo'sion**, a sudden burst or blow-up, with a loud noise. —adj. **explo'sive**, liable to explode: hot-tempered. — n. anything (e.g. gunpowder) that will explode.

ex'ploit, n. a daring deed: a feat.— v. **exploit'**, to make use of selfishly. —n. **exploita'tion**.

explore', v. to make a journey of discovery.—ns. **explora'tion**; **explōr'er**, one who explores.

expō'nent, n. one who shows skill.

export', v. to send out goods, etc. from a country.—ns. **ex'ports**, goods sent out of a country for trade purposes; **exporta'tion**.

expose', v. to place something where all can see it: to show up a hidden evil: to lay open to sun, wind, cold, etc.—ns. **exposi'tion**, a public show: a statement which makes clear a writer's meaning; **exposure** (eks-pō'zhur), act of laying bare : act of showing up an evil : openness to danger, sun, bad weather, etc. : the direction which a place faces (e.g. The garden has a southern *exposure*).

expos'tulate, *v.* to protest : to argue : to object.—*n.* **expostulā'tion.**

expound', *v.* to explain fully and earnestly.

express', *v.* to press out : to put into words : to send off in a hurry.— *adj.* clearly stated (e.g. *express* instructions) : sent in haste (e.g. *express* messenger).—*n.* a very fast train.—*n.* **express'ion,** look in one's face : manner in which anything is spoken, sung, written, etc.—*adj.* **expres'sive,** full of meaning.

exprō'priate, *v.* to take away a person's belongings.

expulsion. See expel.

expunge', *v.* to rub out : to wipe out.

ex'purgate, *v.* to remove nasty parts (e.g. of a book, newspaper, etc.). —*n.* **expurgā'tion.**

exquisite, eks'kwi-zit, *adj.* excellent : of great beauty : (of pleasure or pain) very great.

extant, *adj.* still existing.

extempore, eks-tem'po-re, *adv.* and *adj.* at a moment's notice—without having time to prepare.—*v.* **extem'porise,** to make up (music, a speech, etc.) as one plays, speaks, etc.

extend', *v.* to stretch : to hold out : to last.—*ns.* **exten'sion,** a part added (e.g. to a building, to a holiday) ; **extent',** the space something covers.—*adj.* **exten'sive,** wide : covering a large space.

exten'uate, *v.* to lessen : to make to seem less bad (e.g. He tried to *extenuate* his brother's fault).— *n.* **extenuā'tion.**

extē'rior, *adj.* lying on the outside (e.g. an *exterior* wall).—*n.* the outside : one's appearance.—*adj.* **exter'nal,** lying on the outside.

exter'minate, *v.* to destroy completely, to kill off.—*n.* **extermina'tion.**

extinct', *adj.* dead : no longer active (e.g. an *extinct* volcano) : of a kind no longer found alive (e.g. *extinct* animals).—*v.* **extinguish**

(eks-ting'gwish), to quench, to put out (e.g. a light, fire, etc.).— *ns.* **extinc'tion,** the act of putting out : state of being extinct ; **ex-ting'uisher,** a spray containing chemicals for putting out fires.

ex'tirpate, *v.* to destroy completely **;** to slaughter.—*n.* **extirpā'tion.**

extol', *v.* to praise greatly.

extort', *v.* to take by force or threats. —*n.* **extor'tion,** obtaining money, goods, information, confession, etc. by threats : an overcharge.— *adj.* **extor'tionate,** much too dear.

ex'tra, *adj.* more than usual : additional.—*adv.* unusually.—*n.* anything beyond the usual.

extract', *v.* to draw or pull out by force : to choose out parts of a book, etc.—*ns.* **ex'tract,** a part chosen (e.g. from a book) : the best parts, the strength (e.g. *extract* of beef, of malt) ; **extrac'tion,** act of drawing out : one's descent (e.g. He was of English *extraction*).

extrā'neous, *adj.* having nothing to do with the matter.

extraordinary, eks-tror'di-nar-i, *adj.* not usual : wonderful : special.

extrav'agant, *adj.* wasteful : going beyond proper limits.—*n.* **extrav'agance.**

extreme, eks-trēm', *adj.* farthest off : greatest, very great.—*n.* the far-thest-away place : the end : the limit.—*ns.* **extrem'ity,** farthest-off part or place : great distress or pain ; (*pl.*) farthest-off parts of the body (e.g. nose, ears, toes) ; **extrē'mist,** one who carries ideas foolishly far.

ex'tricate, *v.* to disentangle **:** to set free.—*adj.* **ex'tricable.**

exū'berant, *adj.* overflowing with happiness.—*n.* **exū'berance.**

exūde', *v.* to give off (sweat, resin, gum, etc.).—*n.* **exūdā'tion.**

exult', *v.* to rejoice greatly : to boast about a victory.—*adj.* **exult'ant,** shouting in triumph.— *n.* **exultā'tion.**

eye, ī, *n.* the seeing part of the body : sight : anything like an eye (e.g. the hole in a needle).—*v.* to look or gaze at.—*ns.* **eye'-ball,** the ball of the eye ; **eye'brow,** the hairy ridge above the eye ; **eye'glass,** a glass to help sight; eye'lashes, (pl.) the line of hairs on the edge of the eyelid; eye'let, a small eye or hole for a lace or cord, as in garments, sails, etc.; eye'lid, the lid or cover of the eye; eye'-ōpener,

a startling story; eye'sore, anything that is ugly to the eye; eye'-witness, one who sees a thing done.

eyry, eyrie, ī'ri, n. the nesting-place of eagles or other birds of prey: any secure, lofty place.

F

fā'ble, n. a story (usually of animals, birds, etc.) that has a lesson or moral.—adj. fab'ulous, wonderful (as in the fables): huge beyond belief: false, untrue.

fab'ric, n. cloth: the outside parts (walls, etc.) of a building.

fab'ricate, v. to manufacture: to make up (lies).—n. fabricā'tion.

façade, fa-sad', n. the front or face of a building.

face, n. the front part of the head: front of anything: look.—v. to turn in the direction of: to stand opposite to.

facet, fas'et, n. a small surface or face (e.g. of a diamond).

facetious, fa-sē'shus, adj. funny, witty.—n. facē'tiousness.

facial, fā'shal, adj. having to do with the face.

facility, fa-sil'i-ti, n. ease: skill in doing a thing: (pl.) the means for doing a thing easily.—v. facil'itate, to make easy.

facsimile, fak-sim'i-li, n. an exact copy (e.g. of handwriting, coins).

fact, n. a thing done, a deed: truth.

faction, fak'shun, n. a band of people acting together against others: a gang.—adj. fac'tious, trouble-making, riotous.

factitious, fak-tish'us, adj. made by man, not by nature.

fac'tor, n. one who does business, buys and sells, for another: a number which exactly divides into another (e.g. 3 is a factor of 6).—v. fac'torise, to find factors of.—n. fac'tory, a large workshop where goods are made in large quantities (e.g. sausage factory, motor-car factory): a trading settlement in a far-off country.

fac'ulty, n. a special gift of mind or body, special cleverness: division

of a university, college, or school (e.g. Faculty of Science).

fad, n. an odd like or dislike.

fade, v. to lose colour, strength, or freshness: to go from sight or view.—adjs. fād'ing; fāde'less.

fag, v. to work hard: to weary: to work as a school fag.—n. any tiresome bit of work: a young schoolboy who does jobs for an older one.

fag'got, fag'ot, n. a bundle of sticks.

Fahrenheit, far'en-hīt, n. a thermometer with freezing-point marked 32°, boiling-point 212°.

fail, v. to try without success (e.g. to fail in an examination, to fail in business): to lose strength (e.g. The engine failed. His heart failed. His courage failed): to disappoint (e.g. I will not fail you). —ns. fail'ing, a fault: a weakness; fail'ure, the act of failing: an attempt which has not succeeded: a person who has not done what was expected of him: a breakdown (e.g. of an engine).

fain, adj. glad.—adv. willingly.

faint, adj. wanting in strength, brightness, courage.—v. to become weak: to lose colour: to fall down senseless.—n. a sick turn in which a person loses his senses.—adv. faint'ly, dimly, not clearly.—n. faint'ness.

fair, adj. of a light colour: not dark-haired: free from rain: not favouring one side, just: good enough but not excellent: beautiful: free from fault, pure.—v. (of the weather) to clear.—adv. kindly, honestly (e.g. He spoke him fair).—ns. fair'ness; fair'-way, the deep-water part of a channel, river, etc.: the mown part on a golf-course.—adj. fair'-mind'ed, judging fairly.

fair, n. a large market held at fixed times.

fair'y, *n.* a small creature, in human form, able to do kind or unkind acts.—*n.* **fairy'land,** the country of the fairies.

faith, *n.* trust: belief (e.g. in God, religion): one's word.—*adjs.* **faith'ful,** believing: loyal: keeping one's promises; **faith'less.**

fake, *v.* to cheat by making an imitation.—*n.* a swindle, dodge, sham.

fakir, fa-kēr', *n.* an Indian holy man.

fal'con, *n.* a bird of prey, once used to hunt game.

fall, fawl, *v.* to drop down: to be killed in battle: to become less: (of a fortress) to give in: to happen: (with *on*) to attack: (with *to*) to begin eagerly.—*n.* a dropping down: a rush of water: lowering (in value): autumn (the season when leaves *fall*): a bout at wrestling: the yielding of a city.—*adj.* **fall'en,** having become evil: ruined: killed.

fallacy, fal'a-si, *n.* a wrong opinion or belief: something which seems true but is really false.—*adj.* **fallacious** (fal-ā'shus).

fallible, fal'i-bl, *adj.* apt to make a mistake.—*n.* **fallibil'ity.**

fallow, fal'ō, *n.* land left unsown for a time after being ploughed.

fallow, fal'ō, *adj.* of a yellowish-brown colour.—*n.* **fall'ow-deer,** a yellowish-brown deer smaller than the red-deer.

false, fawls, *adj.* untrue: not real, sham.—*ns.* **falsehood,** a lie, an untruth: **false'ness, fals'ity,** quality of being false.—*v.* **fals'ify,** *v.* to prove to be wrong: to make up account-books wrongly in order to deceive.

falter, fawl'ter, *v.* to be unsteady (in walking, speaking, etc.).

fame, *n.* the quality of being well known: renown. — *adjs.* **famed** (fāmd), **fā'mous,** very well known.

familiar, fa-mil'yar, *adj.* well known (e.g. This is a *familiar* scene): knowing all about (e.g. I am *familiar* with this town): so friendly as to appear cheeky (e.g. He spoke to me in a *familiar* way).—*n.* a spirit.—*n.* **familiar'ity.**—*v.* **famil'iarise,** to make quite accustomed.

fam'ily, *n.* one's children: all those

(parents, children, relatives, etc.) living in one house: a group (e.g. of plants, animals, languages) having some likeness.

famine, fam'in, *n.* great shortage, esp. of food or water.—*v.* **fam'ish,** to suffer great hunger or thirst.

famous. See **fame.**

fan, *n.* an instrument for making a rush of air.—*v.* to cause a rush of air with a fan.—*n.* **fan'light,** a window shaped like an open fan, often over a door.

fanatic, fan'a-tik, *n.* a person who is over-eager about something (esp. religion).— *adj.* **fanatical,** madly keen.

fan'cy, *n.* a whim: a sudden liking: the power of the mind to imagine things (usually pleasant).—*adj.* not plain: ornamented.—*v.* to imagine: to have a liking for: to breed animals, birds, etc.—*n.* **fan'cier,** one whose hobby is to keep prize animals, birds, etc. (e.g. dog-*fancier*, pigeon-*fancier*). —*adj.* **fan'ciful,** full of whims or oddness: imaginary, not real.

fane, *n.* a temple.

fan'fare, *n.* a great blowing of trumpets or bugles.

fang, *n.* the tooth of a wild beast: the poison-tooth of a serpent.— *adj.* **fanged,** having fangs.

fantasia, fan-ta-zē'a, *n.* a light piece of music.

fantasy, phantasy, fan'ta-si, *n.* something full of fancy: a strange dream, a vision.—*adj.* **fantas'tic,** fanciful: unusual, strange.

far, *adj.* and *adv.* to a great distance.—*advs.* **far'ther: far'thest.** —*adj.* **far'-fetched,** very unlikely (e.g. a *far-fetched* story).

farce, *n.* a play full of rough fun and comic doings: anything silly or useless.—*adj.* **farcical** (far'sikal).

fare, *v.* to get on (e.g. He *fared* well (or badly) in the competition): to feed.—*n.* the price of a journey: a person who pays to be carried on a journey: food.—**farewell'!** may you fare well! good-bye!

farinaceous, fa-ri'nā-shus, *adj.* like flour: starchy.

farm, *n.* a country-house, with lands for ploughing, cattle, sheep, hens, etc.—*v.* to work the lands, etc.

of a farm: to buy or sell for a fixed amount the right to gather taxes.—*ns.* **far′mer**; **farm′stead**, a farm and farmhouse.

far′rier, *n.* one who shoes horses and treats their diseases.—*n.* **farr′iery**, the business of a farrier.

farrow, far′ō, *n.* a family of baby pigs.

far′thing, *n.* old coin, ¼ of a penny.

fascinate, fas′i-nāt, *v.* to charm: to put a spell on.—*adj.* **fas′cinating**, charming: delightful.—*n.* **fascinā′tion.**

fashion, fash′un, *n.* the make or cut of a thing (esp. in dress, hats, etc.): way of doing a thing: custom.—*v.* to shape according to a pattern.—*adj.* **fash′ionable**, agreeing with the latest style of dress, way of living, etc.: stylish.

fast, *adj.* firm: fixed: quick-moving.—*adv.* firmly: quickly: close, near.—*v.* **fasten** (fas′n), to fix: to make firm (e.g. by nailing).—*n.* **fast′ness**, a stronghold, fortress, castle.—**fast by**, close to.

fast, *v.* to eat no food for a time.—Also *n.*

fastid′ious, *adj.* difficult to please.

fat, *n.* an oily substance in animals and plants.—*adj.* having much fat: thick (e.g. a *fat* book).—*v.* **fat′ten**, to make, become, fat.

fate, *n.* what the future holds for one: fortune, luck: end or death (e.g. He met his *fate* bravely).—*adj.* **fāt′al**, causing death.—*n.* **fatal′ity**, an accident causing death.—*adjs.* **fāt′ed**, doomed: **fāte′ful**, having important results.

fa′ther, *n.* a male parent: a priest.—*ns.* **fa′ther-in-law**, the father of one's husband or wife; **fa′therland**, one's native land.

fath′om, *n.* a depth-measure (6 ft.).—*v.* to get to the bottom of a mystery.

fatigue, fa-tēg′, *n.* great tiredness.—*v.* to tire out.—*adj.* **fatiguing** (fa-tēg′ing), tiring.

fatuous, fat′ū-us, *adj.* very foolish: silly-looking.

fault, fawlt, *n.* a mistake: a slight wrong-doing.—*adjs.* **fault′less**; **fault′y**, having a fault: not in good order.

faun, fawn, *n.* an imaginary creature, half man, half beast.

fauna, fawn′a, *n.* the animals of a country.

favour, fā′vur, *n.* kindness, a kind deed: a knot of ribbons, or a flower, worn at a wedding.—*v.* to be on the side of: to be helpful to.—*adj.* **fā′vourable**, friendly: helpful to.—*n.* **fā′vourite**, a well-liked person or thing.—Also *adj.*—*n.* **fā′vouritism**, liking one person more than another.

fawn, *n.* a young fallow deer: its colour—light yellowish brown.—*adj.* like a fawn in colour.

fawn, *v.* to make one's self humble in order to get a favour.

fay, *n.* a fairy.

fealty, fē′al-ti, *n.* loyalty: a vow to keep faith.

feasible, fēz′i-bl, *adj.* able to be done: likely.—*n.* **feasibil′ity.**

feast, *n.* a rich and plentiful meal: a joyous or solemn holding of some event.—Also *v.*

feat, *n.* a deed difficult to do.

feather, feth′er, *n.* one of the growths which form the outer covering of a bird.—*n.* **feath′er-weight**, a person (esp. a boxer) of very light weight.—**a feather in one's cap**, a mark to show that one has done something noble; **to show the white feather**, to show signs of being a coward.

feat′ure, *n.* a mark by which anything is known: (*pl.*) a person's face.—*v.* to show.—*adj.* **feat′ureless**, dull, having no important points.

February, feb′roo-ar-i, *n.* the second month of the year.

fec′und, *adj.* fruitful.—*n.* **fecund′ity.**

fed′eral, *adj.* joined by treaty or bargain (e.g. *Federal* States).—*adj.* **fed′erated**, joined after an agreement made about certain matters.—*n.* **federā′tion**, those joined together: a league.

fee, *n.* a price paid for work done, or to get a certain right (e.g. surgeon's *fee*, school *fee*, entrance *fee*).

fee′ble, *adj.* weak.—*n.* **fee′bleness.**

feed, *v.* to give or eat food.—*n.* food for animals (cattle *feed*, horse *feed*): a meal.

feel, *v.* to try by touch: to be aware of: (with *for*) to be sorry for.—*ns.* **feel'ers,** (*pl.*) thread-like parts of an insect's body (on the head) by which it feels danger, etc.; **feeling,** sense of touch: tenderness: softheartedness: (*pl.*) what one feels inside one (e.g. love, kindness, pity, anger).

feign, fān, *v.* to make a pretence of, to sham.

feint, fānt, *n.* a pretence: a sham move to put an enemy off his guard.—Also *v.*

felicity, fe-lis'i-ti, *n.* happiness.—*n.pl.* **felicitā'tions,** good wishes.—*adj.* **felic'itous,** lucky: suiting well.

fē'line, *adj.* cat-like: of the cat kind.

fell, *n.* a barren hill.

fell, *v.* to bring to the ground: to cut down.

fell, *n.* a skin.

fell, *adj.* cruel: fierce.

fellow, fel'ō, *n.* a companion: an equal: one of a pair: a member of a learned society, college, etc.—*n.* **fell'owship,** state of being a partner or a sharer: friendship: a society: an award to a clever university student, giving him the title of *Fellow*.

fel'on, *n.* one who has been in prison for serious crime (called a **felony**).—*adj.* **felō'nious.**

felt, *n.* a rough cloth made of mixed wool and hair.

fem'inine, *adj.* womanly: having to do with women: female.

fē'mur, *n.* the thigh-bone.

fen, *n.* low marshy land, often covered with water: a bog.

fence, *n.* a wall or hedge for closing in animals or land.—*v.* to close in with a fence: to fight with swords.

fend, *v.* to struggle on one's own (e.g. Let him *fend* for himself).

fend'er, *n.* a fire-guard: a rope-ball lowered over a ship's side to act as a buffer against the quay.

fermentā'tion, *n.* the change which takes place when certain substances are brought together (e.g. when yeast is added to the dough in the making of bread, and to the malt liquid in the making of beer).—*n.* **fer'ment,** a substance (e.g. yeast) which causes fermentation: a state of great excitement.—*v.* **ferment',** to change a substance by adding a ferment: (of milk, food, etc.) to go sour or bad: to stir up (e.g. trouble).

ferocious, fe-rō'shus, *adj.* fierce: savage.—*n.* **ferocity** (fer-os'it-i), fierceness.

fer'ret, *n.* a small weasel-like animal used to chase rabbits out of their warrens.—*v.* to search out without ceasing.

ferrule, fer'il, *n.* a metal ring or cap on the tip of a walking-stick or umbrella.

fer'ry, *v.* to carry over water (usually a river or lake) by boat.—*n.* a crossing-place for boats: the boat which crosses.

fer'tile, *adj.* fruitful, producing much: full of ideas.—*v.* **fer'tilise,** to make fertile.—*ns.* **fertilisā'tion;** **fer'tiliser,** stuff for making fields fertile; **fertil'ity,** fruitfulness.

ferule, fer'ool, *n.* a cane for punishment.

fer'vent, fer'vid, *adjs.* very eager: acting with great keenness.—*n.* **fervour.**

fes'tal, *adj.* having to do with a feast or holiday: joyful.

fes'ter, *v.* (of a cut, a sore) to run with pus ('matter'): to become poisoned.

fes'tive, *adj.* in glad mood, joyful.—*ns.* **fes'tival,** a glad occasion (e.g. music *festival*); **festiv'ity,** joyfulness, merry-making.

festoon', *n.* a hanging garland: a looped decoration.—*v.* to decorate as with festoons.

fetch, *v.* to go and get: to bring in (a price).—**to fetch up,** to stop suddenly.

fête, fet, *n.* a big entertainment: a holiday: a saint's day.—*v.* to give a *fête* in honour of someone.

fē'tid, *adj.* having a rotten smell.

fetish, fē'tish, *n.* a charm worshipped by savages: something of which a person is stupidly fond.

fet'lock, *n.* the part of a horse's leg just above the foot.

fet'ters, *n.pl.* chains for the feet.

fettle, fet'l, *n.* readiness: fitness.

feu, fū, *n.* a right to the use of land, houses, etc. for a fixed yearly payment (**feu′-duty**).

feud, fūd, *n.* a private war between families, clans, tribes, etc.: any fierce quarrel.

feudal, fūd′al, *adj.* having to do with **feud′alism,** the system by which, in olden times, service (usually soldier service) was given to the overlord by the tenants, as a return for their lands.—*adj.* **feu′datory,** holding lands under the feudal system.

fē′ver, *n.* an illness causing great body-heat.—*adjs.* **fē′verish, fē′vered,** having a fever: very excited.

fez, *n.* a close-fitting red hat (shaped like a flower-pot) with black tassel, worn in the East.

fiancé, fē-ong′sā, *n.* one engaged to be married—*fem.* **fiancée.**

fiasco, fi-as′ko, *n.* a complete failure.

fibre, fī′ber, *n.* any fine thread or thread-like stuff.—*adj.* **fi′brous.**

fick′le, *adj.* unsteady, not dependable.

fiction, fik′shn, *n.* story which is not true: an untruth.—*adj.* **fictitious (fik-tish′us),** false: not real (e.g. *fictitious* characters in a book).

fid′dle, *n.* a violin.—*v.* to play the violin: to trifle.—**to play second fiddle,** to be second to someone else instead of being first one's self.

fidel′ity, *n.* faithfulness: truth.

fidget, fij′et, *v.* to be restless.

fief, fēf, *n.* land held from an overlord in return for military service.

field, fēld, *n.* land, open country: ground for growing grass or crops, or for playing games—*v.* (in cricket, etc.) to stop a ball and return it.—*ns.* **field′-day,** a day of unusual bustle; **field′fare,** a kind of thrush; **field′-glass,** a small double telescope; **field′-mar′shal,** an officer of the highest rank in the army.

fiend, fēnd, *n.* the Devil: an evil spirit: a wicked person.—*adj.* **fien′dish.**

fierce, fērs, *adj.* very wild-looking, cruel.—*n.* **fierce′ness.**

fiery, fīr′i, *adj.* like fire: easily made angry: high-spirited.

fife, *n.* a small flute.—*n.* **fif′er,** a fife player.

fight, fīt, *v.* to struggle with: **to go to war with.**—*n.* a struggle: a battle.

fig′ment, *n.* a made-up story.

figure, fig′er or **fig′ūr,** *n.* shape: form: number or sign: price (e.g. a high *figure*).—*v.* to write numbers: to imagine: to appear somewhere.—*adj.* **fig′urātive, (of words)** used not in the ordinary meaning but to show likenesses (e.g. 'He was a *lion* in battle ' is a *figurative* way of speaking).—*n.* **fig′urehead,** a person who does little but who serves as a leader.

fil′ament, *n.* a slender, thread-like object—such as the thin wire in an electric-light bulb.

fil′bert, *n.* a hazel-nut.

filch, *v.* to steal.

file, *n.* a folder or other device in which papers are placed in order: line of soldiers one behind another.—*v.* to put in a file: march in file.

file, *n.* a steel tool with a rough surface, for smoothing.—Also *v.*

filial, fil′yal, *adj.* having to do with a son or daughter.

fil′ibuster, *n.* pirate: one who makes very long speech in order to delay passing of a law.—Also *v.*

fil′igree, *n.* very fine gold- or silver-thread lace-work.

fil′let, *n.* a head-band: meat or fish which has had the bones removed before cooking.—Also *v.*

fil′lip, *n.* an urge onwards.

fil′ly, *n.* a young mare.

film, *n.* a thin skin or coating: a thin celluloid sheet on which photographs are taken.—*v.* to photograph on a film.—**the films,** moving pictures, the cinema.

fil′ter, *n.* a strainer: a device for making water pure.—*v.* to purify by a filter: to come in drops.

filth, *n.* dirt.—*adj.* **filth′y,** foul.

fin, *n.* a part of a fish's body by which it balances itself and swims.

fi′nal, *adj.* last: allowing of no argument (e.g. The editor's decision is *final*).—*n.* **final′ity.**

finale, fi-na′lā, *n.* the last part of anything (e.g. a concert).

finance′, *n.* money affairs.—*v.* to supply with sums of money.—*adj.* **financial (fi-nan′shal).**—*n.* **finan′cier,** one who looks after money affairs.

finch, finsh, *n.* a small bird.

find, *v.* to come upon or meet with : to discover : to come to a decision.—*n.* find′ing, a judgment of a court.

fine, *adj.* made up of small drops or parts : not coarse (e.g. *fine* linen) : beautiful : showy : pure (e.g. *fine* gold).—*n.* fin′ery, showy things, esp. in dress.—**fine arts,** painting, sculpture, music.

fine, *n.* money to be paid as a punishment.—Also *v.*

finesse, fi-nes′, *n.* clever bluff (esp. in games) to hide weakness.

finger, fing′ger, *n.* one of the five branching parts of the hand.— *v.* to touch with the fingers.—*n.* fin′gerprint, mark made by the tip of a finger.

fing′ering, *n.* a thick wool used in knitting stockings.

fin′ical, *adj.* fussy : over-careful.

finis, fī′nis, *n.* the end.

fin′ish, *v.* to end, or complete the making of : to put an end to.—*n.* the end (e.g. of a race, a day) : the last touch (e.g. of paint or polish) that makes a perfect job.—*adj.* fin′ished, ended : perfect.

finite, fī′nīt, *adj.* having an end or limit.

fiord, fjord, fyord, *n.* a long, narrow, rock-bound inlet.

fir, *n.* a cone-bearing tree, valuable for its timber.

fire, *n.* the heat and light given off by something burning : eagerness, keenness.—*v.* to set on fire : to make eager : to make to explode : to shoot.—*adj.* fire′proof, unable to go on fire.—*ns.* fire′bomb, a bomb which causes fire ; fire′brand, a piece of burning wood : one who stirs up anger and rebellion ; fire′-brigade, a company of men for putting out fires ; fire′-damp, a dangerous gas found in coal-mines ; it explodes readily when mixed with air : fire′-fly, a glowing insect ; fire′-guard, a framework of wire placed in front of a fireplace ; fire-guard or fire′-watcher, a person who has to watch for fires and try to put them out ; (*pl.*) fire′works, squibs, rockets, etc. sent up at night for show : angry behaviour.

fir′kin, *n.* a small barrel : 9 gallons : 56 lb. of butter.

firm, *adj.* not easily moved or shaken : with mind made up.—*n.* firm′ness.

firm, *n.* a business company.

firm′ament, *n.* the heavens : sky.

first, *adj.* before all others in place, time, or rank.—Also *adv.—ns.* first′-aid′, treatment of a wounded or sick person before the doctor's arrival ; first′-born, the eldest child.—*adj.* first′-hand, direct.

firth, frith, *n.* a narrow arm of the sea, esp. at a river mouth.

fish, *n.* an animal that lives in water, and breathes through gills : —*pl.* fish or fish′es.—*v.* to search for fish : to search.—*ns.* fish′er, fish′erman, one who fishes ; fish′ery, the business of catching fish : a place for catching fish ; fish′monger, a dealer in fish ; fish′plate, an iron plate fitted on each side of the joining of two rails.— *adj.* fish′y, like a fish : doubtful.

fission, fish′on, *n.* splitting.—**fission bomb,** the atom bomb, whose energy comes from splitting atomic nuclei.—*n.* fissure, a crack.

fist, *n.* a tightly-shut hand.—*n.* fist′icuffs, a fight with the fists.

fit, *adj.* suited to a purpose : proper : in good training or health.—*v.* to be of right size or shape.—*n.* fit′ness.—*adj.* fit′ting, suitable.

fit, *n.* a sudden attack or spasm (of laughter, illness).—*adj.* fit′ful, coming in bursts or spasms.

fives, *n.pl.* a handball game played in a walled 'court.'

fix, *v.* to make or become firm.— *adj.* fixed (fixt′), settled : set in position : lasting.—*adv.* fix′edly. —*n.* fix′ture, anything fixed (e.g. a shelf) : a match or race that has been arranged.

flabbergasted, *adj.* overcome with surprise.

flab′by, *adj.* soft to the touch : hanging loose.—*n.* flab′biness.

flaccid, flak′sid, *adj.* soft and weak.

flag, *v.* to become tired or weak.

flag, *n.* a banner, standard, or ensign : a flat paving-stone : a water-plant or reed.

flag′ship, *n.* in a fleet, the admiral's ship, which flies his flag.

flageolet, flaj´o-let, *n.* a kind of flute : a tin whistle.

flag´on, *n.* a large bottle.

flā´grant, *adj.* openly wicked : unashamed.—*ns.* **flā´grance, flā´grancy.**

flail, *n.* a tool for threshing corn, consisting of a wooden bar (the *swingle*) tied to a handle.

flake, *n.* a thin layer or slice of anything : a small loose part (e.g. of snow).—*v.* to form into flakes.

flamboy´ant, *adj.* of wavy shape : splendidly coloured.

flame, *n.* the bright, leaping light of a fire : rage or anger.—*v.* to burst into flame : to be angry.—*adj.* **flām´ing,** burning : red : violent.

flamingo, fla-ming´gō, *n.* a long-legged bird of bright-red colour, found in hot lands.

flamm´able, *adj.* easily set on fire.

flange, flanj, *n.* a raised edge on the rim of a wheel.

flank, *n.* the side of anything (e.g. of a person's or animal's body, of an army).—*v.* to go by the side of : to be placed at the side.

flan´nel, *n.* loosely woven woollen cloth : an article of woollen clothing.—*n.* **flannelette´,** cotton cloth made in imitation of flannel.

flap, *n.* anything broad and loose-hanging : the sound made when such a thing moves.—*v.* to hang down loosely : to move with a flapping noise.

flare, *v.* to blaze up.—*n.* a bright light, esp. one used at night to light up enemy country : torch.

flash, *n.* a sudden burst (e.g. of light, joy, wit) : a moment.—*v.* to shine out suddenly : to pass quickly.—*adjs.* **flash´y,** dazzling for a moment : showy.—*n.* **flash´light,** a light which shines from time to time : a burst of light in which a photograph is taken.

flask, *n.* a bottle.

flat, *adj.* level : uninteresting : not sparkling (e.g. The lemonade was *flat*) : leaving no doubt (e.g. a *flat* denial) : below the right pitch (e.g. to sing *flat*).—*n.* any level stretch (e.g. of land) : a storey of a building : a house which lies on one storey of a building which contains several storeys : a sign in music which lowers a note : a black key of a piano.—*n.* **flat´ness.**—*v.* **flat´ten,** to make or become flat.

flat´ter, *v.* to puff up with false praise : to make out a person (or thing) to be better than he (or it) really is.—*n.* **flat´tery.**

flat´ulence, *n.* wind in the stomach.—*adj.* **flat´ulent.**

flaunt, *v.* to fly or wave in the wind : to show off.

flavour, flā´vur, *n.* a taste : a good taste.—*v.* to give a taste to.—*n.* **flā´vouring,** anything used to give a special taste.

flaw, *n.* a break, a crack : a fault.—*adj.* **flaw´less,** without fault.

flax, *n.* a plant whose fibres are woven into linen cloth.—*adj.* **flax´en,** made of, or looking like flax : fair, long, and flowing.

flay, *v.* to skin : to strip the skin off.

flea, *n.* a small wingless insect having great jumping power.

fleck, *n.* a spot : a speck.—*v.* **fleck´,** to mark with spots.

fledge, flej, *v.* to get feathers for flying.—*n.* **fledg´ling,** a young bird just feathered.

flee, *v.* to run away (e.g. from danger) : to keep away from.

fleece, *n.* a sheep's coat of wool.—*v.* to clip wool from : to rob by cheating.—*adj.* **fleec´y,** soft and fluffy like wool.

fleet, *n.* a number (e.g. of ships, motor-cars, aeroplanes) : the navy.

fleet, *adj.* swift : nimble, light-footed.—*adj.* **fleet´ing,** passing quickly.—*n.* **fleet´ness,** swiftness.—*v.* **fleet,** to pass by quickly.

flesh, *n.* the soft substance (really muscle) which covers the bones of animals : the body : the soft eatable part of fruit.—*adjs.* **flesh´ly,** thinking only of pleasure : **flesh´y,** fat : plump.—*ns.* **flesh´er, flesh´monger,** a butcher.

flex´ible, *adj.* easily bent.—*v.* **flex,** to bend.—*n.* a length of covered wire for electric connections.—*n.* **flexibil´ity,** ease in bending.

flick, *v.* to strike lightly.—*n.*

flick´er, *v.* to flutter : to burn unsteadily.—*Also n.*

flier, flyer, flī´er, *n.* one who flies or flees : an airman.

flight, flīt, *n.* the act of flying: the distance flown: the act of fleeing or escaping: a flock of birds: a number of steps.—*adj.* **flight´y**, changeable: fond of pleasure.

flims´y, *adj.* thin: easily torn: weak (e.g. of an excuse).

flinch, flinsh, *v.* to move back in fear.

fling, *v.* to throw, to cast.—*n.* a throw or cast: heedless behaviour: a lively dance.

flint, *n.* hard kind of stone.—*adj.* made of flint: hard: cruel.—*n.* **flint´-lock**, a gun set-off by sparks from a flint.

flip, *v.* to toss lightly.—*n.* a light toss or stroke: a short journey (e.g. in an aeroplane).—*n.* **flip´-per**, a limb of a seal, walrus, etc.

flip´pant, *adj.* joking, not serious.—*n.* **flipp´ancy**.

flirt, *v.* to play at love-making.—*n.* one who finds fun in much love-making.—*n.* **flirta´tion**.

flit, *v.* to move quickly to and fro.—*n.* **flit´ting**, movement from place to place.

flitch, *n.* the side of a pig, made into bacon.

float, *v.* to keep on the surface of a liquid: to set going (e.g. He *floated* a business).—*n.* a raft: a cork on a fishing-line: a part of a seaplane upon which the machine floats on water: a large van to take animals to market.—*n.* **floating-dock**. See dock.

flock, *n.* a number of beasts or birds together.—*v.* to gather together in a crowd.

flock, *n.* a shred or tuft of wool: wool or cotton waste.—*n.* **flock´-bed**, **-mattress**, one stuffed with flock.

floe, flō, *n.* a sheet of floating-ice.

flog, *v.* to beat: to lash.—*n.* **flog´ging**.

flood, flud, *n.* a great flow (e.g. of water): the rise or flow of the tide.—*v.* to flow freely: to fill too full (e.g. with water).—*n.* **flood´-lighting**, strong lighting from many points.

floor, flōr, *n.* the part of a room on which walking is done: a storey of a building.—*v.* to make a floor: to knock flat: to puzzle.

flop, *v.* to fall plump: to fail badly.—Also *n.*

flor´a, *n.* the plants of a district looked on as a whole: a description of all these.—*ns.* **florescence** (flor-es´ens), a bursting into flower; **flor´ist**, a seller or grower of flowers.—*adjs.* **flō´ral**, made of flowers; **flor´id**, bright in colour: having too many big words (e.g. a *florid* piece of writing).

flor´in, *n.* a coin, silver in colour, worth two shillings.

floss, *n.* fluffy substance found in plant pods: fine silk thread.—*adj.* **floss´y**, silky.

flotil´la, *n.* a fleet of small ships: a small fleet.

flot´sam, *n.* floating goods washed from a ship or wreck.

flounce, *v.* to move impatiently (as in anger).—Also *n.*

flounce, *n.* a plaited strip on the skirt of a dress.

flound´er, *v.* to throw legs and arms about in struggle: to be at a loss for words.

flound´er, *n.* a small flat-fish.

flour, *n.* finely-ground wheat: any substance crushed to powder.—*v.* to sprinkle with flour.—*adj.* **flour´y**.

flourish, flur´ish, *v.* to prosper: to wave something as a show or threat.—*n.* fancy writing: a burst of music: a waving of something (e.g. swords) for show.

flout, *v.* to treat with scorn: to defy rudely.

flow, flō, *v.* (of liquids) to run: (of the tide) to rise.—*n.* a stream or current: plenty.

flow´er, *n.* the blossom: the best of anything.—*v.* to blossom, to bloom.—*adj.* **flow´ery**, made of flowers: richly decorated.

fluctuate, fluk´tū-āt, *v.* to be always changing: to vary.—*n.* **fluctuā´tion**.

flue, floo, *n.* a passage for air and smoke in a stove or chimney.

fluent, floo´ent, *adj.* finding words easily in speaking or writing.—*n.* **flu´ency**.

fluff, *n.* any soft, downy stuff.—*adj.* **fluf´ly**.

fluid, floo´id, *adj.* flowing.—*n.* something which flows (e.g. a liquid).

fluke, flook, *n.* a flounder: a small worm which harms sheep: **the**

part of an anchor which holds fast in sand: a lucky shot.

flunk'ey, *n.* a servant in uniform.

flu'oridate,—idise, *vs.* to add a substance containing the gas fluorine to (water).—*n.* **flu'oridātion.**

flur'ry, *n.* a sudden gust: bustle.—*v.* to excite.

flush, *n.* a rush of blood to the face: freshness, glow.—*v.* to become red in the face: to clean by a rush of water.—*adj.* well supplied with money.

flush, *adj.* having the surface level with the surface around.

flus'ter, *n.* excitement caused by hurry.—Also *v.*

flute, floot, *n.* musical wind instrument: a carved groove on a pillar.—*v.* to play on the flute: to make grooves.—*adj.* **flut'ed,** decorated with grooves.

flut'ter, *v.* to move the wings as if trying to fly: to move about quickly: (of the pulse, the heart) to beat quickly.—*n.* quick beating (e.g. of pulse): nervous excitement.

flux, *n.* a changing flow (e.g. of events): a substance used in making solder joints.

flȳ, *v.* to move through the air on wings or in an aeroplane: to run away.—*n.* a small winged insect: a fish-hook made to look like a fly: a light horse-carriage.—*adj.* sly, knowing.—*ns.* **fly'leaf,** a blank leaf at beginning and end of a book; **fly'wheel,** a wheel, having a heavy rim, which enables a machine to run at a steady speed. —**flying squad,** motor-police.

foal, *n.* young horse.—*v.* to give birth to a foal.

foam, *n.* froth or bubbles on liquids. —*v.* to gather foam: to rage.

fob, *n.* a trick: a small watch-pocket: fancy chain hanging from the watch-pocket.—*v.* to cheat: to brush rudely aside.

fo'c's'le. See **forecastle.**

focus, fō'kus, *n.* meeting-point for rays of light: point on which light, a look, attention, is directed:—*pl.* **fō'cuses** or **foci** (fō'sī).—*v.* to get the right length of ray for a clear picture: to direct to one point.

fod'der, *n.* dried cattle-food (hay, oats, etc.).

foe, fō, *n.* an enemy.

fog, *n.* thick mist.—*v.* to cover in fog: to bewilder.—*adj.* **fog'gy.**—*ns.* **fog-horn; fog-signal.**

fog, fog'gage, *ns.* grass which grows in autumn after the hay is cut.

fō'gy, fō'gey, *n.* a dull old fellow.

foib'le, *n.* a weak point in character.

foil, *v.* to defeat: to puzzle: to disappoint.—*n.* a blunt sword with button at end, used in fencing-practice.

foil, *n.* a thin sheet of metal (e.g. *tin-foil*).

foist, *v.* to pass off as genuine.

fōld, *n.* a part laid over another: an enclosure for sheep, etc.—*v.* to wrap up: to lay one part over another.—*n.* **fold'er,** a folding booklet.

foliage, fō'li-āj, *n.* leaves.

folk, fōk, *n.* people: nation, race: (*pl.*) one's family or relations.—*ns.* **folk-lore,** the study of the customs, beliefs, fairy-tales, etc. of a people; **folk-tale,** a story (e.g. of fairies, giants, gods, heroes) which has been handed down from father to son for hundreds of years; **folk-song,** a song which has been sung by the people of a country for hundreds of years.

fol'low, *v.* to go or come after: to happen as a result: to act according to: to understand: to work at (a trade).—*ns.* **foll'ower; foll'owing,** supporters.

fol'ly, *n.* foolishness: stupid conduct.

foment', *v.* to bathe with warm water: to stirup, encourage growth of (e.g. rebellion).—*n.* **fomentā'tion,** a bathing with warm water.

fond, *adj.* loving: tender: foolish.—*v.* **fond'le,** to caress.—*n.* **fond'ness.**

font, *n.* the basin holding water for baptism.

fool, *n.* a silly person: a court jester.—*v.* to deceive: to play the fool.—*adj.* **fool'ish.**—*ns.* **fool'ishness, fool'ery,** foolish behaviour. —*adjs.* **fool'hardy,** rash: bold and taking foolish risks; **fool'-proof,** (of engines, machinery, etc.) unable to go wrong even though clumsily handled.

fools'cap, *n.* a large size of writing or printing paper.

foot, *n.* the lower part of the leg (from ankle down): the lower part of anything: twelve inches: foot-soldiers :—*pl.* **feet.**—*ns.* **foot'-gear,** boots, shoes, stockings; **foot'hill,** smaller hill at the foot of a mountain; **foot'hold,** place to put the foot in climbing; **foot'ing,** foothold: a beginning; **foot'light,** a light at the front of a stage, shining on the face of an actor; **foot'-note,** a note at the bottom of a page; **foot'-pad,** a highway robber; **foot'-plate,** driver's platform on a railway-engine; **foot'print,** the mark of a foot; **foot'rule,** a ruler twelve inches long; **foot-soldier,** an infantry-man; **foot'step,** the sound of a person walking.—**to foot,** to pay (a bill).

fop, *n.* a person who is vain about dress.—*adj.* **fop'pish.**

for'age, *n.* food for horses and cattle.—*v.* to search for food, fuel, camp necessaries, etc.

forasmuch as, *conj.* because, since.

for'ay, *n.* a sudden raid for plunder.

forbear', *v.* to keep one's self in check: to hold back from.—*n.* **forbear'ance,** control of temper.—*adj.* **forbear'ing,** patient.

forbid', *v.* to order not to.—*adjs.* **forbid'den; forbid'ding,** unpleasant: rather frightening.

force, *n.* strength: violence: the police: a group of soldiers, etc.—*n.pl.* **forces,** soldiers, sailors, airmen.—*v.* to compel: to break open (e.g. a locked door, gate): to hurry on (e.g. He *forced* the pace): to make (flowers, vegetables, etc.) grow more quickly than is natural.—*adjs.* **forced,** done by great effort: unnatural; **force'ful,** acting with power; **forc'ible,** done by force.—**a forced march,** a specially long and hard march.

forceps, *for'seps, n.* a pair of pincers with a strong grip.

ford, *n.* shallow place in a river where one can wade across.—*v.* to cross water on foot.

fore, *adj.* and *adv.* at the front.

fore ! in golf, a warning cry to people in the way.

fore'arm, *n.* the part of the arm between the elbow and the wrist.

forearm, *for-arm', v.* to prepare beforehand.

forebode', *v.* to foretell (usually evil).—*n.* **forebōd'ing,** a feeling of coming evil.

forecast', *v.* to guess beforehand: to predict.—*n.* **fore'cast.**

forecastle, *fōr'kas-l, fo'c'sle, fōk'sl, n.* a raised deck at the fore-end of a ship: the forepart of ship, under the deck, where the crew live.

fore'father, *n.* an ancestor.

fore'finger, *n.* the finger next the thumb.

forefront, *n.* the very front.

forego', *v.* to go before.—**foregone conclusion,** a result that can be guessed rightly long before the finish ; **the foregoing,** something mentioned already.

fore'ground, *n.* the part of a picture or landscape nearest the eye.

forehead, *for'ed, n.* the part of the face above the eyebrows.

foreign, *for'in,* belonging to another country: strange.—*n.* **foreigner** (*for'in-er*), a native of another country.

fore'land, *n.* a headland : a cape.

fore'leg, *n.* one of the front legs of an animal.

fore'lock, *n.* the lock of hair on the forehead.

fore'man, *n.* an overseer of workmen: a leader (e.g. *foreman* of a jury):—*pl.* **fore'men.**

fore'mast, *n.* ship's mast nearest the bow.

fore'most, *adj.* most famous : furthest forward.

fore'noon, *n.* part of the day before noon.

foren'sic, *adj.* having to do with courts of law.

forerun'ner, *n.* one who goes in front to tell of others coming : a sign that something is coming.

foresee', *v.* to see or know beforehand.—*n.* **fore'sight,** wisdom in looking ahead : a fitting on the front of the barrel of a rifle to make correct aiming possible.

fore'shore, *n.* the part of the shore between high and low water marks.

foresight. See **foresee.**

for′est, *n.* large piece of land covered with trees: a stretch of country kept for game (e.g. deer).—*ns.* **for′ester,** a forest worker; **for′estry,** forest-growing.

forestall, fōr-stawl′, *v.* to buy up the whole stock of goods before they are brought to market, so as to sell again at higher prices: to act before someone else.

fore′täste, *n.* a taste beforehand: a warning sample.

foretell′, *v.* to tell before: to prophesy.

forethought, fōr′thawt, *n.* thought or care for the future.

forewarn′, *v.* to warn beforehand.— *n.* **forewarn′ing.**

forewoman, fōr′woom-an, *n.* a woman overseer: a head-woman in a shop or factory.

forfeit, for′fit, *v.* to lose a right by bad conduct.—*n.* that which is given up or taken away for wrongdoing: a fine.—*n.* **for′feiture,** the loss of something as a punishment.

forge, fōrj, *n.* a smith's workshop: a furnace in which metal is heated.—*v.* to hammer (metal) into shape: to imitate for fraud. —*n.* **forg′ery,** the making or altering of any writing for fraud: something imitated.

forge, fōrj, *v.* to move steadily on (e.g. He *forged* ahead through the snow).

forget′, *v.* to lose or put away from the memory.—*adj.* **forget′ful,** apt to forget.—*n.* **forget′fulness.**

forgive, for-giv′, *v.* to pardon: to be merciful.—*n.* **forgive′ness,** pardon: readiness to pardon.—*adj.* **forgiv′ing,** merciful.

forgo′, *v.* to give up: to do without.

fork, *n.* a pronged instrument for lifting things: anything divided like a fork (e.g. a road, treebranch).—*v.* to divide into two branches, etc.

forlorn′, *adj.* quite lost, wretched. —**forlorn′ hope,** a plan which seems to have no chance of success.

form, *n.* shape or appearance: a paper with blank spaces to be filled in: a long seat: a school class: the nest of a hare.—*v.* to

give shape to: to make.—*ns.* **formal′ity,** something done so often in the same way as to become tiring: cold correctness of manner: great show, ceremony; **formā′tion,** the act of forming: arrangement (e.g. of aeroplanes when flying).—*adjs.* **form′al,** (of a person's manner) cold, businesslike: done according to rule.

for′mer, *adj.* at an earlier time: first-mentioned.—*n.* the first of two.—*adv.* **form′erly,** in times past.

for′midable, *adj.* causing fear: likely to make afraid.

for′mūla, *n.* a set of rules to be followed: an arrangement of signs or letters used in chemistry, arithmetic, etc. to express an idea briefly (e.g. H_2O = water).—*pl.* **for′mulæ** or **for′mulas.**—*v.* **for′mulāte,** to set down clearly.

forsake′, *v.* to give up, to desert: to leave.—*adj.* **forsā′ken,** left alone: miserable.

forsooth′, *adv.* in truth: certainly.

forswear, for-swār′, *v.* to deny upon oath: to abandon.

fort, *n.* a place of defence against an enemy.

forte, fort, *n.* that at which one is very good.

forte, for′te, *adv.* (in music) strongly, loudly.—*adv.* **fortis′simo,** very strongly.

forth, *adv.* out: onward in time. —*adj.* **forth′coming,** happening soon: about to appear.—*adv.* **forthwith′,** immediately.

fort′ify, *v.* to strengthen against attack: to build forts round.— *n.pl.* **fortificā′tions,** trenches, dugouts, ramparts, etc. for defence.

fortissimo. See **forte.**

fort′itūde, *n.* courage in meeting danger or bearing pain.

fort′night, *n.* two weeks.—*adj.* and *adv.* **fort′nightly,** once a fortnight.

fort′ress, *n.* a large fortified place (e.g. Gibraltar is a *fortress*).

fortuitous, for-tū′i-tus, *adj.* happening by chance.

for′tūne, *n.* luck (good or bad): wealth.—*adj.* **for′tunate,** lucky.

for′um, *n.* market-place in ancient Rome: any public place where speeches are made.

for'ward, *adj.* near the front : ready : too ready in word or action : early ripe.—*v.* to help on: to send on.—*advs.* **for'ward, for'wards,** onward: towards the front.

foss, fosse, fos, *n.* a ditch round an ancient fort or castle.

fos'sil, *n.* the hardened remains or shape of a plant or animal found in rock: an old, out-of-date person.—*v.* **foss'ilise,** to change into a fossil.

fos'ter, *v.* to bring up or nurse: to help on.— *ns.* **fos'ter-child** (**-brother, -sister**), a boy (or girl) taken into a family and brought up as one of that family; **fos'ter-mother** (**-father**), mother (father) who takes a child into a family and rears it as her (his) own.

foul, *adj.* very dirty: unfair: entangled: (of weather, temper) stormy.—*v.* to soil : to come into collision with: to play unfairly. —*n.* a breaking of the rules of a game.—**foul play,** an evil deed done on purpose; **to fall foul of,** to come against, to quarrel with.

found, *v.* to lay the foundation of: to establish: to leave money with which to start a school, hospital, etc.— *ns.* **founda'tion,** that on which anything rests: money left for special purpose; **founda'tioner,** one who is kept by the funds of a school or college.

found, *v.* to shape by pouring melted metal into a mould. —*ns.* **found'er,** one who does this (e.g. *brassfounder*); **found'ry,** workshop where founding is done.

foun'der, *v.* (of a ship) to sink: (of a horse) to go lame.

foundling, fownd'ling, *n.* a child left by its parents: an orphan.

foun'tain, *n.* a jet of water rising up: the pipe or pipes from which it comes: the beginning of anything.—*n.* **fount,** a spring of water: the beginning of anything.

fowl, *n.* a bird, esp. of the farm-yard or poultry kind.—*ns.* **fowl'er,** one who shoots or snares wild birds; **fowl'ing-piece,** a light gun for shooting wild-fowl.

fox, *n.* a dog-like reddish-brown animal of great cunning: anyone very cunning:—*fem.* **vix'en.**— *ns.* **fox'-earth,** a fox's burrow; **fox'glove,** a beautiful tall wild-flower; **fox'trot,** a dance made up of walking steps and turns.

fracas, fra'ka, *n.* uproar: a noisy quarrel.

fraction, frak'shun, *n.* a fragment or part (e.g. $\frac{1}{2}$, $\frac{2}{3}$, $\frac{5}{6}$, etc.): a very small part.

fractious, frak'shus, *adj.* cross, quarrelsome.

frac'ture, *n.* a break in something hard, esp. in a bone of the body.

fragile, fraj'il, *adj.* easily broken.

frag'ment, *n.* a part broken off: an unfinished part.—*adj.* **frag'-mentary,** broken: made up of pieces.

fra'grant, *adj.* sweet-smelling.—*n.* **frā'grance,** sweet scent : perfume.

frail, *adj.* weak: easily tempted to do wrong.—*n.* **frail'ty,** weakness.

frame, *v.* to put a frame round: to put together, to construct: to plan.—*n.* a case or border round anything: build of body: state (of mind).—*n.* **frame'work,** the outline, shape, or skeleton of anything.

franc. *n.* a French coin.

franchise, fran'chiz *n.* right of voting for member of Parliament.

Fran'co-, prefix meaning French.

frank, *adj.* free: open, speaking one's mind.—*v.* (long ago) to mark a letter so that it went post-free; (to-day) to mark a letter by machine to show that postage has been paid.

frank'incense, *n.* a scented gum.

frank'lin, *n.* an English farmer of olden times, who owned his land.

fran'tic, *adj.* mad.

frater'nal, *adj.* brotherly.—*v.* **frat'-ernise,** to make friends with: to go together like brothers.—*n.* **frater'nity,** a company of persons having the same purpose or ideas : a brotherhood.

fratricide, frat'ri-sīd, *n.* one who kills his brother: the murder of a brother.

fraud, *n.* deceit, dishonest dealing.— *adj.* **fraud'ūlent.**

fraught, frawt, *adj.* filled : laden (e.g. The plan is *fraught* with dangers).

fray, *n.* a fight, a brawl.

fray, *v.* to wear away at the edges.

freak, *n.* a sudden fanciful notion : something very odd.—*adj.* **freak′ish**, apt to change suddenly : very odd.

freck′le, *n.* a brown spot on the skin.

free, *adj.* not bound or shut in : generous : frank (in manner) : costing nothing.—*v.* to set at liberty.—*ns.* **free′booter**, a roving pirate ; **free′dom**, liberty : an honour giving certain rights connected with a city ; **free′lance**, a person working on his own (e.g. a writer who is not engaged by any one newspaper) ; **Free′mason**, a member of a men's society, sworn to secrecy ; **free′stone**, an easily quarried stone.— **Free Trade**, a system of trade in which no taxes are placed on goods coming into a country.

freeze, *v.* to turn into ice : to go stiff (e.g. with cold, fear).

freight, frāt, *n.* load, cargo : charge for carrying a load.—*v.* to load with goods.—*ns.* **freight′-train**, a goods train ; **freighter**, a ship or aircraft that carries cargo.

French, frensh, *adj.* belonging to France or to its people.—*n.* the people or language of France.—*n.* **French-window**, a long window also used as a door.—**to take French leave**, to remain absent without permission.

fren′zy, *n.* a fit of madness : wild excitement.—*adj.* **fren′zied**, mad.

frequent, frē′kwent, *adj.* happening often.—*n.* **frē′quency.**—*v.* **frequent′**, to visit often.

fres′co, *n.* a picture painted on a wall.

fresh, *adj.* new : strong : with new strength : (of butter, water) not salt.—*v.* **fresh′en**, to make fresh : to grow strong.—*ns.* **fresh′et**, a stream of fresh water : overflow of a river from rain or melted snow ; **fresh′man**, **fresh′er**, a first-year university student : a newcomer.

fret, *v.* to wear by rubbing : to be peevish.—*adj.* **fret′ful**, short-tempered.

fretwork, *n.* decorated cut-out work in wood.—*n.* **fret′saw**, a narrow-bladed, fine-toothed saw for fretwork.

fri′able, *adj.* crumbling easily.

fri′ar, *n.* a brother in one of the orders of the Roman Catholic Church.—*n.* **fri′ary**, the friars' house : a monastery.

friction, frik′shun, *n.* rubbing : wear, hindrance, caused by parts rubbing together : bad feeling.

Fri′day, *n.* sixth day of the week.

friend, frend, *n.* one fond of another : a companion : a member of the Society of Friends (a Quaker).— *adj.* **friend′ly**, kind : on good terms.—*ns.* **friend′liness** ; **friend′ship.**—**friendly society**, an insurance society whose members save up for times of sickness and trouble.

frieze, frēz, *n.* coarse woollen cloth.

frieze, frēz, *n.* a part of wall below the ceiling, often ornamented with designs.

frig′ate, *n.* a swift-sailing warship of earlier times, with many guns.

fright, frīt, *n.* sudden fear : terror : an ugly, oddly-dressed person.— *v.* **fright′en**, to make afraid.—*adj.* **fright′ful**, causing terror.

frigid, frij′id, *adj.* frozen, stiffened with cold : cold in manner.— *ns.* **frigid′ity**, coldness ; **frigidaire′** (frij-id-ār′), a very cold safe where food may be stored in hot weather.

frill, *n.* a crimped or ruffled edging (of linen, lace, etc.) : a useless ornament.

fringe, *n.* a border of loose threads : any edge.—*v.* to border round.

frisk, *v.* to skip about playfully.— *adj.* **frisk′y.**

frith. See **firth**.

frit′ter, *n.* meat, pancake, or thin slice of fruit, sweetened, fried, and served hot.—*v.* to waste time.

friv′olous, *adj.* fond of playing : silly.—*n.* **frivol′ity**, fun.

fro, *adv.* from : back or backward.

frock, *n.* a one-piece outer garment worn by women and children : a monk's wide-sleeved garment.— *v.* to clothe with a frock.

frog, *n.* a small land-and-water creature : soft horny substance on the sole of a horse's hoof.

frol′ic, *n.* fun: a wild prank: a merry-making.—*adj.* merry.—*v.* to play wild pranks or merry tricks.—*adj.* **frol′icsome,** gay.

frond, *n.* leaf-like growth, esp. in ferns.

front, frunt, *n.* the forepart of anything: the face: (in war) the fighting line.—*v.* to face, to look towards.—*n.* **front′age,** front part of a building.

frontier, front′ēr, *n.* a boundary between countries.—Also *adj.*

frontispiece, front′is-pēs, *n.* a picture at the very beginning of a book.

frost, *n.* frozen dew: the state of coldness needed to form ice: a cheat, a disappointment.—*v.* to damage by frost: to cover with frost or anything sparkling like it.—*adjs.* **frost′ed; frost′y.**

froth, *n.* foam on liquids.—*v.* to throw up foam: to be very angry.—*adj.* **froth′y.**

fro′ward, *adj.* stubborn.

frown, *v.* to wrinkle the brows.— Also *n.*—**to frown on,** to look upon with dislike.

frow′zy, *adj.* rough and tangled.

fruc′tify, *v.* to make fruitful: to bear fruit.

frugal, froo′gal, *adj.* careful in spending, thrifty.—*n.* **frugal′ity.**

fruit, froot, *n.* that which grows from the earth and is fit for food: the part of a plant containing the seed: result.—*adjs.* **fruit′ful,** bringing forth fruit; **fruit′less,** having no fruit: useless, done in vain (e.g. a *fruitless* errand).—*n.* **fruit′erer,** one who sells fruit.

fruition, froo-ish′un, *n.* ripeness.

frump, *n.* a cross and untidy woman.

frus′trate, *v.* to make useless, to bring to nothing.—*n.* **frustrā′tion.**

frȳ, *v.* to cook by heating in fat.— *n.* anything fried.

frȳ, *n.* young fishes.—**small fry,** people or things of little importance.

fud′dle, *v.* to make stupid with drink.

fudge, fuj, *n.* nonsense.

fū′el, *n.* any substance by which a fire is kept going (e.g. coal, wood, oil).

fugitive, fūj′i-tiv, *adj.* running away: lasting a short time.—*n.* a runaway.

fugue, fūg, *n.* a piece of music.

ful′crum, *n.* the point on which a lever rests: a prop.

fulfil, fool-fil′, *v.* to do fully or well: to put into action.—*n.* **fulfil′ment.**

full, fool, *adj.* holding as much as can be held: having no empty space.—*n.* greatest size (as of the moon).—*v.* to draw up (cloth) on one side more than on another. —*adv.* very: completely (used along with many *adjs.*, e.g. **full-blown,** fully opened out, as a flower).—*ns.* **full-dress,** dress worn on great occasions; **full-moon,** the moon when it appears as a complete circle (i.e. when it is on the side of the earth farthest from the sun).

full, fool, *v.* to press or beat cloth in a mill.—*n.* **fuller′s-earth,** soft earth, which removes grease from cloth.

ful′minate, *v.* to speak with angry threats.—*n.* **fulminā′tion.**

fulsome, fool′sum, *adj.* sickening: overdone (e.g. *fulsome* praise, flattery).

fum′ble, *v.* to grope about awkwardly: to drop a catch or a pass at cricket or rugby.

fūme, *n.* smoke or vapour.—*v.* to give off smoke or vapour: to be in a rage.

fūm′igate, *v.* to kill germs (in a sickroom) by means of strong fumes. —*n.* **fumigā′tion.**

function, fungk′shun, *n.* the doing of a thing: special duty (e.g. of a part of the body): an important meeting.—*v.* to work: to carry out usual duties.—*n.* **func′tionary,** one holding an office, an official.

fund, *n.* sum of money for a special purpose: store or supply.

fundament′al, *adj.* of the greatest importance: going to the very bottom of the matter.—*n.* a necessary part: (*pl.*) the groundwork or first stages.

fū′neral, *n.* burial.—*adj.* **funereal** (fū-nē′re-al), dismal: mournful.

fun′gus, *n.* a soft, spongy plant growth (e.g. toadstool, mushroom): disease-growth on animals and plants:—*pl.* **fungi** (fun´ji) or **fun´guses.**

funic´ular rail´way, *n.* a kind of railway in which carriages are pulled uphill by a rope.

fun´nel, *n.* a wide-mouthed filler by which liquids are poured into bottles: a tube or passage for escape of smoke, air, etc.

fun´ny, *adj.* causing laughter: comical.—*n.* **funny-bone,** the elbow-joint.

fur, *n.* short fine hair of certain animals: their skins covered with fur (used for clothing): a coating on the tongue, on the inside of kettles, boilers, etc.—*v.* to line or cover with fur.—*adj.* **fur´ry.**—*n.* **fur´rier,** one who buys, sells, or works with furs.

fur´below, *n.* the plaited border of a gown or petticoat.

fur´bish, *v.* to rub up until bright.

furious. See **fury.**

furl, *v.* to roll up (a sail, flag).

fur´long, *n.* one-eighth of a mile (220 yards).

furlough, fur´lō, *n.* holiday leave.

fur´nace, *n.* a very hot oven or closed-in fireplace for melting iron ore, etc.

fur´nish, *v.* to fit up (a room or house) completely: to give (e.g. I *furnished* him with a list of names).—*ns.* **fur´nishings** (*pl.*), fittings of any kind; **fur´niture,** movable articles in a house, room, office, etc.

furore, foo-rōr´ā, *n.* a craze: wild eagerness.

furrow, fur´ō, *n.* the trench made by a plough: any groove: a wrinkle.—*v.* to cut deep grooves in: to wrinkle.

fur´ther, *adv.* and *adj.* to a greater distance or degree: in addition.

—*adv.* **fur´thermore,** in addition to what has been said.—*v.* **fur´ther,** to help on.—*n.* **fur´therance,** a helping on.

furtive, fur´tiv, *adj.* done slyly, stealthy.

fury, fū´ri, *n.* rage: violent anger.—*adj.* **fū´rious.**

furze, *n.* a prickly plant with yellow flowers (also called **gorse, whin**).

fuse, fūz, *v.* to melt: to join together.—*n.* easily melted wire put in an electric circuit for safety. (If wires receive too much electricity and are overheated the *fuse-wire* melts first, lights go out, and fire is avoided.).—*n.* **fū´sion,** a melting: close union of things, as if by melting.—**fusion bomb,** the hydrogen bomb, whose energy comes from fusion of nuclei of atoms.

fuse, *n.* any device for causing an explosion to take place at a certain time chosen beforehand.

fuselage, fū´zil-āj, *n.* the body of an aeroplane.

fū´sil, *n.* a flint-lock musket.—*ns.* **fusilier´, fusileer´,** once, a soldier armed with a fusil—now a title borne by a few regiments of the British army; **fūsillade´,** a number of guns fired at same time, a volley.

fuss, *n.* bustle: haste, flurry.—*v.* to be in a bustle.—*adj.* **fuss´y.**

fustian, fust´yan, *n.* coarse, ribbed cotton cloth.

fust´y, *adj.* mouldy: stale-smelling.

fū´tile, *adj.* useless: having no effect.—*n.* **fūtil´ity,** uselessness.

fū´ture, *adj.* about to be: that is to come.—*n.* time to come.—*n.* **futur´ity,** time to come.

fuzz, *n.* fine light dust, down, etc.—*adj.* **fuz´zy,** covered with fuzz, fluffy: curly.

G

gab´ble, *v.* to talk fast, chatter.—Also *n.*

gaberdine, gab-er-dēn´, *n.* a loose cloak: a kind of cloth.

gā´ble, *n.* the end wall of a building.

gad, *v.* to wander about aimlessly.—

n. **gad´about,** a person who loves wandering about.

gad´fly, *n.* a fly which is a pest to animals.

Gael, gāl, *n.* a Scottish Highlander.—*adj.* **Gaelic** (gāl´ik), belonging to the Gaels.—*n.* their language.

gaff, *n.* spear or hook used by fishers for landing fish, such as salmon : a spar from a mast, for raising the top of a sail.

gaf′fer, *n.* an old man : an overseer of workmen.

gag, *v.* to silence by stopping the mouth.—*n.* something put in a person's mouth to silence him.

gage, gāj, *n.* a something (e.g. a glove) given as a sign of a challenge : a pledge.

gaggle, *n.* a flock (of geese).

gaiety, gaily. See gay.

gain, *v.* to win : to earn : to reach. —*n.* something won : profit.

gain′say, *v.* to contradict : to deny.

gait, *n.* way or manner of walking.

gait′er, *n.* a cloth ankle-covering, fitting over the shoe, sometimes reaching to knee.

ga′la, *n.* a feast-day : a time of rejoicing and merry-making.

gal′antine, *n.* fowl, veal, or other meat, boned and pressed, and served cold.

Gal′axy, *n.* Milky Way : (small g) a splendid gathering (e.g. of women, famous people).

gale, *n.* a strong wind.

gall, gawl, *n.* bile (a bitter fluid coming from the liver and stored in **gall-bladder**) : bitter hatred.

gall, gawl, *v.* to hurt by rubbing : to annoy.—*adj.* **gall′ing,** annoying.

gall, gawl, *n.* a growth (caused by insects) on oaks and other trees and plants.

gal′lant, *adj.* brave : noble : paying great attention to ladies.—*n.* a gay dashing person : (gal-ant′) a man who is a favourite with ladies because of his fine manners. —*n.* **gal′lantry,** bravery : politeness to ladies.

galleon, gal′i-un, *n.* a large Spanish vessel of olden times, mostly used for carrying treasure.

gal′lery, *n.* a long passage : the top floor of seats in a theatre : a room for showing paintings, etc. : spectators, e.g. at a golf match.

gal′ley, *n.* a long, low-built ship driven by oars : a place where cooking is done on board ship.— *n.* **galley-slave,** a prisoner who is condemned to work at the oars of a galley.

galliard, gal′yard, *n.* a lively old-time dance.

gallon, gal′un, *n.* a measure for liquids (4 quarts or 8 pints).

gal′lop, *v.* to move by leaps : to move very fast.—*n.* fast pace.

gallows, gal′lōz, *n.* wooden framework on which criminals are hanged.

gal′op, *n.* lively dance : the music for it.

galore′, *adv.* in great plenty.

galosh′, *n.* a rubber shoe or slipper worn over another in wet weather.—Also **golosh′.**

gal′vanism, *n.* electricity got by action of chemicals (usually acids) on metal.—*adj.* **galvan′ic.** —*v.* **gal′vanise,** to stir into activity.—*n.* **galvanom′eter,** an instrument for measuring electric currents.—**gal′vanised iron,** iron coated (by electricity) with zinc to prevent rusting.

gam′bit, *n.* a first move (e.g. in chess) in which something is lost in order to make one's position stronger.

gam′ble, *v.* to play games for money : to risk money on the result of a game : to take a wild chance.—Also *n.*

gamboge, gam-bōj′, *n.* a gum which gives a yellow colour.

gam′bol, *v.* to leap playfully.— Also *n.*

game, *n.* a sport of any kind : the number of points required to win a contest : wild animals and birds hunted for sport.—*adj.* plucky.—*v.* to gamble.—*ns.* **game′keeper,** one who looks after gamebirds, animals, fish, etc. ; **game′ster,** a gambler ; **gām′ing,** gambling.—**big game,** large hunted animals (e.g. lions, deer, etc.).

gam′in, *n.* a rough and ragged street-boy.

gam′mer, *n.* an old woman.

gam′mon, *n.* leg of a pig, salted and smoked.

gamp, *n.* a large, clumsy umbrella.

gam′ut, *n.* a scale in music : the whole extent of anything.

gan′der, *n.* a male goose.

gang, *n.* a company of people met together for evil purpose : a number of labourers.—*ns.* **gang′er,** foreman of a company of workmen (e.g. navvies); **gang′ster,** one of a gang of evil-living people.

gang′rel, *n.* a tramp.—Also *adj.*

gangrene, gang′grēn, *n.* the rotting of some part of the body.—*adj.* **gang′renous.**

gang′way, *n.* a passage between rows of seats : a movable passage-way leading from a quay to a ship.

gan′net, *n.* a large sea-bird (the solan goose).

gan′try, *n.* a platform for a travelling crane : a stand for barrels.

gaol, gaoler. See **jail, jailer.**

gap, *n.* an opening : a deep valley between hills.

gape, *v.* to open the mouth wide (e.g. in surprise).

garage, gar′ij or gar-azh′, *n.* a building for storing a motor-car (or cars) : a shop where motor repairs are done, and petrol, oil, etc. sold.

garb, *n.* dress.—*v.* to clothe.

gar′bage, *n.* waste matter.

gar′ble, *v.* to pick out parts which suit one's purpose : to mix up so as to mislead.

gar′den, *n.* a piece of ground on which flowers or vegetables are grown. — *n.* **gar′dener.** — **garden city,** a town beautifully laid out, with wide streets and gardens ; **garden party,** a large tea-party, held out of doors.

gargan′tuan, *adj.* very large, huge.

gar′gle, *v.* to wash the throat with a soothing or germ-killing liquid, making a bubbling sound in doing so.—*n.* liquid used as a gargle.

gar′goyle, *n.* a jutting-out roof-spout, quaintly carved.

gār′ish, *adj.* showy.

gar′land, *n.* a wreath of flowers : a collection of chosen pieces (e.g. of prose, poetry, songs).—*v.* to decorate with a garland.

gar′lic, *n.* a plant of the onion kind, with a strong smell and burning taste.

gar′ment, *n.* any article of clothing.

gar′ner, *n.* a place where grain is stored up.—*v.* to store as in a garner.

gar′net, *n.* a precious stone, red in colour.

gar′nish, *v.* to adorn : to decorate a table-dish.—*n.* **gar′nishing,** decoration for a table-dish (e.g. parsley with fish).

gar′ret, *n.* a room next the roof of a house.

gar′rison, *n.* a body of troops for guarding a fortress.—*v.* to supply with troops for defence.

garrotte, gar-rot′, *v.* to strangle : to half-strangle and then rob.

gar′rulous, *adj.* fond of talking.—*ns.* **garrul′ity, garr′ulousness.**

gar′ter, *n.* a broad elastic band to keep a stocking up : the badge of the highest order of knighthood in Britain (*Order of the Garter*).

garth, *n.* a yard : a garden.

gas, *n.* matter in the form of vapour : any such matter when used for lighting, heating (*coal-gas,* got from coal), for deadening pain (e.g. the gas used by a dentist), or for poisoning (*poison gas*) : (in America) petrol :—*pl.* **gas′es.**—*adj.* **gā′seous.**—*v.* **gas,** to poison with gas : to talk idly.—*ns.* **gas′-bag,** person who talks much, a chatterbox ; **gaselier′,** a hanging, branched framework of gas-lights ; **gas′-engine,** engine worked by explosions of a gas ; **gas′-mask,** a covering for the face to prevent breathing in of poisonous gas ; **gas′oline,** petrol ; **gasom′eter,** a tank for storing gas.

gash, *v.* to make a deep cut into anything.—*n.* a deep, open wound.

gasp, *n.* the sound made by a sudden catching of the breath.—*v.* to breathe with difficulty : to speak with gasps : to be in great need of, to desire greatly.

gas′tric, *adj.* having to do with the stomach.—*n.* **gastri′tis,** a painful illness of the stomach.

gate, *n.* an opening in a wall, etc. : that which closes the opening : the number of people at a match, or the total sum they pay to get in.—*n.* **gate′way,** an opening containing a gate : an entrance.

gâteau, gat′ō, *n.* a fancy cake.

gath′er, *v.* to bring together, or to come, to one place : to increase : to learn, conclude.—*n.* **gath′ering,** a crowd : an abscess.

gauche, gōsh, *adj.* clumsy.

gaucho, gow'chō, n. a native of S. America, noted for wonderful horse-riding.

gaud'y, adj. showy, gay.—n. gaud'iness.

gauge, gāj, v. to measure how much is in something : to make a guess. —n. a measuring-rod : a guess. —n. gaug'er, a government tax-officer who measures the contents of whisky-casks, etc.—ns. broad-, narrow-gauge, railways having the distance between rails greater or less than the standard gauge (4 ft. 8½ ins.).

Gaul, n. a name of France in olden times : an inhabitant of Gaul.

gaunt, adj. thin, pinched-looking.

gaunt'let, n. the iron glove of armour, which in olden times used to be thrown down as a challenge : a long glove covering the wrist.—to run the gauntlet, to take punishment from all sides ; to throw down the gauntlet, to give a challenge.

gauze, n. thin cloth that can be seen through : any material like this (e.g. wire-gauze).

gavotte, ga-vot', n. a lively dance.

gawk'y, adj. awkward, stupid.

gay, adj. lively : merry, full of fun : bright-coloured.—n. gai'ety.—adv. gai'ly.

gaze, v. to stare at.—n. a fixed look.

gazelle, ga-zel', n. a small, deer-like animal.

gazette, ga-zet', n. a newspaper, esp. one having lists of government notices.—n. gazetteer', a dictionary dealing only with names of places, rivers, etc.

gean, n. a wild cherry.

gear, n. anything needed for a particular job (e.g. harness, tools, clothes) : (in machinery) a connection by means of toothed wheels.—v. to put in gear.—n. gear'ing, toothed wheels, pinions, etc. in a machine.

geese, pl. of goose.

geisha, gā'sha, n. a Japanese dancing girl.

gelatine, jel'a-tin, n. a jelly-like substance made from hooves, animal bones, etc.—adj. gelat'inous, jelly-like.

gelding, n. a name for a kind of horse.

gelid, jel'id, adj. icy cold.

gem, jem, n. any precious stone : anything very valuable.

gendarme, zhong-darm, n. a French armed policeman.

gender, jen'der, n. (in grammar) the difference between nouns according to sex (e.g. ' Boy ' is masculine gender, ' Girl ' is feminine, ' Table ' is neuter).

genealogy, jen-e-al'o-ji, n. history of the descent of families : the list of forefathers of a person or family.—adj. genealog'ical.—n. geneal'ogist, one who studies or traces genealogies.—genealogical tree, the forefathers of a family or person drawn up in the form of a tree with roots, branches, etc.

general, jen'er-al, adj. looked at broadly, not in detail (e.g. He gave me a general idea of his plan): not special : widespread: public.—n. the chief of an army. —v. generalise', to take for granted that what is true for some is true for all.—ns. general'ity, the most part; generalis'simo, the chief general.—adv. gen'erally, in general, in most cases.

generate, jen'er-āt, v. to bring into life: to set going.—n. genera'tion, act of creating or making : a step in family descent (e.g. grandfather=1st generation, father= 2nd generation, son=3rd generation): people born at about the same time; gen'erātor, a machine for making (e.g. electricity).

generous, jen'er-us, adj. giving plentifully: kind.—n. generos'ity.

genesis, jen'e-sis, n. beginning.

genial, jē'ni-al, adj. good-natured.

genius, jēn'yus, n. unusual cleverness: a person who is unusually clever (pl. gē'niuses).—ns. gen'ius or genie, a guardian spirit (pl. genii, jēn'ē-ī).

genteel, jen-tēl', adj. well-bred: graceful : fashionable.

gentile, jen'tīl, n. (in the Bible) anyone not a Jew : a foreigner.

gentle, jen'tl, adj. well-born : soft in manner, not rough.—n. gentil'ity, nobleness of birth : polite manners, good education.

gentleman, jent´l-man, *n.* a man, esp. one of noble birth : a well-mannered man : a man (opposite of *lady*) :— *fem.* **gen´tlewoman.** —*adj.* **gen´tlemanly,** behaving in a polite manner.

gentry, jen´tri, *n.* the class of people just below the nobles in rank.

genuine, jen´ū-in, *adj.* real, not sham.—*n.* **gen´uineness.**

genus, jē´nus or jen´us, *n.* a group made up of a number of kinds (called *species*) :— *pl.* **gen´era.**

geography, jē-og´ra-fi, *n.* the branch of knowledge which deals with the surface of the earth and its inhabitants : a book containing a description of the earth.—*n.* **geog´rapher.** — *adjs.* **geograph´ic,** -al,** having to do with geography.

geology, jē-ol´o-ji, *n.* the branch of knowledge which tells of the rocks of the earth.—*adj.* **geolog´ical.**

geometry, jē-om´e-tri, *n.* the branch of knowledge which deals with the study of lines, angles, and figures.—*adj.* **geomet´rical,** having regular shape.

geranium, je-rā´ni-um, *n.* a plant, with bright-red, pink, or white flowers.

gerfalcon, jer´fawl-kon, *n.* a large falcon.

germ, jerm, *n.* the tiny beginning of a living thing, whether a plant or an animal : a very small living thing which may cause a disease : that from which anything springs. —*n.* **germ´icide,** a germ-killer.— *v.* **ger´minate,** to begin to grow, to sprout.—*n.* **germinā´tion.**

german, jer´man, *adj.* closely related, as *cousins german.*—*adj.* **germane´,** nearly related : suitable.

German, jer´man, *n.* a native of *Germany* : the German language.

gesticulate, jes-tik´ū-lāt, *v.* to wave hands and arms about in excitement.—*n.* **gesticulā´tion.**

gesture, jes´tūr, *n.* a movement of the body : an action, which shows one's feelings.

get, *v.* to obtain : to go or move (e.g. He *got* down ; *Get* up ! = Rise !) : to catch (a disease).

gewgaw, gū´gaw, *n.* a toy.

geyser, gā´- or gī´ser, *n.* a hot spring (as in Iceland) which spouts water into the air : a gas or electric water-heater.

ghastly, gast´li, *adj.* like a ghost, horrible in appearance.—*n.* **ghast´-liness.**

gherkin, ger´kin, *n.* a small cucumber used in pickles.

ghetto, get´ō, *n.* the Jews' district in some cities.

ghost, gōst, *n.* a spirit, usually of a dead person.—*adj.* **ghost´ly,** like a ghost.—*n.* **ghost´liness.**

ghoul, gool, *n.* an evil spirit which plunders dead bodies.—*adj.* **ghoul´-ish,** horrible.

giant, jī´ant, *n.* a person of great height or size (*fem.* **gi´antess**) : anything very large.—*adj.* **huge.**

gibber, jib´er, *v.* to speak nonsense.

gibberish, jib´erish, *n.* quick, gabbling talk : words without meaning.

gibbet, jib´et, *n.* in olden times, a gallows on which criminals were hung up after execution.

gibbon, gib´un, *n.* a tailless, monkey-like animal.

gibbous, gib´us, *adj.* shaped like the moon when it is nearly full.

gibe, jibe, jīb, *v.* to make fun of un-kindly.—Also *n.*

giblets, jib´lets, *n.pl.* eatable parts from the inside of a fowl.

gid´dy, *adj.* unsteady, dizzy : whirling : thoughtless.—*n.* **gidd´iness.**

gift, *n.* something given (e.g. a present) : natural power (e.g. He has the *gift* of prophecy).—*v.* to give as a present.—*adj.* **gift´ed,** given as a present : having special natural power : specially clever.

gig, *n.* a light, two-wheeled carriage.

gigantic, ji-gan´tik, *adj.* huge, of giant size.

gig´gle, *v.* to laugh in a silly manner. —Also *n.*

gigot, jig´ot, *n.* a leg of mutton.

gild, *v.* to cover with gold : to make bright.—*n.* **gilt,** the gold covering used in gilding.—*adj.* covered with thin gold : coloured like gold.—*adj.* **gilt-edged,** very good : having no risk of failure.

gill, jil, *n.* a measure (¼ pint) for liquids.

gil´lie, *n.* a man-servant who acts as a help and guide for one who is fishing or shooting.

gills, *n.pl.* the openings on the side of a fish's head through which it breathes.

gillyflower, jil´i-flow-er, *n.* a common name for stock or wallflower.

gilt. See gild.

gimcrack, jim´krak, *n.* a toy: something cheap and not good.

gim´let, *n.* a small tool for boring holes by turning it with the hand.

gin, jin, *n.* a strong drink got from grain, flavoured with juniper berries.

gin, jin, *n.* a trap or snare: a machine for separating cotton from its seeds.—*v.* to trap or snare: to clear cotton of its seeds.

ginger, jin´jer, *n.* a hot-tasting root, used as a seasoning.—*adj.* having ginger in it: reddish brown in colour (esp. hair).—*n.* gin´gerbread, cake flavoured with ginger.

gingerly, jin´jer-li, *adv.* with soft steps: very carefully.

gingham, ging´am, *n.* a striped or checked cotton cloth.

ginn. See jinn.

gipsy. See gypsy.

giraffe, ji-raf´, *n.* an African animal with very long legs and neck.

gird, *v.* to bind round: to clothe.—*ns.* gird´er, a beam of iron, steel, or wood used in building; gird´le, something which goes round: a waist-belt.

gir´dle, grid´dle, *n.* a flat iron plate for baking cakes, scones, etc.

girl, *n.* a female child: a young unmarried woman.—*n.* girl´hood, the state or time of being a girl.—*adj.* girl´ish, of or like a girl.

girth, *n.* measurement round the middle: a saddle-band.

gist, jist, *n.* the main thought of a matter (e.g. the *gist* of a story).

give, giv, *v.* to hand over: to utter (a shout, cry): to break or crack (e.g. The bridge *gave* under the weight of the train).—*n.* giv´er.— **to give away,** to betray; **to give in,** to yield; **to give over,** to stop (doing something); **to give rise to,** to cause; **to give up,** to hand over: to yield: to cease (fighting); **to give way,** to yield: to break.

giz´zard, *n.* part of a bird's stomach.

glacé, gla´sā, *adj.* iced: glossy (e.g. *glacé* leather).

glacier, glas´i-er, *n.* a slowly moving river of ice, in some countries found in valleys between high mountains.—*adj.* glacial (glā´-shal), having to do with ice or with glaciers.

glacis, glā´sis, *n.* a gently sloping bank in front of a fort.

glad, *adj.* pleased: cheerful: giving pleasure.—*v.* glad´den, to make glad.—*n.* glad´ness.—*adj.* glad´some, glad: gay.

glade, *n.* an open space in a wood.

glad´iātor, *n.* (in olden times) a man who was trained to fight with other men or with animals for the amusement of spectators.

glaive, glāv, *n.* a weapon (a curved blade fixed on wooden pole).

glamour, glam´er, *n.* magic: charm.

glance, *n.* a quick look: a sudden gleam of light.—*v.* to take a quick look at: to gleam: to half-hit and fly off sideways.

gland, *n.* a part of the body which draws off used-up material from the blood (e.g. a kidney), or which makes useful matter for the body (e.g. the liver).—*adj.* glan´dūlar.

glare, *n.* a dazzling light: an angry look.—*v.* to shine with a dazzling light: to look angrily.—*adj.* glār´ing, dazzling: very bad (e.g. a *glaring* mistake).

glass, *n.* a substance made from sand and silica: anything made of glass (e.g. a mirror, a drinking-vessel): (*pl.*) spectacles.—*adjs.* glass, glassy, made of glass.—*ns.* glass´-pā´per, paper covered with finely ground glass, and used like sand-paper; plate´-glass, thick glass made in plates (used for shop windows).

glaze, *v.* to cover with a thin coating (e.g. of glass): to make shiny: to put panes of glass in a window.—*n.* a shiny surface.—*ns.* glāz´er, a workman who puts glaze on paper, pottery, etc.; glā´zier, one who sets glass in window-frames.

gleam, *v.* to glow: to flash.—*n.* a beam: brightness.

glean, *v.* to gather corn in handfuls after the reapers: to collect.

glebe, glēb, *n.* the land belonging to a parish church.

glee, *n.* joy : a song in parts.—*adj.* **glee′ful,** merry.—*n.* **glee′man,** one who sings glees, a minstrel.

glen, *n.* a long narrow valley.

glib, *adj.* speaking smoothly : ready at finding excuses.—*n.* **glib′ness.**

glide, *v.* to move smoothly.—*n.* act of gliding : a sliding kind of dance-step.—*n.* **glīd′er,** an aeroplane without an engine.

glim′mer, *v.* to burn : to appear faintly.—*n.* a faint light.—*n.* **glimm′ering,** a slight idea, a hint.

glimpse, *n.* a hurried view in passing.—*v.* to have a hurried look at.

glint, *v.* to shine, gleam.—Also *n.*

glisten, glis′n, *v.* to sparkle.

glit′ter, *v.* to sparkle.—Also *n.*

gloam′ing, *n.* twilight, dusk.

gloat, *v.* to look at with wicked joy.

globe, *n.* a ball : the earth : a ball with a map of the world drawn on it.—*n.* **glob′ūle,** a drop : a very small ball-shaped piece.—*adj.* **glob′ūlar,** ball-shaped.

gloom, *n.* dullness, darkness : sadness.—*adj.* **gloom′y,** dimly lighted : sad.

glō′ry, *n.* fame : honour : great show, splendour.—*v.* (with *in*) to boast about.—*adj.* **glō′rious,** splendid : deserving great praise.—*v.* **glō′rify,** to make glorious : to praise highly.

gloss, *n.* brightness on the surface.—*v.* to make bright : to explain : to hide a fault.—*adj.* **gloss′y,** shiny, highly polished.—*n.* **gloss′ary,** a list of difficult words, with their meanings.

glot′tis, *n.* the opening to the windpipe.

glove, gluv, *n.* a covering for the hand, having a sheath for each finger : a boxing-glove.

glow, glō, *v.* to shine with great heat.—*n.* great heat : bright light.—*adj.* **glow′ing,** full of praise (e.g. I hear *glowing* accounts of his bravery).—*n.* **glow′worm,** a kind of beetle which shows a tiny light in the dark.

glow′er, *v.* to stare with a frown.

glucose, gloo′kōse, *n.* a kind of sugar, found in juice of fruits : a syrup made from starch by chemicals.

glue, gloo, *n.* a sticky substance got by boiling skins, hooves, etc. of animals.—*v.* to join with glue.—*adj.* **glu′ey,** sticky.

glum, *adj.* sad : frowning.

glut, *v.* to take one's fill greedily : to supply too much.—*n.* too much of something (e.g. a *glut* of fish on the market).

glut′ton, *n.* one who eats too much : the wolverene (a kind of weasel).—*adj.* **glutt′onous,** fond of overeating : eating greedily.—*n.* **glutt′ony,** greediness in eating.

glycerine, glis′er-in, *n.* a colourless, sticky, sweet-tasting liquid.

gnarled, narld, *adj.* knotty, twisted.

gnash, nash, *v.* to grind (the teeth).

gnat, nat, *n.* small biting fly, midge.

gnaw, naw, *v.* to bite at, bit by bit.

gneiss, nīs, *n.* a hard kind of rock.

gnome, nōm, *n.* a goblin who lives underground.

gnu, nū, *n.* a South African antelope.

gō, *v.* to move : to become (e.g. *go* bad, *go* mad).—*adj.* **go-ahead,** eager, pushing.—*n.* **go-cart,** a small folding perambulator.—**Go to it !** Work hard ! ; **to go about,** to set to work doing something ; **to go for,** to attack ; **to go in for,** to decide to use ; **to go on,** to continue ; **to go over,** to tell (a story) bit by bit : to examine ; **to go under,** to be defeated.

goad, *n.* a sharp-pointed stick for driving oxen.—*v.* to urge on.

goal, *n.* the upright posts between which the ball is to be driven in football and other games : the finishing-post of a race : anything aimed at or wished for.

goat, *n.* an animal of the sheep family with horns and long-haired coat.

gob′ble, *v.* to swallow quickly : to make a noise like a turkey.

gob′let, *n.* large cup without handles.

gob′lin, *n.* a mischievous fairy.

God, *n.* the Creator and Keeper of the world.—*n.* **god,** anything worshipped, an idol :—*fem.* **god′dess.** —*adj.* **god′ly,** holy, good-living.— *ns.* **god′father,** a man who, at a child's baptism, says that he will see that the child is brought up according to the beliefs of the Church (*fem.* **god′mother**) ; **god′send,** unexpected good fortune ; **god′speed,** a wish for success, or for a safe journey.

gog'gle-eyed, -id, *adj.* with staring eyes.

gog'gles, *n.pl.* a kind of spectacles.

goitre, goi'ter, *n.* a neck swelling.

gōld, *n.* a precious yellow metal: riches.—*adj.* of, or like, gold.— *adj.* gold'en, of, or like, gold: very fine.—*ns.* gold'field, a place where gold is found; gold'finch, a small beautiful, many-coloured bird, common in Britain during summer; gold'fish, a kind of Chinese carp, golden-yellow, often kept in aquaria; gold'smith, a maker of gold articles.—golden mean, wedding, see mean, wedding.

golf, *n.* a game in which a ball is struck with various clubs round a *course* (usually 18 'holes').

gollywog, gol'i-wog, *n.* a doll with black face and bristling hair.

golosh. See galosh.

gon'dola, *n.* a boat used on Venice canals: the car of an airship.— *n.* gondolier (gon-dol-ēr'), a boatman who rows a gondola.

gong, *n.* a metal plate which, when struck, gives a booming sound; used as a call to meals and by the time-keeper in a boxing-match.

good, *adj.* well-formed: fit: valuable: well-behaved: kind: holy. —*n.pl.* goods, one's belongings: things to be bought and sold.— *n.* good'ness, the quality of being good.—*adjs.* good-for-nothing, useless, lazy; good'ly, of fine appearance: fair-sized: valuable; good-nā'tured, kind, cheerful.— *ns.* Good Friday, Friday before Easter Sunday; good'will, kind wishes: the right to deal with the customers of a shop.—good-mor'ning, good-mor'row (=*good-morning*), good-day', good-aft'er-noon, good-e'vening, good-night', good-bye', words used as greeting when meeting or leaving a friend.

goose, *n.* (*pl.* geese) a web-footed bird larger than a duck: a silly person.—*n.* goose'flesh, a rough feeling in the skin caused by cold or fear.

gooseberry, gooz'ber-i, *n.* an eatable berry.

Gord'ian, *adj.* used in the phrase to cut the Gordian knot, to get out of difficulty by bold means.

gore, *n.* a thick mass of blood: blood. —*adj.* gor'y, covered with blood.

gore, *v.* (of bulls) to pierce with the horns.

gorge, gorj, *n.* the throat: a narrow pass among hills.—*v.* to swallow greedily.

gorgeous, gor'jus, *adj.* showy, splendid: magnificent.

Gor'gon, *n.* a monster of old-time fables, whose glance turned people to stone: any stern-looking person.

gorgonzō'la, *n.* a strong kind of cheese.

goril'la, *n.* the largest kind of ape.

gor'mandise, *v.* to eat greedily.

gorse. See furze.

gos'hawk, *n.* a short-winged hawk.

gos'ling, *n.* a young goose.

gos'pel, *n.* the teachings of Christ: His life-story as told by Matthew, Mark, Luke, or John: absolute truth.

gos'samer, *n.* fine spider-threads floating in the air or lying on bushes: any thin material.

gos'sip, *n.* one who listens to and passes on chatter: idle talk.—*v.* to tell idle tales: to chatter.

Gothic, *adj.* (of buildings) having high-pointed arches, clustered columns, etc.

gouda, gow'da, *n.* a kind of cheese.

gouge, gowj or gooj, *n.* a chisel, with a hollow blade, for cutting grooves.—*v.* to scoop out.

gourd, goord, *n.* a large fleshy fruit: the skin of a gourd used as a drinking-cup.

gourmand, goor'mand, *n.* one who eats greedily: a glutton.—*n.* gourmet (goor-mā), one with a taste for good wines.

gout, gowt, *n.* a painful swelling of the smaller joints, esp. of the great toe.—*adj.* gout'y.

govern, guv'ern, *v.* to rule, control: to put laws into action.—*ns.* gov'ernment, rule: control: the statesmen who rule a country; gov'erness, a lady who teaches girls, young children, at their home; gov'ernor, a ruler: a part of an engine which controls its speed of working.

gown, *n.* a woman's upper garment: a long loose robe worn by clergymen, lawyers, headmasters, teachers, etc.

grab, *v.* to seize or grasp suddenly : to lay hands on, esp. by rough or unjust means.—*n.* a sudden grasp or catch.

grace, *n.* beauty of form : favour : pardon : God's mercy : a short prayer at a meal : the title of a duke or archbishop.—*adjs.* **grace′ful,** beautiful in appearance : done in a neat way ; **gracious** (grā′-shus), kind : polite : coming by God's favour ; **grace′less,** wicked.

grade, *n.* a step or placing according to quality or rank : class : slope.—*v.* to arrange in order (e.g. from easy to difficult).—*ns.* **gradā′-tion,** arrangement in order (e.g. of rank, difficulty, etc.) ; **grā′dient,** a slope (on a road, railway, etc.). —*adj.* **grad′ual,** step by step : going slowly but steadily.— *adv.* **grad′ually.**

grad′uate, *v.* to divide into regular spaces : to pass university examinations and receive a degree.— *n.* one who has done so.— *n.* **graduā′tion,** the act of getting a degree from a university.

Graf, *n.* a German title meaning Count.

graft, *v.* to fix a shoot or twig of one plant upon another, so that it may grow there : to put skin from one part of the body upon another part.

graft, *n.* profit made against the law.—Also *v.*

Grail, *n.* (in old-time stories) the plate used by Christ at the Last Supper.

grain, *n.* a seed (e.g. of wheat, oats) : corn in general : a very small quantity : a very small weight : the run of the marking lines in wood, leather, etc.—*v.* to paint in imitation of the grain of wood.

gram, gramme, *n.* the unit of weight in the metric system.

gram′mar, *n.* the study of the right use of words : a book which teaches grammar.—*ns.* **grammā′-rian,** one with great knowledge of grammar ; **gram′mar-school,** a higher school (in olden times a school in which Latin and Greek grammar were taught).—*adj.* **grammat′ical,** correct according to rules of grammar.

gramme. See gram.

gramophone, gram′o-fōn, *n.* an instrument which produces speech, music, singing, etc. from a record.

gram′pus, *n.* the killer-whale.

gran′ary, *n.* a storehouse for grain.

grand, *adj.* great : noble.—*ns.* **grand′father,** one's father's or mother's father ; **grand′mother,** one's father's or mother's mother ; **grand′child, grand′son, grand′-daughter,** a son's or daughter's child ; **grand′pārents,** one's grandfather and grandmother ; **grandee′,** a man of high rank ; **grand′duke,** a duke of specially high rank ; **grandeur** (grand′ūr), great beauty : greatness ; **grand′piano,** a piano with a large flat top.

grandiloquent, gran - dil′o - kwent, *adj.* speaking in high-sounding language.

grandiose, gran′di-ōz, *adj.* trying to make a great show : boasting.

grange, grānj, *n.* a farmhouse with its stables and other buildings.

granite, gran′it, *n.* a hard rock of greyish or reddish colour.

gran′ny, *n.* a grandmother : an old woman.

grant, *v.* to give : to allow : to admit as true—*n.* something given.

gran′ule, *n.* a tiny grain or part.— *adjs.* **gran′ular,** made up of grains ; **gran′ulāted,** broken into grains.

grape, *n.* the fruit of the vine.—*ns.* **grape′fruit,** a fruit like a large orange ; **grape′shot,** shot which scatters when fired.

graph, grahf, *n.* line (or lines) drawn on squared paper to show changes in quantity (e.g. temperature, rainfall, distance travelled, money spent).—*adj.* **graph′ic,** lively, well told.

graphite, graf′īt, *n.* blacklead (used in making pencils).

grap′nel, *n.* a small anchor with several claws or arms.

grap′ple, *v.* to come to grips (with).

grasp, *v.* to clasp with fingers or arms : to understand.—*n.* handgrip : one's power of understanding.—*adj.* **grasp′ing,** greedy, mean.

grass, *n.* a kind of plant with long narrow leaves (wheat, reeds, bamboo, sugar-cane are *grasses*): the green covering of fields: pasture.—*adj.* **grass′y**, covered with grass: green like grass.— *n.* **grass′hopper**, a jumping insect, like the locust and cricket; **grass-widow**, a woman whose husband is away.

grate, *n.* a framework of iron bars for holding burning coals.—*n.* **grā′ting**, a frame of iron bars.

grate, *v.* to wear away with anything rough: to rub down small: to make a harsh sound: to make angry or displeased.—*n.* **grāt′er**, an instrument with a rough surface for rubbing small.

grateful, **grāt′fool**, *adj.* causing pleasure: thankful.—*v.* **grat′ify**, to please.—*ns.* **gratificā′tion**, pleasure; **grat′itude**, thankfulness: desire to return kindness.

gra′tis, *adv.* for nothing: without payment.

gratuity, **gra-tū′i-ti**, *n.* a money gift in return for something done.— *adj.* **gratuitous** (gra-tū′i-tus), done without payment: done without reason (e.g. a *gratuitous* insult).

grave, *n.* a pit in which to bury the dead.—*n.* **graveyard**, a place where dead are buried: cemetery.

grave, *adj.* important: serious: not gay or showy.—*n.* **grav′ity**.

grav′el, *n.* small stones or pebbles: sand and stones mixed.

grā′ven, *adj.* carved (e.g. image).

grā′ving-dock. See **dock**.

grav′ity, *n.* weight: seriousness: importance: force of attraction (e.g. that force which causes things to fall to the ground).—*v.* **grav′itāte**, to move towards as if strongly attracted.

grā′vy, *n.* the juice got from meat while cooking.

gray. See **grey**.

gray′ling, *n.* a fish of the salmon kind.

graze, *v.* to feed on grass.—*ns.* **grāz′ier**, one who grazes cattle for market; **grāz′ing**, cattle-rearing: grass land fit for cattle.

graze, *v.* to pass lightly along the surface: to touch in passing.—*n.* a flick, a light touch.

grease, *n.* thick animal fat: oily matter of any kind.—*v.* to smear with grease.—*adj.* **greas′y**.

great, **grāt**, *adj.* large: heavy: long-lasting: noble: mighty.—*ns.* **great′ness**; **great′-grand′parents**, the father and mother of a grandfather or grandmother; **great′-grand′child**, the son or daughter of a grandson or granddaughter.

greaves, *n.pl.* old-time armour of leather, etc., for the legs.

grebe, **grēb**, *n.* a short-winged, tailless water-bird.

greed, *n.* great and selfish desire. —*adj.* **greed′y**, wishing for too much (esp. food and money).—*n.* **greed′iness**.

Greek, **Grecian**, **grē′shan**, *adjs.* belonging to Greece.—*n.* **Greek**, the language of the people of Greece.

green, *adj.* of the colour of growing grass: strong and lively: unripe: knowing little, easily taken in.—*n.* the colour of growing grass: ground covered with grass: (*pl.*) green vegetables for food.—*ns.* **green′ery**, green plants; **green′ness**; **green′gāge**, a kind of plum, green but sweet; **green′-grōcer**, one who sells fresh vegetables; **green′horn**, a person who knows little and is easily taken in; **green′house**, a glass-house for growing plants; **green′sward**, smooth turf, green with grass.— *adj.* **green-eyed** (-īd), jealous.

greet, *v.* to speak to a person with kind words, to say 'Hullo,' 'Good-day,' etc.: to send kind wishes to.—*n.* **greet′ing**, words of joy, kindness.

greeve, *n.* a farm-manager.—Also **grieve**.

gregarious, **gre-gā′ri-us**, *adj.* living in flocks and herds.

grenade′, *n.* a small bomb.—*n.pl.* **grenadiers** (gren-a-deers′), once, soldiers who threw grenades; now, the first regiment of foot-guards, the Grenadier Guards.

grey, **gray**, **grā**, *adj.* ash-coloured (white mixed with black): grey-haired, old.—*n.* grey colour: a grey horse.—*ns.* **grey′beard**, an old man: a kind of jug used for drinking; **grey′hound**, a fast-running dog, used for chasing hares and dog-racing.

grid, *n.* a grating of bars : a gridiron : part of a wireless valve : a network of wires carrying electricity through the country.

grid′dle. See gird′le.

grid′iron, *n.* a frame of iron bars for cooking flesh or fish over the fire.

grief, grēf, *n.* sorrow.

grieve. See greeve.

grieve, grēv, *v.* to feel sorrow : to make sorrowful, to vex.—*n.* **griev′ance**, a wrong : a cause for complaining.—*adj.* **griev′ous**, painful : causing grief.

grif′fin, **grif′fon**, *n.* (in fables) an animal, with the body and legs of a lion and the beak and wings of an eagle.

grill, *v.* to cook on a gridiron over a fire : to torment.—*n.* a gridiron : grilled meat.—*n.* **grill′room**, an eating-place where beefsteaks, etc. are grilled to one's order.

grille, gril, *n.* a grating of open-work metal over a door or window.

grilse, *n.* a young salmon.

grim, *adj.* fierce-looking : stern.—*n.* **grim′ness.**

grimace, gri-mās′, *n.* a twisting of the face in fun or pain.—Also *v.*

grime, *n.* dirt.—*adj.* **gri′my.**

grin, *v.* to smile in a silly or cruel manner, showing the teeth.— Also *n.*—**to grin and bear**, to suffer without complaining.

grind, *v.* to rub or crush to powder : to sharpen by rubbing : to study hard.—*n.* hard or unpleasant work : hard study.—*ns.* **grind′er**, one who grinds : a double tooth ; **grind′stone**, a large turning-stone for grinding or sharpening tools.

grip, *n.* firm hold with the hand or mind : the handle or part by which anything is held.—*v.* to take fast hold of.

gripe, *v.* to squeeze : to give pain (e.g. in the stomach).—*n.* a tight hold : a pain in the stomach.

grisly, griz′li, *adj.* frightful : hideous.

grist, *n.* corn for grinding : a supply of something.

gristle, gris′l, *n.* a tough, elastic substance in meat.—*adj.* **grist′ly.**

grit, *n.* small pebbles : dust : firmness of character, pluck.—*v.* to set one's teeth when one is faced with danger.—*adj.* **gritty**, sandy : plucky.

grizzled, griz′ild, *adj.* grey, or mixed with grey.—*adj.* **grizz′ly**, of a grey colour.—*n.* the grizzly bear.

groan, *v.* to utter a moaning sound in trouble.—Also *n.*

groat, *n.* an old silver coin, worth fourpence.

groats, *n.pl.* oat grains without the husks.

grocer, grōs′er, *n.* a dealer in tea, sugar, etc.—*n.pl.* **gro′ceries**, articles sold by grocers.

grog, *n.* a mixture of spirits and cold water, without sugar.—*adj.* **grog′gy**, weak and staggering (from blows or illness).

grog′ram, *n.* a kind of coarse cloth.

groin, *n.* the part of the body where the thigh joins the trunk.

groom, *n.* one who has the charge of horses : a man who is being married.—*v.* to look after (esp. a horse) : to smarten.—*n.* **grooms′-man**, a 'best man,' i.e. one who attends a bridegroom at his marriage.

groove, *n.* a furrow or long hollow.—*v.* to cut a groove.

grope, *v.* to search by feeling.

gross, *adj.* coarse : glaring : stupid : shameful : having nothing taken off (e.g. His *gross* profit was £1000 ; when his debts were paid £500 remained—his *net* profit was £500).—*n.* the whole taken together : twelve dozen (144).—*n.* **gross′ness**, rudeness.

grotesque, grō-tesk′, *adj.* queer : stupidly silly (e.g. a *grotesque* story).

grot′to, *n.* a cave :—*pl.* **grott′os.**

ground, *n.* the soil : a good reason (e.g. Have you any *ground* for complaint ?) : surface on which pictures, etc. are drawn : (*pl.*) lands surrounding a castle, mansion-house, etc. : useless matter lying at the bottom of liquids (e.g. *coffee-grounds*).—*v.* (of ships) to strike the bottom and remain stuck.—*adjs.* **ground′-ed**, having a good foundation ; (aeroplanes) unable to fly ; **ground′less**, without reason.—*ns.* **ground′-floor**, storey at street-level ; **ground′ing**, first steps in learning something ; **ground′-swell**, broad ocean waves ; **ground′-work**, first stages of anything.

ground'sel, *n.* a wild plant with clusters of small yellow flowers.

group, groop, *n.* a number of persons or things together.—*v.* to form into a group.

grouse, *n.* a game-bird hunted on moors and hills.

grove, *n.* a small wood: a shady walk.

grov'el, *v.* to lie flat, esp. in fright: to make one's self humble.

grow, grō, *v.* to become bigger or stronger: to go forward from one state to another: to become: to rear plants, trees, etc.—*n.* **growth.**

growl, *v.* to utter a deep sound like that of a dog.—Also *n.*

grub, *n.* the form of an insect after being hatched from the egg (e.g. caterpillar): (*slang*) food.—*v.* to dig up: (*slang*) to eat.—*adj.* **grub'by,** dirty.—*n.* **grub'ber,** a farm-tool for digging out weeds.

grudge, gruj, *v.* to give unwillingly: to show discontent at another's success.—*n.* cause of quarrel: bad feeling.

gruel, groo'el, *n.* a thin mixture of oatmeal boiled in water.—*adj.* **gru'elling,** very tiring.

gruesome, groo'sum, *adj.* horrible: fearful.

gruff, *adj.* rough in manner.

grum'ble, *v.* to murmur with discontent.—Also *n.*

grum'py, *adj.* cross, peevish.

grunt, *v.* to make a sound like that of a pig.—Also *n.*

guano, gwa'nō, *n.* droppings of sea-birds used as manure.

guarantee, gar-an-tē', *n.* a promise to stand good for another: a statement that a thing (e.g. a watch) will work well: money put down which will be given up if a promise is broken.—*v.* to make sure, to give a guarantee.—*n.* **guar'antor,** one who pays up if a promise is broken.

guard, gard, *v.* to keep safe from danger or attack.—*n.* that which guards: a man or group of men whose duty it is to protect: one in charge of railway-train or coach: a position of defence (in boxing, cricket, fencing, etc.): a watch-chain: (*pl.*) the name for certain regiments.—*adj.* **guard'ed,**

careful.—*ns.* **guard'ian,** one who takes care (e.g. of an orphan); **guards'man,** a soldier of the Guards.

guava, gwa'va, *n.* a tree with yellow pear-shaped fruit.

gud'dle, *v.* to catch fish with the hands.

gudgeon, guj'un, *n.* a small fresh-water fish: a metal pin at the end of a shaft.

guerdon, ger'dun, *n.* a reward.

guerilla, guerrilla, ger-ril'a, *n.* a method of fighting in which many small bands keep on worrying a bigger army but do not fight a battle in the open: a member of such a band.—Also *adj.*

guernsey, gern'zi, *n.* a sailor's closely-fitting knitted woollen shirt: a kind of dairy cow.

guess, ges, *v.* to say without sure knowledge: to say what is likely to be the case.—*n.* a judgment or opinion given without exact counting or working out.

guest, gest, *n.* a visitor: one who is invited.

guffaw', *v.* to laugh loudly.—Also *n.*

guide, gīd, *v.* to show the way to.—*n.* one who shows the way: one who points out interesting things about a place: a book (*guide-book*) telling about a place.—*n.* **guid'ance,** facts or advice which help one to act properly; **guided missile,** an explosive weapon which after being fired can be guided to its target by radio waves.

guild, gild, *n.* a company of persons joined together for a special reason (e.g. *guild* of merchants).

guile, gīl, *n.* clever fraud: deceit.

guillemot, gil'e-mot, *n.* diving bird.

guillotine, gil'ō-tēn, *n.* an instrument for beheading (used in France): a machine for cutting paper.—*v.* to behead with the guillotine.

guilt, gilt, *n.* wickedness: blame for wrong-doing (e.g. for breaking a law).—*adj.* **guilt'y.**

guinea, gin'i, *n.* twenty-one shillings (there was once a gold coin of this amount).—*ns.* **guin'ea-fowl,** a bird, something like a pheasant, having white-spotted feathers; **guinea-pig,** a gnawing animal, about the size of a rabbit.

guise, gīz, *n.* appearance: dress: custom.

guitar, gi-tar′, *n.* a six-stringed musical instrument, something like a banjo.

gulch, *n.* a narrow rocky valley.

gulf, *n.* a large inlet of the sea.

gull, *n.* web-footed sea-bird.

gul′let, *n.* throat: passage by which food goes down into stomach.

gull′ible, *adj.* easily tricked.

gul′ly, *n.* channel worn by water.

gulp, *v.* to swallow eagerly or in large mouthfuls.—Also *n.*

gum, *n.* the firm flesh in which the teeth grow.—*n.* **gum′boil,** a boil on the gum, causing swollen face.

gum, *n.* sticky juice got from some trees and plants.—*v.* to stick with gum.—*adj.* **gum′my,** sticky.

gumption, gum′shn, *n.* good sense.

gun, *n.* any weapon firing bullets or shells: a cannon.—*ns.* **gun′boat,** small warship with heavy guns; **gun′-carriage,** wheeled support for a field-gun: **gun′-cotton,** a powerful explosive; **gun′-metal,** mixture of copper and tin; **gun′nery,** knowledge about firing guns; **gunpowder,** an explosive in powder form; **gun′-running,** bringing guns into a country against the law; **gun′shot,** distance over which a gun can fire.— **to stick to one's guns,** to hold on to one's opinion.

gunwale, gun′el, *n.* the upper edge of a ship's side.

gur′gle, *v.* to flow making a bubbling sound.

gush, *v.* to flow out in a strong stream: to talk too freely, without thinking.—*n.* a strong flow.

gus′set, *n.* a cornered piece of cloth

put into a garment to strengthen some part of it.

gust, *n.* a sudden blast (e.g. of wind): a violent burst of feeling.—*adj.* **gust′y,** stormy.

gust, *n.* pleasure of tasting. — *n.* **gust′o,** taste: eagerness.

gut, *n.* a narrow passage in the body: cord for violin - strings, fishing-hooks, etc.: (*pl.*) the bowels.—*v.* to take out the inner parts: to destroy completely.

gut′ta-perch′a, *n.* the hardened juice of various trees: rubber.

gut′ter, *n.* a water-channel (e.g. on a roof, at the roadside).

gut′tural, *adj.* harsh in sound, as if formed in the throat: having to do with the throat.—*n.* a letter whose sound comes from the throat.

guy, gī, *n.* a steadying rope for tent, etc.

guy, gī, *n.* an image of Guy Fawkes, burned on 5th November: a queerly dressed person.

guz′zle, *v.* to eat or drink greedily.

gymkhana, jim-ka′na, *n.* a games-meeting.

gymnasium, jim-nā′zi-um, *n.* a building or room fitted out for body exercising :—*pl.* **gymnā′sia.** —*n.pl.* **gymnas′tics,** exercises to strengthen the body.—*n.* **gym′nast,** one who teaches or does gymnastics.—*adj.* **gymnas′tic,** having to do with bodily exercises.

gypsum, jip′sum, *n.* a softish chalk-like mineral.

gypsy, gipsy, jip′si, *n.* a wandering person living in a caravan.

gyrate, jī′rāt, *v.* to whirl round.—*n.* **gyrā′tion.**—*adj.* **gy′ratory.**

gyroscope, jī′ro-skōp, *n.* an arrangement, like a large heavy top, sometimes used for steadying ships, torpedoes, etc.

gyves, jīvz, *n.pl.* chains, fetters.

H

haberdash′ery, *n.* such goods as ribbons, tape, etc.—*n.* **haberdash′er,** a person who sells haberdashery.

habil′iment, *n.* a garment.

hab′it, *n.* something one has got

used to doing: one's ordinary behaviour: a person's usual way of dressing: tight-fitting dress (*riding-habit*) worn by ladies on horseback.—*adj.* **habit′ual,** usual, formed by habit.—*v.* **habit′uāte,** to make accustomed.—*n.* **habitué** (hab-it´ū-ā), a regular attender (e.g. He is an *habitué* of the theatre).

hab´itable, *adj.* that may be dwelt in.—*ns.* **hab´itant**, one who dwells in a place ; **hab´itat**, the natural home of an animal or plant ; **habita´tion**, a dwelling-place.

hack, *v.* to cut in pieces.—*n.* a rough cut.—*n.* **hack´saw**, a saw for cutting metal.

hack, *n.* a horse kept for hire : a person who does hard work for another, and is poorly paid.

hackle, *v.* and *n.* See **heckle**.

hack´neyed, *adj.* stale : too much used (e.g. 'Mary had a little lamb . . .' is a *hackneyed* poem). —*n.* **hack´ney-carriage**, a carriage let out for hire.

had´dock, *n.* a small sea-fish.

Hades, hā´dēz, *n.* the dwelling-place of the dead, in old-time stories : hell.

hæmorrhage, hemorrhage, hem´or-āj, *n.* a bleeding.

haft, *n.* a handle.

hag, *n.* an ugly old woman : a witch.

hag´gard, *adj.* tired and weak-looking : wild-eyed with worry.

hag´gis, *n.* a Scottish, pudding-like food, made from the heart, lungs, and liver of a sheep, chopped up with suet, onions, oatmeal, etc., and boiled in a sheep's stomach-bag.

hag´gle, *v.* to be slow and hard in making a bargain.

hail, *v.* to greet : to call to.—*n.* a call : greeting.—**Hail!** a word of welcome ; **to hail from**, to come from.

hail, *n.* frozen raindrops : a shower (e.g. of bullets, shells, etc.).—*n.* **hail´storm**, a storm in which hail falls.

hair, *n.* thread-like growth from the skin of an animal : the whole mass of these (as on the head).— *ns.* **hair´breadth, hair´s´breadth**, a very small distance ; **hair´dresser**, one who cuts hair : a barber ; **hair´-spring**, a very fine spring (e.g. in balance-wheel of a watch). —*adjs.* **hair´y**, covered with hair ; **hair´-raising**, causing great fear.— **to split hairs**, to be very particular over unimportant details.

hake, *n.* a fish something like a cod.

hal´berd, *n.* a weapon (a battle-axe fixed on a long pole).—*n.* **halberdier´**, a soldier armed with a halberd.

halcyon, hal´si-un, *n.* the kingfisher. —**halcyon days**, a time of peace and happiness.

hale, *adj.* healthy : sound in body.

hale, *v.* to drag.

half, hahf, *n.* one of two equal parts: —*pl.* **halves** (hahvz).—*adj.* made up of two equal parts.—*v.* **halve** (hahv), to cut in two.—*ns.* **half-breed, half´-caste** (-kast), a person having father and mother of different races, esp. white and black ; **half´-brothers, half´-sisters**, brothers or sisters having only one parent the same ; **half-crown´**, a silver coin (2½ shillings, not now in use) ; **halfpenny** (hā´-pen-i), a copper coin (not now in use) ; **half´ sovereign**, (-sov´rin), a gold coin (10 shillings); (not used); **half´-truth**, a statement that is only partly true.—*adjs.* **half´-heart´ed**, not caring much, not eager ; **half´-wit´ted**, weak in the mind.—*adv.* **half´-mast**, (of flags) hoisted half-way up the mast, to show that some well-known person has died.

hal´ibut, *n.* the largest kind of flat-fish.

hall, hawl, *n.* a passage or large room at entrance to a house : a large room : a large country house, the home of a squire or land-owner : a college.

Hallelujah, hal-e-loo´ya, *n.* an exclamation meaning ' Praise ye the Lord ' : a song of praise to God.

hall-mark, hawl´-mark, *n.* a mark put on gold and silver articles to show the quality of the gold or silver : any mark which shows that a thing is good.

halloo´, *n.* a cry to draw attention : a huntsman's cry.—Also *v.*

hallow, hal´ō, *v.* to make holy : to set apart for holy use.—*n.* **Hall´ow-e´en**, the evening of Oct. 31st, next day being **Hall´owmas**, the Feast of All-Hallows, or All-Saints.

hallucination, hal-loo-sin-ā´shun, *n.* an idea that one is seeing something (which really is not there): a false idea.

hā′lō, *n.* a circle of light round the sun or moon: a ring of light around the head (as in pictures of saints).

halt, hawlt, *v.* to stop from going on. —*n.* a stop in walking: a stopping-place.

halt, hawlt, *v.* to be lame, to limp: to walk unsteadily: to be uncertain.—*adj.* lame, crippled, limping.

halter, hawlt′er, *n.* a head-rope for holding and leading a horse.

halve. See **half.**

hal′yard, hal′liard, *n.* rope for hoisting or lowering sail, yard, or flag.

ham, *n.* the back of the thigh: thigh of pig, salted and dried.

hamadrȳ′ad, *n.* deadly Indian snake.

ham′let, *n.* a small village.

ham′mer, *n.* a tool for beating, or driving nails: a striking-piece in a clock, piano, pistol, etc.—*v.* to drive or shape with a hammer: to attack fiercely.—**hammer-and-tongs**, violently.

ham′mock, *n.* netting hung up by the corners, and used as a bed.

ham′per, *v.* to hinder.

ham′per, *n.* a large basket.

ham′string, *n.* sinew behind the knee on horse's hind-leg.—*v.* to lame by cutting this.

hand, *n.* the part of the body at the end of the arm: a pointer (e.g. of a clock): a measure (four inches): a workman: one's style of handwriting: side or direction: a player's set of cards.— *v.* to give with the hand.—*ns.* **hand′-bag**, a large purse carried by women; **hand′bill**, a small printed notice; **hand′book**, a small book (e.g. a guide-book); **hand′cuffs**, steel bands, joined by a short chain, put round the wrists of prisoners; **hand′ful**, as much as can be held in one hand; **hand′maid(en)**, a girl servant · **hand′work**, work done by hand; **hand′writing**, writing with pen or pencil.—*adjs.* **hand′-made, hand′-wrought**, made by hand.—**at hand**, near by; **hand-to-hand fighting**, fighting with fists, rifle-butts, bayonets; **out of hand**, out of

control; **to live from hand to mouth**, to use up what one has without thought for the future.

hand′icap, *v.* (in a race or competition) to give all an equal chance of winning by making things a little more difficult for the better ones: to hinder.—*n.* something which keeps back: a race in which the runners are handicapped.

hand′icraft, *n.* skilled work done by hand.—*n.* **hand′icraftsman.**

hand′iwork, hand′ywork, *n.* work done by the hands.

handkerchief, hang′ker-chif, *n.* a cloth for wiping the nose, etc.

hand′le, *v.* to touch, hold, or use with the hand: to manage.—*n.* that part of anything by which it is held in the hand.

handsome, han′sum, *adj.* good-looking: noble: generous.

han′dy, *adj.* clever with the hands: ready to the hand, near.—*ns.* **handi′ness; hand′y-man**, a man for doing odd jobs.

hang, *v.* to fix to some point off the ground: to hover in the air, as a hawk: to put a criminal to death by putting a rope round his neck and dropping him.—*n.* the way in which a thing hangs.—*ns.* **hang′er**, that on which a coat is hung: a short, curved sword; **hang′ing**, the killing of a criminal by hanging: (*pl.*) curtains; **hang′-man**, the man who hangs criminals.—*adj.* **hang′-dog**, mean, low, guilty-looking.—**to hang fire**, (of a gun) to be slow in going off: (of a plan) to be delayed.

hangar, *n.* a shed for housing aeroplanes.

hank, *n.* a coil or loop of string, rope, wool, etc.

hank′er, *v.* to long for.

hank′y-pank′y, *n.* trickery.

han′som-cab, *n.* a light two-wheeled cab with the driver's seat raised behind.

hap, *n.* chance: fortune.—*v.* to happen.—*adjs.* **hap-haz′ard**: relying on luck: happening without planning (also *adv.*); **hap′less**, unlucky.—*adv.* **hap′ly**, perhaps.

happen, *v.* to take place: to do by chance (e.g. I *happened* to find him).—*n.* **happ′ening**, an event.

hap'py, *adj.* lucky: joyful: very suitable.—*adv.* **happ'ily.**—*n.* **hap'piness.**—*adj.* **happ'y-go-luck'y,** easy-going, taking things as they come.

harangue, ha-rang', *n.* a loud speech to a crowd.—Also *v.*

harass', *v.* to vex sorely, to annoy: to make sudden attacks on.

harbinger, har'bin-jer, *n.* a sign of something to come (e.g. The swallow is the *harbinger* of summer).

harbour, har'bur, *n.* a place of refuge or shelter: a port for ships.—*v.* to give refuge or shelter: to store (e.g. unkind thoughts) in the mind. — *ns.* **har'bour-dues,** charges for the use of a harbour; **har'bour-mas'ter,** the officer who has charge of a harbour.

hard, *adj.* solid, firm: not easily broken or put out of shape: not easy to understand: not easy to please: mean about money: having no kind or gentle feelings: (of water) having much lime.—*adv.* close, near (e.g. *hard by,* very near).—*adv.* **hard'ly,** scarcely, not quite: with difficulty.—*v.* **har'den,** to make hard.—*n.* **hard'ness,** the state of being hard.—*adjs.* **hard'-head'ed,** clever, having good sense; **hard'-heart'ed,** having no kind feelings; **har'dy,** daring, brave: able to bear a rough life.—*ns.* **har'diness,** bravery, boldness; **har'dihood,** cheeky boldness; **hard-labour,** tiring work given to prisoners as part of their punishment; **hard'ship,** something not easy to bear (e.g. cold, want of food, money, etc.); **hard'ware,** a name for goods such as pots, pans, grates; **hard'wood,** the wood of the oak, ash, beech, elm, mahogany, and some other trees.—**hard hit,** hurt (e.g. by a loss of money); **hard lines, hard luck; hard of hearing,** pretty deaf; **hard up,** short of money; **to die hard,** to die only after a great struggle for life.

hare, *n.* a timid animal, like a large rabbit, with a divided upper lip and long hind-legs, which runs swiftly by leaps.—*ns.* **hare-and-hounds,** a game in which some set off on a long run across country, dropping pieces of paper (the scent) as they go, and others try to overtake, following their trail; **hare'bell,** a plant with blue bell-shaped flowers; **hare'-lip,** a divided upper lip like that of a hare.—*adj.* **hare'-brained,** careless about what one does: mad.

harem, hā'rem or ha-rēm', *n.* the women's rooms in a Mohammedan's house: the women in these.

hark, *v.* to listen.—**to hark back,** to go back to what was being spoken about.

harlequin, har'le-kwin or -kin, *n.* a clown, in a dress of many colours: a character in a pantomime.

har'lot, *n.* a woman who leads an evil life for money.

harm, *n.* hurt: wrong: mischief.—*v.* to cause damage: to do a wrong to.—*adjs.* **harm'ful; harm'less.**

har'mony, *n.* agreement of one part, colour, or sound with another: pleasant companionship: (in music) the putting together of sounds which go well with each other.—*adjs.* **harmon'ic,** having to do with harmony; **harmōn'ious,** pleasant-sounding: working together peacefully.—*v.* **har'monise,** to agree: to match: (in music) to provide the different parts (e.g. for a song).—*ns.* **harmō'nium,** a musical wind-instrument, like a small organ; **harmon'ica,** a mouth-organ.

har'ness, *n.* the leather and other fittings for a horse at work: armour of man or horse.—*v.* to put harness on a horse: to put armour on.

harp, *n.* a musical instrument played by plucking the strings with the fingers.—*v.* to play the harp.—**to harp on,** to talk much about.—*ns.* **harp'er, harp'ist.**

harpoon', *n.* a spear tied to a rope, used for capturing whales.—*v.* to hit with a harpoon.

harpsichord, harp'si-kord, *n.* an old-fashioned musical instrument something like a piano.

har'py, *n.* (in old fables) a monster with the body of a woman, wings, feet, and claws of a bird of prey : any person living on the wealth or strength of another.

harquebus. See **arquebus.**

har′rier, *n.* a small dog with a keen smell, for hunting hares : (*pl.*) hare-and-hounds runners.

harrow, har′ō, *n.* a frame with iron teeth or spikes for breaking-up clods in ploughed land, or for covering seeds.—*v.* to drag a harrow over : to worry the feelings.—*adj.* **harr′owing,** worrying to the feelings.

har′ry, *v.* to plunder, lay waste.

harsh, *adj.* rough : bitter : unkind.— *n.* **harsh′ness.**

hart, *n.* the stag or male deer from the age of six years :—*fem.* **hind.** —*ns.* **hart′ebeest, hart′beest,** a South African antelope ; **harts′horn,** ammonia (once got from the shavings of a hart's horn) ; **harts′tongue,** a kind of fern.

harum-scarum, hā′rum-skā′rum, *adj.* caring little about what one does or wears.—Also *n.*

har′vest, *n.* the time of gathering in the ripened crops : the crops gathered in.—*v.* to reap and gather in.—*ns.* **har′vester,** a reaper ; **har′vest-feast, har′vesthome,** the feast held at the bringing home of the harvest.

hash, *v.* to chop up.—*n.* a dish (e.g. of chopped meat) : old stuff done up for second use.—**to make a hash of,** to spoil completely.

hasp, *n.* a clasp or catch.—*v.* to fasten (a door) with a catch.

has′sock, *n.* a thick cushion used as a footstool or for kneeling on.

häste, *n.* speed, quickness, hurry. —*vs.* **haste, hasten** (hās′n), to hurry on : to drive forward.— *adj.* **hast′y,** hurried : done without thinking : quick-tempered.

hat, *n.* a covering for the head.—*ns.* **hat′ter,** one who makes or sells hats ; **hat′-trick,** (in cricket) the putting-out of three batsmen by one bowler, with three bowls, one after the other.

hatch, *n.* a roof-door, esp. in the deck of a ship : a lower half-door : a grating.—*n.* **hatch′way,** opening in a floor or ship's deck.

hatch, *v.* to produce young from

eggs : to set a plan working (often an evil plan).—*n.* **hatch′-ery,** a place for hatching eggs (esp. eggs of fish).

hatch, *v.* to shade with fine lines.

hatch′et, *n.* a small axe.—**to bury the hatchet,** to put an end to a quarrel.

hate, *v.* to dislike very much.—*n.* great dislike.—*adj.* **hate′ful,** causing hate.—*n.* **hāt′red,** very bitter feeling against.

haughty, haw′ti, *adj.* proud : looking down on others.—*n.* **haught′-iness.**

haul, *v.* to drag, pull with force.— *n.* a strong pull : that which is caught at one pull (e.g. a *haul* of fish) : a rich find : great profit.— *n.* **haul′age,** money charged for carrying goods.

haunch, hawnsh, *n.* the fleshy part of the hip.

haunt, *v.* to visit often : to hang about a place (e.g. A ghost *haunts* this old house).—*n.* a place often visited.—*adj.* **haunt′ed,** visited by ghosts.

hautboy. See **oboe.**

have, hav, *v.* to own or possess : to hold, contain.—**to have at,** to attack ; **to have done with,** to finish ; **to have out,** to settle (e.g. an argument).

hā′ven, *n.* an inlet of the sea with a safe place for anchoring, a harbour : a refuge.

hav′ersack, *n.* a cloth bag with shoulder-strap, for carrying food, etc.

hav′oc, *n.* great destruction.

haw. See **hawthorn.**

hawk, *n.* a bird of prey of the falcon kind.—*v.* to hunt birds with trained hawks.—*adj.* **hawk′-eyed,** having very good sight.

hawk, *v.* to carry goods about for sale.—*n.* **haw′ker,** a door-to-door merchant.

haw′ser, *n.* a strong rope used in towing ships.

haw′thorn, *n.* a prickly tree, with white flowers (often called *may*) and small red berries (*haws*).

hay, *n.* grass, cut and dried, used as cattle-food.—*ns.* **hay′cock,** a pile of hay in a field ; **hay′-fork,** a long-handled fork used in turning and lifting hay ; **hay'-fever,** an illness like a bad cold which affects some people in summer ; **hay'-rick, -stack,** hay built in a pile.

haz'ard, *n.* a game played with dice : a chance, a risk : (in golf) a difficulty to be played out of (e.g. bunker, road, bushes).—*v.* to risk : to try one's chance.—*adj.* **haz'ardous,** dangerous, risky.

haze, *n.* thin mist.—*adj.* **hāz'y,** overhung with a thin mist : not having clear ideas.—*n.* **haz'iness.**

hā'zel, *n.* a nut-bearing tree.—*adj.* light-brown in colour.

hē, *pron.* some (male) person already spoken about (subject of verb).

head, hed, *n.* uppermost part of the body, containing the brain : chief part, place, or person : a cape.—*v.* to lead : to go in front of : to check : to go straight for : to hit (a ball) with the head.—*ns.* **head'ache,** a pain inside the head ; **head'-dress,** a covering for the head ; **head'er,** a dive, head first, into water ; **head'-gear,** covering or ornament of the head ; **head'ing,** that which stands at the head (e.g. the title of a book or chapter) ; **head'land,** a point of land running out into the sea, a cape ; **head'-light,** a strong light carried in front (e.g. of a motorcar) ; **head'-line,** line at the top of a page in a newspaper ; **head'master,** the principal master of a school :—*fem.* **head'-mis'tress** ; **head'-piece,** a helmet ; **head'quarters,** place where the chief officers of an army stay : the chief office (e.g. of a business) ; **head'way,** forward movement ; **head'-wind,** a wind blowing straight in one's face.—*adjs.* **head'strong,** fond of doing what one likes, no matter what others say ; **head'y,** affecting the head.—*adv.* **head'long,** with the head first : without stopping.

heal, *v.* to make or become healthy or sound : to cure.—*n.* **health** (helth), the state of one's body : soundness of body : a wish (said while drinking) that someone may be well.—*adjs.* **health'ful,** full of health ; **health'y,** in good health.

heap, *n.* a pile of things thrown one on top of another.—*v.* to throw in a pile.

hear, *v.* to receive (sounds, news, music) by the ear : to listen to.—*n.* **hear'ing,** the act or power of listening : attentive listening : a court case.—*n.* **hear'say,** what one hears people say.—**Hear ! Hear !** a cry of applause for a speaker.

hearken, hark'n, *v.* to hear with attention.

hearse, herss, *n.* a carriage for carrying a dead body to burial.

heart, hart, *n.* the part of the body which acts as a blood-pump : the inner or chief part of anything : feelings of love : courage : eagerness : one of the signs on playing-cards.—*v.* **hearten** (hart'n), to cheer on.—*adjs.* **heart'-broken,** nearly dead with sorrow ; **heart'less,** cruel ; **heart-rending,** causing feelings of great sorrow ; **heart'y,** cheery : strong, healthy : done eagerly.—*n.* **heart'burn,** a burning feeling in the stomach after eating : indigestion ; **heart-failure,** death caused by the sudden stopping of the heart's beating.

hearth, harth, *n.* the floor of the fireplace : home.

heat, *n.* warmth : anger : a division of a race (e.g. The race will be run in five *heats*).—*v.* to make hot.— **heat barrier,** difficulty caused by heating of air round aircraft at very high speeds.

heath, *n.* a barren open country : a small-flowered heath plant.

heath'en, *n* one who does not believe in our God, esp. one who worships idols.—*n.* **heath'endom,** lands where heathen people live.—*adj.* **heath'enish,** not civilised : savage : cruel.

heather, heth'er, *n.* a plant with small purple or white flowers growing on moorland.

heave, *v.* to lift by force : to throw : to push : to rise and fall.—*n.* a throw : a push : rise and fall.— **to heave in sight,** come in sight.

heaven, hev'n *n.* the sky : the dwelling-place of God : any place of great happiness.—*adj.* **heav'enly,** dwelling in heaven : delightful.—**heavenly bodies,** the sun, moon, and stars.

heavy, hev'i, *adj.* having great weight: not easy to bear: severe: slow: dull: sleepy.—*n.* **heav'iness.**

Hebrew, hē'broo, *n.* a Jew: the language of the Jews.—Also *adj.*

heck'le, *v.* (in an election) to test a speaker by asking him awkward questions.—*n.* **heck'le,** the long shining feathers on a cock's neck.

hec'tic, *adj.* flushed in the face, fevered: exciting.

hec'tor, *v.* to annoy: to bully.

hedge, hej, *n.* a fence or thicket of bushes, shrubs, etc.—*v.* to shut in with a hedge: to avoid giving a straight answer.—*ns.* **hedge'hog,** a small prickly-backed animal, with a snout like a pig's; **hedge'row,** a row of trees or bushes round a field or along a lane.

heed, *v.* to give attention to, to listen to.—Also *n.*—*adj.* **heed'less,** careless: having no thought of.

heel, *n.* back part of the foot.—*v.* to hit with the heel: to put a heel on (a shoe).—**down-at-heel,** poorly and untidily dressed: **to take to one's heels, to show a clean pair of heels,** to run away.

heel, *v.* (of ships) to lean over.

heifer, hef'er, *n.* a young cow.

height, hīt, *n.* the state of being high: distance upwards: the highest point: a high place.—*v.* **height'en,** to make higher.

heinous, hā'nus, *adj.* very wicked.

heir, ār, *n.* one who by right gets a title or property on the death of the owner:—*fem.* **heiress** (ār'es).—*ns.* **heir'-appā'rent,** one who is expected to succeed to title or property; **heir'loom,** something valuable that has been handed down in the family from generation to generation; **heir'-presumptive,** one who will be heir unless a nearer relative is born.

helicopter, *n.* a flying machine kept in the air by rotating propellers which enable it to go straight up and down.

heliograph, hē'li-o-graf, *n.* a means of signalling, using the sun's rays.

heliotrope, hē'li-o-trōp, *n.* a plant with small, sweet-smelling lilac-blue flowers: a light purple colour.

helium, hēl'i-um, *n.* a very light gas, which does not explode.

hell, *n.* the place of punishment of the wicked after death: the dwelling-place of evil spirits: any place of great wickedness or destruction.

helm, *n.* the wheel or handle by which a ship is steered.—*n.* **helms'man,** the one who steers.

helm, hel'met, *n.* a covering of armour for the head.

help, *v.* to aid: to give the means for doing something: to keep from doing (e.g. I cannot *help* liking him).—*n.* aid: one who aids.—*adjs.* **help'ful,** useful; **help'less,** useless: powerless.—*ns.* **help'ing,** a share (e.g. of food); **help'mate, help'meet,** a partner (e.g. one's husband or wife).

hel'ter-skel'ter, *adv.* in a great hurry.

helve, *n.* the handle of an axe or hammer.

hem, *n.* the border of a garment doubled down and stitched.—*v.* to form a hem on: to edge.—**to hem in,** to surround.

hemisphere, hem'is-fēr, *n.* a half of the globe, or a map of it (*western, eastern, northern, southern hemisphere*).

hem'lock, *n.* a poisonous plant.

hemp, *n.* a plant with a stringy bark used for making ropes, bags, sails, etc.—*adj.* **hemp'en.**

hen, *n.* a female bird.—*n.* **hen'coop,** large cage for fowls.—*v.* **hen'peck,** (of a wife) to worry a husband into always giving way.

hence, *adv.* from this place or time: in the future: for this reason.— **Hence ! Away !**—*advs.* **hence'forth, hencefor'ward,** from now on.

henchman, hensh'—, *n.* follower.

hep'tagon, *n.* a flat figure with seven angles and seven sides.

her, *pron.* a female person already spoken about (object of verb).—*adj.* belonging to such person.

her'ald, *n.* a person who carries and reads important notices: one who sees to coats of arms, crests, etc.: something that goes before and acts as a sign.—*v.* to announce loudly: to be a sign of.—*n.* **her'aldry,** the study of coats of arms, badges, crests, etc.—*adj.* **heral'dic,** having to do with heraldry.

herb, *n.* a plant the stem of which dies every year (a tree or shrub has a lasting stem): a plant used in the making of medicines.—*adj.* **herbā'ceous**, having to do with herbs.—*ns.* **herbage** (herb'āj), green food for cattle: pasture: herbs; **herb'alist**, one who studies, collects, or sells herbs; **herbā'rium**, a collection of plants or herbs dried and divided into their different kinds.—*adj.* **herbiv'orous**, eating or living on grass, etc.

Herculean, her-kū'lē-an, *adj.* very difficult or dangerous: very strong, giant-like. (In Greek stories *Hercules* was a giant who had twelve very difficult tasks to do.)

herd, *n.* a flock of animals of one kind: one who tends sheep or cattle: a mob.—*v.* to go in herds: to tend sheep or cattle.

here, *adv.* in this place.—*advs.* **hereafter**, **hereupon**, after this.

heredity, *n.* the passing on of qualities (appearance, diseases, habits) from parents to children.—*adj.* **hered'itary**, passed on thus.

heresy, *n.* an opinion which goes against what is believed by most people.—*n.* **her'etic**, one who holds or teaches such an opinion.—*adj.* **heret'ical**.

heritage, her'it-āj, *n.* something received by will: something one has because of one's birth.—*adj.* **her'itable**, able to be handed down by will from father to son.—*n.* **her'itor**, (in Scotland) a landholder in a parish.

hermaphrodite, her-maf'rod-īt, *n.* an animal or plant in which are united the qualities of both male and female (e.g. a worm).

hermetically sealed, closed completely (e.g. a glass tube whose opening is closed by melting the glass).

hermit, *n.* one who lives alone.—*n.* **her'mitage**, dwelling of a hermit: a lonely house.

hern. Same as heron.

hēro, *n.* a man of great bravery: the chief male person in a story:—*pl.* **hē'roes**; *fem.* **heroine** (her'ō-in).—*adj.* **herō'ic**, like a hero: brave.—*n.* **heroism** (her'ō-izm), bravery.

heron, her'un, *n.* a large water-bird, with long legs and neck.

Herr, *n.* the German word for Mr:—*pl.* **Her'ren**.

her'ring, *n.* a small eatable sea-fish.—**red herring**, herring salted and dried: a small matter brought up to draw attention away from some more serious matter.

hes'itate, *v.* to be in doubt: to stop, because of uncertainty: to stammer in talking.—*ns.* **hes'itancy**, **hesitā'tion**, doubt: uncertainty: stammering.—*adj.* **hes'itant**.

het'erodox, *adj.* holding opinions different from those held by most people.—*n.* **het'erodoxy**.

heterogeneous, het-er-o-jē'ne-us, *adj.* made up of different kinds.

hew, hū, *v.* to cut in pieces: to shape.—*n.* **hew'er**.

hex'agon, *n.* a figure with six sides and six angles.—*adj.* **hexag'onal**.

hey-day, hā'dā, *n.* the time of greatest strength.

hiatus, hī-ā'tus, *n.* a gap, opening: an awkward pause in a speech: a lost part in an old writing.

hi'bernate, *v.* to pass winter in a kind of sleep, as hedgehogs do.—*ns.* **hibernā'tion**; **hi'bernator**.

hic'cup, *n.* a sharp gasp, caused by laughing, eating, drinking: a fit of such gasping.—Also *v.*

hick'ory, *n.* the tough wood of an American tree.

hidal'go, *n.* a Spanish nobleman.

hide, *v.* to put or keep out of sight.—*adj.* **hid'den**, put out of sight: unknown.—**in hiding**, hidden.

hide, *n.* the skin of an animal.—*v.* to flog or whip.—*n.* **hid'ing**, a thrashing.—*adj.* **hide-bound**, having the mind shut against new ideas.

hideous, hid'e-us, *adj.* frightful: horrible.

hie, hī, *v.* to go quickly: to make one's way.

hierarchy, hī'er-ark-i, *n* a body of church rulers in order of rank: a number of things or persons arranged in order of rank.

hieroglyphic, hī-er-o-glif'ik, also **hi'eroglyph**, *n.* ancient Egyptian writing, in which pictures are used as letters.

hig'gle, *v.* to argue over the price of anything.

hig'gledy-pig'gledy, *adv.* and *adj.* topsy-turvy, in great disorder.

high, hī, *adj.* raised far above: far up in rank: above the rest in price, voice, force: (of meat) slightly bad.—Also *adv.*—*n.* **High'ness,** a princely title.—*adjs.* **high'-born,** high'-bred, of noble birth.—*n.* high'brow, a person of learned tastes.—*adjs.* **high'-explo'sive** (shells, bombs), causing great damage; high-flown (language), full of fine words; high'-handed (actions), done without thought for others; high'-mind'ed, proud; high'-sound'ing, sounding grand but meaning little; high'-spir'ited, bold, daring; high'-strung, nervous: easily excited.—*ns.* high'-day, holiday: day of rejoicing; high'-jinks, pranks; high'land, a land of hills and mountains; High'lands, the north of Scotland; Highlander, one who belongs to the Highlands: a Scottish soldier wearing a kilt; high'road, main road; high-tide, high'-wa'ter, the time at which the tide comes farthest up the shore; high'-trea'son, the crime of acting against one's own country; high'-way, the public road; high'-wayman, a robber who attacks people on the public road.—the high seas, open seas; Highway Code, a set of 'safety-first' rules drawn up by the Government.

hight, hīt, an old word meaning 'was called.'

hike, *n.* a journey on foot.—Also *v.*—*n.* hī'ker.

hila'rious, *adj.* in laughing mood: very merry.—*n.* hilar'ity.

hill, *n.* a mass of high land.—*adj.* hill'y.—*n.* hill'ock, a small hill.

hilt, *n.* the handle, esp. of a sword.

him, *pron.* a male person already spoken about (objective case).

hind, *n.* female deer: farm-servant.

hind, hīnd'er, *adjs.* placed behind.— *adj.* hind'most, farthest behind.

hin'der, *v.* to keep back, to delay.— *n.* hin'drance, something that delays.

Hin'du, Hin'doo, *n.* one whose religion is Hin'duism, one of the chief religions of India.

Hindustan'i, *n.* a language of India.

hinge, hinj, *n.* a joint on which a door or lid turns: that on which anything depends.—*v.* to move on a hinge: to depend on.

hint, *n.* slight mention, inkling.—*v.* to make a slight mention.

hin'terland, *n.* the district lying inland from the coast.

hip, *n.* the fleshy part of the upper leg.

hip, *n.* the fruit of the wild brier.

hip'podrome, *n.* a large ground for horse or chariot-racing: a circus.

hippopot'amus, *n.* a large African animal living in and near rivers: —*pl.* hippopot'amuses or hippopot'ami.

hire, *n.* money paid for work done, or for the use of something belonging to another person.—*v.* to give or get the use of something by paying money.—*ns.* hire'-ling, one who works in order to get money; hire'-purchase, a way of buying an article by paying for it in weekly or monthly parts or *instalments*—the buyer uses the article while paying for it.

hirsūte, *adj.* hairy: shaggy.

his, hiz, *adj.* belonging to him.

hiss, *v.* to make a sound like that of letter *s.*—*n.* such a sound, made to show anger or displeasure.

his'tory, *n.* an orderly account of the events, ways of living, etc. which make up the story of a nation: any account of what has happened.—*n.* histō'rian, one who writes history.—*adjs.* historic, important, likely to be remembered; histor'ical, having to do with history: told in history.

histrionic, his-tri-on'ik, *adj.* having to do with stage-acting or actors. —*n.pl.* histrion'ics, play-acting.

hit, *v.* to strike: to come upon, discover.—*n.* a stroke: a shot which strikes a target: a surprising success.

hitch, *v.* to catch by a hook: to make fast.—*n.* a jerk: an unexpected stop or delay: a knot for making fast (e.g. *clove-hitch*).

hith'er, *adv.* to this place.—*adj.* nearer.—*adv.* hith'erto, up till now.—hither and thither, back and forward: to and from.

hive, *n.* a place where bees live : a busy place.

hoar, *adj.* greyish-white : white with age or frost.—*n.* **hoar'-frost,** white frost.—*adj.* **hoar'y,** white or grey with age : of great age.

hoard, *n.* a hidden store (e.g. of treasure, food, etc.).—*v.* to store up in secret.

hoard, hoard'ing, *ns.* a fence of boards.

hoar'hound, hore'hound, *n.* a plant used in medicine.

hoarse, *adj.* having a harsh, grating voice.

hoax, *n.* a joke meant to deceive people, often (but not always) in fun.—*v.* to play a deceiving trick.

hob, *n.* a small shelf fixed to the front of a fireplace.

hob'ble, *v.* to tie the legs loosely : to walk with a limp.—Also *n.*

hob'by, *n.* a favourite way of passing one's spare time.

hob'by-horse, *n.* a wooden horse on rockers or in a merry-go-round.

hobgob'lin, *n.* a mischievous fairy.

hob'nail, *n.* a big-headed nail used for horse-shoes and heavy boots.

hob'nob, *v.* to be very friendly.

hock, *n.* a kind of white wine.

hock'ey, *n.* an eleven-a-side ball game, played with sticks shaped like the letter J.

hŏ'cus-pŏ'cus, *n.* a juggler's trick.

hod, *n.* a wooden trough on a pole, for carrying bricks and mortar.

hoe, *hō, n.* tool used for weeding, loosening earth.—*v.* to use a hoe.

hog, *n.* pig : young unshorn sheep.

Hog'manay, *n.* in Scotland, Dec. 31st.

hogs'head, *n.* a large cask for wine.

hoist, *v.* to lift.—*n.* lift, elevator.

hōld, *v.* to keep in one's grip : to contain : to think : to carry out (e.g. a party).—*n.* grip : (in ships) a large space where cargo is carried : a fortified place.—**to hold forth,** to make a speech ; **to hold good,** to be true ; **to hold off,** to defend one's self successfully against ; **to hold out,** to offer : to continue to fight ; **to hold over,** to keep till later ; **to hold up,** to support : to hinder : to attack and demand money from ; **Hold!** Stop ! Enough !—*ns.* **hōld'er,** something made to *hold* something else (e.g. *pen-holder*) ;

hold'ing, the amount held (e.g. land, shares in a company) ; **hold'-up,** an attack for robbery.

hole, *n.* an opening in something solid : a difficulty : a poor, dirty house.—*v.* to put into a hole.

hol'iday, *n.* a day on which some event is remembered : a day of rest and amusement. (Really *holy day*.)

hol'land, *n.* a coarse linen cloth.

hollow, *hol'ō, adj.* having empty space inside : not solid : not faithful.—*n.* a hole, sunken place : channel.—*v.* to make a hole in : to scoop out.

hol'ly, *n.* an evergreen shrub with scarlet berries and prickly leaves.

hol'lyhock, *n.* a tall garden plant.

holm'-oak, hōlm or hōm, *n.* the evergreen oak.

hol'ocaust, *n.* a burnt sacrifice : a great destruction by fire.

hōl'ster, *n.* the leather case for a pistol.

hōlt, *n.* a wood or woody hill : an orchard : a refuge : an otter's den.

hō'lus-bō'lus, *adv.* all at a gulp : altogether.

hō'ly, *adj.* pure in heart : religious : set apart for use in worshipping God.—*n.* **hō'liness,** the state of being holy.—**His Holiness,** a title of the Pope.—**holy city,** a city which is a special centre of worship (e.g. *Jerusalem* among Christians, *Benares* among Hindus, *Mecca* among Mohammedans) ; **Holy Grail.** See **Grail ; Holy Land,** the land of Palestine ; **holy orders,** the duties of a clergyman ; **holy war,** a war fought for reasons of religion ; **Holy Writ,** the Bible.

hom'age, *n.* in olden times, service due to an overlord from those below him : respect outwardly shown.

home, *n.* one's usual dwelling-place : a small hospital (often called a *nursing-home*).—*adj.* having to do with one's dwelling or country.—*adv.* to one's home : to the full length (e.g. He drove the nail *home*).—*adjs.* **ho'ming,** (esp. of pigeons) having the habit of making for home ; **home'ly,**

plain but pleasant : comfortable ; home'sick, sick for home. —*ns.* home'-farm, a farm on an estate, belonging to the mansion-house ; hom'er, a homing pigeon ; home'stead (-sted), farmhouse : small farm.—**Home Rule**, ruling of a country by its own people, not by another nation ; **Home Secretary**, the government minister who looks after the police and such matters.

hom'icide, -sīd, *n.* the killing of a human being : one who kills a human being.—*adj.* homici'dal.

hom'ily, *n.* a short, simple sermon.

homogeneous, hŏ-mō-jē'ni-us, *adj.* of the same kind or nature : having its parts all alike.—*n.* homogenē'ity.

hom'onyms, *n.pl.* words having the same sound but a different meaning (e.g. *there, their*).

hone, *n.* a stone for sharpening. —*v.* to sharpen.

honest, on'est, *adj.* just : free from fraud : truthful.—*n.* hon'esty, the state of being honest : a flowering plant.

honey, hun'i, *n.* a sweet, thick fluid made by bees from the *nectar* collected by them from flowers.— *ns.* honeycomb (hun'i-kōm), a network of wax cells in which bees store honey : anything like this.—*v.* to drill with holes like the cells in an empty honeycomb ; hon'eymoon, a holiday spent immediately after marriage ; hon'eysuckle, a climbing shrub with sweet-smelling cream-coloured flowers.

honk, *n.* the cry of the wild goose : the noise of a motor-horn.

honour, on'or, *n.* respect for truth, honesty, fair-dealing : fame : a title which shows respect : a prize. —*v.* to give respect to what is good : to give high rank to : to pay money when due.—*adjs.* hon'ourable, worthy of honour : noble—used as a title of rank, e.g. the *Honourable* (or *Hon.*) John Smith ; hon'orary, done to give honour : acting without payment.—*n.* honorā'rium, a gift or fee for services not paid for by wages.

hood, *n.* a covering for the head : a folding cover over seats in a carriage, car, etc.

hood'wink, *v.* to deceive.

hoof, *n.* horny substance on the feet of certain animals (*e.g.* horses) : —*pl.* hoofs, hooves.

hook, *n.* a bent piece of metal for holding or catching anything (e.g. *fish-hook*) : a curved tool for cutting grain.—*v.* to catch, hold, or drag with a hook.—*adj.* hooked, curved like a hook.—**by hook or by crook**, by one means or another, whatever the cost.

hook'ah, hook'a, *n.* a tobacco-pipe having a long tube, in which smoke is drawn through water, used by Turks and Arabs.

hoo'ligan, *n.* a wild fellow.

hoop, *n.* a ring of thin wood or metal (e.g. round a cask).

hooping-cough. See whoop.

hoopoe, hoop'ō, *n.* a bird with a large crest.

hoot, *v.* to call like an owl : to shout at in contempt.—*n.* hoot'er, a steam-whistle.

hop, *v.* to leap on one leg or both : to walk lame.—*n.* a short jump. —*ns.* hop'per, a box or funnel for shaking down corn to the grinding machinery : a boat with a movable part in the bottom for shaking out dredged mud ; hop-scotch, a hopping-game over ' scotches ' (lines drawn on ground).

hop, *n.* a climbing plant, the bitter cones of which, when ripe, are used in brewing.

hope, *n.* a state of mind in which one expects good to come : something desired.—*v.* to expect good to happen. — *adjs.* hope'ful ; hope'less.

horde, *n.* a wandering tribe or clan.

horehound. See hoarhound.

hori'zon, *n.* the line which seems to be formed by the meeting of the earth and sky : the limit of what a person can see or understand. — *adj.* horizon'tal, lying level.

horn, *n.* a hard growth on the heads of certain animals (e.g. oxen, sheep, deer) : something made of horn or curved like one (e.g.

drinking-horn, hunting-horn): a part of a motor-car which gives a warning sound.—*adjs.* **horned,** having horns (often used of the moon when it is crescent-shaped); **horn'y,** hard like horn.—**horn of plenty,** the sign of plenty (carried by Ceres, the Greek goddess of crops), filled to overflowing with fruits and flowers.

hor'net, *n.* a kind of wasp.

horn'pipe, *n.* a lively dance often done by sailors.

hor'oscope, *n.* the telling of a person's fortune by studying the position of the stars at his birth.

hor'ror, *n.* great fear, terror: something which causes fear.—*adjs.* **hor'rible,** causing horror; **hor'rid,** nasty.—*v.* **hor'rify,** to frighten greatly.

horse, *n.* a well-known four-footed animal: soldiers who go on horses, cavalry: a wooden frame (e.g. a *clothes-horse*).—*ns.* **horse'-chest'nut,** the brown nut or seed of the *horse-chestnut* tree; **horse-cou'per,** one who buys and sells horses; **horse'-fly,** a large fly which stings horses; **horse-play,** rough play; **horse'-pow'er,** the power of a horse: (in measuring the strength of an engine) the amount of power needed to raise 33,000 lb. one foot in one minute; **horse'-race,** a race by horses; **horse'-rad'ish,** a plant with a root of a biting taste; **horse'-sense,** common sense; **horse'-shoe,** a shoe for horses, made of a curved piece of iron.—**Horse Guards,** a regiment of horse-soldiers, sometimes used as a guard for the Queen.

horticul'ture, *n.* the branch of knowledge which deals with gardening.—*adj.* **horticul'tural,** having to do with gardening.—*n.* **horticul'turist,** one who makes a hobby of gardening.

hosan'na, *n.* an exclamation of praise to God.

hose, *n.* a covering for the legs or feet: a rubber tubing for carrying water:—*pl.* **hose.**—*ns.* **hō'sier,** one who sells hose and other knitted goods; **hō'siery,** goods of this kind.

hospice, hos'pis, *n.* a place of refuge (e.g. for travellers caught in a storm), esp. one kept by monks.

hos'pitable, *adj.* showing kindness to guests or strangers.—*n.* **hospital'ity,** a friendly welcome for guests or strangers.

hos'pital, *n.* a building for the treatment of the old, the sick, and hurt.

hōst, *n.* one who gives a welcome to guests, at a hotel, or parties: an innkeeper or hotel-keeper:—*fem.* **hōst'ess.**

hōst, *n.* a very large number: an army.

hōst, *n.* (in the Roman Catholic Church) the holy bread used in the Lord's Supper.

host'age, *n.* a prisoner held by the enemy to make sure that a bargain will be kept to.

hos'tel, *n.* a building where students or scholars live.—*ns.* **hos'telry,** an inn; **hostler** or **ostler** (hos'ler, os'ler), the servant who looks after the horses at an inn.

hos'tile, *adj.* having to do with an enemy: not friendly.—*n.* **hostil'ity,** unfriendliness: the state of being an enemy:—*pl.* **hostil'ities,** acts of warfare.

hot, *adj.* very warm: easily made angry: (of food) having much spice.—*adjs.* **hot'-blood'ed,** easily roused; **hot'-head'ed,** rash: acting without thinking.—*n.* **hot'-bed,** a garden-bed kept specially warm in order to hurry on plants: a place where there is much disease or wickedness; **hot'house,** a heated glass-house for plants.

hotch'potch, **hotch'pot,** *ns.* a kind of broth: a confused mixture.

hōtel', *n.* a building where board and lodging may be obtained by travellers for payment.

hough, hock, hok, *n.* the joint on the hind-leg of an animal, below the knee: in man, the back part of the knee-joint.—*v.* to cut the sinews of this joint.

hound, *n.* a dog used in hunting: a mean rogue.—*v.* to hunt: to pursue.

hour, owr, *n.* sixty minutes, the 24th part of a day: a time or occasion.—*adj.* **hour'ly,** happening or done every hour.—Also *adv.*—*n.*

hour'-glass, an instrument for measuring the hours by the running of sand from one glass into another.

house, *n.* a building in which one lives : a family : a business firm : a building where school-boarders stay : the House of Commons.—*v.* **house** (howz), to provide a house for : to shelter.—*adj.* **housing** (howz'ing), having to do with houses.—*ns.* **house'-ā'gent,** a man who sees to the selling and letting of houses ; **house'-boat,** a river-barge with a deck-cabin for dwelling in ; **house'-breaker,** a day-time burglar : a man who takes down old buildings ; **house'-hold,** the people who usually stay together in a house : a family ; **house'holder,** the chief person in a family ; **house'keeper,** one who looks after the running of a house ; **house'maid,** a maid who works about the house ; **house'-warm'ing,** a party held when a family goes to stay in a new house ; **house'wife,** the mistress of a house : (huz'if) a pocket sewing outfit.—**a house'hold word,** something which everyone is talking about.

housing, howz'ing, *n.* a decorated cover for a horse.

hovel, hov'el or huv'el, *n.* a small dirty dwelling.

hover, hov'er or huv'er, *v.* to remain in the air, keeping in the same spot : to move to and fro near something.

how, *adv.* in what manner : to what extent.—*adv.* **howev'er,** no matter how.—*conj.* but, in spite of that.—*conj.* **howbē'it,** yet.

how'dah, hou'dah, *n.* a seat fixed on an elephant's back.

how'itzer, *n.* a short cannon used to throw a shell into a besieged town or a trench.

howl, *v.* to make a long, loud, whining sound like that of a dog or wolf : to yell (e.g. in pain, anger, joy).—Also *n.*—*n.* **howl'er,** a very silly mistake.

hub, *n.* the centre part of a wheel, through which the axle passes : important town, the centre of much traffic and business.

hub'bub, *n.* a confused sound of many voices : uproar.

huck'aback, *n.* a coarse linen for towels, etc.

huck'ster, *n.* a pedlar.

hud'dle, *v.* to throw or crowd together in confusion.—*n.* a confused crowd : heap.

hue, hū, *n.* colour : tint.

hue, hū, *n.* a shouting.—**hue and cry,** an alarm and general chase (e.g. after a thief).

huff, *n.* fit of pettish anger.—*v.* to take the sulks : to force out breath as in anger.—*adj.* **huf'fy.**

hug, *v.* to hold lightly with the arms : to keep close to (e.g. The ships *hug* the shore).

huge, hūj, *adj.* of great size.—*n.* **huge'ness.**

hulk, *n.* an old ship unfit for use : anything big and clumsy : (*pl.*) old ships used as prisons.—*adj.* **hulk'ing,** big and clumsy.

hull, *n.* a husk or outer covering : the framework of a ship.—*v.* to strip off the outer covering.

hullō', a word of greeting.

hum, *v.* to make a buzzing sound like that of bees : to sing with the lips shut : to be noisily busy.—*ns.* **hum, hum'ming,** the noise of bees : any buzzing, droning sound.

hū'man, *adj.* having to do with man.—*adjs.* **humane',** kind, gentle ; **humanitā'rian,** kind to one's fellow-men.—*n.* **human'ity,** men and women in general, the human race : kindness, gentleness.

hum'ble, *adj.* modest : meek : not of high rank.—*v.* to make to feel low or mean.

hum'ble-bee, *n.* another name for the bumble-bee.

hum'bug, *n.* a fraud : one who makes himself a nuisance to others : a kind of candy.

humdrum, *adj.* dull : not exciting.

hū'mid, *adj.* moist, damp.—*n.* **humid'ity,** moisture : amount of wetness.

hūmil'ity, *n.* lowliness or meekness of mind : modesty.—*v.* **humil'iate,** to make to feel humble : to take silly pride out of.—*adj.* **humil'iat-ing,** causing a feeling of meek-ness.—*n.* **humil'iation,** something which hurts one's pride : shame.

hum'ming-bird, *n.* a bright-feathered bird whose wings make a humming sound.

hum'mock, *n.* a hillock : a ridge or small hill (e.g. of ice).—*adjs.* **humm'ocked, humm'ocky.**

humour, hū'mur or ū'mur, *n.* one's state of mind, temper : the ability to see the funny side of things.—*v.* to coax into pleasant frame of mind : to fall in with another's wishes.—*n.* **hu'morist,** one who can bring out the amusing side of things.—*adj.* **hu'morous,** funny : raising laughter.

hump or **hunch,** hunsh, *ns.* a lump (e.g. upon the back).—*ns.* **hump'-back, hunch'back,** a back with a hump or hunch : a person with a humpback.—*adjs.* **hump'-backed, hunch'backed.**

hū'mus, *n.* rotting leaves, etc. in the soil, which make it rich.

hunch. See **hump.**

hun'dred, *n.* the number of ten times ten : a division of a county.

hun'dredweight, *n.* 112 lbs. (usually written 1 cwt.). 20 cwts. = 1 ton.

hun'ger, *n.* desire for food : strong desire for anything.—*v.* to go without food : to long for.—*adj.* **hung'ry,** lacking food : greedy.—*n.* **hunger-strike,** refusal to eat (e.g. by prisoners, to show discontent).

hunt, *v.* to chase animals as prey or for sport : to search (for).—*n.* a chase of wild animals : a search.—*ns.* **hunt'er** (*fem.* **hunt'ress**), one who hunts : a horse trained for hunting : a watch whose face is protected by a hinged metal cover ; **hunts'man,** a member of a hunt.

hurd'le, *n.* a frame of twigs or branches used as fencing : a brushwood frame over which the runners leap in racing.

hur'dy-gur'dy, *n.* a musical instrument played by turning a handle, hand-organ.

hurl, *v.* to move rapidly : to throw with force.

hur'ly-bur'ly, *n.* a great stir, uproar.

hurrah, a shout of joy.

hur'ricane, *n.* a violent storm of wind (over 80 miles per hour). —*n.* **hur'ricane-lamp,** a lamp specially made to keep alight in strong wind.

hur'ry, *v.* to do or move quickly.—*n.* eagerness to act or move quickly.—*adj.* **hur'ried,** moving in a hurry.

hurt, *v.* to cause pain to : to wound.—*n.* a wound : damage.—*adj.* **hurt'ful,** causing pain or damage.

hurt'le, *v.* to dash against : to move with a whizzing sound.

hus'band, *n.* a married man—opposite of *wife.*—*v.* to spend or use (e.g. one's money, strength) very carefully.—*ns.* **hus'bandman,** a farmer ; **hus'bandry,** the business of farming : care with one's money, thrift.

hush ! silence ! be still !—*v.* **hush,** to make quiet.—*ns.* **hush'aby,** a slumber-song used to sing babies to sleep ; **hush'-mon'ey,** money given as a bribe to make one keep silent.—**to hush up,** to silence awkward questions.

husk, *n.* the dry thin covering of certain fruits and seeds : (*pl.*) what is thrown out as waste. —*adj.* **husked,** having a husk : having the husk taken off.

husk'y, *adj.* (of the voice) hoarse, rough in sound.—*n.* a Canadian sledge-dog : an Eskimo.

hussar, hooz-zar', *n.* a light-armed horse-soldier.

hussif. See **housewife.**

huss'y, *n.* a forward, cheeky girl.

hus'tings, *n.pl.* the platform from which candidates in elections for Parliament used to speak : the voting-places.

hustle, hus'l, *v.* to push rudely : to hurry.—Also *n.*

hut, *n.* a small wooden building : a native dwelling.

hutch, *n.* a box for rabbits : a low wagon in which coal is drawn up out of the pit.

huzza', hurrah ! a shout of joy.

hyacinth, hī'a-sinth, *n.* a sweet-smelling bulb-flower : a precious stone.

hyæna or **hyena,** hī-ē'na, *n.* a wild animal, something like a wolf.

hȳ'brid, *n.* an animal or plant produced from two different kinds (e.g. a mule, which is a *hybrid* from a horse and an ass).

hȳ′dra, *n.* in old-time stories, a water-serpent, with many heads which, when cut off, at once grew again: any evil which is difficult to get rid of.

hȳ′drant, *n.* a water-plug by which a hose or pipe can be screwed to a main-pipe.

hydraul′ic, *adj.* carrying water: worked by water.

hȳ′dro-, a prefix, meaning water.—*ns.* **hydro-electric′ity,** electricity got from water-power (*adj.* **hydroelec′tric**); **hy′drogen,** the lightest gas; with *oxygen* it makes up water (**hydrogen bomb,** exceedingly powerful bomb in which explosion is caused by turning hydrogen into helium); **hydropath′ic** (also **hydro**), large hotel, esp. one where water-treatment for ailments may be had; **hydrophobia** (hĭ-drō-fō′bi-a), a disease caused by the bite of a mad dog; **hy′dro-plane,** a seaplane: a kind of racing motorboat.

hyena. See **hyæna.**

hygiene, hī′jēn, *n.* the study of health and cleanliness.

hymn, him, *n.* a song of praise, esp. one sung to God.—*ns.* **hym′nal, hym′nary,** a hymn-book.

hyperbole, hī-per′bo-lē, *n.* a description or statement which is overdone: an exaggeration.

hypercrit′ical, *adj.* too fond of looking for very small faults.

hyphen, hī′fen, *n.* a short stroke (-) joining two syllables or words, as in *hydro-electric*.

hyp′notise, *v.* to put a person into a kind of deep sleep during which he obeys orders given to him.—*n.* **hyp′notism,** a sleep-like state of this kind.—*adj.* **hypnot′ic.**

hypocrite, hip′o-krit, *n.* a person who pretends to be good but is not.—*n.* **hypocrisy** (hip-ok′ris-i), a false show of goodness.—*adj.* **hypocrit′ical.**

hypoder′mic needle (syringe), *n.* a doctor's instrument (a fine, hollow needle) for giving an injection of a drug just below the skin.

hypot′enuse, *n.* the longest side of a right-angled triangle.

hypoth′esis, *n.* something supposed: something taken as true for the sake of argument:—*pl.* **hypoth′eses.**—*adj.* **hypothet′ical,** supposed.

hys′sop, *n.* sweet-smelling plant.

hyster′ics, hystē′ria, *ns.* an illness of the nerves, causing fits of laughter or crying which the person cannot help.—*adj.* **hyster′ical,** having hysterics: very easily excited.

I′bex, *n.* a wild mountain-goat.

I′bis, *n.* a stork-like wading bird.

ice, *n.* frozen water.—*n.* **ic′ing,** melted sugar, flavoured, and allowed to set.—*adj.* **ic′y,** cold: without love.—*adv.* **ic′ily.**—*ns.* **ice′-age,** the far-off time when our land was mostly covered with ice; **ice′berg,** a huge mass of floating ice; **ice-cream,** a sweet creamy mixture, flavoured and frozen; **ice′-float, ice-floe,** a piece of floating ice.

ichneumon, ik-nū′mun, *n.* a small Egyptian animal which destroys crocodiles' eggs: a kind of fly.

ichthyosaurus, ik-thi-o-sawr′us, *n.* a kind of giant sea-reptile which lived in long-past ages.

i′cicle, *n.* a hanging, pointed piece of ice formed by the freezing of dropping water.

i′con, *n.* an image (e.g. of Christ or of a saint).

icon′oclasm, *n.* act of breaking images.—*n.* **icon′oclast,** a breaker of images: one who goes against a belief held by others.

idē′a, *n.* the image or shape of something as seen in one's mind: a notion, thought.—*adj.* **idē′al,** as perfect as can be thought of: existing in imagination only—opposite of *real.*—*n.* that which is highest and best, nearest perfection.—*v.* **idē′alise,** to think of as perfect: to form ideas.—*n.* **idē′alist,** one who thinks that perfection can be reached.

iden'tify, v. to prove to be the same: to recognise.—*ns.* **identifica'tion; iden'tity,** the state of being the same: name (e.g. The *identity* of the thief was kept secret).—*adj.* **iden'tical,** the very same.

idiocy. See idiot.

ide'ology, n. a set of ideas, esp. new ideas of governing.

id'iom, n. a phrase or sentence in which the words have a special meaning (e.g. *How are you? Be off with you!*).—*adj.* **idiomat'ic.**

idiosyncrasy, id-i-o-sing'kra-si, n. an odd way of doing or thinking.

id'iot, n. a foolish or unwise person.—*n.* **id'iocy,** foolishness: weakness of mind.—*adj.* **idiot'ic,** foolish, stupid.

idle, ī'dl, *adj.* not busy on something: out of work: useless.—*v.* to spend (time) in doing nothing.—*ns.* **id'ler; id'leness.**—*adv.* **id'ly.**

i'dol, n. an image worshipped as a god: a person or thing loved or honoured too much.—*v.* **i'dolise,** to love greatly.—*ns.* **idol'atry,** the worship of images; **idol'ater,** a worshipper of idols.

idyll, ī'dil or id'il, n. a short poem giving happy pictures (e.g. of country life).—*adj.* **idyll'ic,** having to do with a happy simple life.

ig'loo, n. an Eskimo's snow hut.

igneous, ig'ne-us, *adj.* having to do with fire: made by the working of heat (e.g. an *igneous* rock, which has been formed by the great heat in the centre of the earth).

ignite, ig-nīt', v. to set on fire: to take fire.—*n.* **igni'tion,** act of setting on fire: the sparking part of a motor-engine.

ignoble, ig-nō'bl, *adj.* of low birth: mean or worthless.

ignominy, ig'nō-min-i, n. the loss of one's good name: disgrace.—*adj.* **ignomin'ious,** dishonourable: disgraceful.

ignora'mus, n. a person who knows little or nothing.

ignore, ig-nōr', v. to take no notice of.—*adj.* **ig'norant,** not knowing: knowing nothing.—*n.* **ig'norance,** want of knowledge.

iguana, i-gwä'na, n. a tree-lizard.

ilk, *adj.* the same.—**of that ilk, of** the same name or place.

ill, *adj.* evil, bad: unlucky: sick.—*adv.* badly.—*n.* evil: bad luck.—*n.* **ill'ness,** sickness.—*adj.* **ill-at-ease,** unhappy, uncomfortable; **ill'-bred,** badly brought up; **ill-got'ten,** obtained in a bad way; **ill'-na'tured,** cross; **ill'-starred,** unlucky.—*n.* **ill'-will,** dislike: hatred.—*v.* **ill'-treat,** to use roughly.

ille'gal, *adj.* against the law.—*n.* **illegal'ity.**

illegible, il-lej'ibl, *adj.* not easy to read, badly written.

illegitimate, il-le-jit'im-āt, *adj.* born of unmarried parents.

illicit, il-lis'it, *adj.* not allowed by law.

illit'erate, *adj.* not able to read or write, not educated.—*n.* **illit'eracy.**

illogical, il-loj'ik-al, *adj.* against the rules of reason or common-sense.

illu'minate, v. to light up: to decorate with fancy letters or designs (e.g. an *illuminated address,* a decorated piece of writing in praise of a person).—*ns.* **illumina'tion,** a light, esp. a bright light: fancy lettering; **illū'minant,** something which gives light.—*adj.* **illū'minative,** giving light: making clear or easy to understand.—*v.* **illumine** (il-lū'min), to give light to: to make easy to understand.

illusion, il-lū'zhun, n. something which deceives the mind: a false show.—*n.* **illū'sionist,** one who is able to deceive people, a conjuror.—*adjs.* **illū'sive, illū'sory,** deceiving by false show.

il'lustrate, v. to make clear to the mind: to explain by examples: to draw pictures for a book.—*n.* **illustra'tion,** an example which helps to make a matter clear: a picture in a book or magazine.—*adj.* **il'lustrative,** making clear.

illus'trious, *adj.* noble: famous.

im'age, n. a likeness, esp. one made from wood or stone, an idol: a picture in the mind.—*n.* **imagery** (im'aj-ri), word-pictures that help to make an author's writing more interesting or more life-like.

imagine, im-aj'in, v. to form a pic-

ture in the mind: to think.—
adjs. imag'inable, able to be
thought of; imag'inary, fancied,
not real; imag'inative, good at
using one's imagination.

imbecile, im'be-sil, *n.* a weak-
minded person.—*ns.* imbecil'ity,
weak-mindedness, stupidity.

imbibe', *v.* to drink in.

imbue', *v.* to fill the mind with.—
imbued with, full of.

im'itate, *v.* to try to be the same as,
to copy.—*ns.* imita'tion, a copy;
im'itator, one who copies.

immac'ulate, *adj.* spotless.

immate'rial, *adj.* of little importance.

immature, im-ma-tūr', *adj.* not ripe:
not fully grown (in wisdom, size,
strength, etc.): (of a plan) not
ready to be carried out.

imme'diate, *adj.* having nothing
coming between: without delay: direct.—*adv.* imme'diately,
at once, without delay: closely.

immemo'rial, *adj.* going further
back in time than can be remembered.

immense', *adj.* very large.—*n.* im-
mens'ity.

immerse', *v.* to plunge into water:
to interest deeply.—*n.* immer-
sion, the act of dipping completely in water.

im'migrate, *v.* to come into a
country and settle there.—*ns.*
immigra'tion; im'migrant, a settler.

im'minent, *adj.* about to happen.

immo'bile, *adj.* not easily moved.—
n. immobil'ity.

immod'erate, *adj.* going beyond
proper bounds.

immod'est, *adj.* shameless.

immor'al, *adj.* wicked, sinful.—*n.*
immoral'ity.

immor'tal, *adj.* living for ever.—*n.*
immortal'ity, unending life or
fame.—*v.* immor'talise, to make
immortal or famous for ever.

immovable, im-moov'a-bl, *adj.* not
able to be moved or changed.

immune, im-mūn', *adj.* free from:
not likely to take a disease.—*n.*
immu'nity.—*v.* im'munise, to
make a person unlikely to take
a disease by putting into his blood
something to fight the disease.

imp, *n.* a wicked spirit: a mischievous child.—*adj.* imp'ish.

im'pact, *n.* the force of a blow: a
collision.

impair', *v.* to weaken.—*n.* impair'-
ment.

impale', *v.* to pierce with something
sharp.

impal'pable, *adj.* not able to be felt by
touching: not easily understood.

impart', *v.* to tell to others what
one knows.

impartial, im-par'shal, *adj.* not
favouring one more than another, just.—*n.* impartial'ity.

impass'able, *adj.* (of roads, mountains, etc.) not able to be passed
along or over.—*n.* impasse (im'-
pas), a difficulty from which
there seems to be no way out.

impassioned, im-pash'ond, *adj.*
moved by strong feeling.

impas'sive, *adj.* not easily roused,
either by pleasure or pain.

impatient, im-pā'shent, *adj.* not able
to wait: restless.—*n.* impatience.

impeach', *v.* to accuse of wrong-
doing: to bring a high official
before the House of Lords to be
judged.—*n.* impeach'ment.

impec'cable, *adj.* doing no wrong:
faultless.

impecunious, im-pe-kū'ni-us, *adj.*
having no money: poor.

impede, im-pēd', *v.* to hinder, keep
back.—*n.* imped'iment, a hindrance: (in a person's talk) a
stutter.—*n.pl.* impedimen'ta, baggage.

impel', *v.* to urge, to drive on.

impend', *v.* to be about to happen.

impen'etrable, *adj.* not able to be
passed through.

impen'itent, *adj.* not sorry for having done wrong.

imper'ative, *adj.* that must be
obeyed.

impercep'tible, *adj.* not able to be
seen: very small.

imper'fect, *adj.* not as good as possible: having a fault.—*n.* im-
perfec'tion, a fault or flaw.

imperial, im-pē'ri-al, *adj.* having to
do with an emperor or an em-
pire: royal.—*n.* a tuft of hair on
the lower lip and chin.—*n.* im-
pē'rialist, one who believes in
having a strong empire.

imper′il, v. to put in danger.

impérious, adj. showing off one's power, haughty.

imper′ishable, adj. that will not die: everlasting.

impermeable, im-per′mē-able, adj. not able to be passed through (e.g. Clay is *impermeable* by water).

imper′sonal, adj. not living as a person: not connected with a person.

imper′sonate, v. to dress up as, or act the part of someone.—ns. impersonā′tion; imper′sonator.

imper′tinent, adj. not having to do with what is being spoken about: cheeky, bad-mannered.—n. imper′tinence.

impertur′bable, adj. not easily worried, calm.

impervious, im-per′vi-us, adj. able to stand against (e.g. He is *impervious* to insult).

impetī′go, n. a skin disease.

impetuous, im-pet′ū-us, adj. rushing with force: acting without cool thinking, rash.—n. impetuos′ity.

im′petus, n. force (e.g. The *impetus* of the collision was very great).

impinge, im-pinj′, v. to strike against: to touch upon.

impious, im′pi-us, adj. having no respect for holy things.

implā′cable, adj. not able to be soothed or calmed: unforgiving.

implant′, v. to plant in.

im′plement, n. a tool used for work (e.g. a spade, a painter's brush).—v. implement′, to carry out, to fulfil (e.g. a promise).

im′plicate, v. to bring a person into an affair (e.g. Your statement *implicates* you in the crime).—n. implicā′tion, something meant though not actually said.—adj. implicit (im-plis′it), meant though not actually said: complete (e.g. *implicit* faith, *implicit* obedience).

imply′, v. to mean.

impolīte′, adj. not polite: rude.

impol′itic, adj. unwise.

import′, v. to bring goods from abroad: to mean.—ns. im′port, something brought to a country from abroad: meaning: importance; importā′tion, act of importing.

impor′tant, adj. worth taking notice of: special: (of persons) fussy.—n. impor′tance.

importūne′, v. to keep asking for something.—adj. impor′tūnāte, asking again and again.—n. importūn′ity.

impōse′, v. to lay upon (e.g. a duty upon a person): to deceive.—adj. impōs′ing, making much show.—n. imposi′tion, a tax: a burden: an exercise given as a punishment: a fraud.

impos′sible, adj. not able to be done.—n. impossibil′ity.

im′pōst, n. a tax.

impos′tor, n. one who pretends to be somebody else in order to deceive.—n. impos′tūre, the act of deceiving in this way.

im′potent, adj. powerless.—n. im′-potence.

impound′, v. to shut in with a fence: to take possession of something by law (e.g. cattle in payment of a fine).

impov′erish, v. to make poor by too free spending.—n. impov′erishment.

imprac′ticable, adj. not able to be done.—n. impracticabil′ity.

im′precate, v. to call down curses upon.—n. imprecā′tion, a curse.

impreg′nable, adj. (of a fort) too strong to be captured.

impress′, v. to mark by pressing upon: to fix deeply in the mind.—ns. im′press, that which is made by pressure: a stamp: likeness (e.g. the Queen's head on a coin); impress′ion, a mark made by impressing: the number of copies of a book printed at one time: what a person thinks about something.—adjs. impress′ionable, easily moved or affected; impress′ive, having a great effect on the mind: solemn.

impress′, v. to force a person to join the army or navy

imprint′, v. to print: to fix in the mind.—n. im′print, that which is imprinted: the printer's name on a book.

impris′on, v. to shut up as in a prison.—n. impris′onment.

improb′able, adj. not likely to happen.—n. improbabil′ity.

impromp'tū, *adj.* done without preparation (e.g. *impromptu* speech).

improp'er, *adj.* not suitable : wrong : rude.—*n.* **impropri'ety**, something improper (e.g. a rude remark).—**improper fraction**, a fraction greater than 1 (e.g. $\frac{5}{4}$, $2\frac{1}{3}$).

improve, im-proov', *v.* to make or become better : to make good use of.—*n.* **improve'ment**.

improv'ident, *adj.* spending what one has without thinking of the future.—*n.* **improv'idence**.

improvise', *v.* to put together on the spur of the moment (e.g. a roughly *improvised* stretcher ; an *improvised* tune).—*n.* **improvisā'tion**.

imprudent, im-proo'dent, *adj.* unwise.

im'pŭdent, *adj.* having no shame : rude.—*n.* **im'pudence**.

impugn, im-pūn', *v.* to attack by words or arguments.

im'pulse, *n.* sudden force, such as a push : a sudden wish resulting in sudden action.—*adj.* **impuls'ive**, acting suddenly and without calm thinking.—*n.* **impuls'iveness**.

impū'nity, *n.* freedom from punishment, injury, or loss.

impure, im-pūr', *adj.* mixed with other substances : unclean : sinful.—*n.* **impur'ity**.

impute, im-pūt', *v.* to blame for : to think of as belonging to (e.g. Let no one *impute* wicked thoughts to me).—*n.* **impūtā'tion**, blame.

inabil'ity, *n.* lack of power to do something.

inaccessible, in-ak-ses'ibl, *adj.* not able to be reached : lying out of the way.

inac'cūrate, *adj.* not exact : not correct.—*n.* **inac'curacy**.

inactive, in-ak'tiv, *adj.* not working : doing nothing.—*ns.* **inac'tion**, **inactiv'ity**, idleness : rest.

inadequate, in-ad'ek-wāt, *adj.* not enough.—*n.* **inad'equacy**.

inadmis'sible, *adj.* not fit to be allowed to count (e.g. His evidence was *inadmissible*).

inadver'tent, *adj.* not giving full attention : careless : unintentional.—*n.* **inadver'tence**.

inadvī'sable, *adj.* not worthy of being done.

inane', *adj.* very foolish.—*n.* **inan'ity**.

inan'imate, *adj.* without life.

inap'plicable, *adj.* not suitable to the purpose.

inappreciable, in-a-prē'shi-abl, *adj.* so small as not to be worth notice.

inapproach'able, *adj.* not able to be easily reached.

inapprō'priate, *adj.* not suitable.

inapt', *adj.* not fit : dull, not clever.

inartic'ūlate, *adj.* unable to speak clearly.

inartis'tic, *adj.* having no idea of what is beautiful : not pleasing to the eye.

inasmuch as, *conj.* because, since.

inatten'tive, *adj.* not paying attention.

inau'dible, *adj.* not loud enough to be heard.

inau'gūrate, *v.* to make a beginning with something, usually with show or ceremony.—*n.* **inaugurā'tion**.—*adj.* **inau'gural**.

inauspicious, in-aw-spish'us, *adj.* unlucky.

inborn', *adj.* born in one, not learned afterwards : natural.

incal'cūlable, *adj.* not able to be counted or measured : very great.

incandes'cent, *adj.* glowing white with heat (e.g. an *incandescent* gas-mantle).

incantā'tion, *n.* words sung or said as a spell.

incā'pable, *adj.* unable to do what is expected : not fit for a job : drunk.

incapacitate, in-kap-as'i-tāt, *v.* to take away power, strength, or rights : to disable.—*n.* **incapac'ity**, want of ability or power.

incar'cerate, *v.* to imprison.

incar'nate, *adj.* having human form.—*n.* **incarnā'tion**, appearance in the form of a human body.

incautious, in-kaw'shus, *adj.* not careful.

incen'diary, *n.* a person who, on purpose, sets fire to a building, etc.—*n.* **incen'diarism**, the crime of setting fire to buildings.—**incendiary bomb**, a bomb meant to cause damage by fire.

incense, in-sens′, v. to make angry : to perfume with incense. — n. **in′cense,** sweet-smelling spices burned in religious ceremonies.

incen′tive, n. that which drives one to do something.

inception, in-sep′shun, n. a beginning.

incer′tain, adj. not certain.

inees′sant, adj. going on without a pause.

inch, insh, n. one twelfth of a foot.

in′cident, n. a happening.—adj. **in′cident′al,** happening as a result : going along with (e.g. The in-cidental expenses of motoring are heavy).—adv. **incident′ally,** by the way.

incin′erate, v. to burn to ashes.—ns. **incinera′tion;** **incin′erator,** a furnace for burning up anything.

incip′ient, adj. beginning.

incise, insīz′, v. to cut into : to engrave.—n. **incision (in-sish′un),** the act of cutting into something : a cut, a gash. — adj. **inci′sive,** cutting into : sharp (e.g. in the use of words).—ns. **inci′siveness; inci′sor,** a front tooth.

incite, in-sīt′, v. to move to action : to urge on.—n. **incite′ment.**

incivil′ity, n. rudeness.

inclem′ent, adj. unmerciful : (of weather) stormy.—n. **inclem′ency.**

incline′, v. to lean or slope towards : to go right or left from the direct path : to have a liking for.—ns. **in′cline,** an up- or down-slope ; **inclina′tion,** a bending (e.g. of the body in bowing) : a slope or tilt : a liking or fondness.

include, in-klood′, v. to count in, along with others.—n. **inclu′sion.** —adj. **inclu′sive,** counting all in, the ends as well as middle (e.g. From Tuesday to Thursday in-clusive is 3 days).

incog′nito, adj. disguised : under a false name.—n. a disguise.

incohē′rent, adj. not holding together well : (of a story) not well connected.—n. **incohē′rence.**

incombus′tible, adj. not able to be burned by fire.

income, in′kum, n. gain or profit : a person's earnings.—adj. **incom′-ing,** coming in (e.g. the incoming tide).

incommū′nicative, adj. unwilling to tell what one knows : shy.

incom′parable, adj. without equal, matchless.

incompat′ible, adj. not in agreement : unable to exist together.—n. **incompatibil′ity.**

incom′petent, adj. not good enough at one's job.—n. **incom′petence.**

incomplete, in-kom-plēt′, adj. not finished.

incomprehen′sible, adj. not able to be understood : puzzling.

inconceivable, in-kon-seev′able, adj. not able to be imagined : un-thinkable.

inconclusive, in-kon-kloo′siv, adj. not decided : having no definite result.

incongruous, in-kon′groo-us, adj. not matching well : not suitable to the occasion.—n. **incongrui′ty.**

incon′sequent, adj. uncertain in movement or thinking.—adj. **in-consequen′tial,** of little value.

inconsid′erate, adj. not thinking of the rights and feelings of others.

inconsis′tent, adj. changeable : not agreeing with (e.g. His evil life was inconsistent with his high position).—n. **inconsis′tency.**

inconspicuous, in-kon-spik′ū-us, adj. hardly seen.

incon′stant, adj. often changing : unsteady in one's duties towards another.—n. **incon′stancy.**

incontest′able, adj. too clear to be denied.

incon′tinent, adj. unable to check one's passions. — adv. **incon′-tinently,** without delay, immediately.

inconvē′nient, adj. causing a certain amount of trouble : not suitable. —n. **inconvē′nience,** trouble, dis-comfort.—v. to cause trouble to.

inconver′tible, adj. that cannot be changed.

incor′porate, v. to form a society.—adj. formed into a society.

incorrect′, adj. wrong.

incorrigible, in-kor′ij-ibl, adj. too bad to be put right.

incorrupt′, adj. pure : not to be tempted by bribes. — adj. **in-corrupt′ible,** lasting always : that cannot be bribed.

increase', v. to grow, or make to grow (in size or value).—n. **in'crease**, a growing larger: the part added by growth.

incred'ible, adj. beyond belief.—n. **incredibil'ity**.

incred'ulous, adj. refusing to believe what one hears.—n. **incredu'lity**.

in'crement, n. the amount by which a thing is made bigger: a part added.

incrim'inate, v. to show that a person has had a hand in a crime.

in'cubate, v. to sit on eggs to hatch them.—ns. **incuba'tion**, the time a disease takes to develop; **in'cubātor**, a large heated box for hatching eggs.

in'cubus, n. the nightmare: a great worry.

incul'cate, v. to impress something on a person's mind by much repeating.

incul'pate, v. to blame.

incum'bent, adj. lying on as a duty (e.g. It is *incumbent* upon me to warn you).—n. one who has charge of a church.

incur', v. to bring on: to run into (e.g. debt).

incu'rable, adj. unable to be cured.

incu'rious, adj. asking no questions: not interested.

incursion, in-kur'shun, n. a raid (e.g. into an enemy's land).

indebted, in-det'ed, adj. being in debt: obliged by something received.—n. **indebt'edness**.

indē'cent, not fit to look at: rude.—n. **inde'cency**.

indecision, in-de-sizh'un, n. slowness in making up one's mind, hesitation.—adj. **indeci'sive**, not coming to definite result.

indecorous, in-dek'or-us, adj. against good manners.—n. **indeco'rum**, rude or rowdy behaviour.

indeed, adv. in truth, really.

indefat'igable, adj. never tiring.

indefeas'ible, adj. (of one's rights) not to be taken away.

indefen'sible, adj. unable to be defended: (of behaviour) unable to be excused.

indef'inite, adj. having no clear boundary: not certain or fixed.—adj. **indefi'nable**, not able to be stated clearly.

indel'ible, adj. unable to be rubbed out.

indel'icate, adj. not in keeping with polite manners, rude. — n. **indel'icacy**.

indem'nify, v. to pay money to a person in order to make up for damage done or loss suffered.—n. **indem'nity**, the money paid (e.g. by one country to another after a war so that damage may be put right).

indent', v. to notch or dent: to begin a new paragraph by going in from the margin.—n. **in'dent**, a cut or notch in the margin: a dent; **indenta'tion**, a notch or notch-like mark (often used in speaking of bays, river-mouths); **indent'ūre**, a written statement of a bargain (e.g. between an apprentice and his master).

indepen'dent, adj. acting or thinking for one's self, not relying on others: having enough to live on in comfort without working or relying on another for help.—n. **independ'ence**, the power to act or think on one's own: freedom.

indescrib'able, adj. not able to be described.

indestruc'tible, adj. not able to be destroyed.

in'dex, n. anything that points out: the forefinger: alphabetical list which shows the subjects dealt with in a book:—pl. **in'dexes**.

In'dian, adj. having to do with India, or with the first dwellers in America.—Also n.—ns. **In'diaman**, a large ship used in trade with India; **in'dia-rub'ber**, see **rubber**.—Indian corn, maize; Indian file, single file; Indian ink, see ink; Indian summer, a period of warm, dry, calm weather in late autumn; india paper, a thin paper; Red Indians, the natives of North America, so called from the colour of the skin, which is, however, really a yellowish-brown.

in'dicate, v. to point out, to show. —ns. **indica'tion**; **in'dicātor**, something which points out.— adj. **indic'ative**, pointing out.

indict, in-dīt', v. to accuse of a crime. —n. **indictment** (in-dīt'ment), an accusation against a person.

indiff'erent, *adj.* neither very good nor very bad : showing no lively interest.—*n.* **indiff'erence**, lack of interest or feeling.

indigenous, in-dij'en-us, *adj.* belonging to a country, not coming from abroad.

in'digent, *adj.* living in want, poor.—*n.* **in'digence**.

indigestion, in-di-jest'shun, *n.* pain after eating owing to food not being suitable.—*adj.* **indiges'tible**.

indig'nant, *adj.* angry because of hurt feelings.—*ns.* **indignā'tion; indig'nity**, rudeness, with insult added.

in'digo, *n.* a violet-blue dye.

indirect', *adj.* not straight : going by a roundabout way.

indiscreet', *adj.* rash, thoughtless (e.g. An *indiscreet* word or act often causes trouble).—*n.* **indiscretion** (-kresh'n), a rash or unwise saying or act.

indiscrim'inate, *adj.* making no difference between one thing and another : not caring who or what suffers.—*adv.* **indiscrim'inately**.

indispen'sable, *adj.* not able to be done without : necessary.

indispō'sed, *adj.* slightly ill : not willing.—*n.* **indisposi'tion**, a slight illness : unwillingness.

indispū'table, *adj.* not able to be denied.

indistinct', *adj.* not clear.

indite', *v.* to write a song or poem.

individ'ūal, *adj.* having to do with one only of a group.—*n.* a single person, animal, plant, or thing.—*ns.* **individ'ūalism**, belief that 'each for himself' works best ; **individ̄ūal'ity**, separate existence : the special points which make a person or thing different from others.

indivis'ible, *adj.* not able to be divided.

in'dōlent, *adj.* lazy.—*n.* **in'dolence**.

indom'itable, *adj.* not able to be tamed : tireless, unyielding.

in'door, *adj.* done inside a building.—*adv.* **in'doors**.

indū'bitable, *adj.* not to be doubted.

indūce', *v.* to persuade : to bring on (e.g. an illness).—*n.* **indūce'ment**, something which coaxes or persuades (e.g. Money is an *inducement* to work).

induct', *v.* to bring into : to introduce (e.g. a new clergyman to a church).—*n.* **induc'tion**, an introduction to a new position : the producing of electricity in a body by placing it near another body containing electricity.

indulge', *v.* to give way readily to fancies and wishes.—*n.* **indul'gence**, a giving-in to wishes or fancies : a pardon for a sin, after the sinner has repented.—*adj.* **indul'gent**, not strict, kind : yielding to wishes of others.

in'dustry, *n.* steady attention to work : a trade which is concerned with the preparing of goods for market (e.g. coal *industry*, fishing *industry*, cotton *industry*).—*adjs.* **indus'trial**, having to do with the making of goods in factories ; **indus'trious**, hardworking, busily at work.

inē'briate, *v.* to make drunk.—*n.* a drunkard.

ined'ible, *adj.* not eatable.

ineff'able, *adj.* not able to be put into words.

ineffec'tive, *adj.* useless, having no effect.—*adjs.* **ineffec'tūal**, doing no good ; **inefficient** (in-e-fish'ent), not good enough to do the work required.—*ns.* **ineffec'tiveness ; inefficacy** (in-ef'i-kas-i), lack of power to do what is wanted ; **ineffic'iency**.

inel'egant, *adj.* not pretty to look at.—*n.* **inel'egance**.

ineligible, in-el'i-jibl, *adj.* not able to be chosen : not wanted.

inept', *adj.* not fit : clumsy : foolish.—*n.* **inep'titude**.

inequal'ity, *n.* unevenness.

inequitable, in-ek'wit-abl, *adj.* unfair.—*adj.* **ineq'uity**.

inert', *adj.* dull : without the power of moving.—*n.* **inertia** (in-er'shi-a), unwillingness to move.

ines'timable, *adj.* not able to be valued : priceless.

inev'itable, *adj.* not able to be avoided.—*n.* **inevitabil'ity**.

inexact', *adj.* not quite correct.

inexcū'sable, *adj.* not to be excused.

inexhaus'tible, *adj.* very plentiful, not likely to become used up.

inex'orable, *adj.* not able to be moved by prayer or pleading.

inexpe′dient, *adj.* not likely to help: not wise (e.g. The sailors thought it *inexpedient* to remain on the ship any longer).—*n.* **inexpe′diency**.

inexpen′sive, *adj.* cheap in price.

inexpe′rience, *n.* lack of knowledge.—*adj.* **inexpe′rienced**.

inex′pert, *adj.* not skilled.

inex′plicable, *adj.* not able to be explained.

inexpres′sible, *adj.* not able to be told in words.

inex′tricable, *adj.* not able to be disentangled.

infall′ible, *adj.* never making an error: certain to produce the result expected.

infamous, in′fa-mus, *adj.* having a reputation of the worst kind: disgraceful.—*n.* **in′famy**, a bad reputation: public disgrace.

in′fant, *n.* a babe: (in law) a person under twenty-one years of age.—*n.* **in′fancy**, the state or time of being an infant: the beginning of anything.—*adj.* **in′fantile**, having to do with infants.—*n.* **infanticide** (in-fant′i-sīd) child-murder.

in′fantry, *n.* foot-soldiers.

infat′uate, *v.* to fill with foolish love.—*n.* **infatuā′tion**.

infect′, *v.* to pass on (e.g. a disease).—*n.* **infec′tion**, the means (usually germs) by which disease is spread: anything that spreads widely and affects many people.—*adj.* **infec′tious**, apt to spread.

infer′, *v.* to reach a decision by thinking or reasoning: to hint at.—*n.* **in′ference**, the result of one's reasoning: a hint.

infe′rior, *adj.* lower in any way: not of best quality.—*n.* one lower in rank.—*n.* **inferior′ity**.

infer′nal, *adj.* belonging to the lower regions: cursed.—*n.* **infer′no**, hell: any place on fire.

infest′, *v.* (of enemies) to occupy: to swarm over.

in′fidel, *adj.* unbelieving.—*n.* one who does not believe in the religion of Christ.—*n.* **infidel′ity**, unfaithfulness.

infil′trate, *v.* to pass into in small amounts.—*n.* **infiltrā′tion**.

in′finite, *adj.* without end or limit: without bounds.—*adj.* **infinites′-**imal, very small.—*n.* **infin′ity**, space or time, so great in stretch as to be beyond our power of thinking.

infirm′, *adj.* feeble: weak.—*ns.* **infirm′ary**, a hospital for the treatment of the sick and hurt; **infirm′ity**, disease: weakness.

inflame′, *v.* to make hot, painful, or angry.—*n.* **inflammā′tion**, heat in a part of the body, with pain, redness, and swelling.—*adjs.* **inflam′mable**, easily set on fire: easily excited; **inflam′matory**, rousing to anger or excitement.

inflāte′, *v.* to puff up with air or gas, or with foolish pride.—*n.* **inflā′tion**, the act of blowing up (e.g. a tyre): the use of too much paper money, causing high prices.

inflex′ible, *adj.* not yielding.

inflict′, *v.* to lay on (e.g. blows).—*n.* **inflic′tion**, a punishment.

influence, in′floo-ens, *n.* power to affect other persons or things.—*v.* to have power over.—*adj.* **influential** (in-floo-en′shi-al).

influen′za, *n.* a kind of severe cold.

in′flux, *n.* a flowing in.

inform′, *v.* to give knowledge to: (with *against* or *on*) to tell on.—*ns.* **inform′ant**, one who gives news; **informā′tion**, knowledge, news, tidings; **inform′er**, one who tells on another, esp. in a court.—*adj.* **inform′ative**, giving information.

infor′mal, *adj.* not strict about form: free and easy: not requiring full-dress.—*n.* **informal′ity**.

infringe, in-frinj′, *v.* to break a rule or law.—*n.* **infringe′ment**.

infū′riate, *v.* to make mad: to drive into a rage.

infūse′, *v.* to pour upon or over: to fill the mind (e.g. with a desire to do something).—*n.* **infū′sion**, a liquid (e.g. tea) formed by pouring water on something.

in′gathering, *n.* the collecting and storing of the fruits of the earth: harvest.

ingenious, in-jēn′i-us, *adj.* skilful in inventing: cleverly thought out.—*n.* **ingenū′ity**, cleverness: quickness of ideas.

ingenuous, in-jen′ū-us, *adj.* knowing little about life: simple in mind.—*n.* **ingen′uousness**.

ingle-nook, -side, *ns.* a fireside.

inglŏ'rious, *adj.* shameful.

ingot, ing'got, *n.* lump of rough metal, esp. gold or silver.

ingrain. Same as **engrain.**

ingratiate, in-grā'shi-āt, *v.* to get (one's self) into the favour of somebody.

ingrat'itūde, *n.* lack of thanks: unwillingness to give thanks.

ingrē'dient, *n.* one of the things of which a mixture is made.

inhab'it, *v.* to dwell in: to occupy. —*adj.* **inhab'itable,** fit to be lived in.—*n.* **inhab'itant,** a dweller.

inhale', *v.* to draw in (the breath, smoke, etc.).—*n.* **inhalā'tion.**

inhē'rent, *adj.* inborn: natural.

inher'it, *v.* to get something (e.g. property, a title) on the death of a relative: to take certain qualities from one's forefathers (e.g. He *inherited* his father's love of sport).—*n.* **inher'itance,** that which one gets when a relative dies.

inhib'it, *v.* to hold back, to check.

inhos'pitable, *adj.* not kind to strangers.

inhū'man, *adj.* cruel.—*n.* **inhuman'ity.**

inim'ical, *adj.* like an enemy, not friendly.

inim'itable, *adj.* too good to be imitated.

iniquity, in-ik'wi-ti, *n.* wickedness: a sin.—*adj.* **iniq'uitous,** unjust: wicked.

initial, in-ish'al, *adj.* placed at the beginning.—*n.* the letter beginning a word, esp. a name.—*v.* to put the initials of one's name to. —*v.* **init'iate,** to make a beginning: to give first lessons to.— *ns.* **initiā'tion; initiative** (in-ish'i-ā-tiv), the first step: eagerness to make progress.

inject', *v.* to put a drug or other liquid into the veins of the body by means of a needle and **syringe.** —*n.* **injec'tion.**

injudicious, in-joo-dish'us, *adj.* not wise: thoughtless.

injunction, in-jungk'shun, *n.* a command: an order by which a judge stops an unlawful act.

injure, in'joor, *v.* to harm: to damage.—*adj.* **inju'rious,** hurtful:

harming a person's name.—*n.* **in'jury,** wrong: a hurt.

injustice, in-jus'tis, *n.* a wrong or unfair act.

ink, *n.* a coloured liquid used in writing, printing, etc.—*v.* to daub with ink.—*adj.* **ink'y.—Indian ink,** a very black ink used by artists; **invisible ink,** a kind of ink which does not show on paper until it is heated.

ink'ling, *n.* a hint or slight sign.

in'land, *n.* the part of a country away from the coast or boundary. —*adj.* far from the sea: carried on or produced within a country (e.g. *inland* trade).

inlay, *n.* a kind of decoration done by fitting pieces of different shapes and colours into a background.—*v.* to do this kind of work.—*adj.* **inlaid'.**

in'let, *n.* a place of entrance: a small bay.

in'mate, *n.* one who lives in the same house with another: a person in a hospital.

inmost. See **inner.**

inn, *n.* a house for the lodging of travellers, a small country hotel. —*n.* **inn'keeper,** one who keeps an inn.

innate', *adj.* inborn, given by nature.

in'ner, *adj.* farther in.—*adjs.* **inn'ermost, in'most,** farthest in.

in'nings, *n.* a team's turn for batting in cricket: a spell or turn.

innocent, in'ō-sent, *adj.* not guilty: free from blame.—*n.* **in'nocence,** harmlessness: absence of guilt.

innoc'ūous, *adj.* not hurtful.

innovā'tion, *n.* something new.

innoxious, in-nok'shus, *adj.* not hurtful.

innūen'do, *n.* a remark which means to accuse or insult, but does not actually say so (e.g. After you went away, I missed my watch).

innū'merable, *adj.* not able to be counted.

inobser'vant, *adj.* not seeing all that is to be seen.—*n.* **inobser'vance,** failure to notice: failure to obey.

inoc'ūlate, *v.* to give a person a slight attack of a disease (by putting germs in his blood) so that he may not readily take it in the ordinary way.—*n.* inocula'-tion.

inoffen'sive, *adj.* doing no harm: not cheeky.

inopportune', *adj.* coming at a wrong time.

inor'dinate, *adj.* going beyond the limit.

inquest, in'kwest, *n.* an inquiry which the law (in England) says must be made when a person's death is due to an accident or to some unknown cause.

inquietude, in-kwī'e-tūd, *n.* un-easiness of mind: anxiety.

inquire, in-kwīr', *v.* to ask a question: to seek out.—*adj.* inquir'ing, eager to find out.—*ns.* inquir'er; inquir'y, a question: a search for in-formation.—Also spelt **enquire'**, **enquir'ing**, **enquir'er**, **enquir'y**.

inquisitive, in-kwiz'i-tiv, *adj.* fond of asking questions.—*n.* Inquis'i-tion, a Roman Catholic court first set up in Spain in olden times to try and punish those whose be-liefs were thought to be wrong.

in'road, *n.* sudden attack: heavy use (of one's savings, stores, etc.).

insane', *adj.* weak in the mind, mad. —*n.* insan'ity.

insan'itary, *adj.* unhealthy: likely to help the spread of disease.

insatiable, in-sā'shi-abl, *adj.* not able to be satisfied.

inscribe', *v.* to write in or on (e.g. a name on the first page of a book, or on a monument).—*n.* inscrip'-tion, the writing on a book, monu-ment, etc.

inscrutable, in-skroot'a-bl, *adj.* not able to be understood.

in'sect, *n.* any small creature with wings and a body divided into sections.—*n.* insec'ticide, powder or liquid for killing insects.—*adj.* insectiv'orous, (of plants and animals) feeding on insects.

insecure', *adj.* not safe.—*n.* in-secu'rity.

insen'sible, *adj.* not having feeling: too small to be noticed.—*adj.* insen'sitive, having no feeling for finer things.

insep'arable, *adj.* not able to be separated.

insert', *v.* to put in or among.—*n.* inser'tion, something put in.

in'set, *n.* something set in (e.g. a photograph among print).

inshore', *adv.* to or near the shore.

insid'ious, *adj.* likely to trap those who are not careful: treacherous: coming on unnoticed.

insight, in'sīt, *n.* power of looking into a matter and understanding clearly.

insignia, in-sig'ni-a, *n.pl.* signs or badges showing that one holds an office.

insignificant, in-sig-nif'i-kant, *adj.* having no meaning: of little im-portance.—*n.* insignif'icance.

insincere', in-sin-sēr', *adj.* not truth-ful: not to be trusted.—*n.* in-sincer'ity.

insin'uate, *v.* to hint at a fault: to work one's self into favour.—*n.* insinua'tion, a sly hint about a person (e.g. Tommy is always well-behaved when his rich aunt is about).

insip'id, *adj.* tasteless: without liveliness.

insist',*v.* to urge something strongly: to refuse to give way on a matter. —*adj.* insist'ent, holding fast to what one claims: demanding attention at once.—*n.* insist'-ence.

in'solent, *adj.* rude, cheeky.—*n.* in'solence.

insol'uble, *adj.* not able to be melted: not able to be explained. —*adj.* insol'vent, not able to pay one's debts.—*n.* insol'vency.

insom'nia, *n.* sleeplessness.

inspect', *v.* to look into: to examine thoroughly.—*ns.* inspec'tion,care-ful examination; inspec'tor, one who looks into: a person who examines.

inspire', *v.* to put into the mind: to encourage with noble thoughts. —*n.* inspira'tion, an intake of breath: something which gives great encouragement.—*adj.* in-spired', working as if aided by God: full of lofty spirit.

insta'ble, *adj.* not of a steady char-acter.—*n.* instabil'ity.

install, **instal**, in-stawl', *v.* to place in a seat or office: to place in position for use (e.g. Electric light has been *installed*).—*n.* in-stalla'tion.

instal'ment, *n*. a part of a sum of money paid at fixed times until the whole amount is paid: one part of a serial story.

in'stance, *n*. an example.—*v*. to mention as an example.—**at the instance of**, at the request of; **for instance**, to take as an example.

in'stant, *adj*. urgent: quick.—*n*. the present moment of time: any moment of time: (in a date) the present month (e.g. the 5th *instant*, usually *inst.*).—*adj*. **instantān'eous**, done very quickly.

instead, in-sted', *adv*. in place of.

in'step, *n*. the arching part of the foot where it joins the leg.

in'stigate, *v*. to urge on: to stir up.—*n*. **instigā'tion**, the act of stirring up, esp. to evil.

instil', *v*. to put in little by little (esp. ideas into the mind).—*n*. **instillā'tion**.

in'stinct, *n*. a natural feeling or knowledge, which living things seem to have without being taught (e.g. Swallows are led by *instinct* to leave Britain in autumn and return to it in spring).—*adj*. **instinc'tive**, due to instinct, not to thinking out: natural.

in'stitūte, *v*. to set going.—*n*. a law or rule: a society or association, or its meeting-place.—*n*. **institū'tion**, a society set up for some purpose (e.g. providing lifeboats): a building kept up by funds (e.g. *Institution* for Aged Seamen): a settled custom.

instruct', to teach: to order or command.—*n*. **instruc'tion**, teaching: command: (*pl.*) rules showing how something is to be used.—*adj*. **instruc'tive**, containing information or knowledge.—*n*. **instruc'tor**:—*fem.* **instruc'tress**.

in'strument, *n*. a tool: something which produces musical sounds (e.g. a piano, trumpet).—*adj*. **instrument'al**, acting as a cause or a means: helpful: belonging to or produced by musical instruments.—*n*. **instrument'alist**, one who plays on a musical instrument.

insubor'dinate, *adj*. disobedient.—*n*. **insubordinā'tion**.

insuf'ferable, *adj*. not able to be borne.

insufficient, in-suf-fish'ent, *adj*. not enough.—*n*. **insuffic'iency**.

in'sūlar, *adj*. having to do with an island.

in'sūlate, *v*. to cover or separate with rubber, glass, etc. to prevent escape of electricity.—*ns.* **insūlā'tion**; **in'sulator**, a substance through which electricity cannot pass (e.g. rubber, glass).

insult', *v*. to treat with contempt: to hurt feelings by rude acts or words.—*n*. **in'sult**.—*adj*. **insult'ing**, scornful, rude.

insū'perable, *adj*. that cannot be passed over.

insure, in-shoor', *v*. to make sure or secure: to make a payment or payments (carefully worked out according to the amount of risk) which will guard against loss by fire, accident, burglary, death, etc.—*n*. **insur'ance**.

insurgent, in-sur'jent, *adj*. rising up in rebellion.—*n*. a rebel.

insurmoun'table, *adj*. not able to be got over.

insurrection, in-sur-rek'shun, *n*. a rising up in rebellion.

intact', *adj*. untouched: unbroken.

intangible, in-tan'jibl, *adj*. not able to be touched: not clear.

integer, in'te-jer, *n*. a whole number, not a fraction.—*v*. **in'tegrate**, to combine (one group) with another, and treat all individuals in both alike.—*n*. **integ'rity**, honesty: purity.

in'tellect, *n*. the thinking power of the mind.—*adj*. **intellect'ūal**, showing or requiring intellect.

intelligent, in-tel'i-jent, *adj*. having power to understand: well-educated.—*ns.* **intell'igence**, skill of mind, knowledge: information sent, news; **intelligent'sia**, the well-educated people of a place.—*adj*. **intell'igible**, able to be understood.

intem'perate, *adj*. going beyond the usual bounds: drunken in one's habits.—*n*. **intem'perance**.

intend', *v*. to have in mind: to mean to.—*n*. **inten'tion**, what one means to do.—*adjs.* **intent'**, paying close attention: very keen; **inten'tional**, done on purpose.

intense', *adj.* to a high degree: severe.—*n.* **inten'sity**.—*v.* **inten'sify**, to increase.

inter', *v.* to bury.—*n.* **inter'ment**.

intercede, in-ter-sēd', *v.* to act as peacemaker between two persons: to plead with another on behalf of a person.—*ns.* **interces'sion**; **interces'sor**.

intercept', *v.* to stop and seize on its way: to cut off.

interchānge', *v.* to give something and get something, to exchange. —Also *n.*—*adj.* **interchange'able**, able to be used one for the other.

intercourse, in'ter-kōrs, *n.* a coming-and-going among: dealings between people.

interdict', *v.* to forbid.—*n.* **in'terdict**, an order that something must be stopped.

in'terest, *n.* advantage: benefit: special attention: a sum paid for the loan of money.—*v.* **in'terest**, to catch one's attention: to get a person's help.—*adjs.* **in'terested**, having the attention taken up: much concerned with a matter spoken about; **in'teresting**, taking up the attention.

interfēre', *v.* to meddle in what is not one's business: to hinder by coming up against.—*n.* **interfē'rence**, (in wireless) the clashing of two or more stations.

in'terim, *n.* time between: the meantime: one who holds a job only until someone is appointed for good.

intē'rior, *adj.* inner: away from the border or coast.—*n.* the inside of anything: the inland part of a country.

interject', *v.* to throw a remark in.— *n.* **interjec'tion**, word or words of exclamation (e.g. Ah! Oh dear!).

interlace', *v.* to lace or twine together.

interlard', *v.* to scatter in amongst.

interleave', *v.* to put blank leaves among other leaves of a book.

interline', *v.* to write (e.g. corrections) between lines.

interlock', *v.* to lock or clasp together.

interlō'per, *n.* one who trades without right: one who goes in where he has no right.—*v.* **interlope'**.

in'terlūde, *n.* a short piece of music played between the parts of a play, film, etc.: an interval.

intermar'ry, *v.* to marry among members of one tribe or race.

intermē'diate, *adj.* in the middle: coming between.—*n.* **intermediary** (in-ter-mē'di-a-ri), one who acts between two persons (e.g. in trying to settle a quarrel).

inter'ment, *n.* burial.

intermezzo, in-ter-med'zō, *n.* a short musical entertainment between acts.

inter'minable, *adj.* without limit: endless.

intermingle, in-ter-ming'gl, *v.* to mix together.

intermiss'ion, *n.* a stop for a time: a pause.—*adj.* **intermit'tent**, ceasing every now and then.

intermix', *v.* to mix together.

intern', *v.* to keep a person prisoner in a country while a war is going on.—*n.* **intern'ment**.

inter'nal, *adj.* inside: having to do with the inner part:—oppos. of *external*.

international, in-ter-nash'un-al, *adj.* having to do with the dealing between nations: world-wide.—*n.* a match between teams of two countries.

internecine, in-ter-nē'sīn, *adj.* killing each other.

in'terplay, *n.* the working of one part with another, as in a machine.

interpose', *v.* to place or come between: to put in by way of interruption: to interfere.

inter'pret, *v.* to explain the meaning of something said or written: to turn from another language into one that may be understood.— *ns.* **interpreta'tion**, the meaning given by an interpreter: explanation: an actor's way of playing a part: **inter'preter**.

interreg'num, *n.* the time between the end of one reign and the beginning of the next.

inter'rogate, *v.* to examine by asking questions.—*ns.* **interrogā'tion**, act of putting question to: a question: the mark placed after a question (P); **interrog'ative**, a word used in asking a question (e.g. *why, who*).

interrupt′, v. to stop a person while talking or working.—n. **interrup′tion**, a sudden break into talk or work.

intersect′, v. (of lines) to meet and cross.—n. **intersec′tion**, the point where two lines cross.

intersperse′, v. to scatter here and there.—n. **interspersion**.

interstice, in-ter′stis, n. a small space between things closely placed.

intertwine′, v. to twine or twist together.

in′terval, n. time or space between: a short pause in a programme.

intervene′, v. to come or be between: to join in a fight or quarrel between other persons or nations. —n. **intervention**.

interview, in′ter-vū, n. a meeting of one person with one or more others for purposes of business or giving information.—Also v.

intes′tate, adj. dying without having made a will.

intes′tines, n.pl. the inside parts of the body, usually the bowels and passages leading to them.

in′timate, adj. knowing much about: familiar.—n. a close friend.—v. to announce.—ns. **in′timacy**, close friendship; **intima′tion**, notice: announcement.

intim′idate, v. to make afraid, esp. with threats of violence.—n. **intimida′tion**.

intol′erable, adj. not able to be borne.—adj. **intol′erant**, not willing to put up with people of different ideas: harsh in one's treatment of those whom one dislikes.—n. **intol′erance**.

intone′, v. to read (the church service) in a singing manner.—n. **intona′tion**, the rise and fall of the voice.

intox′icate, v. to make drunk: to excite.—n. **intox′icant**, a strong drink.

intract′able, adj. stubborn.

intran′sitive, adj. (of verbs) not of the kind that can take an object (e.g. to go, to fall).

intrep′id, adj. without fear: brave. —n. **intrepid′ity**.

in′tricate, adj. difficult: having many twists and turns.—n. **in′tricacy**.

intrigue, in-trēg′, n. a secret plan: an underhand, mean plot.—v. to form such plot: to catch the interest of.

intrin′sic, adj. lying within: really belonging to the thing.

introduce′, v. to bring in or forward: to make a person known to another.—n. **introduc′tion**, act of making persons or some new thing known: something written at the beginning of a book (e.g. to tell what it is about or tell about the author).—adj. **introduc′tory**, coming at the beginning.

intrude′, in-trood′, v. to thrust one's self in where one has no right.— ns. **intrud′er**; **intru′sion**.—adj. **intru′sive**.

intuition, in-tū-ish′un, n. the power of grasping an idea at once, without thinking: an idea so grasped.

in′undate, v. to flood.—n. **inunda′tion**, a flood.

inūre′, v. to make accustomed.

invade′, v. to enter a country as an enemy.—ns. **inva′sion**, an attack made by an enemy into another country: an attack on the rights of another person; **inva′der**.

inval′id, adj. without value: having no effect.—adj. **in′valid**, sick: weak.—n. one who is weak in health.—vs. to put on the list of sick; **inval′idate**, to destroy the value of.—n. **invalid′ity**, lack of value.

inval′uable, adj. too valuable to be counted or measured.

inva′riable, adj. unchanging.

invasion. See invade.

invec′tive, n. coarse language.

inveigh, in-vā′, v. to speak bitterly against.

inveigle, in-vē′gl, v. to coax, to entice.—n. **invei′glement**.

invent′, v. to make for the first time: to make in the imagination.—ns. **inven′tion**, a new kind of tool, machine, etc.; **inven′tor**.—adj. **invent′ive**, ready in finding out new ways.

in′ventory, n. a list of articles, each mentioned separately (e.g. the goods of a dead person).

invert′, v. to turn upside down: to change the usual order, putting first last.—adj. **inverse′**, in opposite order : opposite in effect.— *n.* inver'sion, a turning upside down : a change of order.

inver'tebrate, *adj.* having no backbone (e.g. worm, limpet).

invest', *v.* to clothe (esp. with robes or decorations that show high position) : to surround, to lay siege to : to lay out money to get more.—*ns.* inves'titūre, the act of giving (with ceremony) a person a high position ; invest'ment, a siege : that for which money has been paid out : the money so paid ; inves'tor, one who invests.

inves'tigate, *v.* to search into with care.—*ns.* investigā'tion, careful search ; invest'igător.

invet'erate, *adj.* firmly fixed by long habit : deep-rooted : (of hatred) bitter.

invid'ious, *adj.* likely to cause ill-will or envy.

invig'orate, *v.* to strengthen, to fill with a feeling of freshness.

invincible, in-vin'sibl, *adj.* not able to be defeated.—*n.* invincibil'ity.

inviolable, in-vī'ol-abl, *adj.* not to be broken, harmed, or misused.—*n.* inviolabil'ity.—*adj.* invī'olate, free from hurt or disgrace.

invis'ible, *adj.* not able to be seen.—*n.* invisibil'ity.

invīte', *v.* to ask a person politely to do something (e.g. come to tea).—*n.* invitā'tion, a polite request to be present : a written notice with such a request.—*adj.* invīt'ing, tempting : attractive.

invocā'tion, *n.* a call or summons, esp. one in the form of a prayer.

in'voice, *n.* a letter, sent with goods, with details of price and quantity.—*v.* to make a list of goods sent, with their prices, etc.

invoke', *v.* to call upon earnestly or solemnly : to address in prayer.

invol'untary, *adj.* not done willingly.

involve', *v.* to have as a consequence : to mix a person up in an affair (e.g. Your presence in the house *involves* you in the burglary).

invul'nerable, *adj.* not able to be harmed.

in'ward, *adj.* placed within : situated in the mind or soul.—*advs.* in'ward, in'wards ; in'wardly, in the parts within : in the heart.

i'odine, *n.* a chemical much used in medicine as a germ-killer.

I O U, *n.* (short for *I owe you*) a note given as a receipt for money borrowed.

ipecacuanha, ip-e-kak-ū-an'a, *n.* a plant whose root yields medicine.

irascible, ir-ass'i-bl, *adj.* easily made angry.—*n.* irascibil'ity.

ire, *n.* anger.—*adj.* irāte', angry.

i'ris, *n.* the rainbow : the coloured part of the eye round the pupil (or centre) : a bulb-flower with large hanging petals :—*pl.* i'rises.—*adj.* iridescent (ir-i-des'ent), coloured like the rainbow : glittering with changing colours.—*n.* irides'cence.

I'rish, *adj.* having to do with Ireland.—*n.* language of the Irish : (*pl.*) the inhabitants of Ireland.—Irish stew, mutton, onions, and potatoes, seasoned and stewed.

irk, *v.* to weary : to distress (e.g. It *irks* me to do this).—*adj.* irk'some, tiresome.

iron, i'rn, *n.* the most widely used of the metals : an instrument of iron (e.g. one for smoothing clothes ; a golf-club, etc.) : (*pl.*) chains.—*adj.* made of iron : like iron : stern : not to be broken.—*v.* to smooth with a smoothing-iron.—*n.* i'ronmonger, a dealer in articles made of iron (called i'ronmongery).—iron curtain, the difficulties barring the way of people who want to find out what is happening in Communist countries.—to have too many irons in the fire, to be trying to do too many things at once.

i'rony, *n.* a way of speaking in which a person says one thing but means the opposite (e.g. 'You *are* smart,' meaning the opposite).—*adj.* iron'ical.

irrational, ir-rash'on-al, *adj.* against the rules of common-sense.

irrefū'table, *adj.* not able to be proved false.

irreg'ūlar, *adj.* against the rules : not coming at stated times : not in the usual form : uneven.—*n.* irregular'ity.

irrel'evant, *adj.* not having to do with what is being spoken about.—*n.* irrel'evancy.

irreli'gious, *adj.* not paying attention to religion : ungodly.

irreme'diable, *adj.* not able to be cured.

irremov'able, *adj.* not able to be removed.

irrep'arable, *adj.* not able to be repaired.

irrepres'sible, *adj.* not able to be kept in check.

irreproach'able, *adj.* free from blame.

irresist'ible, *adj.* not able to be kept off.

irres'olute, *adj.* not able to make up one's mind : not having a fixed purpose or aim.

irrespec'tive, *adj.* taking no account of (e.g. He went every day, *irrespective* of the weather).

irrespon'sible, *adj.* having no sense of what is serious.—*adj.* irrespon'sive, not answering.

irrev'erent, *adj.* having no respect for holy things.—*n.* irrev'erence.

irrev'ocable, *adj.* not to be changed (e.g. My decision is *irrevocable*).

ir'rigate, *v.* to lead water (by canals) to land which is dry, and so make it good for farming.—*n.* irriga'tion.—*adj.* ir'rigable.

ir'ritate, *v.* to make angry : to cause pain to the skin by rubbing.—*n.* irrita'tion, anger : redness of the skin.—*adj.* ir'ritable, cross, easily made angry.

island, i'land, *n.* a mass of land surrounded with water : a small raised space in a busy street where pedestrians may wait.—*n.* islander (i'land-er), an inhabitant of an island.

isle, il, *n.* an island.—*n.* islet (i'let), a little isle.

is'obar, *n.* a line on the map connecting places where the height of the barometer is the same.

i'solate, *v.* to place a person by himself (e.g. so that he may not cause harm to others) : to consider a thing by itself, not with other matters.—*n.* isola'tion.

isothermal, i-so-ther'mal, *adj.* having an equal amount of heat.—*n.* i'sotherm (or isother'mal line), a line on the map connecting places which have the same temperature.

issue, ish'ū, *v.* to go, flow, or come out : to give out.—*n.* a flow : children : the copies of a book, paper, etc. sent out at a time : result, consequence : the actual question which is argued about.

isth'mus, *n.* a narrow neck of land connecting two larger portions.

it, *pron.* something already spoken about (subject or object of verb).

Ital'ian, *adj.* belonging to Italy.

italics, *n.pl.* a kind of type which *slopes to the right* (as in the last four words).—*v.* ital'icise, to print in italics.

itch, *n.* a burning feeling in the skin : a strong desire.—*v.* to have a burning skin : to desire strongly.—*adj.* itch'y.

i'tem, *adv.* likewise : also.—*n.* a separate article or detail in a list.

itin'erant, *adj.* making journeys from place to place : travelling.—*n.* one who travels from place to place : a tramp or gypsy.—*adj.* itin'erary, travelling.—*n.* a guidebook : the road to be travelled.

i'vory, *n.* the hard, white substance which forms the tusks of the elephant, walrus, etc.—*adj.* made of, or like, ivory.

ivy, *n.* a creeping evergreen plant.—*adjs.* i'vied, i'vy-man'tled, overgrown with ivy.

J

jab, *v.* to poke, stab.—Also *n.*

jab'ber, *v.* to talk rapidly.—Also *n.*

jack, *n.* a screw for raising heavy weights such as a motor-car : a knave in cards : the small white ball which is the aiming-mark in bowls.—*ns.* jack'boots, large boots reaching above the knee ; jack'-knife, a large knife ; Jack'-of-all'-trades, one who can turn his hand to anything ; jack'-plane, a large, strong plane used by joiners ; Jack'-tar, a sailor.—every man jack, one and all ; yellow jack, yellow fever.

jackal

jackal, jak'awl, *n.* a wild animal of the dog kind.

jack'anapes, *n.* a cheeky fellow.

jack'ass, *n.* male ass: blockhead.—**laughing jackass**, the Australian giant-kingfisher or kookaburra.

jack'daw, *n.* a kind of small crow.

jack'et, *n.* a short coat: a loose paper cover for a book.

jade, *n.* worn-out horse: worthless woman: dark-green precious stone.—*adj.* **jā'ded**, tired.

jag, *n.* a notch: a splinter: a slight prick.—*v.* to mark with notches: to prick.—*adjs.* **jag'ged**, **jag'gy**.

jaguar, jag'ū-ar, *n.* a South American animal, like a leopard.

jail or **gaol**, jāl, *n.* a prison.—*ns.* **jail'-bird**, **gaol'-bird**, a person who has been in jail; **jail'er**, **jail'or**, **gaol'er**, one who has charge of a jail or of prisoners.

jam, *n.* fruit boiled with sugar to preserve it.

jam, *v.* to press or squeeze tight: to stick and so be unable to move (e.g. This wheel has *jammed*): (in wireless) to 'cut into' another station and make an unpleasant noise.

jamb, jam, *n.* the side-post of a door, fireplace, etc.

jamboree', *n.* a great and lively meeting of Boy Scouts.

jangle, jang'gl, *v.* to sound harshly: to quarrel.

jan'itor, *n.* a doorkeeper: a caretaker:—*fem.* **jan'itress**.

jan'izary, *n.* a Turkish soldier.

Jan'uary, *n.* the first month of the year.

Japanese', *adj.* belonging to Japan or its people.—*n.* the language of the Japanese.

japan', *v.* to varnish: to make black and glossy.

jar, *v.* to make a harsh sound: to be unpleasant: to hurt by shaking or dashing.

jar, *n.* an earthen or glass bottle with a wide mouth.

jar'gon, *n.* hurried talk, difficult to understand.

jarl, yarl, *n.* a noble, chief, earl.

jas'mine, **jes'samine**, *ns.* a plant with very sweet-smelling flowers.

jas'per, *n.* a precious stone.

jaundice, jawn'dis, *n.* a disease which causes yellowness of the eyes and skin.

jaunt, *v.* to go from place to place.—*n.* a journey, esp. one for pleasure.—*adj.* **jaun'ty**, showy: lively.

jav'elin, *n.* a long spear for throwing.

jaw, *n.* the bones of the mouth in which the teeth are set: the side of the face.

jay, *n.* a gay-coloured bird of the crow kind.—**jay-walker**, one who walks carelessly among traffic.

jazz, *n.* kinds of dance music of American Negro origin.

jealous, jel'us, *adj.* wanting to have what belongs to another, envious: carefully looking after what one thinks much of: allowing of no rival.—*n.* **jeal'ousy**.

jeer, *v.* to make fun of: to scoff.—Also *n.*

jel'ly, *n.* the juice of fruit boiled with sugar: anything in a half-solid state.

jem'my, *n.* a burglar's iron tool.

jen'net, *n.* a small horse.

jen'neting, *n.* a kind of early apple.

jen'ny, *n.* a female bird (e.g. *jenny wren*): a machine for spinning thread.

jeopardy, jep'ard-i, *n.* danger.—*v.* **jeop'ardise**, to put in danger.—*adj.* **jeop'ardous**.

jerbo'a, *n.* a small animal, with very long hind-legs.

jerk, *v.* to throw quickly: to give a sudden movement.—*n.* a short, sudden movement.—*adj.* **jerk'y**, moving or coming in jerks.

jer'kin, *n.* a short coat.

jer'sey, *n.* a close-fitting knitted jacket or under-vest.

jes'samine. See jasmine.

jest, *n.* a joke: fun: something made fun of.—*v.* to make fun.—*n.* **jest'er**, one who jests: (in olden times) a king's fool.

jet, *n.* a hard black mineral substance, used for ornaments.—*adj.* **jet'-black**.

jet, *n.* a spout of flame, air, or water.—*n.* **jet aeroplane**, one driven by air, which is sucked in, heated, and forced out backwards.

jet'sam, *n.* goods thrown overboard to lighten a vessel.—*v.* **jet'tison**, to throw goods overboard.

jet'ty, *n.* a small pier.

Jew, joo, *n.* one who is of the race of the Israelites :—*fem.* **Jew′ess.** —*adj.* **Jew′ish**, belonging to the Jews.—*n.* **Jew′s-harp**, a small harp-shaped musical instrument played between the teeth by striking a spring with the finger.

jewel, joo′el, *n.* a precious stone : anything or anyone highly valued.—*v.* to adorn with jewels. —*ns.* **jew′eller**, one who deals in jewels; **jew′ellery, jew′elry,** jewels.

jib, *n.* a three-cornered sail in front of a ship's foremast : the jutting-out arm of a crane.—*v.* to shift (a sail) from one side to the other.

jib, *v.* (of a horse) to shy : to refuse to do something.

jibe, jigot, jimcrack. See **gibe**, etc.

jig, *n.* a lively dance.—*n.* **jigsaw**, a puzzle consisting of many differently shaped parts which, when fitted together, form a picture.

jilt, *v.* to cast aside (a lover).

jingle, jing′gl, *n.* a clinking sound (e.g. of rattling metal): sameness of sound in words.—Also *v.*

jinn, *n.pl.* spirits formed of fire, sometimes appearing as men of great size and ugliness.—Also **djinn, ginn.** (The singular is **jin′nee**.)

jinrick′sha, *n.* in Eastern countries, a two-wheeled carriage drawn by a man.—Also **rick′sha, -shaw.**

job, *n.* a person's daily work : any piece of work.—*adj.* **job′bing**, doing odd jobs of work for payment (e.g. a *jobbing* gardener).— *ns.* **job′bery**, unfair means used for one's own gain; **job′-lot**, a collection of odds and ends.

Job's comforter, a person who, by his gloomy manner, adds to the trouble of the person he wishes to soothe.

jock′ey, *n.* one who rides horses in a race.—*v.* to bump against: to worry or bully a person into doing something.

joc′ular, *adj.* joking, merry.—*adjs.* **jocose′**, merry, playful; **jocund′,** cheerful.—*ns.* **jocular′ity; jocos′-ity; jocun′dity.**

jog, *v.* to push slightly : to travel slowly.

join, *v.* to put or grow together so as to make one piece : to become a member of.—*ns.* **join′er**, a wood-

worker, a carpenter ; **joint**, the place where two or more things join (e.g. two rails, two pieces of wood): that which holds things together: hinge: place where two bones are joined : animal flesh for cooking, esp. when containing joint-bone.—*adj.* united : shared among more than one.—*adv.* **joint′ly**, together.—**to join battle,** to engage in battle.

joist, *n.* the beam to which the boards of a floor or the laths of a ceiling are nailed.

joke, *n.* anything said or done to raise a laugh.—Also *v.*

jol′ly, *adj.* merry.—*n.* **jollifica′tion**, noisy feasting and merriment.— *ns.* **joll′iness, joll′ity**, merriment.

jol′lyboat, *n.* a small boat belonging to a ship.

jolt, *v.* to shake or go forward with sudden jerks.—*n.* a sudden jerk.

jonquil, jonkwil, *n.* a kind of lily, like a narcissus.

jō′rum, *n.* a drinking bowl : a drink.

joss, *n.* a Chinese idol.—*ns.* **joss′-house**, a temple ; **joss′-stick**, a stick of sweet-smelling gum burned by Chinese as an offering to their gods.

jostle, jos′l, *v.* to push against.

jot, *n.* a very small part.—*v.* to make rough notes.—*n.* **jot′ter**, a book for note-taking.

journal, jur′nal, *n.* a book containing each day's doings : a newspaper : a magazine.—*ns.* **jour′-nalism**, the business of running, or writing for, papers and magazines ; **jour′nalist**, one who writes for newspapers, etc.

journey, jur′ni, *n.* a distance travelled.—*v.* to travel.—*n.* **jour′ney-man**, one whose apprenticeship is now finished.

joust, joost, *n.* in olden times, the meeting of two knights on horseback at a tournament.—*v.* to fight on horseback at a tournament.

jō′vial, *adj.* full of joy and happiness.—*n.* **jovial′ity.**

jowl, *n.* the jaw or cheek.

joy, *n.* gladness.—*v.* to be glad.— *adjs.* **joy′ful, joy′ous,** full of joy.

jubilant, joo′bi-lant, *adj.* shouting or singing for joy.—*n.* **jubila′tion**, a shouting for joy.

jubilee, joo´bi-lē, *n.* joy-making in memory of some event (e.g. a wedding, the coming of a king to the throne) which happened fifty years ago.—**Silver Jubilee**, the 25th year; **Diamond Jubilee**, the 60th year.

judge, juj, *v.* to hear a question and decide according to the laws: to form an opinion.—*n.* (in the courts of law) one who hears cases and decides on them according to the country's laws: one skilled in finding out good and bad points.—*n.* **judg´ment**, a decision: a sentence passed: an opinion: good sense in forming opinions.

judicature, joo´di-kā-tūr, *n.* the law-system (judges, courts, etc.) of a country.

judicial, joo-dish´al, *adj.* having to do with a judge or court of justice.

judiciary, joo-dish´i-ar-i, *n.* the judges taken as a whole.

judicious, joo-dish´us, *adj.* wise.

judo, joo͞´dō, *n.* modern ju-jitsu.

jug, *n.* a dish for liquids, with a handle and a shaped mouth.

jug´gernaut, *n.* an idol of a Hindu god beneath whose chariot worshippers sacrificed themselves: any dangerous force or vehicle.

jug´gle, *v.* to toss a number of things (balls, clubs, etc.) into the air and catch them: to cheat by quickness of action.—*n.* **jug´gler**.

jug´ular vein, *n.* the large vein at the side of the neck.

juice, joos, *n.* the liquid in vegetables and fruits: sap.—*adj.* **juic´y**.

ju-jitsu, jiu-jitsu, joo-jit´soo, *n.* a Japanese kind of wrestling.

jujube, joo´joob, *n.* a jellied sweet.

July´, *n.* the seventh month. (From *Julius Cæsar*, who was born in it.)

jum´ble, *v.* to throw together without order.—*n.* a confused mixture.—*n.* **jum´ble-sale**, a sale of odds and ends, cast-off clothing, etc.

jump, *v.* to move by leaps.—*n.* a bound: a sudden movement.—*adj.* **jump´y**, easily startled.—**to jump to conclusions**, to decide that something is so, without waiting to make sure.

jump´er, *n.* a loose-fitting blouse or jersey.

junc´tion, *n.* a place or point of joining (e.g. of railway lines).

junc´ture, *n.* point, state of affairs (e.g. At this *juncture* he collapsed).

June, joon, *n.* the sixth month.

jungle, jung´gl, *n.* thick-growing trees, brush-wood, and tall grasses.

junior, joon´yur, *adj.* younger: in a lower class or rank.—Also *n.*

juniper, joo´ni-per, *n.* an evergreen shrub.

junk, *n.* a Chinese sailing-ship, high in the bow and stern.

junk, *n.* pieces of old rope: rubbish generally: salt meat supplied to vessels for long voyages.

junk, *n.* a thick piece, chunk.

jun´ket, *n.* curds mixed with cream, sweetened and flavoured: a feast or merrymaking.—*v.* to hold a feast.

jurisdiction, joo-ris-dik´shun, *n.* the district over which a judge or court has power.

jurisprudence, joo-ris-proo´dens, *n.* the science or knowledge of law.

jurist, joo´rist, *n.* one learned in the science of law.

jury, joo´ri, *n.* a number (not less than twelve) of men or women (or both) who decide in important law cases whether a prisoner is guilty or not.—*ns.* **ju´ror**, **ju´ryman**, one who serves on a jury.

just, *adv.* judging fairly, not favouring one more than another: exact: keeping within one's rights.—*adv.* exactly: not long since.

just´ice, *n.* fairness in making judgments: what is right or rightly deserved: a judge.—**Justice of the Peace** (shortened to **J.P.**), a citizen who acts as a judge for certain matters.

jus´tify, *v.* to prove or show to be just or right: to clear from blame.—*adj.* **justifi´able**, able to be justified or defended.—*n.* **justifica´tion**, good reason.

jut, *v.* to stand or stick out.

jute, joot, *n.* coarse cloth used for sails, sacks, etc.; made from the Indian plant fibre called **jute**.

juvenile, joo´ve-nīl, *adj.* young: suited to young people.—*n.* a young person.

jux´taposi´tion, *n.* nearness.

K

kale, kail, *n.* a cabbage with open curled leaves : broth made chiefly from kale.

kaleidoscope, ka-lī'do-skōp, *n.* a peep-show with great variety of beautiful colours and forms.—*adj.* **kaleidoscop'ic**, with many changing colours, changing quickly.

kangaroo, kang-gar-oo', *n.* a large and timid Australian animal with very long hind-legs and great power of leaping (the female carries its young in a pouch on the front part of its body).

kap'ok, *n.* a very light waterproof fibre fluff (got from the seeds of a tree) used for stuffing pillows, life-belts, etc.

kauri-pine, kow'ri-pīn, *n.* a forest-tree of New Zealand, yielding **kau'ri-gum** (used in making varnish).

ka'yak, *n.* an Eskimo canoe, made of seal-skins stretched on a frame.

kedge, *n.* a small anchor.

keel, *n.* the part of a ship stretching along the bottom and supporting the whole frame.—*v.* **keel'haul**, to punish by hauling under the keel of a ship by ropes from the one side to the other.

keen, *adj.* eager : very sharp : biting cold.—*n.* **keen'ness.**—**keen prices**, very low prices.

keep, *v.* to look after : to feed and clothe : to have or use : to fulfil (one's promise) : to remain in any position or state : (of food) to remain in good condition.—*n.* a castle stronghold.—*ns.* **keep'er**, one who looks after something (e.g. housekeeper, gamekeeper) ; **keep'ing**, care : charge ; **keep'sake**, a gift in memory of the giver.—**in keeping with**, suited to (e.g. His conduct was not *in keeping with* his position).—**to keep on**, to continue ; **to keep out**, to resist : to stay outside ; **to keep up**, to support : to continue ; **to keep up with**, to go as fast as.

keg, *n.* a small cask or barrel.

kelp, *n.* sea-weed : ashes of sea-weed, used for making iodine, etc.

kel'pie, kel'py, *n.* a water-sprite haunting fords in the form of a horse.

ken, *v.* to know.—*n.* the amount of one's knowledge.—*adj.* **ken'-speckle**, easily seen : outstanding.

ken'nel, *n.* a house for dogs.

kerb, *n.* the edge of a pavement : a fender.

kerchief, ker'chif, *n.* any loose cloth used in dress : a cloth worn by women to cover the head.

ker'nel, *n.* the substance in the shell of a nut : the stone of a pulpy fruit : the important part of anything.

ker'osēne, *n.* paraffin-oil.

ker'sey, *n.* a coarse woollen cloth.

kes'trel, *n.* a small kind of falcon.

ketch, *n.* a small two-masted vessel.

ketch'up, *n.* a flavouring sauce.— Also **catch'up, cat'sup.**

ket'tle, *n.* a metal pot, usually with a spout, for heating liquids.— *n.* **kett'le-drum**, a drum made of a half-globe of brass covered in with stretched skin.

key, kē, *n.* that by which something (e.g. a door-lock, a nut) is screwed or turned : the middle stone of an arch : in musical instruments, one of the small parts for sounding the notes : the chief note of a piece of music : that which explains a mystery : a book containing answers to exercises, etc. —*adj.* **keyed** (kēd), tightened up : standing ready.—*ns.* **key'board**, the keys in a piano or organ arranged along a flat board ; **key'hole**, the hole in which a key of a door, etc. is placed ; **key'-note**, the chief note of a piece of music : the chief point about anything (e.g. The *keynote* of his speech was ' Let us prepare ! ') ; **key'stone**, the stone at the highest point of an arch holding the rest in position.

khaki, ka'ki, *adj.* dust-coloured.—*n.* a light-brownish cloth used for soldiers' uniforms.

khalif. See **calif.**

khan, kan, *n.* a prince, chief, or governor.

kick, v. to hit with the foot: to show resistance: (of a gun) to spring back violently when fired.—n. a blow with the foot: the springing-back of a gun when fired.

kid, n. a young goat: goatskin: (slang) a child.—adj. made of kid leather.

kid'nap, v. to carry off a human being by force.—n. kid'napper.

kid'neys, n.pl. a pair of glands, placed in the lower part of the back, one on each side: sort or kind (e.g. The boys were of the same kidney).

kill, v. to put to death.—n. the animal killed by a hunter.

kiln, n. a large oven for baking bricks, baking lime, drying hops.

kil'ogramme, n. a measure of weight —1000 grammes (about 2¼ lbs.).

kil'omètre, n. a measure of length— 1000 metres (about ⅝ of a mile).

kilt, n. a plaited skirt reaching to the knee, forming part of the Highland dress.—adj. kil'ted, dressed in a kilt.

kimō'no, n. a loose robe, fastened with a sash.

kin, n. persons of the same family: relationship, either by birth or by marriage.—**next of kin**, one's nearest relative.

kind, adj. having good feelings towards others: fond of making gifts.—adv. kind'ly.—n. kind'ness. —adj. kind'ly, gentle, loving.— n. kind'liness.—adj. kindheart'ed, fond of treating others in a gentle manner.

kind, n. sort: race (e.g. The tiger is an animal of the cat kind): goods, not money (e.g. He was paid in kind).

kin'dergarten, n. a school for young children, where teaching is done by games.

kin'dle, v. to light a fire: to stir up (feelings).

kin'dred, n. one's relatives.—adj. of the same sort: related.

kine, n.pl. cows.

king, n. the name given in some countries (e.g. Britain, Belgium) to their chief male ruler.—n. king'dom, the country ruled by a king: one of the three great divisions of Nature (animal, vegetable, and mineral kingdoms). —adj. king'ly, like a king, royal. —ns. king'cup, buttercup: marsh marigold; king'fisher, a bird with bright-coloured feathers.

kink, kingk, n. a twist in a string, rope, etc.—v. to go into twists.

kins'man, n. a man of the same race or family:—fem. kins'woman.— n.pl. kins'folk (-fōk), one's own people, relations.

kiosk, kē-osk', n. a small out-of-doors roofed stall for sale of papers, sweets, etc.: a telephone-box.

kip'per, n. a smoked and dried herring.

kirk, n. (in Scotland) a church.— n. kirkyard', a graveyard.

kir'tle, n. a gown or petticoat.

kiss, v. to touch lovingly with one's lips: to touch gently.—Also n.

kit, n. a soldier's, sailor's, workman's outfit of clothes, tools, etc.

kitch'en, n. a room where food is cooked.—n. kitch'en-garden, a vegetable garden.

kite, n. a bird of the hawk kind: a light frame, covered with paper, for flying in the air.

kith and kin, friends and relatives.

kit'ten, n. a young cat.

kit'tiwake, n. a kind of gull.

kiwi, kē'wi, n. a swift-running, almost wingless bird of New Zealand.

kleptomā'nia, n. mad desire to steal.

knack, nak, n. a clever trick: a toy: tricky skill.—adj. knack'y, cunning: clever with one's hands.

knapsack, nap'sak, n. bag for food, clothes, etc., slung on the back.

knave, nāv, n. a cheating rogue: (in cards) the card between ten and queen.—n. knāv'ery, dishonesty. —adj. knāv'ish, cheating, wicked.

knead, nēd, v. to work by pressing with the fingers.

knee, nē, n. the joint at the bend of the leg.—adj. knee-deep, sunk to the knees (e.g. in snow).

kneel, nēl, v. to go down on one or both knees.

knell, nel, n. the sad sound of a bell as at a funeral: the end (e.g. War is the knell of happiness).

knickerbockers, nik′er-bok′ers, *n.pl.* loose breeches tucked in at the knee.

knife, nīf, *n.* a tool for cutting :—*pl.* **knives** (nīvz).—*v.* to stab.

knight, nīt, *n.* one of noble birth, trained to use arms : a rank, with the title *Sir*, which does not go down from father to son.—*v.* to raise to the rank of knight.—*adj.* **knight′ly,** having to do with a knight : full of courage : of good manners to ladies.—*ns.* **knight′-err′ant,** (in olden times) a knight who travelled in search of adventures ; **knight′hood,** the rank of a knight.—**knight of the road,** a highwayman.

knit, nit, *v.* to weave together by means of needles : to join closely. —*n.* **knitting,** woollen work, done by knitting.

knob, nob, *n.* a hard rounded part standing out from the main part (e.g. the *knob* of a door-handle).

knock, nok, *v.* to strike with something hard or heavy : to drive or be driven against : to tap on a door to have it opened.—*n.* a sudden stroke : a tap (on a door). —*n.* **knock′er,** the hammer on a door for making a knock.—*adj.* **knock′-kneed,** having knees that knock or touch in walking.—**to knock out,** in a boxing-match, to

hit an opponent so that he is unable to rise before ten is counted : to knock senseless.

knoll, nōl, *n.* a small rounded hill.

knot, not, *n.* a tight joint in string or rope, made by tying : the hard part in the wood of a tree where a branch shoots out : a small gathering, cluster (e.g. of people) : a speed-measure for ships (1 knot =about 6080 feet per hour).—*v.* to tie in a knot.—*adjs.* **knot′ted,** full of knots ; **knot′ty,** having knots : difficult.

knout, knoot, *n.* a whip.

know, nō, *v.* to be aware of : to recognise.—*adj.* **know′ing,** clever : cunning.—*n.* **knowledge** (nol′ej), that which is known : information : skill.

knuckle, nuk′l, *n.* a joint of the fingers.—*v.* to bend the fingers : (with *under*) to give in.

koala bear, kō-ah′la, *n.* Australian tree-climbing animal, like a 'teddy-bear' but not really a bear.—Also spelt **kō′la bear.**

kook′aburra. See **jackass.**

kopje, kop′i, *n.* (in South Africa) a low hill.

Kōran′, *n.* the holy book of the Mohammedans.

kraal, krahl, *n.* a South African native village.

kū′dos, *n.* fame : glory.

L

lā′bel, *n.* a small written note fixed on to something (to tell its contents, owner, etc.).—*v.* to fix a label to.

lā′bial, *adj.* having to do with the lips.

lab′oratory, *n.* a chemist's or scientist's workroom.

lā′bour, *n.* hard work.—*v.* to work hard : to move slowly.—*adjs.* **labō′rious,** toilsome : wearisome : hard-working ; **lā′boured,** made with much labour : clumsy.— *n.* **lā′bourer,** one who does work requiring little skill.—**labour of love,** work done for the love of doing it, without hope of payment ; **hard labour,** see under **hard.**

labur′num, *n.* a tree with large

hanging clusters of beautiful yellow or purple flowers.

lab′yrinth, *n.* a place full of windings, a maze.—*adj.* **labyrinth′ine,** like a labyrinth : causing confusion by twists and turns.

lac, *n.* a dark-red gum which comes from the East and is used in dyeing.

lace, *n.* a string or cord, for fastening shoes, leggings, footballs, etc. : fine open-work done with silk, linen, or cotton thread.—*v.* to fasten with a lace.

lacerate, las′er-āt, *v.* to tear : to hurt.

lack, *v.* to be in want : to be without. —*n.* want, need : shortage.—*adj.* **lack′-lus′tre,** without brightness.

lackadai′sical, *adj.* with a bored or

tired look : half-hearted, lacking in energy.

lack'ey, *n.* a man-servant.

lacon'ic, *adj.* using few words (but meaning much).

lacquer, lak'er, *n.* a varnish made of lac.—*v.* to cover with lacquer.

lacrosse', *n.* a twelve-a-side ball-game played with sticks having a shallow net at the end.

lac'tic, *adj.* having to do with milk.

lad, *n.* a boy : a youth.—*fem.* **lass.**

lad'der, *n.* a frame made with steps placed between two upright pieces, by which one may go up or down.

lade, *v.* to load.—*n.* a channel for leading water to a mill-wheel.—*n.* **lād'ing,** that which is loaded: cargo.

lā'dle, *n.* a large spoon (with long handle) for lifting out liquid.—*v.* to lift with a ladle.

lā'dy, *n.* a woman of good manners : a title of the wives of knights, and ranks above them, and of the daughters of noblemen :—*pl.* **ladies** (lā'diz).—*n.* **lā'dybird,** a small beetle, usually bright red or yellow.—**her lā'dyship,** the title of a lady.

lag, *v.* to move slowly and fall behind.—*n.* **lag'gard,** one who hangs back : a slow and lazy worker.

lagoon', *n.* a shallow pond or lake separated from the sea by low sand-banks, or shut in by rocks.

lair, *n.* the den of a wild beast.

laird, *n.* (in Scotland) a land-owner, squire.

laity. See **lay,** *adj.*

lake, *n.* a reddish colour.

lake, *n.* a large stretch of water surrounded by land.

lakh, lak, *n.* an Indian money measure (100,000 rupees, i.e. about £7500).

lam, *v.* to beat.

la'ma, *n.* a priest of Tibet.

lamb, lam, *n.* a young sheep : one gentle as a lamb.—*v.* to bring forth lambs.—*n.* **lamb'kin,** a little lamb.

lam'bent, *adj.* gliding over : flickering.

lame, *adj.* unable to walk, crippled : not good enough (e.g. a *lame* excuse).—*v.* to make lame.—*n.* **lame'ness.**

lament', *v.* to mourn, to wail for : to show grief.—*n.* a show of grief : a mournful poem or piece of music (also **lamentā'tion**).—*adj.* **lam'entable,** sad : pitiful : very bad.

Lam'mas, *n.* the harvest-feast rejoicings, held on 1st August.

lamp, *n.* a glass-covered light.—*n.* **lamp'black,** the black substance formed by the smoke of a lamp.

lampoon', *n.* an attack (in writing) upon a person.

lam'prey, *n.* an eel-like fish.

lance, *n.* a long shaft of wood, with a spear-head.—*v.* to pierce with a lance : to open with a *lancet* (see below).—*ns.* **lance'-cor'poral,** a soldier with rank just below a corporal ; **lan'cer,** a light cavalry soldier armed with a lance : (*pl.*) an old-fashioned dance ; **lan'cet,** a knife used by a doctor for cutting the body.

land, *n.* the solid portion of the earth's surface : a country : a district.—*v.* to set or come on land or on shore.—*adj.* **land'ed,** owning land : consisting of lands and estates (e.g. *landed* property).—*ns.* **land'-breeze,** a breeze blowing from the land towards the sea ; **land'fall,** an approach to land after a voyage : the land approached ; **land'-hold'er,** an owner of land ; **land'ing,** a coming ashore or to ground : a place for getting on shore : the level part of a staircase between the flights of steps ; **land'lord,** the owner of land or houses : the master of an inn :—*fem.* **land'-lady ; land'-lubb'er,** a landsman (a term of scorn used by sailors) ; **land'mark,** any object on land that serves as a guide to seamen ; **land'rail,** the corncrake ; **land'scape,** a beautiful view of inland scenery : a picture of such a scene ; **land'slide, land'-slip,** land that falls down from the side of a hill, usually due to the effect of water ; **lands'-man, land'man,** one who lives or serves on land : one who knows little about the sea.—*adjs.* **land'-locked,** almost shut in by land.

lan'dau, landaulette, lan-daw(-let'), *ns.* a carriage with a top which may be opened and folded back.

lane, *n.* a narrow road : a narrow street.

language, lang'gwāj, *n.* that which is spoken by means of the tongue : the speech of a nation : any manner of showing thought.— dead language, one no longer spoken ; living language, one still spoken.

languid, lang'gwid, *adj.* slack or feeble : wanting in liveliness.— *v.* languish (lang'wish), to grow weak or feeble.—*adj.* lang'uishing, longing for comfort : growing weak.—*n.* languor (lang'wur), state of being languid or faint : dullness.

laniard. See lanyard.

lank, *adj.* shrunken : (of hair) not wavy.—*adj.* lank'y, lean and tall.

lan'tern, *n.* a case for holding or carrying a light : the light chamber of a lighthouse : an opening on top of a dome to let in light.— *adj.* lant'ern-jawed, thin-faced.

lan'yard, lan'iard, *n.* a short rope or cord used for fastening, or as a handle (e.g. in firing a gun).

lap, *v.* to lick up with the tongue : to wash or flow against.

lap, *n.* the loose or overhanging flap of anything : the front part (from waist to knees) of a person seated : a round of the track in racing.—*n.* lap-dog, pet dog small enough to sit in its owner's lap.

lapel', *n.* the part of the breast of a coat which laps over and is folded back.

lap'idary, *n.* one who cuts and shapes precious stones.

lapse, *v.* to fall (into evil ways or careless habits) : to cease to exist (e.g. As his subscription is still unpaid, his membership has *lapsed*). —*n.* a mistake : a passing away.

lap'wing, *n.* the name of a bird of the plover family ; also called peewit.

lar'board, *n.* the left side of a ship looking from the stern, now called port.

larceny, lar'sen-i, *n.* stealing : theft.

larch, *n.* a kind of cone-bearing tree.

lard, *n.* the melted fat of the pig.— *v.* to smear.

lar'der, *n.* a room or place where meat, etc. is kept : stock of food.

large, *adj.* great in size.—*n.* large'ness.—at large, having escaped from prison.

largesse, lar-jes', *n.* a bountiful giving of money.

lar'go, *n.* a piece of music played in a slow and stately manner.

lar'iat, *n.* a rope for fastening horses while grazing : a lasso.

lark, *n.* a well-known singing-bird.

lark, *n.* a trick, a frolic.—*v.* to play tricks : to make fun.

lar'va, *n.* an insect in its first stage after coming out of the egg (i.e. in the caterpillar state).

larynx, lar'ingks, *n.* the upper part of the windpipe : the throat.— *n.* laryngitis (lar-in-ji'tis), a disease causing sore throat.

las'car, *n.* an Indian sailor.

lascivious, las-siv'i-us, *adj.* of bad mind.

lash, *n.* a thong or cord of a whip : a stroke with a whip.—*v.* to strike with a whip or lash : to fasten with a rope or cord : to hurt by bitter words.

lass, *n.* (*fem.* of lad) a girl : a sweetheart.

las'situde, *n.* faintness : weariness.

lasso', *n.* a long rope with a running noose for catching wild horses, etc. :—*pl.* lass'oes.—*v.* lasso', to catch with a lasso.

last, *n.* a foot-like shape on which boots and shoes are repaired.

last, *v.* to continue, go on : to remain in good condition.

last, *adj.* coming after all the others : final : most recent.—at last, in the end ; first and last, altogether ; on one's last legs, completely worn out, about to collapse ; to the last, to the end.

latch, *n.* a small piece of wood or iron to fasten a door.—*v.* to fasten with a latch.—*ns.* latch'et, a strap or buckle for fastening a shoe ; latch'key, a key to raise the latch of a door.

late, *adj.* slow : coming after the expected time : far on : recently dead : towards the close : not long past.—*n.* late′ness, state of being late.—of late, recently.

lā′tent, *adj.* lying hidden.

lat′eral, *adj.* coming from, or placed on, the side.

lā′tex, *n.* the milky juice of plants.

lath, *n.* a thin narrow strip of wood.

lathe, lăth, *n.* a machine which shapes articles of wood, metal, etc. by turning them against cutting edges.

lath′er, *n.* a foam or froth (e.g. from soap and water).—*v.* to cover with lather.

Lat′in, *n.* the language of ancient Rome. — Latin races, French, Italians, Spanish, Portuguese.

lat′itude, *n.* the distance, measured in degrees on the map, of a place north or south from the equator: freedom from worrying rules.

lat′ter, *adj.* coming after: the last of two mentioned: recent.—*adj.* latt′er-day, belonging to recent times.—*adv.* latt′erly, recently.

lattice, lat′is, *n.* a network of crossed wooden strips (also lattice-work).—*adj.* lat′ticed, like a lattice.

laud, *v.* to praise.—Also *n.*—*adjs.* laud′able, worthy of being praised; laud′atory, expressing praise.

laud′anum, *n.* a drug made from poppy-seeds.

laugh, lahf, *v.* to show joy by sound of the voice and look of face: to be gay or lively: (with *at*) to scorn.—*n.* the sound caused by merriment.—*adj.* laugh′able, raising laughter: comical.—*ns.*

laughter (lahf′ter), the act or noise of laughing; laugh′ing-stock, an object of scornful laughter.

launch, lawnsh, *v.* to throw (a lance or spear): to send forth: to cause a new ship to slide into the water.—*n.* act of moving a ship into the water.

launch, lawnsh, *n.* a large boat driven by petrol or steam-engine.

laun′dress, *n.* a woman who washes and irons clothes.—*v.* laun′der, to wash and iron clothes.—*n.* laun′dry, a place where such work is done.

laureate, law′re-āt, *n.* a person crowned with a wreath of the *laurel-tree* (i.e. the bay-tree) as a sign of high honour (e.g. the Poet Laureate of Britain, who writes poems about important events).

la′va, *n.* melted rock thrown out by a volcano.

lav′atory, *n.* a place where one may wash the face and hands.—*v.* lave, to wash: to bathe.

lav′ender, *n.* a plant with pale-purple, sweet-smelling flowers: a pale-purple colour.

lav′erock, *n.* a lark.

lav′ish, *v.* to spend freely: to waste.—*adj.* too free in giving or spending.

law, *n.* the collection of rules (some made by Parliament, others by custom) according to which a country is governed: any set of rules: (in science) a rule which says that in certain conditions certain things always happen.—*adjs.* law′-abid′ing, obeying the law; lawful, allowed by law; law′less, paying no heed to the laws.—*ns.* law′-giver, one who makes laws; law′suit, a quarrel to be settled by a court of law; law′yer, one whose work it is to give advice in matters of law.

lawn, *n.* fine linen.

lawn, *n.* a grassy space.—*n.* lawn′-mow′er, a machine for cutting the grass on a lawn; lawn′-tennis, a game played with a ball and rackets on an open lawn.

lax, *adj.* slack: not strict in keeping order.—*ns.* lax′ity, lax′ness; lax′ative, a medicine, having the power of loosening the bowels.

lay, *v.* to cause to lie down: to place or set down in position: to beat down: (of hens) to produce eggs.—*n.* lay′er, that which lays (e.g. a hen): a thickness or covering (e.g. There was a *layer* of ice on the pond): a shoot of a plant from which a new plant is grown.—to lay about one, to deal blows on all sides; to lay heads together, to plan together; to lay on, to strike, to act with vigour; to lay up, to store up: to put a ship in dock after unloading.

lay, *n.* a poem sung or told.

lay, *adj.* having to do with people who are not clergymen.—*ns.* lā′ity, ordinary people, not clergymen; lay′man, one of the laity.

lay′er. See **lay**, *v.*

layette, lä-yet′, *n.* a baby's complete outfit.

lay-fig′ūre, *n.* a model of a human figure used by artists.

laz′ar, *n.* one with a dreadful disease (usually leprosy).—*ns.* la′zar-house, **lazaret′to,** a hospital for lepers.

lā′zy, *adj.* not caring for work: idle.—*v.* **laze,** to be lazy.—*n.* lā′ziness.

lea, *n.* a meadow.

lead, *v.* to show the way by going first: to direct: to go through, to pass (e.g. He *leads* a busy life).—*n.* first or front place: a direction given by going in front—*ns.* lead′er, one who leads or goes first: a chief: an important part of a newspaper, in which the editor gives his opinions of the day's news (also called a **leading-article**); **lead′ership,** state of being a leader; **leading-strings,** strings used to lead children when beginning to walk: fussy care.

lead, led, *n.* a soft bluish-white metal: the part of a pencil which writes (short for *black-lead*, and really not lead but *graphite*): a weight used for sounding depths at sea: (*pl.*) sheets of lead for covering roofs.—*adj.* lead′en, made of lead: dull, heavy.

leaf, *n.* a part of a plant, usually a green blade growing from the side of a stem: anything thin like a leaf: a page of a book: a hinged flap or movable extra part of a table :—*pl.* **leaves.**—*n.* **leaf′let,** a little leaf: a small, printed sheet.—*adj.* **leaf′y,** full of leaves.—**to turn over a new leaf,** to begin afresh, and do better.

league, lēg, *n.* a measure of distance —3 miles.

league, lēg, *n.* a union of persons, nations, etc. for the benefit of each other, an association of clubs for games.—*v.* to join in a league.

leak, *n.* a hole through which liquid passes. — Also *v.* — *ns.* leak′age, that which enters or escapes by leaking.—*adj.* leak′y, having leaks.

leal, *adj.* true-hearted, faithful.

lean, *v.* to slope over to one side:

to rest (against).—*ns.* lean′ing, a liking for something; **lean′-to,** a shed whose supports lean upon another building or wall.

lean, *adj.* thin: bringing little profit.—*n.* flesh without fat.—*n.* lean′ness.

leap, *v.* to move with bounds: to jump.—*n.* a jump.—*ns.* leap′-frog, a game in which one boy places his hands on the back of another stooping in front of him, and leaps over his head; **leap′-year,** every fourth year (it has 366 days, February having 29).

learn, lern, *v.* to get to know: to gain skill.—*adj.* **learned** (lern′-ed), having great knowledge.—*n.* learn′ing, knowledge.

lease, *n.* an agreement giving the use of house, shop, farm, etc. for a number of years on payment of rent.—*v.* to let for a number of years.—*n.* lease′hold, property, or land, held by lease.

leash, *n.* a line by which a dog is held.—*v.* to put on a leash.

least, *adj.* smallest.—*adv.* in the smallest or lowest degree.—**at least,** or **at the least,** at the lowest reckoning: at any rate.

leather, leth′er, *n.* the skin of an animal, prepared (by tanning) for use in boots, bags, etc.—*v.* to beat. —*n.* leath′ering, a thrashing.— *adjs.* leath′ern, made of leather; leath′ery, like leather: tough.

leave, *n.* permission to do something (e.g. to be absent): parting of friends: farewell: a holiday (esp. of soldiers, sailors).

leave, *v.* to allow to remain: to forsake: to depart from: to make a gift to a person by one's will: to give to a person's charge or care.—*n.pl.* leav′ings, things left over.

leaven, lev′n, *n.* a substance (e.g. yeast) which makes dough rise in a light and spongy form.

lech′erous, *adj.* having a filthy mind.

lec′tern, *n.* a reading-desk in a church.

lec′tūre, *n.* something written or read to an audience, on a certain subject: a scolding.—*v.* to deliver a lecture: to scold.—*n.* lec′-turer, one who lectures.

ledge, lej, *n.* a shelf.

ledger, lej′er, *n.* the chief book of accounts of an office or shop.

lee, *n.* the side away from the wind, the sheltered side.—*n.* lee′way, the distance a ship is driven by wind off her true course : a falling behind.—*adj.* lee′ward, going in the direction toward which the wind blows.—*adv.* towards the lee.

leech, *n.* a blood-sucking worm : an old name for a doctor.

leek, *n.* a vegetable of the onion family.

leer, *n.* a sly, sideways look.—*v.* to look with a sly sideways glance.

lees, *n.pl.* dregs that settle at the bottom of liquid.

leet, *n.* a chosen list of candidates for a job.

left, *n.* the side opposite to the right. —Also *adj.* and *adv.*—*adj.* left′-hand′ed, using the left hand rather than the right : (of right-handed people) awkward. — **left-handed compliment,** one that hurts rather than pleases (e.g. Your father has done your homework well).

leg, *n.* one of the limbs by which animals walk : a long, slender support of anything (e.g. of a table). —*n.* leg′ging, an outer gaiter-like covering for the legs.—*adj.* leg′gy, having legs that look too long for body.—**on one's last legs,** at the end of one's strength, money, etc. ; **to pull a person's leg,** to tease him.

leg′acy, *n.* that which is left by will. —*n.* legatee′, one to whom a legacy is left.

lē′gal, *adj.* allowed by law, lawful : having to do with law.—*v.* le′gal-ise, to make lawful.—*n.* legal′ity, the state of being legal.

leg′ate, *n.* a person who has power to act for another : a person (an *ambassador*) who lives in a foreign country and looks after his own country's affairs there.—*n.* legā′-tion, the headquarters, staff of workers, and house of a legate.

legatee. See legacy.

legend, lej′end, *n.* a wonderful story handed down from olden time.—*adj.* leg′endary, told as a legend : not backed up by facts.

legerdemain, lej-er-dē-mān′, *n.* con-juring by quickness of the hand : sleight-of-hand.

legible, lej′i-bl, *adj.* (of writing) easily read.—*n.* legibil′ity.

legion, lē′jun, *n.* in ancient Rome, a body of soldiers of from three to six thousand : a great number (of people or soldiers).—*n.* lē′gion-ary, a soldier of a legion.

legislate, lej′is-lāt, *v.* to make laws. —*n.* legisla′tion, the action of making laws.—*adj.* leg′islative, having power to make laws.—*ns.* leg′islator, one who makes laws ; leg′islature, the part of the government which has the power of making laws.

legitimate, le-jit′i-māt, *adj.* lawful : born of married parents : genu-ine.—*n.* legit′imacy, lawfulness of birth : agreement with rule.

leisure, lezh′oor, *n.* time free from work : spare time. — *adj.* lei′-sured, not occupied with business. —*adj.* and *adv.* lei′surely, taking plenty of time.

lem′ming, *n.* a small rat-like animal.

lem′on, *n.* an oval fruit with yellow rind and very sour juice : the tree that bears lemons : a pale yellow colour.—*n.* lemonade′, a drink made from sweetened lemon juice and water.

lē′mur, *n.* a monkey-like animal of Madagascar.

lend, *v.* to give use of something for a time : to let for hire : (with *itself*) to be suitable for.

length, *n.* measurement from end to end : the time an action lasts. —*v.* length′en, to make or grow longer.—*advs.* length′wise, length′ways, in the direction of the length. — *adj.* length′y, of great length.—**at length,** at last.

lē′nient, *adj.* merciful : dealing punishment lightly.—*ns.* lē′nience, lē′niency.

lens, *n.* a piece of glass with curved surface or surfaces, used in spectacles, magnifying glasses :— *pl.* lens′es.

Lent, *n.* a fast of forty days (from Ash-Wednesday to Easter) in memory of Christ's fasting in the wilderness (Matthew iv. 2).—*adj.* Lent′en, having to do with Lent : simple, scanty.

len'til, *n.* the seed of a pod-bearing plant, used in soups, etc.

lē'onine, *adj.* like a lion.

leopard, lep'ard, *n.* an animal of the cat kind, with a spotted skin.

lep'er, *n.* a person with **lep'rosy,** a skin disease which slowly eats into the flesh.

less, *adj.* smaller.—*adv.* not so much.—*n.* a smaller portion.—*v.* **less'-en,** to make smaller.—*adj.* **less'er,** smaller.

lessee', *n.* one who has a house, shop, farm, etc. for a number of years, paying rent for it.

les'son, *n.* that which is learned or taught : a part of the Bible read in church.

let, *v.* to allow : to grant use of (e.g. a house, shop, farm) in return for payment.

let, *v.* to prevent.—*n.* hindrance.

lē'thal, *adj.* causing death.

leth'argy, *n.* dullness, sleepiness.—*adjs.* **lethar'gic, -al,** sleepy : moving slowly, as if drugged.

let'ter, *n.* a sign or mark for a sound (e.g. the *letters* of the alphabet) : a written message : meaning, exactly as stated (e.g. He carried out his orders to the *letter*) : (*pl.*) learning (e.g. a man of *letters*).—*v.* to mark with letters.—*adj.* **let'tered,** marked with letters : well educated.—*ns.* **let'tering,** the way in which letters are printed ; **let'ter-press,** reading matter printed from type ; **lett'ers-pat'ent,** a written statement giving certain rights (e.g. to make and sell something which has been invented).

lettuce, let'is, *n.* a plant whose leaves are used as a salad.

levee, lev'ā or le-vē', *n.* an afternoon meeting held by the Queen (or by someone acting for her) : a meeting at which some great person (e.g. the Queen) receives visitors, who pay her respect : a river bank.

lev'el, *n.* a flat, smooth surface : state of being even or equal with : an instrument for showing when a thing is lying perfectly flat.—*adj.* flat, even, smooth.—*v.* to make flat or smooth : to make equal : to take aim.—*adj.* **lev'el-head'ed,** having good sense.—*n.*

lev'el-crossing, a place where a road crosses a railway-track, usually having gates which are closed when a train is passing.

lē'ver, *n.* a bar of iron, wood, etc. used to raise up, or shift, something heavy : a bar or handle by which a machine may be started, stopped, etc.—*n.* **lē'verage,** the power gained by the use of a lever.

lev'eret, *n.* a young hare.

levi'athan, *n.* any huge monster, esp. a sea-monster.

lev'ity, *n.* lack of seriousness of temper or behaviour : thoughtlessness.

lev'y, *v.* to collect by order (e.g. a tax, men for an army).—*n.* money or troops collected by order.

lewd, lūd or lood, *adj.* taking delight in dirty thoughts or acts.—*n.* **lewd'ness.**

lex'icon, *n.* a dictionary.—*n.* **lexicog'rapher,** a maker of a dictionary.

lī'able, *adj.* likely to suffer from (e.g. an illness, attack of an enemy) : bound to answer for something (e.g. I am *liable* for the money you spend ; He is *liable* for service in the army).—*n.* **liabil'ity,** a debt.

liaison-of'ficer (li-ā'zong), *n.* an officer who goes between two forces on the same side, carrying information, etc.

liana, li-an'a, *n.* a climbing twining plant in the jungle.

lī'ar, *n.* one who tells lies.

libā'tion, *n.* the pouring forth of wine or other liquid in honour of a god.

lī'bel, *n.* anything written with the purpose of hurting a person's reputation. — Also *v.* — *adj.* **lī'bellous.**

lib'eral, *adj.* giving much or often : fond of giving money, gifts, etc. : not narrow-minded : (of education) all-round, not for one trade or profession only.—*n.* **liberal'ity,** kindness (in giving away money, gifts, etc.) : nobleness of mind.—*v.* **lib'er'ate,** to set free.—*n.* **liberā'tion.**

lib'ertine, *n.* one who lives a wicked, drunken life.

lib′erty, *n.* freedom to do as one pleases: permission: an impudent act.

libid′inous, *adj.* foul-minded, evil-living.

li′brary, *n.* a building or room containing a collection of books.—*n.* **libra′rian**, the keeper of a library.

libret′to, *n.* a book of the words of a musical play.

lice, plural of louse.

li′cence, *n.* a written permission giving right to do something (e.g. to keep a dog, gun, wireless set, sell stamps, tobacco, etc.): too great use of freedom.—*v.* **li′cense**, to give a right to: to permit.—*ns.* **licensee′**, one to whom a licence is given; **licen′tiate**, a person who has a right to carry on a profession.—*adj.* **licen′tious**, giving way to evil passions, evil-living.—*n.* **licen′tiousness**.

lichen, **li′ken**, *n.* a flowerless plant like moss, which grows on the surface of rocks, etc.

lich′-gate, *n.* a churchyard gate with a porch.

lick, *v.* to pass the tongue over: to take in by the tongue: to beat with blows.—*n.* the act of passing the tongue over: a tiny amount: a blow.—*n.* **lick′ing**, a thrashing.—**to lick the dust**, to be beaten and humbled: to be killed.

licorice. Same as liquorice.

lid, *n.* a cover for a box, pot, etc.

lie, *n.* false statement meant to deceive.—*v.* to tell a lie.—*n.* **li′ar**. —**to give the lie to**, to accuse of lie-telling.

lie, *v.* to rest in a flat position: to remain in a state or position.— **to lie in wait**, to rest in hiding in order to spring out on someone and take him by surprise.

lief, lēf, *adv.* willingly—now chiefly used in the phrases, *I had as lief go as stay*, I would as soon go as stay; *I had liefer go than stay*, I would rather go than stay.

liege, lēj, *n.* a true subject, a vassal. —*n.* **liege-lord**, an overlord.

lien, lē′en, *n.* a right to another's property until the owner pays a debt.

lieu, lū, used in the phrase *in lieu of*, instead of.

lieutenant, lef-ten′ant, *n.* an officer in the army next below captain, in the navy (pron. let-en′ant) next below a lieutenant-commander: rank below a higher officer, as lieutenant-colonel.

life, *n.* state of being alive: liveliness: manner of living: the story of a person's life :—*pl.* **lives**. —*ns.* **life′-belt**, a cork belt for keeping a person afloat; **life′-boat**, a boat for saving shipwrecked persons; **life′-time**, the length of time during which a person or thing lasts; **life′-work**, the work to which one gives up one's life.—*adjs.* **life′less**, dead: wanting in liveliness; **life′-like**, like a living person; **life′-long**, lasting as long as a life; **life′-size**, full size (e.g. a *life-size* painting of a man).

lift, *v.* to raise: to carry away.— *n.* a platform which moves up and down a building, carrying goods or persons: a rise in rank.

lig′ament, *n.* a tough substance which connects the movable bones of the body.

lig′ature, *n.* something which binds: a bandage.

light, līt, *n.* that which shines, and makes it possible for us to see (e.g. *light* of the sun, moon, lamps): day: a flame: a window: knowledge, learning.—*adj.* not dark, bright: whitish.—*v.* to give light to: to set fire to. —*v.* **light′en**, to make clear by giving light or knowledge: to shine clearly (like lightning). —*ns.* **light′house**, a tower-like building, with a flashing light to warn or guide ships or airships; **light′ship**, a ship with a warning light, anchored at a dangerous place.

light, līt, *adj.* not heavy: easy to bear or to do: lively: amusing (e.g. *light* reading).—*v.* **light′en**, to make less heavy.—*n.* **light′er**, a large open boat used in unloading and loading ships.— *adjs.* **light′-fin′gered**, apt to steal; **light′-foot′ed**, nimble, active;

light'-hand'ed, clever with one's hands: carrying little or nothing; light'-head'ed, thoughtless, silly; light'-heart'ed, cheerful; light'some, gay, lively.—ns. light'cav'alry, -horse, -in'fantry, lightly armed cavalry, etc.—to make light of, to think little of.

light, līt, v. (with on, upon) to come down to a landing-place, to settle on: to find by chance.

light'ning, n. an electric flash in the clouds.—ns. light'ning-conductor, a metal rod and wire which catches the electricity of lightning and carries it harmlessly to the earth, thus saving the building.

lig'nite, n. brown woody coal.

like, adj. the same or something the same (in appearance, amount, etc.).—n. something which is like, or equal to another thing.—v. li'ken, to say a thing is like something else.—adj. like'ly, like the thing required, suitable: probable.—adv. probably.—ns. like'lihood, the state of being probable; like'ness, that which is like a thing or person (e.g. a photograph).—adv. like'wise, in the same way: also.

like, v. to be pleased with, or fond of.—n. li'king, a fondness.—adj. likeable, of a kind nature.

li'lac, n. a small tree with hanging bunches of pale purple (sometimes white) flowers.—n. and adj. pale purple.

Lilliputian, adj. tiny. (In Swift's book Gulliver's Travels, the people of Lilliput were very small.)

lilt, n. a cheerful tune.—Also v.

lil'y, n. a plant grown from a bulb, with a large beautiful flower.—n. lily-of-the-valley, a plant with small white bell-shaped flowers.

limb, lim, n. a leg or arm.

lim'ber, n. a two-wheeled part of a gun-carriage holding ammunition, tools, etc.

lim'ber, adj. easily bent.

lim'bo, n. a place where things are thrown aside.

lime, n. the white substance (quicklime) left after heating limestone, used in making cement: any sticky stuff (e.g. bird-lime).—n. lime'kiln, a furnace in which limestone is burned to lime.—adj. lim'y, sticky: like or containing lime.—in the lime-light, being greatly spoken about.

lime, n. a kind of lemon tree, growing in America: the fruit of this tree: a well-known European tree (really linden), with small, sweet-smelling flowers.—n. lime'-juice, the juice of the lime, used as a drink.

lim'it, n. farthest point or place: a boundary.—v. to set bounds to.—n. limita'tion, that which limits: a weak point about a person or thing.

limn, lim, v. to draw or paint.—n. lim'ner, a portrait-painter.

limousine, lim-oo-zeen', n. a kind of closed motor-car.

limp, adj. lacking stiffness: weak.

limp, v. to walk lamely.—Also n.

lim'pet, n. a small shellfish that clings to rocks.

lim'pid, adj. clear: allowing light to shine through.

linchpin, linsh'pin, n. a pin used to keep a wheel on an axle.

lin'den, n. the lime-tree found in Europe.

line, v. to cover on the inside.—n. lin'ing.

line, n. a thread, string, cord, rope: a long pen-stroke: a row (of print, ships, soldiers, etc.): a business company running ships or liners: a railroad: telephone wire: a short letter or note: the equator: (pl.) trenches, etc. for defence of an army, town, etc.—v. to mark out with lines: to place in a row or by the side of.—adjs. lineal (line-al), descended in a direct line (from father to son); lin'ear, made of lines.—ns. lineage (lin'e-āj), one's descent, traced back to one's forefathers; lineament (lin'e-a-ment), a mark or line of the face by which a person is recognised; li'ner, a ship or aeroplane working on a regular service.—ship of the line, a regular warship; regiment of the line, a regiment of the regular army.

lin'en, n. cloth made of flax: articles made of linen (e.g. table-linen, bed-linen).

ling, *n.* a long slender fish like the cod.

ling, *n.* a kind of heather.

linger, ling'ger, *v.* to remain long: to dawdle.

lingerie, lang-zhe-rē, *n.* linen goods, esp. women's underclothing.

ling'ua fran'ca, *n.* a mixed language used by Europeans in dealing with Arabs, Moors, and other Eastern peoples.

ling'uist, *n.* one who knows or studies languages.—*adj.* **linguis'tic.**

lin'iment, *n.* a kind of thin ointment for rubbing away stiffness of the body.

li'ning, *n.* the cover of the inside of anything.

link, *n.* a ring of a chain : the $\frac{1}{100}$th part of a chain (7·92 inches): anything connecting.—*v.* to connect as by a link : to join closely.

link, *n.* a torch.—*ns.* **link'boy**, **link'-man**, one who carries a torch.

link, *n.* a crook or winding of a river.—*n.pl.* **links**, a stretch of flat or slightly hilly ground, esp. one where golf is played.

linn, **lin**, *n.* a waterfall or the pool beneath.

lin'net, *n.* a small song-bird.

lino'leum, *n.* a floor-cloth made mostly from linseed-oil.

li'notype, *n.* a machine which makes solid lines of type for printing.

lin'seed, *n.* lint or flax seed.—*n.* **lin'seed-oil**, oil from flax-seed.

lint, *n.* linen scraped into a soft wool for putting over wounds.

lin'tel, *n.* the timber or stone over a doorway.

lion, li'un, *n.* a fierce four-footed animal of great strength, the male of which has a shaggy mane : —*fem.* **li'oness.**—*v.* **li'onise**, to make a great fuss over a person.—**lion's share**, the largest share.

lip, *n.* the fleshy rim of the mouth : the edge of anything.—*v.* to touch lightly as with the lips.—*adj.* **lipped**, having edges like lips. —*ns.* **lip'-read'ing**, reading what a person says from the movement of the lips ; **lip'-serv'ice**, saying one thing but believing another.

liquefy, lik'we-fī, *v.* to make or become liquid.—*n.* **liquefac'tion.**

liqueur, lik-ūr', *n.* specially prepared strong drink, flavoured, perfumed, and sweetened.—*n.* **liqueur-glass**, a very small drinking-glass.

liquid, lik'wid, *adj.* flowing : (of sound) soft and clear.—*n.* a flowing substance.—*v.* **liq'uidate**, to settle up a debtor's affairs : to close down a business company. —*ns.* **liquida'tion** ; **liq'uidātor**, a man who sees to the closing down of companies.

liquor, lik'ur, *n.* anything liquid, esp. for drinking : strong drink.

liquorice, lik'ur-is, *n.* a plant with a sweet root used in medicine.

lira, lē'ra, *n.* an Italian coin.

lisp, *v.* to say *th* for *s* or *z* in speaking : to speak imperfectly, like a child.—Also *n.*

lissome, lis'som, *adj.* nimble, bending easily.—*n.* **liss'omeness.**

list, *n.* names, numbers, prices, etc. written down one after the other. —*v.* to write down in this way.

list, *v.* to like, please, choose : (of a ship) to lean over to one side. —*n.* a slope to one side.

list, **listen**, lis'n, *vs.* to hear or attend to: to follow advice.—*n.* **list'ener.** —*adj.* **list'less**, having no interest : weary.—*n.* **list'lessness.**—**listen in**, to listen to radio : to overhear intentionally.

lists, *n.pl.* the ground enclosed for a battle between knights.

lit'any, *n.* a set form of prayer.

lit'eral, *adj.* following the exact meaning word for word.—*adv.* **lit'erally**, exactly as stated (e.g. He was *literally* blinded by the flash, i.e. he actually lost the power of sight).

lit'erary, *adj.* having to do with books, authors, or learning : skilled in learning.—*adj.* **lit'erate**, able to read and write.—*n.* **lit'eracy**, ability to read and write.

lit'erature, *n.* the books that are written in any language, esp. those of the great authors : all that has been written on a subject.

lithe, *adj.* easily bent : active.

lithograph, lith'o-graf, *n.* a picture made from a drawing done on stone.—*n.* **lithog'rapher.**

lit'igate, v. to carry on a law-case.—ns. **lit'igant,** a person engaged in a law-case; **litiga'tion,** a law-case.—adj. **litigious** (lit-ij'us), fond of taking one's troubles to court: quarrelsome.

litre, lē'tr, n. metric measure of liquids, equal to nearly one quart.

lit'ter, n. a heap of straw, etc., as bedding for animals: an untidy mess of paper-wrappings, etc.: a bed for carrying the sick and injured: the young of an animal, born at one time (e.g. a *litter* of puppies, pigs).—v. to scatter carelessly about: to produce a litter of young.

littérateur, lē-tā-ra-ter', n. a man who is fond of books and writing.

lit'tle, adj. small in quantity or extent: brief.—n. that which is small in quantity or extent: a small space.—adv. in a small quantity or degree: not much.

lit'toral, adj. belonging to the sea-shore.—n. the sea coast.

liturgy, lit'ur-ji, n. the form of service of a church.

live, liv, v. to have life: to be fed or kept: to dwell.—**to live and let live,** to go one's own way and leave others to go theirs; **to live on,** to get one's food from; **to live down** (one's past), to live quietly until one's evil past is forgotten; **to live up to,** to be as good as expected.

live, adj. having life: active: apt to burn, explode, or give an electric shock.—v. **liv'en,** to make lively.—ns. **live'-stock,** farm animals; **live-wire,** a very active person.

live'lihood, n. one's means of living (e.g. one's daily work).

livelong, liv'long, adj. very long.

live'ly, adj. full of life, high spirits, movement.—n. **live'liness.**

liv'er, n. part of the body that purifies the blood.

liv'ery, n. uniform of men-servants.

liv'id, adj. black and blue: of a lead colour.

liv'ing, adj. having life: active, lively.—n. means of living (esp. that of a clergyman of the Church of England).—**living room,** a sitting-room for general use;

living wage, a wage on which it is possible to live comfortably.

liz'ard, n. a four-footed scaly reptile, with long body and tail.

llama, la'ma, n. a South American humpless animal of the camel kind, used for carrying loads.

llano, la'nō, n. one of the vast plains in the northern part of South America:—pl. **lla'nos.**

lo! look! behold!

loach, n. a small river-fish.

load, v. to put on as much as can be carried: to put on too much: to charge a gun.—n. as much as can be carried at once: cargo.—n. **load-line,** a line along a ship's side to mark the water-line when fully loaded. Often called the **Plimsoll Mark** (after Samuel Plimsoll, M.P., who thought of the idea).

loadstar. Same as **lodestar.**

loadstone. Same as **lodestone.**

loaf, n. a shaped mass of bread:—pl. **loaves.**—n. **loaf-sugar,** white sugar in square-shaped lumps.

loaf, v. to loiter, to pass time idly.—n. **loaf'er.**

loam, n. a rich soil of clay, sand, rotted plants.—adj. **loam'y.**

loan, loan'ing, ns. an open space between fields.

loan, n. anything lent: money lent for interest.—v. to lend.

loath, loth, lōth, adj. unwilling.

loathe, lōth, v. to dislike greatly.—n. **loath'ing,** great hate or disgust.—adj. **loath'some,** causing loathing or disgust.

lob, n. (in cricket and tennis) a slow ball bowled or hit underhand.—v. to send such a ball.

lob'by, n. a small hall: a passage off which rooms open.

lobe, n. the hanging-down part of an ear: a division of a leaf.

lob'ster, n. a shellfish with large claws, used for food.

lob'worm, n. a sea worm.

lo'cal, adj. of or belonging to a certain place (e.g. Wednesday is a *local* holiday in Little Mudford).—vs. **lo'calise,** to keep from spreading; **locate',** to place: to find where something is situated.—ns. **local'ity,** a district; **loca'tion,** situation: a dwelling-place for natives.—**local colour**, details in a story which make it fit a certain place.

loch, lohh, *n.* a lake: an arm of the sea.

lock, *n.* a catch to fasten doors, etc.: a part of a canal for raising or lowering boats: the part of a gun by which it is fired: a tight hold.—*v.* to fasten with a lock: to become fastened.—*ns.* **lock'er**, a hinged box that may be locked; **lock'et**, a little decorated case of gold or silver, usually containing a photograph; **lock'jaw**, a disease (*tetanus*) which stiffens the jaw muscles and keeps the mouth from opening; **lock'out**, the refusal of an employer to admit his work-people within the works, usually in a quarrel about wages; **lock'smith**, a smith who makes locks; **lock'up**, prison: section of a garage.—**lock, stock, and barrel**, with all one's goods.

lock, *n.* a tuft or curl of hair.

locomo'tive, *n.* a railway-engine.—*n.* **locomo'tion**, movement from place to place.

lo'cum-ten'ens, *n.* one taking another's place (esp. a doctor, or a dentist) for a time.

lo'cust, *n.* an insect, like the grasshopper, which feeds on and destroys growing plants.

lode, *n.* a water-course or channel: a vein of a metal in the earth.

lode'star, *n.* the star that guides, the pole-star.

lode'stone, *n.* a piece of iron ore which has the properties of a magnet. (In olden days the lodestone was used by sailors as a compass.)

lodge, loj, *n.* a small house (e.g. of a gatekeeper): a beaver's dwelling: a society (e.g. Freemasons) meeting privately.—*v.* to dwell in *lodgings* (see below): to become fixed (in): to put in safe place: to make known (a complaint).—*ns.* **lodg'er**, one who stays in lodg'ings, i.e. in hired rooms in another person's house; **lodg(e)'ment**, ground gained in attack: a resting-place, a refuge.

loft, *n.* a room or space just under a roof: a gallery in a hall.—*adj.* **loft'y**, high up: noble: proud.—*n.* **loft'iness**.

log, *n.* a bulky piece of wood (e.g. a felled tree): a device for measuring a ship's speed: a list of events, day by day, in a book (**logbook**).—*v.* to write down events (e.g. in a logbook).—*ns.* **log'-cab'in**, **log'-house**, **log'-hut**, a building made of rough logs.—**at loggerheads**, quarrelling.

lo'ganberry, *n.* a fruit like a large raspberry.

logic, loj'ik, *n.* the knowledge of the rules of reasoning correctly.—*adj.* **log'ical**, according to the rules of logic: according to common-sense.

loin, *n.* the back of an animal cut for food: (*pl.*) the lower part of the human back.—*n.* **loin'-cloth**, a piece of cloth for wearing round the loins.—**to gird up the loins**, to prepare for quick action.

loi'ter, *v.* to delay: to be slow of movement.

loll, *v.* to lie lazily about.

lone, **lonely**, lōn'li, *adjs.* alone: standing by itself.—*n.* **lone'liness**. —*adj.* **lone'some**, lying far from other people or their dwellings.

long, *adj.* not short: lasting much time: slow to come.—*adv.* for a great time.—*v.* to wish for very much.—*ns.* **long'boat**, the largest and strongest boat of a ship; **long'-bow**, a bow bent by the hand in shooting (i.e. different from the *cross-bow*); **long'ing**, an eager desire; **long'shoreman**, one who lives on the coast or shore. —*adjs.* **long-head'ed**, wise; **long-range**, able to reach or hit from a great distance; **long'-sight'ed**, able to see far but not close at hand: wise about things yet to happen; **long'-suff'ering**, putting up with troubles for a long time without complaining; **long'-wind'ed**, using many words but meaning very little.

longevity, lon-jev'it-i, *n.* great length of life.

longitude, lon'jit-ūd, *n.* distance east or west of the Greenwich meridian (see *meridian*). The longitude of any place is found by taking its meridian and measuring its distance from the Greenwich meridian, in degrees along the Equator.

look, *v.* to turn the eye towards so as to see : to seem : to face (e.g. this room *looks* south).—*n.* the act of looking : the expression on one's face : appearance.—*ns.* **look'ing-glass,** a glass which shows the image of the person looking into it, a mirror ; **look'-out,** careful watch : a high watching place (e.g. on a ship's mast). —**to look down on,** to despise ; **to look on,** to stand by and watch ; **to look over,** to examine (e.g. figures).—**Look out !** Be careful !

loom, *n.* machine for weaving cloth.

loom, *v.* to appear large or dimly.

loop, *n.* a doubled-over part in a piece of rope, string, etc.—**to loop the loop,** to drive an aeroplane upwards, backwards, and down, in a loop-shaped course.

loop'hole, *n.* a hole in a wall, for firing through : means of escape.

loose, *adj.* slack, free : unbound : not closely packed : careless.— *adv.* **loose'ly.**—*vs.* **loose, loos'en,** to make loose : to slacken.— **loose box,** a part of a stable where horses are kept untied.

loot, *n.* plunder.—*v.* to plunder.

lop, *v.* to hang down limply.—*adjs.* **lop'-eared,** having drooping ears ; **lop'-sid'ed,** heavier or bigger on one side than the other.

lop, *v.* to cut off the top or ends (e.g. of a tree).

lope, *v.* to run with a long stride.

loquacious, lo-kwā'shus, *adj.* talkative.—*ns.* **loquā'ciousness, loquac'ity.**

lord, *n.* a master : a ruler : the owner of an estate : a title given to noblemen, bishops, and judges. —*n.* **Lord,** God.—*v.* to rule harshly.—*ns.* **lord'ling,** a little lord ; **Lord's'-day,** Sunday ; **lord'ship,** power : rule : district under a lord ; **Lord's'-sup'per,** Holy Communion.—*adj.* **lord'ly,** like, or belonging to, a lord : noble, proud.

lore, *n.* learning.

lorgnette, lorn-yet', *n.* eye-glasses with a handle : an opera-glass.

lorn, *adj.* lost, forsaken.

lor'ry, *n.* a four-wheeled wagon for carrying goods.

lose, looz, *v.* to cease to have : to put something where it cannot be found : to waste (time) : to miss (the train, a chance, etc.) : to fail : to be beaten in a fight.— *ns.* **loser** (loo'zer), one who loses ; **loss,** harm : that which is lost : waste.—*adj.* **lost,** not able to be found : thrown away : ruined.— **to lose one's head,** to act stupidly owing to excitement.

lot, *n.* one's fortune or fate : a large number.—**to cast (or draw) lots,** to decide by methods of chance (e.g. by drawing names out of a hat) who is to do something.

loth. Same as loath.

lō'tion, *n.* a liquid for healing wounds or cleaning the skin.

lot'tery, *n.* the sharing-out of money or of prizes by chance.

lō'tus, *n.* the water-lily of Egypt : a tree whose fruit was said to bring on forgetfulness.

loud, *adj.* making a great sound : noisy : showy.—*advs.* **loud, loud'ly.**

lough, lohh, *n.* the Irish form of *loch*.

louis, loo'ee, *n.* an old French gold coin.

lounge, lownj, *v.* to lie back at one's ease : to move about lazily.— *n.* a kind of sofa : a room for lounging in.—*n.* **loung'er,** a lazy fellow.

louse, *n.* a small insect often found on bodies of animals :—*pl.* **lice.**

lout, *n.* a clumsy, awkward fellow.

love, luv, *n.* fondness : great affection : sweetheart, person loved : (in games, such as tennis) no score, nothing.—*v.* to be fond of : to delight in.—*adjs.* **lov'able,** worthy of love ; **love'lorn,** cast aside by one's sweetheart ; **love'ly,** beautiful : delightful ; **lov'ing,** full of love.

low, lō, *v.* to make the loud noise of oxen : to bellow.—*n.* **low'ing.**

low, lō, *adj.* not high : (of rivers) shallow : cheap : humble : sad (e.g. in *low* spirits).—*adv.* cheaply : not loudly.—*n.* **low'ness.**— *v.* **low'er,** to bring low : to haul down : to sink.—*adj.* **low'ly,** meek, humble. — *ns.* **low'liness ; low'land,** low or level country, without hills ; **low'lander,** a native of lowlands.

low'er, *v.* (of the sky) to become

dark and cloudy : to frown.—
adj. low'ering.

loy'al, *adj.* faithful to one's king,
country, duty.—*ns.* loy'alist, one
who is true to his king and
country ; loy'alty.

lozenge, loz'enj, *n.* a diamond-
shaped figure : a small sweetmeat, so shaped.

lub'ber, lub'bard, *n.* an awkward,
clumsy, or lazy fellow.

lubricate, loo'bri-kāt, *v.* to make
smooth or slippery, esp. with oil.
—*ns.* lu'bricant, oil ; lubrica'tion.

lucerne, loo-sern', *n.* a plant used
for feeding cattle.

lucid, loo'sid, *adj.* shining : easily
understood.—*n.* lucid'ity.

lucifer, loo'si-fer, *n.* a match.

luck, *n.* fortune, good or bad.—
adjs. luck'y, fortunate ; luck'less,
unfortunate : unhappy.

lucre, loo'ker, *n.* gain : money, esp.
money valued for its own sake
as by a miser.—*adj.* lu'crative,
giving gain or profit.

ludicrous, loo'di-krus, *adj.* silly
enough to be laughed at.

luff, *v.* to turn a ship towards the
wind.

lug, *v.* to pull or drag with effort.—
ns. lug'gage, the trunks and other
baggage of a traveller ; lug'ger,
a small sailing-vessel.

lugubrious, loo-goo'bri-us, *adj.*
mournful : dismal.

lug'worm, *n.* large worm found in
the sand on the sea-shore, much
used for bait by fishermen.

lukewarm, look-warm, *adj.* neither
hot nor cold : not very eager.

lull, *v.* to soothe or calm.—*n.* a
season of calm.—*n.* lull'aby, a
song to lull children to sleep, a
cradle-song.

lumbā'go, *n.* a sharp pain in the back.

lum'ber, *n.* useless material occupying space : tree-wood sawed or
split.—*v.* to fill with useless things.
—*ns.* lum'ber-man, lum'ber-jack,
one who cuts down trees and
brings the wood from the forest.

lum'ber, *v.* to move heavily.

luminary, loo'min-ar-i, *n.* any body
which gives light (e.g. the sun or
moon) : a person noted for his
knowledge.—*adj.* lu'minous, giving light : well lighted : clear.

lump, *n.* a shapeless mass : a swelling.—*v.* to throw together into
a mass.—*adjs.* lump'ish, heavy :
dull ; lum'py, full of lumps.—
a lump sum, an amount of money
given at one time.

lunar, loo'nar, *adj.* having to do
with the moon.—lunar month,
the time from one full moon to
the next, about 29 days.

lunatic, loo'na-tik, *n.* a madman.—
adj. mad : very foolish.—*n.*
lu'nacy.—lunatic asylum, an older
name for a hospital for persons
who are mentally ill.

lunch, lunsh, luncheon, lunsh'on, *ns.*
a midday meal.—*v.* lunch.

lung, *n.* a part of the body by which
breathing is done.

lunge, lunj, *n.* a sudden thrust or
push (e.g. with a sword).—*v.* to
thrust with a sword, fist, boot,
etc.

lupin, loo'pin, *n.* a garden plant
with flowers on long spikes.

lurch, *v.* (of a ship) to roll or pitch
suddenly to one side.—to leave in
the lurch, to leave in a difficult
position without help.

lūre, *n.* that which entices or leads
on, bait.—*v.* to entice : to lead
on.

lū'rid, *adj.* pale and sick-looking :
gloomy : terrifying.

lurk, *v.* to lie in wait : to keep out
of sight.—*adj.* lurk'ing, lying hid.

luscious, lush'us, *adj.* very sweet in
taste or smell : too sweet.

lush, *adj.* (of grass) rich and juicy.

lust, *n.* great desire, esp. for things
that are wrong.—*v.* (with *after,
for*) to desire eagerly : to have
evil desires.

lustre, lus'ter, *n.* brightness : glory :
a thin glossy dress material.—
adjs. lus'treless, without gloss ;
lus'trous, bright : shining.

lust'y, *adj.* lively : strong.

lute, loot, *n.* a stringed musical
instrument.

luxury, luks'ū-ri, *n.* something
pleasant but not necessary (e.g.
fine food, fine clothes) : a life of
pleasure, fine clothes and food,
etc.—*adjs.* luxur'iant, having very
great growth of leaves, branches,
etc. ; luxu'rious, fond of a life
of pleasure and good things.

lyddite, lid'it, *n.* a powerful explosive.

lỹ'ing, *adj.* in the habit of telling lies.—*n.* the habit of telling lies.

lỹ'ing, *adj.* being in a flat position.

lymph, limf, *n.* water: a colourless fluid in the body.

lynch, linsh, *v.* to judge and put to death without legal trial.

lynx, lingks, *n.* a wild animal of the cat kind, noted for its keen sight.

lyre, lir, *n.* a musical instrument like the harp.—*n.* **lyre-bird,** Australian bird with lyre-shaped tail.

lyric, lir'ik, *n.* a short poem, full of feeling.—*adj.* **lyr'ical,** full of joyful feeling.

M

macad'amise, *v.* to make a road out of small broken stones mixed with tar.

macaro'ni, *n.* wheat paste made into long tubes : a dandy.

macaroon', *n.* a sweet cake made chiefly of almonds and sugar.

macaw', *n.* a long-tailed, showy bird, of the parrot kind.

mace, *n.* a war-club, often spiked : a heavy staff with ornamental head (carried as a sign of office before certain officials, e.g. a mayor).—*ns.* **mace'bear'er,** **ma'cer,** one who carries the mace.

machination, mak-i-nā'shun, *n.* a plan for doing evil.

machine, ma-shēn', *n.* a working arrangement of wheels, levers, or other parts (e.g. a *sewing-machine, flying-machine*) : an engine.—*ns.* **machin'ery,** machines : the working parts of a machine ; **machin'ist,** one who makes or tends machinery ; **machine-gun,** a gun, mounted on a stand, which fires bullets very quickly one after the other.

mack'erel, *n.* a sea-fish like the herring.

mack'intosh, *n.* a waterproof overcoat.

mad, *adj.* out of one's mind : wildly foolish : furious with anger : insane.—*ns.* **mad'ness ; mad'cap,** a rash, hot-headed person ; **mad'house,** a house for mad persons : a lunatic asylum ; **mad'man,** one who is mad.—*v.* **mad'den,** to make mad or angry.

mad'am, *n.* a polite title given to a lady.—*n.* **madame** (ma-dam'), French for *Mrs.*

mad'der, *n.* a plant whose root gives a red dye.

madeira, ma-dē'ra, *n.* a white wine made in Madeira (Canary Islands).—*n.* **madei'ra-cake,** a kind of large sponge cake.

mademoiselle, mad-mwa-zel', *n.* French for *Miss* : a young lady.

Madon'na, *n.* the Virgin Mary : the picture of the Virgin Mary.

mad'rigal, *n.* a part song for five or six voices : a love song.

maelstrom, māl'strom, *n.* a whirlpool : any disturbance causing great confusion.

magazine, mag-a-zēn', *n.* a store for war materials, rifles, gunpowder, etc.: a weekly or monthly paper containing articles by different authors.

magenta, ma-jen'ta, *n.* a colour between pink and red.

mag'got, *n.* a small worm (e.g. of the kind found in rotten meat or fruit).—*adj.* **magg'oty,** full of maggots.

magic, maj'ik, *n.* the art of producing wonders by using secret powers: witchcraft.—*adjs.* **ma'gic, ma'gical,** having to do with magic : very wonderful, as if done by magic.—*n.* **magician** (ma-jish'an), one skilled in magic. —**black magic,** magic which is done by evil spirits and witchcraft ; **magic lantern,** a lantern which throws pictures on a screen.

magistrate, maj'is-trāt, *n.* a person who has the power of putting the law in force : a judge.—*adj.* **magistē'rial,** of the rank of magistrate : proud and stately.

magnanim'ity, *n.* greatness of mind : nobleness of nature : kindness.— *adj.* **magnan'imous,** not mean or selfish.

mag'nate, *n.* a person of high rank or great wealth.

magnē′sium, *n.* a white metal which burns with a dazzling white light, and forms a white powder called *magnesia.*

mag′net, *n.* a piece of iron which attracts iron, and if hung on a thread points north and south.—*adj.* **magnet′ic,** having the powers of a magnet: attractive (e.g. His *magnetic* nature won him many friends).—*v.* **mag′netise,** to make magnetic: to attract.—*n.* **mag′netism,** the power of the magnet: the science which deals with and describes magnets: charm in a person's nature.

magnē′to, *n.* the part of a car which makes the electric sparks that work the engine:—*pl.* **magnē′tos.**

magnif′icent, *adj.* great in deeds or in appearance: noble: splendid.—*n.* **magnif′icence.**

mag′nify, *v.* to make great: to make something appear larger than it is by looking at it through a magnifying-glass (a glass with curved surfaces).—*n.* **magnificā′tion,** the act of magnifying.

mag′nitude, *n.* greatness: size.

magnō′lia, *n.* a North American tree with beautiful leaves, and large white or purplish sweet-scented flowers.

magpie, mag′pī, *n.* a black-and-white chattering bird of the crow kind.

mahara′jah, *n.* the title given to a great Indian prince:—*fem.* **mahara′ni, mahara′nee.**

mahog′any, *n.* the hard reddish-brown wood of an American tree, much used for furniture.

Mahomedan, Mahometan. Same as **Mohammedan.**

mahout, ma-howt′, *n.* the keeper and driver of an elephant.

maid, maid′en, *ns.* an unmarried woman: a young girl: a female servant.—*adj.* unmarried: first (e.g. a *maiden* speech; a *maiden* voyage of a new ship).—*adj.* **maid′enly,** gentle, like a maid.—*n.* **maid′enhair,** a fern with fine hair-like stalks and leaves.—**maiden name,** the family name of a married woman before her marriage (e.g. The *maiden name* of Mrs Jenny Smith was Jenny

Brown); **maiden over,** in cricket, an over in which no runs are made.

mail, *n.* armour of steel rings or plates to defend the body: armour.

mail, *n.* letters carried by post.—*v.* to post.—*ns.* **mail′-bag,** a bag in which letters are carried; **mail-boat, -train,** a boat, train, which carries letters.

maim, *v.* to lame or cripple: to hurt.

main, *n.* strength (often used in the phrase *with might and main*).

main, *adj.* chief, principal.—*n.* the ocean: a large gas or water pipe in a street.—*ns.* **main′-deck,** the principal deck of a ship; **main′-land,** a country, without its neighbouring islands; **main′-mast,** the principal mast of a ship; **main′sail,** the principal sail, usually attached to the mainmast; **main′sheet,** the rope attached to the lower corner of the mainsail; **main′spring,** the spring which causes the wheels to move (esp. in a watch or clock): chief cause of action; **main′stay,** the rope which stretches forward from the top of the mainmast: chief support; **main′top,** a platform on the top of the mainmast.

maintain′, *v.* to keep anything as it is: to keep in good working order: to support: to hold (an opinion).—*n.* **main′tenance,** means of support (food, clothing, etc.).

maize, *n.* Indian corn.

maj′esty, *n.* greatness of rank or manner: a title of kings (used esp. in the forms *His* or *Her Majesty, Your Majesty,* etc.).—*adj.* **majes′tic,** stately.

mā′jor, *adj.* greater in number, quantity, or size: more important: older (e.g. Brown *major,* whose younger brother is Brown *minor*).—*n.* a person 21 years of age: an officer in rank between a captain and lieutenant-colonel.—*ns.* **mā′jor-dō′mo,** an official who looks after the household affairs of a palace or large house: a house-steward; **major′ity,** the greater number: the amount between the greater and the less number (e.g. Fifty voted for Smith, forty for Brown; Smith was appointed by a *majority* of ten): 21 years of age.

make, *v.* to form : to cause to be : to bring about : to amount to : to earn : to force : to pretend.— *n.* kind : shape.—*ns.* **mak′er**; **make-believe,** something pretended (also *v.*); **make′shift,** a thing used for a time for want of something better; **make′-up,** cosmetics for a woman, or for an actor or actress preparing for a part; **make′-weight,** small quantity thrown in to make up weight.—**to make good,** to prove one's self worthy of trust ; **to make out,** to discover, see in the distance : to declare, prove (e.g. He *made out* that Jones could not possibly have done it); **to make up,** to form a whole, along with other things (e.g. The three Houses *make up* the School): to put together a false story : to put powder and paint on the face : (with *for*) to give a thing in return for something lost or taken away (e.g. This money *makes up for* the books I have lost): (with *to*) to become friendly.

maladministra′tion, *n.* bad management, esp. of public affairs.

maladroit′, *adj.* clumsy : careless in what one says.

mal′ady, *n.* illness : disease.

malaise, ma-lez′, *n.* a feeling of sickness.

mala′ria, *n.* a fever caused by mosquito bites.

mal′content, *n.* a discontented person.—Also *adj.*

male, *adj.* masculine.—Also *n.*

maledic′tion, *n.* evil-speaking : a curse.

mal′efactor, *n.* an evil-doer : a criminal.

malev′olent, *adj.* wishing ill to others : finding pleasure in another's misfortune.—*n.* **malev′olence.**

malforma′tion, *n.* bad or wrong shape.

malice, mal′is, *n.* ill-will : spite.— *adj.* **malicious** (mal-ish′us), spiteful.

malign, ma-lin′, *adj.* harmful : malicious.—*v.* to speak evil of, to slander.—*n.* **malig′nity,** great hatred : deadly evil.—*adj.* **malig′nant,** wishing to do great harm : feeling great spite towards: dangerous to life (e.g. a *malignant* disease).

malinger, ma-ling′ger, *v.* to pretend illness in order to escape work.

mal′ison, *n.* a curse.

mall, mawl or mal, *n.* a large wooden hammer.

mall, mal, *n.* a level shaded walk : a public walk.

mal′lard, *n.* a wild duck (esp. the male).

malleable, mal′i-abl, *adj.* able to be beaten out by hammering.

mal′let, *n.* a small wooden hammer: the long-handled hammer for driving the balls in croquet.

mallow, mal′ō, *n.* a plant with soft, downy leaves.

malmsey, mam′ze, *n.* a strong, sweet wine.

malnutrition, mal-nū-trish′un, *n.* underfeeding.

malo′dorous, *adj.* having a bad smell : stinking.

malpractice, mal-prak′tis, *n.* wrongdoing.

malt, mawlt, *n.* barley or other grain prepared for making beer or whisky.—*v.* to make into malt. —*ns.* **malt′ster, malt′man,** one whose work it is to make malt.— *adj.* **malt′y.**

maltreat′, *v.* to use roughly or unkindly.—*n.* **maltreat′ment.**

mamma′, mama′, *n.* mother.

mam′mal, *n.* an animal that feeds its young with its own milk.

mam′mon, *n.* riches : the god of riches.

mam′moth, *n.* a large elephant, not now found living.—*adj.* huge.

man, *n.* a human being : the human race : one of the male sex : a husband : a man-servant : a piece in chess or draughts :—*pl.* **men.**—*v.* to supply with men : to guard (e.g. Here are soldiers to *man* the walls).—*ns.* **man′-at-arms,** a soldier ; **man′-eat′er,** a cannibal : a tiger ; **man′-hole,** a hole in a drain large enough to admit a man ; **man′hood,** state

of being a man : manly quality ;
man'kind, the human race ;
man'-of-war, a warship ; **man'-
slaughter,** the killing of a man
unlawfully but without meaning
to kill him.—*adjs.* **man'ly,** like
a man : full of courage ; **man'-
nish,** man-like in appearance.

man'acle, *n.* a handcuff.—*v.* to put
manacles on.

man'age, *v.* to conduct : to have
control of : to succeed.—*adj.*
man'ageable, easily managed
or controlled.—*ns.* **man'agement,**
skilful treatment : the persons
who look after a business ; **man'-
ager,** a person who looks after a
business :—*fem.* **man'ageress.**

man'darin, *n.* a Chinese official :
a small orange.

man'date, *n.* a command : power
given to person or nation to act
in name of another (e.g. Australia
administers New Guinea by *mandate* of the United Nations).—*adj.*
man'datory, having a mandate :
governed under a mandate.

man'dible, *n.* the lower jaw-bone.

mandoline, man'do-lin, *n.* a round-
backed stringed musical instrument—a kind of guitar.

man'drake, *n.* a plant which, when
eaten, brings on sleep.

man'drill, *n.* a large kind of baboon
found in Western Africa.

mane, *n.* the long hair on the neck
of the horse and the lion.

manganèse', *n.* a hard easily-
broken metal of a greyish-white
colour.

mange, mānj, *n.* a skin disease of
dogs, cats, etc.—*adj.* **mān'gy,**
scabby.

mangel-wurzel, man'gel-wur'zel, *n.*
a kind of beetroot, grown as food
for cattle.

manger, mān'jer, *n.* a trough to
hold food for horses and cattle.—
dog in the manger, one who will
neither enjoy something himself
nor let others do so.

mangle, mang'gl, *v.* to tear in
cutting : to hack or crush to
pieces.

mangle, mang'gl, *n.* a rolling-
machine for smoothing and pressing cloth.—*v.* to smooth with a
mangle.

man'go, *n.* an Indian tree and its
fruit.

man'grove, *n.* a tree which grows on
muddy shores and river-banks in
hot countries.

mā'nia, *n.* madness : too great
fondness for something (e.g. He
has a *mania* for old books).—*n.*
mā'niac, a madman.

man'icûre, *n.* the care of hands and
nails. — Also *v.* — *ns.* **man'icûre,
man'icurist,** one who sees to
hands and nails.

man'ifest, *adj.* easily seen or understood : evident. — *v.* to show
plainly.—*ns.* **manifestā'tion,**something shown plainly : a display ;
manifest'o, a public announcement of what is going to be
done.

man'ifōld, *adj.* of many kinds :
many in number.

man'ikin, *n.* dwarf : little fellow.

manil'a, manil'la, *n.* a fibre used in
making ropes : a kind of cigar.

mān'ioc, *n.* tapioca.

manip'ûlate, *v.* to handle : to
manage skilfully or cunningly.

man'na, *n.* the Israelites' food in
the wilderness (see *Exodus* xvi.).

mannequin, man'i-kin or -kwin, *n.*
a woman in a clothes shop, who
wears clothes to show buyers
how they look.

man'ner, *n.* the way in which anything is done : the way in which a
person behaves.—*n.* **mann'erism,**
an odd point about one's speaking, writing, or behaviour.—*adj.*
mann'erly, showing good manners.
—**all manner of,** all kinds of.

manœuvre, ma-noo'ver or ma-nū'-
ver, *n.* a clever movement of an
army or fleet : a trick : a cunning plan : (*pl.*) practice battles
and exercises (e.g. of troops, warships, aeroplanes).—*v.* to perform
a manœuvre : to move or manage
cunningly.

man'or, *n.* the land belonging to a
lord or squire.—*adj.* **manō'rial.**

manse, *n.* (in Scotland) the house
of a clergyman.

mansion, man'shun, *n.* a large dwelling-house.

man'tel, *n.* the shelf over a fireplace.—Also **man'tel-piece, man'-
tel-shelf.**

mantil′la, *n.* a kind of veil covering the head and falling down upon the shoulders.

man′tle, *n.* a covering: a loose, sleeveless cloak: a network round a gas-jet to give a white light.

man′ual, *adj.* having to do with the hand (e.g. *manual labour*, work done by the hand).—*n.* a small book: a handbook: an organ keyboard.

manufac′ture, *v.* to work up raw materials into useful articles.—*n.* the making of an article, either by hand or machinery: an article so made.—*ns.* **manufact′ory**, a factory or place where goods are manufactured; **manufact′urer**, one who runs a factory.

manūmit′, *v.* to set free from slavery.—*n.* **manumiss′ion**.

manūre′, *v.* to add something (e.g. dung) to land so as to make it more fertile.—*n.* anything that makes the land give better crops.

man′ūscript, *n.* a book or paper written by the hand: the written-out matter for a book before it is printed.

Manx, *adj.* having to do with the Isle of Man or its people.

many, *men′i, adj.* not few: a large number.—**many a man (woman, etc.)**, many men (women, etc.).

Maori, *mow′ri, n.* a native of New Zealand :—*pl.* **Mao′ris**.

map, *n.* a flat drawing of the earth's surface or of part of it.—*v.* to draw in the form of a map: to plan.

ma′ple, *n.* a tree, like the sycamore, whose leaf is the national sign of Canada; sugar is made from one kind of maple.

mar, *v.* to spoil: to ruin.

marabou, marabout, *mar′a-boo, n.* an Indian stork, whose feathers are used to make ladies' necklets, etc.

maraud′, *v.* to plunder.—*n.* **maraud′er**, a plundering robber.

mar′ble, *n.* a fine stone that takes a high polish, used for statues: a little ball of stone or glass.—*n.* **marble-gall**, a small, hard, brown ball which grows on oak-twigs and contains a tiny insect.

March, *n.* the third month.

march, *n.* a boundary of a country : —used chiefly in *pl.* **march′es**.—*v.* to border: to lie next to.

march, *v.* to walk with regular step: to go on steadily.—*n.* the movement of troops: a piece of music fitted for marching to : the distance passed over: a going forward (e.g. the *march* of events).

marchioness. See **marquis**.

mare, *n.* the female of the horse.—*n.* **mare's′-nest**, a discovery which turns out to be a fraud.

margarine, *mar′gar-ēn, n.* a substance like butter, and sometimes used instead of it.

margin, *mar′jin, n.* an edge, border: the blank edge on the page of a book: something extra, beyond what is needed.—*adj.* **mar′ginal**, placed in the margin.

marguerite, *mar′ge-rēt, n.* the ox-eye daisy.

mar′igōld, *n.* a plant with a yellow flower.

marine, *ma-rēn′, adj.* having to do with the sea.—*n.* a soldier serving on board a ship : shipping as a whole (e.g. the *mercantile marine*, the trading ships of a country).—*n.* **mar′iner**, a sailor.—**tell that to the marines !**=I do not believe you !

marionette′, *n.* a doll-like figure moved by strings.

mar′ital, *adj.* having to do with a husband, or with marriage.

mar′itime, *adj.* having to do with the sea or ships : lying near the sea.

mar′joram, *n.* a sweet-smelling plant used as a flavouring.

mark, *n.* a sign that can be seen: a target, a thing aimed at: high position (e.g. a man of *mark*): trace.—*v.* to make a mark on: to observe, watch (e.g. *Mark* what I say and do).—*adj.* **marked**, easily noticed.—*adv.* **mark′edly**.—*ns.* **mar′ker**, one who writes down the score at games (e.g. billiards); **marks′man**, one who shoots well.—**to mark time**, to move the feet up and down, as if marching, but without going forward; **beside the mark**, not connected with what is being spoken about; **trade mark**, a

mark put on goods, etc., to show by whom they were made.

mark, *n.* an old English coin= 13s. 4d. : a coin of Germany.

mar'ket, *n.* a public place for buying and selling : a chance for trade (e.g. There is a good *market* for cotton goods in India).—*v.* to buy and sell.—*adj.* **mar'ketable**, fit to be bought and sold.—*ns.* **mar'ket-cross**, a cross set up in olden times where a market was held ; **mar'ket-day**, the fixed day on which a market is held ; **mar'ket-gar'den**, a garden in which fruit and vegetables are grown for market ; **mar'ket-gar'dener; mar'ket-place**, the open space in a town where markets are held ; **mar'ket-price**, the price at which anything is sold in the market ; **mar'ket-town**, a town having fixed market-days.

marl, *n.* a rich soil (clay and lime).

mar'linespike, *n.* an iron tool, like a spike, for separating the strands of a rope in splicing.

mar'malade, *n.* a jam made from oranges, grape-fruit, or lemons.

mar'moset, *n.* a small American monkey.

mar'mot, *n.* an animal of the squirrel kind, about the size of a rabbit, found in the Alps.

maroon', *n.* a brownish-red colour : a kind of firework.—*v.* to leave a person on an island without means of escape.

marquee, mar-kē′, *n.* a large tent.

marquis, mar'kwis, **marquess**, mar'kwes, *n.* a nobleman next in rank to a duke :—*fem.* **mar'chioness** (mar'shon-es).

marriage. See **marry**.

marrow, mar'ō, *n.* the soft matter in the hollow parts of bones.—**vegetable marrow**, a large thick-skinned fruit used for food.

mar'ry, *v.* to join (or be joined) together, as husband and wife.—*n.* **marriage** (mar'ij), the ceremony by which a man and woman become husband and wife.—*adj.* **marr'iageable**, old enough to be married.

mar'ry! Indeed!

Marseillaise, mar-se-lāz′, *n.* the French national anthem.

marsh, *n.* a piece of low-lying wet ground.—*adj.* **marsh'y.**—*ns.* **marsh'-mal'low**, **marsh'-mar'i-gōld**, names of flowers which grow in damp places.

mar'shal, *n.* a high officer in the army or air-force (e.g. *Field-Marshal*, *Air-Marshal*) : one who directs processions, etc.— *v.* to arrange in order.

marsū'pial, *n.* any animal which carries its young in a pouch (e.g. the kangaroo, opossum).

mart, *n.* a market.

martel'lo, *n.* a round coast-fort.

mar'ten, *n.* a kind of weasel valued for its fur.

martial, mar'shal, *adj.* warlike : brave.—**martial law**, the government of a country by army rules and rulers (e.g. in times of sudden trouble or rebellion).

mar'tin, *n.* a bird of the swallow kind.

mar'tinet, *n.* one who keeps strict order.

Mar'tinmas, *n.* November 11th.

martyr, mar'ter, *n.* one who suffers death or hardship for what he believes.—*v.* to put a person to death for his belief: to torture. —*n.* **mar'tyrdom**, the death of a martyr: torture.

mar'vel, *n.* wonder.—*v.* to wonder: to feel surprise.—*adj.* **mar'vellous**, very wonderful.

mar'zipan, *n.* a mixture of ground almonds, sugar, etc., used in the making of sweets and cakes.

mas'cot, *n.* a person or thing that brings good luck.

mas'cūline, *adj.* of the male sex: manly.

mash, *v.* to beat into a mixed mass. —*n.* a mixture, esp. one of bran, meal, etc., beaten and stirred, as food for cattle or horses.

mask, masque, mask, *n.* a cover for the face, for a disguise: something pretended: a kind of theatre show.—*v.* to cover the face with a mask: to hide.

mā'son, *n.* a worker in stone: a freemason.—*adj.* **mason'ic.**—*n.* **mā'sonry**, stone-work.

masque. See **mask.**

masquerade, mask-er-ād′, *n.* a dance at which masks are worn.— *v.* to pretend to be someone else.

mass, *n.* a lump of matter: a quantity: the main body.—*v.* to form into a mass.—*adj.* **mass′ive**, bulky: heavy.

Mass, *n.* (in the Roman Catholic Church) the service of the Lord's Supper.

massacre, mas′a-ker, *n.* a great slaughter.—*v.* to slaughter.

massage, ma-sazh′, *n.* the rubbing of parts of the body (muscles, knees, etc.) to remove pain or stiffness.—Also *v.*—*n.* **masseur** (mass-er′), one who massages:—*fem.* **masseuse** (mass-erz′).

mast, *n.* a long upright pole for bearing the yards, rigging, etc. in a ship.—*n.* **mast′-head**, the head or top of the mast of a ship.

mast, *n.* the nuts of the oak, beech, chestnut, etc., on which swine feed.

mas′ter, *n.* an employer: a teacher: the commander of a merchant-ship: an expert: one who has passed certain high examinations of a university (e.g. *Master of Arts*).—*v.* to overcome: to become able to do a thing thoroughly.—*adjs.* **mas′terful**, strong-willed; **mas′terly**, showing very great skill, like that of a master. —*ns.* **mas′ter-key**, a key which is so made that it opens a number of different locks; **mas′terpiece**, a piece of work worthy of a master: the best example of an artist's work: a very fine picture, book, piece of music, etc.; **mas′terstroke**, a clever act; **mas′tery**, the power to command: power to understand or manage. —**passed** (or **past**) **master**, anyone who has great knowledge of some subject; **the old masters**, a name for the great painters of long ago.

mas′ticate, *v.* to chew.—*n.* **mastica′tion**.

mas′tiff, *n.* a large dog much used as a watch-dog.

mas′todon, *n.* a kind of elephant, not now found living.

mat, *n.* a material of plaited fibre, straw, etc. on which to clean the feet: a covering put below dishes at table.—*adj.* **mat′ted**, twisted together: thick or tangled.—*n.* **mat′ting**, material from which mats are made.

mat′ador, **mat′adore**, *n.* the man who kills the bull in bull-fights.

match, *n.* a small piece of wood, wax, etc. tipped with a substance which easily takes fire when rubbed.—*ns.* **match′-box**, a box for holding matches; **match′lock**, an old kind of gun fired with a match; **match′wood**, wood broken into small pieces.

match, *n.* anything which agrees with or suits another thing: an equal: a marriage: a contest or game.—*v.* to be of the same make, size, colour, etc.: to join in marriage: to hold one's own with. —*adj.* **match′less**, having no equal.

mate, *n.* a companion: a husband or wife: one of a pair of birds: a ship's officer, next in rank to the captain.—*v.* to marry.

mā′ter, *n.* a mother.

matē′rial, *adj.* made of matter: important.—*n.* that out of which anything is made: cloth.—*adv.* **matē′rially**, to a large extent, greatly.—*v.* **matē′rialise**, to happen: to be fulfilled.—*ns.* **matē′rialism**, the belief that nothing exists but matter, i.e. but what we can see or feel; **matē′rialist**, one who holds this belief.

mater′nal, *adj.* having to do with a mother (e.g. *maternal love*, love like that of a mother to her child; *maternal aunt*, one's mother's sister).—*n.* **mater′nity**.

mathemat′ics, *n.* branch of knowledge which deals with measurements and numbers—arithmetic is one division of mathematics. —*adj.* **mathemat′ical**, done by mathematics: very exact.—*n.* **mathematician** (math-e-ma-tish′an), one good at mathematics.

mat′ins, *n.pl.* morning prayers.—*n.* **matinée** (mat′ē-nā), an afternoon performance (e.g. in a theatre).

matricide, mat′ri-sīd, *n.* the killing of one's own mother: one who kills his own mother.

matric′ulate, *v.* to enter a person's name on the register of a university: to pass an examination (**matriculā′tion**) which gives the right to enter a university.

mat′rimony, *n.* marriage.—*adj.* **matrimō′nial**.

mā´trix, *n.* a mould in which metals, etc. are shaped:—*pl.* **mat´rices.**

mā´tron, *n.* a rather old married woman: a lady or nurse in charge of a hospital, school, boarding-house, or hostel.—*adj.* **mā´tronly,** (of a woman) not young: quiet and noble.

matted, *adj.* See mat.

mat´ter, *n.* that out of which anything is made: a subject written or spoken about: business: yellowish liquid coming from a sore or wound.—*v.* to be of importance.—*adj.* **matt´er-of-fact,** not fanciful: uninteresting.

mat´tock, *n.* a tool like a pickaxe.

mat´tress, *n.* a large flat bag, stuffed with wool or horse-hair, forming part of a bed.

matūre´, *adj.* fully grown: ripe, ready for use.—*v.* to ripen.—*n.* **matūr´ity,** ripeness.

maud´lin, *adj.* silly, soft: half-drunk.

maul, *v.* to beat: to hurt badly by rough treatment.—*n.* a heavy wooden hammer.

maun´dy money, the money given away on **Maundy Thursday,** the Thursday before Good Friday.

mausolē´um, *n.* a very fine tomb or monument.

mauve, mōv, *n.* a beautiful purple colour.

mā´vis, *n.* the song-thrush.

maw, *n.* the stomach.

mawk´ish, *adj.* sickening: (of a story) weak and silly.

max´im, *n.* a rule (e.g. for one's behaviour): a wise saying.

max´im, max´im-gun, *ns.* a light, quick-firing machine-gun.

max´imum, *adj.* the greatest.—*n.* the greatest number: the highest point reached:—*pl.* **max´ima.**

May, *n.* the fifth month of the year.—*ns.* **may,** hawthorn blossom; **May´day,** the first day of May; **may´pole,** a decorated pole for dancing round on Mayday; **May´-queen,** a young woman crowned with flowers as queen on Mayday.

may´be, *adv.* perhaps.

May´day, a distress signal.

mayonnaise´, *n.* a sauce of eggs, oil, vinegar or lemon juice, etc.

may´or, *n.* the chief member of a town council:—*fem.* **may´oress.**

maze, *n.* a place full of windings: a puzzle: a state of not knowing what to do.—*v.* to puzzle greatly.

mazur´ka, *n.* a lively dance.

mē, *pron.* the person who is speaking —objective case.

mead, *n.* a drink (honey and water).

meadow, med´ō, **mead,** *n.* grass land.—*n.* **meadow-sweet,** a wild-flower with cream-coloured blossoms.

meagre, mē´ger, *adj.* having little flesh: scanty.—*n.* **mea´greness.**

meal, *n.* the food taken at one time (e.g. breakfast, dinner, supper).

meal, *n.* grain ground to powder.—*adjs.* **meal´y,** covered with meal: **meal´y-mouthed,** using flattering words but not meaning much.

meal´ie, *n.* a South African name for maize.

mean, *adj.* low in thought or action, not noble: low-born, humble: greedy, esp. with money.—*n.* **mean´ness.**

mean, *adj.* middle: coming midway between other things.—*n.* something lying between: an average.—**the golden mean,** a midway course (e.g. Neither hesitate nor be too rash: strike the *golden mean*).—*n.pl.* **means,** that by which anything is caused: money, property, etc.—**a man of means,** a wealthy man.—*n.* **mean´-time,** the time between two happenings.—*advs.* **mean´time, mean´while.**

mean, *v.* to have in the mind: to intend.—*n.* **mean´ing.**—*adj.* showing feelings by one's looks.

meander, mē-an´der, *v.* to flow in a winding course.

meas´les, *n.sing.* a spreading disease, with red rash.—*adj.* **mea´sly,** ill with measles: miserable: greedy, giving little away.

measure, mezh´ur, *n.* something (e.g. a ruler, quart-jug) by which size or quantity is judged: size or amount: a slow dance: a tune: a plan of action: a law brought before parliament to be considered.—*v.* to find out size, quantity, etc. by using some measure: to mark out.—*adjs.* **meas´urable,** able to be measured; **meas´ured,** steady; **meas´ureless,** having no limits.—*n.* **meas´urement.**

meat, *n.* flesh used as food : any food.—*adj.* **meat'y**, full of meat.

mechanic, mechanical, mek-an'-ik(al), *adjs.* having to do with, or worked by, machinery : done without thinking.—*ns.* **mechan'ic,** machine-workman ; **mech'anism,** machinery, works (e.g. of a clock) ; **mechanised troops,** troops with tanks, motor lorries, etc.

med'al, *n.* a piece of metal in the form of a coin, with a figure or inscription stamped on it, given in memory of an event or as a reward of merit.—*ns.* **medall'ion,** a large medal ; **med'allist,** one who has gained a medal.

med'dle, *v.* to take to or do with something that does not belong to one.—*n.* **medd'ler,** one who meddles.—*adj.* **medd'lesome,** fond of meddling.

mediæval. See medieval.

mē'diate, *adj.* middle : lying between.—*v.* to act as a peacemaker between enemies.—*ns.* **mediā'tion,** peace-making : a request on behalf of another ; **mē'diator,** one who tries to make peace between persons who are quarrelling.

medicine, med'sin, *n.* something given to a sick person in order to make him better : the kind of work done by a doctor.—*adjs.* **med'ical,** having to do with doctors or with healing ; **medicinal** (me-dis'in-al), having power to heal (e.g. *medicinal* water).—*v.* **med'icate,** to mix with medicine.—*n.* **medic'ament,** a medicine.

medieval, mediæval, mē-di-ē'val, *adj.* having to do with the *Middle Ages* (i.e. the years between A.D. 500 and A.D. 1500).

mediocre, mē'di-ō-ker, *adj.* neither good nor bad, middling.—*n.* **medioc'rity.**

med'itate, *v.* to think deeply over : to plan.—*n.* **meditā'tion,** deep thought : worshipping God in silence by thinking deeply about Him.—*adj.* **med'itative,** thoughtful.

mē'dium, *n.* the means used to do something(*pl.* **mē'dia** or **mē'diums**): a person through whom spirits are said to speak (*pl.* **mē'diums**).

—*adj.* lying between : of middle-size (e.g. neither large nor small).—**the happy medium,** a way of acting which lies between (e.g. Do not spend all your money, do not save it all : strike a *happy medium*).

med'lar, *n.* a small tree with a sour fruit.

med'ley, *n.* a mixture : a piece of music put together from a number of other pieces.

meed, *n.* wages : reward.

meek, *adj.* mild and gentle.—*n.* **meek'ness.**

meerschaum, mēr'shawm, *n.* a fine white clay used to make tobacco pipes.

meet, *adj.* right and proper (e.g. It is *meet* that you should stay).

meet, *v.* to come face to face : to come together : to pay (e.g. I cannot *meet* my bills): to be suitable for (e.g. This box *meets* my purpose).—*ns.* a meeting of huntsmen ; **meet'ing,** a coming together, esp. of people.

meg'alith, *n.* a huge stone.

megaphone, meg'a-fōn, *n.* a large speaking-trumpet.

melancholy, mel'an-kol-i, *n.* lowness of spirits, sadness.—*adj.* sad.

mêlée, mel'ā, *n.* a confused fight : a mix-up.

mellow, mel'ō, *adj.* soft and ripe : pleasant to bear or taste.—*v.* to become soft and ripe : to become pleasant.—*n.* **mel'lowness.**

melodram'a, *n.* an exciting play, which moves the feelings.—*adj.* **melodramat'ic,** rather too full of feeling.

mel'ody, *n.* an air or tune : sweetness of sounds.—*adj.* **melō'dious,** pleasing to the ear : tuneful.—*n.* **melō'deon,** a musical instrument having keys and bellows.

mel'on, *n.* a large juicy fruit.

melt, *v.* to make a substance into a liquid by heating or by mixing it with water : to soften : to disappear : to become tender.

mem'ber, *n.* a limb of the body : one who belongs to any group of persons (e.g. a *member* of a football club, a *member* of Parliament).—*n.* **mem'bership,** the members of a club, etc. : the state of being a member.

mem′brane, *n.* a thin skin which covers or lines parts of the body.

memen′to, *n.* something by which an event is remembered:—*pl.* **memen′tōs.**

memoir, mem′war, *n.* a written statement of what has happened : (*pl.*) the story of a person's life.

memoran′dum, *n.* a note which helps one to remember:—*pl.* **memoran′da.**

mem′ory, *n.* the power to remember : something remembered.— *adj.* **mem′orable,** worthy of being remembered, famous.—*n.* **memō′rial,** something (e.g. a monument) which helps us to remember persons or events of the past.—*v.* **mem′orise,** to learn by heart.— **in memory of,** in honour of.

men′ace, *n.* harm or danger that may happen : a threat.—*v.* to be a danger to : to threaten.— *adj.* **men′acing,** evil-looking : threatening.

menagerie, men-aj′er-i, *n.* a collection of wild animals (e.g. in a circus).

mend, *v.* to put right something broken or torn : to make or grow better.—*n.* a part which has been mended.—**on the mend,** getting better.

mendacious, men-dā′shus, *adj.* untruthful.—*n.* **mendac′ity** (men-das′it-i).

men′dicant, *n.* a beggar.

menial, mēn′yal, *n.* a household servant.—*adj.* (of work) humble, as if done by a servant.

mensūrā′tion, *n.* the branch of knowledge dealing with measuring length, height, etc.

men′tal, *adj.* having to do with the mind : done in the mind, not written down (e.g. *mental* arithmetic) : not put into words. —*n.* **mental′ity,** the qualities which make up a person's mind. —**mental home,** one for patients who are ill in mind.

men′thol, *n.* a kind of camphor.

mention, men′shun, *v.* to speak of : to name.—Also *n.*

men′tor, *n.* a wise giver of advice.

men′ū, *n.* a card with a list of dishes to be served at a meal.

mer′cantile, *adj.* having to do with buying and selling, trading.— **mercantile marine,** the ships and sailors which carry on a country's trade.

mercenary, mer′sen-ar-i, *adj.* working for money : greedy in money matters.—*n.* a soldier who is paid by a foreign country to fight in its army.

mer′cer, *n.* one who sells silk and woollen cloth.

mer′chant, *n.* one who carries on a large business in the buying and selling of goods.—*adj.* having to do with a merchant's work, trading.—*ns.* **mer′chandise,** goods to be bought and sold ; **mer′chantman,** a merchant : a trading ship.

merciful, merciless. See **mercy.**

mer′cury, *n.* a heavy, silvery liquid metal (*quicksilver*).—*adj.* **mercūr′ial,** lively : often changing.

mer′cy, *n.* kindness or tenderness towards an enemy : pity : a bit of good luck.—*adjs.* **mer′ciful,** willing to forgive or to punish only lightly ; **mer′ciless,** cruel.

mēre, *n.* a lake.

mēre, *adj.* pure, complete (only in such phrases as *mere nonsense*).— *adv.* **mēre′ly,** only.

meretricious, mer-e-trish′us, *adj.* showy but false.

merge, *v.* to join together : to be swallowed up by.—*n.* **mer′ger,** a joining together of a number of business firms.

merid′ian, *n.* a circle drawn round the globe passing through the North and South Poles (meridians are numbered in degrees to show longitude east and west of Greenwich, whose meridian is numbered 0) : the highest point of success.

meringue, mer-ang′, *n.* a sweet or cake made of sugar and white of egg.

merino, mer-ēn′o, *n.* a sheep which has very fine wool : soft cloth made from its wool.

mer′it, *n.* that which deserves honour or reward : goodness : that which is deserved : (*pl.*) the good points.—*v.* to deserve. —*adj.* **meritō′rious,** deserving honour or reward.

merk, *n.* an old Scottish silver coin.

merle, *n.* the blackbird.

mer′lin, *n.* a kind of small hawk.

mer′maid, *n.* an imaginary sea-creature, with the upper part of its body like that of a lovely woman, the lower part like that of a fish :—*masc.* **mer′man.**

mer′ry, *adj.* full of fun : causing laughter : lively. — *ns.* **mer′riment,** fun and frolic ; **mer′ry-andrew,** a clown ; **mer′ry-go-round,** a ring of hobby-horses or seats on which people ride round at fairs ; **mer′ry-thought,** the forked breast-bone ('wish-bone') of a fowl.

mesh, *n.* the opening between the threads of a net : network.

mes′merise, *v.* to lull a person into a sort of sleep so that one can make him do what one wishes.—*n.* **mes′merism.**

mess, *n.* an untidy sight : disorder, confusion.—*v.* to make untidy.

mess, *n.* (esp. in the army and navy) a number of persons who take their meals together : a portion of food (e.g. 'a *mess* of pottage,' a portion of boiled vegetables). —*v.* to eat food along with others. —*n.pl.* **mess′mates,** those who eat together.

mes′sage, *n.* a piece of news or information sent from one person to another : an errand.—*n.* **mes′senger,** a person who carries a message or who does an errand.

Messi′ah, *n.* Christ.

messmate. See mess.

met′al, *n.* a substance (got usually from rocks) such as gold, silver, iron, etc. : broken stones used in making and mending roads (also called **met′alling**).—*adj.* **metal′lic,** made of metal, like metal.—*n.* **metal′lurgy,** the study of metals. —*adj.* **metallur′gical,** having to do with metal-working.

metamorphosis, met-a-mor′fō-sis, *n.* a change in form or appearance (e.g. from tadpole to frog, from caterpillar to pupa).—*adj.* **metamor′phic,** (of certain kinds of rock) affected by heat and pressure so that they are changed (e.g. clay becomes slate, limestone becomes marble).

metaphor, met′a-for, *n.* a way of describing something by saying that it is something else (e.g. The camel is the *ship* of the desert ; A cheerful friend is a *light in our path*).—*adj.* **metaphor′ical.**

mete, mēt, *v.* to measure.

mē′teor, *n.* a bright star-like body seen for a few moments sailing in the sky.—*adj.* **meteor′ic,** like a meteor : rising to fame for a short time (e.g. He had a *meteoric* career).—*ns.* **mē′teorite,** a meteor which falls to the earth in the form of a piece of rock ; **meteorology** (mē-te-or-ol′o-ji), the branch of knowledge which has to do with the study of the weather ; **meteorol′ogist,** one who studies the weather.—*adj.* **meteorolo′gical.**

mē′ter, *n.* an instrument for measuring (e.g. the amount of gas, electricity, or water used in a house).

mēthinks′, *v.* it seems to me.

meth′od, *n.* orderly arrangement, according to some plan : the way of doing something.—*adj.* **method′ical,** orderly, done according to some plan.

methought, mē-thawt′, *v.* it seemed to me.

methylated spir′it, meth′il-ā-ted, *n.* a blue-coloured liquid, which quickly turns to vapour, used for burning, cleaning, etc.

metic′ulous, *adj.* paying too great care to small matters.

metre, mē′ter, *n.* a measure of length (39½ inches) used in many foreign countries : (in poetry) the regular arrangement of the syllables in a verse.—*adjs.* **met′ric,** having to do with the metric system (see below) ; **met′rical,** (in poetry) having the syllables arranged in regular order.—*n.* **metricā′tion,** change over to the metric system.—**metric system,** the tables of weights and measures based on the system of tens (e.g. 1 metre = 10 decimetres = 100 centimetres).

met′ronome, *n.* an instrument used for tapping out the beat in music practice.

metrop′olis, *n.* the capital of a country : the town where a chief bishop has his seat.—*adj.* **metro-**

pol′itan, having to do with the capital.—*n.* a chief bishop.

met′tle, *n.* high spirit, courage, pluck.—**on one's mettle,** out to do one's best.

mew, *n.* a gull.

mew, *n.* the cry of a cat.—Also *v.*

mew, *v.* to shut up (e.g. in a cage).—*n.* a cage.—*n.pl.* mews, stables.

mias′ma, *n.* poisonous gas (e.g. from a rotting substance, marsh).

mi′ca, *n.* a glittering mineral which divides easily into thin plates or layers.

Michaelmas, mik′el-mas, *n.* the day (Sept. 29) on which the Church remembers St Michael.

mi′crobe, *n.* a very tiny living thing (esp. one causing disease), a germ.

microm′eter, *n.* an instrument used for measuring very small distances or angles.

mi′crophone, *n.* (in a telephone, and in a wireless station) the instrument into which the talking, singing, etc. is done.

mi′croscope, *n.* an instrument (containing magnifying glasses) which makes very small objects easily seen.—*adj.* microscop′ic, very tiny.

mid, *adj.* placed or coming in the middle.—*n.* mid′day, noon.—*adj.* mid′land.—*ns.* mid′night, twelve o'clock at night ; mid′shipman, in the past, a junior officer on board a warship ; mid′summer, the time about June 21 ; mid′winter, the time about December 21.—*advs.* mid′ships, in the middle part of the ship ; mid′way, half-way.

mid′den, *n.* a rubbish-heap.

mid′dle, *adj.* equally distant from both ends.—*n.* the point equally distant from the ends : the centre point.—*adjs.* mid′dle-aged, about 35-45 years of age ; mid′dling, of fair size or quality : not very good or very bad.—*ns.* mid′dleman, a merchant who buys goods to sell them again to small shops ; middle-watch, (on ships) the time between midnight and 4 a.m.— Middle Ages, the time between the years A.D. 500 and A.D. 1500 ; middle class, people who are better off than workmen but are not noblemen or very rich.

mid′dy, *n.* short for midshipman.

midge, *n.* a small fly, a gnat.—*n.* midget (mij′et), a person who has not grown up to the ordinary size.

midst, *n.* the middle.

mid′wife, *n.* a woman who assists a mother when a baby is born :— *pl.* mid′wives.

mien, mēn, *n.* the look or appearance of a person (e.g. The knight was a man of proud *mien*).

might, *n.* power : strength : armed forces.—*adj.* might′y, strong : very great : important. — *adv.* very.—*n.* might′iness, greatness.

mignonette, min-yon-et′, *n.* a plant with small, sweet-smelling flowers.

mi′grate, *v.* to go from one place to another (esp. from one part of the world to another, as certain birds and fishes do).—*n.* migrā′tion.—*adjs.* mi′grant, mi′gratory.

Mika′do, *n.* the emperor of Japan.

milch, milsh, *adj.* giving milk.

mild, *adj.* gentle : not sharp or bitter : soft, calm : (of weather) not cold.—*n.* mild′ness.

mildew, mil′dū, *n.* a mark on plants, cloth, leather, etc., caused by the spreading growth of very tiny living things.

mile, *n.* a measure of length (1760 yards).—*ns.* mileage (mīl′age), distance in miles ; mile′stone, a stone beside a road showing the distance to a certain place : something which marks an important step (e.g. Magna Carta was a *milestone* in our history).

mil′itary, *adj.* having to do with soldiers or with warfare.—*adj.* mil′itant, fighting : warlike.—*v.* mil′itate, (with *against*) to fight against.—*n.* militia (mil-ish′a), a body of men trained to fight as soldiers if their country is attacked : (in Britain) conscripts. —*n.* militia-man, a militia soldier.

milk, *n.* a white liquid produced by female animals as food for their young.—*v.* to draw milk from.— *adj.* milk′y, having to do with milk : soft, gentle.—*ns.* milk′maid, a woman who milks ; milk′man, a man who sells milk ; milk′sop, a soft, girl-like fellow ; Milk′y Way, a bright band of stars stretching across the sky.

mill, *n.* a machine for grinding or crushing (e.g. corn, coffee, etc.): a place where such machines work: a factory where things are made.—*v.* to grind: to stamp a coin, putting a rough marking round the edge (as on a new shilling).—*ns.* **mill′board,** thick cardboard; **mill′dam, mill′pond,** a small lake whose waters are used for driving a mill; **mil′ler,** one who runs a corn-mill; **mill′race,** the stream of water which turns a mill′wheel, and so drives the machinery of a mill; **mill′stone,** a heavy stone with which corn is ground to flour: a great trouble or difficulty which keeps one from making progress.

millen′nium, *n.* a thousand years: the thousand years during which, the Bible says, Christ will reign on the earth.

mil′let, *n.* a grain, much used for food in India.

mil′liard, *n.* a thousand millions.

mil′liner, *n.* one who makes and sells hats, ribbons, gloves, etc. for women.—*n.* **mil′linery,** the goods sold by a milliner.

million, *mil′yon, n.* a thousand thousands (1,000,000).—*n.* **millionaire** (mil-yon-ār′), a person who has a million pounds (or dollars) or more.

mime, *n.* a play in which actions or dancing take the place of speaking: an actor in such a play.—*v.* **mimic** (mim′ik), to imitate, esp. in a mocking way.—*n.* one who copies another closely.—*adj.* imitating: pretended (e.g. The soldiers took part in a *mimic* battle).—*n.* **mim′icry,** close imitation: a likeness of one animal to another or to some thing.

mimo′sa, *n.* a tree with bunches of yellow, scented flowers.

min′aret, *n.* a slender tower on a Mohammedan mosque.

mince, *v.* to cut or chop into small pieces.—*n.* meat cut up small by a machine (min′cer).—*ns.* **mince′-meat,** meat cut up small: the orange-peel, raisins, suet, put inside small pastries; **mince-pie,** a pie filled with mince.—**to mince matters,** to try to soften an un-pleasant statement by using gentle words.

mind, *n.* the power by which we feel and think: memory: belief, opinion: intention (e.g. I have a *mind* to tell him so; to change one's *mind*).—*v.* to see to, to look after: to watch out for (e.g. *Mind* the step): to object to (e.g. I don't *mind* your saying so).—*adj.* **mind′ful,** thinking much about.—**to mind one's p′s and q′s,** to act carefully; **out of one's mind,** mad.

mine, *adj.* belonging to me.

mine, *n.* a place from which metals or coal are dug: a heavy charge of explosive material for blowing up (e.g. a fort, ship, etc.).—*v.* to dig for metals or coal: to blow up with a mine.—*ns.* **mine-layer,** a ship used for placing mines in the sea; a **mine-sweeper** searches for enemy mines and destroys them; **mi′ner,** one who works in a mine.

min′eral, *n.* a substance found in the earth, esp. a metal; **mineral′ogy,** the study of minerals.

mingle, *ming′gl, v.* to mix together.

mini-, small, as in **min′ibus,** etc.

min′iature, *n.* a very small painting.

min′imise, *v.* to make as little as possible.—*n.* **min′imum,** the smallest possible quantity.

min′ion, *n.* favourite: agent.

min′ister, *n.* a statesman: the head of one of the divisions of the government (e.g. the Minister of Education, of Health, of War, etc.): a clergyman.—*v.* to serve: to supply necessary things.—*adj.* **ministe′rial,** having to do with a minister.—*n.* **min′istry,** the work of a minister: the place where a government minister has his headquarters.

mink, *n.* a small weasel-like animal, valued for its fur.

minnow, *min′ō, n.* a very small river or pond fish.

mi′nor, *adj.* smaller, younger: of less importance.—*n.* a person under 21 years of age.—*n.* **minor′ity,** a number less than half—oppos. of *majority.*—**in the minority,** forming the smaller part of those taking part.—See also **major.**

min′ster, *n.* a large church, esp. a cathedral.

min'strel, *n.* in olden days, one who went about amusing others by singing and playing : a singer of negro songs.—*n.* **min'strelsy**, a collection of songs.

mint, *n.* the place where coins are made by the government.—*v.* to make coins.

mint, *n.* a plant (used for flavouring) with sweet-smelling leaves.—*n.* **mint-sauce**.

minuet, min-ū-et', *n.* a slow, graceful dance.

mi'nus, *adj.* less than nothing : being without (e.g. He came *minus* his hat).—*n.* the sign (—) of subtraction (e.g. 6—4=2).

minute, min'it, *n.* the sixtieth part of an hour : the sixtieth part of a degree (e.g. of latitude or longitude) : (*pl.*) the notes taken at a meeting.—*adj.* **minute** (min-ūt'), very small : very exact.

minx, *n.* a cheeky young girl.

mir'acle, *n.* a wonderful act or happening, beyond the power of men (e.g. the *miracles* of Jesus) : a wonderful escape from death or danger.—*adj.* **mirac'ulous**, very wonderful.

mirage, mir-azh', *n.* a strange sight often seen in the desert and elsewhere—the appearance of water, trees, etc. in the air. It is really a reflection from a distant place.

mire, *n.* deep mud.—*adj.* **mi'ry**.

mirk, *n.* dark.—*adj.* **mir'ky**.

mir'ror, *n.* a looking-glass.—*v.* to show up as in a mirror.

mirth, *n.* merriment, laughter.—*adjs.* **mirth'ful**; **mirth'less**.

misadven'ture, *n.* an unlucky happening.

mis'anthrope, *n.* one who hates mankind—also **misan'thropist**.—*adj.* **misanthrop'ic**.—*n.* **misan'thropy**.

misapprehend', *v.* to take a wrong meaning from.—*n.* **misapprehen'sion**.

misappro'priate, *v.* to put to a wrong use : to use for one's self what does not belong to one.

misbehāve', *v.* to behave badly.—*n.* **misbehā'viour**.

miscar'ry, *v.* to go wrong : to be unsuccessful.—*n.* **miscar'riage**, a going wrong, failure.

miscellaneous, mis-el-ān'e-us, *adj.* mixed, made up of several kinds. —*n.* **miscel'lany**, a mixture of things of different kinds (e.g. a collection of writings on different subjects).

mischance', *n.* an unlucky happening.

mischief, mis'chif, *n.* evil : harm : damage.—*adj.* **mischievous** (mis'-chiv-us), wicked : fond of playing pranks.

misconcep'tion, *n.* a wrong opinion.

miscon'duct, *n.* wrong behaviour.

misconstrue, mis-kon-stroo', *v.* to put a wrong meaning on.

miscount', *v.* to count wrongly.

miscreant, mis'kre-ant, *n.* a very wicked person.

misdeal', *v.* to make a mistake in dealing out cards.

misdeed', *n.* a bad deed : a crime.

misdemean'our, *n.* bad conduct.

misdirect', *v.* to send in the wrong direction.

mi'ser, *n.* one who stores up money because of greed : a mean person.—*adj.* **mi'serly**, very mean.

mis'ery, *n.* great unhappiness : great pain.—*adj.* **mis'erable**, very unhappy : very poor : worthless.

misfire', *v.* (of guns, revolvers) to fail to go off.—Also *n.*

misfit', *n.* (of clothes) a bad fit, a wrong size.

misfor'tune, *n.* bad luck : an accident.

misgiv'ing, *n.* a feeling of fear or doubt.

misgovern, mis-guv'ern, *v.* to rule badly or unjustly.

misguided, mis-gī'ded, *adj.* led into doing wrong : (of advice) likely to lead one astray.

mishan'dle, *v.* to treat badly.

mishap, mis-hap', *n.* an accident.

mislay', *v.* to put a thing aside and forget where it is.

mislead', mis-lēd', *v.* to cause to make mistakes.—*adjs.* **mislead'ing**, deceiving : likely to be understood in a wrong way (e.g. a *misleading* sentence) ; **misled** (mis-led'), having been made to believe something which is not true.

misnō'mer, *n.* a wrong name, a name which does not suit.

misplace', *v.* to put in a wrong place.

misprint', *n.* a mistake in printing.

misquote, mis-kwōt', *v.* to make a mistake in repeating what someone has written or said.—*n.* **misquotā'tion.**

misrepresent', *v.* to give a wrong meaning to what a person does.

misrule, mis-rool', *n.* unjust rule: disorder.—*v.* to govern badly.

miss, *n.* an unmarried woman, esp. a young one :—*pl.* **mis'ses.**

miss, *v.* to fail to hit or reach: to find that one has not got something: to go without.—*n.* a failure to hit the mark: a loss.—*adj.* **mis'sing**, lost.

mis'sal, *n.* the Mass book of the Roman Catholic Church.

misshā'pen, *adj.* badly shaped.

missile, mis'īl, *n.* anything (e.g. spear, shell) that is thrown or fired.

mission, mish'on, *n.* the act of sending someone, or of being sent, to do a certain task (e.g. The officers were sent on a *mission* of peace-making): a branch of a church set up (esp. in foreign lands) in order to try to win people over to its religion: one's purpose in life.—*n.* **mis'sionary,** a preacher at a church mission.

missive, mis'iv, *n.* a letter.

misspell', *n.* to spell wrongly.—*n.* **misspel'ling.**

mist, *n.* a cloud of moisture seen in the air: very fine drops of rain.—*adj.* **mist'y**, dim: full of mist.

mistake', *v.* to understand wrongly: to take one thing or person for another.—*n.* an error.—*adj.* **mis-tāk'en**, making an error.

mistletoe, mis'l-tō, *n.* a climbing plant (with white, sticky berries) much used as a Christmas decoration.

mis'tress, *n.* a woman who has power or control: the head of a school or family: a woman well skilled in anything: a woman loved and courted: a title of respect given to a married woman (usually written **Mrs,** mis'iz).

mistrust', *n.* want of trust.—*v.* to doubt.

misunderstand', *v.* to take a wrong meaning from what is said or done.—*n.* **misunderstand'ing**, a mistake in meaning: a slight quarrel.

misuse, mis-ūs', *n.* bad use.—*v.* **misuse** (mis-ūz'), to use for a wrong purpose or in a wrong way: to treat ill.

mite, *n.* anything very small (e.g. a child): a very small insect: a very small coin.

mit'igate, *v.* to make (e.g. trouble, evil) less severe.—*n.* **mitigā'tion.**

mitre, mī'ter, *n.* a pointed crown worn by archbishops and bishops: a slanting joint between two pieces of wood.

mit'ten, for short **mitt**, *n.* a kind of glove, without fingers.

mix, *v.* to unite two or more things to form one mass.—*adj.* **mixed**, jumbled together: made up of different kinds.—*n.* **mix'ture**, a number of things jumbled together: a medicine.

mizz'en-mast, *n.* the mast nearest the stern of the ship.

mnemonic, nē-mon'ik, *n.* something which helps one to remember a thing (e.g. The rhyme 'Thirty days hath September . . .' etc. is a *mnemonic* for the number of days in each month).

moan, *v.* to make a low sound of grief or pain.—Also *n.*

moat, *n.* a deep trench round a castle or fortified place, sometimes filled with water.

mob, *n.* a noisy crowd.—*v.* to treat roughly: to crowd upon.

mobile, mō'bil, *adj.* easily moved: changing quickly.—*n.* **mobil'ity**, readiness to move.

mō'bilise, *v.* to gather troops for war.—*n.* **mobilisā'tion.**

moc'casin or **moc'assin**, *n.* a shoe of deerskin or other soft leather, worn by the North American Indians.

mock, *v.* to laugh at: to make sport of: to deceive.—*adj.* sham, false (e.g. a *mock* battle).—*ns.* **mock'ery**, the act of making fun of somebody or something; **mock'ing-bird**, a kind of thrush (found in North America), which mocks or imitates the notes of birds and other sounds; **mock-turtle,** a kind of soup (made from calf's-head not from turtle-flesh).

mode, *n.* manner: custom: fashion.

mod′el, *n.* a copy, design, or pattern, to be followed: a copy of something made in a small size: a living person used as a copy by an artist.—*adj.* fit to be copied, perfect.—*v.* to make a copy of: to form.

mod′erate, *v.* to keep from being too great or severe: to become less severe.—*adj.* kept within bounds: not going to extremes.—*adv.* **mod′erately,** fairly.—*ns.* **modera′tion,** freedom from going too far in anything: calmness of mind; **mod′erator,** (in some churches) the chairman at a meeting of clergymen.

mod′ern, *adj.* belonging to the present or to a time not long past: not old.—*n.* **modern′ity.**—*v.* **mod′ernise,** to bring up to date.

mod′est, *adj.* shy: humble, not boastful: not very large.—*n.* **mod′esty.**

mod′icum, *n.* a small quantity.

mod′ify, *v.* to set bounds to: to make a change in.—*n.* **modifica′tion.**

mod′ulate, *v.* to change the tone of voice so as to give expression.—*ns.* **modula′tion,** raising or lowering of the voice; **mod′ulator,** a chart from which singing is sometimes taught.

mohair′, *n.* the white silken hair of a long-haired kind of goat.

Moham′medan, *n.* one who follows the religion set up by Mohammed (A.D 570–632). Arabs are Mohammedans.—Also *adj.*

moiety, moi′e-ti, *n.* half: a small share.

moil, *v.* to work wearily, to toil.

moist, *adj.* damp.—*v.* **mois′ten,** to make slightly wet.—*n.* **mois′ture.**

mō′lar, *n.* a back tooth, which grinds one's food.

molas′ses, *n.sing.* a syrup left when sugar is made: treacle.

mole, *n.* a dark-brown mark on the skin.

mole, *n.* a small burrowing animal, with very small eyes and soft fur.—*n.* **mole′hill,** a little hill or

heap of earth cast up by a mole.

mole, *n.* a breakwater: a stone pier.

molecule, mol′e-kūl, *n.* the smallest possible part of a substance.

molest′, *v.* to trouble, to vex, to annoy.—*n.* **molesta′tion.**

mol′lify, *v.* to make soft or tender: to make calm.

mollusc, mol′usk, *n.* a boneless animal with a hard shell (e.g. shellfish).

mōl′ten, *adj.* melted: made of melted metal.

mō′ment, *n.* a very short space of time: importance or value (e.g. Nothing of *moment* has happened). —*adjs.* **mō′mentary,** lasting for a moment or for a very short time: short-lived; **mōment′ous,** of great importance.—*n.* **moment′um,** the force of a moving body.

monarch, mon′ark, *n.* a king, a ruler. — *n.* **mon′archy,** a kingdom.

mon′astery, *n.* a house for monks.—*adj.* **monas′tic,** having to do with monks.—*n.* **monas′ticism,** life in a monastery.

Monday, mun′dā, *n.* the second day of the week.

money, mun′i, *n.* the coins and notes which are used for payments: wealth:—*pl.* **mon′eys.**—*adjs.* **mon′etary,** having to do with money; **moneyed** (mun′ēd), wealthy.—**money order,** a letter by which a person sends money from one post-office to another.

mon′goose, *n.* a small weasel-like animal which kills snakes:—*pl.* **mon′gooses.**

mongrel, maung′grel, *adj.* of a mixed breed.—*n.* an animal (esp. a dog) of a mixed breed.

mon′itor, *n.* a man who advises: an older pupil who looks after younger ones in a school: a warship with revolving gun-turrets:—*fem.* **mon′itress.**

monk, mungk, *n.* a man who takes religious vows and lives apart from the world, usually in a *monastery.*—*adj.* **monk′ish.** — *n.* **monk′s-hood,** a poisonous plant (*aconite*) with a flower like a monk's hood.

monkey, mungk´i, *n.* an animal somewhat resembling man : a mischievous child :—*pl.* **monk´-eys.**—*v.* to meddle with anything. —*ns.* **mon´key-puz´zle,** a tree (really a South American pine) with very prickly branches ; **mon´key-wrench** (-rensh), a screw-key with a movable jaw.

mon´ocle, *n.* a single eyeglass.

monog´amy, *n.* marriage to one wife or husband only.—*adj.* **monog´-amous.**—*n.* **monog´amist.**

mon´ogram, *n.* two or more letters made into a single design.

monologue, mon´ō-log, *n.* a speech uttered by one person.

mon´oplane, *n.* an aeroplane having only one pair of wings—a *biplane* has two pairs.

monop´oly, *n.* the full right, not shared by others, of doing, making, or selling something (e.g. This firm has a *monopoly* in the making of engines).—*v.* **monop´-olise,** to have the full rights in anything : to take up the whole of something (e.g. He *monopolises* my attention).

monosyllable, mon-ō-sil´la-bl, *n.* a word of one syllable.—*adj.* **mono-syllab´ic.**

monotheism, mon´ō-thē-izm, *n.* the belief that there is only one God.

mon´otone, mon´ō-tōn, *n.* a single, unchanging tone of voice.—*adj.* **monot´onous,** uttered in one unchanging tone : dull.—*n.* **monot´-ony,** lack of change : dullness.

mon´otype, *n.* a machine which makes and puts together type for printing.

monseigneur, mong-sen-yer´, *n.* my lord : a title (written *Mgr.*) in France given to a person of high rank, esp. to bishops, etc.

monsieur, mis-ya, *n.* sir : a title (often written *M.*) in France = *Mr* in English :—*pl.* **messieurs** (mes-yer : *MM.*).

monsoon´, *n.* a wind that blows in the Indian Ocean, from the south-west in summer, from the north-east in winter.

mon´ster, *n.* anything of unusual size or appearance : a huge creature, causing fear : a very wicked person.—*v.* **monstros´ity,** something not natural.—*adj.* **mon´strous,** huge : horrible.

month, munth, *n.* twelfth part of a year.—*adj.* and *adv.* **month´ly,** happening once a month.—*n.* a paper published once in a month.

mon´ument, *n.* a building, pillar, tomb, etc. built in memory of a person or an event.—*adj.* **monument´al,** acting as a monument : very great in size.

moo, *n.* the sound made by a cow.

mood, *n.* the state of a person's feelings, temper : manner.—*adj.* **mood´y,** often changing one's temper or mood : gloomy.

moon, *n.* the heavenly body which travels round the earth once each month and reflects light from the sun : a month.—*v.* to wander : to gaze at absently.— *ns.* **moon´beam,** a beam of light from the moon ; **moon´light,** the light of the moon (really the light of the sun on the moon); **moon´shine,** the shining of the moon : rubbish ; **moon-stone,** a precious stone with a pearly reflection from within.—*adj.* **moon´-struck,** weak in the mind.

moor, moor´land, *ns.* a large stretch of ground, often covered with heather or marsh.—*ns.* **moor´-cock, moor´fowl,** the red grouse found in moors ; **moor´hen,** the water-hen.

moor, *v.* to fasten a ship by ropes or by anchor : to fix firmly.—*n.* **moor´ing,** act or means of fastening a ship : (*pl.*) the place where a ship is fastened.

Moors, *n.pl.* the Arab people of the north of Africa.—*adj.* **Moor´ish.**

moose, *n.* a large deer-like animal, found in North America.

moot, *v.* to mention a subject to be talked about.—*adj.* doubtful, not settled.—*n.* in early English history, a meeting called to discuss matters.

mop, *n.* a bunch of rags, etc. fixed on a handle for washing floors, windows, etc.—*v.* to rub or wipe with a mop.

mope, *v.* to grieve and look sad.

moraine, mo-rān´, *n.* a line of rocks and gravel cast aside along the edges of a glacier.

mor'al, *adj.* having to do with right and wrong behaviour, esp. with right behaviour.—*n.* the lesson of a fable or story: (*pl.*) one's manners and behaviour.—*v.* **mor'alise**, to draw a lesson from a story or happening.—*ns.* **mor'alist**, one who studies questions of behaviour; **moral'ity**, the quality of being right in manners and behaviour.—**a moral victory**, a failure more honourable than success.

morale, mo-ral', *n.* spirit and confidence (e.g. in an army).

morass', *n.* a marsh.

mor'bid, *adj.* sickly, not healthy: thinking gloomy or low thoughts.

more, a greater number, amount, extent (e.g. *more* eggs, *more* beautiful).—*adv.* **moreover** (mor-ō'ver), besides.

mor'ibund, *adj.* in a dying state.

morn, mor'ning, *n.* the first part of the day.—*adj.* taking place in the morning.—*ns.* **morn'ing-star**, Venus, when it rises before the sun; **morn'ing-watch**, the watch between 4 and 8 a.m.

moroc'co, *n.* a fine goat-skin leather, first brought from Morocco.

morose', *adj.* gloomy.

morphia, mor'fi-a, *n.* a drug which causes sleep or deadens pain.—Also **mor'phine**.

morr'is-dance, *n.* a country dance in which the dancers wear fancy-dress clothes, decorated with bells.

morrow, mor'ō, *n.* to-morrow: the time just after any event.

morse, *n.* a code of signals (made up of dots and dashes) used in signalling and telegraphy.

mor'sel, *n.* a small piece, esp. of food.

mor'tal, *adj.* liable to die: causing death.—*n.* a human being.—*n.* **mortal'ity**, the number of deaths (e.g. The *mortality* in small-pox is high): the human race. — *adv.* **mor'tally**, fatally.

mor'tar, *n.* a basin in which substances are ground down small: a short gun for throwing shells: a mixture of lime, sand, and water, used for fixing stones in a building, etc.

mortgage, mor'gāj, *n.* a sum of money loaned on the security of buildings, land, etc. (the borrower promises to give up the buildings to the lender if he fails to repay the loan).—*v.* to pledge buildings, etc. as security.—*n.* **mortgagee'**, one to whom property is pledged.

mor'tify, *v.* to vex, to humble.—*n.* **mortifica'tion**, vexation, annoyance: a poisoned wound, which makes the flesh rot.

mortise, mor'tis, *n.* a hole made in a piece of wood to receive the end of another piece.

mor'tuary, *n.* a building where dead bodies are kept before burial.

mosaic, mō-zā'ik, *n.* a kind of work in which small pieces of coloured material (e.g. stone or glass) are formed into patterns or pictures.

Mos'lem, *adj.* and *n.* Mohammedan.

mosque, mosk, *n.* a Mohammedan place of worship.

mosquito, mos-kē'to, *n.* a biting gnat which carries malaria.

moss, *n.* very small flowerless plants, found in moist places: a bog.—*adjs.* **moss'y**, **moss'-grown**.

mōst, the greatest number, amount, extent (e.g. *most* boys, *most* happy).—**at most ten men** = certainly not more than ten men.

mote, *n.* a speck (e.g. of dust).

moth, *n.* a family of insects like butterflies, seen mostly at night.

mother, muth'er, *n.* a female parent: the female head of a convent.—*v.* to act as a mother towards, to care for as a mother.—*adj.* **moth'erly**, like a mother. — *ns.* **moth'er-coun'try**, **-land**, the country of one's birth; **moth'erhood**, state of being a mother; **moth'er-in-law**, the mother of one's husband or wife; **moth'er-of-pearl**, the shining, hard, smooth substance which forms inside certain shells; **moth'er-tongue**, a person's native language.

motion, mō'shun, *n.* movement from one place to another: a plan put before a meeting.—*v.* to make a sign.—*adj.* **mo'tionless**, without movement.

motive, mō'tiv, *adj.* causing motion. —*n.* that which causes a person to act or do something, reason.— *v.* **mo'tivate**, to act as a motive.

mot'ley, *adj.* of different colours.— *n.* the many-coloured dress of a jester or fool.

mō'tor, *n.* that which gives motion: an engine (e.g. of a motor-car, aeroplane, gramophone): short for **motor-car.**—*v.* to go by motor-car.—*ns.* **mo'tor-bicycle, -boat, -bus, -car,** a bicycle (boat, etc.) driven by a petrol engine; **mo'torist,** one who uses a motor-car.

mottled, mot'ld, *adj.* marked with spots of many colours.

mot'tō, *n.* a short sentence or phrase, which acts as a guiding idea (e.g. ' Honesty is the best policy ' is my *motto*): a phrase on a coat of arms :—*pl.* **mot'toes.**

mould, mōld, *n.* earth : soil containing rotted leaves, etc.: a growth (of very tiny plants) found on damp substances.—*v.* to become **mould'y,** i.e. overgrown with mould.

mould, mōld, *n.* a shape into which a liquid substance is poured so that when it cools or sets it takes on the form of the shape (e.g. a *mould* for jellies).—*v.* to shape, fashion.—*n.* **mould'ing,** a decorated border (e.g. that of a picture frame).

moult, mōlt, *v.* (of birds) to cast the feathers.

mound, *n.* a bank of earth or stones.

mount, *n.* a mountain : a piece of cardboard on which anything (e.g. a photograph) is pasted : a horse.—*v.* to go up : to get up on horseback : to fit in or on a mount : to set a precious stone in a metal holder.

mount'ain, *n.* a high hill : anything very large.—*ns.* **mount'ain-ash,** the rowan-tree; **mountaineer',** a climber of mountains; **mountain-lion,** the puma.—*adj.* **mount'-ainous,** having many mountains: huge.—**to make a mountain out of a molehill,** to fancy that a small trouble is a big one.

mount'ebank, *n.* a sham doctor who boasts of his cures : a pretender.

mourn, mōrn, *v.* to be sorrowful.—*n.* **mourn'er.**—*adjs.* **mourn'ful,** sad; **mourn'ing,** showing one's sorrow by weeping and wearing black.—

n. feeling of sorrow or grief : the dress of mourners.

mouse, *n.* a little gnawing animal found in houses and in the fields : —*pl.* **mice.**

moustache, mus-tash', *n.* the hair upon the upper lip of men.

mouth, *n.* the opening in the head of an animal by which it eats and utters sound : that part of a river where it falls into the sea : opening or entrance (e.g. of a bottle).—*v.* to speak in a silly way.—*ns.* **mouth'ful,** as much as fills the mouth :—*pl.* **mouth'fuls ; mouth'piece,** the part of a musical instrument or tobacco-pipe held in the mouth : one who speaks for others.

move, moov, *v.* to change from one place to another : to set in motion, to stir into action : to persuade : to make a proposal.— *n.* a going forward : a change of playing-pieces (e.g. at chess, draughts). — *ns.* **move'ment,** a change of position, from one place to another : a division of a piece of music; **moving-picture** (*slang* movie, moo'vi), a cinema show.—*adjs.* **mov'able,** able to be moved, lifted, changed, etc.; **mov'ing,** in motion : causing pity.

mow, mō, *v.* to cut grass, hay, etc. with a scythe or machine : to cut down in great numbers.— *n.* **mow'er,** machine for mowing.

much, a great amount, extent (e.g. *much* bread, *much* higher).

muck, *n.* dirt : anything filthy.

mū'cus, *n.* the slimy fluid from the nose.—*adj.* **mu'cous,** like mucus.

mud, *n.* wet soft earth. — *adj.* **mud'dy.**

mud'dle, *v.* to work without a plan : to make stupid.—Also *n.*

muezzin, moo-ez'in, *n.* in a Mohammedan mosque (church), the priest who calls out the hour of prayer.

muff, *n.* a warm, soft cover for the hands in winter (worn by women).

muff, *n.* a stupid fellow.—*v.* to fail in doing something : to miss a catch at cricket.

muf'fin, *n.* a soft, light cake to be eaten hot with butter.

muf'fle, v. to wrap up against cold : to deaden sound (e.g. of a bell, drum) by wrapping with cloth.— n. **muf'fler,** a scarf.

muf'ti, n. the plain clothes worn by an officer when off duty.

mug, n. a thick cup for drinking from : a jug : a foolish fellow.

mug'gy, adj. (of the weather) close and damp, foggy.

mŭlat'to, n. a person one of whose parents was black, the other white.

mul'berry, n. a purple berry growing on a tree on whose leaves silkworms are fed.

mulct, n. money paid as a punishment, a fine.—v. to take money from a person as a punishment.

mūle, n. an animal whose parents are a horse and an ass : an instrument for cotton-spinning : a stubborn person.—n. **mūleteer',** one who drives mules.

mull, n. a cape : a snuff-box.

mull, v. to warm, spice, and sweeten wine, ale, etc.—adj. **mulled.**

mulligatawny, mul-i-ga-taw'ni, n. an Indian curry-soup.

multi-, many, as in adjs. **mul'ticoloured,** having many colours; **multifā'rious,** made up of many kinds; **multira'cial,** of many different races of men.

mul'tiple, adj. having many parts : repeated many times.—n. a number or quantity which contains another an exact number of times.

mul'tiplȳ, v. to increase : to increase a number (e.g. to twice, three times, four times its size—4 multiplied by 3 = three times 4, i.e. 12). —ns. **multiplicity** (mul-ti-plis'i-ti), a great number ; **multiplicand',** a number to be multiplied ; **multiplicā'tion,** the act of multiplying ; **mul'tiplīer,** the number by which another is to be multiplied.

mul'titūde, n. a great number : a crowd.—adj. **multitūd'inous,** very many.

mum, adj. silent.

mum'ble, v. to speak softly with the lips close.

mum'mer, n. a masked player : a performer in a dumb show.—n. **mum'mery,** great show without doing anything.

mum'my, n. a body kept whole by wrapping in bandages and treating with wax, spices, etc.—v. **mum'mifȳ,** to make into a mummy.

mumps, n. a disease of the glands of neck, causing swollen face and neck.

munch, munsh, v. to chew with the mouth shut.

mun'dane, adj. belonging to the world.

municipal, mū-nis'i-pal, adj. belonging to a city or town : carried on by a city or town (e.g. a municipal bank).—n. **municipal'ity,** a town or city with its own magistrates.

mūnif'icent, adj. fond of giving away money or gifts.—n. **munif'icence.**

munitions, mūn-ish'unz, n.pl. materials used in war (guns, rifles, shells, etc.).

mū'ral, adj. having to do with a wall.

mur'der, n. the killing of a human being on purpose.—v. to kill on purpose. — adj. **mur'derous.** — n. **mur'derer.**

mur'ky, adj. dark : gloomy.

mur'mur, n. a low, confused sound, like that of running water : a complaint, uttered in a low, muttering voice.—v. to complain, to grumble : to speak in a low voice.

mur'rain, n. a quickly-spreading disease among cattle.

muscle, mus'l, n. fleshy parts of the body which, by drawing together, cause the movements of arms, legs, jaws, etc.—adj. **mus'cūlar,** having to do with the muscles : strong.

muse, mūz, v. to think over a matter quietly.

Muse, mūz, n. (in olden stories) one of the nine goddesses who were supposed to have power over poets and artists : poetry.

museum, mū-zē'um, n. a building in which interesting things (e.g. things of olden times, stuffed animals, pieces of rock, coins) are set out for show.

mush'room, n. a stool-shaped growth which may be eaten.—adj. springing up very quickly.

music, mū′zik, *n.* an arrangement of sweet sounds : the study of such arrangements.—*adj.* **mu′sical,** having to do with music : pleasing to the ear.—*n.* **musician** (mū-zish′an), one skilled in music.

musk, *n.* a strong perfume, obtained from the male **musk-deer** (a small hornless deer found in Central Asia) : a kind of plant with the smell of musk.—*n.* **musk-rat,** a kind of large water-rat (noted for its fur) found in North America.

musket, *n.* a gun once used by foot-soldiers.—*ns.* **musketeer′,** a soldier armed with a musket ; **mus′ketry,** a body of troops armed with muskets : instruction in rifle-firing.

muslin, *n.* a fine, soft cotton cloth.

musquash, mus′kwosh, *n.* fur of the musk-rat.

mus′sel, *n.* a shellfish enclosed within two shells ; used for food.

Mussulman, *n.* a Mohammedan.

mus′tang, *n.* the wild horse of the American prairies.

mus′tard, *n.* a plant with a nipping taste : the seeds of this plant powdered to make a hot seasoning (for meat, etc.).

mus′ter, *v.* to gather together (e.g. troops, courage).—*n.* a collection of troops.—**to pass muster,** to be accepted as satisfactory.

mus′ty, *adj.* mouldy : having a damp smell.

mūte, *adj.* dumb : silent : not sounded.—*n.* a dumb person.

mū′tilate, *v.* to cut off (e.g. a limb or other part of the body) : to harm greatly.—*n.* **mutilā′tion.**

mū′tiny, *v.* to rise against those in power : to refuse to obey the commands of officers in army or navy.—*n.* refusal to obey commands, esp. in the army or navy. —*n.* **mutineer′,** one who takes part in a mutiny.—*adj.* **mu′tinous.**

mut′ter, *v.* to speak words in a low voice : to murmur.

mut′ton, *n.* the flesh of the sheep.

mū′tūal, *adj.* (of two persons) given and received by each to the other (e.g. *mutual* help, *mutual* friendship).

muz′zle, *n.* the nose and mouth of an animal : a fastening placed over the mouth of an animal to prevent biting : the open end of a gun.—*v.* to put a muzzle on : to prevent from speaking.

mȳ, *adj.* belonging to me.—**Oh my !** an exclamation of surprise.

myopia, mī-ō′-, *n.* short-sightedness.

myriad, mir′i-ad, *n.* a very great number.—*adj.* numberless.

myrmidon, mer′mi-don, *n.* a paid follower or servant.

myrrh, mer, *n.* a gum with a bitter taste, used in medicines, perfumes, etc.

myrtle, mer′tl, *n.* an evergreen shrub with beautiful and sweet-smelling leaves.

mystery, mis′ter-i, *n.* something which man cannot explain : a deep secret.—*adjs.* **mystē′rious,** puzzling, difficult to understand ; **mystic** (mis′tik), **mystical,** hidden, secret : having a sacred or secret meaning.—*v.* **mys′tify,** to puzzle greatly : to confuse.

myth, mith, *n.* a story about old-time gods or heroes : a fable : an untrue story.—*adj.* **myth′ical.** —*ns.* **mythol′ogy,** a collection of myths ; **mythol′ogist,** one who writes about myths.

N

nab, *v.* to catch suddenly.

nā′bob, *n.* a title given to certain Indian princes : a very rich man.

nag, *n.* a small horse.

nag, *v.* to find fault with constantly.

naiad, nī′ad, *n.* a goddess of rivers.

nail, *n.* a horny covering, protecting the tips of the fingers and toes : the claw of a bird or other animal : a thin pointed piece of metal for fastening wood.—*v.* to fasten with nails : to pin down.

naïve, na-ēv′, *adj.* simple in thought, manner, or speech.— *n.* **naïveté** (na-ēv′tā).

nā′ked, *adj.* without clothes: having no covering.—*n.* **nā′kedness.**

nam′by-pam′by, *adj.* not manly.

name, *n.* a word by which a person or a thing is known or called: fame (e.g. He had a *name* for honest dealing): authority (e.g. I arrest you in the *name* of the king).—*v.* to give a name to: to call by name.—*adj.* **name′less,** without a name.—*adv.* **name′ly,** that is to say.—*ns.* **name′-plate,** a plate of metal having on it the name of a person; **name′sake,** one having the same name as another.

nann′y-goat, *n.* a female goat.

nap, *n.* a short sleep.—**caught napping,** taken unawares.

nap, *n.* woolly surface of cloth.

nap, *n.* a game of cards.

nape, *n.* the back of the neck.

nā′pery, *n.* table-linen.

naphtha, naf′tha, *n.* a clear liquid which readily catches fire, obtained from petroleum.

nap′kin, *n.* a small towel.

narcissus, nar-sis′us, *n.* a plant something like a daffodil, with a white star-shaped flower:—*pl.* **narciss′ī, narciss′uses.**

narcot′ic, *adj.* producing sleep or deadening pain.—*n.* a medicine which does these things.

narrate′, *v.* to tell a story.—*ns.* **narrā′tion,** the telling of a story; **nar′rative,** a story; **narrā′tor,** one who tells a story.—*adj.* **nar′rative,** telling a story.

narrow, nar′ō, *adj.* of small extent from side to side: selfish: seeing only one point of view (also **narr′ow-mind′ed**).—*n.pl.* **narr′ows,** a sea passage of little width, a strait.—*v.* **nar′row,** to make or become narrow.—*n.* and *adj.* **nar′row-gauge** (gāj), a name given to a railroad of less width than 4 ft. 8½ ins.

nar′whal, nar′wal, *n.* a kind of whale, with a large tusk.

nā′sal, *adj.* belonging to the nose: sounded through the nose.

nasturtium, nas-tur′shum, *n.* a climbing plant, with broad, flat leaves and brightly-coloured flowers.

nas′ty, *adj.* dirty, filthy: disagreeable to the taste or smell: unfriendly, unkindly.—*n.* **nas′tiness.**

nā′tal, *adj.* having to do with one's birth (e.g. one's *natal* day, one's birthday).

nation, nā′shun, *n.* the people living in the same country, or under the same government: a race of people (e.g. the Jewish *nation*).—*adj.* **national** (nash′un-al), belonging to a nation or race.—*ns.* **nat′ional,** a person belonging to a nation, usually in *pl.*, **nationals.**—*v.* **nat′ionalise,** to make something the property or possession of a nation (e.g. coalmining is a *nationalised* industry).—*ns.* **nat′ionalist,** one who seeks to bring people of a nation together under their own government (e.g. a Scottish *nationalist*); **national′ity,** birth in a particular country.—**Nat′ional Anth′em,** the popular song by which a people expresses its love for its country, king, etc. ('God save the Queen' is the British *National Anthem*); **Nat′ional Debt,** money borrowed by the government and not yet paid back.

native, nā′tiv, *adj.* born in a person (e.g. one's *native* intelligence): having to do with one's birth (e.g. my *native* land). — *n.* a person born in a certain place: one of the first inhabitants: a black person.—**The Nativ′ity,** the birth of Christ.

nat′ty, *adj.* trim, tidy, neat.

nā′ture, *n.* the qualities (hates, likes, passions, etc.) of men and women (e.g. *human* nature): the world around us (animals, trees, grass, streams, mountains, etc.): the qualities which make a thing what it is (e.g. The ground is of a hilly *nature*).—*adj.* **nā′tured,** having a certain temper (e.g. *good-natured*).—*n.* **nā′ture-wor′ship,** worship of the powers of nature.—*adj.* **nat′ural,** in one at birth, not learned afterwards: simple, without airs.—*n.* an idiot.—*adv.* **nat′urally,** simply: of course.—*v.* **nat′uralise,** to give the rights of a citizen to one born in another country.—*n.* **nat′uralist,**

one who studies animal and plant life.—nat'ural his'tory, that branch of study which deals with rocks, animals, and plants.

naught, nawt, n. nothing.

naughty, naw'ti, adj. wicked, misbehaving.—n. naught'iness.

nausea, naw'si-a, n. a feeling of sickness.—v. nau'seàte, to fill with disgust, to make sick.—adj. nau'seous, sickening.

naut'ical, adj. having to do with ships or sailors.—nautical mile, 6080 ft.

naut'ilus, n. a small sea-creature of the cuttle-fish family.

nā'val. See navy.

nave, n. the middle or main part of a church.

nave, n. the central part of a wheel through which the axle passes.

nā'vel, n. the small hollow in the centre of the front of the body.

nav'igate, v. to steer or pilot a ship, aircraft, etc.: to sail upon.—adj. **nav'igable**, able to to be used by ships (e.g a navigable channel).—ns. **naviga'tion**, the sailing of ships: a canal; **nav'igàtor**, one who steers or sails a ship.

nav'vy, n. a labourer working on roads, etc.: a digging machine.

nā'vy, n. a nation's ships-of-war.—adjs. **nā'val**, having to do with warships; **navy-blue**, dark blue.

nawab'. Same as nabob.

nay, no.—to say a person nay, to say no to him.

naze, n. a cape.

neap tide, n. the time of very low tide of the sea.

near, adj. not far away in place or time: mean (in money matters).—v. to approach.—adj. **near'-sight'ed**, short-sighted.

neat, adj. trim, tidy, well-shaped.

neb'ūla, n. a misty appearance produced e.g. by very distant stars:—pl. **nebū'læ.**—adj. **neb'ulous**, hazy: vague.

necessary, nes'es-ar-i, adj. not able to be done without or escaped.—n.pl. **ne'cessaries**, food, clothing (e.g. the necessaries of life).—n. **neces'sity**, that which cannot be done without: great need, poverty.—v. **necess'itate**, to make

necessary: to force.—adj. **necess'-itous**, very poor: in great want.

neck, n. the part between the head and body: anything like the neck (e.g. the neck of a bottle, a neck of land).—ns. **neck'lace**, a string of beads or precious stones worn by women round the neck; **neck'tie**, a tie or cloth for the neck.—**neck and crop**, completely; **neck and neck**, side by side.

nec'romancer, n. one who deals in magic.—n. **nec'romancy**.

necrop'olis, n. a cemetery.

nec'tar, n. the drink of the ancient Greek gods: a delicious drink: the honey of flowers.

nec'tarine, n. a kind of peach.

née, nā, adj. born ('Jessie Brown née Jessie Black,' i.e. Mrs Brown was Miss Black before marriage).

need, n. want: poverty.—v. to be in want of.—adjs. **need'ful**, necessary; **need'y**, poor.—**needs must that**, it had to be that; **he must needs go**, he decided he must go.

need'le, n. a small, sharp piece of steel, with an eye for a thread, used in sewing: (in a compass) the moving pointer: (pl.) the long, sharp-pointed leaves of pines, firs, and other such trees.

nefā'rious, adj. very wicked.

negā'tion, n. a saying 'no': denial.—adj. **neg'ative**, meaning or saying 'no' (e.g. a negative answer).—n. a word or statement by which something is denied: (in photography) an image on a glass or film, in which the lights and shades are the opposite of those in nature.—v. to prove the opposite: to cast aside by vote (e.g. The proposal was negatived by the meeting).

neglect', v. to treat carelessly: to fail to give proper attention to: to fail to do.—n. want of care or attention.—adj. **neglect'ful**.

négligé, nā'glē-zhā, n. free and easy dress.

negligence, neg'li-jens, n. want of proper care.—adjs. **neg'ligent**, careless; **neg'ligible**, not worth thinking about: very small.

negotiate, ne-gō'shi-āt, v. to arrange

a bargain, either a buying or a sale: to carry through: to travel safely over or through.—*ns.* negotiā′tion; negō′tiator.—*adj.* negotiable (ne-gō′shi-a-bl), able to be arranged, or to be used in trade: passable.

ne′gro, *n.* a woolly-haired, black-skinned person :—*fem.* ne′gress.

neigh, nā, *v.* to cry like a horse.— Also *n.*

neighbour, nā′bur, *n.* one who lives near.—*n.* neigh′bourhood, district in which one lives: people living near one.—*adjs.* neigh′bouring, lying or living close to; neigh′-bourly, friendly.

nem′esis, *n.* punishment that is bound to follow wrong-doing.

nephew, nev′ū or nef′ū, *n.* the son of a brother or sister.

nerve, *n.* one of the fibres which carry feeling from all parts of the body to the brain: courage: boldness: impudence.—*v.* to collect courage for.—*adj.* nerv′ous, easily excited or frightened.

nest, *n.* bed or place in which birds rear their young (also used of squirrels, mice, rats, etc.): shelter.—*v.* to build a nest and live in it.—*v.* nestle (nesl), to lie close together, like birds in a nest: to settle comfortably.—*n.* nest′ling, a young newly hatched bird.

net, *n.* cord or twine, knotted into meshes for catching birds, butterflies, fish, etc.—*v.* to catch with a net: to cover with a net.—*n.* net′work, any work showing lines crossing one another (e.g. a *network* of roads).

net, nett, *adj.* lowest (e.g. *net price,* a price from which nothing will be taken off). See gross.

neth′er, *adj.* lower.—*adj.* neth′er-most, lowest.

net′tle, *n.* a plant covered with hairs which sting sharply.—*v.* to make angry, provoke.—*n.* nett′le-rash, a skin rash, like that caused by a sting from a nettle.

neuralgia, nū-ral′ji-a, *n.* a pain in the nerves, esp. in those of the head and face.

neurotic, nū-rot′ik, *n.* one who has bad nerves.

neuter, nū′ter, *adj.* (in grammar) neither masculine nor feminine (e.g. the nouns *table, pencils*).

neutral, nū′tral, *adj.* taking no side in a quarrel or war.—*n.* a person or nation that takes no side in a war.—*n.* neutral′ity.—*v.* neu′tral-ise, to make of no effect.

nevertheless′, *adv.* in spite of that.

new, nū, *adj.* recent: not before seen or known: different: not worn.—*adv.* new′ly.—*ns.* new′-ness; new′comer, one who has lately arrived.—*adj.* newfangled (-fang′gld), newly brought out and not thought much of.

news, nūz, *n.sing.* a first account of a recent event.—*ns.* news′-agent, a shopkeeper who sells newspapers; news′monger, one who collects and spreads news; news′paper, printed sheets containing news; news′vendor, a seller of newspapers.

newt, nūt, *n.* a small land-and-water animal, shaped something like a lizard.

nib, *n.* a pen point: (*pl.*) cocoa or coffee beans broken in pieces.

nib′ble, *v.* to take little bites of.— *n.* a little bite.

nice, *adj.* agreeable: delightful: very small, fine.—*n.* nicety (nīs′-it-i), great exactness or fineness in measurement.

niche, nich, *n.* a hollow in a wall for a statue, vase, etc.

nick, *n.* a notch: the moment which is 'just in time.'—*v.* to cut notches in: to cut short.

nick′el, *n.* a greyish-white metal used esp. for mixing with other metals and for plating (*nickel-plating*): (in America) a 5-cent coin (=2½d.).

nick′-nack, *n.* a trifle.

nick′name, *n.* an added name, usually given in fun or scorn.

nicotine, nik′o-tēn, *n.* a poisonous juice in tobacco.

niece, nēs, *n.* the daughter of a brother or sister.

nig′gard, *n.* a mean, stingy person. —*adjs.* nigg′ard, nigg′ardly.

nig′ger, *n.* a black man, a negro.

nig′gling, *adj.* of little account, trifling: mean: fussy.

nigh, nī, *adj.* near.

night, nīt, *n.* the end of the day: the period of darkness between sunset and sunrise.—*ns.* **night'-bird**, a bird that flies only at night; **night'-fall**, close of the day: dusk; **night'-shade**, a plant (often found in shady woods) with poisonous berries; **night'-watch'man**, one who looks after a building during the night.—*adjs.* and *advs.* **night'ly**, done by night: done every night; **night'-long**, lasting all night.

nightingale, nīt'ing-gāl, *n.* a small bird, the male of which sings by night a sweet love-song.

nightmare, nīt'mār, *n.* a very real and frightening dream.

nil, *n.* nothing.

nimble, *adj.* light and quick in motion: active.—*n.* **nim'bleness.**

nin'compoop, *n.* a weak, foolish person.

nine'pins, *n.* a game in which nine pins are set up to be knocked down by a ball.

nin'ny, *n.* a fool.

nip, *v.* to pinch: to cut off: to check the growth of: to destroy.—*n.* a pinch: (of weather) a sharp cold. —*n.* **nip'per**, a small sharp lad: (*pl.*) a sharp tool like pincers.

nit, *n.* the egg of a louse or other small insect.

nitre, nī'ter, *n.* saltpetre.—*n.* **ni'tro-gly'cerine**, a powerful explosive. —*adjs.* **ni'tric**, **ni'trous.**

nitrogen, nī'tro-jen, *n.* a gas forming nearly four-fifths of the air we breathe.—*adj.* **nitro'genous.**

nō'ble, *adj.* brave, good: high in rank, birth, or title: splendid.— *n.* a person of high rank, title, or birth.—*adv.* **nō'bly.**—*adj.* **nō'ble-mind'ed**, having a lofty mind.— *ns.* **nobil'ity**, the nobles of a country: goodness of mind or character; **no'bleman**, a man of high rank.

nō'body, *n.* no one: a person of no account.

nocturne, nok'turn, *n.* a piece of music describing a night scene. —*adj.* **noctur'nal**, happening by night.

nocuous, nok'ū-us, *adj.* hurtful.

nod, *v.* to bend the head forward quickly (often as a sign of agree-ment): to let the head drop in weariness.—*n.* a slight bow.

nod'dle, *n.* the head.

node, *n.* the swollen part of a branch or twig where leaf-stalks join in it.—*n.* **nod'ule**, a small rounded lump.

Noël, nō-el', *n.* Christmas.

noise, *n.* a sound, esp. one which is loud or harsh.—*v.* to spread by tales.—*adjs.* **noise'less**; **nois'y.**

nōm'ad, *n.* a tribesman who wanders about in search of pasture: wanderer.—*adj.* **nomad'ic**, wandering.

nōmen'clature, *n.* method of naming (e.g. flowers): names as a whole.

nom'inal, *adj.* existing only in name: very small (e.g. He was fined the *nominal* sum of one penny).

nom'inate, *v.* to appoint: to mention someone's name for a post or an election.—*ns.* **nomina'tion**; **nominee'**, one whose name is put forward for a post.

non-, *prefix*, not—used in a great many words to change their meaning to the opposite, e.g. *ns.* **non-attend'ance**, absence; **non-com'batant**, a soldier who does not fight (e.g. an army doctor); **non-conduc'tor**, a substance which does not allow heat or electricity to pass easily through or along; **nonconform'ist**, one who does not worship according to the rules of the Church of England.—*adjs.* **non-commis'-sioned**, belonging to the lower ranks of army officers, below the rank of a second-lieutenant; **non-commit'tal**, unwilling to take side in a quarrel, or to give an opinion; **non'-stop**, going without a stop.

nonagenarian, non-a-je-nā'rian, *n.* one who is ninety years of age.

nonce, in the phrase *for the nonce*, for the present time.

nonchalant, non'shal-ant, *adj.* not caring, cool.—*n.* **non'chalance.**

non'descript, *adj.* not easily described: odd.

nonen'tity, *n.* a person of no importance.

non'plus, *v.* to puzzle: to bewilder.

non'sense, *n.* that which has no sense or meaning.—*adj.* **non-sen'sical**, silly.

noon, *n.* midday, twelve o'clock in the day.—*ns.* noon'day, noon'-tide, the time about midday.

noose, *n.* a running loop, tightening when pulled.

norm, *n.* a rule : a standard or pattern to judge other things from.—*adj.* nor'mal, ordinary, according to rule.

north, *n.* one of the four chief points of the compass : the part of the world within the Arctic Regions (the *North Pole* is the central point of the Arctic Regions) : the part of a country lying nearest the Arctic.—*adjs.* north, north'ern, north'erly, having to do with, lying in or near, coming from, the north ; north'-most, north'ernmost, nearest the north ; north'ward, in the direction of the north (also *adv.*).—*ns.* north'-east, the point of the compass midway between north and east ; north'-west, the point of the compass midway between north and west.—See also pole (2).

nose, *n.* the part of the face by which we smell : a jutting-out part of anything (e.g. the front of an aeroplane).—*v.* to track by smelling : to pry into.—*ns.* nose'gay, a bunch of flowers ; nose'-dive, an aeroplane's dive or plunge to the earth.

nos'tril, *n.* one of the openings of the nose.

nos'trum, *n.* a medicine, esp. one sold with the promise of a wonderful cure.

nō'table, *adj.* worth taking notice of : remarkable.—*n.* notabil'ity, a well-known person.

nō'tary, usually no'tary pub'lic, *n.* a person who draws up certain written statements in a way required by law and sees to having them properly signed.

nōtā'tion, *n.* the showing of numbers, musical sounds, etc., by signs (e.g. the *decimal notation* ; *sol-fa notation*).

notch, *n.* a small V-shaped cut.—*v.* to make a notch.

note, *n.* a sign or piece of writing to draw someone's attention : a short explanation : a short letter : a bank-note : a single sound in music (e.g. a high *note*) : fame (e.g. a person of *note*).—*v.* to mark : to notice : to set down in writing.—*adjs.* nō'ted, famous, well known ; note'worthy, worthy of being noted.

nothing, nuth'ing, *n.* no thing : a trifle.

notice, nōt'is, *n.* a statement, esp. one pasted up on a board, put in a newspaper, etc. : attention (e.g. May I draw your *notice* to this error ?) : a warning or command to leave a job or house.—*v.* to see : to pass a remark on.—*adj.* not'iceable, worthy of attention.

nō'tify, *v.* to make known : to give notice to.—*adj.* nō'tifiable, that must be reported (e.g. a *notifiable* disease).—*n.* notifica'tion.

notion, nō'shun, *n.* idea : a whim or queer fancy.

notō'rious, *adj.* well known because of badness (e.g. a *notorious* thief).

notwithstand'ing, *prep.* in spite of.—*conj.* in spite of the fact that.—*adv.* in spite of everything.

nought, nawt, *n.* nothing : the figure 0.

noun, *n.* (in *grammar*) the name of any person or thing.

nourish, nur'ish, *v.* to feed or bring up : to keep in the mind (e.g. He *nourished* the hope that he would succeed).—*n.* nour'ishment, food.

nov'el, *adj.* new : unusual, strange.—*n.* a long story, or book containing one.—*ns.* nov'elist, a writer of novels ; nov'elty, something new.

Novem'ber, *n.* the eleventh month.

novice, nov'is, *n.* a beginner.

now'adays, *adv.* at the present time.

nō'where, *adv.* not in any place.

noxious, nok'shus, *adj.* harmful.

noz'zle, *n.* open end fitted to pipe or tube (e.g. bellows, hose).

nuance, nū-ongs', *n.* a very fine difference in colour, meaning, etc.

nucleus, nū'klē-us, *n.* the central part : point round which a number of persons or things collect.—*pl.* nu'clei.—**nuclear energy,** atomic energy ; **nuclear reactor,** apparatus for producing nuclear energy.

nūde, *adj.* naked.—*ns.* **nū′dist,** one who goes naked ; **nū′dity,** nakedness.

nudge, nuj, *n.* a gentle push.—Also *v.*

nū′gatory, *adj.* trifling.

nug′get, *n.* a lump of gold, silver, etc.

nuisance, nū′sans, *n.* something which annoys or hurts.

null, *adj.* having lost its worth : of no effect (esp. in phrase *null and void*).—*v.* **nulli′fȳ,** to make useless or of no effect.

numb, num, *adj.* having lost (because of cold) the power to feel or move.—*v.* to take away the power of feeling or moving.

num′ber, *n.* a collection or company of things or persons (usually a good many) : a word or figure showing how many.—*v.* to count : to amount to.—*adjs.* **num′berless,** more than can be counted ; **nū′meral,** expressing a number ; **nūmer′ical,** telling how many (e.g. The *numerical* strength of the battalion was . . .) ; **nū′merous,** many.—*ns.* **nū′meral,** a figure used to express a number (e.g. 1, 2, 3 . . .) ; **nū′merātor,** the upper number of a vulgar fraction.

nūmis′matist, *n.* one who collects and studies coins and medals.

num′skull, *n.* a stupid fellow.

nun, *n.* a holy woman who lives in a convent.—*n.* **nun′nery,** a convent for women.

nuptial, nup′shal, *adj.* having to do with marriage.—*n.pl.* **nup′tials,** a wedding.

nurse, *n.* a woman who looks after infants or sick persons.—*v.* to look after an infant or sick person : to keep in the mind (e.g. hope, anger).—*ns.* **nur′sery,** a room for children : a place where young plants are reared ; **nursery-school,** a school for very young children ; **nursing-home,** see **home.**

nur′tūre, *n.* food : the bringing up of children.—*v.* to bring up : to feed : to educate.

nut, *n.* a fruit having a hard shell and, in it, a kernel : a small block of metal for screwing on the end of a bolt : a showily dressed person.—*v.* to gather nuts.

nut′meg, *n.* a hard seed from the East, a spice used in cooking.

nū′triment, *n.* nourishing food.—*adjs.* **nutritious** (nū-trish′us), **nū′tritive,** valuable as food.

ny′lon, *n.* material made of artificial threads made from chemicals.

nymph, nimf, *n.* a goddess of the rivers, trees, etc. : a girl.

O

oaf, *n.* a foolish child left by the fairies : a silly, simple fellow.

oak, *n.* a well-known forest-tree, with hard, valuable wood.—*adj.* **oak′en.**—*ns.* **oak′-apple, oak′-gall,** a spongy growth on the leaves and twigs of oaks, caused by insects ; not the same as **marble-gall.**

oak′um, *n.* old rope untwisted, used for caulking (i.e. stopping up).

oar, *n.* a pole with a flat, blade-like end for rowing.—*v.* to row.—*n.* **oars′man,** rower.

oasis, ō-ā′sis, *n.* in a desert, a place where water is found, and trees, etc. grow :—*pl.* **oases** (ō-ā′sēz).

oast, *n.* a large oven to dry hops.

oat, *n.* (often in *pl.* **oats**), a grassy plant and its seeds, much used as food.—*ns.* **oat′cake,** a thin,

flat cake consisting of **oat′meal,** which is made by grinding down oat grains.—*adj.* **oat′en.**

oath, *n.* a solemn promise to speak the truth, to keep one's word, to be loyal, etc. : a swear word :—*pl.* **oaths.**

ob′dūrate, *adj.* stubborn : hard-hearted

obedient, ob-ē′di-ent, *adj.* ready and willing to do what one is told, dutiful.—*n.* **obē′dience.**—*v.* **obey.**

obeisance, ō-bā′sans, *n.* obedience : a bow or curtsy showing respect.

ob′elisk, *n.* a tall, four-sided pillar, with pointed top.

obese, ō-bēs′, *adj.* very fat.

obey, ō-bā′, *v.* to do as one is told.—*adj.* **obē′dient.**—*n.* **obē′dience.**

obit´uary, *n.* a notice (e.g. in a newspaper) of a person's death.

ob´ject, *n.* anything set before the eyes or mind : an aim or purpose : in a sentence, the word which stands for the person (or thing) on whom the action of the verb is performed (see **subject**).— *v.* **object´**, to give a reason against. — *n.* **objec´tion**. — *adj.* **objec´tionable**, nasty, disagreeable.— *n.* **objec´tive**, that which one aims at doing or reaching.

oblation, ob-lā´shun, *n.* a sacrifice or offering.

oblige, ō-blīj´, *v.* to force or compel (e.g. I was *obliged* to go home) : to do a favour or service to.— *n.* **obliga´tion**, a promise or duty (e.g. I am under an *obligation* to help him).— *adjs.* **oblig´atory**, necessary : imposing a duty ; **oblig´ing**, ready to do a good turn.

oblique, ob-lēk´, *adj.* slanting.

oblit´erate, *v.* to blot out : to destroy.— *n.* **obliterā´tion**.

oblivion, ob-liv´i-un, *n.* state of being forgotten.— *adj.* **obliv´ious**, forgetful.

oblong, *n.* a figure of this shape : □.—Also *adj.*

obnoxious, ob-nok´shus, *adj.* hurtful : causing dislike or offence.

oboe, ō´bō, **hautboy**, ō´-boi, *ns.* a high-pitched wooden wind-instrument.— *n.* **o´bōist**, a player on the oboe.

obscene, ob-sēn´, *adj.* filthy : disgusting.— *n.* **obscen´ity**.

obscūre´, *adj.* dark : not easily understood : unknown : humble. — *v.* to darken : to make less clear.— *n.* **obscū´rity**.

obsequies, ob´se-kwiz, *n.pl.* funeral.

obsequious, ob-sē´kwi-us, *adj.* going out of one's way to win favour.

observe´, *v.* to notice : to say in passing : to obey (e.g. the law, a command).— *n.* **observ´ance**, act of keeping (e.g. a law, a day —Sunday *observance*) : a habit or custom.— *adj.* **observ´ant**, good at noticing.— *ns.* **observā´tion**, act or habit of seeing and noting : attention : remark ; **observ´atory**, a place where the skies are looked at through telescopes ; **observ´er**, one who observes : a

member of an aeroplane crew whose work it is to spy out the enemy's land, movements, etc.

obsession, ob-sesh´n, *n.* a belief or idea from which the mind cannot get away.— *v.* **obsess´**, to fill the mind completely.

ob´solēte, *adj.* gone out of use.— *adj.* **obsoles´cent**, going out-of-date.

ob´stacle, *n.* something which stands in the way and hinders.— *n.* **ob´stacle-race**, a race in which obstacles have to be passed.

ob´stinate, *adj.* stubborn : not yielding to treatment (e.g. an *obstinate* disease).— *n.* **ob´stinacy**, stubbornness.

obstrep´erous, *adj.* noisy.

obstruct´, *v.* to block up, to keep from passing : to hold back.— *n.* **obstruc´tion**, anything which hinders.

obtain´, *v.* to get : to hold : to be in use (e.g. This custom no longer *obtains* in Turkey).— *adj.* **obtain´able**, able to be got.

obtrude, ob-trood´, *v.* to come in when not wanted : to force something upon somebody.— *ns.* **obtrud´er** ; **obtru´sion**.— *adj.* **obtrus´ive**, forward, impudent.

obverse´, *n.* the side of a coin on which is the head.

obviate, ob´vi-āt, *v.* to remove : to prevent (e.g. This *obviates* the difficulty).

obvious, ob´vi-us, *adj.* plain : seen or understood at a glance.

occasion, o-kā´zhun, *n.* a happening : a special time : a cause or reason : opportunity.— *v.* to cause, to give rise to.— *adj.* **occā´sional**, happening now and then.— *adv.* **occā´sionally**.

Occident, ok´si-dent, *n.* the West.

occult´, *adj.* secret : mysterious.

oc´cupȳ, *v.* to dwell in : to keep busy : to take up space or time. — *ns.* **oc´cupancy**, the time during which one occupies a house, office, etc. ; **oc´cupant**, **oc´cupier**, one who has possession (of a house, etc.) ; **occupā´tion**, possession : one's trade or job.

occur´, *v.* to come into the mind : to happen : to be found here and there.— *n.* **occur´rence**, a happening or event.

ocean, ō′shin, *n.* the stretch of salt water surrounding the land of the globe : also one of its five great divisions (Atlantic, Pacific, Indian, Arctic, Antarctic).

ochre, ō′ker, *n.* a fine pale-yellow clay, used for colouring.

oc′tagon, *n.* a shape or figure having eight straight sides and eight angles.—*adj.* **octag′onal.**

oc′tave, *n.* (in music) a stretch of eight sounds (e.g. from *low doh* to *high doh*).

Octō′ber, *n.* the tenth month of the year.

octogenarian, ok-tō-je-nā′ri-an, *n.* one who is eighty years old.

oc′tōpus, *n.* a sea-creature of the cuttle-fish kind, with eight arms.

oc′ūlist, *n.* an eye-doctor.

odd, *adj.* (of a number) not even, leaving a remainder when divided by two (e.g. the numbers 1, 17, 315) : unusual, strange.—*ns.* **odd′ity,** something strange : a queer person :—*pl.* **odd′ments,** odds and ends, scraps.

ode, *n.* a song.

odious, ō′di-us, *adj.* hateful.—*n.* **o′dium,** dislike, hatred.

odour, ō′dur, *n.* smell (pleasant or unpleasant).—*adjs.* **odorif′erous,** spreading smell, pleasant or unpleasant ; **o′dorous,** sweet-smelling.

off, *adv.* and *prep.* not on : away from.—*adj.* farther away.—*n.* the side of a cricket field opposite to that on which the batsman stands (i.e. to the right of the wicket-keeper when the batsman is right-handed).

off′al, *n.* waste : the parts of an animal unfit for use as food, etc.

offend′, *v.* to displease : to make angry : to sin.—*ns.* **offence′,** a hurt to a person's feelings : a crime ; **offen′der** ; **offen′sive,** the position of one who attacks (e.g. The army took up the *offensive*) : an attack.—*adj.* annoying : disgusting.

off′er, *v.* to put forward (e.g. a gift, a price) : to lay before : to say that one is willing to do something : to occur (e.g. If the opportunity *offers* . . .).—*n.* a bid of

money : something proposed.—*ns.* **off′ering,** a gift : a church collection ; **off′ertory,** that which is read or sung while a church collection is being taken : the collection.

off′hand, *adj.* said or done without thinking.

office, of′is, *n.* one's job, duty, or work : a place where the letters, accounts, etc. of a business are dealt with : a service or kindness : an act of worship.—*n.* **off′icer,** one who holds an office : a person holding a position of trust in the army, navy, air-force, etc.—*adj.* **official** (of-fish′al), given out by those in power (e.g. an *official* notice, i.e. a government notice) : forming part of one's task when holding a job or office (e.g. his *official* duties).—*n.* one who holds a position of trust with the government or with a large company (e.g. a customs *official*, a bank *official*).—*adj.* **officious** (of-fish′us), fussy, fond of interfering.—*v.* **officiate** (of-fish′i-āt), to perform a duty or service (e.g. The clergyman *officiated* at the funeral).

off′ing, *n.* the part of the sea some distance from the shore, but in sight of it.

off′set, *v.* to weigh against, to make up for.

off′shoot, *n.* a shoot growing out of the main stem.

off′spring, *n.* one's child or children.

of′ten, oft, oft-times, *adv.* many times.

ō′gle, *v.* to make eyes at.

ogre, ō′ger, *n.* a man-eating giant of fairy tales :—*fem.* **o′gress.**

oil, *n.* fatty liquid, often easily set on fire, got from plants (e.g. palm-oil), animals (e.g. whale-oil), and minerals (e.g. paraffin).—*v.* to apply oil to.—*ns.* **oil′-cloth,** a painted floorcloth of canvas coated with hardened oil ; **oil′-painting,** a picture painted in oil-colours ; **oil′skin,** cloth made waterproof by means of oil.—*adj.* **oil′y,** greasy : messy.

oint′ment, *n.* a greasy substance for healing hurts or sores.

ōld, *adj.* aged : not new : belonging to far-off times.—*adj.* **old'en**, belonging to long ago.

oleaginous, ō-lē-aj'in-us, *adj.* oily.

olive, ol'iv, *n.* an evergreen tree, yielding a fruit (the olive), from which oil (olive-oil) is pressed : a yellowish-green colour.—**olive branch**, a sign of peace.

om'elet, **om'elette**, *n.* eggs beaten up, and fried in a pan.

ō'men, *n.* a sign of future events, either good or evil.—*adj.* **om'in-ous**, likely to bring trouble.

ōmit', *v.* to leave out.—*n.* **omis'sion**.

om'nibus, *n.* a large public motor-car for passengers—now short-ened to **bus**.—**omnibus volume**, a book of long stories by one author.

omnip'otent, *adj.* able to do every-thing.—*n.* **omnip'otence**.

omniscient, om-nish'-yent, *adj.* knowing everything.—*n.* **omni'-science**.

omniv'orous, *adj.* feeding on all kinds of food.

once, wuns, *adv.* at a former time : for one time only.—**once for all**, once only and not again ; at once, without delay.

oncoming, on'kum-ing, *n.* an ap-proach.—Also *adj.*

on'erous, *adj.* heavy, hard to bear or do.

one-sided, wun-sī'ded, *adj.* seeing only one side of an argument.

ongoings, on'gō-ingz, *n.pl.* strange and unusual behaviour.

onion, un'yun, *n.* a plant growing from a bulb ; it has a sharp taste and smell.

on'looker, *n.* one who looks on.

on'set, *n.* a fierce attack.

on'shore, *adj.* going towards the shore : happening on the land.

onslaught, on'slawt, *n.* a fierce at-tack.

ō'nus, *n.* a burden.

on'ward, *adj.* going forward.—*advs.* **on'ward**, **on'wards**.

onyx, on'iks, *n.* a precious stone with layers of different colours.

ooze, n. soft mud : a gentle flow.—*v.* to flow gently.

ō'pal, *n.* a precious stone, bluish white in colour, remarkable for its changing rainbow colours.—*adj.* **opales'cent**, pearly-white with changing rainbow colours.

opaque, ō-pāk', *adj.* not able to be seen through : dark.

ō'pen, *adj.* not shut : free from trees : not frozen up : public : frank : clear.—*v.* to make open : to begin : to unlock.—*adjs.* **open-handed**, giving away money, etc. freely ; **open-hearted**, frank ; **open-minded**, ready to take up new ideas.—*n.* **o'pening**, an open place : opportunity : chance.

op'era, *n.* a play set to music.

op'erate, *v.* to work so as to bring about a certain effect : to per-form an operation.—*n.* **operā'-tion**, action : the cutting of a part of the human body in order to cure disease : (*pl.*) movements of armies, troops.—*adj.* **op'erātive**, working, in action : having effect. —*n.* a workman in a factory. —*n.* **op'erātor**, one who works a machine.

operet'ta, *n.* a short musical play.

ophthalmia, of-thal'mi-a, *n.* an ill-ness causing soreness of the eyes.

opiate, ō'pi-āt, *n.* a sleep drug.

opinion, ō-pin'yun, *n.* belief : what one thinks : judgment.—*v.* **opine'**, to think, to have an idea.

opos'sum, *n.* a small American marsupial (i.e. an animal that carries its young in its pouch).

oppō'nent. See **oppose**.

opportūne', *adj.* coming at the right time.—*ns.* **opportū'nity**, a chance to do something ; **opportū'nist**, one who seizes his chances.

oppose', *v.* to stand against or in the way of : to struggle against. —*ns.* **oppō'nent**, an enemy : a rival ; **op'posite**, something as different as possible (e.g. black is the *opposite* of white ; ' yes ' is the *opposite* of ' no ') ; **opposi'-tion**, those who resist : (in Parlia-ment) the party which is against the government (i.e. the most powerful) party.—*adj.* **op'posite**, facing, right in front of : lying on the other side : as different as possible.

oppress', *v.* to govern harshly : to treat cruelly : to load with burdens.—*adj.* **oppress'ive**, cruel, harsh : tiring.—*n.* **oppres'sion**.

opprō'brium, *n.* great disgrace.—*adj.* **opprō'brious**.

op'tic, op'tical, *adjs.* having to do with the eye or sight (e.g. *an optical illusion*, a mistake due to the way one looks at a thing).— *n.* **optician** (op-tish'an), one who makes or sells spectacles.

op'timism, *n.* the belief that all is for the best: the habit of taking a bright, hopeful view of things. —*n.* **op'timist**, one who takes a cheerful view of things.—*adj.* **optimist'ic**.

option, op'shun, *n.* choice.—*adj.* **op'tional**, left to one's choice.

op'ulent, *adj.* wealthy.—*n.* **op'ulence**, riches.

or'acle, *n.* in far-off times, a holy place where a god was thought to give answers to difficult questions—the answer (also called an *oracle*) was often of double meaning: a person famed for wisdom. —*adj.* **orac'ular**, very wise: of double meaning.

ō'ral, *adj.* spoken, not written.

or'ange, *n.* a juicy fruit, with a thick, golden-colour skin: a reddish-yellow colour.

ōrang'-utan', or **-outang**, oo-tan(g'), *n.* a large, man-like ape.

oration, ō-rā'shun, *n.* a public speech, esp. one in fine language.—*ns.* **or'ator**, a public speaker: a fine speaker; **or'atory**, the art of speaking well in public.

oratō'rio, *n.* a sacred story set to music.

orb, *n.* a sphere or globe: a heavenly body (moon, star, etc.).

or'bit, *n.* the path of a planet, etc., round another heavenly body, or of a space capsule round the earth, etc.—*v.* to send round, or go round, the earth, etc., in space.

orch'ard, *n.* a garden of fruit trees.

orchestra, or'kes-tra, *n.* a group of musicians playing together.

orchid, or'kid, *n.* a plant with a showy flower.

ordain', *v.* to put in order: to declare something to be law: to receive (a clergyman) into the Church.—*adj.* **or'dinal**, showing the order of (first, second, third, etc. are the *ordinal* numbers).— *ns.* **or'dinance**, a law; **ordinā'tion**, the receiving of a clergyman into the Church.

ordeal, or'dē-al, *n.* a hard trial or test: suffering.

or'der, *n.* regular arrangement: rank or position: a command: a society or brotherhood (e.g. of monks, Templars): an honour, esp. one given by a king.—*v.* to arrange: to command.—*adj.* **or'derly**, in proper order: well behaved.—*n.* **or'derly**, a soldier who carries the orders and messages of an officer.

or'dinary, *adj.* common, usual: plain. —*n.* the common run of things.

ord'nance, *n.* the branch of the army which sees to the supply of heavy guns and ammunition, soldiers' stores, etc.: big guns.— **ordnance survey**, a government office which produces very carefully drawn maps.

ore, *n.* a mineral from which a metal is got (e.g. iron *ore*).

or'gan, *n.* part of the body (e.g. the nose, the *organ* of smell): a large musical wind-instrument: a means of spreading information, such as a newspaper.—*adj.* **organ'ic**, produced by the organs: made up of parts all having their own work to do: living.—*ns.* **or'ganism**, any living thing; **or'ganist**, one who plays the organ.

or'ganise, *v.* to arrange: to get up (e.g. a concert).—*n.* **organisā'tion**, the act of arranging: a body of people working together for a purpose.

orgy, or'ji, *n.* a drunken feast.

oriel, ō'ri-el, *n.* a window that juts out.

Orient, ōr-i-ent, *n.* the East.—*adj.* **Orien'tal**, Eastern. — *n.* a native of the East.—*n.* **Orient'alist**, one who studies the language, customs, etc. of peoples of the East. —*v.* **o'rientate**, to find one's bearings: to set or place in a certain way.—*n.* **orientā'tion**.

orifice, or'i-fis, *n.* an opening.

origin, or'i-jin, *n.* the starting-point: cause. — *adj.* **orig'inal**, first in order: not copied: able to think or do something new.— *n.* a first copy: a model from which other things are made.— *v.* **orig'inate**, to bring into being: to produce.—*n.* **original'ity**, the ability to think out new ideas or to do things on one's own.

or'ison, *n.* a prayer.

or'nament, *n.* any thing that adorns or adds beauty.—*v.* to adorn.—*n.* ornamentā'tion.—*adj.* ornate', richly decorated.

ornithologist, ŏr-ni-thŏl'o-jist, *n.* one who makes a special study of birds.—*n.* ornithol'ogy.

orographical, or-o-graf'ik-al, *adj.* showing the mountains of a country (e.g. an *orographical* map).

orphan, or'fan, *n.* a child who has lost one or both parents.—*adj.* having lost one or both parents.—*n.* or'phanage, a home for orphans.

or'rery, *n.* a clockwork model of the stars, sun, earth, and moon, showing their positions and motions.

orth'odox, *adj.* holding views (esp. religious views) that are generally believed.—*n.* orth'odoxy.

orthography, or-thog'ra-fi, *n.* correct spelling : spelling in general.

oscillate, os'sil-lāt, *v.* to swing to and fro, like the pendulum of a clock : (of a wireless set) to make a ' howling ' noise.—*n.* oscil-lā'tion.

osier, ōzh'yir, *n.* willow twigs used in making baskets, etc.

osprey, os'prā, *n.* the sea-eagle.

os'sify, *v.* to turn into bone.

osten'sible, *adj.* not real : pretended (e.g. His illness was the *ostensible* cause of his absence, his laziness the real cause).

ostentā'tion, *n.* the making of a great show in order to attract attention.—*adj.* ostentā'tious, fond of show.

ostler, os'ler, *n.* stableman at an inn.

ostracise, os'tra-sīz, *v.* to banish from the company of other people : to exile.

os'trich, *n.* a large, swift-running bird, whose feathers are sometimes of great value for dress purposes.

otiose, ō'shi-ōz, *adj.* lazy : idle.

ot'ter, *n.* a water-animal living on fish.

Ottoman, o'tō-man, *n.* and *adj.* Turk.—*n.* ottoman, a low, cushioned seat without back—a kind of couch.

ounce, *n.* one-sixteenth of a pound avoirdupois : small quantity.

ounce, *n.* a spotted flesh-eating animal, sometimes called snow-leopard.

our, *adj.* belonging to us.

oust, owst, *v.* to drive out, expel.

outbid', *v.* to offer a higher price than somebody else.

outbreak, owt'brāk, *n.* a beginning (e.g. of a war, of disease).

outbuilding, owt'bild-ing, *n.* a shed.

out'burst, *n.* a bursting out, esp. of angry feelings.

out'cast, *adj.* driven away from friends and home.—*n.* a homeless person.

outclassed, owt-klast', *adj.* thoroughly beaten : very poor in comparison.

outcome, owt'kum, *n.* the result.

out'cry, *n.* a loud cry of distress, anger, etc.

outdis'tance, *v.* to leave a rival behind (e.g. in a race).

outdo, owt-doo', *v.* to do better than.

out'door, *adj.* done *out of doors,* i.e. in the open air (e.g. *outdoor* games, exercises, sports).

out'fall, *n.* the mouth of a river.

out'fit, *n.* a collection of necessary articles (e.g. tools for a motor-car ; clothes, etc. for a voyage). —*n.* out'fitter, a merchant who sells outfits, esp. men's clothes.

outflank', *v.* to stretch out the side of one army beyond that of another : to get the better of.

outgrow, owt-grō', *v.* to grow more than : to get too big (e.g. for one's clothes). — *n.* out'growth, an offshoot.

out'house, *n.* a shed.

out'law, *n.* someone outside the protection of the law : a robber or brigand.—*v.* to place someone beyond the protection of the law.

out'lay, *n.* money paid out.

out'let, *n.* a passage outwards : a means of letting something out (e.g. Football was an *outlet* for his high spirits).

out'line, *n.* the outer line : a sketch showing only the main lines, a rough plan or sketch.—*v.* to draw in outline : to sketch roughly.

outlive, owt-liv', v. to live longer than.

out'look, n. a view (e.g. from a window): what is likely to happen (e.g. the weather *outlook*).

outly'ing, adj. far from the centre: distant.

outnum'ber, v. to be greater in number than.

out-of-the-way, adj. not easily reached: unusual.

out'post, n. a military guard in front of the main army: a settler's camp in the wilds.

out'put, n. the goods turned out by a machine, factory, etc.

outrage, owt'rāj, n. a wicked act of great violence: an act which does harm to feelings, rights, etc. —v. to injure: to insult.—adj. **outrā'geous**, very wrong: violent.

out'rider, n. a servant who rides in front of a carriage.

outright, owt'rīt, adv. completely.

outrun', v. to run faster than.

out'set, n. beginning.

out'side, n. the surface: the furthest limit.—Also adj., adv.—n. **outsi'der**, stranger: a runner whom no one expected to win a race.

out'size, n. a very large size.

out'skirts, n.pl. the outer border of a city: the suburbs.

outspan', v. to loosen oxen from a wagon.

outspo'ken, adj. bold in speech.

outstand'ing, adj. well-known: easily seen: (of accounts, debts) unpaid.

outstrip', v. to leave behind in running.

outvote', v. to defeat (e.g. in an election) by a greater number of votes.

out'ward, adj. on the outside or surface.—advs. **outwards** (or **out'wardly**).—adj. **out'ward-bound**, sailing to a foreign port.

outweigh, owt-wā', v. to be more important than.

outwit', v. to be too clever for: to baffle.

out'work, n. a fort outside the main defences.

ouzel, oo'zl, n. a kind of thrush.

ō'val, adj. having the shape of an egg.—Also n.

ō'vary, n. the part of the body in which eggs are formed: (in plants) the seed-case.

ōvā'tion, n. an outburst of cheering, hand-clapping, etc.: a hearty welcome.

oven, uv'n, n. a covered place, above or beside a fire, for baking.

o'veralls, n.pl. a garment worn over ordinary clothes to protect them against dirt or weather.

overawe, ō-ver-aw', v. to make silent by fear or wonder.

overbalance, ō-ver-bal'ans, v. to lose one's balance and fall: to push over.

overbearing, ō-ver-bār'ing, adj. haughty.

o'verboard, adv. out of a ship into the water.

overbur'den, v. to weigh down with too great a load.

overcast', v. to cloud: to cover with gloom: to sew over the edges of a piece of cloth slightly. —adj. (of the sky) cloudy.

overcharge, ō-ver-charj', v. to load too heavily: to charge too great a price.—n. **o'vercharge**, a price which is too high.

overcome, ō-ver-kum', v. to get the better of: to conquer.

overdo, ō-ver-doo', v. to do too much: to carry too far: to cook too long.—adj. **overdone'**, carried too far: cooked too much.

overdraw', v. to draw more money from the bank than is standing at one's name: to go beyond the truth.—n. **o'verdraft**, the amount of money overdrawn from a bank.

overdue, ō-ver-dū', adj. behind the stated time (e.g. The train is *overdue*): still unpaid though the time for payment has passed.

overflow, ō-ver-flō', v. to be so full as to run over: to be very plentiful.—n. **o'verflow**.

overgrown, ō'ver-grōn, adj. covered with grass or leaves: too big for one's age.

overhang', v. to jut out over.

overhaul, ō-ver-hawl', v. to examine carefully and carry out repairs: to catch up with.—n. **o'verhaul**.

overhear', v. to hear what was not meant to be heard.

overjoyed', adj. filled with great joy.

o'verland, adj. going overland, not by sea.

overlap', v. to cover and stretch a little beyond.

overload', v. to load or fill too much.

overlook', v. to look down upon from a higher point : to fail to see : to pardon : to be in charge of.

o'verlord, n. a lord, esp. one who is over other lords.

overmuch', adv. too much.

overnight', adv. during the night.

overpow'er, v. to defeat by greater force.—adj. **overpow'ering**, unable to be resisted.

overrate', v. to value too highly.

overreach', v. (with one's self) to go too far with a matter and so fail in one's purpose.

override', v. to trample down : to set aside (e.g. The wicked ruler overrides the wishes of his people).

overrule', o-ver-rool', v. to set aside by using higher authority.

overrun', v. to grow or spread over (e.g. The garden is overrun with weeds and the house with mice) : to take possession of, and lay waste a country (e.g. The Scottish army overran the north of England).

oversea, overseas, adj. and adv. beyond the sea.

oversee', v. to watch over.—ns. **o'verseer**, one who oversees ; **o'versight**, a mistake (as when something has been left out).

overshad'ow, v. to throw a shadow over : to take the importance from.

overshoot', v. to shoot beyond a mark : to say more than is true.

overstate', v. to say more than is true.

overstep', v. to go further than one should.

overt, ō'vert, adj. open to view : not hidden.

overtake', v. to come up with, to catch up.

overthrow', v. to throw down or upset : to defeat.

o'vertime, n. time spent in working beyond one's set hours.

o'verture, n. a proposal or offer (e.g. overtures of peace) : a piece of music played as an introduction to an opera, etc.

overturn', v. to throw down or over : to conquer : to ruin.

overween'ing, adj. thinking too highly of one's powers, haughty.

overwhelm', v. to defeat utterly.

overwork', v. to work beyond one's powers.—adjs. **overworked'**; **overwrought'** (-rawt'), excited : tired out.

ovip'arous, adj. bringing forth young by laying eggs which hatch out (e.g. hens, most snakes and fishes).

ō'vum, n. an egg :—pl. **ova**.

owe, ō, v. to be bound to pay : to be in debt : to be obliged for.—**owing to**, because of.

owl, n. a bird of prey well known by its hooting call.—n. **owl'et**, a young owl.

own, ōn, v. to possess : to confess to be true.—adj. belonging to a certain person.—ns. **own'er**, one who possesses ; **own'ership**, possession.

ox, n. the male of the cow, esp. one used for drawing loads :—pl. **ox'en**. — **ox-eye daisy**, a well-known wild flower (marguerite), like a large daisy.

oxygen, oks'i-jen, n. a gas without taste, colour, or smell, forming part of the air and of water (it is necessary for life).

O'yes, O'yez, Hear ye !

oys'ter, n. a double-sided shellfish, used as food.

ozone', n. a kind of oxygen : pure, healthy air.

P

pab'ulum, n. food.

pace, n. a step : rate or manner of walking.—v. to measure by steps : to walk backwards and forwards.

pacify, pas'i-fī, v. to bring back peace to : to calm.—adj. **pacif'ic**, fond of peace.—n. **pac'ifist**, one who hates war and works for peace.

pack, n. a bundle, esp. that of a pedlar or soldier : a set of cards : a number of animals (e.g. hounds) : a mass of floating and broken ice.—v. to collect and store (clothes, etc.) in a case or trunk : to crowd : to fill a meeting with one's own friends.—*ns.* pack′age, a bundle ; pack′et, a small parcel ; packet-steamer, a ship used for carrying letters and passengers ; pack′-horse, a horse used to carry packs ; pack′-man, one who goes from door to door, selling small articles from a pack : a pedlar ; pack′-saddle, a saddle for packs or burdens.

pact, *n.* something fixed or agreed upon : a bargain or contract.

pad, *n.* a soft, or firm, cushion-like mass : sheets of paper fixed together : a rocket-launching platform.—*v.* to stuff with anything soft : to fill up (e.g. a book) with useless material.—*n.* pad′ding, stuffing material : (in writing) matter put in just to fill space.

pad, *n.* a thief, robber (more usually foot′-pad) : a slow-going horse.—*v.* to trudge along.

pad′dle, *v.* to row : to dabble in water with the feet.—*n.* a short, broad, spoon-shaped oar. — *n.* paddle-steamer, a steamer driven not by propellers but by two large wheels made up of paddles.

pad′dock, *n.* a toad or frog.

pad′dock, *n.* a small closed-in field.

pad′dy, *n.* growing rice : rice in the husk.—*n.* padd′y-field, a muddy field in which rice is grown.

pad′lock, *n.* a movable lock with hinged hook.

pæan, pē′an, *n.* a song of triumph or joy.

pā′gan, *n.* a heathen.—*n.* pa′ganism.

page, *n.* a boy attending on a person of rank : a boy servant (e.g. in hotels).

page, *n.* one side of a written or printed leaf of paper.

pageant, paj′int, *n.* a show or procession made up of scenes from the history of a place : any fine show.—*n.* pa′geantry, splendid show or display (e.g. The coronation took place with great *pageantry*).

pagō′da, *n.* an Eastern temple, esp. in China and India.

pail, *n.* an open vessel of tin, zinc, or wood, for holding or carrying liquids.

pain, *n.* suffering which hurts either mind or body : punishment (e.g. under *pain* of death) : (*pl.*) care (e.g. He takes great *pains* with his work).—*v.* to cause suffering to.—*adjs.* pain′ful ; pain′less ; pains′taking, very careful.

paint, *v.* to cover with colour : to describe in words.—*n.* something used for colouring.—*ns.* paint′er, one whose trade is painting : an artist ; paint′ing, a painted picture.

paint′er, *n.* a rope used to fasten a boat.

pair, *n.* two of a kind : a set of two.—*v.* to join in couples : to go two and two.

pal′ace, *n.* a large and fine house, such as that of a king, queen, archbishop, or nobleman.

pal′adin, *n.* one of the twelve peers of Charlemagne's household : an old-time knight.

palæolithic, pa-lē-ō-lith′ik, *adj.* belonging to the early Stone Age (i.e. when man used stone tools).

palanquin, palankeen, pal-an-kēn′, *n.* a light covered carriage, carried on the shoulders of men.

pal′ate, *n.* the roof of the mouth.—*adj.* pal′atable, pleasant to the taste.

palatial, pa-lā′shi-al, *adj.* like a palace : magnificent.

pala′ver, *n.* light, idle talk : a talk with native chiefs.

pale, *n.* a piece of wood (a stake) used in making a fence (called a pā′ling) to enclose ground : a fence : an enclosed space or district.—*n.* pal′isade, a fence of pointed stakes.

pale, *adj.* light or whitish in colour : not ruddy or fresh.—*v.* to make or turn pale.

palette, pal′et, *n.* a little oval board on which an artist mixes his colours.

palfrey, pal′fri, *n.* a horse for riding (not a war-horse).

paling, palisade. See pale.

pall, pawl, *n.* a cloak : the cloth over a coffin at a funeral.

pall, pawl, *v.* to become dull or uninteresting.

pal′let, *n.* a straw bed.

palliasse, pa-li-as´, *n.* a small bed made of straw.

palliate, pal´i-āt, *v.* to make excuses for: to lessen.—*adj.* **pal´liative**, making less severe.—*n.* something which lessens pain, disease, etc.

pal´lid, *adj.* pale.—*n.* **pal´lor**, paleness.

palm, pahm, *n.* a tall tree, with broad, spreading, fern-like leaves, which grows in hot countries: a leaf of this tree, shown as a sign of victory.—*ns.* **palmer** (pah´mer), a pilgrim from the Holy Land, carrying a branch of palm; **palm-oil**, an oil made from the fruit of palms.—*adj.* **palmy**, flourishing: full of prosperity.

palm, pahm, *n.* the inner part of the hand.—*ns.* **palmist** (pah´mist), one who claims to tell fortunes by the lines and marks of the palm of the hand; **palmistry** (pah´mis-tri), the telling of fortunes in this way.—**to palm off**, to give something with the intention of cheating (e.g. He *palmed* off a bad shilling on me).

pal´pable, *adj.* able to be touched or felt: easily noticed.

pal´pitate, *v.* (of the heart) to beat rapidly, to throb.—*n.* **palpitā´tion**, uncomfortable throbbing of the heart.

palsy, pawl´zi, *n.* a loss of power and feeling in the muscles.

paltry, pawl´tri, *adj.* of little value: mean.

pam´pas, *n.pl.* a name for the vast treeless plains of South America.

pam´per, *v.* to feed with fine food: to spoil by giving way to.

pamphlet, pam´flet, *n.* a small book, clasped together but not bound in a cover.

pan, *n.* a broad, shallow pot used in cooking.—*v.* to wash gold-bearing soil with water: to turn out (well, badly, etc.).—*n.* **pan´cake**, a thin cake of eggs, flour, sugar, and milk, fried in a pan.

panacea, pan-a-sē´a, *n.* a cure for all things.

pandemō´nium, *n.* a noisy meeting: a meeting of evil spirits.

pan´der, *v.* to be anxious to give way to other people or their wishes.

pane, *n.* a sheet of glass.

panegyric, pan-e-jir´ik, *n.* a speech praising highly some person or event.

pan´el, *n.* a flat piece of wood such as that let into a door or wall: a jury: a list of insured persons under a doctor.

pang, *n.* a sudden, sharp pain.

pan´ic, *n.* sudden and great fright.

pannier, pan´yer, *n.* a basket, esp. one slung on a horse's back.

pan´oply, *n.* a full suit of armour.

panora´ma, *n.* a wide view: a picture giving views of objects in all directions.

pan´sy, *n.* a flower like the violet but larger.

pantaloon´, *n.* (in pantomimes) a foolish old man whom the clown makes fun of: (*pl.*) a kind of trousers.

pantechnicon, pan-tek´ni-kon, *n.* a place for storing furniture: a large van for removing furniture.

pan´theon, *n.* a building with tombs or memorials of many of the famous men of a country.

pan´ther, *n.* a leopard.

pan´tomime, *n.* dumb show: a Christmas play, usually founded on a fairy tale.

pan´try, *n.* a room for storing food.

papacy, pā´pa-si, *n.* the office or power of the Pope.—*adj.* **pā´pal**.

papaw´, *n.* a tree with a yellow eatable fruit; grows in America and elsewhere.

pā´per, *n.* a material (made from rags, grass, wood, etc.) used for writing, wrapping, etc.: a newspaper: an essay on a learned subject.—*v.* to cover with paper. —*ns.* **pa´perback**, a book bound in a paper cover; **paper-chase**, game in which one runner leaves a trail of paper so that others may track him; **paper-hanger**, one who papers walls of rooms; **paper-money**, bank notes.

papier-mâché, pap´yä-mah´shā, *n.* a substance consisting of paper-pulp, shaped (by moulding) into trays, boxes, etc.

pā´pist, *n.* a scornful word for a Roman Catholic.

papoose´, *n.* a Red Indian's baby.

papyrus, pa-pī′rus, *n.* a reed from which the people of olden times made their paper :—*pl.* **papy′rī,** very old writings on papyrus paper.

par, *n.* the state of being equal : normal state of health (e.g. Being below *par*, he caught a chill).

parable, par′a-bl, *n.* a story or fable which teaches a lesson.

parachute, par′a-shoot, *n.* an arrangement shaped like an umbrella, to make possible a safe landing from an aeroplane.—*n.* **par′achutist,** a soldier dropped by parachute from an aeroplane.

parade′, *n.* show, display : an orderly arrangement of troops for inspection or exercise : a seaside roadway.—*v.* to show off : to arrange (troops) in order : to march in a procession.

Par′adise, *n.* Heaven : any place or state of great happiness.

par′adox, *n.* a saying which seems to be nonsense but is really true (e.g. 'The rule of the road is a *paradox* quite : If you keep to the left you're sure to be right ').

par′affin, *n.* a white waxy substance (got from shale) yielding an oil (*paraffin-oil*) which is easily set on fire.

par′agon, *n.* a pattern or model (e.g. This boy is a *paragon* of good manners).

paragraph, par′a-graf, *n.* a division of a piece of writing.

par′allel, *adj.* side by side.—**parallel lines,** lines that remain the same distance apart (e.g. railway lines). —*n.* comparison : (*parallel of latitude*) a line drawn east and west across a map or round a globe at a set distance from the equator to mark latitude. —*n.* **parallel′ogram,** a four-sided figure, the opposite sides of which are parallel and equal lines.

paralyse, par′a-līz, *v.* to make helpless : to strike with paralysis.— *n.* **paral′ysis,** loss of the power to move and feel in any part of the body.—*adj.* **paralyt′ic,** suffering from paralysis.—*n.* a paralysed person.

par′amount, *adj.* above all others.

par′apet, *n.* a wall on a bridge or balcony, to prevent persons from falling over.

paraphernalia, par-a-fer-nāl′i-a, *n. pl.* one's belongings.

paraphrase, par′a-frāz, *v.* to put the thoughts or contents of a piece of writing into other words.— Also *n.*

parasite, par′a-sīt, *n.* an animal, plant, or person which lives on another—the flea, the mistletoe, and a son who lives on the money his father makes, are *parasites*.

par′asol, *n.* a small umbrella used as a sunshade.

par′boil, *v.* to boil slightly.

par′cel, *n.* a small packet or bundle : a quantity.—*v.* to divide into portions.

parch, *v.* to dry up : to scorch.

parch′ment, *n.* the skin of a goat or sheep scraped, dried, and smoothed for writing on : paper something like real parchment.

pard, *n.* a panther.

par′don, *v.* to forgive : to set free from punishment.—*n.* forgiveness.—*adj.* **par′donable,** able to be forgiven.—*n.* **par′doner,** in olden days, one who sold pardons from the Pope.

pare, *v.* to peel off (e.g. the skin of an apple).

pā′rent, *n.* a father or mother.—*n.* **par′entage,** birth (e.g. of noble *parentage*, of noble birth, born of noble parents).—*adj.* **parent′al,** having to do with parents : tender, loving.

parenthesis, pa-ren′the-sis, *n.* a word, phrase, or sentence put in another phrase or sentence, often inside brackets, e.g. His father (*so he said*) was dead.— *adj.* **parenthet′ical.**

pariah, pār′i-a, *n.* (esp. in India) a person of low birth : an outcast : a wandering dog living on rubbish.

par′ish, *n.* a division or district of a county.—*n.* **parish′ioner,** a member of a parish or of a parish church.

par′ity, *n.* the state of being equal.

park, *n.* a grass field : a large enclosed piece of land surrounding a country house or mansion : a piece of ground enclosed for sports : a place (*car park*) where motor-cars, etc. may be left for a time.—*v.* to enclose : to leave in a car park.

par′kin, perkin, *n.* a kind of biscuit made of oatmeal and treacle.

parlance, *n.* a way of speaking.

par′ley, *v.* to hold a conference.— *n.* a meeting between enemies to talk over terms (e.g. of peace).

parliament, par′li-ment, *n.* the chief law-making council of a nation—in Britain, the House of Commons and House of Lords.

par′lour, *n.* a sitting-room in a house.

par′lous, *adj.* perilous : hard to deal with.

parochial, par-ō′ki-al, *adj.* having to do with a parish : not broad-minded, narrow.

par′ody, *n.* an imitation of a poem in which its words and ideas are changed so as to produce a funny effect.—*v.* to make a parody of.

parole, par-ōl′, *n.* word of honour (esp. that given by a prisoner-of-war not to escape) : a password.

paroxysm, par′oks-izm, *n.* a fit of pain, rage, passion, etc.

parquet, par′ket, **parquetry,** par′-ket-ri, *n.* a flooring, made of wooden blocks, arranged in a pattern.

parr, *n.* a young salmon.

parricide, par′ri-sīd, *n.* the murder of one's parent : one who murders his parent.

par′rot, *n.* a bird (found in warm countries) with brilliant feathers and a hooked bill, well-known for its skill in imitating the human voice.

par′ry, *v.* to keep off (e.g. a blow).

parse, *v.* to tell the parts of speech of words in a sentence, and how the words are connected with each other.

par′simony, *n.* great care in spending one's money : meanness.

pars′ley, *n.* a small, bright-green herb, used in cookery.

pars′nip, *n.* a plant, with an eatable yellowish root shaped like a carrot.

par′son, *n.* a clergyman.

part, *n.* a portion or share : char-

acter taken by an actor in a play : (*pl.*) skill : talents.—*v.* to divide : to put or keep apart.—*n.* **part′-pay′ment,** the payment of part of what one owes.

partake, par-tāk′, *v.* to take a part or share in : to eat (e.g. He *partook* of a hearty supper).

partial, par′shal, *adj.* having to do with a part only : showing favour to one side, person, or thing : unfair : fond (of).

participate, par-tis′i-pāt, *v.* to have a share in.—*ns.* **partic′ipant, partic′ipator,** one who takes part in.

par′ticiple, *n.* an adjective formed from a verb.

par′ticle, *n.* a little part : a very small portion : a small word, such as a preposition.

particular, par-tik′ū-lar, *adj.* having to do with a single person or thing : special : very exact : difficult to please.—*n.pl.* the facts or details about anything (e.g. These are the *particulars* of the accident). — *v.* **partic′ularise,** to give details.

part′ing, *adj.* putting apart : going away.—*n.* a point or a line of division : the act or moment of going away.

par′tisan, *n.* a faithful member of a party or side : a weapon like a long spear.

partition, par-tish′un, *n.* a division : a wall between rooms.—*v.* to divide into parts : to divide by making a wall.

part′ner, *n.* one who shares : one working with another in business : one of a pair in games or dancing : a husband or wife.—*v.* to go with somebody as a partner.—*n.* **part′-nership,** two or more people working (or playing) together.

partridge, par′trij, *n.* a moorland bird, which is shot for sport.

par′ty, *n.* a number of persons having the same plans or ideas (e.g. the Labour *Party*): a gathering of guests (e.g. a birthday *party*): a person taking part in an affair (e.g. He was a *party* to the crime). —**party line,** a shared telephone line : policy laid down by the leaders of a political party.

parvenu, par´ve-nū, *n.* a person who has suddenly become well known or wealthy.

pasha, *n.* a title given to Turkish governors, leaders, etc.

pass, *v.* to move from one place to another: to travel: (of time) to go by: to disappear: to die: to put (a law) into force: to be successful (in an examination or inspection): to declare something to be suitable.—*n.* a narrow passage, esp. over or through a range of mountains: a ticket allowing one to go somewhere: success in an examination.—*adj.* **pass´able,** fairly good: (of a river, ford, etc.) able to be crossed.—*ns.* **pass´er-by** (*pl.* **pass´ers-by**), one who happens to walk that way; **pass´port,** written permission to travel abroad; **pass´word,** a secret word, which allows those who know it to pass.—*adv.* **pass´ing,** very.—**a pretty pass,** a fine state of affairs; **to pass muster,** see muster.

pass´age, *n.* a passing: a journey (e.g. in a ship): a long and narrow way (esp. between rooms in a house): a part of what is written in a book.—**bird of passage,** a bird which goes to warm lands for the winter.

passenger, pas´en-jer, *n.* a traveller in a train, aeroplane, etc.

passion, pash´un, *n.* anger: strong feeling: love.—*n.* **Passion,** the sufferings (esp. the death) of Christ.—*adj.* **pass´ionate,** easily moved to anger: full of feeling.—*ns.* **Passion-flower,** a flower which gets its name because it is said to be like Christ's ' crown of thorns '; **Passion-play,** a religious play, showing the sufferings and death of Christ; **Passion-week,** the week before Easter.

pass´ive, *adj.* making no resistance: acted upon, not acting.

Passover, pas´ō-ver, *n.* a solemn feast of the Jews, in remembrance of the *passing* of the destroying angel *over* the doors of the Israelites when he killed the children of the Egyptians (see Exodus xi. xii.).

past, *adj.* having happened or occurred in time gone by (e.g. He thanked me for *past* kindness).—*n.* time gone by.—*prep.* after: farther than: beyond.—*adv.* by (e.g. to march *past*).

paste, *n.* flour and water used as dough for pies, pastry, etc.: a sticky liquid for sticking paper, etc. together: any soft mixture (e.g. *meat-paste*): a fine kind of material used in making imitation pearls.—*n.* **paste´board,** cardboard.

pas´tel, *n.* a coloured crayon.

pas´tern, *n.* the lowest part of a horse's leg, just above the hoof.

pasteurise, pas´ter-īz, *v.* to heat food (esp. milk) in order to kill harmful germs in it.

pastille, pas-tēl´, *n.* a small sweet.

past´ime, *n.* something which serves to pass the time away (e.g. a game, a hobby).

pas´tor, *n.* a clergyman of a church.—*adj.* **pas´toral,** having to do with shepherds and their life, or with country life in general.—*n.* a poem describing the scenery and life of the country.

pās´try, *n.* crust of pies, tarts, etc.

past´ūre, *n.* ground covered with grass for cattle to graze on.—*v.* to put cattle to pasture.—*n.* **past´-ūrage,** grazing land.

pās´ty, *adj.* like paste: pale.—*n.* a meat-pie.

pat, *n.* a light, quick blow, as with the hand: a tap: a small lump (e.g. of butter).—*v.* to strike gently: to tap.

pat, *adv.* at the right time or place: off by heart.

patch, *v.* to mend by putting in a new piece.—*n.* a piece sewed or put on: a small piece of ground.—*adj.* **pat´chy,** uneven: mixed in quality.—*n.* **patch´work,** work formed of patches or pieces sewed together: work clumsily done.

pate, *n.* the top of the head.

pā´tent, *adj.* open: easily seen: protected by a patent—i.e. a written statement which gives to one person or business firm the right to make or sell something (esp. a new invention).—*v.* to obtain a patent for.—*n.* **patentee´,** one who holds a patent.—*adv.* **pa´-** *tently,* openly, clearly.

pater'nal, *adj.* fatherly: on one's father's side of the family (e.g. *a paternal grandfather*, one's father's father).—*n.* pater'nity, state of being a father.

pāt'ernoster, *n.* the Lord's Prayer.

path, path'way, *ns.* a way trodden out by the feet: a track.—*adj.* **path'less**, having no path: little known.

pā'thos, *n.* pity, deep feeling.—*adj.* **pathet'ic**, causing pity.

patient, **pā'shint**, *adj.* suffering delay, pain, discomfort, etc. without complaint or murmuring. —*n.* a sick person.—*n.* **pat'ience**, power to be patient: contentedness in spite of delay, pain, etc.: a card game for one person.

patois, **pat'wa**, *n.* a language as spoken by the common people.

patriarch, **pā'tri-ark**, *n.* the head of a family or tribe: a head of the Greek Church.—*adj.* **patriarch'al**.

patrician, **pa-trish'an**, *n.* a Roman nobleman in olden times.—*adj.* of noble birth.

patricide, **pat'ri-sīd**, *n.* the murder of one's own father: one who commits such a murder.

pat'rimony, *n.* property handed down from one's father or from one's ancestors.

patriot, **pā'tri-ot**, *n.* one who loves his country.—*n.* **pā'triotism**, love of one's country.—*adj.* **patriot'ic**.

patrōl', *v.* to keep guard or watch by marching or sailing to and fro.— *n.* the guard thus kept: the men or ships keeping watch.

pā'tron, *n.* one who protects: a customer of a shop: one who has the right to appoint a person to an office, esp. to appoint a clergyman to a church.—*n.* **patronage** (pat'-), the support given by a patron: the right of appointing to a church, etc.—*v.* **patronise** (pat'-), to act as a patron toward: to encourage, support, or protect: to treat a person as if one is above him.

patronymic, **pat-rō-nim'ik**, *n.* a name taken from one's father or ancestor: a surname.

pat'ten, *n.* a clog.

pat'ter, *v.* (of falling rain or hail) to make a sharp tapping sound: to make the sound of short, quick steps.—*n.* the sound of falling rain, footsteps, etc.: chatter: a great many words sung or spoken very rapidly.

patt'ern, *n.* a model: an example to be copied: a design.—*v.* to shape something according to a model.

pat'ty, *n.* a little pie.

paucity, **paw'sit-i**, *n.* fewness: scarcity.

paunch, *n.* the belly.

pau'per, *n.* a very poor person: one who lives on money supplied by taxes.

pause, *n.* a short stop: an interval: a break in speaking or writing.— *v.* to stop: to wait.

pave, *v.* to lay a street or pathway with stone, concrete, etc., to form a level surface for walking on.— *n.* **pave'ment**, a paved road.—to **pave the way for**, to prepare the way for.

pavilion, **pa-vil'yun**, *n.* a large tent: a building in which players of outdoor games change their clothes: a large building.

paw, *n.* the foot of an animal having claws.—*v.* to scrape with the forefoot: to handle roughly.

paw'ky, *adj.* quiet and clever: sly, cunning.

pawl, *n.* a short bar lying against a toothed wheel to prevent it from running back.

pawn, *v.* to hand an article of value to a money-lender and receive a loan of money for it—when the money is repaid the article is given back. — *n.* something pawned, a pledge.—*n.* **pawn'-broker**, one who lends money for pawned articles.

pawn, *n.* (in chess) a small piece of the lowest rank: a person of no account used by another for a purpose.

pay, *v.* to give money for something: to reward: to suffer the penalty of: to punish: to give out rope, line, etc.—*n.* money given or received for work, etc., wages: reward.—*adj.* **pay'able**, requiring to be paid.—*ns.* **payee'**, one to whom money is paid; **pay'ment**, act of paying: money paid (or its value in goods, etc.).

pay'nim, *n.* a heathen.

pea, *n.* a climbing plant, bearing round seeds (*peas*) in pods.—*n.* **pease-meal**, meal made by grinding dried peas.

peace, *n.* calm: quietness, rest: freedom from war: a treaty bringing this about.—*adjs.* **peace'-able**, of a quiet nature, fond of peace; **peace'ful**, quiet: calm.—*ns.* **peace'maker**, one who brings about peace between enemies; **peace'-off'ering**, something offered, to bring about peace.

peach, *n.* a juicy, velvet-skinned fruit.

pea'cock, *n.* a large bird, noted for its splendid feathers, esp. in its tail :—*fem.* **pea'hen**.

peak, *n.* the pointed top of a mountain or hill : the highest point: the jutting-out part of the brim of a cap.—*adj.* **peaked**, pointed : having a sickly look (also **peak'y**).

peal, *n.* loud sound (e.g. of laughter): a set of bells tuned to each other. —*v.* to sound loudly.

pear, pār, *n.* a juicy fruit.

pearl, perl, *n.* a gem found in the oyster and several other shellfish: something very precious. — *n.* **pearl-fisher**, a diver who searches for oysters containing pearls.

peasant, pez'ant, *n.* a countryman: one who works and lives on the land.—*n.* **peas'antry**, country-folk.

peat, *n.* a kind of turf, cut out of boggy places, dried, and used as fuel.

peb'ble, *n.* a small, roundish stone. —*adj.* **pebb'ly**, full of pebbles.

peccadil'lo, *n.* a trifling fault.

peck, *v.* to strike with the beak : to pick up with the beak : to nibble at (food).—*n.* a sharp blow with the beak : a measure (2 gallons) for grain, etc. — *adj.* **peck'ish**, somewhat hungry.

peculiar, pē-kūl'yar, *adj.* one's own, belonging to no other : special : strange, odd.—*n.* **peculiar'ity**, that which marks a person off from others : something odd. — *adv.* **pecul'iarly**.

pecuniary, pē-kū'ni-ar-i, *adj.* having to do with money.

pedagogue, ped'a-gog, *n.* a teacher.

ped'al, *n.* a lever worked by the foot,

as in a cycle, piano, etc. : (in an organ) a key worked by the foot.

ped'ant, *n.* one who makes a great show of learning.—*adj.* **pedant'ic**. —*n.* **ped'antry**, a boastful show of learning.

ped'dle, *v.* to travel from door to door selling small objects : to trifle.—*n.* **ped'lar**, one who peddles, a hawker.

ped'estal, *n.* the foot of a pillar, statue, etc.

pedes'trian, *adj.* going on foot : dull. —*n.* one who goes on foot, a walker : one who goes in for walking races.

ped'igree, *n.* a list of the ancestors from whom one has descended : one's descent.—*adj.* **ped'igreed**, of good birth.

ped'lar. See peddle.

pedom'eter, *n.* an instrument for measuring the distance covered by a walker.

peel, *v.* to strip off the skin or bark : to bare: to lose the skin.—*n.* skin : rind : bark.

peel, peel'-tow'er, *ns.* a small, square fortress.

peel'er, *n.* a policeman.

peep, *v.* to look through a narrow opening : to look slyly or carefully : to begin to appear.—*n.* a sly look : the first light (of day) : a narrow view.

peer, *n.* one's equal in rank or merit : a nobleman : a member of the House of Lords.—*n.* **peer'age**, a peer's title : the whole number of the peers.—*adj.* **peer'less**, without an equal, matchless.

peer, *v.* to look closely : to look into darkness.

pee'vish, *adj.* ill-natured, cross, fretful.

pee'wit, *n.* the lapwing.

peg, *n.* a small wooden pin.—*v.* to fasten with a peg : (with *away*) to work very hard.

pelf, *n.* money, riches.

pel'ican, *n.* a large water-bird, with a pouched bill for storing fish.

pelisse, pe-lēs', *n.* a child's coat : a cloak of silk or other cloth, with long sleeves, worn by ladies.

pell, *n.* a skin or hide.

pel'let, *n.* a little ball (e.g. of shot): a small pill.

pell-mell', *adv.* in great confusion.

pellucid, pe-lū'sid, *adj.* perfectly clear.

pelt, *n.* a raw skin or hide.

pelt, *v.* to throw things at: (of rain) to fall heavily.

pem'mican, pem'ican, *n.* dried meat, pressed hard, used as food by explorers.

pen, *n.* an instrument for writing in ink.

pen, *v.* to shut up, to enclose.—*n.* a small enclosure: a fold for animals, sheep, cattle, etc.

pē'nal, *adj.* having to do with punishment.—*v.* pē'nalise, to punish.—*ns.* pen'alty, punishment: fine; pen'ance, punishment which one chooses to suffer to make up for wrong-doing.—**penal servitude**, imprisonment with hard labour as an added punishment.

pence. See penny.

pencil, pen'sil, *n.* an instrument (containing a black substance called graphite) for writing, drawing, etc.: a small paint-brush.

pen'dant, *n.* an ornament hung from a necklace: an ear-ring: a lamp, or lights, hanging from the roof.

pen'ding, *adj.* awaiting a decision.

pen'dūlum, *n.* a swinging weight (e.g. in a clock).

pen'etrate, *v.* to pierce into: to enter.—*adj.* pen'etrating, piercing: sharp.—*n.* penetrā'tion, the act of breaking through or into: cleverness in understanding.

penguin, pen'gwin, *n.* a large sea-bird of Antarctic regions.

penicill'in, *n.* a substance, got from mould, which kills many disease germs (e.g. pneumonia).

penin'sūla, *n.* a piece of land almost surrounded by water.

pen'itent, *n.* one who is sorry for his sins.—Also *adj.*—*n.* penitentiary (pen-i-ten'shi-a-ri), a prison.

penknife, pen'nīf, *n.* a pocket-knife.

pen'nant, *n.* a long flag coming to a point at the end.—Also pen'non.

pen'ny, *n.* a coin worth $\frac{1}{12}$ shilling: (new penny) $\frac{1}{100}$ of £1:—*pl.* pennies, used for the number of coins (e.g. I have ten *pennies*):—pence, the amount of pennies in value (e.g. This ball costs *tenpence*).—**penny-wise but pound-foolish**,

saving small sums but not caring about large amounts.

pension, pen'shun, *n.* a sum of money given weekly, monthly, or yearly to a person, because of past services or old age.—*v.* to give a pension to.—*n.* pen'sioner, one who receives a pension.

pensive, pen'siv, *adj.* thoughtful, sad.

pen'tagon, *n.* a five-sided figure.

pent'house, *n.* a shed, with its roof sloping from the wall of a building.—*n.* pent'roof, a roof with a slope on one side only.

penult'imate, *adj.* last but one.

pen'ūry, *n.* poverty, want.—*adj.* penū'rious, poor: mean: stingy.

peony, pē'o-ni, *n.* a garden plant with large red or white flowers.

people, pē'pl, *n.* the men, women, and children of a country or nation: persons generally.—*v.* to fill with living beings.

pep'per, *n.* a plant whose berries are powdered and used as seasoning (*pepper*).—*v.* to sprinkle with pepper: to hit or pelt as with shot.—*n.* pep'percorn, the berry of the pepper plant.—*adj.* pep'pery, containing much pepper: hot-tempered.—*n.* pep'permint, a sweet with a sharp taste.

peradven'ture, *adv.* by chance.

peram'bulate, *v.* to walk up and down.—*n.* peram'bulator, a baby-carriage (often shortened to pram).

perceive, per-sēv', *v.* to understand: to see.—*adj.* percep'tible, able to be seen or understood.—*n.* percep'tion, power to understand.

percentage, per-sen'tāj, *n.* the rate per hundred (e.g. *five per cent.*, written 5%, five out of every hundred).

perch, *n.* a fresh-water fish.

perch, *n.* a rod on which birds roost: any high seat or position: a measure of length (5½ yards): a measure of area (30¼ sq. yards).—*v.* to place upon: to roost.

perchance', *adv.* by chance: perhaps.

per'colate, *v.* to strain through.

percussion, per-kush'un, *n.* a striking of one body against another: the striking of drums, tambourines, etc.

perdition, per-dish'un, *n.* utter loss or ruin : everlasting punishment.

per'egrinate, *v.* to travel about from place to place.—*n.* **per'egrine,** a falcon used in hawking.

peremp'tory, *adj.* urgent : to be obeyed at once.

perennial, per-en'i-al, *adj.* lasting through the year : (of plants) growing from year to year without replanting or sowing.

per'fect, *adj.* complete : finished : faultless : thoroughly learned or trained.—*v.* (per-fekt') to make perfect : to finish.—*n.* **perfec'tion,** the state of being perfect : complete freedom from flaws : the highest state or degree.

perfer'vid, *adj.* very eager.

perfid'ious, *adj.* treacherous. — *ns.* **perfid'iousness,** per'fidy.

perforate, *v.* to make a hole or holes through.—*adj.* **per'forated,** pierced with holes.

perform', *v.* to do or act : to act a part, as on the stage : to play upon (a musical instrument).—*ns.* **perfor'mance,** an entertainment (in a theatre, etc.) ; **perfor'mer,** one who acts or performs.

per'fume, *n.* sweet scent : fragrance.—*v.* (per-fūm') to put scent on or in : to give fragrance to.—*ns.* **perfu'mer,** a maker of perfume ; **perfu'mery,** the shop or factory of a perfumer.

perfunc'tory, *adj.* done carelessly or half-heartedly.

perhaps', *adv.* it may be.

per'il, *n.* great danger.—*adj.* **per'ilous,** very dangerous.—**at one's peril,** at one's own risk.

perim'eter, *n.* the outside line enclosing a figure : fortified line built round a town for its defence.

period, pē'ri-ud, *n.* an age : a stretch of time : the time during which something (e.g. a revolution of the earth round the sun) takes place : a complete sentence : a full stop (.).—*adjs.* **period'ic,** **period'ical,** happening again and again at regular intervals (e.g. every month, year).—*n.* **period'ical,** a magazine which appears at regular intervals (e.g. every month or week).

peripatet'ic, *adj.* walking about.

periphrasis, per-if'ra-zis, *n.* a round-about way of speaking.

per'iscope, *n.* an instrument (a kind of mirror) by which an observer in a trench or submarine is able to see objects on the surface.

per'ish, *v.* to pass away completely : to waste away : to die : to rot.—*adj.* **per'ishable,** liable to go bad quickly.

per'iwig, *n.* a small wig.

periwink'le, *n.* a small shellfish, shaped like a small snail, boiled and eaten as food : a creeping, evergreen plant, with a small blue flower.

perjure, per'joor, *v.* to tell a lie when one has sworn to tell the truth (e.g. He *perjured* himself at the trial).—*ns.* **per'jurer** ; **per'jury.**

perk, per'ky, *adjs.* neat : trim : jaunty.

per'kin. See **parkin.**

per'manent, *adj.* lasting : fixed, not to be moved (e.g. the *permanent way,* the railroad).—*ns.* **per'manence,** **per'manency.**

permeate, per'mē-āt, *v.* to pass through the pores of : to go through and through.—*adj.* **per'meable.**

permit', *v.* to allow : to give leave to.—*n.* (per'mit) a written order, allowing a person to do something (e.g. to fish in private waters).—*n.* **permis'sion,** leave : freedom given to do something.—*adjs.* **permiss'ible,** allowable ; **permiss'ive,** allowing something but not ordering it to be done.

permūtā'tion, *n.* the arrangement of things, numbers, letters, etc. in every possible way.

pernicious, per-nish'us, *adj.* very hurtful : destructive.

perorā'tion, *n.* the closing part of a speech.

perpend', *v.* to consider carefully.

perpendic'ular, *adj.* standing upright : at right angles.—*n.* a line at right angles to another.

per'petrate, *v.* to commit (e.g. a sin, an error).—*ns.* **perpetrā'tion** ; **per'petrātor.**

perpet'ual, *adj.* never ceasing, everlasting, unending.—*adv.* **perpet'ually.**—*v.* **perpet'uate,** to cause to last for ever or for a very long time.—*n.* **perpetu'ity,** endless time or duration.

perplex', v. to puzzle.—n. **per'plex'ity**, a puzzled state of mind: trouble.

perquisite, per'kwiz-it, n. something one is allowed to have over and above one's payment.

per'secute, v. to punish: to ill-treat, esp. on account of religious beliefs.—ns. **persecu'tion**; **per'secutor**.

persevere, per-se-vēr', v. to keep trying to do a thing: to work hard and steadily (e.g. at a design or plan).—n. **persevē'rance**, the habit of trying hard until one is successful.

persist', v. to hold fast to something (e.g. to an idea): to continue to do something in spite of difficulties: to persevere.—adj. **persis'tent**, pushing on, esp. against difficulties: obstinate.—ns. **persis'tence, persis'tency**.

per'son, n. a human being: one's body: a character in a play.—adj. **per'sonable**, good-looking; **per'sonal**, one's own: private: (of remarks) unkind.—ns. **per'sonage**, a well-known person; **per'sonality**, that which makes one person different from another: (pl.) nasty remarks about someone; **per'sonalty**, personal property.—adv. **per'sonally**, as far as I am concerned.—vs. **per'sonate**, to pretend to be someone else; **person'ify**, to talk about qualities, seasons, etc., as if they were living persons (e.g. Truth is a mighty queen. Summer spreads her blooms).—n. **personifica'tion**.

perspective, per-spek'tiv, n. a scene or view: the art of drawing objects as they appear to the eye (e.g. nearer things or parts larger than those farther off).

perspicacious, per-spi-kā'shus, adj. of clear or sharp understanding: quick-sighted.—n. **perspicacity** (per-spik-as'i-ti), keenness of sight or of understanding.

perspicuous, per-spik'ū-us, adj. easily understood: clear.—n. **perspicu'ity**, clearness in expressing one's thoughts.

perspire', v. to sweat.—n. **perspira'tion**, sweat.

persuade, per-swād', v. to bring a person to do or think something, by arguing with him or advising him: to convince.—n. **persua'sion**, act of persuading: a religious belief, or a body of people holding such (e.g. He is of the Wesleyan persuasion).—adj. **persua'sive**, having the power to win over by argument, etc.—n. **persua'siveness**.

pert, adj. saucy: cheeky.

pertain', v. to belong: to have to do with.—adj. **per'tinent**, having a close connection with the subject spoken about: to the point.

pertinacious, per-ti-nā'shus, adj. holding strongly to an idea: obstinate: unyielding.—n. **pertinacity** (per-tin-as'i-ti).

perturb', v. to disturb greatly: to make anxious.—n. **perturba'tion**, great worry of mind.

perūke', n. a wig.

perūse', v. to read with attention: to examine carefully.—n. **perū'sal**, reading.

pervade, v. to go or spread through.

perverse', adj. stubborn: obstinate in holding to the wrong.—ns. **pervers'ity, perverse'ness**, stubbornness: wickedness.

pervert', v. to turn to a wrong use: to lead astray: to turn from what is true.—n. (per'vert) one who gives up his religion for another and is thought by his friends to be doing wrong.—n. **perver'sion**, misuse: a turning from truth.

pervious, per'vi-us, adj. having a way through.

peseta, pe-sā'ta, n. a Spanish coin.

pes'ky, adj. annoying.

pessimism, pes'i-mizm, n. the habit of looking on the dark side of things.—n. **pess'imist**, one who believes that everything is for the worst.—adj. **pessimis'tic**.

pest, n. a troublesome person, animal, or thing: a deadly disease.—adj. **pestif'erous**, spreading disease or infection: foul.—n. **pest'ilence**, plague: deadly and spreading disease.—adjs. **pest'ilent**, very unhealthy: troublesome; **pestilential** (pes-ti-len'shal), causing disease: destructive.

pes′ter, *v.* to worry a person continually : to trouble.

pestle, pes′l, *n.* a chemist's tool for grinding things to powder.

pet, *n.* a tame animal which is fondly looked after : a favourite child : a fit of sulks.—*v.* to fondle : to sulk.—*adj.* **pet′tish**, sulky.

pet′al, *n.* a flower-leaf.

petard′, *n.* a shell filled with gunpowder, for breaking down walls, gates, doors, etc.

petition, pet-ish′un, *n.* a request, esp. one signed by many people and sent to a government asking for something special : a prayer. —*v.* to ask as a favour : to ask humbly.—*n.* **petit′ioner**, one who offers a petition.

pet′rel, *n.* a small, long-winged seabird.

pet′rify, *v.* to turn into stone: to turn stiff with fear.—*n.* **petrifac′tion**.

petro′leum, *n.* a mineral oil, coming from the depths of the earth in various parts of the world.—*n.* **pet′rol**, purified petroleum, used in motor-cars, etc.

pet′ticoat, *n.* an underskirt, worn by women.

pet′tifogger, *n.* a lawyer who takes up only trifling cases : one who uses mean and crooked methods. —*adj.* **pett′ifogging**, trifling.

pet′ty, *adj.* small : trifling.

pet′ulant, *adj.* peevish : fretful.—*n.* **pet′ulance**.

pew, pū, *n.* a seat in a church.

pewter, pū′ter, *n.* a mixture of tin and lead.

phaeton, fā′ton, *n.* an open four-wheeled carriage.

phalanx, fal′angks, *n.* a company of foot-soldiers, drawn up for battle in an oblong-shaped body.

phantasm, fan′tasm, *n.* an image of an object, seen in the fancy : a ghost.—*n.* **phantasmago′ria**, a magic-lantern picture-show : a crowd of shadowy, fanciful figures.

phantasy. See **fantasy.**

phantom, fan′tom, *n.* a ghost.

Pharaoh, fā′ro, *n.* a king of Egypt in olden times.

pharmaceutical, far-ma-kū′ti-kal, *adj.* having to do with the making up and sale of medicines and drugs.—*ns.* **pharmacy** (far′ma-si), the art of preparing medicines : a chemist's shop ; **phar′macist**, a chemist.

pharos, fā′ros, *n.* a lighthouse.

pharynx, far′ingks, *n.* the back part of the throat.

phase, fāz, *n.* appearance (e.g. Full moon is a *phase* of the moon) : period, stage (e.g. The war has entered upon a new *phase*).

pheasant, fez′ant, *n.* a moorland bird, hunted for sport, with brilliant feathers and eatable flesh.

phenomenon, fē-nom′e-non, *n.* anything remarkable or very unusual : something in nature which attracts our wonder (e.g. a rainbow, comet, etc.) :—*pl.* **phenom′ena.**—*adj.* **phenom′enal**, uncommon : striking.

phial, fī′al, *n.* a small glass bottle.

philander, fil-an′der, *v.* to make love.—*n.* **philan′derer**.

philanthropy, fi-lan′thro-pi, *n.* the love of doing good to all men, esp. by giving one's money for good purposes : love of mankind.— *adj.* **phil′anthropic**, doing good to others.—*n.* **philan′thropist**, one who does good to others.

philately, fi-late′e-li, *n.* stamp-collecting.—*n.* **philat′elist**.

philology, fil-ol′o-ji, *n.* the study which deals with the growth and history of languages.—*n.* **philol′ogist**.

philosopher, fi-los′o-fer, *n.* a lover of wisdom : one who keeps his head and acts calmly in difficulties.— *adjs.* **philosoph′ic, -al**, calm : not easily upset or disturbed.—*n.* **philos′ophy**, the study of wisdom : reasoning : calmness of temper.— *v.* **philosophise′**, to think deeply and talk wisely about a matter.

philtre, philter, fil′ter, *n.* a magic drink.

phlegm, flem, *n.* the thick slimy matter brought up from the throat by coughing : coolness of temper.—*adj.* **phlegmatic** (fleg-mat′ik), not easily excited.

phlox, floks, *n.* a well-known garden plant.

phœnix, phenix, fē′niks, *n.* in old-time fables, a bird which was said to burn itself and to rise afresh from its ashes.

phone, short for **telephone.**

phonetic, fō-net′ik, *adj.* having to do with the sound of the voice: spelt according to sound (e.g. *fonetik*).

phonograph, fō′nō-graf, *n.* an old name for a gramophone.

phosphorus, fos′fo-rus, *n.* a yellow-ish substance, like wax, burning easily and giving out light in the dark. — *ns.* **phos′phate,** a chemical used for manuring ground; **phosphores′cence,** faint glow of light in the dark. — *adj.* **phosphores′cent.**

photography, fō-tog′ra-fi, *n.* the art of taking pictures by means of a camera, making use of the action of light on special films or plates. — *n.* **phō′tograph,** a picture so made. — *v.* to take a picture with a camera. — *n.* **phōtog′rapher.**

phrase, frāz, *n.* a small group of words telling a single thought: a short, clever saying. — *v.* to say in words. — *n.* **phraseol′ogy,** manner of putting phrases together.

phrenology, fren′ol-o-ji, *n.* the study of the outside of the skull, believing that a person's cleverness may be judged from the shape of his head. — *n.* **phrenol′ogist.**

phthisis, thī′sis, *n.* consumption.

physic, fiz′ik, *n.* the study of medicine: a medicine. — *n.* **physician** (fi-zish′an), a doctor. — *adj.* **phys′-ical,** having to do with the forces of nature: having to do with the body, not with the mind. — *adv.* **phys′ically.** — *ns.* **physicist** (fiz′i-sist), a student of science; **physics** (fiz′iks), the branch of learning which includes the study of heat, electricity, magnetism, etc.

physiognomy, fiz-i-on′o-mi, *n.* the expression on one's face.

physiography, fiz-i-og′ra-fi, *n.* knowledge of the earth: description of rivers, mountains, etc.

physiology, fiz-i-ol′o-ji, *n.* the study of the way in which living bodies work (e.g. blood circulation, food digestion, breathing of plants). — *n.* **physiol′ogist.**

physique, fiz-ēk′, *n.* the build of one's body: bodily strength.

piano, pi-a′no, **pianoforte,** pi-a-no-for′te, *ns.* a musical instrument played by striking keys. — *ns.* **pianist** (pē′a-nist), one who plays on a piano; **piano′la,** a self-playing piano. — *advs.* **pia′no,** softly; **pianis′simo,** very softly.

piazza, pi-ats′a, *n.* a place or square surrounded by buildings: a walk under a pillared roof.

pibroch, pē′brohh, *n.* a kind of bag-pipe music.

picador′, *n.* a mounted bull-fighter.

piccanin′ny, pickanin′ny, *n.* a negro baby.

pic′colo, *n.* a small, shrill flute.

pick, *v.* to choose : to seek (quarrel): to pull or pluck (flowers, fruit, feathers) : to open a lock (with a tool, not a key) : to steal (e.g. from a pocket). — *n.* choice : the best. — *ns.* **pick′axe,** an axe for breaking up hard soil, etc.; **pick′-pocket,** one who robs people's pockets. — **to pick up,** to lift from the ground: to learn (e.g. language.)

pick′et, *n.* a pointed stake : a small sentry-post or guard : a number of men on strike who prevent others from working. — *v.* to fasten (e.g. a horse) to a stake : to set a guard of soldiers, strikers.

pick′le, *n.* a liquid in which food is preserved : an unpleasant situation : (usually in *pl.*) vegetables preserved in vinegar. — *v.* to preserve with salt, vinegar, etc.

pic′nic, *n.* a pleasure party or outing, in which meals are taken outside. — Also *v.*

pic′ture, *n.* a painting or drawing : a portrait : (*pl.*) a film show. — *v.* to call up an image or likeness in the mind. — *adjs.* **pictō′rial,** having pictures; **picturesque** (pik-tū-resk′), such as would make a good or striking picture. — *n.* **pic′ture-house,** a place where film shows are given.

pidgin (pij′in) **English,** talk used by English people in speaking and dealing with Chinese.

pie, pī, *n.* meat or fruit baked in a covering of paste: a magpie.

piebald, pī′bawld, *adj.* having white and black in patches : spotted.

piece, pēs, *n.* a part of anything : something put together (in writing, music, art, theatre, etc.): a coin : a gun.—*v.* to put together : to patch.—*adv.* **piece′meal,** by pieces, little by little.—*n.* **piece′-work,** work paid for as each piece is done, not by the hour, week, etc.

pied, pīd, *adj.* spotted : of mixed colours.

pier, pēr, *n.* pillar (e.g. supporting an arch): a stone or wooden platform stretching from the shore into the sea : a wharf.

pierce, pērs, *v.* to make a hole through : to enter into.—*adj.* **pierc′ing,** keen : high-sounding.

pierrot, pē′er-ō, *n.* a comic entertainer or minstrel, with white face and white dress.

piety, pī′e-ti, *n.* holiness : love and duty towards one's parents.

pig, *n.* a farm animal, from whose flesh ham and bacon are made : a rough piece of smelted metal (e.g. *pig-iron*): a stone bottle.—*v.* to live in filth or untidiness.—*ns.* **pig′gery, pig′sty,** a place where pigs are kept ; **pig′-skin,** pig's leather : saddle ; **pig′-tail,** tail of hair as worn by Chinese.—*adj.* **pig′-headed,** stubborn.—**pig in a poke** (=bag), something bought without being examined.

pigeon, pij′un, *n.* a well-known bird, the dove.—*adj.* **pig′eon-heart′ed,** timid.—*n.* **pig′eon-hole,** a small division in a case or desk for papers, etc.

pig′ment, *n.* paint : colouring matter.

pigmy. Same as **pygmy.**

pike, *n.* a fresh-water fish : a weapon, like a spear, with a long shaft and a sharp head.

pil′chard, *n.* a small sea-fish, often called *sardine.*

pile, *n.* a heap : a large building.—*v.* to heap up.

pile, *n.* a pillar : a large stake driven into the earth as a foundation for a building, bridge, etc.

pile, *n.* the nap or woolly surface of cloth.

pil′fer, *v.* to steal small things.

pil′grim, *n.* a traveller to a holy place.—*n.* **pil′grimage,** a journey to a holy place.

pill, *n.* a little ball containing medicine.

pil′lage, *n.* plunder, spoil, esp. that taken in war.—*v.* to take by force and robbery, to plunder.

pil′lar, *n.* a standing support for roofs, arches, etc.: anything that supports.

pillion, pil′yun, *n.* a cushion on which a woman sat when, in days gone by, she rode behind a man on horseback : a seat for a passenger on a motor-cycle.

pil′lory, *n.* in days of old, a wooden frame (with holes for the head and hands) for the punishment of wrong-doers.—*v.* to mock.

pillow, pil′ō, *n.* a cushion for the head.—*v.* to rest on a pillow.

pi′lot, *n.* one who steers a ship in or out of a harbour : the person flying an aeroplane : a trusted guide.—*v.* to steer, to guide.

pim′pernel, *n.* a plant, of the primrose family, with small pink or scarlet flowers.

pim′ple, *n.* a small pointed swelling on the skin.

pin, *n.* a short piece of thin wire, pointed at one end and rounded at the other, used for fastening : a wooden or metal peg or nail.—*v.* to fasten as with a pin : to seize and hold fast (e.g. the arms).

pin′afore, *n.* a little apron.

pince-nez, pins′-nā, *n.* a pair of eye-glasses with a spring for gripping the nose.

pinch, pinsh, *v.* to grip hard : to nip : to squeeze the flesh so as to give pain : to be sparing.—*n.* a nip : a small amount : need, distress.—*n.* **pin′cers,** a tool with jaws for gripping firmly, esp. for drawing out nails.—**to feel the pinch,** to be in hunger or want.

pinchbeck, pinsh′bek, *n.* a yellow metal (a mixture of copper and zinc).—*adj.* sham : flashy.

pine, *n.* a cone-bearing tree : a pine-apple.—*n.* **pine′-apple,** a fruit (growing in hot countries) shaped like a large pine-cone.

pine, *n.* to waste away (with pain, grief, distress, etc.): to long for.

ping, *n.* the whistling sound of a bullet.—*n.* **ping-pong,** table-tennis.

pinion, pin′yon, *n.* a bird's wing : a small toothed wheel.—*v.* to hold back by binding the arms : to fasten the wings (of a bird).

pink, *n.* a garden flower : a light-red colour : very good state (e.g. the *pink* of health).

pin′nace, *n.* a small vessel with oars and sails : warship's small boat.

pin′nacle, *n.* a turret : a high point like a spire : the highest point.

pint, *n.* the eighth part of a gallon, half a quart.

pioneer, pī-ō-nēr′, *n.* one who goes before to clear the way for others : an explorer.—Also *v.*

pious, pī′us, *adj.* religious : godly : good-living.—*n.* **pī′ety.**

pip, *n.* a seed (of fruit) : a spot (e.g. on dice, cards, an officer's tunic).

pipe, *n.* a musical instrument in which the note is made by blowing : a tube (of earthenware, metal, etc.) which carries water, gas, etc. : a tube with bowl at the end, for tobacco-smoking : a wine measure : bird's note.—*v.* to play upon a pipe : to whistle, to chirp : to utter shrilly.—*ns.* **pipe′clay,** a kind of white clay, used for making clay-pipes, also for whitening steps, etc. ; **pipe′-line,** a long line of pipes such as carry oil from an oil-field.—**pīp′ing hot,** boiling hot.

pipette, pi-pet′, *n.* a small glass tube.

pip′it, *n.* a small bird, like a lark.

pip′pin, *n.* a kind of apple.

piquant, pē′kant, *adj.* sharp : rousing the appetite or interest.

pique, pēk, *n.* spite : a feeling of anger caused by wounded pride.—*v.* to wound the pride of : to offend.

pirate, pī′rat, *n.* a sea-robber, a buccaneer : one who, without permission, prints what another has written.—*n.* **pī′racy,** robbery on the sea.—*adj.* **pirat′ical.**

pirn, *n.* a reel or bobbin.

pirouette, pir-oo-et′, *n.* a rapid whirling on the toes in ballet dancing.—Also *v.*

piscatōr′ial, *adj.* having to do with fishing.

pis′til, *n.* the seed-bearing part of a flower.

pis′tol, *n.* a small gun, held in one hand when firing.

pis′ton, *n.* a plate or plug of metal, fitting the bore of a cylinder, in which it moves up and down.—*n.* **pis′ton-rod,** the rod to which the piston is fitted.

pit, *n.* a hole in the ground : a place from which minerals are dug : the ground-floor of a theatre.—*v.* to lay or store in a pit : to set against each other.—*adj.* **pit′ted,** (of the skin) marked with small holes.

pit′apat, *adj.* fluttering : sounding like falling rain-drops.

pitch, *n.* a thick dark substance obtained by boiling down tar.

pitch, *v.* to fix (e.g. a tent) in the ground : to throw : to strike the key-note of a tune : (of a ship) to rise and fall with the waves.—*n.* a throw : the height or depth of a note : (in cricket) ground between wickets.—*n.* **pitch′fork,** a fork for pitching hay : a tuning-fork.—*v.* to throw suddenly into any position.—*n.* **pitch′-pine,** a North American tree from which tar and pitch are made.

pitch′er, *n.* a large jug.

piteous. See **pity.**

pitfall, pit′fawl, *n.* a trap.

pith, *n.* the soft substance in the centre of the stems of plants : marrow : energy, force.—*adj.* **pith′y,** very full of meaning (e.g. a *pithy* saying).

pit′tance, *n.* a very small allowance.

pit′y, *n.* a feeling for the sufferings of others.—*v.* to feel sorry for.—*adjs.* **pit′eous,** **pit′iable,** deserving pity : wretched ; **pit′iful,** sad.

piv′ot, *n.* the pin or centre on which anything turns or depends.—*adj.* **piv′otal,** holding an important position.

pix′y, *n.* a fairy.

plac′ard, *n.* a printed notice placed on a wall (e.g. as an advertisement).

placate′, *v.* to make friendly.

place, *n.* an open space in a town : city, town, village : one's home : rank : passage in a book.—*v.* to put or set : to settle : to remember who a person is.

placid, plas´id, *adj.* calm: not easily disturbed.

plagiarise, plā´ji-ar-īz, *v.* to steal or borrow from the writings or ideas of another.—*ns.* **pla´giarism; pla´giarist.**

plague, plāg, *n.* a deadly, spreading disease: a nuisance.—*v.* to pester or annoy.

plaice, *n.* a broad, flat fish, like the flounder.

plaid, plad or plād, *n.* a large loose shawl, part of the special dress of the Highlanders of Scotland.

plain, *adj.* level: smooth: simple: clear: without ornament.—*n.* a level stretch of land.—*adj.* **plain´-spo´ken**, speaking one's thoughts.

plaint, *n.* a sad song: a cry of distress: a complaint.—*n.* **plaint´iff**, a person who brings another to court to settle a dispute.—*adj.* **plaint´ive**, sad: sorrowful.

plait, *n.* a fold (e.g. of a dress): twined hair.—*v.* to fold: to twine (hair) together.

plan, *n.* a drawing of a building as if seen from above: a map: an arrangement to do something.—*v.* to make a sketch or plan: to arrange to do something.

plane, *n.* a level surface: a joiner's tool for smoothing wood: short for *aeroplane.*—*v.* to smooth.—*adj.* smooth: level.

plane, *n.* a tree with broad leaves.

plan´et, *n.* one of the heavenly bodies which move round the sun.—*adj.* **plan´etary.**

plank, *n.* a long flat piece of timber.

plant, *n.* anything growing from the ground, having stem, root, and leaves: machinery used in a factory.—*v.* to put into the ground for growth: to set down firmly: to settle (e.g. colonists in a new country).—*ns.* **planta´tion**, a wood: a colony: an estate for growing cotton, sugar, rubber, tobacco, etc.; **plant´er**, the owner of a plantation.

plan´tain, *n.* a small plant, with broad leaves and seed-bearing spikes: a kind of banana: the plane-tree.

plaque, plak, *n.* a decorated metal tablet (e.g. on a wall).

plash, *n.* a puddle: a sudden downpour.—*v.* to splash.

plas´ter, *n.* a mixture of lime, water, and sand for covering walls: a sticky substance used for dressing wounds.—**plaster of Paris**, a quick-hardening plaster (first found near Paris).

plas´tic, *adj.* easily moulded or shaped.—*n.* a chemical substance which is moulded when soft and sets hard (e.g. Bakelite).

plate, *n.* a flat piece of metal, china, glass, etc.: a shallow dish for holding food: gold and silver articles: a sheet of metal (copper, lead, etc.) used in printing: a fine book-illustration.—*v.* to cover with a coating of metal (e.g. *nickel-plated*).—*ns.* **plā´ting**, a thin covering of metal; **plate-glass**, a fine kind of glass, in thick sheets, used for shop-windows, mirrors, etc.; **plate´-layer**, a workman who lays the rails of a railway.

plateau, pla-tō´, *n.* a broad level stretch of high land.

plat´form, *n.* a raised level surface, such as that for passengers at a railway station: a part of a floor raised above the rest to form a standing-place for speakers, workmen, etc.

plat´inum, *n.* a heavy and very valuable steel-grey metal.

plat´itude, *n.* an empty remark made as if it were important.

platoon´, *n.* (in the army) a body of soldiers, the quarter of an infantry company.

plat´ter, *n.* a large flat plate or dish.

plaud´it, *n.* applause—used often in *pl.* **plaud´its.**

plausible, plawz´i-bl, *adj.* seeming to be worthy of praise: seeming to be true.—*n.* **plausibil´ity.**

play, *v.* to take part in a game, or in gambling, or in a theatre play: to trifle: to carry out a trick: to perform upon a musical instrument: to direct upon (e.g. The firemen *played* their hoses on the burning building): (of a fountain) to splash up.—*n.* an amusement: any exercise for amusement: gambling: a story for acting: (in machinery) freedom to move (e.g. This wheel has too much *play*).—*ns.* **play′er**, an actor: a sportsman: a musician; **play′-fellow**, **play′mate**, a friend with whom one plays; **play′thing**, a toy; **play′wright**, a writer of plays.—*adj.* **play′ful**, fond of playing.—**to play the game**, to act fairly and honestly.

plea, *n.* an excuse: a prisoner's answer in a law-court: urgent request.—*v.* **plead**, to state one's case, esp. in a law-court: to beg earnestly: to offer as an excuse. —**to plead guilty**, or **not guilty**, (in a law-court) to admit, or deny, one's guilt.

please, *v.* to give joy or delight to: to be willing.—*adj.* **pleasant** (plez′ant), giving joy or delight. —*ns.* **pleas′antness**; **pleas′antry**, good-humoured joking; **pleasure** (plezh′oor), joy or delight: what one wishes to be done (e.g. I shall do your *pleasure*).

plebeian, plē-bē′an, *adj.* having to do with the common people (who in old-time Rome were called the *plebs*).—*n.* a person of low birth.— *n.* **plebiscite** (pleb′i-sīt), a system of deciding a matter by asking everybody to give his vote, for or against.

pledge, *n.* something given or put down to make sure a person will do a thing: a solemn promise: a drinking toast.—*v.* to give as security, to pawn: to promise solemnly to do something (e.g. He *pledged* himself to carry out the plan): to drink to the health of.

plē′nary, *adj.* full: complete.

plenipotentiary, plen-i-po-ten′shi-a-ri, *n.* an ambassador with full powers.—Also *adj.*

plen′ish, *v.* to furnish.

plen′ty, *n.* a full supply: abundance (of food, money, etc.).—*adjs.* **plen′teous**, **plen′tiful**, not scarce: abundant.

pleth′ora, *n.* the state of having too much of anything.

pleurisy, ploo′ri-si, *n.* inflammation of part of the lung.

pli′able, **pli′ant**, *adjs.* easily bent or folded: easily persuaded.

pli′ers, *n.pl.* small pincers.

plight, plīt, *v.* to promise solemnly.

plight, plīt, *n.* condition: state (e.g. The marooned sailors were in a sad *plight*).

Plim′soll mark. See **load-line**.

plimsolls, *n.pl.* light rubber-soled shoes with canvas uppers.

plinth, *n.* the square slab at the foot of a column.

plod, *v.* to travel slowly and steadily: to work on steadily.— *n.* **plod′der**, a dull, slow, but hard-working person.

plot, *n.* a small piece of ground.

plot, *n.* a plan, esp. for doing evil: the story of a play, novel, etc.— *v.* to plan (esp. mischief): to work out secret plans: to mark out on paper.—*n.* **plot′ter**.

plough, plow, *n.* a farmer's tool for turning up the soil.—*v.* to turn up the ground in furrows.—*n.* **plough′share**, the blade of the plough.—**The Plough**, a group of seven stars—*The Great Bear*.

plover, pluv′er, *n.* the lapwing.

pluck, *v.* to strip off (e.g. the feathers of a bird): to snatch.

pluck, *n.* the heart, liver, and lungs.

pluck, *n.* courage, bravery.—*adj.* **pluck′y**, brave.

plug, *n.* a block or peg used to stop a hole: a stopper.—*v.* to stop with a plug.

plum, *n.* a well-known stone-fruit.

plumage, ploom′āj, *n.* the feathers of a bird.

plumb, plum, *n.* a lead weight hung on a string (**plumb-line**), used to test if a wall has been built straight up.—*adj.* standing straight up.—*v.* to test the depth (of the sea, etc.).

plumber, plum′er, *n.* a workman who fits and mends pipes, taps, etc. in a house: a worker in lead.—*n.* **plumb′ing**, the plumber's trade.

plume, ploom, *n.* a feather, esp. one worn as an ornament: a crest.—*v.* to adorn with feathers: to boast (e.g. He *plumed* himself on his success).

plum′met, *n.* a weight of lead hung on a line, for taking depths at sea.

plump, *adj.* fat: in good condition. —*v.* to grow fat: to swell.

plump, *adv.* falling straight downward.—*adj.* direct, straightforward.—*n.* a heavy shower of rain.—*v.* (in an election) to give all one's votes for one person: to fall or sink suddenly.

plun'der, *v.* to steal by force.—*n.* that which is seized by force.

plunge, plunj, *v.* to dive: to throw suddenly into water or other liquid: to rush into danger.—*n.* an act of plunging: dive.

plural, ploo'ral, *adj.* more than one.—*n.* (in *grammar*) the form which shows more than one (e.g. 'Mice' is the *plural* of 'mouse').

plus, *adj.* more: to be added.—*n.* the sign (+) denoting that numbers are to be added.— **plus-fours,** baggy golfing-trousers.

plush, *n.* a cloth of cotton or silk, with a soft velvety top.

plutocrat, ploo'to-krat, *n.* a wealthy person: one who throws his money about.—*adj.* **plutocrat'ic.**

ply, *v.* to work at steadily: to make regular journeys (e.g. The ship *plies* between London and Glasgow).

ply'wood, *n.* a board made up of thin sheets of wood glued together.

pneumatic, nū-mat'ik, *adj.* filled with air: moved by air.

pneumonia, nū-mō'ni-a, *n.* a disease of the lungs.

poach, *v.* to cook eggs, without the shell, in boiling water.

poach, *v.* to trespass and steal game (hares, deer, salmon, etc.).—*n.* **poach'er,** one who steals game.

pock, *n.* a small blister.

pock'et, *n.* a small bag (e.g. in a garment, suit, billiard-table).—*v.* to put in the pocket: to steal.—*n.* **pock'et-book,** a book for holding papers or money carried in the pocket.

pod, *n.* the long seed-case of pea, bean, etc.

podgy, poj'i, *adj.* short and fat.

poem, pō'em, *n.* a piece of writing set out in striking language; it is arranged in lines which usually have a regular beat and often have rhyming words at the end. —*ns.* **po'etry, po'esy,** the art of writing poems: poems as a whole; **po'et,** one who writes

poetry:—*fem.* **po'etess.**—*adj.***poet'-ic,** having to do with poetry.

pogrom', *n.* cruel treatment of people because of their beliefs.

poignant, poin'ant, *adj.* sharp: very painful.

point, *n.* a sharp end: a cape: a dot: a stop: a place, spot: exact moment: the chief matter of an argument: a mark (e.g. in a competition): (*pl.*) the joining of railway lines: chief marks of character (e.g. He has many good *points*).—*v.* to sharpen: to aim: to call attention to (e.g. to *point out* a building, a person, a mistake): to fill the joints (of a wall) with cement.—*adjs.***point'ed,** sharp: keen: outspoken (e.g. *pointed* remarks); **point'less,** having no meaning.—*n.* **point'er,** a rod for pointing: a dog trained to look for game.—*adj.* **point-blank,** fired from very close range: direct, straight to the point (e.g. a *point-blank* question).

poise, *v.* to balance: to hang over (in the air).—*n.* state of balance.

poison, *n.* something which, when taken in by a living body (man, animal, plant), kills or harms.—*v.* to give poison to: to kill with poison: to make bitter or bad.—*adj.* **poi'sonous,** harmful because having poison in it: causing evil.

poke, *v.* to thrust at: to grope or feel.—*n.* a thrust: a pocket: a sack.—*n.* **po'ker,** an iron rod for stirring up the fire: a card-game.

polar. See pole.

pōl'der, *n.* (in Holland) land below the level of the sea.

pole, *n.* a long rod or piece of wood: a measure of length and area (same as **perch**).—*v.* to push with a pole.—*n.* **pole'-axe,** a battle-axe having a long handle.

pole, *n.* the point around which anything turns (e.g. the *North Pole, South Pole,* the earth's farthest north and farthest south points, around which it turns. Also the point in the sky around which the stars *seem* to turn—the star near this point is called the *Pole-star* or *North Star*): the sky: (*pl.*) opposite points of a magnet.—*adj.* **po'lar,** having to do with the N. or S. Pole.

pole'cat, n. a large kind of weasel.

police, pō-lēs', n. the body of men and women whose work it is to keep order and see that the laws are obeyed.—v. to keep law and order in (a place).

policy, pol'i-si, n. a course of action: an agreement with an insurance company.

polio (or **poliomyelitis,** pol-i-ō-mī-e-lī'tis), n. a disease also known as infantile paralysis.

pol'ish, v. to make smooth by rubbing.—n. smoothness: anything used to produce a polish: fine manners.

polite', adj. having good manners, courteous.—n. **polite'ness.**

pol'itic, adj. wise: cunning.—adj. **polit'ical,** public: having to do with government.—ns. **pol'itics,** the study of government: **politician** (pol-it-ish'an), one whose business is politics (e.g. a member of Parliament).—**political map,** a map coloured to show the land held by different nations.

pōl'ka, n. a kind of dance.

pōll, n. the head: a counting of voters at an election: the place of an election.—v. to cut or clip off (hair, horns, branches, etc.): to vote.—ns. **poll'ing-booth,** a place where election votes are given; **poll-tax,** a tax on each head, that is, on every person.

pol'lard, n. a tree having the whole top cut off, so that new branches grow from the top of the stem: a hornless animal.

pol'len, n. the fertilising dust of flowers.—v. **pol'linate,** to fertilise with pollen.

pollūte', v. to make dirty.—n. **pollū'tion,** dirt.

pō'lō, n. a game (like hockey), played on horseback.

poltroon', n. an idle, lazy fellow: a coward.

polygamy, pol-ig'a-mi, n. the custom of having more than one wife or one husband at the same time.—n. **polyg'amist.**—adj. **polyg'amous.**

pol'yglot, adj. written in many languages: speaking many languages.

pol'ygon, n. a figure of many angles and sides.

polysyllable, pol'i-sil'a-bl, n. a word of three or more syllables.

polytechnic, pol-i-tek'nik, adj. deal-with many arts or subjects.—n. **polytechnic (institution),** a college in which such subjects as engineering, building, etc. are taught.

polytheism, pol'i-thē-izm, n. a belief in many gods.

pomade', n. an ointment for the hair.

pom'egranate, n. a large fruit with thick skin and many seeds.

pommel, pum'el, n. the knob on a sword-hilt: the high part of a saddle.—v. to beat soundly.

pomp, n. great show: splendour.—adj. **pomp'ous,** grand: boastful.

pon'cho, n. a South American cloak (blanket with hole for the head).

pond, n. a pool of standing water.

pon'der, v. to think over.—adj. **pon'derous,** weighty: clumsy: sounding very important.

poniard, pon'yard, n. a small dagger.

pon'tiff, n. a bishop: the Pope.—adj. **pontif'ical,** belonging to a pontiff: pompously forcing one's opinion on others.—n. a service-book of a pontiff or bishop: (pl.) robes of office.

pontoon', n. a flat kind of boat used in forming a **pontoon'-bridge** (that is, a platform or roadway across a river supported upon a number of pontoons).

pō'ny, n. a small horse.

poo'dle, n. a kind of dog, with curly hair (often fancifully clipped).

pool, n. a small stretch of water: a deep part of a stream of water: a collection of wheat, milk, etc. in one place in order to give greater profit in selling: the money played for in a game.—v. to put together one's money, wheat, milk, etc. in a pool.

poop, n. the back part (or stern) of a ship.

poor, adj. having little or no money or goods: weak: not good: trifling.—adj. **poor'ly,** in weak health.

pop, v. to make a sharp, quick sound: to move quickly and unexpectedly.—n. a sharp, quick, banging sound.—adv. suddenly: with a sharp sound.

Pope, *n.* the bishop of Rome, head of the Roman Catholic Church.

pop'injay, *n.* a parrot: a target, like a parrot: a dandy or fop.

pop'lin, *n.* a kind of cloth, made of silk and worsted.

pop'py, *n.* a plant with large showy flowers. (From one kind of poppy opium is got.)

pop'ulace, *n.* the common people.

pop'ular, *adj.* pleasing to most people: widely or commonly used or liked: common.—*v.* **pop'ularise,** to make popular: to spread among the people.—*n.* **popular'ity,** favour with everybody (e.g. This soap enjoys great *popularity*).

population, pop-ū-lā'shun, *n.* the people who live in a place.—*n.* **pop'ulate,** to fill with people.—*adj.* **pop'ulous** full of people.

porcelain, pors'lān, *n.* a fine kind of china.

porch, *n.* a covered-in doorway of a building.

por'cūpine, *n.* one of the largest of gnawing animals, covered with sharp quills.

pore, *n.* a tiny hole (e.g. in the skin).—*adj.* **po'rous,** having pores through which liquid may pass.

pore, *v.* to study closely.

pork, *n.* the flesh of the pig.—*adj.* **pork'y,** fat.

porphyry, por'fir-i, *n.* a kind of marble, speckled white and purple.

porpoise, por'pus, *n.* a sea animal, blunt-nosed, about five feet long.

por'ridge, *n.* meal boiled in water or milk.

porringer, por'in-jer, *n.* a small dish (for holding porridge).

port, *n.* a harbour: a gate or entrance: the left side of a ship as one faces the prow: a small window-like opening in the side of a ship for light or air (usually called **port-hole**): the way one carries one's self, one's manner of walking: a dark-red wine (named from Oporto in Portugal).—*v.* to turn (e.g. the helm of a ship) to the left: to hold a rifle in a slanting direction across the body.—*n.* **por'ter,** a door-

keeper: luggage bearer: **a dark-brown bear.**

port'able, *adj.* able to be lifted and carried (e.g. *portable* wireless set).

por'tal, *n.* gate: arched doorway.

portcul'lis, *n.* a sliding doorway of crossed woodwork or ironwork, which can be let down in a moment to keep out an enemy.

portend', *v.* to foretell the future.—*n.* **por'tent,** that which foretells: an evil sign of the future.—*adj.* **porten'tous,** foretelling ill: wonderful: dreadful.

por'ter. See port.

portfolio, port-fō'li-ō, *n.* a case for carrying papers, drawings, etc.: a collection of such papers.

port-hole. See port.

port'ico, *n.* a porch in front of the entrance to a building: a row of columns in the front of a building: a covered walk.

portion, pōr'shun, *n.* a part, a share: a helping: a wife's fortune: fate.—*v.* to divide into parts: to give as a share.—*adj.* **por'tionless,** having no money or property.

port'ly, *adj.* bulky: stately.

portmanteau, port-man'to, *n.* a large leather trunk.

por'trait, *n.* a drawing, painting, or photograph of a person, esp. of his face: a description.—*v.* **portray',** to paint or draw a person: to describe in words.

pose, *n.* a position: one's manner of behaviour, esp. an unnatural manner.—*v.* to place one's self so as to produce an effect: to pretend to be what one is not (e.g. He *poses* as a great writer): to put forward a problem.—*n.* **pos'er,** one who poses: a difficult question.

position, po-zish'un, *n.* place: situation: job: rank.—*v.* to place.

pos'itive, *adj.* clearly said in words: real: confident: decisive.

posse, pos'i, *n.* a force or body (e.g. of constables).

possess', *v.* to have or hold as one's own: to seize. — *adjs.* **possessed** (poz-est'), in the power of an evil spirit: **possess'ive,** showing possession (e.g. the *possessive* case in grammar).—*ns.* **posses'sion,**

the act of possessing : something owned ; **posses'sor**, the owner.

pos'set, n. hot milk, curdled with wine, ale, or vinegar.

pos'sible, adj. able to happen : able to be done.—n. **possibil'ity**, something that may happen or that may be done.—adv. **poss'ibly**, perhaps.

post, n. a pole (of wood, iron, etc.) fixed in the ground.—v. to fix (e.g. a notice) on a post or board. —n. **post'er**, a large bill or placard.

post, n. place of duty (e.g. The soldier remained at his *post*) : a settlement, camp, or station (e.g. a military *post*, trading *post*) : a job, situation : (before the time of railways) a stage or division of a journey which was covered without changing horses (**post-horses**) : the carrying of letters, parcels, etc. by a branch of the government (**post-office**).—v. to put (a letter, parcel) in the post-office : to set or place in position : to travel with post-horses : to travel quickly : to supply with news.—ns. **post'age**, money paid for the carrying of a letter ; **post'-chaise** (-shāz), a travelling carriage ; **post'man, post'woman**, one who delivers letters ; **post'mark**, the mark put on a letter at a post-office ; **post'-master**, master of a post-office.— adv. **post-haste**, at top speed.

post-, after (e.g. *post-war*).

poste'rior, adj. situated behind.

poster'ity, n. our descendants (our children, their children, and so on) : people of the future.

post'ern, n. a back-door or gate.

posthumous, post'ū-mus, adj. (a child) born after the father's death : (a book) printed after the author's death.

postilion, postillion, pōs-til'yun, n. one who guides the horses of a carriage, and rides one of them.

post-mort'em, n. an examination of a dead body (to find out the cause of death).

postpone', v. to put off to a future time : to delay.—n. **postpone'-ment**.

post'script, n. a part added at the end of a letter, after the sender's name.

pos'tulate, v. to lay down as correct : to take for granted without proof.—n. anything taken for granted without proof.

pos'ture, n. manner of standing, appearance : feeling.

pō'sy, n. a bunch of flowers : a motto on a ring.

pot, n. a jar of baked clay, metal, or glass.—v. to put (e.g. flowers) into pots : to preserve.

pō'table, adj. fit for drinking.

pot'ash, n. a substance first obtained from the ashes of plants.

pōtā'tion, n. drinking : a drink.

pōtā'to, n. a plant whose tubers (*potatoes*) are used as food.

pō'tent, adj. strong : able to do much.—n. **po'tency**, power.—adj. **pōten'tial**, possible.—ns. **potential'ity** ; **po'tentate**, a prince : one who possesses power.

poth'er, n. bustle, stir.—Also v.

pō'tion, n. a dose (esp. of medicine) : a drink.

pot-pourri, pō-poo'ri, n. a mixed dish : a mixed perfume : anything greatly mixed.

potsherd. See pottery.

pottage, pot'aj, n. a thick soup : porridge.

pot'tery, n. cups, dishes, vases, etc. of baked clay : a place where such things are made.—ns. **pot'ter**, one who makes such things ; **pot'sherd**, a piece of a broken flower-pot.

pouch, n. a pocket or bag.

poultice, pōl'tis, n. a dressing (of meal, bran, etc. and hot water) put on the body to lessen pain. —v. to put a poultice on.

poultry, pōl'tri, n. fowls.—n. **poul'terer**, one who buys and sells fowls.

pounce, v. to fall upon and seize with the claws : to swoop down upon suddenly.—n. the claw of a bird.

pound, n. 16 ounces : formerly, 20 shillings : now 100 new pence.

pound, v. to shut up or confine (e.g. strayed animals).—n. a pen in which animals are confined.

pound, v. to beat into very small pieces or powder : to beat : to walk with heavy steps.

pour, pōr, v. to flow or make to flow in a stream.

pout, v. to push out the lips crossly.

pov´erty, n. the state of being poor: want.

pow´der, n. fine dust: gunpowder. —v. to sprinkle with dust: to grind down to powder.—adjs. **pow´dered,** in the form of a fine dust: **pow´dery,** covered with powder: like powder.

pow´er, n. strength: force: ability to do things: a strong nation: rule: force used for driving machines (e.g. electric power, steam power, etc.).—adjs. **pow´erful; pow´erless.** —ns. **pow´er-house, -station,** a building where electricity is made.

pow-wow, n. a talk with Red Indians: a friendly talk.

practice, prak´tis, n. habit: the act of doing: exercise by which one prepares for a race, match, etc.: a doctor's or lawyer's business.— adjs. **prac´ticable,** able to be used or done; **prac´tical,** able to be carried out: learned by practice (e.g. He has a practical knowledge of carpentry).—v. **practise** (prak´tis), to do exercises (e.g. piano): to perform: to follow one's profession.—n. **practitioner** (prak-tish´un-er), one engaged in a profession—usually a doctor or lawyer.

prairie, prā´ri, n. a stretch of level land, without trees and covered with grass.

praise, v. to speak highly of a person or thing: to give glory (e.g. by singing hymns of praise). —n. an expression of honour, glory: hymn-singing.—adj. **praise´-worthy,** deserving to be spoken highly of.

pram. See **perambulator.**

prance, v. to strut or jump about in a showy or warlike manner.

prank, v. to dress one's self up showily.—n. a trick played for mischief.

prate, v. to talk foolishly.

prat´tle, v. to talk much without much sense: to talk childishly. —Also n.

prawn, n. a shellfish like the shrimp.

pray, v. to ask earnestly: to beg: to offer up a prayer.—n. **pray´er,** an earnest request for something:

that part of worship in which we ask for forgiveness, blessing, mercy, and give thanks for goodness, etc.

pre-, before (e.g. pre-war).

preach, v. to give a sermon: to keep saying (e.g. that something should be done).—n. **preach´er.**

preamble, prē-am´bl, n. something said by way of introduction (esp. in an Act of Parliament).

prearrange, prē-ar-rānj´, v. to arrange beforehand.

preb´end, n. the share of the income of a cathedral paid to a clergyman who takes part in its services.—n. **preb´endary,** a clergyman who receives a prebend, a canon.

precarious, prē-kā´ri-us, adj. uncertain: risky.

precaution, prē-kaw´shun, n. care taken beforehand (e.g. to avoid a mishap, a disease, etc.).—adj. **precau´tionary.**

precede, prē-sēd´, v. to go before in time, rank, or importance.— adj. **prece´ding,** coming before: previous.—ns. **precedence** (prē´-sed-ens), the act of going before in time: higher rank: a place of honour; **precedent** (pres´ed-ent), a past action which may serve as an example or rule in the future.

precentor, prē-sen´tor, n. the leader of the singing in a church.

precept, prē´sept, n. a rule to guide one's action: a commandment. —n. **precep´tor,** a teacher.

precinct, prē´singkt, n. the ground around a cathedral: (pl.) grounds of a house or building.

precious, presh´us, adj. of great price or worth: highly valued.

precipice, pres´i-pis, n. a steep cliff. —adj. **precip´itous,** very steep: hasty.

precipitate, prē-sip´i-tāt, v. to hasten: to throw head-foremost: to bring on too suddenly.—adj. headlong: hasty, rash.—n. that which settles at the bottom of a liquid.—n. **precipitā´tion,** great hurry: rash haste: rainfall.

précis, prā´sē, n. a summary of a piece of writing.

precise, prē-sīs´, adj. definite : exact :

clear in meaning : very particular.
—*n*. precision (prē-sish´un).

preclude, prē-klood´, *v*. to prevent:
to make impossible.

precocious, pre-kō´shus, *adj*. too
wise for one's years : forward.—
n. precocity (pre-kos´it-i).

precur´sor, *n*. a forerunner : a person
or thing which is a sign of something to come (e.g. A wet summer
is the *precursor* of a bad harvest).

pred´atory, *adj*. of plundering habits.

predecessor, prē-dē-ses´or, *n*. a
former holder of an office or
position.

predes´tine, predes´tinate, *vs*. to
decide or fix beforehand.—*n*.
predestina´tion, the belief that
God has decided beforehand all
that is to happen.

predeter´mine, *v*. to settle beforehand.

predic´ament, *n*. an unfortunate or
unpleasant situation.

pred´icate, *v*. to declare.—*n*. (*grammar*) what is said about the subject of a sentence (i.e. what the
subject does).

predict´, *v*. to foretell, prophesy.—
ns. predic´tion ; predic´tor, an
instrument used by anti-aircraft-
gunners to make aim more sure.

predilection, prē-di-lek´shn, *n*. a
preference for something.

predispose´, *v*. to turn a person in
favour of something beforehand :
to make liable to.—*n*. predisposi´-
tion, a leaning towards : liability
to take a disease.

predom´inate, *v*. to be strongest :
to rule over.—*n*. predom´inance,
greater power or influence.—
adj. predom´inant, ruling : most
noticeable.

pre-em´inent, *adj*. standing above
all others.—*n*. pre-em´inence.

preen, *v*. to arrange feathers, as
birds do.

pref´ace, *n*. an introduction to a
book.—*v*. to put at the beginning
(e.g. He *prefaced* his speech with
an appeal for silence).

pre´fect, *n*. one set in authority over
others : (in schools) a senior boy
or girl having certain powers.

prefer´, *v*. to choose one thing rather
than another : to like better : to
put forward (a claim or request).

—*adj*. pref´erable, more desirable.
—*ns*. pref´erence, the choice of one
thing before another ; prefer´-
ment, promotion.—*adj*. preferen´-
tial, giving or receiving preference.

pre´fix, *n*. a letter, syllable, or word
put at the beginning of a word
to affect its meaning. (The *pre-*
of this word is a *prefix* meaning
'before.' See p. 375.)

preg´nant, *adj*. fruitful: full of
meaning.

prehensile, prē-hen´sil, *adj*. suitable
for seizing or holding.

prehistor´ic, *adj*. belonging to a very
early age, before history was
written down.

prejudge, prē-juj´, *v*. to judge or
decide something before hearing
the facts of a case.

prejudice, prej´oo-dis, *n*. an unfair
feeling for or against anything :
an opinion formed without careful thought : harm, injury.—*v*.
to fill with prejudice : to damage the chances of : to injure.
—*adj*. prejudicial (-dish´al), causing prejudice : harmful.

prel´ate, *n*. a bishop or archbishop.
—*n*. prel´acy, the office of a
prelate.

prelim´inary, *adj*. going first : preparing the way.—*n*. a first step :
preface.

prel´ude, *n*. a piece of music played
as an introduction to the main
piece : something that goes before and acts as an introduction.

prem´ature, *adj*. ripe too soon:
coming before the right or
proper time.

premed´itate, *v*. to think out beforehand.—*n*. premedita´tion.

premier, prem´ē-er, *adj*. first : leading, foremost. — *n*. a prime-
minister.

prem´ises, *n.pl*. a building, along
with its outer buildings, yard, etc.

pre´mium, *n*. a reward : payment
on an insurance policy : the
money paid by an apprentice to
learn a trade or profession.

preoccupy, prē-ok´ū-pī, *v*. to take
up a person's attention : to
occupy beforehand.—*adj*. prē-
oc´cupied, lost in thought.—*n*.
preoccupa´tion, something which
takes up one's time and attention.

prepare', *v.* to get ready : to fit out. —*n.* **prepara'tion**, the act of getting or making ready : something made ready (e.g. a medicine, face-cream).—*adj.* **prepar'atory**, made ready for some purpose: acting as an introduction or first step (e.g. a *preparatory* school).

prepay', *v.* to pay before or in advance.—*n.* **prepay'ment**.

prepon'derate, *v.* to be greater in weight, power, or number.—*n.* **prepon'derance**, greater weight, power, or number.

preposition, prep-ō-zish'un, *n.* (in *grammar*) a word such as *of*, *to*, *in*.

prepossess', *v.* to fill the mind beforehand with some opinion : to bias. —*adj.* **prepossess'ing**, pleasant. —*n.* **prepossess'ion**, an opinion formed beforehand.

prepos'terous, *adj.* very foolish : absurd.

prerequisite, prē-rek'wi-zit, *n.* something necessary before a thing can be done.

prerog'ative, *n.* a privilege or right enjoyed by a person because of his rank or position.

presage, prē-sāj', *v.* to foretell : to warn.

Presbytēr'ian, *adj.* (a church) having business and other affairs managed by presbyteries, i.e. groups of ministers and elders.

prescience, prē'shi-ens, *n.* knowledge of something beforehand.

prescribe', *v.* to lay down as a rule : to order (usually in writing) the taking of a medicine.—*n.* **prescrip'tion**, an order by a doctor for the preparing of a medicine.— *adj.* **prescrip'tive**, holding good by reason of custom or long-continued habit.

pres'ence, *n.* the state of being present (opposite of absence): one's personal appearance.—*adj.* **pres'ent**, being here : ready at hand : belonging to the time in which we are.—*n.* the time in which we live.—**presence of mind**, the power to think calmly and act wisely in a difficulty.

prēsent', *v.* to hand over a gift : to offer : to set forth : to point or aim (e.g. a rifle) : to introduce a person.—*ns.* **pres'ent**, a gift ;

presenta'tion, act of handing over a present : the present itself : the setting forth of a statement.— *adj.* **present'able**, fit to be seen or presented.—*adv.* **pres'ently**, after a little, by-and-by.

prēsen'timent, *n.* a feeling that something unpleasant is about to happen, a foreboding.

prēserve', *v.* to keep safe from harm or injury : to defend : to treat food in such a way that it will not go bad.—*n.* private ground : a place where game (deer, grouse, etc.), animals, birds, etc. are protected : (*pl.*) jam.— *ns.* **preserva'tion**, the act of preserving or keeping safe ; **preser'vative**, something which prevents food from going bad.

prēside', *v.* to be chairman at a meeting.—*ns.* **pres'ident**, a chairman at a meeting : the leading member of a club, institution, etc. : the head of a republic ; **pres'idency**, the office or rank of a president.

press, *v.* to push on : to squeeze out : to urge : to smooth out (e.g. clothes).—*n.* a crowd : a printing-machine : a cupboard.—*adj.* **pressing**, requiring action at once. —*n.* **pressure** (presh'ur), force : strong persuasion : difficulties : the reading of a barometer.

press'gang, *n.* a body of men once employed to carry off men by force into the army or navy.

prestige, pres'tēzh, *n.* good name, reputation.

prēsume', *v.* to take for granted : to take upon one's self : to act without right.—*n.* **presumption** (pre-zum'shun), something supposed : strong likelihood.—*adj.* **prēsump'tuous**, bold, forward: taking much for granted.

pretend', *v.* to make believe : to offer as true something that is not so : to lay claim to. —*ns.* **pretence'**, false show : a false claim ; **preten'sion**, the act of pretending : something pretended : a claim (whether true or not) ; **preten'der**, one who lays claim to something (e.g. to the title of king).—*adj.* **preten'tious**, making great claims : claiming more than is right.

pre´text, *n.* an excuse.

pretty, prit´i, *adj.* pleasing to the eye: neat.—*adv.* quite, fairly (e.g. *pretty* good).—*n.* prett´iness.

prevail´, *v.* to get the better of: to be victorious: to persuade (e.g. He *prevailed* upon me to stay): to be in general use.—*n.* prev´alent, common: wide-spread.—*n.* prev´alence.

prevar´icate, *v.* to avoid telling the truth by saying first one thing then another.—*ns.* prevarica´tion; prevar´icator.

prevent´, *v.* to hinder: to stop.—*ns.* preven´tion; preven´tive, something which keeps disease away.

previous, prē´vi-us, *adj.* going before in time: former.

prey, prā, *n.* booty: plunder: animals killed by others for food.—*v.* to seize and eat (e.g. The hawk *preys* upon smaller birds).—beast (bird) of prey, an animal (or bird) which lives on other beasts (or birds) which it kills.

price, *n.* money for which a thing is bought or sold: reward.—*adj.* price´less, of very great value.

prick, *v.* to pierce slightly: to pain sharply.—*n.* a sharp point: a sting: a thorn.—*n.* prick´le, a sharp point growing on a plant or animal.—*adj.* prick´ly.

pride, *n.* too great an opinion of one's self: a feeling of pleasure: dignity.—*v.* to take pleasure in (e.g. I *pride myself* on my writing).

priest, prēst, *n.* a clergyman.—*n.* priest´hood, the state of being a priest: those who are priests.

prig, *n.* a vain person.—*adj.* prig´gish.

prim, *adj.* exact and correct in manner, dress, talking, etc.

prima-donna, prēma-don´a, *n.* a woman singer of world fame.

pri´mary, *adj.* first: chief.

pri´mate, *n.* an archbishop.—*n.* pri´macy.

prime, *adj.* first in time, rank, or importance (e.g. *Prime Minister*, the head of the government): of highest quality, excellent.—*n.* the time of greatest health and strength (e.g. He was in the *prime* of life).—*v.* to prepare (a gun) for firing: to prepare one's self with full information about something.—*n.* pri´ming, powder in a gun.

primer, prim´er or pri´mer, *n.* a first book: an infant's reading-book.

prime´val, *adj.* having to do with the first age of the world: very old.

primitive, prim´i-tiv, *adj.* very old: clumsy: out-of-date.

prim´rose, *n.* an early pale-yellow spring flower common in woods and hedges.—*adj.* yellow: gay.

prince, *n.* the son of a king: a royal ruler:—*fem.* princess´.—*adjs.* prince´ly, grand: fit for a prince.

principal, prin´si-pal, *adj.* chief, taking the first place.—*n.* the head of a school or college or university: money (put into a bank) on which interest is paid.—*n.* principal´ity, a country under a prince.

principle, prin´si-pl, *n.* rule by which one guides one's actions: a fixed rule or law.

print, *v.* to mark letters on paper with types: to write in big, clear letters: to bring out as a book: to stamp patterns on cloth: to make a finished photograph.—*n.* a mark made by pressure: a copy (of a photograph, etc.): a printed cloth.—*n.* print´er, one who prints books, newspapers, etc.

pri´or, *adj.* earlier: former.—*n.* the head of a pri´ory (=a religious house below an abbey in rank):—*fem.* pri´oress; prior´ity, the right to be first (e.g. The fire-engine must have *priority* in traffic.

prise. See prize.

prism, *n.* a solid body whose two ends are the same shape and size.

pris´on, *n.* a building where law-breakers are locked up, a jail.—*n.* pris´oner, one locked up in jail: a captured enemy soldier.

pris´tine, *adj.* as in days gone by.

privacy, pri´va-si or priv´a-si, *n.* secrecy: undisturbed quietness (e.g. Let us talk in the *privacy* of my house).

pri´vate, *adj.* having to do with a person's own affairs, not public: hidden from view: secret.—*n.* an ordinary soldier of the ranks.

privateer', *n.* an armed private vessel with orders from a government to seize and plunder enemy ships.

priva'tion, *n.* want: poverty: hardship.

priv'et, *n.* a shrub used for hedges.

privilege, priv'i-lej, *n.* a favour or right enjoyed by one person only, or by a few only.—*v.* to grant a right to.

priv'y, *adj.* private: secret: hidden.—**Privy Council**, statesmen who act as the Queen's advisers.

prize, *n.* reward of merit: something won in a competition: a captured vessel.—*adj.* very fine, worthy of a prize.—*v.* to value highly.—*ns.* **prize'-crew**, sailors who take charge of a captured ship: **prize'-fight**, a boxing match.

prize, **prise**, *v.* to force open with a tool or lever.

prob'able, *adj.* likely: that may happen or be true.—*n.* **probabil'ity**, likelihood.—*adv.* **prob'ably**, very likely.

proba'tion, *n.* the testing of a person's conduct, powers, or character: a test or trial.—*n.* **proba'tioner**, one who is on trial (e.g. a person starting out to be a clergyman or nurse).

probe, *n.* a long, thin instrument used by doctors to examine a wound.—*v.* to examine very carefully.

prob'ity, *n.* honesty: goodness of character.

prob'lem, *n.* a question or difficulty to be solved.—*adjs.* **problemat'ic**, **-al**, doubtful: difficult to settle.

proboscis, prō-bos'is, *n.* the nose of an animal or insect: the trunk of an elephant.

proceed, prō-sēd', *v.* to go forward: to go on with, to continue.—*ns.* **proce'dure**, order or method of doing business: conduct; **proceed'ing**, a step: an action: (*pl.*) things done (e.g. at a meeting): a law action; **pro'ceeds**, (*pl.*) the money taken at a sale, concert, etc.

process, prō'ses, *n.* method used in manufacturing goods: course: a gradual going-forward: a law-court case.

procession, prō-sesh'un, *n.* a line of persons or vehicles moving in order, one after the other.—*adj.* **proces'sional**, having to do with a procession.—*n.* a hymn sung during a procession.

proclaim', *v.* to cry aloud: to announce publicly.—*n.* **proclama'tion**, a notice or announcement, such as that of a king or government.

procliv'ity, *n.* a leaning towards something: an inclination.

procrastinate, prō-kras'ti-nāt, *v.* to put off till some other time.—*n.* **procrastina'tion**.

procure', *v.* to obtain: to bring about.—*n.* **proc'urator**, a lawyer.

prod, *v.* to prick: to urge on.

prod'igal, *adj.* spending one's money without care or thought: wasteful.—*n.* **prodigal'ity**.

prodigy, prod'i-ji, *n.* a very clever person: a marvellous thing.—*adj.* **prodigious** (prod-ij'us), very wonderful: huge.

produce', *v.* to bring forth: to yield: to cause.—*ns.* **prod'uce**, yield: crops, farm-products; **prod'uct**, the result of numbers multiplied together: effect: a thing produced: (*pl.*) the goods which a country yields; **produc'tion**, the act of producing: that which is produced.—*adj.* **produc'tive**, fruitful: bringing forth results.

profane', *adj.* not sacred: treating God's name or holy things without respect: wicked.—*n.* **profan'ity**, swearing: want of respect for sacred things.

profess', *v.* to own freely: to declare strongly: to claim skill in.—*adv.* **profess'edly**, according to one's own statement.—*n.* **profess'ion**, an open declaration: an occupation calling for special knowledge (e.g. the work of a doctor, lawyer, etc.).—*adj.* **profess'ional**, having to do with a profession: making money out of games (opposite of *amateur*, who plays only for amusement).—*n.* a paid player of a game.—*n.* **profess'or**, a name for one of the principal teachers in a university.

prof'fer, *v.* to bring forward: to offer.—*n.* an offer.

proficiency, prō-fish'en-si, *n.* skill.—*adj.* **profi'cient,** well-skilled: expert.

prō'file, *n.* an outline: a side-view of a head or portrait.

prof'it, *n.* gain: benefit: the money got by selling an article for a higher price than was paid for it.—*v.* to gain or receive benefit: to bring good.—*adj.* **prof'itable,** yielding gain.—*n.* **profiteer',** one who makes large profits unfairly.

prof'ligate, *adj.* living in an evil way.—*n.* **prof'ligacy.**

prōfound', *adj.* very deep: deeply felt, heartfelt: difficult to understand or solve (e.g. a *profound* problem).—*n.* **profund'ity,** depth.

prōfūse', *adj.* pouring out freely (e.g. He was *profuse* in his thanks): spending too freely.—*n.* **profūs'ion,** great abundance.

progenitor, prō-jen'it-or, *n.* an ancestor.—*n.* **pro'geny,** children.

prognosticate, prog-nos'ti-kāt, *v.* to foretell.—*n.* **prognostica'tion.**

programme, prō'gram, *n.* a list showing what is to take place: a plan.—*v.* to prepare the series of operations to be carried out by a machine.

prōg'ress, *n.* advance, forward movement: increase: improvement.—*v.* **progress',** to go forward: to improve.—*n.* **progres'sion,** onward movement: regular and gradual advance.—*adj.* **progres'sive,** going forward: improving: keen to improve.—*adv.* **progress'ively,** without stopping (e.g. He became *progressively* worse).

prōhib'it, *v.* to forbid.—*n.* **prohibi'tion,** forbidding: the forbidding by law of the making of strong drinks. — *adj.* **prohib'itive,** so high in price as to make buying impossible.

project, proj'ekt, *n.* a plan, scheme.—*v.* **project',** to throw forward: to form a plan: to jut out.—*ns.* **projec'tile,** a body (e.g. a shell) thrown by force through the air; **projec'tion,** something which juts out; **projec'tor,** a lantern for throwing pictures on a screen.

prōletā'riat, *n.* the working people.

prōlif'ic, *adj.* very fruitful.

prō'lix, *adj.* long and wordy: tiresome.—*n.* **prolix'ity.**

prologue, prō-log, *n.* a preface: the introductory lines before a play.

prolong', *v.* to make longer.—*n.* **prolongā'tion,** a lengthening, in time or space.

promenade, prom-e-nad', *n.* a walk for pleasure: the place for this walk.—*v.* to walk for pleasure.

prom'inent, *adj.* standing out and above others: easily seen: famous.—*n.* **prom'inence.**

promiscuous, prō-mis'kū-us, *adj.* mixed: paying no heed to differences between one thing or person and another.—*n.* **promiscū'ity.**

promise, prom'is, *v.* to say that one will do or will not do something: to show signs of (e.g. To-morrow *promises* to be a fine day).—*n.* one's word to do or not to do something: a sign of something to come (e.g. His paper showed great *promise*).—*adjs.* **prom'ising,** showing signs of turning out well.—**promiss'ory note,** a bank-note.

prom'ontory, *n.* a headland or high cape, jutting out into the sea.

prōmote', *v.* to move up to a higher position: to help onwards.—*n.* **promō'tion.**

prompt, promt, *adj.* ready: done at once: quick.—*n.* to move to action: to help a speaker when he has forgotten what to say.—*ns.* **prompt'itūde, prompt'ness.**

prō'mulgate, *v.* to make widely known: to publish.—*n.* **promulgā'tion.**

prone, *adj.* lying face downward: inclined to do something.

prong, *n.* the spike of a fork.—*adj.* **pronged.**

prō'noun, *n.* a word used instead of a noun (e.g. *I, you, who?, this*).

prōnounce', *v.* to utter: to speak: to give judgment.—*adj.* **pronounced',** easily noticed: decided.—*ns.* **pronounce'ment,** a statement (e.g. of a government) of what is going to be done; **pronunciā'tion,** the way a word is said.

proof, *n.* a test or trial, making

something clear beyond doubt : a copy of a printed sheet for correction before printing.

prop, n. a support.—Also v.

prop′agate, v. to spread : to produce plants, seedlings, young of animals, etc.—ns. **propagan′da,** news and opinions given out with the intention of winning people over to one's own side or way of thinking ; **propagan′dist,** one who spreads such news.

propel′, v. to drive forward.—n. **propel′ler,** a set of leaf-shaped blades on a shaft which, by turning, drive ships and aircraft.

propen′sity, n. a leaning towards (good or evil) : inclination.

prop′er, adj. one's own : right : suitable : correct.—adv. **prop′erly,** in the right way : thoroughly.

property, prop′er-ti, n. that which one owns : an estate : a quality (e.g. Hardness and brilliance are well-known *properties* of the diamond) : (pl.) furniture, etc. required by actors in a play.

prophesy, prof′e-sī, v. to foretell.—ns. **prophecy** (prof′e-si), something foretold ; **prophet** (prof′it), one who tells beforehand of things to come : one who tells the will of God :—fem. **proph′etess.**

propinquity, prō-ping′kwi-ti, n. nearness.

propitiate, prō-pish′i-āt, v. to gain the favour of : to calm the anger of.—adj. **propi′tious,** favourable.

proportion, prō-por′shun, n. a part or share : the size of a part as compared with other parts or with the whole (e.g. The *proportion* of the class who passed the examination was very small) : suitability in the size of the different parts (e.g. An elephant's feet are in *proportion* to the rest of its body) : a kind of sum in which parts are compared with the whole.—adjs. **propor′tional, proportionate,** in proportion.

propose, prō-pōz′, v. to put forward (e.g. a plan) for consideration : to intend : to offer marriage.—ns. **propo′sal,** anything put forward for consideration : an offer ; **proposi′tion,** a statement : an offer : something to be done.

propound, prō-pound′, v. to set forth for consideration.

proprietor, prō-prī′e-tor, n. an owner : —fem. **propri′etress, propri′etrix.**

propriety, pro-prī′e-ti, n. rightness : fitness : decency.

propulsion, prō-pul′shun, n. a driving forward.

prorogue, prō-rōg′, v. to bring the meetings of parliament to an end for a time.—n. **proroga′tion.**

prosaic, prō-zā′ik, adj. dull, not interesting.

proscribe, prō-skrīb′, v. to send into exile, to banish : to forbid.—n. **proscrip′tion,** a sentence to death or exile.

prose, prōz, n. writing which is not in verse.—adj. **pro′sy,** dull, uninteresting.

prosecute, pros′e-kūt, v. to carry on (e.g. He *prosecutes* his studies earnestly) : to bring before a court.—ns. **prosecu′tion,** the act of bringing a court case against another ; **pros′ecutor,** the law officer who leads a court case against a prisoner.

proselyte, pros′e-līt, n. one who has come over from one religion or opinion to another : a convert.

prospect, pros′pekt, n. a view : what one may expect to happen (e.g. Having few troops, the general was faced with the *prospect* of a defeat ; This job has good *prospects*).—v. **prospect′,** to make a search for minerals : to explore. ns. **prospec′tor,** one who searches for new mineral deposits ; **prospec′tus,** a handbook giving information about a business which is to be started.—adj. **prospec′tive,** likely to be or to happen.

pros′per, v. to get on well, to succeed.—n. **prosper′ity,** success : good-fortune.—adj. **pros′perous,** making good progress : successful.

pros′trate, adj. lying face down on the ground : worn out (e.g. by sorrow).—v. **prostrate′,** to throw down (e.g. The generals *prostrated* themselves before the king).—adj. **prostra′ted,** worn out (by grief or tiredness).—n. **prostra′tion.**

protag′onist, n. a leader : a champion.

prŏtect′, v. to shield from danger, to keep safe.—ns. **protec′tion**, sheltering care: defence: the taxing of foreign goods in order to give home industries a better chance; **protec′tionist**, one who believes in taxing foreign imports; **protec′tor**, a guardian; **protec′torate**, a country which is governed and defended by another country.

protégé, prot-ā-zhā, n. a person who is under the care of another.

prŏtest′, v. to declare solemnly: to speak strongly against something.—ns. **prō′test**, a strong statement showing displeasure; **protestā′tion**, a solemn statement of what one thinks.

Prot′estants, n.pl. those who broke away from the Church of Rome at the time of the Reformation.—n. **Prot′estantism**, the Protestant religion.

prototype, prō′tō-tīp, n. the first or original type or model from which anything is copied: a pattern.

protract′, v. to draw out or lengthen in time, to prolong.—adj. **protrac′ted**, drawn out, tiring.—n. **protrac′tor**, an instrument for measuring angles in drawings.

protrude, prō-trood′, v. to stick out.—n. **protru′sion**.—adj. **protru′sive**.

protŭ′berance, n. a swelling: a bulging mass.—adj. **protu′berant**, swelling: sticking out.

proud, adj. haughty: thinking too highly of one's self: determined to refuse help from others.—n. **pride**.

prove, proov, v. to try by testing or by suffering: to show that something is true: to turn out (to be).—e.g. His remarks *proved* to be correct.—n. **proof**.

prov′ender, n. food, esp. for horses and cattle.

prov′erb, n. a short saying full of wise meaning (e.g. *A rolling stone gathers no moss*).—adj. **prover′bial**, spoken about by everybody (e.g. His kindness is *proverbial*).

provide, v. to make ready beforehand: to supply.—conj. **provi′ded (that)**, on condition (that), if.

prov′idence, n. foresight: thrift: the care of God over all His creatures.—adjs. **prov′ident**, showing foresight for the future: thrifty; **providen′tial**, fortunate, coming as if from the hand of God (e.g. He had a *providential* escape).

prov′ince, n. a division of a country: the extent of one's knowledge (e.g. Gardening is outside my *province*): (pl.) the part of a country outside the capital.—adj. **provin′cial**, belonging to a province: rough in manners.

provision, pro-vizh′un, n. preparation: an arrangement: (pl.) food.—adj. **provisional**, lasting for the time being.—n. **provi′so**, a condition on which something is done.

provoke, v. to call forth: to rouse to anger.—n. **provocā′tion**, an act which rouses anger.—adjs. **provoc′ative**, calling forth (e.g. anger, thought); **provō′king**, annoying.

prov′ost, n. (in Scotland) the leading magistrate of a town, the mayor: the head of a college.

prow, n. the fore-part of a ship.

prow′ess, n. bravery, esp. in war.

prowl, v. to go about stealthily in search of prey or plunder.

proxim′ity, n. nearness.

prox′y, n. one who acts or votes for another.

prude, prood, n. a woman who wishes herself to be thought very modest and good.—n. **pru′dery**.—adj. **pru′dish**.

prudent, proo′dent, adj. careful: wise in conduct.—n. **pru′dence**.

prune, proon, n. a dried plum.

prune, proon, v. to cut twigs off a tree: to shorten (e.g. a story).

prŷ, v. to look closely into: to lift with a lever.

psalm, sahm, n. a sacred song, esp. one in the Book of Psalms.—ns. **psalmist**, a writer of psalms; **psalter** (sawl′ter), a book of psalms; **psal′tery**, a stringed instrument of olden times.

pseudo, sū′dō, a prefix meaning false.—n. **pseudonym**, sū′do-nim, a false name used by an author (e.g. 'Lewis Carroll' was the *pseudonym* of Rev. Charles L. Dodgson).

psychic, sī'kik, *adj.* having to do with the mind or soul, or with spirits—also **psy'chical.**—*ns.* **psychol'ogy**, the science which studies the human mind ; **psychol'ogist**, one who studies psychology.

ptarmigan, tar'mi-gan, *n.* a kind of grouse, which turns white in winter.

ptomaine, tō-mān, *n.* a poison which often forms in stale food and causes serious illness.

pub'lic, *adj.* open to, or concerning, people in general : known by everybody.—*n.* the people in general.—*ns.* **pub'lican**, the keeper of a *public-house* (i.e. a place where strong drink is sold): (in the Bible) a tax-gatherer ; **publicity** (pub-lis'i-ti), the state of being well known : advertisement.—*v.* **pub'lish**, to make known : to put out a book for sale.—*ns.* **pub'lisher**, one who sees to the preparing of books ; **publica'tion**, the act of publishing : a book or magazine for sale to the public.

puce, *adj.* a brownish-purple.

puck'er, *v.* to gather into wrinkles or folds.—*n.* a wrinkle or fold.

pudding, pood'ing, *n.* a soft kind of food made of flour, milk, eggs, etc.

pud'dle, *n.* a small pool of muddy water.

pū'erile, *adj.* childish : of small importance, silly.

puff, *v.* to breathe heavily (as after running): to blow up : to praise a person too much.—*n.* a short, sudden blast of wind : a piece of light pastry : a light ball or pad for dusting powder on the skin.—*adj.* **puf'fy**, blown out, flabby.

puf'fin, *n.* a water-bird, having a short, thick beak.

pug, *n.* a monkey : a little dog.

pugilist, pū'jil-ist, *n.* a boxer.—*n.* **pu'gilism**, boxing.

pugnacious, pug-nā'shus, *adj.* quarrelsome, fond of fighting.—*n.* **pugna'city**, readiness to fight.

pūke, *v.* to vomit.

pull, pool, *v.* to draw with force : to tear, to pluck.—*n.* the act of pulling : a drink : an advantage in a contest (e.g. The older boxer's extra weight gave him a decided *pull* over his opponent).

pullet, pool'et, *n.* a young hen.

pulley, pool'i, *n.* a grooved wheel fitted with a cord and set in a block—often used for raising weights : (in machinery) a wheel which drives or is driven by another wheel, with which it is connected by means of a belt or cord passing round the rim.

pul'monary, *adj.* of the lungs.

pulp, *n.* the soft fleshy part of a fruit : a soft mass (made of esparto, wood, etc.) which is made into paper.—*v.* to reduce to pulp.

pulpit, pool'pit, *n.* an enclosed platform in a church, for the preacher.

pulse, *n.* the beating or throbbing of the blood-vessels of the body as blood flows through them.— *v.* to beat or throb—also **pul'sate.**

pulse, *n.* beans, pease, etc.

pul'verise, *v.* to make into powder.

pū'ma, *n.* a wild animal of America, like a large cat.

pumice, pum'is, *n.* a light, rocky substance thrown up by volcanoes, used for rubbing away stains or for polishing.

pum'mel, *v.* to beat with the fists.

pump, *n.* an instrument used for raising water and other liquids : an instrument for drawing out or forcing in air.—*v.* to work a pump : to draw out information from a person by cunning questions.

pump, *n.* a thin-soled shoe worn in dancing.

pump'kin, *n.* a large roundish, thick-skinned, yellow fruit, used for food.

pun, *n.* a play upon words (e.g. ' They went and *told* the sexton, and the sexton *tolled* the bell.'— Hood).—*v.* to make a pun.—*n.* **pun'ster**, one who makes puns.

punch, punsh, *v.* to beat with the fist : to make a hole with a sharp tool.—*n.* a blow with the fist : a tool used for punching holes.

punch, punsh, *n.* a mixture of spirits, water, sugar, lemon-juice, and spice.

punctil′ious, *adj.* paying great care to small points, esp. in one's behaviour.

punc′tual, *adj.* up to time, not late. —*n.* **punctual′ity.**

punc′tuate, *v.* to divide up sentences by commas, full-stops, etc.—*n.* **punctua′tion,** commas, full-stops, etc.

punc′ture, *n.* a small hole.

pun′dit, *n.* a learned man.

pungent, pun′jent, *adj.* sharp-tasting or smelling : hurting (e.g. He made some *pungent* remarks).

pun′ish, *v.* to cause to suffer for fault or crime : to inflict pain. —*n.* **pun′ishment,** pain or unpleasantness inflicted for a fault or crime.—*adj.* **pū′nitive,** inflicting punishment.

punt, *n.* a flat-bottomed boat with square ends.—*v.* to drive a punt with a pole.

pū′ny, *adj.* little and weak.

pup, *n.* a young dog—also **puppy.**

pū′pa, *n.* a stage in the growth of an insect (e.g. a butterfly caterpillar becomes a *pupa* ; from the *pupa* comes the winged butterfly).

pū′pil, *n.* one who learns : a child under a teacher : the round opening in the middle of the eye.

pup′pet, *n.* a small doll moved by wires : one who does as another tells him.

pup′py, *n.* a young dog.

purchase, pur′chis, *v.* to buy.—*n.* that which is bought : the power got by using a lever.—*n.* **pur′chaser,** one who buys.

pūre, *adj.* clean : spotless : unmixed.—*adv.* **pure′ly,** merely.—*n.* **pū′rity.**

pur′gatory, *n.* a place where a soul is made pure before entering heaven : a severe trouble.

purge, purj, *v.* to make clean or pure.—*n.* **pur′gative,** a medicine which drives harmful matter out of the body.

pū′rify, *v.* to make pure, to cleanse. —*ns.* **purifica′tion ; pūr′ist,** one who is very particular in the choice of words.

Pū′ritan, *n.* one who believes in keeping religion and behaviour pure.—*adj.* **puritan′ical.**

pū′rity, *n.* cleanness : freedom from wicked thoughts or actions.

purl, *v.* to flow with a rippling sound.—Also *n.*

purl, *n.* a knitting stitch worked upside-down, giving a ribbed pattern.—Also *v.*

purloin′, *v.* to steal.

pur′ple, *n.* a dark colour formed by the mixture of blue and red : the robe of an emperor or high officer of the Church.

pur′port, *n.* meaning.—*v.* **purport′,** to mean.

pur′pose, *n.* an aim or plan kept before the mind : intention.—*v.* to plan to do.—*adj.* **pur′poseful,** knowing what one wants to do.— **on purpose,** intentionally ; **to no purpose,** in vain.

purr, pur, *n.* the sound a cat makes when pleased.—Also *v.*

purse, *n.* a small bag for carrying money : a sum given as a present or prize.—*n.* **purs′er,** the officer who looks after a ship's money.

purse, *v.* to close (lips) tightly.

pursue, pur-sū′, *v.* to follow after in order to overtake or capture : to chase : to be engaged in.—*ns.* **pursu′er,** one who pursues : a person who brings another to court ; **pursuit′,** the act of pursuing : an occupation or hobby (e.g. Gardening is an interesting *pursuit*).

purvey, pur-vā′, *v.* to provide (food, etc.)—*n* **purvey′or.**

pus, *n.* yellow matter from a wound.

push, poosh, *v* to press against with force : to shove : to urge on : to make an effort.—*adj.* **push′ing,** anxious to get on.

pusillan′imous, *adj.* cowardly.

pus′tūle, *n.* a small pimple containing pus.

put, poot, *v.* to place in a position : to express in words (e.g. I will *put* the question thus).—**put about,** vexed ; **to put by,** to save ; **to put down** (rebels), to make to cease fighting ; **to put into** (a port), to sail into ; **to put up,** to lodge ; **to put up with,** to bear patiently.

pū′trefy, *v.* to rot.—*n.* **putrefac′tion.** —*adj.* **pū′trid,** rotten : stinking.

putt, *v.* to send a ball forward.

put′ty, *n.* paste of whiting and oil.

puz'zle, *v.* to worry a person by making him think hard : to think long and carefully.—*n.* a difficulty which causes much thought : a toy or riddle to test one's thinking.

pygmy, pigmy, pig'mi, *n.* a dwarf.

pyja'mas, *n.pl.* a sleeping-suit.

py'lon, *n.* a pillar or tower built at an aerodrome to serve as a guide : a pillar for carrying wires with electric current.

pyr'amid, *n.* a solid shape having flat sides which come to a point at the top.

pyre, pīr, *n.* a pile of wood on which a dead body is burned.

pyrotechnics, pī-rō-tek'niks, *n.* fire-works.

Pyrrhic (pir'ik) **victory,** a victory gained at so great a cost that it is as bad as a defeat.

py'thon, *n.* a large but not poisonous snake which crushes its victims.

Q

quack, *n.* the cry of a duck : a person who has no training as a doctor but pretends to be able to cure.—*v.* to make the noise of a duck.

quadran'gle, *n.* a figure having four equal sides and angles : a square surrounded by buildings.—*adj.* **quadrang'ular.**

quad'rant, *n.* the fourth part of a circle : an instrument used in measuring heights.

quadrille, kwod-ril', *n.* a square dance for four couples.

quad'ruped, *n.* a four-footed animal.

quadruple, kwod'roo-pl, *adj.* fourfold. —*v.* to make four times greater.— *n.pl.* **quad'ruplets,** four children born of one mother at one birth.

quaff, *v.* to drink in large draughts.

quag'ga, *n.* a zebra-like animal, found in South Africa.

quag'mire, *n.* wet, boggy ground.

quail, *v.* to shrink back in fear.

quail, *n.* a small bird of the partridge kind.

quaint, *adj.* odd, unusual : old-fashioned.

quake, *v.* to shake with cold or fear.

Quā'kers, *n.pl.* a name for the religious group called the *Society of Friends,* who believe in a plain, peace-loving life.

qual'ify, *v.* to become fit for following a profession or trade, or for holding a position : to lessen the force of a statement by adding something.—*n.* **qualifica'tion,** something which qualifies : a quality that fits a person for a post.

qual'ity, *n.* an outstanding point in a person or thing (e.g. Kindness is a *quality* admired by all; Hardness is a well-known *quality* of the diamond) : worth, rank (e.g. cloth of poor *quality*) : good birth (e.g. a man of *quality*).

qualm, kwahm, *n.* a sudden attack of illness : doubt whether one is doing right.

quan'dary, *n.* a state of difficulty or uncertainty.

quan'tity, *n.* the amount of anything : size, bulk : a measure.

quarantine, kwor'an-tēn, *n.* a system under which persons who have, or may have, a fever are kept apart, in order to prevent the spread of disease (e.g. The ship, on which there were ten cases of small-pox, was put in *quarantine*). —*v.* to keep apart in order to check disease.

quarrel, kwor'el, *n.* an angry dispute : a breaking-off of friendship.—*v.* to find fault : to disagree : to fight.—*adj.* **quarr'elsome,** fond of quarrelling.

quarry, kwor'i, *n.* a place from which stone is cut for building, road-making, etc.—*v.* to dig from a quarry.

quarry, kwor'i, *n.* a hunted animal : prey.

quart, kwort, *n.* a measure of liquids (two pints or the fourth part of a gallon).

quarter, kwor'ter, *n.* a fourth part : a fourth part of an hour, year : 28 lbs. : 8 bushels : direction (e.g. No help came from any *quarter*) : a division of a town : mercy granted to an enemy

(e.g. No *quarter* !) : (*pl.*) lodgings.
—*v.* to divide into four equal parts : to provide with lodgings.
—*adj.* and *adv.* **quar'terly,** happening every three months.—*ns.* **quar'ter-deck,** the part of the deck of a ship between the stern and the hind-mast ; **quar'terly,** a magazine published every quarter of a year, i.e. every three months ; **quar'termaster,** an officer who looks after the lodging, and attends to the supplies, of soldiers ; **quar'tern-loaf,** a loaf weighing about four pounds ; **quar'ter-staff,** a long staff, grasped by both hands, used in fencing ; **quartet',** **quartette** (kwor-tet'), a company of four players or singers, also the music written for them.

quartz, kworts, *n.* a hard substance often found in rocks.

quash, kwosh, *n.* to crush : to wipe out (e.g. a judge's decision).

quassia, kwash'i-a, *n.* a South American tree, used to make a bitter medicine.

quatrain, kwot'rān, *n.* a verse of four lines.

quaver, kwā'ver, *v.* to shake, shiver : to speak in a shaking voice.—*n.* a trembling : a note in music.

quay, kē, *n.* a landing-place, for the loading and unloading of boats.

queasy, kwē'zi, *adj.* inclined to be sick.

queen, *n.* the wife of a king : a female ruler : a playing-card : a piece in chess.—*adj.* **queen'ly,** like a queen.—*ns.* **queen'-bee,** the only female bee in a hive—it is larger than an ordinary bee ; **queen'-con'sort,** the wife of the reigning king ; **queen'-dow'ager,** the widow of a dead king ; **queen'-moth'er,** the mother of the reigning king or queen.

queer, *adj.* odd, strange : not feeling very well.—*v.* to spoil (e.g. He has *queered* my pitch, i.e. he has upset my plans).

quell, *v.* to crush : to put down (e.g. fears, suspicions).

quench, kwensh, *v.* to drink and so satisfy one's thirst : to put out a fire.

querulous, kwer'ū-lus, *adj.* complaining : fond of quarrelling.

query, kwē'ri, *n.* a question : a question mark (?).

quest, *n.* a search.—*v.* to go in search of.

question, kwes'chn, *n.* the act of asking about something : a problem, a difficult matter : a subject of talk or voting.—*v.* to ask questions of : to doubt.—*adj.* **quest'ionable,** doubtful : not very good.—*n.* **questionnaire** (kest-yon-ār'), a written list of questions to be answered.

queue, kū, *n.* line of persons waiting (e.g. to enter a picture-house).—*v.* to stand in a queue.

quib'ble, *n.* a clever use of words, esp. to avoid telling the full truth.—Also *v.*

quick, *adj.* living : lively : keen : clever.—*n.* a very tender part of the body, esp. under the nails.—*v.* **quick'en** to give life to : to hasten.—*ns.* **quick'lime,** lime which has not been mixed with water ; **quick'sand,** loose, wet sand sinking under the feet ; **quick'set,** a living plant (esp. hawthorn) planted as a hedge ; **quick'silver,** mercury.

quiescent, kwē-es'ent, *adj.* lying at rest.

quiet, kwī'et, *adj.* calm, smooth : gentle : not noisy : (of colours) not glaring.—*n.* calm : peace.—*v.* to calm, to silence.—*v.* **qui'eten,** to make quiet, calm.—*ns.* **qui'etness,** **qui'etude,** rest : stillness ; **quietus** (kwī-ē'tus), a finishing stroke : death.

quill, *n.* the feather of a goose or other bird used as a pen : one of the sharp spines of a hedgehog or porcupine.

quilt, *n.* a padded bed-cover.—*v.* to stitch together two pieces of cloth with something soft between.—*adj.* **quilt'ed,** padded.

quince, *n.* a pear-like fruit.

quinine, kwin-ēn', *n.* a bitter drug made from the bark of a tree, used as medicine in cases of fever.

quinquennial, kwin-kwen'i-al, *adj.* happening once in five years : lasting five years.

quinquereme, kwin'kwe-rēm, *n.* a ship of olden times, driven by five rows of oars.

quin'sy, *n.* a painful disease of the throat.

quintes'sence, *n.* something in its best and purest form.

quintet, quintette, kwin-tet', *n.* a company of five singers or players, also the music written for them.

quip, *n.* a quick, smart saying.

quire, *n.* a measure for paper (24 sheets).

quirk, *n.* a trick : a clever or witty saying.

quit, *v.* to give up : to leave.—*adj.* clear : freed from a duty.—*ns.* **quit'-rent**, a rent by which the tenants are freed from all other services ; **quit'tance**, a freeing from debt.—**to be quits**, to be even with each other, to owe nothing to each other.

quite, *adv.* completely : entirely.

quiv'er, *n.* a case for arrows.

quiver, kwiv'er, *v.* to shake.

quixot'ic, *adj.* having noble but foolish aims which cannot be carried out. (From *Don Quixote*.)

quiz, kwiz, *v.* to make fun of.—*n.* a test of knowledge, esp. on radio.

quoit, koit, *n.* a heavy flat ring (of iron or rubber), for throwing at a *hob* (or pin), in the game of quoits.

quon'dam, *adj.* that was formerly (e.g. my *quondam* friend).

quō'rum, *n.* the least number of people who must be present at a meeting before any business can be done.

quō'ta, *n.* a part or share to be given or received by each member of a group.

quote, *v.* to repeat the words of anyone (in writing this is done within **quotation-marks** (" "), e.g. He said " I am going away "): to state a price for.—*n.* **quōtā'tion**, the repeating of something said or written : a price stated.

quoth, *v.* said (e.g. ' Quoth Mrs Gilpin, " That's well said." ').

quotient, kwō'shent, *n.* the answer to a division sum.

R

rabbi, rab'ī, *n.* a Jewish teacher or doctor of the law.

rab'bit, *n.* a small burrowing, long-eared animal.—*n.* **rab'bit-warr'en**, a place where wild rabbits live.

rab'ble, *n.* a disorderly, noisy crowd ; a mob.

rab'id, *adj.* mad : (of dogs) sick with **rabies** (rā'bi-ēz), a disease which causes madness.

raccoon', racoon', *n.* a small fur-bearing animal of North America.

race, *n.* living beings of the same kind (e.g. the human *race*, all mankind ; the black *races*, peoples whose colour is black, negroes).—*adj.* **racial** (rā'shal).

race, *n.* a trial of speed : a strong and swiftly-flowing current.—*v.* to run swiftly : to run for a prize.—*adj.* **ra'cy**, (of stories) full of action and brightly written.

rack, *n.* a framework for holding articles (e.g. letters, plates, hats) : an instrument for torturing victims by stretching their joints.—

v. to torture on the rack : to put a great strain on (e.g. He *racked* his brain for a plan).

rack, *n.* flying, broken clouds.

racket, racquet, rak'et, *n.* a bat for playing tennis, badminton, etc. : (*pl.*) a game something like tennis.

rack'et, *n.* din : great noise.

raconteur, ra-kong-ter', *n.* a teller of stories.

racy. See **race**.

rādar, *n.* a means used to detect objects through darkness or fog, or at great heights ; it depends upon the 'echo' of wireless waves.

radiant, rā'di-ant, *adj.* sending out rays of light or heat : shining : beaming with joy and happiness. —*n.* **ra'diance**, splendour, brilliance.—*v.* **ra'diate**, to send out rays of light or heat : to send out a wireless message : to shine : to spread out or send out from a centre (e.g. Four roads *radiate* from this town).—*ns.* **rādiā'tion** ; **rā'diātor**, an electric or gas fire or bunch of hot-water pipes, which send out heat; the part of a motor-engine which does the cooling.

rad´ical, *adj.* going to the root or bottom (e.g. a *radical* change, a very thorough change).—*n.* a root: one who desires to makes great changes in the government.

rā´dio, *n.* wireless.—*v.* to send a wireless message.—*n.* radiogram, a wireless set and gramophone in one cabinet.—radio telegraphy, telephony. See telegram.

rādioactive, *adj.* giving off dangerous rays.

rad´ish, *n.* a sharp-tasting root, served raw in salads.

rā´dium, *n.* a very rare metal which sends out rays that are used in the treatment of some diseases.

rā´dius, *n.* a straight line from the centre to the circumference of a circle:—(*pl*) radii (rā´di-ī).

raf´fle, *n.* the selling of a number of marked tickets, one of which is picked out by chance, and the buyer receives a prize.—*v.* to sell by means of a raffle.

raft, rahft, *n.* a number of logs, planks, or barrels, fastened together and used as a roughly made boat.

rafter, rahft´er, *n.* one of the sloping beams supporting a roof.

rag, *n.* a torn piece of cloth: (*pl.*) worn-out, shabby clothes.—*n.* **rag´amuffin**, a ragged, dirty person.—*adj.* rag´ged, torn and tattered: shaggy.

rag, *v.* to torment: to play rough jokes upon.—*n.* a rough joke.

rage, *n.* great anger, fury: something very much in fashion.—*v.* to be wild and furious (e.g. with anger).

raid, *n.* a short, sudden attack.— Also *v.*—*n.* raid´er.

rail, *n.* a strip of wood or iron, as in fences, staircases, etc.: (*pl.*) strips of steel, forming the track on which trains or trams run.— *v.* to enclose with rails: to send by railway.—*ns.* rail´ing, a fence of posts and rails; rail´road, rail´-way, a road or way laid with steel rails on which trains run.

rail, *v.* to use impudent or angry language.—*n.* rail´lery, jesting.

rai´ment, *n.* clothing.

rain, *n.* water falling from the clouds in drops.—*v.* to pour or fall in drops.—*ns.* rain´bow, the brilliant coloured bow or arch seen opposite the sun when rain is falling; rain´fall, the amount of rain that falls in a certain time; rain´-gauge (-gāj), an instrument for measuring rainfall.

raise, *v.* to lift up: to bring up (a matter) for consideration: to breed (e.g. He *raises* dogs): to collect (money): to give up (a siege).

rai´sin, *n.* a dried grape.

ra´jah, ra´ja, *n.* an Indian prince.— *n.* raj, rule.

rake, *n.* an instrument, like a large comb, for smoothing earth, drawing hay, etc.—*v.* to gather together with a rake: to search very carefully: to fire at a ship, from one end to the other.

rake, *n.* a person who lives a wicked life.—*adj.* rā´kish, of a bad character.

ral´ly, *v.* to gather again (e.g. The general *rallied* his troops after the defeat): to recover a little from an illness.—*n.* a gathering: recovery (e.g. of strength, order, prices): (in tennis) a long-continued piece of play before the point is lost.

ral´ly, *v.* to make fun of a person in a kindly way.

ram, *n.* a male sheep: something used for battering down a wall, knocking in heavy pillars, etc.— *v.* to beat down hard: to strike with a ram: (of ships) to run into and cause damage (e.g. The destroyer *rammed* the submarine).

ram´ble, *v.* to walk without hurry: to speak in a careless, round-about way.—*n.* a wandering walk.

ram´ify, *v.* to make or divide into branches: to spread out.—*n.* ramifica´tion.

ramp, *v.* to leap or bound.—*n.* a leap: a slope: the upward bend in a stair-rail.—*n.* rampāge´, a state of anger or excitement.— *v.* to storm at violently.—*adj.* ram´pant, going unchecked (e.g. This crime is *rampant*): standing on the hind-legs (e.g. a *lion rampant* in a coat of arms).

ram´part, n. a mound or wall surrounding a fortified place.

ram´rod, n. a rod for ramming down the charge in a gun.

ramshackle, ram´shakl, adj. badly made : falling to pieces.

ranch, ransh, n. in America, a farm for cattle-rearing.

rancid, ran´sid, adj. smelling or tasting stale : sour : disgusting.

rancour, rang´kur, n. bitter ill-feeling—adj. ran´corous.

rand, n. standard S. African coin.

ran´dom, adj. aimless : done without any purpose.—**at random,** without any plan or purpose.

range, rānj, v. to set in a row : to place in proper order : to wander at liberty : to extend.—n. a line or row (e.g. a range of mountains) : extent, number (e.g. He could talk on a wide range of subjects) : a piece of ground with targets : the distance which a shot carries : a cooking-stove.—n. rān´ger, a keeper who looks after a forest or park.

rank, n. a row or line, esp. of soldiers : class or order : high position (e.g. a man of rank) : (pl.) the classes of soldiers below officers.—v. to place in a line : to put, or to be, in a certain order. —n. rank´er, an officer who has risen from the ranks.

rank, adj. coarse : growing plentifully : strong-tasted : utter (e.g. rank nonsense).

ran´kle, v. to cause painful feelings.

ran´sack, v. to plunder : to search thoroughly.

ran´som, n. price paid for the freeing of a captive person.

rant, v. to use fine-sounding but silly language : to talk noisily.

rap, n. a sharp blow.—v. to strike with a quick, sharp blow.

rapacious, ra-pā´shus, adj. greedy : eager to seize as much as possible. —n. rapa´city, greed.

rape, v. to carry away by force.

rape, n. a plant of the turnip kind, whose seeds yield oil.

rap´id, adj. hurrying along : speedy. —n.pl. rap´ids, a part in a river where the current flows swiftly and roughly.—n. rapid´ity, swiftness.

rapier, rā´pi-er, n. a light sword with a narrow blade.

rap´ine, n. plunder.

rapt, adj. having the mind fully occupied (e.g. in thought, wonder).—n. rap´ture, great delight. —adj. rap´turous.

rare, adj. thin : seldom met with, uncommon : especially good.—v. **rarefy** (rar´i-fī), to make rare, thin, or less dense.

ras´cal, n. a rogue, scamp : a dishonest fellow.—adj. ras´cally.

rash, adj. too bold, acting without thought.—n. rashness.

rash, n. a redness on the skin (e.g. in scarlet-fever, measles).

rash´er, n. a thin slice of bacon or ham.

rasp, rahsp, v. to rub with a rasp (a coarse file).—adj. rasp´ing, (of the voice) rough and unpleasant.

raspberry, raz´ber-i, n. a well-known red or yellow berry.

rat, n. a gnawing animal, larger than the mouse.—v. to hunt or kill rats.

ratch´et, n. a wheel with a toothed edge and a catch allowing winding in one direction only (e.g. in a watch).

rate, n. amount, proportion (e.g. the birth-rate, death-rate, i.e. the number of births, deaths, in every thousand of the people of a place) : the sum of money to be paid by the owner of a house, shop, etc. to the council of his town or county (often in pl.— rates).—v. to work out an amount or proportion : to value.—ns. rā´tings, in the navy, sailors below the rank of officers ; rate-payer, one who pays rates.

rate, v. to scold.

rather, rah´ther, adv. more truly : more willingly : in some degree.

rat´ify, v. to agree to (e.g. The parliament ratified the treaty).— n. ratifica´tion.

ratio, rā´shi-o, n. the proportion of one thing to another :—pl. rā´tios.

ration, ra´shon, n. a measured amount of food given out each day to a person or animal : an allowance.—v. to deal out (e.g. food) in measured amounts.

rational, rash´on-al, adj. able to reason : sensible.

rat′tan, *n.* a tall palm-tree: a walking-stick made from it.

rat′tle, *v.* to give out short, sharp sounds, to clatter: to speak quickly.—*n.* a sharp noise, quickly repeated: a clatter: a noisy toy. —*n.* **rat′tlesnake,** a poisonous snake having, in its tail, bones which rattle.

rav′age, *v.* to lay waste: to destroy. —*n.* ruin.

rave, *v.* to be mad: to talk wildly.

rav′el, *v.* to twist (e.g. threads) together and mix up.

ra′ven, *n.* a kind of crow.

rav′enous, *adj.* very hungry: greedy.

ravine, ra-vēn′, *n.* a deep, narrow hollow between hills.

rav′ish, *v.* to carry away by violence: to rob: to thrill with delight.—*adj.* **rav′ishing,** filling with delight.

raw, *adj.* uncooked: as gathered in a wild state, not made up (e.g. *raw* cotton, *raw* sugar): sore: knowing little: (of weather) chilly and damp.

ray, *n.* a line of light or heat: a faint gleam (e.g. of hope, of knowledge).

ray, *n.* a flat fish.

ray′on, *n.* a name for artificial silk (i.e. silk made from wood).

raze, *v.* to destroy a town or wall so that it lies level with the ground.

ra′zor, *n.* a sharp-edged instrument for shaving.—*ns.* **ra′zor-bill,** a kind of bird, common on the coasts of North America; **ra′zor-fish,** a long narrow shellfish.

reach, *v.* to stretch or extend: to stretch out the hand: to arrive at: to go as far as.—*n.* the distance something covers: the distance one can stretch the arm: a straight part of a stream between bends.

react, rē-akt′, *v.* to act or behave in response to something done.— *n.* **reac′tion,** behaviour as result of action or stimulus: a return to things as they were.—*adj.* **reac′tionary,** trying to go back to the old state of things—*n.* one who tries to do so.—**nūclear (or atomic) reactor.** See **nucleus.**

read, rēd, *v.* to utter aloud written or printed words: to study for

a profession (e.g. He₀ is *reading* law).—*adj.* **read′able,** interesting.—*ns.* **read′er,** one who reads: a person who reads carefully the type of a book before it is printed.

ready, red′i, *adj.* prepared: willing: quick to act.—*adv.* **read′ily.**—*adj.* **ready-made,** (clothes) made for sale to anyone whom they will fit.—*ns.* **ready-money,** payment in cash; **ready-reckoner,** a book giving lists of answers of multiplication sums; used in offices to save working out such sums.

real, rē′al, *adj.* actually existing: not a fraud: sincere: (of property) consisting of lands or houses.—*v.* **re′alise,** to make real, to accomplish (e.g. The soldier *realised* his ambition when he became a general): to understand completely: to sell something and get money for it.—*ns.* **re′alism,** the habit of showing things as they are; **re′alist,** one who looks upon things as they are; **real′ity,** that which is real and not imaginary: truth.—*adj.* **realis′tic,** life-like.—*adv.* **re′ally,** in fact.—**really!** I am surprised!

realm, relm, *n.* a kingdom, a country: a name sometimes given to any branch of man's life (e.g. the *realm* of sport, of music, of learning).

ream, *n.* a measure for paper.

reap, *v.* to cut down (e.g. corn): to receive a reward (e.g. for work done).—*n.* **reap′er,** a person who reaps: a machine for reaping.

rear, *n.* the back part of anything: the last part of an army or fleet.— *ns.* **rear′-ad′miral,** an officer who commands the rear division of the fleet; **rear′-guard,** troops which protect the rear of an army.

rear, *v.* to bring up (children): to breed (animals): (of horses) to stand on the hind-legs.

rea′son, *n.* cause: excuse: purpose: the power of the mind by which man forms opinions, and judges right and truth: common-sense. —*v.* to think out opinions: to try to persuade a person by arguing.—*adj.* **reas′onable,** sensible: fair.

reassure, rē-a-shoor , *v.* to drive away doubts or fears.

rē′bate, *n.* a part of a payment or tax which is given back to the payer.

reb′el, *n.* one who fights against those in power.—*v.* **rebel′**, to take up arms against those in power : to revolt.—*n.* **rebell′ion**, an open or armed fight against those in power : a revolt.—*adj.* **rebell′ious**, unwilling to be ruled : discontented.

rebound′, *v.* to spring back.—Also *n.*

rēbuff′, *n.* an unexpected, blunt refusal : a check.

rēbūke′, *v.* to scold, to blame.—*n.* a scolding.

rēbut′, *v.* to drive back : to deny what has been said.

recalcitrant, rē-kal′si-trant, *adj.* stubborn : disobedient.

recall, rē-kawl′, *v.* to call back : to call back to mind, to remember. —*n.* a signal to soldiers to return.

rēcant′, *v.* to take back what one has said : to give up a religion which one has followed.—*n.* **rēcantā′tion**.

rēcapit′ūlate, *v.* to go over again quickly the chief points of anything : to summarise. — *n.* **recapitūlā′tion**.

rēcap′ture, *v.* to get possession of once again.

rēcast′, *v.* to fashion or shape anew.

rēcēde′, *v.* to go back.—*adj.* **rēcēd**- ing, sloping backward.

receipt, rē-sēt′, *n.* a written note saying that money has been received : a recipe.—*v.* to give a receipt for money received.

receive, rē-sēv′, *v.* to take what is offered : to accept : to welcome : to take goods, knowing them to be stolen.—*n.* **receiv′er**, one who receives stolen goods : a telephone or a wireless set with which messages are heard.

recent, rē′sent, *adj.* happening a short time ago : fresh, new : modern.—*adv.* **rē′cently**, lately.

receptacle, rē-sep′ta-kl, *n.* a place to receive or hold things in.—*n.* **recep′tion**, a welcome (e.g. The new boy had a good *reception*) : a large meeting of welcome.

recess, rē-ses′, *n.* part of a room formed by a curving away of the wall : an out-of-the-way spot : the time during which parliament or the law-courts do not meet.

recession, rē-sesh′un, *n.* a giving back.

recipe, res′i-pē, *n.* a statement of the substances which make up a dish, and the way of cooking : a doctor's prescription.

recipient, rē-sip′i-ent, *n.* one who receives.

reciprocal, rē-sip′rō-kal, *adj.* acting in return : given and received.— *v.* **rēcip′rocāte**, to return kindness for kindness, etc.

recite, rē-sīt′, *v.* to repeat aloud from memory.—*ns.* **reci′tal**, a musical performance, either singing or playing : the facts of a story told one after the other : **recitā′tion**, a poem, or other piece, recited.

reck, *v.* to care for : to heed.—*adj.* **reck′less**, rash.

reck′on, *v.* to count : to regard (e.g. I *reckon* him a first-class shot) : to believe.—*n.* **reck′oning**, a settlement of accounts, etc. : a bill : a sum.

rēclaim′, *v.* to win back land from the sea by draining, building banks, etc. : to make waste land fit for ploughing.—*n.* **reclamā′- tion**.

rēcline′, *v.* to lean back or sideways : to rest.

recluse, rē-kloos′, *n.* one who shuts himself off from company, and who lives by himself.

recognise, rek′og-nīz, *v.* to know again : to know or greet a person in passing : to see the truth of.— *n.* **recogni′tion**, act of recognising.—*adj.* **rec′ognisable**.

rēcoil′, *v.* to shrink from, in horror or fear : (of guns) to jump back after a shot is fired.—*n.* a rebound.

recollect′, *v.* to remember.—*n.* **recollec′tion**, memory : something remembered.

recommend′, *v.* to advise : to say that a person or thing is good.— *n.* **recommendā′tion**, act of praising : a good point.

re′compense, *v.* to repay, to reward : to make up for loss.—Also *n.*

reconcile, rek′on-sĭl, *v.* to bring together in friendship, after a quarrel : to make to agree.—*n.* **reconcilia′tion,** a renewing of friendship.

rec′ondite, *adj.* secret : little known.

reconnaissance, re-kon′i-sans, *n.* a scouting-out of a stretch of country before a battle.

reconnoitre, rek-o-noi′ter, *v.* to spy out the number, position, movements, of enemy troops.

rēcord′, *v.* to put a matter down in writing so that it may be read afterwards : to make a gramophone record.—*v.* **rec′ord,** a register : a written report of any fact or facts : something that records (e.g. a gramophone *record*) : past history : (in races, games, etc.) the best-known performance.—*ns.* **record′er,** one who records : judge in certain courts ; **record-player,** gramophone run by electricity, not spring-wound.

rēcount′, *v.* to count again : to tell the story of.—*n.* **rē′count,** a second count (e.g. of votes).

recoup, rē-koop′, *v.* to make up for losses.

recourse, rē-kōrs′, *n.* used in the phrase **to have recourse to,** to make use of, to turn to.

recover, rē-kuv′er, *v.* to get possession of again : to cure : to become well again.—*adj.* **recov′erable,** able to be regained.—*n.* **recov′ery,** a return to health, or to any former state.

recreant, rek′rē-ant, *adj.* cowardly : false.—*n.* a cowardly, mean-spirited person.

recreate, rek′rē-āt, *v.* to cheer or amuse.—*n.* **recrea′tion,** amusement apart from one's work : sport.

recriminate, rē-krim′in-āt, *v.* to accuse one's accuser in return.—*n.* **recrimina′tion.**

recruit, rē-kroot′, *n.* a newly-enlisted soldier or supporter.—*v.* to enlist a soldier : to recover in health.—*n.* **recruit′ing-ser′geant,** a sergeant who enlists recruits.

rec′tangle, *n.* a four-sided figure with all its angles right angles and its opposite sides equal.

rec′tify, *v.* to put right.

rec′titude, *n.* correctness of behaviour.

rec′tor, *n.* a clergyman of the Church of England : (in Scotland) the headmaster of a large higher school.—*n.* **rec′tory,** the house of a Church of England rector.

rēcum′bent, *adj.* lying down.

rēcū′perate, *v.* to get back strength or health.

rēcur′, *v.* to happen again : to come back to the mind.—*adj.* **recur′rent.**—*n.* **recur′rence.**

rec′usant, *n.* one who refuses to accept the rules of the government in religious matters.

red, *n.* and *adj.* the colour of blood.—*ns.* **red′breast,** the robin ; **red′lead,** lead of a fine red colour, used in painting, etc. ; **red′shank,** a red-legged bird of the snipe family ; **red′skin,** a Red Indian ; **red′wing,** a kind of thrush.—*v.* **red′den,** to make red : to blush.—*adjs.* **red′-hand′ed,** caught in the act of doing wrong (e.g. The police caught the thief *red-handed*) ; **red-let′ter,** standing out from the rest (e.g. His birthday is a *red-letter* day for him).—**Red Cross,** the badge and flag of the ambulance services in time of war ; **Red Ensign,** the flag of all British vessels not belonging to the navy, i.e. of all British merchant ships ; **Red Indian,** see under **Indian** ; **red tape,** unnecessary and bothersome rules about how things are to be done.

rēdan′, *n.* a kind of rampart.

rede, rēd, advice.

rēdeem′, *v.* to buy back (e.g. articles from a pawnbroker) : to carry out a promise : to deliver from sin.—*adj.* **redeem′ing,** making up for other faults (e.g. Good spelling was the *redeeming* feature of his composition).—*ns.* **Redeem′er,** Jesus Christ ; **redemption** (re-dem′shun).

red′olent, *adj.* sweet-smelling : smelling (of).

redoubt, rē-dowt′, *n.* a kind of field fortification.— *adj.* **redoubt′able,** brave, bold.

rēdound′, *v.* to add to (e.g. Everything he does *redounds* to his advantage).

rĕdress', v. to set right : to make up for.—n. something done or given to make up for a loss or wrong.

rĕduce', v. to make smaller : to weaken : to subdue.—n. reduc'tion.—adj. redū'cible.

redun'dant, adj. more than what is needed.—n. redun'dance.

reed, n. a tall grass, with a straight stalk, growing in moist or marshy places : a pipe which gives a musical sound.

reef, n. a chain of rocks lying at or near the surface of the sea.

reef, n. a portion of a sail rolled or folded up.—v. to take in a reef or reefs of a sail.

reek, n. smoke.—v. to smoke : to smell unpleasantly.

reel, n. a lively Scottish dance.

reel, n. a bobbin (for cotton, for fishing-lines, etc.).—v. to wind on a reel : to stagger or stumble. —to reel off, to tell a story without stopping.

rĕfec'tion, n. a meal : refreshment. —n. refec'tory, a dining-hall.

rĕfer', v. to take (e.g. a matter, difficulty) to another person : to make mention of : to look up a book.—ns. referee', one to whom a matter is taken for settlement : (in games) a judge ; ref'erence, a mention : a note about a person's character and abilities ; referen'dum, a vote given by the people of a country about some important matter.—reference library, a library containing books to be looked at but not to be taken away.

rĕfine', v. to make clear, to purify.— adj. refined', purified : polite in one's manners.—ns. refine'ment, good manners, taste, learning ; refin'ery, a place where such things as sugar and oil are refined.

rĕfit', v. to repair damages.

rĕflect', v. to throw back (e.g. light) : to think over something carefully : to pass a hurtful remark.—ns. reflec'tion or reflex'-ion, the act of throwing back (e.g. of a ray of light) : careful thought : blame ; reflec'tor, something which throws back light (e.g. a mirror).—adj. reflec'tive, thoughtful.

rĕ'flex, n. an action which we cannot help doing (e.g. jerking the leg when the knee-cap is struck).

rĕform', v. to make better : to give up sins and evil ways and follow a better way of living.—n. change for the better : an improvement. —ns. reformā'tion, a change for the better (e.g. in a person's character) ; Reformation, the great religious movement in the 16th century from which the Protestant Church arose ; refor'-matory, a school for reforming young wrong-doers ; refor'mer, one who wishes to bring about improvements : one of the leaders of the Reformation.

rĕfrac'tory, adj. breaking rules wilfully : not easily led.

rĕfrain', n. a chorus coming at the end of each verse of a song.

rĕfrain', v. to check one's self from doing something.

rĕfresh', v. to give new strength, power, or life : (of the memory) to bring facts back to mind.— adj. refresh'ing, bringing back strength : cooling.—n. refresh'-ment, that which refreshes (e.g. food and drink).

refrigerator, rĕ-frij'e-rā-tor, n. a machine which keeps food cool and so prevents it from going bad.

refuge, ref'ūj, n. a place of shelter (from attack, danger, etc.).—n. refugee', one who seeks shelter in another country.

rĕfund', v. to pay back.

rĕfūse', v. to be unwilling (e.g. He refused to leave the room) : to say 'no.'—ns. refu'sal ; ref'use, that which is thrown aside as worthless.

rĕfūte', v. to prove that what has been said is wrong.—n. refutā'tion.

rĕgain', v. to win back again.

rĕ'gal, adj. kingly, royal : very grand.—n.pl. regā'lia, certain marks or signs of royalty (e.g. crown and sceptre).

rĕgale', v. to entertain in a fine manner : to give delight to.

rĕgard', v. to look at carefully : to look upon with respect or affection : to consider (e.g. I regard you as a nuisance).—n. atten-

tion, care: (*pl.*) good wishes.—
adj. regard′less, paying no care
or attention.—with (or in) regard
to, regarding, concerning.

regat′ta, *n.* a race for yachts or
other small boats.

regency. See regent.

regenerate, rē-jen′er-āt, *v.* to make
new and good again, to reform.—
adj. reformed.—*n.* regenera′tion.

regent, rē′jent, *n.* one who governs
in place of a king.—*n.* rē′gency,
rule by a regent.

regicide, rej′i-sīd, *n.* the murder
of a king: the murderer of a king.

régime, rā-zhēm′, *n.* form of government.

regimen, rej′i-men, *n.* rule: diet and
habits to be followed.

regiment, rej′i-ment, *n.* a body of
soldiers, commanded by a colonel.
—*adj.* regiment′al.

region, rē′jun, *n.* a portion of land:
a stretch of country: neighbour-
hood.—*adj.* rē′gional.

register, rej′is-ter, *n.* a written list
(e.g. of attendances at school, of
people who have votes, of people
who are looking for work): the
distance between the highest and
lowest notes of a voice or instrument.—*v.* to set down in writing
(e.g. in a register): to vote: (in
the post-office) to pay a small
extra sum as postage so that
special care may be taken of a
letter.—*ns.* reg′istrar, one whose
duty it is to keep a register of
births, deaths, marriages; reg′is-
try, an office where a register is
kept.

regret′, *v.* to be sorry for.—*n.*
sorrow for anything.—*adjs.* re-
gret′ful; regret′table, unfortunate:
unwelcome.

reg′ular, *adj.* done according to rule:
arranged in order: happening at
certain fixed times: belonging to
the *regular army* (see below).—
n. a soldier of the *regular army.*
—*n.* regular′ity.—*v.* reg′ulāte, to
control by rules: to adjust the
works of a clock or watch so that
it may keep the right time.—*ns.*
regula′tion, a rule or order; reg′-
ulātor, a lever that controls the
speed, power, etc. of a machine.
—regular army, the part of the

army which is kept always in
training, even in peace time.

rehabil′itate, *v.* to give back rights
and powers which have been lost.

rehearsal, rē-hers′al, *n.* a private
practice of a play, concert, etc.
before performance in public.—
v. rehearse′, to hold a private
practice of a play, etc.: to mention a number of facts one after
the other.

reign, rān, *n.* rule: time during
which a king or queen rules.—
v. to rule.

reimburse, rē-im-burs′, *v.* to repay.

rein, rān, *n.* one of two straps attached
to a bridle for guiding a horse.—
v. to keep back, to hold in check.

reindeer, rān′dēr, *n.* a kind of deer
found in the Far North.

reinforce, rē-in-fors′, *v.* to support
and strengthen an army with
extra men: to add stronger
material to (e.g. *reinforced concrete,*
cement with a steel backbone to
strengthen it).—*n.* reinforce′ment,
an extra force, esp. of troops.

reinstate, rē-in-stāt′, *v.* to put back
in a former position of power.—
n. reinstate′ment.

reiterate, rē-it′e-rāt, *v.* to repeat
again and again.

reject′, *v.* to throw away, to cast
aside: to refuse to take.—*n.*
rejec′tion.

rejoice′, *v.* to be glad: to make glad.
—*n.* rejoi′cing.

rejoin′, *v.* to join again: to give an
answer to a reply.—*n.* rejoin′der,
an answer to a reply.

rejuvenate, rē-joo′ve-nāt, *v.* to make
young again.

relapse′, *v.* to fall back (e.g. into
ill-health, evil ways).—Also *n.*

relate′, *v.* to show how one thing is
connected with another: to tell
a story.—*ns.* rela′tion, rel′ative,
one who is of the same family,
either by birth or marriage:
connection between two or more
things; rela′tionship, connection.
—*adj.* rela′ted, of the same
family; rel′ative, having a connection with.

relax′, *v.* to slacken: to make
(laws, rules) less severe.—*n.* rē-
laxa′tion, a slackening: amusement, rest from work.

rělay', *n.* a supply of horses or men to relieve others on a journey.— *v.* to receive and pass on a wireless message or programme.—**relay race**, a race in which one runner goes a certain distance, a new runner continuing from there.

rêlease', *v.* to set free.—Also *n.*

rel'egate, *v.* to put away or lower.

rělent', *v.* to become less severe.— *adj.* **relent'less**, without pity.

rel'evant, *adj.* having to do with what is being spoken about.— *n.* **rel'evancy**.

rěli'able, *adj.* worthy of being trusted.—*n.* **reli'ance**, trust.

rel'ic, *n.* something which is left over: an old ruin: (*pl.*) a dead body or part of one.

relief, rê-lêf', *n.* a lessening of pain or anxiety: the coming of fresh soldiers to take the place of those who have been on duty, or to help those who are being attacked by an enemy: help given to a poor person: a way of carving in which the design stands out from its background.—*v.* **relieve** (rê-lêv'), to lessen pain or anxiety: to take over a duty from someone else: to come to the help of a town or army attacked by an enemy.

religion, rê-lij'un, *n.* the beliefs which are behind a person's way of worship: the worship of God. —*adj.* **reli'gious**, holy.

relinquish, rê-ling'kwish, *v.* to give up.

rel'ish, *v.* to like the taste of: to enjoy.—*n.* a good taste: appetite: a sauce.

rěluc'tant, *adj.* unwilling.—*n.* **reluc'tance**.

rěly', *v.* to have full trust in.—*n.* **reli'ance**, trust.

rěmain', *v.* to stay, to be left behind: to stay on in the same place: to last.—*ns.* **remain'der**, that which is left behind after the removal of the rest; **remains'** (*pl.*), that which is left: a dead body.

rěmand', *v.* to put a person back in prison until a full trial is made.

rěmark', *v.* to say: to notice.—*n.* something said.—*adj.* **remark'able**, deserving notice: famous.

rem'edy, *n.* a cure for an illness or evil.—*v.* to cure.

rěmem'ber, *v.* to keep in mind: to recall to the mind.—*n.* **remem'brance**, memory.

rěmînd', *v.* to bring a matter back to a person's mind.—*n.* **remind'er**, one who, or that which, reminds.

reminiscence, rem-i-nis'ens, *n.* the remembering of some event of the past: (*pl.*) a telling of the events, friendships, etc. of one's life.—*adj.* **reminis'cent**, reminding one of the past.

rěmit', *v.* to pardon: to do away with (e.g. a debt, a person's punishment): to send (money): to hand over (e.g. a prisoner to a higher court).—*ns.* **remis'sion**, pardon; **remit'tance**, money sent.—*adj.* **remiss'**, careless: not punctual.

rem'nant, *n.* a small remaining piece.

rěmon'strate, *v.* to set forth strong reasons against.—*n.* **remon'strance**.

rěmorse', *n.* sorrow for a fault: bitter repentance.—*adjs.* **remorse'ful**, filled with regret; **remorse'less**, cruel.

rěmote', *adj.* far distant in time or place: out of the way.

rěmount', *v.* to mount (e.g. a horse) again.

remove, rê-moov', *v.* to take from its place: to dismiss (a person from a post): to change one's dwelling-place: to dismiss.—*n.* a change to a higher class.—*n.* **remo'val**, a moving from one place to another.—*adj.* **remov'able**.

rěmū'nerate, *v.* to pay for something done.—*n.* **remūnera'tion**, pay, salary.—*adj.* **remū'nera'tive**, profitable.

rend, *v.* to split.

ren'der, *v.* to give up, to hand over: to translate into another language.—*n.* **ren'dering**, a translation.

rendezvous, ron'de-voo, *n.* a meeting-place fixed beforehand.

ren'egade, *n.* one who deserts his side, religion, or beliefs.

renew, rê-nū', *v.* to make new again: to begin again: to repair.—*n.* **renew'al**.

ren'net, *n.* a substance used in curdling milk for making junket.

rēnounce', *v.* to give up.—*n.* renun'ciation.

ren'ovate, *v.* to make like new again: to clean.—*n.* renovā'tion.

rēnown', *n.* fame.—*adj.* renowned (rē-nound'), famous.

rent, *n.* a tear, a split.

rent, *n.* a payment made for the use of a house, shop, land, etc.—*v.* to pay or receive rent for a house, etc.—*n.* ren'tal, money paid as rent.

renunciation. See renounce.

rēor'ganise, *v.* to put in a different and better order.

rep, repp, *n.* a kind of cloth with a fine, ridged surface.

rēpair', *v.* to mend: to make up for a wrong: to go (e.g. He *repaired* once more to his house).—*n.* the condition in which a thing is (e.g. The house is in bad *repair*).—*n.* reparā'tion, something which makes up for a wrong.

repartee', *n.* a smart, ready answer.

rēpast', *n.* a meal.

rēpā'triate, *v.* to send war prisoners back to their own country.

rēpay', *v.* to pay back.—*n.* repay'ment, that which is paid back.

rēpeal', *v.* to do away with a law that has been passed.—Also *n.*

rēpeat', *v.* to say or do over again: to say from memory.—*adv.* repeat'edly, again and again.—*ns.* repeat'er, an alarm-clock that rings several times: a gun firing several shots; repetition (rep-et-ish'n), act of repeating: saying of poetry from memory: copy.

rēpel', *v.* to drive back or away.—*adj.* repel'lent, disgusting.

rēpent', *v.* to be sorry for what one has done.—*n.* repent'ance.—*adj.* repent'ant.

repercussion, rē-per-kush'un, *n.* a jumping-back: an echo: an effect of something which has happened.

repertoire, rep'er-twar, *n.* the list of works that a performer, singer, etc. is ready to perform.

repetition. See repeat.

rēplace', *v.* to put something back where it was, or where it belongs: to put one thing in place of another, esp. something new in the place of something which has been broken.

rēplen'ish, *v.* to fill up one's supply again.

rēplete', rē-plēt', *adj.* full.

rep'lica, *n.* an exact copy (e.g. of a picture).

rēplȳ', *v.* to answer.—*n.* an answer: a hitting back.

rēport', *v.* to give an account of: to tell about: to write down and take notes of (a speech, meeting, etc.), esp. for a newspaper.—*n.* an account, description: a rumour: the sound made by the firing of a gun.—*n.* repor'ter, one who writes news articles for a newspaper.

rēpose', *v.* to rest.—*n.* sleep, rest.—*n.* repos'itory, a place where things are stored for safe-keeping: a shop.

reprehend', *v.* to blame.—*adj.* reprehen'sible, deserving blame.—*n.* reprehen'sion, blame.

represent, rep-rē-zent', *v.* to claim to be, to declare to be: to stand in place of: to act a part (e.g. in a play).—*n.* representā'tion, an image, picture: a strong claim.—*adj.* represent'ative, typical: standing for all of its kind.—*n.* one who stands for a district in Parliament, i.e. a member of Parliament: a commercial traveller.

rēpress', *v.* to keep down.—*n.* repres'sion.

reprieve, rē-prēv', *v.* to pardon a criminal.—Also *n.*

rep'rimand, *n.* a severe scolding.—*v.* to scold severely.

rēprint', *v.* to print again.—*n.* rē'print, another printing of a book.

rēpri'sal, *n.* the act of paying back wrong for wrong: revenge.

rēproach', *v.* to blame severely.—*n.* blame: something that brings blame.—*adj.* reproach'ful, bearing disgrace or shame.

rep'robate, *n.* a person of evil habits.—Also *adj.*

rēprōdūce', *v.* to produce again: to produce a copy of.—*n.* reproduc'tion.

rēproof', *n.* a scolding, blaming.—*v.* reprove (rē-proov'), to blame.

rep′tile, *n.* a crawling or creeping animal.

repub′lic, *n.* a form of government in which the rule is in the hands of the representatives of the people; the head is usually a president, and there is no king. France and the United States of America are republics.

repudiate, rĕ-pū′di-āt, *v.* to refuse to look upon as one's own: to deny.—*n.* repudiā′tion.

repug′nant, *adj.* hateful: distasteful (to person).—*n.* repug′nance.

repulse′, *v.* to drive back (an enemy).—*n.* a defeat.—*adj.* repul′sive, causing disgust, loathsome.—*n.* repul′sion, disgust.

repūtā′tion, repute′, *ns.* the name or character which a person has in the eyes of other people (e.g. a man of bad *reputation*, good *reputation*): fame.—*adjs.* rep′ūt-able, looked on as good or honourable; repū′ted, looked upon, considered (e.g. He is *reputed* to be very rich).—*adv.* repū′tedly, in the opinion of most people.

request′, *v.* to ask for earnestly.—*n.* an earnest asking for something: the thing asked for.

requiem, rek′wi-em, *n.* a hymn or mass sung for the dead.

require′, *v.* to ask: to need: to ask for as a right.—*n.* require′ment, a thing needed: a demand.

requisite, rek′wi-zit, *adj.* needed.—*n.* that which is needed.—*n.* requisi′tion, demand: an order to provide supplies (e.g. for a school, army).

requite′, *v.* to repay.—*n.* requit′al, payment in return.

rescind, rĕ-sind′, *v.* to do away with an order or law.

rescue, res′kū, *v.* to free from danger or harm: to deliver.—*n.* an act which saves from harm or danger.

research, rĕ-serch′, *n.* a careful search: close and careful study in order to find out new facts.

rēsem′ble, *v.* to look like: to say one thing is like another.—*n.* resem′blance, likeness.

resent, rĕ-zent′, *v.* to be angry at.—*n.* resent′ment, bitter feelings.

reserve, rĕ-zerv′, *v.* to keep back (for future use): to book a seat.—*n.* something kept back: (*pl.*) troops kept ready to help those already fighting: a piece of country set apart for natives or wild animals: want of frankness.—*adj.* reserved (rĕ-zervd′), shy.—*n.* reservā′tion, something kept back: a condition upon which a thing is done.

reservoir, rez′erv-war, *n.* a place where anything (esp. water) is kept in store.

reside, rĕ-zīd′, *v.* to have one's home (in).—*n.* res′idence, house, place where one lives: act, or period, of living in a place: a large house.—*adj.* res′ident, living in a place for some time.—*n.* one who has his home in a place.—*adj.* residen′tial, containing a large number of fine houses.

residue, rez-i-dū, *n.* what is left over.

resign, rĕ-zīn′, *v.* to give up one's office or post: to accept calmly (e.g. He *resigned* himself to his fate).—*adj.* resigned (rĕ-zīnd′), not complaining.

resil′ient, *adj.* springing back easily, elastic.

resin, rez′in, *n.* a sticky substance that oozes out from certain plants (firs, pines, etc.).—*adj.* res′inous.

resist, rĕ-zist′, *v.* to struggle against.—*n.* resis′tance, a strong stand against.

resolute, rez′ō-lūt, *adj.* bold: with mind made up.—*n.* resolū′tion, firmness of mind or purpose: a proposal put before a public meeting: the opinion of the meeting on any matter.

resolve, rĕ-zolv′, *v.* to decide: to separate into parts.—*n.* a fixed purpose, a firm plan.

res′onant, *n.* echoing.—*n.* res′on-ance, a deep, echoing tone.

resort, rĕ-zort′, *v.* to go: to turn to, make use of (e.g. He *resorted* to trickery to win the battle).—*n.* a holiday place.—**in the last resort**, as a last hope.

resound′, *v.* to echo: to be much mentioned.

resource, rĕ-sōrs′, *n.* a source of help: (*pl*) money, wealth of any kind.—*adj.* resource′ful, ready at thinking out the right thing to do.—**as a last resource**, as a last hope.

rĕspect', v. to honour : to pay attention to.—n. honour : (pl.) good wishes.—**with respect to this, in this respect**, concerning this matter.—adjs. respec'table, worthy of honour : worthy of notice ; respect'ful, showing respect ; respec'tive, used thus—John and Peter went to their respective homes, i.e. John went to John's home, Peter to Peter's.—adv. respec'tively, used thus—John and Peter had six books and three books respectively, i.e. John had six books, Peter had three books.

rĕspire', v. to breathe.—ns. respirā'tion, breathing ; res'pirātor, a mask worn over mouth and nose to purify the air breathed in.

respite, res'pit, n. a pause : rest.

rĕsplen'dent, adj. very bright.—n. resplen'dence.

rĕspond', v. to answer.—n. response', a reply : the answer made by the people to the priest during church services.—adj. respon'sible, liable to be called to account : trustworthy : important (e.g. He occupies a responsible position in the school).—n. responsibil'ity.

rest, n. sleep : peace : death : a pause.—v. to cease from action or work : to be still : to sleep : to be dead : to lean on or against a support.—adjs. rest'ful, quiet ; res'tive, rest'less, unable to keep still.

rest, n. what is left, the remainder.

restaurant, res'tŏr-ong, n. a place where meals may be bought and eaten.—n. restaurateur (res-tŏr-a-ter'), the keeper of a restaurant.

restitū'tion, n. the giving back of what has been lost or taken away.

restive. See rest.

rĕstore', v. to put back : to give back : to do up (e.g. an old building, a picture) and put it in a good condition.—ns. restorā'tion ; restŏr'ative, a medicine that brings back strength.

rĕstrain', v. to hold back, to check.

—n. restraint', want of liberty : self-control.

rĕstrict', v. to hem in : to keep in check.—n. restric'tion, something (e.g. a law or rule) which keeps one in check.

rĕsult', n. a happening which is due to something already done : the figure or answer got by working out a sum : (in games) the score.—v. to end up (e.g. The match resulted in a victory for us).

rĕsume', v. to take up again : to begin again.—n. resumption (rĕ-zump'shun), a new start.

résumé, rez'ū-mā, n. a short summary.

resurrection, rez-ur-ek'shun, n. the rising from the dead.—v. resurrect', to bring back to life or to use.

resuscitate, rĕ-sus'i-tāt, v. to bring back to life.—n. resuscitā'tion.

rĕtail', v. to sell goods in small amounts to the person who is going to use them : to tell a story fully.—ns. rē'tail, the sale of goods in small quantities to the actual user ; retail'er, a shopkeeper.

rĕtain', v. to keep possession of : to engage a person's services by paying a fee beforehand.—ns. retent'ion (see below) ; retain'er, a fee for services paid beforehand : a follower.

retaliate, rĕ-tal'i-āt, v. to return like for like, to hit back.—n. retaliā'tion.

rĕtard', v. to keep back : to make slow or late.

retch, v. to try to vomit.

rĕten'tion, n. the act of holding in.—adj. reten'tive, able to hold (e.g. a retentive memory, a memory which does not easily forget).

reticent, ret'i-sent, adj. not saying much, shy in speaking.—n. ret'icence.

retinue, ret'i-nū, n. the attendants who follow a person of rank.

rĕtire', v. to go back : to go to bed : to give up one's work and live on the money one has laid aside.—adjs. retired', out-of-the-way, quiet : having given up work ; retir'ing, shy.—n. retire'ment, quiet, loneliness : life after one has given up one's business.

rĕtort′, v. to make a sharp reply.— n. a ready and sharp reply: a bottle of thin glass.

rĕtrace′, v. to go back by the same way.

rĕtract′, v. to take back what one has said.

rĕtreat′, v. (of an army) to move backwards because of the pressing forward of the enemy.—n. a backward march: an out-of-the-way, little-known spot.

retrench, rē-trensh′, v. to cut down expenses.

retribution, ret-ri-bū′shun, n. punishment.

retrieve, rē-trēv′, v. to find again: to search for and fetch (e.g. The dog *retrieved* the shot bird).—n. **retriev′er**, a dog trained to find and fetch birds which have been shot.

ret′rŏgrade, adj. going backward: falling from better to worse.

ret′rŏspect, n. a view of the past.— adj. **retrospec′tive**, looking back on past happenings.

rĕturn′, v. to go or come back: to pay back.—n. a going back: profit: a paper giving facts and figures (e.g. a person's income-tax *return*).

reunion, rē-ūn′yun, n. a happy meeting of old friends.

rĕveal′, v. to make known: to show. —n. **revelation** (rev-el-ā′shun), that which is made known: a surprising piece of information.

reveille, rev-el′i, n. a bugle-call at daybreak to waken soldiers.

rev′el, v. to make merry: to take great delight in.—n. merrymaking, with dancing.—ns. **rev′eller**; **rev′elry**, noisy merrymaking.

revelation. See **reveal.**

revenge, rē-venj′, n. harm done to another person in return for harm which he has done.—adj. **revenge′ful**, full of a desire to get revenge.

revenue, rev′en-ū, n. money received as payments, income.

rĕver′berate, v. to echo.—n. **reverberā′tion.**

rĕvēre′, v. to look upon with great respect.—n. **rev′erence**, great respect.—adjs. **rev′erend**, worthy of respect: a title given to clergymen; **rev′erent**, showing respect: humble.

rev′erie, n. a day-dream.

rĕverse′, v. to turn upside down or the other way round: to back (a car).—n. the opposite: a defeat: the back, esp. of a coin or medal.—n. **rever′sal**, the act of reversing.—adj. **rever′sible**, (of clothes, rugs, etc.) able to be turned over and worn inside out.

rĕvert′, v. to come back to what was being spoken about: to turn back.—n. **rever′sion.**

review, rē-vū′, v. to give an opinion of (e.g. a book): to inspect (troops).—n. an opinion (e.g. of a book, of an event): an inspection of troops, etc.: a magazine giving opinions on books, events, etc.

rĕvile′, v. to say harsh things about.

rĕvise′, v. to examine and correct faults: to change (one's opinion). —n. **revision** (rē-vizh′un), the act of revising.

rĕvive′, v. to return to life, strength, or fame.—ns. **revi′val**, a return to life: a new interest shown (e.g. in a religion, in a trade); **revi′valist**, one who helps on a religious revival.

rĕvoke′, rē-vōk′, v. to do away with a rule that has been made: (in cards) to fail to follow suit.

rĕvŏlt′, v. to rise up against: to feel disgust.—n. a rising against those in power.—adj. **revol′ting**, causing disgust, sickening.

revolution, rev-o-lū′shun, n. a turning round a centre: rising of a people or party against those in power, causing a change in government: a complete change (e.g. in ideas, way of doing things). —adj. **revolu′tionary**, bringing about great changes (e.g. in government, ideas).—v. **revolu′tionise**, to bring about a complete change.

rĕvolve′, v. to roll or turn round.— ns. **revolu′tion** (see above); **revol′ver**, a small pistol the chamber of which holds a number of bullets and *revolves* after each shot is fired.

revue, rĕ-vū′, *n.* a light, musical theatre show.

revul′sion, *n.* disgust: a sudden change of feeling.

reward′, *n.* what one gets for one's labours: pay.—*v.* to repay.

rhapsody, rap′sod-i, *n.* wild and excited music, poetry, or speaking.—*v.* **rhap′sodise**, to talk wildly.

rhetoric, ret′or-ik, *n.* the art of good speaking or writing: fine, but rather empty, talk.—*adj.* **rhetor′ical**.

rheumatism, room′a-tism, **rheumati′cs**, *ns.* a disease which causes swelling and pain of one's joints.—*adj.* **rheumat′ic**.

rhinoceros, ri-nos′er-os, *n.* a large, thick-skinned animal, with one horn (or two) on the nose, found in Africa and India:—*pl.* **rhino′ceroses**.

rhododendron, rō-do-den′dron, *n.* a flowering shrub, with thick green leaves and large beautiful flowers, something like roses.

rhubarb, roo′barb, *n.* a plant, the stalks of which are used in cooking, and the root in medicines.

rhyme, **rime**, rīm, *n.* (in poetry) a likeness in the sound of the words at the ends of the lines of a verse: a short poem.—*v.* to sound like (e.g. 'Star' *rhymes* with 'are'): to write poetry.—*n.* **rhy′mer**, a poet.

rhythm, rithm, *n.* a smooth, flowing graceful motion: (in writing, esp. in poetry) a regular flow of words and phrases.—*adjs.* **rhyth′mic**, **-al**, smooth-flowing.

rib, *n.* one of the bones from the backbone which protect the chest: a spar of wood which strengthens the side of a ship.

rib′ald, *adj.* (of jokes, songs, etc.) low, vile, dirty.

rib′bon, *n.* a narrow strip or band of silk.

rice, *n.* the seeds of a plant, grown in well-watered ground in India and some other countries.

rich, *adj.* wealthy: containing much feeding material.—*n.pl.* **rich′es**, wealth.—*adv.* **richly**, greatly.

rick, *n.* a stack (e.g. of hay).

rick′ets, *n.sing.* a disease of children, causing softening and bending of the bones.—*adj.* **rick′ety**, unsteady.

rick′shaw, *n.* a two-wheeled carriage, pulled by a man.

ricochet, rik′ō-shā, *n.* bullet which skips along the ground, or glances off other objects.—Also *v.*

rid, *v.* to free: to drive away.—*n.* **rid′dance**, a clearing away.

rid′dle, *n.* a puzzling question: a kind of tray for sifting.—*v.* to make many holes in.

ride, *v.* to be carried on a horse, bicycle, or in a car, train, etc.: to manage a horse: to float at anchor.—*n.* a journey on horseback, bicycle, etc.—*n.* **ri′der**, one who rides: something added to what has already been said.

ridge, rij, *n.* a raised part between furrows: a mountain range.

rid′icule, *v.* to laugh at, to mock.—Also *n.*—*adj.* **ridic′ulous**, deserving to be laughed at, very silly.

rife, *adj.* very common.

riff-raff, *n.* rough, low people.

rif′le, *v.* to rob: to plunder.

rif′le, *n.* a musket with a grooved barrel.

rift, *n.* a crack.—**rift valley**, a long valley formed by the falling down of part of the earth's crust.

rig, *v.* to clothe, to dress: to fit a vessel with sails and ropes.—*ns.* **rig′ging**, ship's spars, ropes, etc.; **rig-out**, one's dress.

right, rīt, *adj.* correct, true: just: straight: on the side opposite to the *left* side.—*n.* that which is correct or good, and which ought to be done: something which we expect to be allowed to do: a fair and just claim: **right-hand side**.—*v.* to mend, to set in order: to put back in the proper position.—*adjs.* **righteous** (rīt′yus), living a good life, just (*n.* **right′eousness**): **right′ful**, having a just claim: **right′-handed**, using the right hand more easily than the left.—*ns.* **right-angle**, an angle of 90 degrees, i.e. like one of those in a square; **right-of-way**, a road or path, over private land, along which people may pass without being stopped.

rigid, rij′id, *adj.* not easily bent: stiff: strict.

rig′marole, *n.* a long, meaningless string of words.

rig′our, *n.* strictness: harshness.

rill, *n.* a small stream.

rim, *n.* an outside edge (e.g. the outer ring of a wheel, top of a cup).

rime, *n.* thick white frost.—See also **rhyme.**

rind, *n.* the skin of fruit: the bark of trees.

ring, *n.* a circle: a small hoop, often of gold, worn on the finger: a roped-in space for boxing.—*n.* **ring′leader,** the head of a wicked gang.

ring, *v.* to sound with a clear note (like that of a bell): to echo.— *n.* the sound of a bell.

rink, *n.* a sheet of ice for skating or curling.

rinse, rins, *v.* to wash lightly: to clean (e.g. a cup) by putting in and emptying out water.

rī′ot, *n.* a noisy disorder among a crowd of people.—*adj.* **rī′otous,** noisy.—**to run riot,** to become wildly excited, to run mad.

rip, *v.* to tear: to strip off.—*n.* a tear.

ripe, *adj.* (of fruit, grain, etc.) ready to be gathered in or eaten: (of plans) ready to be carried out: having lived and seen much (e.g. *ripe* age, experience).—*v.* **rī′pen,** to become ripe.—*n.* **ripe′ness.**

rip′ple, *n.* a little wave.—Also *v.*

rise, riz, *v.* to get up: (a river) to have its beginning or source: to fly upwards: to rebel: to increase. —*n.* a slope upwards: an increase in wages, prices, etc.—*n.* **rī′sing,** rebellion.—**to give rise to,** to cause; **to rise to the occasion,** to show that one is able to deal with a difficulty; **to rise above,** to find better to do than.

risk, *n.* chance of loss or injury: a danger.—*v.* to take the chance of.—*adj.* **risk′y,** dangerous.

ris′sole, *n.* meat minced and fried.

rite, *n.* something done as part of a religion.—*n.* **rit′ual,** the way of carrying out worship.

rī′val, *n.* one who is seeking the same object as another: an opponent, a competitor.—*v.* to seek to equal.—*n.* **rī′valry.**

riv′en, *adj.* split.

riv′er, *n.* a large running stream of water.

riv′et, *n.* a bolt for fastening plates of metal together by hammering both ends flat.—*v.* to fasten with a rivet: to fasten one's eyes upon.

riv′ulet, *n.* a small stream.

roach, *n.* a fresh-water fish.

road, *n.* a public way for travelling on.—*ns.* **road′stead, roads,** a place where ships may lie at anchor.

roam, *v.* to wander about.

roan, *n.* a horse with a dark-brown coat mixed with grey.

roar, *v.* to utter a loud sound: to cry aloud.—Also *n.*

roast, *v.* to cook before a fire, or in an oven.—*n.* meat roasted.

rob, *v.* to steal.—*ns.* **rob′ber; rob′-bery,** the act of stealing.

robe, *n.* a long gown or outer garment: (*pl.*) the dress which shows one's rank or position (e.g. the Lord Mayor's *robes*).—*v.* to dress.

rob′in, rob′in-red′breast, *ns.* a small bird, known by its red breast.

rō′bot, *n.* a working figure of a man: a person who does his work by habit, without thinking.

rōbust′, *adj.* strong, healthy.

roc, *n.* (in fables) a great bird, able to carry off an elephant.

rock, *n.* a large piece of stone.— *ns.* **rock′salt,** salt in solid form; **rock′ery,** a pile of small rocks with earth for growing plants on.

rock, *v.* to move backward and forward, or from side to side.—*n.* **rock′er,** curved support on which e.g. a rocking-horse swings.

rock′et, *n.* a tube containing materials which, when set on fire, give off a jet of gas driving the tube forward, used in a firework, for signalling, for launching a spacecraft: a spacecraft.

rod, *n.* a long, slender stick or bar.

rō′dent, *n.* any gnawing animal (e.g. rat, beaver, squirrel, rabbit, etc.).

rodeo, rō-dā′o, *n.* a round-up of cattle for marking: a show of riding by cowboys.

roe, *n.* the eggs of fishes.

roe, *n.* a female deer: a small kind of deer.—*n.* **roe′buck,** the male of the roe.

rogue, rōg, *n.* a dishonest person : a rascal.—*n.* **rog′uery**, dishonesty : mischief.—*adj.* **rog′uish**, wicked : full of mischief.

rôle, *n.* a part to be performed (e.g. by an actor in a play).

rōll, *v.* to turn like a wheel : (of a ship, or a person's walk) to rock or move from side to side : to rumble like thunder.—*n.* a bundle made by turning over and over (e.g. *roll* of cloth) : a small loaf : a rocking movement : a list of names : a long, rumbling sound.—*ns.* **roll′-call**, the calling of the names on the *roll*, to find who are present and absent ; **roll′er**, anything cylinder-shaped (e.g. *roller* of a mangle) : a long, swelling wave ; **roll′ing-stock**, railway engines, carriages, waggons, etc.

rol′licking, *adj.* noisy and full of fun.

rō′ly-pō′ly, *n.* a jam-roll pudding.

Roman, rō′man, *adj.* having to do with Rome.—*n.* a native of, or dweller in, Rome.—**Rom′an Cath′-olic Church**, the Church whose earthly head is the Pope, the Bishop of Rome.

rōmance′, *n.* an imaginary tale, with happenings which pass beyond those of real life.—*v.* to write or tell wild, fanciful tales.—*adj.* **roman′tic**, full of feeling and fancy : dealing with love.

romp, *v.* to skip about in play.—*n.* **romp′er**, a child's overall.

rood, *n.* a measure of area (the fourth part of an acre) : a cross carrying an image of Christ.

roof, *n.* the top covering of a house, building, coach, etc. :—*pl.* **roofs**.

rook, *n.* a kind of crow : a cheat. —*v.* to cheat : to take a person's money.—*n.* **rook′ery**, a place where rooks make their nests.

room, *n.* an inside division in a house : empty space.—*adv.* **room′y**, having plenty of empty space.

roost, *n.* a pole on which a bird rests at night.—*v.* to sit or sleep on a roost.—*n.* **roost′er**, a cock.

root, *n.* the part of a plant which is fixed in the earth, and which draws up sap from the soil : the real cause of any trouble : a word from which other words have grown (see also page 377).—*v.* to take root : to tear up by the root.—*adj.* **root′ed**, firmly planted : greatly felt (e.g. a *rooted* dislike).

rope, *n.* a thick cord, made by twisting strands of hemp, wire, etc.—*v.* to fasten or catch with a rope.

rorqual, ror′kwal, *n.* a very large whale.

rō′sary, *n.* a prayer to the Virgin Mary : a string of beads used in saying a rosary prayer.

rose, *n.* a white, yellow, pink, or red flower, with a sweet scent, which grows on a prickly bush : a light-red colour—the colour of the rose.—*adjs.* **roseate** (rō′zi-et), rosy : rose-coloured ; **rōs′y**, red : blushing.—*n.* **rose′-water**, scent made from rose leaves.

rosemary, rōz′mā-ri, *n.* an evergreen sweet-smelling shrub.

rosette, rō-zet′, *n.* a badge, shaped like a rose, made of ribbons : (in buildings) a rose-shaped ornament.

ros′in, *n.* resin (the sticky sap of some trees) in a hard form.

ros′trum, *n.* the platform from which a speaker speaks.

rot, *v.* to become or make rotten : to go bad from want of use.—*n.* decay : a disease in sheep.

rō′tary, *adj.* turning round like a wheel.

rōtate′, *v.* to turn round like a wheel (e.g. The earth *rotates* on its axis). —*n.* **rotā′tion**, turn : (of crops) a regular order in which various kinds are grown, one after another.

rote, *n.* used in phrase **by rote** = by heart, without understanding what is said.

rot′ten, *adj.* (of meat, fruit, etc.) having gone bad.

rōtund′, *adj.* round : plump.

rouge, roozh, *n.* a powder used to give colour to the cheeks or lips.

rough, ruf, *adj.* not smooth : uneven : not polished : coarse, harsh : hasty (e.g. a *rough* guess) : stormy.—*n.* a bully.—*v.* **roughen** (ruf′en), to make rough.—*adjs.* **rough′-cast**, covered with plaster and fine gravel ; **rough′-shod**, shod with roughened shoes (to prevent horses slipping on roads in frosty weather).—*n.* **rough′-rid′er**, one who breaks in horses.

roulette, rool-et', *n.* a game of chance, played with a ball and a board which turns like a wheel.

round, *adj.* shaped thus—◯: ball-shaped: plump.—*n.* a circle: a single bullet or shell (e.g. Each man had 10 *rounds* of ammunition): a burst of firing, cheering, etc. : a part-song (e.g. ' London's burning . . .') in which the singers, when finished, go back to the beginning: a division of a boxing-match: one game of golf.—*adv.* and *prep.* on every side: in a circle.—*ns.* **round about**, a merry-go-round: a meeting-place of roads, where traffic must move in a circle; **round'el**, a circle-dance; **round'elay**, a short song with a chorus; **round'ers**, a well-known ball-game.—*adj.* **round'about**, taking the long way of doing what is to be done.—*adv.* **round'ly**, boldly: plainly.

rouse, *v.* to raise or stir up: to awaken.—*adj.* **rous'ing**, stirring.

rout, *n.* a large party of merry-makers: a rabble.

rout, *v.* to defeat and drive away in disorder.—*n.* a confused flight.

route, root, *n.* the course to be followed: a road.

routine, roo'-tēn, *n.* a fixed, unchanging order of things.

rove, *v.* to wander.—*n.* **ro'ver**, a wanderer: a robber or pirate.

row, rō, *n.* a line of objects: a rank.

row, rō, *v.* to drive a boat by oars.—*n.* an outing in a rowing-boat.

row, *n.* a noisy quarrel: a noise.—*adj.* **row'dy**, noisy and quarrelsome.—*n.* a rough, noisy person.

row'an, *n.* the mountain-ash (a tree with bright-red berries).

row'el, *n.* the little sharp-pointed wheel in a spur.

:owlock, rŏ'lok, *n.* the oar-rest on the side of a rowing-boat.

roy'al, *adj.* kingly.—*ns.* **roy'alist**, one who supports a king; **roy'alty**, a royal person, or royal persons as a whole: a sum paid to the owner of the land containing a mine (so much for each ton), or to the author of a book (so much for each copy sold).

rub, *v.* to clean, polish: to wipe.—*n.* a wipe: a difficulty.

rub'ber, *n.* a tough elastic substance, used in bicycle tubes, tyres, etc.: (*india-rubber*) a piece of rubber used for rubbing out marks.

rub'ber, *n.* an odd number of games (three, five) in cards, cricket. etc.

rub'bish, *n.* waste matter: nonsense.

rub'ble, *n.* small, rough stone used in building.

rubicund, roo'bi-kund, *adj.* reddish, rosy-faced.

ruby, roo'bi, *n.* a red-coloured precious stone.—*adj.* red.

ruck, *n.* a wrinkle or crease.

ruck, *n.* a crowd: the crowd (e.g. of competitors) who never come to the front in a race.

rucksack, *n.* a bag carried on the back.

rud'der, *n.* the flat piece of wood or metal, fixed to the stern of a boat, by which it is steered.

rud'dy, *adj.* red: having the face a healthy red colour.

rude, rood, *adj.* rough in manners: not polite: roughly made.

rudiments, roo'di-ments, *n.pl.* the first steps in a subject. — *adj.* **rudimen'tary**, not going beyond the beginnings of a subject.

rue, roo, *n.* a bitter-leafed plant.

rue, roo, *v.* to be sorry for.—*adj.* **rue'ful**, sorrowful.

ruff, *n.* a frilled collar, worn in olden times.

ruffian, ruf'i-an, *n.* a coarse, cruel fellow.—*adj.* **ruff'ianly**.

ruf'fle, *v.* to wrinkle: to vex.

rug, *n.* a mat for the floor: a woollen cover (e.g. a travelling-*rug*).

rug'by, *n.* a form of football in which the ball may be carried—usually 30 players (15 on each side) take part in the game.

rug'ged, *adj.* rough: uneven: sturdy.

ruin, roo'in, *n.* downfall: destruction: (*pl.*) the remains of a building that has been pulled down, or has fallen to pieces.—*v.* to destroy: to make very poor.—*n.* **ruinā'tion**, overthrow: destruction.—*adj.* **ru'inous**, wasteful: lying in ruins.

rule, rool, *n.* government: a law (e.g. for the carrying on of business, playing of games, etc.):

a marked wooden or metal strip for measuring length.—v. to govern: to decide: to mark with lines.—n. ru'ler, one who governs: an instrument for drawing lines; ru'ling, a decision about some question.

rum, n. a spirit made from sugar-cane.

rum, adj. odd, queer.

rum'ble, v. to make a loud, dull noise.

ruminant, roo'mi-nant, adj. chewing the cud (like a cow).—n. an animal that chews the cud.—v. ru'minate, to chew the cud: to be deep in thought.

rum'mage, v. to turn things over in search: to ransack.—Also n.

rumour, roo'mur, n. talk which one hears but which may not be true. —v. to tell as a rumour.

rump, n. the end of the back-bone.

rum'ple, v. to crease.

run, v. to move swiftly, to hasten: to take part in a race: to flow: to smuggle (e.g. arms into a country).—n. the act of running: a flow: a pen for fowls: a drive: distance travelled: a scoring move in cricket.—ns. run'nel, a little river or stream; run'ner, messenger; run'ner-up, one who is second in a race or competition; run'ning-board, the footboard by the side of a motor-car or railway-engine.—to run out, (of stores) to become finished: (cricket) to hit a batsman's wicket while he is running and so put him out.

run'agate, n. a vagabond.

rune, roon, n. a letter used in certain old writing.

rung, n. a step or a ladder.

runnel. See run.

rupee, roo-pē', n. a coin of India, Pakistan, Ceylon (worth about 1s. 6d.).

rup'ture, n. a breaking (esp. of friendship): a painful trouble in the lower part of the body.—v. to break or burst.

rural, roo'ral, adj. having to do with the country.

ruse, rooz, n. a trick.

rush, n. a tall plant (growing in damp or marshy places) with a straight stem.

rush, v. to move forward in haste: to take (e.g. a fort) by a quick, sudden attack: to make a person hurry.—n. a quick, forward movement: a charge.

rusk, n. a kind of light biscuit.

rus'set, adj. reddish-brown.—n. an apple of russet colour.

rust, n. the reddish-brown coating which comes on iron and steel (caused by air and moisture).— v. to gather rust.—adj. rust'y, covered with rust: out of practice.

rus'tic, adj. belonging to the country. —n. a countryman.—v. rus'ticate, to live in the country: to banish a student (who has done wrong) for a time from a college.

rustle, rus'l, v. (of silk, straw, etc.) to make a soft, whispering sound.

rut, n. a deep track made by a wheel.

ruthless, rooth'les, adj. without pity, cruel.

rye, rī, n. a grain.—n. rye'-grass, a kind of grass grown for hay and cattle-feeding.

ryot, rī'ut, n. an Indian farmer.

S

Sab'bath, n. (among the Jews) the seventh day of the week, set apart for rest: (among Christians) the first day of the week, Sunday.

sa'ble, n. a small furred animal, like the weasel, valued for its dark-brown or blackish fur (called sable): black: (pl.) mourning clothes.—adj. black.

sabot, sab'ō, n. a wooden shoe.

sabotage, sab'ō-tazh, n. deliberate destruction of machinery, etc.

sabre, sā'ber, n. a cavalry sword.

sac, sak, n. (in plants and in animals' bodies) a bag for a liquid.

saccharine, sak'a-rin, n. a very sweet substance.

sacerdotal, sas-er-dō'tal, adj. having to do with priests.

sach′et, _n._ a small bag (e.g. for scent, handkerchiefs).

sack, _n._ a large bag of coarse cloth for holding grain, flour, etc.: dismissal from one's job.—_v._ to put a person out of his job, to dismiss.—_ns._ **sack′cloth,** cloth for sacks: coarse cloth once worn as a sign of mourning or sorrow for sin; **sack′ing,** coarse cloth or canvas used for sacks.

sack, _v._ to attack and plunder.— Also _n._

sack, _n._ a Spanish wine.

sack′but, _n._ a kind of trumpet.

sac′rament, _n._ (in Christian churches) the name given to certain important parts of the service (e.g. the _sacrament_ of the Lord's Supper, that is, Holy Communion; the _sacrament_ of Baptism).

sā′cred, _adj._ holy.

sac′rifice, _n._ an offering to God (in olden times the offering was usually an animal): something given up in order to benefit another person.—_v._ to kill and offer an animal to God in worship: to give up something for someone else.—_adj._ **sacrificial** (sak-ri-fish′al), having to do with a sacrifice.

sacrilege, sak′ri-lej, _n._ the using of a holy thing or place in a wicked way.—_adj._ **sacrile′gious.**

sac′rist, sac′ristan, _ns._ an official who has the care of the sacred cups, robes, etc. of a church.

sac′rosanct, _adj._ very sacred: not to be harmed.

sad, _adj._ full of sorrow: unhappy.— _v._ **sad′den,** to make sad.

sad′dle, _n._ a seat (usually of leather) on the back of a horse or on a bicycle.—_v._ to put a saddle on: to put a load on a person (e.g. His son _saddled_ him with many debts).—_n._ **sadd′ler,** a maker of saddles and harness (called **sadd′lery**).

safar′i, _n._ a hunting journey in East Africa.

safe, _adj._ free from harm or danger: sure.—_n._ a cupboard for foodstuffs: a strong heavy chest or steel box in which money and jewels may be locked away. —_ns._ **safe-conduct,** a passport

given to a person, so that he may travel in safety; **safe′guard,** protection: a passport to protect a traveller; **safe′ty,** freedom from danger or loss: **safe′ty-lamp,** a lamp (used by miners) which does not set on fire the dangerous gases of a coal-mine; **safety-razor,** a razor with a protected blade.—**safety first,** the motto of those whose aim is more careful use of the roads.

saf′fron, _n._ a crocus from which is obtained a yellow dye.

sag, _v._ to droop in the middle.

sa′ga, _n._ an old-time story of Norway or Iceland.

sagacious, sa-gā′shus, _adj._ very wise, quick at understanding.—_n._ **saga′city.**

sage, sāj, _n._ wise: a wise man.

sage, sāj, _n._ a plant of the mint kind, used for flavouring.

sā′go, _n._ a white, starchy substance (got from certain Eastern palms) used in puddings.

sah′ib, _n._ a term of respect given in India to persons of rank and to Europeans.

sail, _n._ a sheet of canvas spread to catch the wind: a journey in a ship: an arm of a windmill.— _v._ to travel by boat: to float along.—_n._ **sail′or,** a seaman.

saint, _n._ a person who is well known for holiness: a title given (by the Roman Catholic Church) after death to very holy persons (e.g. _Saint_ Patrick)—it is usually shortened to **St** (_St_ Patrick).— _adj._ **saint′ly,** very holy.

sake, _n._ cause: purpose (e.g. He did it for the _sake_ of making money; He did it for my _sake_).

salaam, sal-ahm′, _n._ an Eastern greeting: a deep bow.—Also _v._

sal′ad, _n._ a dish of lettuce, celery, mustard and cress, tomatoes, etc., cut up and served raw.

salaman′der, _n._ a small lizard-like animal (people used to think that it could live in fire).

sal′ary, _n._ the name given to the wages of teachers, bankers, clerks, etc.

sale, _n._ the act of selling: the selling-off of goods at lower prices than usual.—_v._ **sell.**

salient, sā'li-ent, *adj.* pointing outwards : standing out, chief (e.g. the *salient* points of a speech).— *n.* a jutting-out part (e.g. of a line of battle).

sa'line, *adj.* salty.—*n.* a salt spring.

sali'va, *n.* spittle.

sallow, sal'ō, *n.* a low shrub of the willow kind.

sallow, sal'ō, *adj.* of a pale, yellowish colour.

sal'ly, *n.* a sudden rushing forth (e.g. of troops to attack besiegers): an attack in words.—*v.* to rush out suddenly : to go for a walk.

salmon, sam'un, *n.* a large fish with fine-tasting reddish-orange flesh. —*n.* **salm'on-trout**, a large trout like the salmon.

salon, sal-ong, *n.* a drawing-room : a show of paintings.

saloon', *n.* a large room : a passengers' dining-room or sitting-room in a ship : (in a train) a car or carriage for dining or sleeping : a covered-in motor-car : (in America) a public-house.

salt, sawlt, *n.* a substance used for seasoning, usually found in the earth : an old sailor.—*v.* to sprinkle with salt.—*adj.* tasting of salt : bitter.—*ns.* **salt'-cellar**, a small table dish for holding salt ; **salt'-pan**, a dried-up salt lake.—**the salt of the earth**, the best kind of people.

salubrious, sa-loo'bri-us, *adj.* healthy (e.g. This is a *salubrious* place).

sal'utary, *adj.* having a good effect.

salute, sal-oot', *v.* to greet a person : to honour a person by a firing of guns.—*n.* an action of respect (e.g. a private soldier raising his hand to an officer as a mark of respect): a firing of guns as a welcome to a person.—*n.* **salūtā'tion**, a warm greeting.

salvage, sal'vāj, *n.* goods saved from destruction or waste : payment made for saving a ship from fire, wreck, or capture.—*v.* to save goods which are in danger.

salvā'tion, *n.* the saving of man from evil and its results.

salve, *n.* a healing ointment.—*v.* to heal : to save from damage by fire or wreck.

sal'ver, *n.* a tray.

sal'vo, *n.* a great burst of gun-fire, of bombs, or of clapping.

Sam Browne, *n.* an army-officer's belt.

same, *adj.* exactly like.—Also *n.*

sam'ite, *n.* a heavy silk cloth.

sam'pan, *n.* a small boat used in Far Eastern countries.

sam'ple, *n.* a small part taken from something to show what the whole is like : a specimen.—*v.* to take a sample of : to test the qualities of.

sam'pler, *n.* a piece of needlework to show one's skill.

sanatō'rium, *n.* a hospital, esp. for people suffering from disease of the lungs.

sanct'ify, *v.* to make sacred or holy : to free from sin.—*ns.* **sanctifica'tion** ; **sanc'tity**, holiness ; **sanc'tuary**, a sacred place : a place where one can be safe from pursuers.—*adj.* **sanctimo'nious**, making a show of holiness.

sanction, sangk'shun, *v.* to permit. —*n.* permission : a punishment for the breaking of a law.

sand, *n.* the fine powder of crushed or worn rocks : (*pl.*) stretch of sand on the seashore.—*adj.* **sand'y**, having much sand : like sand : (of hair) yellowish-red in colour.—*ns.* **sand-bag**, a bag filled with sand, used against bullets and fire-bombs ; **sand'-dune** (-doon), a ridge of sand blown up by the wind ; **sand'-glass**, a glass which measures time by the running of sand ; **sand'-martin**, a small swallow, which nests in sandy banks ; **sand'-paper**, paper (covered with a kind of sand) for smoothing and polishing ; **sand'piper**, a wading bird ; **sand'-shoe**, a light shoe, usually with a rubber sole ; **sand'stone**, a rock made of layers of sand pressed together.

san'dal, *n.* a shoe in which the sole is bound to the foot by straps.

sand'wich, *n.* two slices of bread with meat, ham, lettuce, etc. between.—*v.* to fit something between two other objects.—*n.* **sand'wich-man**, a man who walks the streets between two advertising boards.

sane, *adj.* healthy : of sound mind : sensible.—*n.* **san'ity,** soundness of mind or body : good-sense.

sanguine, sang'gwin, *adj.* blood-red : hopeful : cheerful. — *adj.* **san'guinary,** bloody.

san'itary, *adj.* helping on health.— *n.* **sanita'tion,** the branch of knowledge which has to do with health and cleanliness.

sanity. See sane.

sap, *n.* the juice of plants.—*v.* to drain of sap : to use up (e.g. to *sap* one's strength).—*n.* **sap'ling,** a young tree.

sap, *v.* to destroy by digging underneath.—*n.* a trench or tunnel by which the enemy's position may be approached.—*n.* **sap'per,** a private in the Royal Engineers.

sapphire, saf'īr, *n.* a precious stone of a beautiful blue colour.

sar'casm, *n.* a hurting remark, said in scorn.—*adj.* **sarcas'tic,** scornful.

sarcoph'agus, *n.* a stone coffin.

sardine, sar-dēn', *n.* a small fish of the herring kind.

sardon'ic, *adj.* bitter, mocking.

sar'i, *n.* the robe of Indian women—made by wrapping round the body a long piece of cloth.—*n.* **sarong',** kind of skirt worn by Malays.

sash, *n.* a band, ribbon, or scarf, worn as an ornament.

sash, *n.* a window-frame.

Sā'tan, *n.* the Devil.—*adj.* **Satan'ic,** having to do with Satan : devilish.

satch'el, *n.* a small bag for carrying books, papers, etc.

sate, *v.* to give more than enough.

sateen', *n.* a glossy-looking cotton or woollen cloth.

sat'ellite, *n.* a smaller body moving round a larger—as moon round earth : an object or vehicle fired into space to travel round a planet : one who hangs round an important person : a state strongly influenced by a more powerful one.

satiate, sā'shi-āt, *v.* to fill full : to give more than enough.—*n.* **satiety** (sa-tī'i-ti), over-fullness.

sat'in, *n.* a closely woven silk with a glossy surface.—*n.* **sat'inwood,** a smooth wood.

sat'ire, *n.* a piece of writing which makes a fool of certain people or of their ways.—*adj.* **satir'ical.**— *v.* **sat'irise,** to make certain persons or their ways look silly.

sat'isfy, *v.* to give enough to : to please : to free from doubt (e.g. His explanation *satisfied* me that he had nothing to do with the robbery).—*n.* **satisfac'tion,** a feeling of pleasure or fullness.— *adj.* **satisfac'tory,** good enough to please.

sat'rap, *n.* (in old-time Persia) a governor of a province.

sat'ūrate, *v.* to make overfull with moisture.—*n.* **satūra'tion.**

Sat'urday, *n.* the seventh day of the week.

sat'urnine, *adj.* gloomy, angry.

satyr, sat'er, *n.* a god of the woods—half man, half goat.

sauce, *n.* a liquid seasoning added to food, to give a sharp flavour : impudence.—*adj.* **sau'cy,** cheeky.

sau'cer, *n.* a small, deep plate, placed under a tea-cup.

saun'ter, *v.* to stroll about without hurry.—Also *n.*

sau'sage, *n.* minced meat stuffed into a skin.

sav'age, *adj.* wild : fierce and cruel. —*n.* a human being in a wild state : a fierce or cruel person.— *v.* to attack very fiercely.—*n.* **sav'agery,** cruelty.

savan'nah, *n.* a grassy, treeless plain.

savant, sav'ong, *n.* a learned man.

save, *v.* to bring out of harm or danger : to put by (money) : to keep safe.—*prep.* except (e.g. All were broken *save* one).—*ns.* **saviour** (sāv'yer), one who saves from harm ; **Saviour,** Jesus Christ ; **sā'vings,** money put by ; **sā'vings-bank,** a bank where people put by small amounts of money.

savour, sā'vur, *n.* taste.—*v.* to flavour : to taste of.—*adj.* **sā'voury** having a pleasant taste or smell. —*n.* a small course at the beginning or end of a meal.

savoy', *n.* a winter cabbage.

saw, *n.* a tool, with a toothed edge, for cutting wood, etc.—*v.* to cut with a saw.—*ns.* **saw'dust,** wood-dust, made in sawing ; **saw'-mill,** a mill where wood is sawn up ; **saw'yer,** one who saws wood.

saw, *n.* an old and wise saying.

sax'ifrage, *n.* a rock plant.

saxophone, sax'o-fōn, *n.* a kind of trumpet, with many keys.

say, *v.* to speak: to tell: suppose (e.g. Some boys, *say* ten, were in the hall).—*n.* right to speak (e.g. I have no *say* in the matter).—*n.* say'ing, a common remark.—**I say!** Dear me!

scab, *n.* a crust formed over a sore.

scab'bard, *n.* the sheath in which the blade of a sword is kept.

scabies, skā'bi-ēz, *n.* an itchy skin-disease.

scaf'fōld, *n.* a platform on which people are put to death.—*n.* scaf'folding, the poles and wooden platforms used by workmen when a building is being put up, repaired, or painted.

scald, skawld, *v.* to burn with hot liquid.—*n.* a burn so caused.

scale, *n.* a measure (e.g. the *scale* of a map): a number of musical notes following each other.—*v.* to climb.—**large (or small) scale,** dealing in large (or small) amounts (e.g. The making of motor-cars is carried on on a *large scale*).

scale, *n.* one of the small, thin flakes on the skin of a fish or snake: a thin layer.—*v.* to peel off in thin layers.—*adj.* scā'ly, covered with scales.

scale, *n.* a weighing-machine—often in *pl.*

scal'lop, *n.* a shellfish.—*adj.* scal'-loped, (in sewing) having an edge of a wavy appearance.

scalp, *n.* the skin and hair of the top of the head.

scal'pel, *n.* a doctor's knife.

scamp, *n.* a rascal.—*v.* to do work carelessly.—*v.* scam'per, to run about gaily: to run off in fear.

scan, *v.* to count the beats in a line of verse: to examine carefully.—*n.* scan'sion, the measuring of beats in a line of verse.

scan'dal, *n.* talk that runs down a person: that which breaks the ordinary rules of good conduct.—*v.* scan'dalise, to shock: to disgrace.—*n.* scan'dal-monger, one who spreads wicked stories about a person.—*adj.* scan'dalous, shameful, disgraceful.

scant, scant'y, *adjs.* not plentiful: hardly enough.

scape'goat, *n.* one who bears the blame for the wrong-doing of others.—*n.* scape'grace, a good-for-nothing fellow, a rascal.

scar, *n.* the mark left by a wound.—*v.* to mark with a scar.—*adj.* scarred.

scar, *n.* a bare rocky place on the side of a hill.

scarce, skārs, *adj.* not plentiful: not enough.—*adv.* hardly.—*n.* scarc'ity, want: shortage.

scare, *v.* to drive away by frightening: to strike with sudden terror. —*n.* a sudden fear.—*n.* scare'-crow, a dummy man set up to scare away crows or birds.

scarf, *n.* a strip of cloth, worn round the neck or on the shoulders:— *pl.* scarfs or scarves.

scar'ify, *v.* to scratch (e.g. the skin).

scarlatina, skar-la-tē'na, *n.* scarlet-fever.

scar'let, *n.* a bright-red colour.— Also *adj.*—*ns.* scar'let-fē'ver, a spreading fever, known by the scarlet rash; scar'let-run'ner, a bean-plant, with scarlet flowers, which climbs supports.

scarp, *n.* a steep slope.

scāth'ing, *adj.* (of talking or writing) bitter: saying cruel things.—*adj.* scatheless (skāth'les), without hurt or harm.

scat'ter, *v.* to throw loosely about: to send in all directions: to flee in all directions.—*n.* scat'terbrain, a thoughtless person.

scaur, *n.* a steep bank or rock.

scav'enger, *n.* a person who cleans streets: an animal which feeds on dead flesh.

scene, sēn, *n.* the place where an action happens: a painting: a small division of a play: a show of bad temper.—*n.* scē'nery, the painted background on a theatre stage: the general appearance of a stretch of country (mountains, rivers, lakes, cliffs, etc.).—*adj.* scēn'ic, having to do with scenery. —**scenic railway,** a small railway (e.g. at a fair) running through imitation scenery.—**behind the scenes,** happening privately.

scent, sent, *v.* to discover by the smell : to cause to smell pleasantly.—*n.* a smell (esp. a pleasant smell) : the trail of smell by which an animal may be tracked. —**off the scent**, on the wrong track.

sceptic, sceptical, skep'tik (-al), *adjs.* doubtful.—*n.* scep'tic, one who doubts (esp. in matters of religion).

sceptre, sep'ter, *n.* the rod which is the sign of a king's rule.

schedule, shed'ūl, *n.* a list of articles : a programme : a time-table.

scheme, skēm, *n.* a plan : a number of small houses arranged together according to some plan.— *v.* to make plans (often for evil purposes).—*n.* sche'mer.

schism, sizm, *n.* a breaking away of some persons from the main party (e.g. in a church).

schist, shist, *n.* a rock formed when clay is pressed together very hard.

scholar, skol'ar, *n.* a pupil : a man of great learning.—*n.* schol'arship, learning : a sum of money given to help a clever student to carry on further studies.—*adj.* scholas'tic, having to do with schools or scholars.

school, skool, *n.* a place of learning, esp. for children : a group of thinkers or artists who have the same ideas.—*ns.* school'days, the part of a person's life during which he attends school ; school'fel'low, one taught at the same school ; school'master ; school'mistress.

school, *n.* a large number of fish (or whales) of the same kind, swimming about together.

schooner, skoon'er, *n.* a sailing-ship with two masts.

schottische, sho-tēsh', *n.* a dance like the polka.

sciatica, sī-at'i-ka, *n.* a severe pain in the upper part of the leg.

science, sī'ens, *n.* all that is known about a subject, carefully arranged so that it may be studied : knowledge : the study of the facts of nature (e.g. heat, light, electricity, etc.) : trained skill in games.—*adj.* scientif'ic, having

to do with science : done in a way which shows careful thinking.— *n.* sci'entist, one who studies science (esp. the science of nature).

scimitar, sim'i-tar, *n.* a short, single-edged, curved sword.

scintillate, sin'til-ate, *v.* to sparkle.

scion, sī'on, *n.* a young member of a family : a descendant.

scissors, siz'orz, *n.pl.* a cutting instrument with two blades.

scoff, *v.* to make fun off, to mock.

scold, *v.* to find fault with, to blame. —*n.* a bad-tempered woman.— *n.* scold'ing.

sconce, *n.* a candlestick, fixed to a wall.

scone, skon, *n.* a kind of small cake.

scoop, *v.* to lift up (e.g. water) with something hollow : to dig out.— *n.* a large, short-handled hollow spoon, or ladle : a coal-scuttle : an exciting piece of news which one newspaper prints before other papers have heard about it.

scope, *n.* room to act or see or move : matters spoken or written about (e.g. What is the *scope* of this book ?).

scorch, *v.* to burn slightly, to singe : to dry up with heat : to ride a bicycle or drive a car at a very high speed.—*adj.* scorch'ing, burning on the surface : very hot.

score, *n.* a mark or notch for keeping count : a line drawn : an account : (in games) runs, points, or goals made : a written-out piece of music.—*v.* to write down (e.g. debts, points, etc.) : (in games) to make runs, goals, etc.—*n.* sco'rer, one who writes down the score : one who makes a run, kicks a goal, etc.—**to score out**, to remove from a list.

scorn, *v.* to look down on, to despise : to refuse to consider.—Also *n.*— *adj.* scorn'ful, full of contempt.

scorpion, skor'pi-un, *n.* a creeping beast like a small lobster, with a poisonous sting in the tail.

Scot, *n.* a native of Scotland.—*adjs.* Scots, Scot'tish, Scotch.—*n.* Scots, the dialect spoken in the Lowlands of Scotland.

scotch, *v.* to wound slightly.

scot-free, *adj.* unhurt : unpunished.

scoun′drel, *n.* a rascal, a worthless person.

scour, *v.* to clean (e.g. a pot) by rubbing with something rough.

scour, *v.* to run swiftly through a place in search of something.

scourge, skurj, *n.* a whip: a plague.

scout, *n.* one sent out to spy and bring in information: a Scout.—*v.* to act as a scout: to search out: to laugh at something, treating it with scorn.

scow, *n.* a flat-bottomed boat.

scowl, *v.* to wrinkle the brows and look angry.—Also *n.*

scrag′gy, *adj.* thin and rough: uneven, rugged.

scram′ble, *v.* to struggle to seize something before others: to wriggle along on hands and knees.—*n.* a rush and struggle to get something.—**scrambled eggs,** eggs beaten up with milk and butter and heated until stiff.

scrap, *n.* a small piece: a picture suited for pasting in a book: a short fight: (*pl.*) small pieces, odds and ends.—*v.* to throw away as useless.—*ns.* **scrap′-book,** a blank book for scraps or cuttings: **scrap′-heap,** a place where old iron is collected: rubbish-heap.—*adj.* **scrap′py,** (of writing, talking) made up of odds and ends, and not well put together.

scrape, *v.* to make a harsh or grating noise: to rub, polish, or clean with something sharp: to collect (e.g. money) with difficulty: to rub lightly.—*n.* a troublesome difficulty.

scratch, *v.* to mark with something pointed: to tear or to dig with the claws: to rub out: to take one's name out of the list of those entering a competition.—*n.* a mark or tear made by scratching: a slight wound.—*adj.* (in golf) very good (and so getting no allowance in competitions): (of a team) not made up of regular players.—**up to scratch,** as good as is wanted.

scrawl, *v.* to write untidily or hastily.—*n.* bad writing.

scrawn′y, *adj.* thin-looking.

scream, *v.* to utter a shrill, piercing cry, to shriek.—Also *n.*

scree, *n.* loose stones lying at the foot of a cliff.

screech, *v.* to utter a harsh, shrill, and sudden cry.—Also *n.*—*n.* **screech′-owl,** the barn-owl.

screed, *n.* a long tiresome speech or letter.

screen, *n.* that which shelters (e.g. from danger, from view, heat, cold, or the sun): a wooden division inside a building: the sheet on which a cinema- or lantern-picture is shown: a coarse sieve for sifting coal, etc.—*v.* to shelter or hide: to pass through a coarse sieve.

screw, skroo, *n.* a kind of nail with a winding groove or ridge (called the *thread*) on its surface, used for fastening and holding things together: a propeller of a steamer: a turn or twist to one side.—*v.* to fasten with a screw: to twist: to squeeze.—*n.* **screw′-driver,** tool for driving or turning screw-nails.

scrib′ble, *v.* to write carelessly.—*n.* careless writing.

scribe, *n.* writer: clerk: teacher of the law among the Jews.

scrim′mage, *n.* a disorderly struggle. See also **scrum.**

scrimp, *v.* to make too small or too short.—*adj.* short, scanty.

scrip, *n.* a note which shows that one has money in a business.

scrip, *n.* a small bag.

script, *n.* type like written letters.

Scrip′ture, *n.* the Bible (often in *pl.*).—*adj.* **scrip′tural.**

scriv′ener, *n.* a kind of clerk.

scroll, *n.* a piece of paper rolled up (in far-off times books were written on *scrolls* not on pages): an ornament like a scroll.

scrub, *v.* to rub hard, esp. with something rough.—*n.* brushwood: a low bush.—*adj.* **scrub′by,** mean.

scruff, *n.* the skin at the back of the neck.

scrum, *n.* (short for *scrimmage*). In rugby, a struggle for the ball by the forwards bunched together.

scruple, skroo′pl, *n.* a small weight: hesitation or doubt about what one ought to do.—*v.* to hesitate in deciding.—*adj.* **scru′pulous,** careful over the smallest details.

scrutiny, skroo'ti-ni, *n.* careful examination : careful second counting of the votes given at an election.—*v.* scru'tinise, to search very closely.

scud, *v.* to run quickly (e.g. The ship *scuds* before the gale ; The clouds *scud* across the sky).—*n.* misty clouds driven by the wind.

scuf'fle, *v.* to struggle at close quarters.—*n.* a hand-to-hand fight.

scull, *n.* a short oar.—*v.* to drive a boat onward with one oar, worked at the back of the boat.

scul'lery, *n.* the place for washing up and storing dishes, pots, pans, etc.—*n.* scullion (skul'yun), a servant who works in the kitchen.

sculp'ture, *n.* the carving of figures in wood, stone, etc.—*n.* sculp'tor, one who carves figures :—*fem.* sculp'tress.

scum, *n.* foam or froth that rises to the surface of liquids : the worst part of anything : worthless people.—*v.* to take the scum from, to skim.

scup'per, *n.* a hole in the side of a ship to carry off water from the deck (often used in *pl.*).

scurf, *n.* small flakes of skin sometimes found among the hair of the head.

scurrilous, skur'ril-us, *adj.* using low or foul words: insulting.—*n.* scurril'ity, low or foul talk.

scur'ry, *v.* to hurry along.—Also *n.*

scur'vy, *n.* a skin disease due to a lack of fresh food.—*adj.* suffering from scurvy: mean, low-down (e.g. a *scurvy* trick).

scutcheon, skuch'un, *n.* a short form of escutcheon.

scut'ter, *v.* to run quickly.

scut'tle, *n.* a metal or wooden box for holding coal.

scut'tle, *n.* a small opening (with a lid) in the deck, side, or bottom, of a ship.—*v.* to sink a ship by cutting holes in it.

scut'tle, *v.* to hurry away.

scythe, sīth, *n.* a large curved blade, on a long handle, for mowing grass, etc.—*v.* to cut with a scythe.

sea, *n.* a stretch of salt water : the swell of the sea in a storm : a great quantity or number (e.g. a *sea* of troubles).—*ns.* sea'-

board, land along the edge of the sea ; sea'-breeze, a breeze blowing from the sea towards the land ; sea'coast, the shore of the sea ; sea'-dog, the common seal: the dog-fish: an old sailor: a pirate ; sea'farer, a traveller by sea, a sailor ; sea'-fight, a battle between ships at sea ; sea'-gull. Same as gull ; sea'horse, the walrus ; sea'kale, a eatable vegetable of the cabbage kind ; (*pl.*) sea'-legs, ability to walk on a ship's deck when it is pitching or rolling ; sea'-lev'el, the level or surface of the sea ; sea'-lion, a large kind of seal ; sea'man, a sailor ; sea'manship, the art of steering and looking after ships at sea ; sea'-mew, the common gull ; sea'-plane, an aeroplane which can rise from and alight on water ; sea'port, a town with a harbour ; sea'-rob'ber, sea'-rō'ver, a pirate ; sea'scape, a picture of a scene at sea ; sea'-ser'pent, an imaginary sea monster ; sea'shore, the land close to the sea ; sea'sickness, sickness caused by the rocking movement of a ship ; sea'side, the land beside the sea ; sea'-trout, a name for a large trout, which spends part of its life in the sea ; sea'-ur'chin, a small sea-creature ; sea'weed, sea'-wrack (-rack), plants growing in the sea.—*adjs.* sea'faring, going to sea ; sea'-girt, surrounded by the sea ; sea'sick ; sea'-worthy, (of boats) in a good enough condition to go to sea.—at sea, on the sea ; quite puzzled.

seal, *n.* a stamp, with a raised design, for marking wax (sealing-wax) which closes a letter : the wax so marked.—*v.* to fasten with a seal: to close up completely: to make certain (e.g. They *sealed* the bargain with a handshake).

seal, *n.* a sea animal, hunted for its oil and furry skin, which is used for women's coats.

seam, *n.* the line formed by the sewing together of two pieces of cloth: a vein or layer of metal, ore, coal, etc.—*adj.* seam'y, having seams: unpleasant (e.g. the *seamy* side of life).—*ns.* seam'-

stress, semps′tress, a woman who sews for a living.

séance, sā′ongs, *n.* a meeting of people who believe that it is possible to receive messages from the spirits of dead people.

sear, *v.* to scorch.—*adj.* dry.

search, serch, *v.* to look around (for something): to explore.—*n.* an attempt to find: an examination.—*adj.* search′ing, looking over closely: going deeply into a matter (e.g. a *searching* question, inquiry).—*ns.* search -light, a very powerful electric light which may be turned in any direction; search′-warr′ant, permission from a court to search (e.g. in a house) for stolen goods.

sea′son, *n.* one of the four periods of the year: the usual or proper time for anything: any particular time: a short time.—*adjs.* sea′sonal, having to do with the seasons; sea′sonable, happening at the proper time: fitted for the season (e.g. Snow at Christmas is *seasonable*).—**in season,** suitable: fit to be eaten; **out of season,** unsuitable: unfit to be eaten; **season ticket,** a ticket which can be used over and over again for a certain time.

sea′son, *v.* to prepare for use: to flavour: to become ready for use (e.g. well *seasoned* wood, i.e. wood which has been cut and allowed to dry).—*n.* sea′soning, something (e.g. salt, pepper) added to food to give it more taste.

seat, *n.* something on which one sits: a mansion: a place in Parliament or a council: place where something is situated (e.g. the *seat* of government).—*v.* to place on a seat: to have seats for.

secede, sē-sēd′, *v.* to break away (from).—*n.* seces′sion.

seclude, sē-klood′, *v.* to keep apart, or away from people's notice.—*adj.* sēclud′ed, placed away from public notice.—*n.* seclu′sion.

sec′ond, *adj.* following the first.—*n.* one who is second: one who acts as attendant to a person who boxes or fights a duel: the 60th part of a minute of time, or of a degree (in measuring angles).—

v. to act: to support: to act as a supporter or attendant.—*adjs.* sec′ondary, second in position: not in the first rank: of less importance; sec′ond-best, best except one; sec′ond-hand, not new: that has been used by another; sec′ond-rate, not of the best quality.—*n.* second-sight, power of seeing into the future.— secondary school, a school for higher education.

se′cret, *adj.* kept from notice: hidden: private.—*n.* something hidden: something which, when told, explains a mystery.—*n.* se′crecy, darkness, mystery (e.g. There is an air of *secrecy* about his actions).—secret service, a body of men employed by a country to spy out the secret plans of another country.

sec′retary, *n.* one who writes letters for another: a high government official (e.g. the *Secretary of State for War*).—*adj.* secretā′rial, having to do with a secretary's work.

secrete, sē-krēt′, *v.* to hide: to give forth a juice or liquid (e.g. milk, saliva, resin, rubber, all of which are called secrē′tions).

se′cretive, *adj.* fond of doing things secretly: saying little to others about what one knows.

sect, *n.* a group of people who hold certain views, esp. in religious matters.—*adj.* sectā′rian, having to do with sects.

section, sek′shun, *n.* a part or division: the view of the inside of anything when it is cut open from top to bottom.

sec′tor, *n.* a part of a circle.

sec′ūlar, *adj.* having to do with the things of this world: not sacred: happening once in a hundred years.—*v.* sec′ularise, to turn something from sacred to common use.

secure, sē-kūr′, *adj.* free from fear or danger: safe.—*v.* to make safe: to seize and hold fast.— *n.* secū′rity, safety: property or goods which a lender of money may keep until his loan is paid back: (*pl.*) shares of money in a business.

sedan', *n.* a covered chair for one person, carried on two poles by two bearers.

sedate', *adj.* calm, cool: serious.— *n.* **sed'ative**, soothing medicine; **seda'tion**, use of sedatives.

sed'entary, *adj.* requiring much sitting (e.g. A typist's work is a *sedentary* occupation).

sedge, *n.* a coarse grass growing in swamps and rivers.

sed'iment, *n.* the grains or solid parts which settle at the bottom of a liquid: dregs.

sedition, sē-dish'un, *n.* action or speech which may lead to rebellion.—*adj.* **sedi'tious**.

seduce', *v.* to lead astray.—*ns.* **sedu'cer**; **seduc'tion**.—*adj.* **seduc'tive**, attractive.

sed'ulous, *adj.* trying hard.—*n.* **sedū'lity**.

see, *n.* the district of a bishop.— **Holy See**, the Pope's court.

see, *v.* to notice by the eye: to discover: to understand: to visit.— *conj.* **see'ing that**, since, because. —to see about, to find out about; **to see (a matter) through**, to work until it is finished; **to see through** (a person, a trick), to know enough not to be deceived by (him, it); **to see eye to eye with**, to agree completely with; **to see to** (e.g. tea), to prepare (tea).

seed, *n.* the grain or nut from which a new plant may be grown: children: (in a competition) a very good entrant picked to play in later rounds only.—*n.* **seed'ling**, a young plant from seed.

seed'y, *adj.* sickly.

seek, *v.* to look for: to try.

seem, *v.* to appear to be.—*adjs.* **seem'ing**, having the appearance of: **seem'ly**, (of behaviour) fitting, decent.

sē'er, *n.* a prophet.

see'saw, *n.* a game in which two children, seated one at each end of a board laid over a support (e.g. a barrel), move up and down with a swinging movement.— *adj.* moving up and down, or backwards and forwards.

seethe, sēth, *v.* to boil: to be very angry.—*adj.* **seeth'ing**.

seg'ment, *n.* a part cut off: the part of a circle cut off by a straight line.

seg'regate, *v.* to separate from others.—*n.* **segrega'tion**.

seigneur, sen-yer', *n.* (in old-time France) a title given to the lord of a great estate.

seine, sān, *n.* a large fishing-net.

seismic, sīs'mik, having to do with earthquakes.—*n.* **seismograph** (sīs'-mo-graf), an instrument which shows the place or direction of an earthquake and measures its force.

seize, sēz, *v.* to take by force: to grasp.—*n.* **sei'zūre**, the act of taking by force: something captured: a sudden attack (e.g. of illness).

sel'dom, *adv.* not often.

select', *v.* to pick out, to choose.— *adj.* picked out: the best.—*ns.* **selec'tion**, the act of choosing: something chosen; **selec'tor**, one who chooses.—*adj.* **selec'tive**, picking out: (of wireless sets) able to separate stations from each other.

self, *n.* one's own person:—*pl.* **selves**.—*adj.* **sel'fish**, caring only for one's own affairs.—*n.* **sel'fishness**.—*adjs.* **self-act'ing**, working by itself; **self-centred** (-sen'terd), looking after one's own affairs and forgetting other people: selfish; **self-con'fident**, full of trust in what one can do; **self-conscious** (-kon'shus), thinking too much about one's self and so acting strangely; **self-contain'ed**, not showing one's feelings: (of a house) complete in itself, not sharing anything with other houses; **self-ed'ūcated**, having taught one's self; **self-ev'ident**, clear enough to need no proof; **self-made**, owing one's rise to one's own efforts; **self-possessed** (-poz-est'), calm in mind or manner; **self-righteous** (-rī'chus), thinking a lot of one's own goodness; **self-sac'rificing**, giving up one's own good in order to do good to others; **self-same**, the very same; **self-sat'isfied**, quite pleased with what one has done; **self-seek'ing**, eager to make profit for one's self; **self-sufficient**

(-suf·ish'ent), needing no help: haughty; **self-willed**, fond of having one's own way.—*ns.* **self-control'**, the power of holding one's feelings in check: calmness; **self-defence'**, the art of defending one's self: boxing; **self-deni'al**, the saying of 'no' to one's own desires; **self-esteem'**, a good opinion of one's self; **self-gov'ernment**, the power given to a country to make its own laws and look after itself: home rule.

sell, *v.* to hand over and get money for.—*ns.* **sale**, the act of selling; **sell** (*slang*), a fraud; **sel'ler**, one who sells goods.

sel'vage, *n.* the side of a piece of cloth which does not pull away.

semaphore, sem'a-for, *n.* signalling by means of two arms which form different positions for each letter.

sem'blance, *n.* likeness: appearance.

sem'i, prefix meaning *half*.—*ns.* **sem'icircle**, half of a circle; **semico'lon**, a stop used in writing (;).—*adj.* **semidetached'**, (of a house) joined to another house on one side, but separate from other houses on the other.

sem'inary, *n.* a school or college.

Semit'ic, *adj.* Jewish.

semolina, sem-ō-lē'na, *n.* a floury food made from wheat.

semp'stress, *n.* a woman who sews.

sen'ate, *n.* in some countries (e.g. U.S.A.) the upper house of parliament: the council of law-makers in old-time Rome.—*ns.* **sen'ator**, a member of a senate; **senā'tus**, council ruling over a university.

send, *v.* to make to go.—*ns.* **sen'der**; **send'-off**, a joyful farewell.—to **send for** (a person, thing), to order (him, it) to be brought; **to send** (a person) **to Coventry**, to refuse to deal with him.

seneschal, sen'e-shal, *n.* steward in an old-time nobleman's household.

senile, sē'nīl, *adj.* having to do with old age (e.g. *senile decay*, weakness due to old age).—*n.* **senil'ity**, old age.

senior, sēn'yor, *adj.* older in age or rank.—*n.* one older in age or

S.D.—10

service.—*n.* **senior'ity**, state of being older in years or higher in rank or office.

sen'na, *n.* the dried leaves of a plant, used as medicine.

señor, sen-yōr', *n.* the Spanish word for Mr.—*ns.* **seño'ra**, Mrs; **señorita** (sen-yor-ē'ta), Miss.

sensation, sen-sā'shun, *n.* feeling by the senses: strong excitement.—*adj.* **sensā'tional**, causing great excitement.

sense, *n.* a power by which we feel or take notice (e.g. We have five *senses*—hearing, tasting, seeing, smelling, touching): wisdom (e.g. He usually acts with *sense*): meaning.—*v.* to feel.—*adjs.* **sense'less**, stunned (e.g. by a blow): foolish; **sen'sible**, wise: big enough to be noticed; **sen'sitive**, having feelings that are easily moved: quickly changed by light; **sen'sual**, pleasing the senses: wicked; **sen'suous**, moving the senses.

sen'tence, *n.* a number of words which together make a sensible statement: the punishment which a judge gives to a breaker of the law.—*v.* to state what a lawbreaker's punishment is to be.—*adj.* **sententious** (sen-ten'shus), full of meaning: high-sounding.

sen'timent, *n.* a thought: feeling: a thought expressed in words.—*adj.* **sentimen'tal**, showing too much feeling.

sen'tinel, sentry, sen'tri, *ns.* a soldier on guard.

sep'als, *n.pl.* the green leaves beneath the petals of a flower.

sep'arate, *v.* to set apart: to divide anything into parts.—*adj.* divided: not connected.— *n.* **separā'tion**, a dividing or putting apart.

sepia, sē'pi-a, *n.* a brown colour.

se'poy, *n.* an Indian soldier in the British army in India.

sept, *n.* a clan.

Septem'ber, *n.* the ninth month of the year.

septen'nial, *adj.* lasting seven years: happening every seven years.

sep'tic, *adj.* (of a wound) poisoning the blood.

septuagenarian, sep-tū-aj-e-nā'ri-an, *n.* a person seventy years old.

sepulchre, sep'ul-ker, *n.* a place of burial : tomb.—*adj.* **sepul'chral,** having to do with sepulchres : (of a voice) deep or gloomy in tone.

sequel, sē'kwel, *n.* that which follows : result, consequence.

sequence, sē'kwens, *n.* a number of things following each other.

sequestered, sē-kwes'terd, *adj.* lying out of the way : lonely, quiet.

sequestrate, sē-kwes'trāt, *v.* to take a person's goods and sell them in order to get money to pay his debts.

sequin, sē'kwin, *n.* a sparkling ornament worn on dresses.

sequoia, sē-kwoi'a, *n.* a giant tree, growing in the west of America.

seraglio, se-ral'yō, *n.* a Turkish palace : the women's place in a palace.

seraph, ser'af, *n.* an angel of the highest rank :—*pl.* **seraphs, seraphim.**—*adj.* **seraph'ic,** like an angel : pure.

sere, sēr, *adj.* dry, withered.

serenade, ser-e-nād', *n.* evening music in the open air, esp. under a lady's window : soft music.—*v.* to sing or play a serenade.

serene, sē-rēn', *adj.* calm : bright : not worried.—*n.* **seren'ity,** calmness, peace.

serf, *n.* a slave bought and sold with the land on which he works.—*n.* **serf'dom,** slavery.

serge, serj, *n.* a strong cloth.

sergeant, sar'jent, *n.* a rank in the army above corporal : a policeman above the ordinary rank.—*n.* **ser'geant-ma'jor,** an army rank, above ordinary sergeant.

serial, sē'rial, *n.* a tale printed, a part at a time, in a magazine or newspaper.

series, sē'rēz, *n.* a number of things of the same kind following each other :—*pl.* **series.**

serious, sē'ri-us, *adj.* not joyful : in earnest : important : thoughtful : apt to cause danger.

sermon, ser'mon, *n.* a talk about a verse from the Bible : a speech.

serpent, ser'pent, *n.* a snake.—*adj.* **ser'pentine,** wave-shaped, like a moving serpent.—*n.* a mineral of a greenish colour.

serried, ser'rid, *adj.* crowded together.

serum, *n.* a liquid put into a person's blood to fight against disease germs.

serve, *v.* to work for and obey : to attend or wait upon at table, etc. : to give out food, goods, etc. : to be used as (e.g. The cave will *serve* as a shelter from the storm) : (in tennis) to throw up the ball and hit it with the racket.—*ns.* **ser'vant,** one who works for, and obeys a master : a person paid to do house-work ; **service** (ser'vis), duty of a servant : worship : use : time spent in army, navy, air force : the first hit in each point of a tennis game.—*adj.* **ser'viceable,** useful.—**Serves him right !** He deserves it.

serviette, ser-vi-et', *n.* a table-napkin.

servile, ser'vīl, *adj.* like a slave : following without thinking.—*ns.* **servil'ity ; ser'vitor,** a man-servant, esp. one who looks after a college ; **ser'vitude,** slavery.

session, sesh'un, *n.* a meeting of a court or council.

set, *v.* to place : to put together (e.g. the broken parts of a limb, type for printing) : (of the sun) to sink out of sight at the end of the day : (of a jelly) to become firm.—*adj.* fixed : firm : (of the sun) sunk out of sight.—*n.* a number of persons or things that are alike : a number of games in tennis (not less than six) : small paving block (also **sett**).—*ns.* **set'-back,** a movement in the wrong direction : a defeat ; **set'-square,** a three-cornered ruler ; **set'ting,** background : music written to suit certain words ; **set'-to,** a fight.—**to set about,** to begin (to do) ; **to set in,** to begin (e.g. Winter *set in*) ; **to set off** (or **out**), to depart ; **to set upon,** to attack.

settee', *n.* a kind of sofa.

set'ter, *n.* a hunting dog.

set'tle, *v.* to place in a fixed position : to agree over a matter : to become calm or quiet : (with *down*) to make one's home in a place : to bring people to live in a country : to pay a bill.—*n.*

set′tlement, the act of settling: the decision which ends an argument: payment for a bill: money given to a woman on her marriage: a number of people who have come to live in a place (the people are called **set′tlers**).

set′tle, n. a long seat, with a high back.

sev′er, v. to cut apart or away.—n. **sev′erance**.

sev′eral, adj. more than one or two, a good many: different (e.g. The boys went their *several* ways).

severe, se-vēr′, adj. serious: harsh: strict: (of weather) very stormy or cold.—n. **sever′ity**.

sew, sō, v. to join together with a needle and thread.

sewer, soo′er, n. an underground drain for carrying off water and waste matter.—ns. **sewage** (soo′āj), water and waste matter; **sewerage**, a system of draining by sewers.

sex, n. a word used when speaking of the difference between male and female (e.g. A boy is of the male *sex*, a girl of the female *sex*).—adj. **sex′ual**, having to do with matters of sex.

sex, prefix meaning *six*.—ns. **sexagenā′rian**, a person sixty years old; **sexcenten′ary**, the six-hundredth year since some event took place (e.g. 1914 was the *sexcentenary* of the Battle of Bannockburn).

sex′tant, n. an instrument used for measuring angles.

sex′ton, n. a man who works about a church, and sees to the ringing of the bell and to the digging of graves.

shab′by, adj. worn-looking: poorly dressed: mean, low-down.

shack, n. a roughly-built cabin, usually of wood.

shack′le, v. to fasten with a chain: to hold in check.—n.pl. **shackles**, chains fastening the limbs.

shad, n. a fish of the herring family.

shade, n. half darkness: a cool place, out of the sun: a shelter from the sun or light: the deep-ness of a colour: a ghost.—v. to shelter from the sun or light: to darken.—adj. **shā′dy**, sheltered from the sun: likely to be evil.—ns. **shād′ing**, the marking of the darker places in a picture; **shadow** (shad′ō), a dark patch caused by some object coming in the way of a light: a person who follows another about everywhere: a ghost.—v. to follow a person about and watch him closely.—adj. **shad′owy**, full of shadows: not real, fanciful: likely to be evil.

shaft, n. the long rod on which the head of an axe, spear, arrow, etc. is fixed: an arrow: a rod which turns a machine: the pole of a carriage to which the horses are tied: the deep, narrow passage-way leading to a mine: a ray of light: the main part of a pillar.

shag, n. rough woolly hair: tobacco cut in fine shreds: a diving bird (the cormorant).—adj. **shag′gy**, rough, hairy, or woolly.

shagreen′, n. green leather made of horse, seal, or shark skin.

shah, n. the king of Persia.

shake, v. to move quickly backwards and forwards: to tremble: to disturb.—n. trembling: a shock: a drink mixed by shaking or stirring quickly.—adj. **shā′ky**, not firm, weak.—n. **shake′-down**, a hastily made bed.—**to shake hands**, to clasp hands in greeting (to show pleasure, end a quarrel); **to shake one's faith (in)**, to make one have doubts (about).

shako′, n. soldier's cap, with peak.

shale, n. a kind of rock, from which oil is got.

shal′lop, n. a light boat.

shallot′, n. a kind of onion.

shallow, shal′ō, n. a place where the water is not deep.—adj. not deep: not wise.

sham, n. something which is not what it appears to be.—adj. false: pretended.—v. to pretend.

sham′ble, v. to walk in a shuffling manner.

sham′bles, n. a slaughterhouse: a battle-field on which many lie killed and wounded.

shame, *n.* a painful feeling caused by wrong-doing, disgrace, mockery, etc.—*v.* to cause to blush: to bring disgrace on.—*adjs.* **shame'faced,** very shy; **shame'ful,** disgraceful; **shame'less,** having no shame: cheeky. — **for shame!** a phrase meaning 'You should be ashamed!'

sham'my, *n.* chamois-leather.

shampoo', *v.* to wash the hair thoroughly with soap and water.

sham'rock, *n.* a small plant, with leaves divided in three—the national plant of Ireland.

shanghai, shang-hī', *v.* to give a person a sleeping-medicine and carry him off before he wakens.

shank, *n.* the part of the leg between the knee and the foot: the part of a tool joining the handle to the head.

shan'ty, *n.* a roughly-made dwelling-place: a sailors' song (also spelt **chanty**).

shape, *n.* the form or outline of anything: a dish or tin for making a pudding: a jelly-like pudding. —*v.* to make in a certain form: to show how one is likely to act (e.g. He *shapes* well at football). —*adjs.* **shape'less,** not regularly shaped; **shape'ly,** regular in form: of good appearance.

share, *n.* one of the parts into which a thing is divided: one of the parts into which the money of a business firm is divided (the profits are paid by paying a certain amount for every share). —*v.* to divide out among a number of people, giving each a share: to have a part in.—*n.* **share'holder,** a person who has one or more shares, or parts, in the money of a business company.

shark, *n.* a large, very fierce, and greedy sea-fish: a wicked and greedy person.

sharp, *adj.* having a thin cutting edge or fine point: quick at understanding: hurting, stinging, biting (e.g. *sharp* wind, *sharp* words). —*adv.* punctually (e.g. 10 a.m. *sharp*).—*n.* a sign (♯) used in music to show that a note is to be raised half a tone.—*v.* **shar'pen,**

to make sharp.—*ns.* **shar'pener,** an instrument for sharpening; **shar'per,** a cheat (esp. at cards); **sharp'shooter,** a rifleman with a good aim.—*adjs.* **sharp-sight'ed,** having keen sight; **sharp-wit'ted,** quick-thinking.—**sharp practice,** cheating; **Look sharp!** = Hurry!

shat'ter, *v.* to break in pieces: to upset (e.g. a person's hopes).

shave, *v.* to cut away hair with a razor: to cut away (e.g. wood) with a plane or knife: to pass very near without touching.—*n.* act of shaving: a narrow escape. —*n.* **shā'ving,** a very thin slice.

shawl, *n.* a loose-knitted woollen covering for the shoulders.

she, *pron.* some (female) person already spoken about; subject of verb.

shay, *n.* a chaise.

sheaf, *n.* a bundle (e.g. corn, papers) tied together:—*pl.* **sheaves.**

shear, *v.* to cut with scissors (esp. the wool from a sheep's back). —*ns.* **shear'er;** **shears** (*pl.*), large scissors.

sheath, *n.* a close-fitting case for a sword or dagger.—*v.* **sheathe** (sheath), to put into a sheath.

shed, *v.* to throw or cast off (e.g. The moon *sheds* its light; The girl *sheds* tears; The trees *shed* their leaves).

shed, *n.* a small building outside a house, an out-house: a parting (e.g. of the hair).

sheen, *n.* brightness: gloss.

sheep, *n.* a well-known animal from whose wool clothing is made: a very meek person, afraid to think for himself.—*adj.* **sheep'ish,** shy and frightened.— *ns.* **sheep'-cote,** a shelter for sheep; **sheep'-dog,** a dog trained to look after sheep; **sheep'-run,** **sheep'walk,** a feeding-ground for sheep; **sheep'shank,** a sailor's knot, used for shortening a rope.

sheer, *adj.* very steep: pure, not mixed (e.g. *sheer* delight, *sheer* nonsense).—*v.* to turn aside from a straight line.

sheet, *n.* a large thin piece of anything (e.g. cotton cloth, glass, paper); a stretch of water or ice: the rope fastened to the

lower corner of a sail: a sail.—
ns. sheet'ing, material used for
making sheets; sheet-light'ning,
lightning which appears in great
sheets or flashes; sheet'-anchor,
the largest anchor of a ship, only
used in cases of great danger:
something upon which one can
trust fully in time of danger.

sheikh, shāk, *n.* an Arab chief.

shek'el, *n.* an old-time Jewish
weight and coin, mentioned in
the Bible.

shelf, *n.* a board fixed on a wall, for
laying things on: a sand-bank:
—*pl.* shelves.

shell, *n.* a hard outer covering (e.g.
of an egg, nut, pea-pod): a
metal case, filled with powder
and shot, fired from a gun.—*v.*
to take the shell from: to fire
shells at.—*adj.* shel'ly, covered
with shells.—*n.* shell'fish, a water
creature covered with a shell (e.g.
oyster, limpet, mussel).

shellac', *n.* a kind of resin, sold in
thin flakes, and used for making
varnish, polish, and gramophone
records.

shel'ter, *n.* something which acts as
a protection from harm, rain,
sun, etc.—*v.* to give protection
to.

shelve, *v.* to put up shelves: to put
something (e.g. a plan) aside for
the time being: to slope gently
(e.g. The land *shelves* towards
the sea).

shepherd, shep'erd, *n.* a man who
looks after sheep:—*fem.* shep'-
herdess.—*v.* shep'herd, to watch
over carefully, to guide.

sher'bet, *n.* a fizzing drink, made
from fruit juices.

sher'iff, *n.* an important law official
in a county: (in Scotland) a judge.

sher'ry, *n.* a kind of wine, which
gets its name from the Spanish
town of Jerez.

Shet'land pony, a small shaggy
pony; Shetland wool, a very
fine wool, made from the wool
of the sheep of the Shetland
Isles.

shew, shō, *v.* another spelling of
show.—*n.* shewbread. See show-
bread.

shib'boleth, *n.* a word for testing

whether a person belongs to a
certain party: an old-fashioned
belief. (The story of the word
is told in Judges xii. 4–6.)

shield, shēld, *n.* (in olden times) a
piece of armour (of metal or
strong leather) carried for defence—usually worn on the left
arm, to keep off blows: anything which protects from harm.
—*v.* to protect from harm, to
defend.

shift, *v.* to change: to remove: to
do a job for one's self (e.g. He
will have to *shift* for himself).
—*n.* a change (e.g. of clothes,
house): a group of workers on
duty at the same time (e.g. I am
on the *day-shift*): a plan to get
out of a difficulty, a dodge.—
adjs. shift'less, having no set
plan: unable to think for one's
self: shif'ty, not to be trusted.

shilla'lah, *n.* an Irish name for a
wooden club.

shil'ling, *n.* a coin (before 1971),
$\frac{1}{20}$th of £1.

shil'ly-shal'ly, *v.* to hesitate in making up one's mind.

shim'mer, *v.* to shine with a quivering
light.—Also *n.*

shin, *n.* the large bone in the leg,
below the knee.—*v.* (with *up*) to
climb.

shin'dy, *n.* a noise, uproar.

shine, *v.* to give out a steady light:
to be bright or beautiful: to be
very good at (e.g. He *shines* at
arithmetic.—*n.* brightness: sunny
weather. — *adj.* shi'ny, bright,
glossy.

shing'le, *n.* a thin strip of wood,
used in making roofs: coarse
gravel on the shores of rivers or
of the sea: a way of cutting
women's hair, so that it is short
at the back.—*n.pl.* shingles, a
painful disease, often causing
skin trouble round the waist.—
v. to cut the hair short at the
back.

shin'ty, *n.* a Scottish ball game,
something like hockey.

ship, *n.* any large boat which goes
on sea voyages.—*v.* to take on
to a ship (e.g. goods for sending
away, water during a storm):
to go by ship.—*ns.* ship'-breaker,

one who takes old ships to pieces and sells the parts; **ship'-brōker,** one who sells and buys ships, and does various other kinds of business connected with them; **ship'-builder,** one who makes ships; **ship'-canal,** a canal deep enough for sea-going ships (e.g. the *Manchester Ship Canal*); **ship'-chandler,** one who buys and sells ships' stores; **ship'master,** a ship's captain; **ship'mate,** a fellow-sailor; **ship'ment,** goods put on a ship; **ship'ping,** ships looked on as a whole; **ship'-wreck** (-rek), the loss of a ship at sea; **ship'wright** (-rīt), a carpenter at the building of a ship; **ship'-yard,** the yard in which ships are built.—*adj.* **ship-shape,** in good order, trim, tidy.

shire, *n.* a county.

shirk, *v.* to avoid doing one's duty.—*n.* **shirk'er.**

shirt, *n.* a garment, having sleeves, worn by men on the upper part of the body.—*n.* **shirt-blouse,** a woman's blouse, with collar and cuffs.

shiv'er, *v.* to tremble (e.g. with cold or fear): to break into small pieces.—*n.* a small broken piece.

shoal, *n.* a great number together (e.g. a *shoal* of herring).—*v.* to travel in shoals.

shoal, *n.* a shallow place, a sand-bank.—*v.* to become less deep.

shock, *n.* a sudden blow, coming with great force: unexpected bad news: sudden illness caused by blood clogging the brain: sudden shaking caused by an electric current: an earthquake.—*v.* to shake with force: to upset with bad news or bad behaviour.—**shock troops,** soldiers specially trained for hard fighting.

shock, *n.* a heap of sheaves of corn: tangled hair.—*adj.* **shock-headed,** having long and untidy hair.

shod, *adj.* wearing shoes.

shod'dy, *adj.* cheap and badly made.—*n.* old wool and cloth pulled to pieces and used for the making of new material.

shoe, **shoo,** *n.* a covering for the foot, not reaching above the ankle.—*v.* to put shoes on (e.g. a horse).—*ns.* **shoe'black,** one who cleans shoes on the street; **shoe'horn,** a curved piece of horn or metal used for making one's shoe slip easily over one's heel; **shoe'maker,** one who makes and mends shoes.

shoo! Go away!

shoon, *n.pl.* an old name for shoes.

shoot, *v.* to let fly with force: to send a bullet from a gun, or an arrow from a bow: to kick for a goal: (of plants) to send forth new twigs: to make a cinematograph film.—*n.* a hunting outing: a new twig.—*ns.* **shooting-gallery,** a place indoors for shooting practice; **shooting-star,** a 'falling star'—really a rock (from some heavenly body) which becomes red-hot when flying through the air.

shop, *n.* a place where goods are sold: a place where work is done.—*v.* to visit a shop and buy goods.—*ns.* **shop'lifter,** one who steals things from a shop which he visits; **shop'walker,** one who walks about a shop and sees that customers are being served.—**to talk shop,** to talk about one's work when one is off duty.

shore, *n.* the land beside sea, river, or lake.—*adj.* **shore-going,** living on, or belonging to, the land.

shore, *n.* a prop or support.—*v.* to support with wooden beams.

shorn, *adj.* with hair or wool cut.

short, *adj.* lacking in length or weight: (of the voice) sharp, rude: crumbling away easily.—*n.pl.* **shorts,** trousers reaching only to the knee.—*adv.* **short'ly,** very soon.—*v.* **shor'ten,** to make less in length. — *adjs.* **short-handed,** having fewer helpers than usual; **short-sighted,** able to see clearly only a short distance: thinking only of the present; **short - tempered,** easily made angry.—*ns.* **shor'tage,** an amount that is not enough for the needs; **short'bread,** rich tea-cake, like biscuit; **short-cir'cuit,** an escape of electricity by a short cut, often causing sparking and fire; **short'-coming,** a fault, sin; **short-commons,** small supply of food; **short'hand,** a way of writing, using strokes and dots to show sounds — much quicker than ordinary writing; **short-shrift,** quick punishment.—**in short,** in a few words; **to make short work of,** to settle a difficulty very quickly; **short cut,** a quicker way than usual; **the long and short of the matter,** the matter put in a few words.

shot, *n.* something which is shot or fired : small lead bullets, used in cartridges : the noise made by a gun : the distance covered by a bullet, ball, arrow, etc.: a throw or cast or turn at a game : one who fires a rifle : one scene in a cinematograph film.

shot, *adj.* having colours which seem to change quickly.

shoulder, shōl′der, *n.* the part of the body between the neck and the upper arm : a fore-limb.—*v.* to carry on the shoulder : to bear the full weight of a burden.—*ns.* **shoul′der-blade,** the broad, flat bone of the shoulder; **shoul′der-strap,** a strap or tape passing over the shoulder : braid worn on the shoulder of a uniform.

shout, *n.* a loud and sudden cry.— Also *v.*

shove, shuv, *v.* to push with force.— Also *n.*

shovel, shuv′el, *n.* a kind of spade, with a broad blade, used for lifting coal, gravel, etc.—*v.* to lift with a shovel.

show, shō, *v.* to put something forward so that it may be seen : to come into sight : to point out : to make clear.—*n.* something seen : a performance (e.g. a circus, theatre) : a place where flowers, dogs, cattle, etc. are collected so that people may see them.—*adj.* **show′y,** fine to look at : pretty but not good.— *ns.* **show′bread,** among the Jews, twelve holy loaves presented to God in His Temple; **show′room,** a room where goods are laid out for people to see; **show′man,** a person who arranges circuses, etc.

show′er, *n.* a short fall of rain.—*v.* to drop in a fluttering stream : to pour (e.g. blessings, curses, etc.). —*adj.* **show′ery,** rather rainy.—

ns. **show′er-bath,** a bath with a spray overhead; **show′erproof,** a light raincoat.

shrap′nel, *n.* a shell in which are bullets which scatter with the explosion : shell or bomb splinters.

shred, *n.* a long, narrow piece, cut or torn off.—*v.* to cut or tear in small pieces.

shrew, shroo,*n.* an insect-eating, long-nosed animal, something like a mouse : a noisy, quarrelsome woman.—*adjs.* **shrewd** (shrood), quick and wise in judging : cunning; **shrew′ish,** quarrelsome.

shriek, shrēk, *v.* to utter a scream. —Also *n.*

shrift, *n.* a confession made to a priest : mercy.—*n.* **short-shrift.** See **short.**

shrill, *adj.* having a very high, piercing sound.

shrimp, *n.* a small, eatable shellfish : a small, withered-looking person.

shrine, *n.* a holy altar or temple.

shrink, *v.* to make or grow smaller : to draw back in fear or disgust.— *n.* **shrink′age,** the amount by which a thing grows smaller.

shrive, *v.* to hear a confession and give pardon.

shriv′el, *v.* to dry up and become wrinkled.

shroud, *n.* the cloth round a dead body : anything which covers (e.g. The mist came down like a *shroud*) : (*pl.*) the ropes from the mast-head to a ship's sides.—*v.* to cover up as with a shroud.

Shrove-tide, *n.* the name given to the days just before Ash-Wednesday.—*n.* **Shrove-Tuesday,** the day before Ash-Wednesday (which is the first day of Lent).

shrub, *n.* a small tree-like bush or plant.—*n.* **shrub′bery,** a place where many shrubs grow.

shrug, *v.* to show surprise or doubt by drawing up the shoulders.— Also *n.*

shrunk′en, *adj.* grown smaller.

shud′der, *v.* to tremble from cold, fear, disgust.—Also *n.*

shuf′fle, *v.* to mix cards before dealing them : to make a scraping noise with the feet.—Also *n.*

shun, *v.* to keep clear of.

shunt, v. (of railway engines) to move to and fro at a station (e.g. in order to pick up trucks).

shut, v. to close a door, window, lid, etc.—n. **shut'ter,** a cover for a window, or for a camera lens.

shut'tle, n. the part of a weaving-loom which carries the cross-thread from side to side.—n. **shut'tle-cock,** a rounded cork, stuck with feathers, used instead of a ball in badminton.

shy, adj. easily frightened : afraid to speak out.—v. to start aside in fear.—n. **shy'ness.**—adv. **shy'ly.**

shy, v. to throw.—Also n.

sibyl, sib'il, n. in old-time stories, a woman able to tell the future.

sick, adj. ill with disease : wanting to vomit : having had enough (of).—v. **sick'en,** to make or become sick.—adjs. **sick'ening,** causing sickness, disgust, weariness ; **sick'ly,** unhealthy : feeble. — n. **sick'ness,** illness.

sick'le, n. a hooked knife for cutting grain.

side, n. an edge or border : the part between the hip and shoulder : any party, team : spinning motion given to a ball by striking it sidewise : (slang) pride.—adj. on or towards the side.—v. to take up the cause of one party against another.—ns. **side'board,** a piece of furniture on one side of a dining-room for holding dishes, etc. ; **side'-glance,** a glance to one side ; **side'-is'sue,** a less important matter aside from the main business ; **side'light,** something which throws light upon a matter ; **side'-line,** an extra bit of business, outside what one is really concerned with ; **side'-show,** a less important show in a larger one ; **side-slip,** a sudden slip to right or left in flying ; **sid'ing,** a short line of rails on which wagons are shunted from the main-line.—v. **si'dle,** to go or move side-foremost.—adj.and adv. **side'long,** in a side direction.

sidereal, sī-dē'rē-al, adj. having to do with the stars.

siege, sēj, n. the settling down of an army round or before a fort or town in order to capture it.

sienna, si-en'a, n. a browny-yellow or reddish-brown colour.

sierra, si-er'a, n. a range of mountains with jagged peaks.

siesta, si-es'ta, n. a short sleep or rest taken in the heat of the day.

sieve, siv, n. a round box (with a meshwork bottom) used to separate the coarse parts of anything (e.g. flour, sand) from the fine.—v. to put through a sieve.

sift, v. to separate with a sieve : to examine closely.

sigh, sī, v. to take a long, deep-sounding breath, as in love or grief.—Also n.

sight, sit, n. act or power of seeing : that which is seen : that which is worth seeing : (on a gun) a guide to the eye in taking aim.—v. to catch sight of.—adj. **sight'ly,** pleasing to the sight or eye.—ns. **sight'-read'er,** one who is able to play or sing from music he has not seen before ; **sight'-seeing,** the act of seeing the chief buildings, monuments, etc. of a place.

sign, sīn, n. a mark by which a thing is known (e.g. + is the sign of addition) : a nod, wave of the hand, to show one's meaning : advertisement of coloured lights : something which shows what is going to happen (e.g. A red sunset is a sign of good weather).—v. to make a nod, or wave of the hand : to write one's name.—ns. **sign'board,** a shopkeeper's notice ; **sign'post,** a post showing the direction and distances of certain places.

sig'nal, n. a sign for giving a message from a distance : the message given.—v. to make signals to.—adj. worthy of notice.—v. **sig'nalise,** to make notable.

sig'nature, n. the name of a person written by himself : (in music) the flats and sharps which show the key.—n. **sig'natory,** one who has written his name as a promise to do something.

sig'net, n. a private seal.—n. **sig'net-ring,** a ring with one's initials on it.

sig'nify, v. to mean. — ns. **sig'nificance, significa'tion,** meaning :

importance.—*adj.* **signif'icant,** meaning much.

signor, sēn'yor, *n.* the Italian for Mr.—*ns.* **signo'ra,** Mrs ; **signorina** (sēn-yor-ē'na), Miss.

si'lence, *n.* absence of sound or speech : quietness.—*v.* to cause to be quiet or still.—*adj.* **si'lent,** free from noise : not speaking.— **the silent service,** tho navy.

silhouette, sil-oo-et', *n.* a shadow-outline (usually coloured black).

sil'ica, *n.* a white or colourless substance, of which flint and sandstone are mostly made up.

silk, *n.* very fine, soft thread spun by silkworms : cloth woven from it.—*adjs.* made of silk ; **silk'en, silk'y,** made of silk : like **silk.**—*ns.* **silk'-mercer, a silk-seller; silk'worm,** a moth caterpillar which spins a silken cocoon.

sill, *n.* a ledge or shelf, such as that below a window.

sil'ly, *adj.* foolish : of weak mind : simple.

si'lo, *n.* a tower-like building for storing grain, or for keeping green crops for cattle-food.

silt, *n.* sand left when water flows away.—*v.* (with *up*) to become blocked by mud.

sil'van, *adj.* dwelling in woods : wooded.

sil'ver, *n.* a soft white metal, able to take on a high polish : money made of silver.—*adjs.* **sil'ver, sil'very,** made of silver : looking like silver : having a soft and clear tone.—*v.* to make or become white, like silver.—*n.* **sil'versmith,** a smith who works in silver.— *adj.* **sil'ver-tongued,** pleasing in speech.—**silver jubilee, silver wedding.** See **jubilee, wedding.**

sim'ian, *adj.* ape-like.

sim'ilar, *adj.* like or nearly like.— *ns.* **similar'ity ; simile** (sim'i-le), a striking comparison : a way of making one's meaning clearer by comparing one thing to another—e.g. The aeroplane soared *like a bird.*

sim'mer, *v.* to boil with a gentle, hissing sound.

simoom', *n.* a hot, dry wind blowing from the deserts of Northern Africa and Arabia.

sim'per, *v.* to smile in a silly manner.

sim'ple, *adj.* easy : plain : not cunning : too trusting, easily cheated. —*n.* a healing plant.—*ns.* **sim'pleton,** a person who is easily cheated ; **simplicity** (sim-plis'-i-ti), easiness : plainness ; **simplifica'tion,** the act of making simple.—*v.* **sim'plify,** to make easier.—*adv.* **sim'ply,** in simple manner : putting the matter shortly and simply.

sim'ulate, *v.* to pretend.—*n.* **simula'tion.**

simultaneous, sim-ul-tā'nē-us, *adj.* happening at the same time.

sin, *n.* a wicked act, esp. one which breaks the laws of one's religion. —*v.* to do wrong.—*adj.* **sin'ful,** wicked.—*n.* **sin'ner.**

sincere, sin-sēr', *adj.* honest in word and deed : frank.—*n.* **sincer'ity.**

sinecure, sin'ē-kūr, *n.* a job in which one receives money but has little or no work to do.

sinew, sin'ū, *n.* a tough string-like substance which joins a muscle to a bone.—*adj.* **sin'ewy,** having sinews : strong.

sing, *v.* to make musical sounds with one's voice : to write a poem in praise of some person or his actions.

singe, sinj, *v.* to burn slightly.—Also *n.*—*adjs.* **singe'ing; singed.**

single, sing'gl, *adj.* made up of one only, not double : alone : not married : honest.—*v.* (with *out*) to pick out.—*adv.* **sing'ly,** one by one. — *adjs.* **sin'gle-breast'ed,** with one row of buttons ; **sing'le-hand'ed,** working by one's self ; **sin'gle-heart'ed,** having a sincere heart.—*ns.* **sing'lestick,** a stick or cudgel for one hand : a fight or game with singlesticks ; **sing'let,** an undershirt.

sing'ular, *adj.* unusual, uncommon : strange, odd : (in grammar) the form of a word which shows that only one of a thing is being spoken of (e.g. the word *Boy* is *singular,* the word *Boys* is plural).—*n.* **singular'ity,** strangeness, queerness.—*adv.* **sing'ularly,** strangely.

sin'ister, *adj.* evil-looking : unlucky.

sink, *v.* to go lower: to fall, or cause to fall, to the bottom, or below the surface: to lose strength.—*n.* a basin, with a drain for carrying off dirty water: a foul or dirty place.—*ns.* **sink′er,** a weight fixed to a fishing-line; **sink′ing-fund,** money put aside every year for the purpose of paying off debt.

sinuous, sin′ū-us, *adj.* bending in and out: winding: crooked.—*n.* **sinuos′ity,** a bend.

sip, *v.* to drink in small quantities.—Also *n.*

siphon, sī′fon, *n.* a bent tube for drawing off liquids from one dish into another: a glass bottle, for lemonade, soda-water, etc., fitted with a glass tube up which liquid is driven by gas.

sir, *n.* a word of respect used in speaking or writing to a man: the title of a knight or baronet (e.g. *Sir* Walter Scott).

sire, *n.* a father: a forefather: a father-animal (esp. among horses): title used in speaking to a king.

si′ren, *n.* a loud hooter (used by ships, factories, and as air-raid warning): a woman who attracts people, often leading them to harm and evil.

sir′loin, *n.* the upper part of the loin of beef.

siroc′co, *n.* a name given in Italy to a dusty dry wind coming over sea from Africa: any south wind.

sir′rah, *n.* sir (used in anger).

sis′al-grass, *n.* a grass, much grown in East Africa, used for making ropes.

sis′kin, *n.* a small bird of the finch family.

sis′ter, *n.* a female born of the same parents as one's self: a woman, belonging to a church society, who does good work among the poor and sick: a nun: a nurse of higher rank.—*adj.* **sis′terly,** like a sister.—*ns.* **sis′terhood,** women who join together for purposes of religion, good works, etc.; **sis′ter-in-law,** the sister of one's husband or of one's wife: the wife of one's brother.

sit, *v.* to rest on a seat: (of birds) to rest on eggs in order to hatch them: to hold a meeting.—*n.* **sit′ting,** one's seat in a church: eggs which are to be hatched: a meeting (e.g. of Parliament): a visit to a photographer or painter, so that he may take a photograph or paint a picture.— **to sit tight,** to be unwilling to move; **to sit up,** to sit with one's back straight: to remain out of bed.

site, *n.* a place chosen for some purpose (e.g. a building): a place where a building once stood, or where some event took place.

situated, sit′ū-āt-ed, *adj.* placed.— *n.* **situā′tion,** the place where anything stands: a job: state of affairs (e.g. We are in a difficult *situation* about money).

six′pence, *n.* a silver coin, worth six pennies.—*adj.* **six′penny,** costing sixpence.

size, *n.* space taken up by anything.—*v.* to arrange according to size.—**to size up,** to form an opinion about a person: to consider carefully.

size, *n.* a kind of weak glue, used as varnish.

siz′zle, *v.* to make a hissing sound.

skate, *n.* a steel blade with clips and screws for fastening it to the boot, for moving on ice.—*v.* to move on skates.

skate, *n.* a large flat-fish.

skean-dhu, skēn′doo, *n.* a Highlander's knife or dagger.

skein, skān, *n.* a coil of thread or yarn, loosely tied in a knot.

skel′eton, *n.* the bony framework of an animal, without the flesh: any framework or outline.—*ns.* **skeleton-crew,** a small crew consisting of necessary men only; **skeleton-key,** one which may be used for opening many different locks—it has only the outer shape, the inner parts being cut away.—**skeleton in the cupboard,** some hidden sorrow or shame.

skep, *n.* a beehive made of straw or wicker-work.

sker′ry, *n.* a rocky isle.

sketch, *n.* a rough plan or painting or drawing, to be done more fully later: a drawing in pencil or ink: a short play.—*v.* to make a rough plan of : to give the chief points of : to draw in pencil or ink.— *adj.* sketch'y, roughly done.

skew, skū, *adj.* off the straight : not at right angles.—Also *adv.*

skewer, skū'er, *n.* a pin of wood or iron for keeping meat in shape while roasting.

ski, skē, *n.* a long, narrow, wooden snow-shoe :—*pl.* ski or skis.—*v.* to travel on skis.—*n.* ski'ing.

skid, *n.* a wedge or drag put under a wheel to check it on a steep place : a side-slip.—*v.* to check with a drag : (of wheels) to slide along without turning : to slip sideways.

skiff, *n.* a small light boat.

skill, *n.* cleverness at doing a thing —either from practice or as a natural gift.—*adjs.* skil'ful, clever and quick at doing something ; skilled, clever at a trade because one has been trained to it.

skillet, *n.* a small metal dish with a long handle.

skim, *v.* to clear off scum : to move swiftly along the surface of something : to pass over lightly : to glide along near the surface.— *n.* skim'-milk, milk from which the cream has been skimmed.

skimp, *v.* to give hardly enough : to do a thing imperfectly.—*adj.* scanty.

skin, *n.* the outer covering (e.g. of an animal's body, of a fruit).— *v.* to strip the skin from : to peel. —*adjs.* skin'ny, very thin ; skin-deep, as deep as the skin only, on the surface.—*n.* skin'flint, a very greedy person.—by the skin of one's teeth, very narrowly ; to save one's skin, to escape without injury : to save one's self in a cowardly way.

skip, *v.* to leap lightly and joyfully : to pass over.—*n.* a light leap : the captain of a side at bowls.—*n.* skip'ping, a game in which the players jump over a turning rope.

skipper, *n.* the captain of a ship or aeroplane.

skirmish, *n.* a fight between two small forces.—Also *v.*

skirt, *n.* the part of a garment below the waist : a woman's garment like a petticoat : the outer edge or part.—*v.* to be on the border. —*ns.* skir'ting, cloth made up in lengths for women's skirts ; skirt'ing-board, the narrow board next the floor round the walls of a room.

skit, *n.* a piece of writing which makes fun of a person, play, book, etc.

skittish, *adj.* frisky : easily frightened.

skittles, *n.pl.* a game in which standing pins are bowled at : ninepins.—*v.* skit'tle, to knock down easily, as in skittles.

skulk, *v.* to sneak out of the way.

skull, *n.* the bones which hold the brain : the head part of a skeleton. —*n.* skull'cap, a cap which fits closely to the head.—skull and cross-bones, the sign of death : the sign on a pirate's flag.

skunk, *n.* a kind of weasel, which defends itself by giving out an evil-smelling liquid : mean rogue.

sky, *n.* the heavens.—*v.* to hit a ball high into the air.—*ns.* sky'lark, a lark which sings while hovering far overhead ; sky'larking, mischievous behaviour ; sky'light, a window in a roof or ceiling ; sky'line, the horizon ; sky'scrāp'er, a high building of many storeys.—*adv.* sky'ward(s), towards the sky.

slab, *n.* a thin cake of anything (e.g. of stone, toffee).

slack, *adj.* not firmly held or holding : careless : not busy.—*n.* the loose part of a rope : (*pl.*) trousers. —*vs.* slack, slack'en, to become or make loose : to become slower : to give up trying.—*n.* slack'er, one who is not trying.

slack, *n.* coal-dust.

slag, *n.* cinders from iron-smelting works.

slake, *v.* to quench thirst : to mix lime with water.

slam, *v.* to shut with a bang.

slam, *n.* (in cards) the winning of every trick.

slander, *n.* words spoken with the purpose of doing harm to a person's reputation.—*v.* to do harm to a person's reputation by wilful untruth.—*adj.* slan'derous:

slang, *n.* a homely way of speaking, not to be used in correct speaking or writing (e.g. 'Copper' and 'Bobby' are *slang* words for 'Policeman').—*v.* to scold.—*adj.* **slang'y**, using slang.

slan'ting, *adj.* sloping.—*n.* **slant**, a slope.—*v.* to turn in a sloping direction : to be placed in a sloping manner, like the roof of a house.—*adv.* **slant'wise**, in a sloping manner.

slap, *n.* a blow with the hand.—*v.* to strike with the open hand or anything flat.—*advs.* **slap'-bang**, with force, all at once ; **slap'-dash**, in a bold, careless way.

slash, *v.* to strike at and make long cuts.—*n.* a long cut.

slat, *n.* a thin strip of wood, slate, stone, etc.

slate, *n.* an easily split rock, dull-blue, grey, purple, or green in colour (used for roofing or for writing upon).—*v.* to cover with slate.

slate, *v.* to say harsh words about.

slat'tern, *n.* an untidy woman (esp. in dress or appearance).—*adj.* **slatt'ernly**, dirty, untidy.

slaughter, slaw'ter, *n.* great destruction of life.—*v.* to kill : to slay.—*n.* **slaugh'terhouse**, a place where animals are killed in order to be sold for food.

slave, *n.* one who is forced to work with little or no reward, at the will of the master to whom he belongs.—*v.* to work like a slave. —*ns.* **slave'-dri'ver**, one who urges on slaves at their work : one who treats his workpeople like slaves ; **slā'ver**, a ship employed in the slave-trade : a person who buys and sells slaves ; **slā'very**, the state of being a slave : bondage : drudgery.— *adj.* **slā'vish**, slave-like : without thinking or acting for one's self.

slā'ver, *n.* spittle running from the mouth.—*v.* to let the saliva run out of the mouth.

slay, *v.* to put to death.

sled, **sledge**, slej, *n.* a carriage with runners made for sliding upon snow.

sledge, slej, **sledge'-hammer**, *ns.* a large heavy hammer used by smiths.

sleek, *adj.* smooth, glossy : polite in order to deceive, speaking cunningly.

sleep, *n.* a rest, with the eyes closed, in which one's senses are dulled for the time being.—*v.* to rest the senses.—*adjs.* **sleep'y**, tired and wanting to rest one's senses ; **sleep'less**, not able to sleep.—*ns.* **sleep'er**, one who sleeps : a stout wooden or steel beam supporting railway-lines : a railway-carriage in which there are beds for passengers ; **sleep'ing-draught**, a drink to bring on sleep ; **sleep'ing-part'ner**. See **partner** ; **sleep'-walk'er**, one who walks while asleep ; **sleep'y-head**, a lazy person.

sleet, *n.* rain mixed with snow or hail.

sleeve, *n.* the part of a garment which covers the arm. — *n.* **sleeve'-link**, two buttons, joined by a link, for holding together the two edges of the cuff.—**to have something up one's sleeve**, to have something hidden for use if the need arises ; **to laugh in one's sleeve**, to laugh to one's self.

sleigh, slā, *n.* a sledge.—*v.* to travel on a sledge.

sleight, slīt, *n.* cleverness or trickiness.—*n.* **sleight'-of-hand**, quickness of hand.

slen'der, *adj.* thin : narrow : small in amount.

sleuth, slooth, *n.* a tracker, a detective.—*n.* **sleuth'-hound**, a bloodhound.

slew, sloo, *v.* to swing round.

slice, *v.* to divide into thin pieces.— *n.* a thin broad piece : a broad knife for serving food (e.g. fish).

slick, *adj.* smooth-tongued : smart : quick in movement.

slide, *v.* to move quickly over a smooth surface : to slip, move.— *n.* a slippery track : a smooth slope : a strip of glass on which an object or a picture is mounted ready to be used with a microscope or lantern.

slight, slīt, *adj.* of little value, importance, or amount : slender in build.—*v.* to insult by paying little heed to.—*n.* an insult.

slim, *adj.* gracefully thin : slender, not stout.—*v.* to arrange one's food and exercise so that one may make one's weight less.

slime, *n.* sticky mud : wet filth.—*adj.* **slim′y,** muddy : filthy.

sling, *n.* a strap or pocket with a string attached to each end, for hurling a stone : a bandage hanging from the neck or shoulders to support a wounded limb : a rope with hooks, used in hoisting and lowering objects.—*v.* to throw with a sling : to move or swing by means of a rope.

slink, *v.* to sneak away.

slip, *v.* to move quietly or stealthily : to move out of position : to move by sliding.—*n.* act of slipping : an error, a slight mistake : a twig : a strip or narrow piece of anything (e.g. paper) : a smooth slope, on which a ship is built (also *slipway*) : any loose covering (e.g. a garment, a pillow-cover) : a fielding position in cricket.—*ns.* **slip′-knot,** a knot which slips along ; **slip′per,** a loose shoe easily put on.—*adjs.* **slip′pery,** smooth, not giving a firm grip : deceitful, unable to be trusted ; **slip′shod,** having shoes worn away at the heel : careless.—**to slip off,** to go off noiselessly or hastily ; **to slip on,** to put on loosely or in haste ; **to slip up,** to make a mistake ; **to give a person the slip,** to escape stealthily from him.

slit, *v.* to make a long narrow cut in : to cut into strips.—*n.* a long narrow cut or opening.

slith′er, *v.* to slide.—*adj.* **slith′ery,** slippery.

sli′ver, *n.* a long thin strip or paring.

slob′ber, *v.* to let spittle dribble from the mouth.

sloe, *slō, n.* the blackthorn : its fruit.

slog, *v.* to hit or work hard.—*n.* **slog′ger,** a hard hitter or worker.

slō′gan, *n.* a war-cry among the old-time Highlanders of Scotland : a catchy phrase (e.g. ' Eat more fruit ').

sloop, *n.* a light boat : a one-masted sailing-vessel.

slop, *v.* to overflow : to spill.—*n.pl.* **slops,** dirty water.—*adj.* **slop′py,** wet : too full of silly feeling.

slope, *v.* to lie in a direction that is not level.—*n.* something which is higher at one end than at the other (e.g. a hill-side, roof of a house).

slot, *n.* a slit or groove.

slōth, *n.* laziness : a slow-moving animal (which lives in trees) of South America. — *adj.* **sloth′ful,** lazy.

slouch, slowch, *n.* a hunched-up body position.—*v.* to walk with shoulders rounded and head hanging.—*n.* **slouch′-hat,** a hat with broad, soft, flapping brim.

slough, slow, *n.* a bog or marsh.

slough, sluf, *n.* the cast-off skin of a serpent.—*v.* to cast a coat or skin.

sloven, sluv′n, *n.* a person carelessly or dirtily dressed.—*adj.* **slov′enly,** untidy, careless.

slow, slō, *adj.* taking much time : not hurrying : behind in time : not quick in learning : dull.—*v* to slacken speed.—*n.* **slow′coach,** one who is slow of movement.—**slow-motion film,** one which shows movements very slowly.

sludge, sluj, *n.* soft mud.

slug, *n.* a kind of snail, with no shell.—*adj.* **slug′gish,** moving slowly.—*n.* **slug′gard,** one who is slow and lazy in his habits.

slug, *n.* a small piece of metal used as a bullet.

sluice, sloos, *n.* a sliding gate for holding back a flow of water : the stream which flows through it.—*v.* to clean out with a strong flow of water.

slum, *n.* a crowded part of a town where the houses are dirty and unhealthy.

slum′ber, *v.* to sleep.—*n.* sleep.

slump, *v.* to fall or sink suddenly.—*n.* a sudden fall of prices.

slur, *v.* to pass over lightly (e.g. He *slurs* his words in speaking).—*n.* a bad mark against one's name : (in music) a mark (⌢) showing that notes are to be sung to the same syllable.

slush, *n.* watery mud : melting snow.—*v.* to throw water, thin paint, whitewash, etc. upon.

slut, *n.* a dirty, untidy woman.—*adj.* **slut'tish,** dirty : careless.

slȳ, *adj.* cunning : wily.—*adv.* **slȳ'ly.**—*n.* **slȳ'ness.—on the sly,** secretly.

smack, *n.* taste : flavour.—*v.* (with *of*) to have a taste (of).

smack, *n.* a small fishing-vessel.

smack, *v.* to strike smartly, to slap loudly.—*n.* a sharp sound : a crack.—*adv.* sharply.

small, smawl, *adj.* little (in size, worth, importance).—*n.* lower part (of the back).—*ns.* **small'-arms** (*pl.*), muskets, rifles, pistols, etc. (i.e. weapons that can be carried by a man) ; **small'-beer,** a weak kind of beer ; **small'-hours** (*pl.*), the hours just after midnight ; **small'pox,** a serious fever, causing small *pocks* or hollows on the skin ; **small'-talk,** trifling conversation.

smart, *adj.* quick in thought or action : well-dressed.—*n.* a sharp, stinging pain.—*v.* to feel or cause sharp pain.

smash, *v.* to break in pieces.—*n.* the act of breaking with force : a railway, motor, or aeroplane accident : the ruin of a business firm.—**smashing victory,** a complete victory.

smat'tering, *n.* a very slight knowledge of a subject.

smear, *v.* to spread with anything sticky.

smell, *n.* the sense, or power, of noticing things through one's nose : that which may be noticed thus (e.g. the *smell* of a flower) : a perfume.—*v.* to use one's sense of smell : to give off a smell.—*n.* **smelling-salts,** strong-smelling chemicals in bottle, used to revive fainting persons.—**to smell a rat,** see **rat** ; **to smell out,** to find out by prying.

smelt, *n.* a fish of the salmon kind.

smelt, *v.* to melt ore in order to separate the metal from dirt.

smile, *v.* to show pleasure by the face : to be favourable.—*n.* act of smiling.

smirch, *v.* to stain.—Also *n.*

smirk, *v.* to smile in an unnatural manner.—Also *n.*

smite, *v.* to hit hard.

smith, *n.* a worker in metals.—*n.*

smith'y, the workshop of a smith.

smit'ten, *adj.* having been hit hard.

smock, *n.* loose outer garment of coarse white linen, etc., worn over the other clothes as a protection.

smog, *n.* smoky fog.

smoke, *n.* the cloud-like substance which is given off by anything burning.—*v.* to give off smoke : to draw in and puff out the smoke of tobacco : to apply smoke to (e.g. bees).—*adjs.* **smō'ky ; smoke'-less.**—*ns.* **smōker,** one who smokes : a concert at which smoking is allowed ; **smoke'-screen,** a heavy cloud of smoke used in war to hide ships, factories, etc. ; **smoke'-stack,** a factory or steamer chimney.

smōlt, *n.* a young salmon.

smooth, *adj.* not rough : having an even surface : having no difficulties in the way. — *v.* **smooth, smoothe,** to make even or level : to soften : to calm.—*adv.* **smooth'ly.**—*n.* **smooth'ness.**—*adj.* **smooth'-tongued** (-tungd), flattering.

smother, smuth'er, *v.* to kill or be killed by want of air.

smoulder, smōl'der, *v.* to burn slowly without bursting into flame.

smudge, smuj, *n.* a spot, a stain.—*v.* to soil with spots or stains.—*adj.* **smud'gy.**

smug, *adj.* well satisfied with one's self : having an air of smartness.

smug'gle, *v.* to bring certain goods into a country without paying the taxes fixed by law : to send secretly.—*n.* **smugg'ler,** one who smuggles : a vessel used in smuggling.

smut, *n.* a spot of dirt or soot : a plant disease which blackens ears of corn, heads of grasses, etc.—*v.* to blacken.—*adj.* **smut'ty,** stained with smut : (of talk) dirty, rude.

snack, *n.* a light, hasty meal.

snag, *n.* a hidden log in a river : a stumbling-block : a difficulty.

snail, *n.* a soft-bodied, small, crawling animal, with a shell : a person who is very slow.—**snail's pace,** a very slow speed.

snake, *n.* a legless, crawling creature: a serpent.—*adj.* **snak'y,** cunning: deceitful.

snap, *v.* to break suddenly, with a sharp sound: to bite at.—*n.* a sudden bite, break, or crack: a sharp sound: liveliness: a short period of weather (e.g. a cold *snap*).—*adj.* **snap'py,** sharp in manner: acting quickly.

snare, *n.* a running noose of string or wire, etc., for catching an animal: a trap: a hidden danger.—*v.* to catch by a snare.

snarl, *v.* to growl: to speak in a rude or gruff manner.—*Also n.*

snatch, *v.* to seize quickly.—*n.* a hasty catching or seizing: a small piece (e.g. of poetry, music).

sneak, *v.* to creep or steal away meanly: to behave meanly.—*n.* a mean fellow.—*adjs.* **sneak'ing,** mean: secret; **sneak'y,** behaving meanly.

sneer, *v.* to show contempt by the tone of one's voice.—*n.* a remark which shows contempt.

sneeze, *v.* to make a sudden, cough-like noise through the nose.—*Also n.*

snick, *v.* to cut off a small piece.—*Also n.*—*n.* **snickersnee',** big knife.

snick'er, *v.* to giggle.—*n.* a giggle.

sniff, *v.* to draw in air through the nose: to find out by the sense of smell: (with *at*) to treat with scorn.—*n.* a sharp breath taken in through the nose: a faint smell.—*adj.* **sniff'y,** slightly scornful.

snig'ger, *v.* to laugh in a quiet sly manner.—*Also n.*

snip, *v.* to cut off sharply: to cut off.—*n.* a cut with scissors: a small piece: something certain or easy.—*n.* **snip'pet,** a little piece cut off.

snipe, *n.* a bird with a long straight bill, found in marshy places: a mean fellow.

sni'per, *n.* a rifleman who lies in hiding and shoots from a long distance.—*v.* **snipe.**

sniv'el, *v.* to run at the nose: to whine.—*n.* a pretended cry.

snob, *n.* a person who looks down on others and thinks that he belongs to a better class than they.—*adj.* **snob'bish,** full of silly pride.—*ns.* **snob'bery, snob'-bishness.**

snood, *n.* a band round a girl's hair.

snook'er, *n.* billiard game using twenty-two coloured balls.

snoop, *v.* to go about sneakingly.

snooze, *v.* to sleep lightly.—*Also n.*

snore, *v.* to breathe roughly and hoarsely in sleep.—*Also n.*

snort, *v.* to force air noisily through the nostrils.—*Also n.*

snout, *n.* the nose of an animal.

snow, snō, *n.* frozen moisture falling in soft flakes.—*v.* to fall in soft flakes.—*adjs.* **snow'y,** full of snow; **snow'-blind,** dazzled by the light reflected from the snow; **snow'-bound,** closed in by snow; **snow'-capped,** with tops covered in snow.—*ns.* **snow'ball,** a ball of snow pressed together; **snow'-boot,** a boot to protect the foot and ankle when walking in snow; **snow'drift,** a bank of snow blown together by the wind; **snow'drop,** a small white bulb-flower, blooming in early spring; **snow'-flake,** a single piece of snow; **snow'-line,** the height up a mountain above which there is always snow; **snow'-plough,** a machine for clearing snow from roads and railways; **snow'-shoe,** a long, broad shoe for walking on the top of snow; **snow'-wreath,** a snowdrift.—**snow-leopard.** See **ounce.**

snub, *v.* to check sharply (e.g. by a rude remark).—*n.* a rude, stinging remark.—*adj.* **snub'-nosed,** having a short and fat nose.

snuff, *v.* to draw in through the nose: to smell at anything: to take snuff into the nose.—*n.* powdered tobacco for drawing up into the nose: a sniff.—*ns.* **snuff'-box, snuff'-mull,** a box for snuff.—*v.* **snuf'fle,** to breathe heavily or speak through the nose.

snuff, *v.* to nip off the burnt part of a candle-wick.—*n.* **snuff'ers,** a kind of scissors for trimming the wick of a candle.

snug, *adj.* lying close and warm: comfortable.—*v.* **snug'gle,** to cuddle, nestle.

sō, adv. thus: to such an extent (e.g. so big).

soak, v. to suck up: to wet through and through.—n. **soak′ing,** a wetting through (e.g. by rain).

soap, n. a mixture containing oils or fats and other substances, used as a help in washing.—adj. **soap′y,** like soap: full of soap: fond of flattering.—n.pl. **soap′-suds,** soapy water worked into a frothy foam.

soar, v. to fly into the air: (of prices) to rise quickly.

sob, v. to weep with catchings of the breath.—Also n.

sō′ber, adj. not drunk: having a serious mind: dark in colour.—ns. **sō′berness, sobriety** (sō-brī′e-ti), the state of being sober.

sobriquet, sō′brē-kā, n. a nickname.

sō′-called, adj. bearing a name or title to which one has no right (e.g. The so-called doctor was a cheat).

sociable, sō′sha-bl, adj. fond of the company of others.

society, sō-sī′et-i, n. a number of persons joined together for some special purpose (e.g. dramatic society, for the acting of plays; debating society, for talking about matters): friendship with other people (e.g. He is fond of society): a name for the noble and wealthy people of a place (e.g. He is a member of London society).—adj. **social** (sō′shal), having to do with society: having to do with the everyday life of the people (e.g. social history).—ns. **so′cialism,** the belief that a country's wealth (its land, mines, industries, railways, etc.) should belong to the people as a whole, not to private owners: a system in which the state runs the country's wealth; **so′cialist; sociology** (sō-shi-ol′ō-ji), branch of knowledge which has to do with study of the everyday life of people.

sock, n. a short stocking.

sock′et, n. a hollow into which something is fitted.

sod, n. a piece of earth grown with grass: turf.

sō′da, n. a substance, something like salt, used in washing, baking, etc.

—ns. **so′da-fountain,** a counter at which lemonade and iced drinks are sold; **so′da-water,** a fizzing liquid, containing soda, water, and gas.

sod′den, adj. soaked through and through.

sō′fa, n. a long, stuffed seat with back and arms.

soft, adj. easily put out of shape when pressed: not hard: not loud: full of feeling, easily moved.—adv. gently: quietly.—v. **soften** (sof′n), to make or grow soft: to make less strong.—ns. **soft′-goods** (pl.), cloth, and cloth articles; **soft′wood,** the wood of a cone-bearing tree (e.g. fir, larch).

sog′gy, adj. soaked with water.

soil, n. the ground, esp. that in which plants grow: dirt.—v. to dirty.

soirée, swor′ā, n. an evening party: a tea party.

sojourn, sō′jurn, v. to stay for a time.—Also n.

sol′ace, n. something which makes pain or sorrow easier to bear.—v. to comfort.

sō′lan-goose, n. the gannet (a seabird, like a large gull, found on a few rocky islands).

sō′lar, adj. having to do with the sun.—n. **solar-system,** a name for the star-like bodies, or planets, which move round the sun as a centre (e.g. The earth is a planet in the solar system).

sōl′der, n. melted lead used for making metal-joints.—v. to join two metals with solder.—ns. **sol′dering-bolt, -iron,** a tool with pointed copper end for use in soldering.

soldier, sōl′jer, n. a man who serves in an army.—n. **soldier-of-fortune,** one ready to serve anywhere so long as there is something to be gained.

sole, n. the underside of the foot or of a boot.—v. to put a sole on (a boot).

sole, n. a small flat-fish.

sole, adj. alone: only: single.—adv. **sole′ly.**

solecism, sol′e-sizm, n. a bad mistake (in writing, speaking, behaviour).

solemn, sol'em, *adj.* serious-looking : turning the mind to serious thoughts.—*n.* solem'nity, seriousness.—*v.* sol'emnise, to carry out (e.g. a wedding) with suitable show.

sol-fa', *n.* (in music) singing from notes named *doh, ray, me,* etc.

solicit, sō-lis'it, *v.* to ask earnestly : to try to obtain.—*adj.* solic'itous, anxious : careful : asking questions.—*ns.* solic'itor, a lawyer who advises people what to do, and gets the facts ready for a court case ; solic'itude, care : anxiety about a matter.

sol'id, *adj.* hard right through : firm (e.g. Ice is *solid* ; water is *liquid*): able to be depended on.—*n.* a substance which is hard right through.—*n.* solid'ity, the state of being solid.—*v.* solid'ify, to make or become solid.

soliloquy, sol-il'ō-kwē, *n.* a speech to one's self.—*v.* solil'oquise, to speak to one's self.

sol'itary, *adj.* alone or lonely : living alone, far off from other people or places.—*n.* one who lives alone—a hermit.

sol'itude, *n.* want of company : a lonely place.

sō'lō, *n.* a musical piece for one singer or player.—*n.* sō'lōist, one who plays or sings a solo.

solstice, sol'stis, *n.* the time of longest daylight (*summer solstice,* about 21st June) or longest dark (*winter solstice,* about 21st December).

sol'uble, *adj.* able to be melted in a liquid : (of difficulties, problems, etc.) able to be got over.—*n.* solubil'ity.

solution, sol-ū'shun, *n.* a liquid with something melted in it : an answer to a problem, puzzle, etc.

solve, *v.* to clear up or explain : to work out an answer for.—*adj.* sol'vent, able to pay all debts.—*n.* anything that makes another melt.—*n.* sol'vency, the state of being able to pay all debts.

sombre, som'ber, *adj.* dull : gloomy.

sombrero, som-brā'rō, *n.* a broad-brimmed felt hat.

somersault, sum'er-sawlt, *n.* a leap in which a person turns with his heels over his head.

some, sum, *adj.* and *pron.* a number or quantity (of).—*prons.* some'body ; some'one ; some'thing.—*advs.* some'how ; some'times ; some'what, rather, a little (e.g. He was *somewhat* sad) ; some'where.

somnam'bulist, *n.* a sleep-walker.

som'nolence, *n.* sleepiness.

son, sun, *n.* a male child.—*n.* son'-in-law, one's daughter's husband.

sona'ta, *n.* a piece of music.

song, *n.* words set to music : the notes of a bird.—*n.* song'ster, a singer : a bird that sings :—*fem.* song'stress.—**bought for an old song,** bought very cheaply.

son'net, *n.* a poem in fourteen lines. —*n.* sonneteer', a writer of sonnets.

sonorous, sō-nō'rus, *adj.* giving a clear, loud sound.

soon, *adv.* in a short time from now : early : readily, willingly.—**sooner or later,** at some time to come.

soot, *n.* the black powder left by smoke.—*adj.* soot'y, like soot : choked with soot.

sooth, *n.* truth.—*adv.* indeed.—*n.* sooth'sayer, one who is able to tell the future.

soothe, sooth, *v.* to please with soft words : to make pain less hurtful.

sop, *n.* bread dipped in soup or some other liquid before being eaten : something (e.g. money) given to keep a person quiet.—*v.* to soak.

sophisticated, so-fis'ti-kā-ted, *adj.* knowing all there is to know about life, evil as well as good (e.g. Once he was a simple country boy ; now he is a *sophisticated* man of the town).—*ns.* soph'ist, one who tries to deceive by false reasoning ; soph'istry, false reasoning.

soporif'ic, *adj.* causing sleep.—*n.* something which causes sleep.

sopra'no, *n.* a singing voice of high pitch.

sorcerer, sor'ser-er, *n.* one who works magic spells : a wizard :—*fem.* sor'ceress.—*n.* sor'cery, magic.

sor'did, *adj.* dirty, filthy : mean.

sore, *adj.* causing pain.—*n.* a wound, cut, or blister, which causes pain. —*n.* **sore'ness.**—*adv.* **sore'ly,** in a way that causes pain: very greatly.

sor'rel, *n.* a plant, like the dock, with sour-tasting leaves.

sor'row, *n.* pain of mind: sadness. —*v.* to be sad.—*adjs.* **sor'ry,** sad because one has done wrong: feeling pity: miserable, unhappy (e.g. a *sorry* state of affairs); **sor'rowful,** sad because one is suffering.

sort, *n.* a number of persons or things of the same kind.—*v.* to separate articles into different lots, putting each in its place (e.g. They *sort* letters at the post-office).—*n.* **sor'ter.**—**out of sorts,** not feeling very well.

sortie, sor'ti, *n.* a sudden attack made by the defenders of a place upon those who are trying to take it.

sot, *n.* a drunken fellow.—*adj.* **sot'-tish,** foolish: stupid with drink.

sot'to voce, vō'che, *adv.* said in a low voice.

sou, soo, *n.* a French halfpenny.

soufflé, soof'lā, *n.* a kind of pudding made by whisking whites of eggs.

sough, sow, *v.* (of the wind) to make a sighing sound.

soul, sōl, *n.* the spirit: nobleness of mind: a person.—*adjs.* **soul'ful,** full of feeling; **soul'less,** having no fine feeling: mean.

sound, *adj.* healthy: safe, not harmed: free from mistake.— *adv.* completely (*sound* asleep).

sound, *n.* a noise.—*v.* to make a noise: to listen carefully in order to find out something (e.g. The doctor *sounded* the boy's chest): to ask a person questions to find out what he thinks: to test depth of water by dropping lead weight tied to a string.— **sound barrier,** difficulty in increasing speed which aeroplane meets about speed of sound.

soup, soop, *n.* a liquid food, made by boiling meat and vegetables.

sour, *adj.* having a taste like that of vinegar: bad-tempered.

source, sors, *n.* the place where something has its beginning: a

spring, esp. one from which a river flows.

souse, *v.* to dip in salted water.

south, *n.* one of the four chief directions—the direction in which the sun is seen at midday.— *adjs.* **southern** (suth'ern), **southerly** (suth'er-li), having to do with the south.—*ns.* **south-east,** the direction half-way between south and east; **south-west,** the direction half-way between south and west; **south-wes'ter,** a wind blowing from the south-west; **sou'wester,** a water-proof hat with a broad flap behind.—*adjs.* **south-eas'tern;** **south-eas'terly;** **south-wes'tern;** **south-wes'terly.**

souvenir, soo-ve-nēr', *n.* a small object which will help one to remember a person or place.

sovereign, sov'rin, *n.* a king or queen: (in Britain) a gold coin worth twenty shillings.—*adj.* above all others.—*n.* **sovereignty** (sov'rin-ti), highest power.

sow, *n.* a female pig.

sow, sō, *v.* to scatter seed so that it may grow.—*n.* **sow'er.**

soy or **soy'a,** *n.* a kind of bean, grown in China and Japan.

spa, spah, *n.* a place where people go to drink health-giving waters.

space, *n.* the distance between objects: an uncovered part: the region above the earth in which are the moon, sun, and stars: a length of time.—*v.* to put things apart from each other, leaving room between them.—*adj.* **spacious** (spā'shus), having plenty of room: wide.—*ns.* **space-man,** a man equipped to travel in space, e.g. to the moon; **space-ship,** a vessel of a special kind made to carry man through space.

spade, *n.* the tool with which a gardener digs: one of the four kinds of marks used on playing-cards (♠).—**to call a spade a spade,** to say plainly what one thinks.

spaghetti, spa-get'ti, *n.* wheat paste made into long cords.

spake, *v.* spoke (only used in old-fashioned writing).

span, *n.* the distance between the tips of a man's little finger and thumb (about nine inches): the full time anything lasts : an arch of a bridge : a number of horses or oxen pulling a wagon or plough.—*v.* to stretch across (e.g The bridge *spans* the river).

span'gle, *n.* a small sparkling ornament.

spaniel, span'yel, *n.* a kind of dog (brown, black, sometimes partly white) with large, hanging ears.

Span'ish, *adj.* having to do with Spain.—*n.* the language spoken in Spain.—*n.* **Spaniard** (span'yard), a person who belongs to Spain.

spank, *v.* to strike with the hand : to move along quickly.

spank'er, *n.* the hind-sail of a ship.

span'ner, *n.* a tool used to tighten the nut of a screw.

spar, *n.* long piece of wood : ship's mast or cross-piece.

spar, *v.* to fight with the fists.

spare, *v.* to use in small amounts : to do without : to deal gently with : to save from death.—*adj.* not needed for use at the time : thin (e.g. a tall, *spare* man).

spark, *n.* a small red-hot part shot off from something that is burning : a small portion (e.g. a *spark* of love, courage) : the tiny electric flash which makes a motor-engine work : a lively fellow.—*v.* to make sparks.—*n.* **spar'kle**, brightness.—*v.* to shine in a glittering way.

sparrow, spar'ō, *n.* a small dull-coloured bird.—*n* **spar'row-hawk**, a short-winged hawk.

sparse, *adj.* thinly scattered : scarce. —*n.* **spar'sity.**

spasm, *n.* a sudden jerk of the muscles, as in hiccup and cramp : a sudden movement.—*adj.* **spasmod'ic**, coming now and again, not regularly : uneven.

spate, *n.* flood (e.g. The river is in *spate*).

spats, *n.pl.* small coverings for the ankles.

spat'ter, *v.* to splash with mud, paint, etc.

spat'ula, *n.* a broad knife-blade (often made of wood) used for spreading.

spav'in, *n.* a leg-disease of horses.

spawn, *n.* the eggs of fish or frogs.

—*v.* (of fishes and frogs) to lay eggs.

speak, *v.* to say in words.—*ns.* **speak'er**, one who speaks : the member of the House of Commons who sees that the talking there is done in an orderly manner ; **speech**, that which is said.—**to speak fair**, to talk to a person in a friendly way.

spear, *n.* a long weapon, with an iron or steel point, used in war and in hunting.—*v.* to stick with a spear.

special, spesh'al, *adj.* not common : more than usual : meant for a certain purpose.—*n.* an extra train, run for a certain purpose (e.g. for a football match).—*v.* **spe'cialise**, to mark out as different : to give one's self up to the study of one particular job.— *ns.* **spe'cialist**, one who makes a very deep study of one branch of work (e.g. Dr Brown is a heart *specialist* ; Dr White is an ear *specialist* ; I am a radio *specialist*) ; **spe'cialty** or **speciality** (spesh-i-al'it-i), something to which one gives more than the usual amount of thought : something for which a person or shop is well known (e.g. Muttonpies are this baker's *speciality*) ; **species** (spē'shis), a group of plants or animals which are alike in certain ways : a kind ; **specie** (spē'shi), gold and silver coins ; **specific** (spes-if'ik), a cure which will not fail.—*adj.* **specif'ic**, giving all the details clearly.—*v.* **spe'cify**, to set down or tell clearly what is wanted : to make particular mention of.—*n.* **specifica'tion**, a written account telling about the plan of a building, motor-car, ship, etc., and giving all the details.

specimen, spes'i-men, *n.* a sample : an item in a collection (e.g. a stamp in an album).

specious, spē'shus, *adj.* showy but not good : false.

speck, *n.* a small spot : a grain of dust.—*n.* **speck'le**, a spot on a different-coloured background. —*adj.* **speck'led**, dotted with speckles.

spec′tacle, n. a sight, esp. one which is striking or wonderful:—n.pl. **spec′tacles,** glasses which a person wears to help his eyesight.— adj. **spectac′ular,** making a great show.

spectā′tor, n. one who looks on.

spectre, spek′ter, n. a ghost.—adj. **spec′tral,** ghostly.

spec′trum, n. the rainbow colours which light shows when passed through a specially shaped glass. —n. **spec′troscope,** an instrument by means of which a spectrum can be seen.

spec′ulate, v. to help one's thinking by guessing: to wonder: to buy goods in order to sell them again at a profit.—adj. **spec′ulative,** letting one's thought wander widely: running the risk of making either a great profit or a great loss.

speech, n. the power or way of speaking: the words which a person speaks in talking to a meeting. — adj. **speech′less,** so surprised that one cannot speak.

speed, n. quickness of moving.—v. to move along quickly: to drive very fast in a motor-car: to go well.—adj. **speed′y,** going quickly. —n. **speedom′eter,** an instrument that shows how fast one travels.

spell, n. a few words which, when spoken, are supposed to act like magic: a charm: a short space of time: a turn (at work, rest, play).—v. to give the letters which make up a word.—adj. **spell′-bound,** charmed, held in wonder.—n. **spell′ing-bee,** a spelling competition.

spel′ter, n. zinc (a grey metal).

spen′cer, n. a light jersey.

spend, v. to use (money) for buying: to use up: to pass time (e.g. I *spent* a week there).—adj. **spent,** unable to do more.—n. **spend′-thrift,** one who spends money freely and carelessly.

sperm′-whale, n. a kind of whale from which is got **spermaceti** (sper-ma-set′i), a waxy substance used for making fine candles.

sphagnum, sfag′num, n. a kind of moss sometimes used for dressing wounds.

sphere, sfēr, n. a ball: one's daily work: the rank or position which one holds among other people. —adj. **spher′ical,** round like a ball.

Sphinx, sfingks, n. in tales of old-time Greece, a monster with the head of a woman and the body of a lioness, which gave riddles to travellers, and strangled those who could not solve them (there is a well-known image of the Sphinx in Egypt): a puzzling person: one whose looks do not show his feelings.

spice, n. a sweet-smelling, sharp-tasting substance used for flavouring (pepper, nutmeg, vanilla are *spices*): anything that adds liveliness, interest.—v. to season with spice.—adj. **spicy** (spī′si), full of spices: sharp, lively.

spi′der, n. a creature with eight long thin legs, that spins a web in which to snare flies.—adj. **spī′dery,** like a spider: very thin.

spike, n. a small pointed rod: a large nail: an ear of corn: a head of flowers.—v. to pierce with a spike: to thrust a spike into a gun and break it off, making the gun useless: to make useless.

spikenard, spik′nard, n. an Indian plant which gives a sweet-smelling oil.

spill, v. to allow liquid to run out or overflow.—n. a fall.

spill, n. a thin strip of wood or twisted paper for lighting a candle, a pipe, etc.

spin, v. to draw out cotton, wool, silk, etc., and make it into threads: to whirl quickly.—ns. **spin′ner,** one who spins; **spin′-ning-wheel,** a machine for spinning, made up of a wheel driven by the hand or by a foot-treadle, which drives spindles.—**to spin a yarn,** to tell a long story.

spin′ach, n. a vegetable with thick juicy leaves, which are boiled and used for food.

spin′dle, n. the pin from which the thread is twisted in spinning wool or cotton: a pin on which anything turns.

spin′drift, n. the spray blown from the tops of waves.

spine, *n.* the backbone : any ridge running lengthways : a thorn.— *adj.* **spine′less,** having no spine : weak.

spin′et, *n.* an old kind of piano.

spin′ney, *n.* a small bushy wood.

spin′ster, *n.* a woman who is not married.—*n.* **spin′stress,** a woman who spins.

spi′ral, *adj.* coiled round like a spring or the lines on a screw.—Also *n.*

spire, *n.* a tall, sharp-pointed tower (e.g. on the roof of a church).

spir′it, *n.* life : the soul : a ghost : bravery, boldness : liveliness : real meaning : strong drink such as whisky or brandy.—*v.* (with *away*) to carry off secretly.— *adjs.* **spir′ited,** lively ; **spir′itless,** not lively, sad ; **spir′itual,** having to do with the soul ; **spir′ituous,** having to do with strong drink.— *ns.* **spir′itual,** a kind of hymn, sung by the dark-skinned people of America ; **spir′itualist,** one who believes that the souls of dead people go on living, and are able to talk to persons who are still alive—the belief is called **spir′itualism.**—**in high spirits,** very lively ; **spirit lamp,** a lamp which burns *methylated spirit* (a purple liquid).

spit, *n.* an iron bar on which meat is roasted : a long piece of land running into the sea.

spit, **spit′tle,** *ns.* the liquid which forms in a person's mouth.—*v.* **spit,** to throw this liquid out from the mouth : to rain slightly.—*ns.* **spit′fire,** a hot-tempered person ; **spittoon′,** a dish into which people may spit.

spite, *n.* grudge : ill-will : hatred.— *v.* to vex.—*adj.* **spite′ful.**—**in spite of,** taking no notice of (e.g. He went off *in spite of* his father's command that he was to stay).

splash, *v.* to spatter with water or mud.—*n.* water or mud thrown on anything.

splay, *v.* to put a bone out of place. —*adj.* turned outward (e.g. *splay-foot*).

spleen, *n.* a soft part inside the body, near the stomach : gloominess of mind : bad temper.—*adj.* **splenet′-ic,** easily made angry or gloomy.

splen′did, *adj.* very fine : shining bright.—*n.* **splendour** (splen′dur).

splice, *v.* to join two ends of a rope by twining the threads together : to join together two pieces of wood by fitting them into each other.—*n.* a joint so made.

splint, *n.* a piece of wood tied to a broken arm or leg to keep the parts together.—*n.* **splint′er,** a sharp broken piece of wood, metal, pottery, etc.

split, *v.* to cut or break lengthways : to be broken in pieces : to give away secrets.—*n.* a long crack or break : (*pl.*) in dancing, the trick of going down on the floor with the legs spread out sideways.—*adj.* **split′ting,** very bad (e.g. a *splitting* headache).— **to split one's sides,** to laugh very loudly.

spoil, *v.* to make bad or useless : to become bad or useless : to take by force and rob.—*n.* plunder taken from a captured town, ship, etc.—*n.* **spoil′er,** a plunderer, robber.

spoke, *n.* one of the ribs or bars from the centre to the rim of a wheel.—**a spoke in one's wheel,** a difficulty in one's way.

spoke′shave, *n.* a tool for shaping wood.

spokes′man, *n.* one who speaks for others.

spoliā′tion, *n.* plundering robbery.

sponge, spunj, *n.* the soft frame-work of a kind of sea-animal, used for washing the body because it sucks up and holds water.—*v.* to wipe with a sponge : to live by getting money and favours from others.—*adj.* **spongy** (spun′ji), soft like a sponge : soft and damp.—**to throw up the sponge,** to give up a fight.

spon′sor, *n.* one who gives his word that another person will do something : a god-father or god-mother.

spontaneous, spon-tā′ne-us, *adj.* done readily, without being forced : seeming to happen of its own accord.—*n.* **spontanē′ity.**

spook, *n.* a ghost.

spool, *n.* a reel for thread, photograph film, etc.

spoon, *n.* a hollow-shaped piece of metal, wood, horn, fixed to a handle, and used for lifting liquid foods to the mouth: a wooden golf-club.—*v.* to lift with a spoon.

spoor, *n.* the footmarks or trail left by an animal.

sporad'ic, *adj.* happening here and there, or now and again.

spore, *n.* the seed of plants such as ferns.

spor'ran, *n.* a fancy hanging pocket, with tail-like ornaments, worn in front of a kilt.

sport, *n.* games such as football, cricket, fishing, hunting: something which gives fun: a jest: a person who is fond of fun and games.—*v.* to have fun.—*adjs.* **sport'ing**, liking sport: believing in fair play: having a chance of success: **sport'ive**, playful, merry. —*ns.* **sports'man**, one who enjoys open-air games: one who likes to see fair play: **sports'manship**, a liking for fair play.

spot, *n.* a small round mark or stain (of mud, paint, etc.): a place (e.g. This is the *spot* where Nelson fell).—*v.* to mark with spots: to catch sight of.—*adjs.* **spot'ted**, **spot'ty**, full of spots: **spot'less**, very clean and tidy.—*n.* **spot'light**, a light that is shone on an actor on the stage.

spouse, *n.* a husband or wife.

spout, *n.* a mouth like that of kettle or tea-pot: strong jet of liquid. —*v.* to pour out: to talk a lot.

sprain, *n.* a painful twist.—Also *v.*

sprat, *n.* a small fish.

sprawl, *v.* to throw the limbs about carelessly when lying or resting.

spray, *n.* a fine mist of water like that made by a waterfall or by a dashing wave: a shower-bath. —*v.* to squirt with a mist of water or some other liquid.

spray, *n.* a small twig or shoot of a plant.

spread, spred, *v.* to scatter in all directions: to put the cloth, knives, forks, cups, etc. on a table: (of an illness such as fever) to go from one person to another.—*n.* a table full of fine things to eat: a cover for a bed:

the space covered by whatever is spread or scattered.—*adj.* **spread-eagled** (-ē'gild), with arms and legs spread out: scattered widely.

spree, *n.* a merry party.

sprig, *n.* a small twig: a young person: a nail without a head: a piece of lace.

sprightly, sprīt'li, *adj.* lively.—*n.* **spright'liness**.

spring, *v.* to jump: to come up from under ground: to come from (e.g. His bravery *springs* from his love of adventure): to explode a mine.—*n.* a leap: a coil of wire, such as that used to make a clock go: a small stream flowing out from the ground: the season when plants begin to grow (in Britain, the months of March, April, and May).—*adj.* **spring'y**, jumping up quickly.—*ns.* **spring'-board**, a jumping-off board from which swimmers dive; **spring'-bok**, a deer found in South Africa; **spring'er**, a dog used in hunting; **spring'-tide**, the season of spring: the time of very high tide of the sea.—**to spring a leak**, to become leaky; **to spring a surprise**, to give a surprise.

sprink'le, *v.* to scatter in small drops or pieces.—*ns.* **sprink'ling**, a few here and there; **sprink'ler**, something which sprinkles water or some other liquid (e.g. to put out a fire).

sprint, *v.* to run a short race at full speed.—Also *n.*

sprite, *n.* a fairy.

sprout, *v.* to begin to grow.—*n.* a young bud.

spruce, sproos, *adj.* neat, smart.

spruce, sproos, *n.* a kind of fir-tree.

sprȳ, *adj.* lively, gay.

spūme, *n.* froth, foam.

spunk, *n.* match-wood: pluck.

spur, *n.* a sharp point worn by a horse-rider on his heel and used to drive on his horse: anything that urges a person on to do something: a small line of mountains running off from a larger range.—*v.* to use spurs on a horse: to urge on.—**on the spur of the moment**, (said or done) without thinking beforehand: in rash haste.

spurious, spū'ri-us, *adj.* false.

spurn, *v.* to cast aside with scorn.

spurt, *v.* to spout in a sudden stream.—*n.* a sudden stream pouring out: a sudden effort.

sputter, *v.* to spit or spill over in small drops (like the wax of a burning candle).

spy, *n.* one who is sent into the country or camp of an enemy in order to find out secrets.—*v.* to catch sight of: to watch secretly.—*n.* **spy'glass**, a small telescope.

squabble, skwob'il, *v.* to quarrel noisily.—Also *n.*

squad, skwod, *n.* a group of soldiers or workmen.—*n.* **squad'ron**, a number of warships under an admiral: a number of aeroplanes (usually about 12) under a **squadron-leader** (=major): a number (120 to 200) of horse-soldiers.

squalid, skwol'id, *adj.* very dirty, filthy.—*n.* **squal'or**.

squall, skwawl, *n.* a strong and sudden gust of wind.—*v.* to cry out loudly.—*adj.* **squal'ly**.

squander, skwon'der, *v.* to waste one's money, goods, strength, etc.

square, skwār, *n.* a figure shaped thus, □: a large open space in the middle of a town: (in arithmetic) the answer when a number is multiplied by itself.—*adj.* shaped like a square: fair, honest (e.g. a *square* deal, i.e. a fair or just action or offer): (in games) equal in scores: enough to satisfy (e.g. a *square* meal): facing one, right in front.—*v.* to make like a square: to pay what one owes: to multiply a number by itself.—**square root**, the number which, multiplied by itself, gives a certain other number (e.g. 4 is the *square root* of 16).

squash, skwosh, *v.* to crush together.—Also *n.*

squash'-rack'ets, *n.* a ball-game played in a four-walled court.

squat, skwot, *v.* to sit down on the heels: to come to live on a piece of land without right.—*adj.* short and thick.—*n.* **squat'ter**, one who comes to live on a piece of land

without right: one who gets land from the government.

squaw, skwaw, *n.* the wife of a Red Indian.

squawk, skwawk, *v.* to give a harsh cry.—Also *n.*

squeak, skwēk, *v.* to give a high, shrill cry.—Also *n.*

squeal, skwēl, *v.* to give a loud, shrill cry.—Also *n.*

squeamish, skwēm'ish, *adj.* a little bit sick: easily sickened.

squeegee, skwē-jē, *n.* a rubber roller for pressing photographs dry.

squeeze, skwēz, *v.* to press together tightly: to force through.—*n.* the act of squeezing: a crowd of people crushed together.

squib, skwib, *n.* a small firework.

squid, skwid, *n.* a fast-swimming sea-creature of the cuttle-fish kind.

squint, skwint, *v.* to twist the eyes in looking at something: to have the eyes looking different ways.—*n.* a fault in eyesight (eyes looking in different ways). —*adj.* off the straight.

squire, skwīr, *n.* a country gentleman who owns a large stretch of land: in olden times, a knight's servant.

squirm, skwirm, *v.* to wriggle the body, esp. in pain.

squirrel, skwir'el, *n.* a little animal, usually reddish-brown in colour, with a bushy tail, and living mostly in trees.

squirt, skwirt, *v.* to shoot out a narrow stream of water.—Also *n.*

stab, *v.* to stick a sharp point into.— *n.* a wound made by a sharp-pointed weapon: a sharp pain.

sta'ble, *n.* a building for horses. —*adj.* standing firm, steady: lasting a long time.—*n.* **stabil'ity**, steadiness.

stacca'to, *adj.* (in music) with the notes played in a sharp, jerky manner, each being clearly sounded.

stack, *n.* a large pile of straw, hay, wood, etc.: a number of things standing together (e.g. a *stack* of chimneys, rifles).—*v.* to pile in a stack.

sta'dium, *n.* a large sports-ground or race-course.—*pl.* **sta'dia**.

staff, stahf, *n.* a stick: a flag-pole: the five lines and four spaces on which music is written: workers under a head (e.g. *staff* of a school).

stag, *n.* a male deer:—*fem.* **hind.**

stage, *n.* a platform (e.g. in a theatre): the distance that may be travelled for a particular fare (e.g. From High Street to Low Street is a penny *stage*): period, step in development (e.g. the first *stage* of a war).—*v.* to act a play: to perform.—*ns.* **stage'-coach,** a coach running every day with passengers; **stage'-fright,** an actor's fear when he acts in public for the first time; **stage'-whisper,** loud whisper.

stag'ger, *v.* to sway from side to side: to surprise greatly.

stag'nant, *adj.* (of water) standing still, not flowing.—*v.* **stag'nate,** to remain still, without movement. —*ns.* **stag'nancy; stagna'tion.**

staid, *adj.* serious in manner.

stain, *v.* to give a different colour to: to mark with blobs of colour: to cover with guilt or shame.— *n.* a thin kind of paint (e.g. *floor-stain*): a mark which stains, and which will not wash out: a bad mark in one's character.— *adj.* **stain'less,** (of metals) not marking easily, not rusting.

stair, *n.* a number of steps one after the other, by which one can reach a higher or lower level. —*n.* **stair'case,** a stretch of stairs with rails on one or both sides.

stake, *n.* a strong stick pointed at one end: the stout post to which, in olden times, witches and other persons were tied to be burned.

stake, *n.* the money that one puts down as a bet.—*v.* to bet money: to risk.—**at stake,** to be won or lost: in great danger (e.g. My life is *at stake* if I do that).

stal'actite, *n.* a stalk of lime hanging from the roof of a cave (it is formed by the dripping of water containing lime).—*n.* **stal'agmite,** a stalk of lime, like a stalactite, but rising from the floor of a cave.

stale, *adj.* no longer fresh, because too long kept: no longer interesting.

stale'mate, *n.* (in a quarrel or argument) a position in which neither side can win.

stalk, stawk, *n.* the stem of a plant: a tall chimney.

stalk, stawk, *v.* to walk with long, slow steps: (in hunting) to go quietly up to animals (e.g. deer) in order to shoot at close range. —*n.* **stalk'er,** one who stalks animals.

stall, stawl, *n.* a place where a horse or other animal stands and is fed: a stable: a place on which articles are laid out for sale (e.g. a *fruit-stall, book-stall*): a seat in a church (for choir or clergy): a theatre seat on the ground floor: (flying) loss of speed and control.—*v.* (flying) to lose speed and get out of control: (in motoring) to stop the engine by mistake.

stallion, stal'yon, *n.* a male horse.

stalwart, stawl'wart, *adj.* tall and strong.—Also *n.*

sta'mens, *n.pl.* the small-headed stalks in the middle of a flower which bear the pollen.

stam'ina, *n.* strength, power of lasting out.

stam'mer, *v.* to have difficulty in saying the first letter of words in speaking. — *n.* difficulty in speaking.

stamp, *v.* to make a noise by hitting the floor or ground with the foot: to set or stick a mark on. —*n.* a mark made or stuck on letters or papers to show that money has been paid: something which makes a mark or pattern (e.g. on cloth, coins, books, etc.): the mark so made: a heavy steam-hammer for crushing: kind, sort (e.g. He is a man of a different *stamp*).

stampede, stam-pēd', *n.* a wild rush of frightened animals.—Also *v.*

stanch or **staunch,** *v.* to stop blood from flowing.

stanchion, stan'shun, *n.* a standing-up iron bar used as a support.

stand, *v.* to stop moving: to be in a certain position: to be on the feet or on end (not lying or sitting down): to bear, to suffer (e.g. I cannot *stand* this heat): to offer to pay for (e.g. I will *stand* you tea).—*n.* something on which anything is placed: lines of raised seats from which people may see games: an attempt to defend (e.g. a *stand* for freedom; The enemy made a *stand* on the hill).—*n.* stand'ing, one's rank or position among others (e.g. He has no *standing* among such clever men).—*adj.* placed on foot or on end: not moving or flowing: lasting (e.g. a *standing* joke): settled, fixed by rules.—*ns.* stand'point, one's point of view; stand'still, a stop (e.g. The car came to a *standstill*).—*adjs.* stand-off'ish, rather proud in manner; stand-up, fierce, bitter (e.g. a *stand-up* fight).—to stand by, to be ready to help; to stand fast, to refuse to give in; to stand for, to try to get into (e.g. I am *standing for* parliament); to stand up for, to be ready to fight for; to stand up to, to bear bravely: to fight against.

stan'dard, *n.* something which stands and is fixed (e.g. a *lamp-standard*): a rule by which other things may be judged: a large flag on a staff: a school class. —*adj.* according to rule, usual (e.g. One shilling is the *standard* charge).—*v.* stan'dardise, to make all of one kind or size.

stan'za, *n.* a number of lines making up a part of a poem—a verse.

stā'ple, *n.* a loop-shaped iron nail: the chief product of a place: a market.—*adj.* chief, main.

star, *n.* one of the bright bodies in the sky at night (except the moon): anything shaped with a number of points: the chief actor or actress in a play or film. —*v.* to act the chief part in a play.—*adj.* star'ry, full of stars.— *ns.* star'fish, a small sea-creature, with five points; star'-gazer, one who studies the stars; Stars-and-Stripes, the flag of the United States of America.

star'board, *n.* the right side of a ship, as one looks towards the bow (or front).—Also *adj.*

starch, *n.* a white flour-like food substance (found in potatoes, bread, biscuits, etc.): a kind of jelly used for stiffening clothes.—*adj.* starch'y, stiff with starch: cold and unfriendly in manner.

stare, *v.* to look at with a fixed look —Also *n.*

stark, *adj.* stiff: naked.—*adv.* quite (e.g. *stark* naked, *stark* mad).

star'ling, *n.* a small bird, with dark glossy feathers.

start, *v.* to begin to move: to jump back in surprise.—*n.* a beginning: the act of going away from a place (e.g. We had an early *start*): a fright: a help given to the weaker ones in a race (e.g. The youngest runner got a *start* of five yards).—*v.* star'tle, to give a fright to.

starve, *v.* to suffer greatly from hunger, cold, or lack of money: to die for want of food or heat.— *ns.* starva'tion; star'veling, a starved creature.

state, *n.* the condition in which something is (e.g. the bad *state* of the roads): the people of a country under a government: the government and its officials: great show, pomp (e.g. The king drove in *state*).—*adj.* having to do with the government.—*v.* to tell, say, or write fully.—*adj.* state'ly, noble-looking, proud.— *ns.* state'ment, that which is said or written; state'room, a large cabin in a ship; states'man, a man whose work it is to see to the governing of a country.

station, stāsh'n, *n.* a place where trains, buses, etc. stop to pick up or set down passengers: a place which is the centre for work or duty of any kind (e.g. *wireless-station, fire-station, military station*): one's rank in life.— *v.* to order a person to stay in a place.—*adj.* stā'tionary, standing still, not moving.—*n.* station-master, the man at the head of a railway station.

stationery, stā'shn-er-i, *n.* writing paper, envelopes, pens, inks, etc. —*n.* stā'tioner, one who sells these.

statis'tics, *n.pl.* figures and facts set out in order (e.g. *statistics* of trade for a year).—*n.* statistician (stat-is-tish'an), one who makes up or studies statistics.

statue, stat'ū, *n.* a copy of a person or animal carved in stone or metal.—*ns.* stat'uary, a collection of statues: statuette (stat-ū-et'), a small statue.—*adj.* statuesque (stat-ū-esk'), like a statue.

stat'ure, *n.* a person's height.

stā'tus, *n.* rank.

stat'ute, *n.* a written law of a country.—*adj.* stat'utory, according to law.

staunch, *adj.* firm in one's beliefs: able to be trusted.—*v.* See stanch.

stave, *n.* the lines on which music is written: a small piece of music or song: a verse.—*v.* (with *off*) to drive off, to keep away.

stay, *v.* to remain: to dwell: to cause to stand still: to keep from falling.—*n.* time spent in a place: a strong rope running from the side of a ship to the mast-head: (*pl.*) a woman's under-garment which supports the waist.

St Ber'nard, *n.* a large dog of the kind kept by the monks of the Great St Bernard Pass (in the Alps).

stead, sted, *n.* place (e.g. I shall go in your *stead*): use, help (e.g. This will stand you in good *stead*, i.e. this will be of great help to you).

steadfast, sted'fast, *adj.* firm: faithful and true.

steady, sted'i, *adj.* firm, not moving: regular: living a sensible life.—*n.* stead'iness.

steak, stāk, *n.* a slice of meat for cooking.

steal, *v.* to take what does not belong to one: to move quietly, so as not to be seen or heard.—*n.* stealth (stelth), the act of stealing.—*adj.* stealthy (stelth'i), done in a secret manner.

steam, *n.* vapour from hot liquid, esp. from boiling water.—*v.* to give off steam: to cook in steam: to move by steam.—*adj.* steam'y, too fast.—*ns.* steam'boat,

steam'er, steam'ship, a ship driven by a steam-engine; **steam-engine,** an engine worked by the force of steam: a railway engine; **steam'-roller,** a steam-driven engine, with large and very heavy wheels, used for flattening roads.

steed, *n.* a horse, esp. one which can run swiftly.

steel, *n.* iron mixed with carbon to make it very hard: a bar of steel on which knives may be sharpened: a piece of steel with which flint is struck to make sparks: a sword.—*v.* (with *one's self*) to harden one's courage.

steep, *adj.* going up or down with a great slope.—*n.* a cliff-like slope.

steep, *v.* to dip or soak in a liquid.

steep'le, *n.* a tower of a church rising to a point.—*ns.* steep'le-jack, one who climbs steeples and chimney-stalks to make repairs; steep'lechase, a race run across open country, over hedges, ditches, walls, etc.

steer, *n.* a young ox.

steer, *v.* to guide a ship, motor-car, etc.—*ns.* steer'age, the part of a ship set aside for the passengers who pay the lowest fares; steers'-man, one who steers; steer'ing-gear, the parts of a ship, motor-car, etc. which have to do with the steering.

stel'lar, *adj.* having to do with the stars.

stem, *n.* the part of a plant which supports the leaves and flowers, and through which the sap rises from the roots: the little branch on which are leaves or fruit: a family or branch of a family: the front part of a ship: the part of a word to which an end-part (called a *suffix*) may be added.—*v.* to stop or hold in check.

stench, stensh, *n.* a strong bad smell.

sten'cil, *n.* a sheet of metal, cardboard, etc., with a pattern cut out: the drawing or design made by rubbing ink over the cut-out pattern.—*v.* to make a design in this way.

stenography, sten-og´ra-fi, *n.* a kind of writing (called also *shorthand*) by which one can write down words as quickly as they are spoken.—*n.* **stenog´rapher**.

stentō´rian, *adj.* (of the voice) very loud.

step, *n.* one movement of the leg in walking or running : the mark of a person's foot : the sound made by the foot in walking : one of the parts of a stair or ladder on which one stands : (*pl.*) a flight of stairs.—*v.* to walk.—*ns.* **step´-dance**, a dance in which there are very tricky movements of the feet ; **step´- ping-stone**, a stone (e.g. in a stream) on which one may place the foot in crossing ; **step´-ladder**, a ladder with a support on which it rests.—**out of step**, not stepping with the same foot at the same time as other people ; **to step out**, to walk quickly ; **to take steps**, to begin to do something for a certain purpose (e.g. I shall *take steps* to have the guilty person punished).

step´-child, *n.* a child by a first marriage. (If John Smith's mother dies and his father marries again, John Smith is the *step-child* of the second Mrs Smith, and she is John's **step-mother**. If she has any sons or daughters they are John's **step-brothers** or **step-sisters**.)

steppe, step, *n.* a great plain, without trees.

stereoscope, ster´e-o-skōp, *n.* an instrument (with two glasses) for looking through, by means of which two pictures of the same object are made to look like one, which stands out very clearly.

stereotype, ster´e-o-tīp, *n.* a lead copy of a page of printing type which can be used many times over for printing.—*adj.* **ster´eo-typed**, fixed, not changing much (e.g. He has *stereotyped* ideas).

ster´ile, *adj.* bringing forth no fruit or crops : barren.—*n.* **steril´ity**.—*v.* **ster´ilise**, to make barren : to kill germs (e.g. in milk) by boiling or by other means.

ster´ling, *n.* a name for British money (e.g. one pound *sterling*).—*adj.* pure : of good quality.

stern, *adj.* angry or displeased in look, manner, or voice : showing no pity.

stern, *n.* the back part of a ship.—*n.* **stern´sheets**, the part of a boat between the stern and the rowers.

stertorous, ster´tō-rus, *adj.* snoring.

stethoscope, steth´ō-skōp, *n.* an instrument by means of which a doctor listens to the beats of a person's heart or tests his breathing.

stevedore, stēv´e-dōr, *n.* one who loads and unloads ships.

stew, stū, *v.* to cook by slow boiling.—*n.* meat stewed : worry.

steward, stū´ard, *n.* a ship's officer who sees to the stores and the serving of meals : a ship's waiter : one who shows people to their seats at a concert or meeting : a chief official at a race meeting : one who manages an estate or farm for someone else : —*fem.* **stew´ardess**.

stick, *v.* to pierce with something sharp : to fix or remain fixed : to hesitate.—*adj.* **stick´y**, clinging closely (like glue, treacle, fly-paper).—*ns.* **stick´ing-plas´ter**, a kind of tape with a sticky substance on one side, used for putting on cuts ; **stick´-in-the-mud**, a person who cannot get on in life.—**to stick in**, to keep hard at work ; **to stick pigs**, to hunt wild pigs on horseback and pierce them with spears.

stick, *n.* a small branch : a long thin piece of wood : a long piece of toffee, etc.

stick´leback, *n.* a small river-fish with prickles on its back.

stick´ler, *n.* one who pays great attention to small matters.

stiff, *adj.* not easily bent : not able to move without pain : thick, not flowing easily : cold in one's manner : hard (e.g. a *stiff* examination).—*v.* **stiff´en**, to make or become stiff.—*adj.* **stiff´-necked**, proud, hard to move.

sti´fle, *v.* to kill by keeping away fresh air : to keep back (e.g. a cry, tears).—*adj.* **stif´ling**, very hot and stuffy.

stig′ma, *n.* a mark of disgrace : (in a flower) the top of the *pistil*.—*v.* **stig′matise**, to mark with disgrace : to give a bad name to.

stile, *n.* a set of steps for climbing over a wall or fence.

stilet′to, *n.* a long thin knife.

still, *adj.* without movement : silent : (of sounds) soft : (of water) calm.—*v.* to make calm or quiet.—*adv.* always : for all that.—*adjs.* **still′y**, quiet, calm ; **still′-born**, dead when born.

still, *n.* a vessel in which whisky or brandy is made.

stilt′ed, *adj.* not natural in manner.

stilts, *n.pl.* long poles with footrests on which a person may walk clear of the ground.

stim′ulant, *n.* something which stirs up the feelings : whisky, brandy. —*v.* **stim′ulate**, to stir up to action.—*n.* **stim′ulus**, something which stirs up action or quickens working :—*pl.* **stim′uli**.

sting, *v.* to prick with a sharp point : to cause pain or grief to.—*n.* the part of bee, wasp, scorpion, etc. with which it defends itself by pricking : the pain caused by a sting.

stingy, stin′ji, *adj.* mean, greedy.

stink, *n.* a bad smell.—*v.* to give out a bad smell.

stint, *v.* to give hardly enough.

sti′pend, *n.* pay (esp. of a clergyman).—*n.* **stipendiary** (stī-pen′-di-ar-i), a kind of judge.

stip′ulate, *v.* to set down conditions : to ask for.—*n.* **stipulā′tion**, condition : something asked for.

stir, *v.* to set in movement : to move one's self.—*n.* disturbance, fuss.—*adj.* **stir′ring**, exciting.

stirk, *n.* a young ox or cow.

stir′rup, *n.* a metal loop hung from a saddle as a support for the horseman's foot.—*n.* **stir′rup-cup**, a cup (of wine) drunk by a horseman before he leaves.

stitch, *n.* the loop made by a sewing-needle or by knitting-pins : a sharp, sudden pain in one's side.—*v.* to fasten with stitches. —**a stitch in time saves nine**, a small cure used early saves much trouble later on.

stith′y, *n.* a blacksmith's shop.

stī′ver, *n.* an old coin of small value.

stoat, *n.* a name for the weasel (a small rat-like animal).

stock, *n.* the trunk or stem of a tree : a block of wood : the handle of a whip, rifle, etc. : one's forefathers : a store of goods (e.g. a grocer's *stock*) : shares in a business : the animals of a farm (often called live‑**stock**) : liquid (used for soup) in which meaty bones have been boiled : a garden flower : —*pl.* **stocks**, a wooden frame, with holes for the ankles and wrists, in which, in olden times, breakers of the law were fastened as a punishment : the great wooden framework upon which a ship is supported when being built.—*v.* **stock**, to keep a supply of : to supply a cattle-farm with animals.—*adj.* lasting, known by everyone (e.g. a *stock* joke).— *adjs.* **stock′-still**, quite still ; **stock′y**, short and stout in build.—*ns.* **stockade′**, a fence of strong posts stuck close together in the ground ; **stock′broker**, a person who buys and sells shares in business companies ; **stock-in-trade**, the goods of a shopkeeper ; **stock′-market**, a place where men meet to buy and sell business shares ; **stock′-whip**, a whip with a short handle and long lash ; **stock′-yard**, a yard for the animals at a cattle-market or slaughterhouse.—**to take stock**, to make a list of all the goods in a shop : to look carefully at something.

stock′ing, *n.* a knitted covering for the leg and foot.

stodgy, stoj′i, *adj.* (of food) very heavy : (of people, writing) having no brightness.

stoic, stō′ik, *n.* one who bears pain or excitement without showing any signs of it.—*adj.* **stō′ical**.

stoke, *v.* to put coal, wood, or other fuel on a fire.—*n.* **stō′ker**, one who looks after a furnace ; **stoke′-hole**, the space, at the mouth of a furnace, where stokers work.

stole, *n.* a long robe reaching to the feet : a narrow shoulder-strip of silk or linen worn by priests.

stol′id, *adj.* dull : heavy : not easily

excited.—*ns.* stolid'ity, stol'id-ness.

stomach, stum'ak, *n.* the bag-like part of the body into which the food passes when swallowed: courage, pride.—*v.* to put up with, to bear.

stone, *n.* a hard piece of rocky matter: a shaped piece of stone for a certain purpose (e.g. *grind-stone, paving-stone*): a diamond, ruby, etc.: the hard seed of some fruits (e.g. peach, cherry): a measure of weight (=14 lb.).—*v.* to pelt with stones: to take the seeds out of fruit.—*adj.* made of stone.—*adjs.* ston'y, like stone: hard: fixed (e.g. a *stony* stare); stone'-blind, quite blind; stone'-deaf, quite deaf.—*ns.* stone'-fruit, a fruit which has a hard seed or seeds; stone'ware, a kind of pottery made out of coarse clay.— **to leave no stone unturned,** to do everything that can be done.

stook, *n.* a number of corn-sheaves standing together in a cornfield.

stool, *n.* a low seat without a back. **—to fall between two stools,** to lose both things because one could not decide which of them to choose.

stoop, *v.* to bend forward: to be mean enough to do a certain thing (e.g. He *stooped* to copying his neighbour's sums).—*n.* a bending forward of the body.

stop, *v.* to stuff or close up a hole: to cause to stand still: to cease from moving or from doing something: to prevent (a person) from doing something.—*n.* a pause: a standing still: a place where a train, bus, etc. stands for a little during a journey: a mark of punctuation: a knob on an organ for making a sound of a certain kind.—*ns.* stop'page, a state of no movement: something which blocks a tube: a strike of workmen; stop'per, a cork; stop'-cock, a short pipe with a tap; stop'-gap, something which serves a purpose for the time being or until something better is found; stop'-watch, an accurate watch used in timing races—it is started at the beginning of the race and stopped at the end.—**stop-press news,** (in a newspaper) news that has come in at the last minute, and is put in a column by itself.

store, *n.* a large amount: a supply of goods laid by to be used later: a place where goods are kept: a shop (esp. one with many different parts).—*v.* to put aside for use in the future.—*ns.* stor'age, the placing of goods in a store: money paid to a person who looks after stored goods; store'-house, store'room, a place where goods are stored.—**to set great store by,** to look upon as very good or valuable.

stor'ey, *n.* all the rooms on the same floor of a building (the second *storey* is one stair up, the third *storey* is two stairs up):—*pl.* stor'eys.—*adj.* stor'eyed, built in floors, one above the other.

stork, *n.* a wading bird with long bill, long neck, and long legs.

storm, *n.* a sudden burst of bad weather (e.g. with heavy rain, lightning, thunder, high wind): a burst of anger.—*v.* to be in great anger: to make a strong attack on a fort.—*adjs.* storm'y; storm'-bound, unable to leave a place because of a bad storm.— **to take by storm,** to capture a fortress by a sudden, strong attack.

stor'y, *n.* an account of something that has taken place: a tale.— *adj.* stor'ied, told in stories: famous.

stout, *adj.* fat, thick: strong: brave. —*n.* a strong kind of beer.—*n.* stout'ness.

stove, *n.* a fireplace (using coal, gas, oil, or electricity) used for warming a room or for cooking.

stove, *adj.* (with *in*) broken in.

stow, stō, *v.* to pack: to put away in a suitable place.—*n.* stow'-away, one who hides himself in a ship so that he may sail without paying a fare.

strad'dle, *v.* to stand or walk with the legs apart: to sit with one leg on each side (e.g. of a chair or horse).

strag´gle, v. to stray from the main body: to fall behind: to lie scattered.—n. **strag´gler**, one who wanders away from the rest and falls behind.—adj. **strag´gly**, spread out: untidy.

straight, strāt, adj. not bent or curved: fair, honest.—adv. in the shortest way: at once: plainly (e.g. I told him *straight* . . .).—v. **straighten** (strāt´en), to make straight.—adj. **straight-for´ward**, not turning to right or left: without any difficulties: honest, frank.—adv. **straight´way**, at once.—n. **straight-edge**, a kind of ruler.

strain, v. to stretch out tight: to hurt a muscle or other part of the body (e.g. by lifting a heavy weight): to wear out (a person's patience, friendship, etc.): to pass through a sieve.—n. a hurt to a muscle or other part of the body: something hard to bear or do: a tune or song: kind (e.g. a *strain* of fowls; a remark in the same *strain*).—n. **strain´er**, a small sieve such as that used for catching tea-leaves.

strait, adj. strict: narrow.—n. a narrow strip of sea between two pieces of land: (pl.) difficulties, hardships.—adjs. **strait´ened**, having become poor and needy; **strait´-laced**, very strict in thought and behaviour.—ns. **strait´-jacket**, **-waistcoat**, a jacket which can be tightly laced, sometimes used for binding prisoners and mad persons.

strand, n. the shore.—v. to run on to the shore.—adj. **strand´ed**, left helpless (e.g. without money or friends).

strand, n. one of the threads that make up a string or rope.

strange, strānj, adj. not well known: queer: having to do with lands beyond the sea.—ns. **strange´ness**; **stranger** (strān´jer), a person who is not known: a visitor.—a **stranger to the truth**, a liar.

stran´gle, v. to choke the life out by gripping the throat tightly.—n. **strangulā´tion**.

strap, n. a narrow strip of leather, cloth, etc.—v. to bind with a strap: to beat with a strap.—adj. **strap´ping**, tall and handsome.—n. **strap´-hanger**, one who stands in a bus, etc. and holds on by a strap above his head.

stratagem, strat´a-jem, n. a cunning trick.—ns. **strategy** (strat´e-ji), the art of guiding the movements of troops before a battle; **strat´egist**, a good general.—adjs. **stratē´gic**, **-al**.

strath, n. in Scotland, a wide valley.—n. **strathspey** (strath-spā´), a Scottish dance.

stratosphere, strat´ō-sfēr, n. a layer of the earth's atmosphere, about five miles above the earth.

strā´tum, n. a layer of rock (such as is seen in a quarry):—pl. **strā´ta**.—v. **strat´ify**, to set out in layers.

strā´tus, n. low clouds, spread out.

straw, n. the stalk on which corn grows, and from which it is thrashed: a quantity of these when thrashed: anything worthless.—n. **straw´berry**, a small, juicy, red fruit.

stray, v. to wander: to become lost.—adj. lost: happening here and there.—n. a wandering person or animal.

streak, n. a line or stripe different in colour from that which surrounds it.—v. to mark with streaks.—adjs. **streaked**, **streak´y**, having streaks.

stream, n. a flow of water, air, light, etc.: a small river.—v. to flow or pour out.—ns. **stream´er**, a narrow flag blowing in the wind: a beam of light in the sky; **stream´let**, a small stream of water.—adj. **stream´lined**, (of a motor-car, train, aeroplane, etc.) shaped so that it may cut through the air as easily as possible.

street, n. a road (in a town) lined with houses.

strength, n. power: the number of men in an army or part of it.—v. **strength´en**, to make strong.

strenuous, stren´ū-us, adj. making great efforts: requiring much strength.—n. **stren´uousness**.

stress, n. force: importance: the extra weight laid on the part of a word which is sounded most (e.g. *but*'ter): difficulty, trouble (e.g. We live in times of *stress*).—*v.* to make out to be important.

stretch, *v.* to draw out: to reach out: to lie spread out.—*n.* an unbroken length of space or time. —*n.* stretch'er, a light folding bed for carrying persons who are too ill to walk.

strew, stroo, *v.* to spread by scattering.

strick'en, *adj.* hurt, sorrowful (because of grief, old age, etc.).

strict', *adj.* paying great heed to correct behaviour, obedience to rules, etc.: exact.—*ns.* strict'ness; strict'ure, something harsh said or written about a person.

stride, *v.* to walk with long steps.— *n.* a long step: a step forward.

stri'dent, *adj.* making a harsh, unpleasant sound.

strife, *n.* a fight: a time of quarrelling.

strike, *v.* to give a blow to: to hit with force: (of clocks) to sound the hours and half-hours: to light (a match): to take down (a flag, tent, or sail): to find an unknown mine, oil-well, etc.: to stop work as a sign of displeasure (e.g. because wages are not high enough).—*n.* the stopping of work when workers strike.—*adj.* stri'king, splendid, unusual to look at.—to strike up, to begin to play (a tune); to go (come out) on strike, to strike work.

string, *n.* a thick thread: a piece of wire or gut in a violin, banjo, harp, etc.: a number of things coming one after the other.—*v.* to put on a string.—*adj.* stringy (string'i), like string.

stringent, strin'jent, *adj.* strict: allowing no freedom to choose.— *n.* strin'gency, strictness.

strip, *v.* to pull off in strips: to take off a covering (e.g. one's clothes).—*n.* a long narrow piece of anything: a change of clothes.

stripe, *n.* a band of different colour from that on which it stands: a blow with a whip or rod.—*adj.* striped (stript), having stripes.

strip'ling, *n.* a growing youth.

strive, *v.* to try hard to do something: to fight.—*n.* strife, fighting or quarrelling.

stroke, *n.* a blow (e.g. with a hammer, whip): something unlooked-for (e.g. a *stroke* of illness, a *stroke* of good luck): one movement of anything (e.g. *stroke* of a pen, *stroke* of a clock-chime, *stroke* of an oar in rowing): in a boat, a rower with whom the other rowers keep time.

stroke, *v.* to rub gently with the hand.

ströll, *v.* to wander on foot.—Also *n.*

strong, *adj.* powerful: easily noticed (smell): bitter (taste): able to stand against attack: healthy: moving with force.—*ns.* strength; strong'hold, a place which is built to stand against the attack of an enemy, a fortress; strong'-room, a room with strong door and walls in which money or jewels may be put for safety. —strong drink. See drink.

strop, *n.* a strip of leather on which a razor is sharpened.—*v.* to sharpen a razor.

struc'ture, *n.* a building, esp. one of large size: the way the parts of anything are arranged (e.g. the *structure* of a flower, the *structure* of a story).

strug'gle, *v.* to try hard (e.g. to free one's self, to do something): to fight.—*n.* a hard effort: a life with little money.

strum, *v.* to play a piano in a coarse, noisy manner.

strut, *v.* to walk about proudly (like a peacock).—Also *n.*

strut, *n.* a support (e.g. between the wings of an aeroplane).

strychnine, strik'nin, *n.* a bitter poisonous drug.

stub, *n.* a small stump (e.g. of a pencil, cigarette).—*v.* to knock one's foot against something hard.

stub'ble, *n.* the stumps of the stalks of corn left in the ground after corn is cut: a short and stiff beard.

stub'born, *adj.* unwilling to give way: headstrong.—*n.* stub'bornness.

stuc'co, *n.* a kind of plaster (used for covering walls, making ornaments, etc.).

stuck, *adj.* fixed on (by gum, glue, etc.).—*adj.* **stuck-up,** proud, haughty.

stud, *n.* a nail with a large head: a button with a head for fastening a collar.—*v.* to fasten studs in.—*adj.* **stud′ded,** thickly sprinkled with (e.g. The meadow is *studded* with flowers).

stud, *n.* a number of horses kept for breeding purposes.

stu′dent, *n.* one who studies.

studio, stū′di-o, *n.* the workshop of an artist or photographer: a building or room in which cinema films are made: (in broadcasting or television) a room where the talking, singing, etc. is done.

stud′y, *v.* to read books in order to learn a subject: to pay heed to (e.g. I shall *study* all your needs).—*n.* the learning of a subject (e.g. the *study* of history, botany): a room where one does one's reading: a photograph or painting.—*adj.* **stud′ied,** well thought out: done on purpose.

stuff, *n.* the material of which anything is made: cloth: nonsense.—*v.* to pack full: to fill the skin of a dead animal so that it may be kept.—*adj.* **stuf′fy,** hot, making breathing difficult.—*n.* **stuf′fing,** breadcrumbs, onions, etc. packed inside a fowl or other meat and cooked with it.

stul′tify, *v.* to make stupid.

stum′ble, *v.* to trip in walking: to do wrong.—*n.* a trip.—*n.* **stum′bling-block,** a difficulty in the way of a plan.

stump, *n.* the root left after the main part has been cut away (e.g. the *stump* of a tree, tooth, arm): one of the wickets in cricket.—*v.* (in cricket) to knock down a batsman′s wicket while he is outside his mark: to walk with a heavy tread: to puzzle greatly.—*adj.* **stump′y,** short and thick.

stun, *v.* to knock senseless (by a blow): to surprise very greatly.

stunt, *n.* a daring trick: a trick to attract attention.

stunt′ed, *adj.* small and badly shaped.

stū′pefy, *v.* to make stupid or senseless: to make speechless with surprise.—*n.* **stūpefac′tion.**

stupendous, stū-pen′dus, *adj.* wonderful, amazing (because of size or power).

stū′pid, *adj.* foolish: dull at learning: struck senseless: silly.—*ns.* **stupid′ity; stū′por,** the state of being senseless or having no feeling.

stur′dy, *adj.* strong: well built, healthy.

sturgeon, stur′jun, *n.* a large fish.

stutter, *v.* to utter one's words in a jerky way, to stammer.—*n.* a jerky way of speaking.—*n.* **stut′terer.**

stȳ, *n.* a pimple on the eyelid:—*pl.* **sties.** (Sometimes spelt **stye,** *pl.* **styes.**)

stȳ, *n.* a closed-in pen for pigs:—*pl.* **sties.**

Stygian, stij′i-an, *adj.* black, dark. (From the old-time story of the river *Styx,* the river of darkness.)

style, *n.* way, manner: one's manner of writing or speaking: a pointed tool for writing.—*adj.* **stȳ′lish,** well-dressed, smart, up-to-date.

styptic, stip′tik, *n.* something which stops bleeding.

suasion, swā′zhn, *n.* advice.

suave, swāv or swahv, *adj.* pleasant: agreeable.—*n.* **suav′ity,** pleasing manner.

subaltern, sub′l-tern or sub-ol′tern, *n.* an officer in the army under the rank of captain.

subconscious, sub-kon′shus, *adj.* only faintly aware of what one is doing.

subdivide, sub-di-vīd′, *v.* to divide into smaller parts.—*n.* **subdivi′sion,** a part made by subdividing.

subdue, sub-dū′, *v.* to conquer: to tame.

subed′itor, *n.* one who assists the editor of a paper.

sub′ject, *adj.* under the power of another: liable to suffer from (e.g. I am *subject* to colds).—*n.* one under the power of another: a member of a nation: something spoken or written about: (in grammar) the noun or pronoun in a sentence which does the action stated in the predicate (e.g. in *The boy reads the book,* '*boy*' is the *subject,* '*book*' is the *object*).—v. **subject'**, to bring under the power of : to conquer.

subjoin', v. to add at the end.

subjugate, sub'joo-gāt, v. to bring under one's power : to conquer.

sublet', v. to let a house for which one is paying rent one's self.

sublieutenant, sub-loo-ten'ant, n. an officer in the navy below the rank of lieutenant.

sublime', adj. very noble : grand.— n. sublim'ity.

submarine, sub'-ma-rēn, n. a warship which can travel under water.—adj. found under water, in the sea.

submerge, sub-merj', v. to cover with water : to sink.—n. submer'sion.

submit', v. to give in, to yield : to place a matter before someone so that he can give his opinion.— n. submis'sion, a surrender.—adj. submis'sive, meek, yielding easily.

subor'dinate, adj. lower in rank or importance.—n. one who serves under another.—v. to look upon as of less importance : to place in a lower rank.

suborn', v. to give a person money so that he will do a wrong (e.g. tell an untruth).

subpœna, sub-pē'na, n. an order for a person to appear in court.

subscribe', v. to write one's name at the end of a statement : to help towards something (e.g. by giving money).—n. subscrip'tion, money given towards something.

subsequent, sub'sē-kwent, adj. following, coming after.

subservient, sub-ser'vi-ent, adj. weak-willed, ready to do as one is told.

subside', v. to settle down : to get less and less (e.g. The flood *subsided*) : to die away (e.g. The noise has *subsided*).—n. sub'si-dence, a falling down (e.g. of the ground above a mine).

sub'sidy, n. money paid by a government to help a trade or some other nation.—v. sub'sidise, to give money as a help.—adj. sub-sidiary (sub-sid'i-ar-i), acting as a help : of less importance.

subsist', v. to live : to live on (e.g. I *subsist* on milk and eggs).—n. subsist'ence, means of living.

S.D.—11

sub'soil, n. the earth just beneath the surface.

sub'stance, n. matter that can be seen and felt (e.g. Glue is a sticky *substance*) : real meaning (e.g. The *substance* of his speech was this . . .) : wealth (e.g. He is a man of *substance*).—adj. substantial (sub-stan'shal), able to be seen and felt : fairly big.—n. sub'stantive, (in grammar) a noun.—v. substantiate (sub-stan'-shi-āt), to tell what one knows in order to prove that a matter is true.

substitute, v. to put in place of (e.g. The cricket captain *substituted* John Smith for Tom Brown).—n. a person or thing acting or used instead of another.—n. substitū'tion.

substrā'tum, n. a layer lying underneath : a foundation.

subterfuge, sub'ter-fūj, n. a cunning trick to get out of a difficulty.

subterranean, sub-ter-rā'ne-an, adj. found under the ground.

subtle, sut'l, adj. not easy to understand : full of hidden meaning : cunning.—n. subtlety (sut'il-ti), cunning cleverness.

subtract', v. to take one number from another.—n. subtrac'tion.

sub'urb, n. a part of a town lying away from the centre.—adj. subur'ban, having to do with a suburb or suburbs.

subvention, sub-ven'shn, n. money given as a help.

subvert', v. to overthrow, destroy (e.g. the government of a country) : to take away a person's loyalty.—adj. subver'sive, likely to cause the overthrow of a government, or to take away loyalty.

sub'way, n. an underground passage (e.g. under a busy street) : an underground railway.

succeed, suk-sēd', v. to manage to do what one has been trying to do : to get on well : to take the place of (e.g. The prince *succeeded* his father on the throne) : to become the next holder of (e.g. The prince *succeeded* to the throne).—ns. success (suk-ses'), the doing of what one has been trying to do : a person or thing that turns out well ; **succession** (suk-sesh'un), the right of becoming the next holder (e.g. of a throne) : a number of things coming one after the other (e.g. Napoleon won a *succession* of victories, or, three victories *in succession*) ; **success'or**, one who comes after : an heir.—*adj.* **success'ful**, turning out well, or as planned : having done as one had planned ; **success'ive**, following each other without a break (e.g. Monday, Tuesday, and Wednesday are three *successive* days).

succinct, suk-singt', *adj.* short, brief.

succour, suk'ur, *v.* to help in time of distress.—*n.* help.

suc'culent, *adj.* juicy.

succumb, suk-um', *v.* to yield : to die.

suck, *v.* to draw in with the mouth (e.g. milk from a mother) : to put something in one's mouth and make a licking noise.—*n.* the taking of a mouthful by sucking : a noisy lick.—*ns.* **sucker**, a side shoot rising from the root of a plant : a wet pad (of leather, rubber, etc.) which sticks firmly to a surface ; **suck'ling**, a baby or young animal which still sucks its mother's milk ; **suction** (suk'-shun), the act of drawing in something by sucking (e.g. A water-pistol is filled by *suction*).—*v.* **suck'le**, to give milk to young.

sud'den, *adj.* happening without being expected : done in haste.—*adv.* **sud'denly.**—*n.* **sud'denness.**

suds, *n.pl.* frothy soapy water.

sue, sū, *v.* to start a law-case against

suède, swād, *n.* a kind of leather with a soft, dull surface.

suet, soo'et, *n.* hard animal fat.

suf'fer, *v.* to feel pain : to bear : to allow.—*ns.* **suf'fering**, pain : trouble ; **suf'ferance**, permission (e.g. He stays with us on *sufferance*, i.e. we allow him to stay with us, but shall send him away if he misbehaves).

suffice', *v.* to be enough.—*adj.* **sufficient** (suf-fish'ent), enough.

suf'fix, *n.* a small part added to the end of a word (e.g. *-ly*, added to *quick*, gives *quickly*). See p. 375.

suf'focate, *v.* to choke by stopping the breath or by keeping out fresh air.—*n.* **suffoca'tion.**

suffrage, suf'raj, *n.* a vote in an election, esp. for Parliament.

suffuse', *v.* to spread over (e.g. A blush *suffused* her face.—*n.* **suffu'sion.**

sugar, shoo'gar, *n.* a sweet substance got mostly from **sugarcane** (a tall grass which grows in hot countries) and **sugar-beet** (a vegetable which grows in Britain and elsewhere).—*adj.* **sug'ary**, sweet : full of sugar grains.

suggest, suj-est', *v.* to bring forward (an idea) : to hint : to make a remark.—*n.* **suggestion** (suj-es'-chn), an idea put forward : a helping hint.—*adj.* **suggestive** (suj-es'tiv), giving helpful ideas : rather rude.

suicide, soo'i-sīd, *n.* the taking of one's own life on purpose : one who kills himself on purpose.—*adj.* **suici'dal**, likely to cause one's own death.

suit, soot, *v.* to be pleasing to (e.g. This country *suits* me) : to look well on (e.g. That hat *suits* you). —*n.* a set of clothes (jacket, waistcoat, and trousers) : a trial in a law-court : the act of making love to a lady : one of the four divisions (spades, hearts, diamonds, clubs) of playing-cards.—*adj.* **suit'able**, fitting the purpose : just what is wanted.—*ns.* **suit'-case**, a large leather bag for carrying clothes ; **suit'or**, a man who visits a lady hoping that some day he may marry her.—**to follow suit**, to play the same kind of card : to do just as someone else has done.

suite, swēt, *n.* the body of attendants who go with an important person : a number of rooms : a set of furniture : a number of musical pieces connected with each other.

sulk, *v.* to keep silent because one is displeased.—*adj.* **sulk'y.**—**the sulks**, silence because one is displeased.

sul'len, *adj.* angry and silent : looking gloomy.—*n.* **sul'lenness.**

sul'ly, *v.* to dirty : to spoil (one's good name).

sulphur, sul′fur, *n.* a yellow substance found in the ground; when burnt it gives off a choking smell.—**sulphu′ric acid,** a burning liquid used in electric batteries.

sul′tan, *n.* the name for a king in some Eastern countries.—*n.* **sultan′a,** a sultan's wife: a kind of raisin.

sul′try, *adj.* very hot and close.

sum, *n.* the answer when two or more things are added together: a quantity of money: a question in arithmetic.—*v.* to add together: (with *up*) to gather together shortly all that has been said (e.g. At the end of the trial the judge *summed up* the evidence).—*v.* **sum′marise,** to re-tell a story shortly.—*n.* **sum′mary,** a short re-telling of a story, book, etc.—*adj.* short: done with haste, without wasting time.—*adj.* **sum′marily** (e.g. The judge dealt *summarily* with the prisoners, i.e. ordered them to be punished right away).

sum′mer, *n.* the warmest season of the year (in Britain, the months June, July, and August).—*n.* **sum′mer-house,** a small house in a garden.—**Summer Time,** time as on our clocks in summer, showing 12 noon 1 hour before the sun is at its highest point.

sum′mit, *n.* the top (e.g. of a hill): the highest point.—**summit conference,** a conference between heads of governments.

sum′mon, *v.* to order a person to come (e.g. to one's self, to a court of law).—*n.* **sum′mons,** an order to a person to go to be tried by a judge.—*v.* to give such an order.

sump′ter, *n.* a horse or mule for carrying loads.

sumptuary, sump′tū-ar-i, *adj.* checking expense or too fine living.—*adj.* **sumptuous** (sump′tū-us), very costly to buy: splendid.

sun, *n.* the round body in the sky from which the earth gets its light and heat.—*v.* (with *one's self*) to sit in the sunshine.—*adjs.* **sun′ny,** full of sunshine: cheerful; **sun′burned, sunburnt,**

having the body coloured red or brown by the heat of the sun.—*ns.* **sun′beam,** a ray of light from the sun; **sun′burn,** a red or brown colour of the skin, caused by the heat of the sun; **sundial** (sun′dī-al), a kind of clock (often found in gardens) on which the time is shown by a shadow cast by the sun; **sun′flower,** a large yellow flower whose petals are spread out like rays of the sun; **sun′rise,** the time in the morning when the sun is first seen; **sun′set,** the time in the evening when the sun goes out of sight; **sun′shine,** warm light from the sun: cheerfulness; **sun′stroke,** an illness caused by the rays of the sun striking one's head.

sun′dae, *n.* a large fancy ice-cream, with fruit, etc.

Sun′day, *n.* the first day of the week.

sun′der, *v.* to cut apart, to separate.

sundry, sun′dri, *adj.* several, more than one or two: various.—*n.pl.* **sundries** (sun′drēz), odds and ends: different small things.

sup, *v.* to eat one's evening meal: to eat with a spoon.

superabundant, soo-per-a-bun′dant, *adj.* more than enough.—*n.* **superabun′dance.**

superannuate, soo-per-an′ū-āt, *v.* to take away a person's job because he is too old, and give him a pension instead.

superb, soo-perb′, *adj.* very fine, showy: excellent.

supercilious, soo-per-sil′i-us, *adj.* full of pride: looking down on others.

superficial, soo-per-fish′i-al, *adj.* showy but not really good: not sincere (e.g. His kindness is *superficial*).—*n.* **superficial′ity.**

superfluous, soo-per′floo-us, *adj.* more than enough: not needed.—*n.* **superflu′ity.**

superhuman, soo-per-hū′man, *adj.* greater than would be expected of an ordinary man (e.g. He made a *superhuman* effort).

superintend, soo-per-in-tend′, *v.* to look after, to be in charge of (e.g. a school, or the building of a bridge).—*n.* **superinten′dent,** one who is in charge of people at work.

superior, soo-pēr'i-or, *adj.* higher in rank : better than others.— *n.* a person who is above others.

superlative, soo-per'la-tiv, *adj.* better than all others : (in grammar) an adjective with an ending which means ' more than all others ' (e.g. The *highest* hill of all).

supernatural, soo-per-nat'ū-ral, *adj.* not able to be explained in the ordinary way.— *n.* the world of wonders beyond our knowledge.

superscription, soo-per-skrip'shn, *n.* the markings on a coin.

supersede, soo-per-sēd', *v.* to take the place of someone (e.g. because one is better at that job): to give a person's job to someone who will do it better.

superstition, soo-per-stish'n, *n.* a belief in wonders, magic, good and bad luck, and in things which cannot be explained : a silly belief.— *adj.* **superstitious** (soo-per-stish'us), believing in such things.

superstructure, soo-per-struk'tūr, *n.* a building on the top of something else.

supervene, soo-per-vēn', *v.* to happen.

supervise, soo-per-vīz', *v.* to be in charge of some work and see that it is properly done.— *ns.* **supervision** (soo-per-vizh'n); **supervisor.**

supine, soo'pīn, *adj.* lying on the back.

supper, *n.* the evening meal.

supplant', *v.* to take the place of somebody, esp. by unfair or cunning means.

supple, *adj.* bending easily, springy (like a thin cane).— *n.* **suppleness.**

supplement, sup'le-ment, *n.* something added : extra pages added to a newspaper or magazine for some special reason.— *v.* **supplement',** to add something in order to make up for what is lacking.— *adj.* **supplementary,** added as an extra.

suppliant, sup'li-ant, *adj.* asking earnestly.— *n.* one who asks earnestly.— *v.* **supplicate,** to ask earnestly for something (e.g. by praying).— *n.* **supplication,** an earnest prayer.

supply', *v.* to provide what is wanted.— *n.* an amount of something that is wanted (e.g. a *supply* of writing-paper).— *n.pl.* **supplies** (sup-līz'), a stock of necessary things, esp. food or money.

support', *v.* to hold up : to provide food, clothes, etc. for a person : to help a person to do something (e.g. by giving him money, praise).— *n.* something which holds up : one who provides food, clothes, etc. for another (e.g. He is my only *support*).— *n.* **supporter,** one who helps and takes an interest (e.g. a *supporter* of a football club).

suppose', *v.* to look upon a statement as true (e.g. Let us *suppose* I had £100): to think (e.g. What do you *suppose* I did ?).— *n.* **supposition,** a statement taken as true : something imagined.— *adj.* **supposititious** (sup-pos-i-tish'-us), false.

suppress', *v.* to crush, put down (e.g. a rebellion): to keep back (e.g. a yawn, a piece of news).— *n.* **suppression,** the act of suppressing.

suppurate, *v.* to fester.

supreme, soo-prēm', *adj.* highest : greatest : most powerful.— *n.* **supremacy,** chief power.

surcharge, *n.* extra postage.

surcingle, ser'sing-gl, *n.* strap fastening a saddle on a horse.

sure, shoor, *n.* certain : not likely to fail : strong. — *advs.* **surely,** without doubt.— *n.* **surety** (shoor'ti), certainty : person who promises that another person will do something : pledge money.— *adj.* **sure'-footed,** able to walk in dangerous places without slipping or falling.— **to be sure !** certainly !

surf, *n.* the foam made by the dashing of waves.

surface, *n.* the outside or top of anything (e.g. the *surface* of the earth).— *n.* **surface-man,** a man who helps to keep a railway-track in good order.

surfeit, sur'fit, *n.* too much of anything.— *v.* to give or take too much of anything.

surge, *v.* to rise high : to move like

waves.—*n.* the rising of a large wave : waves.

surgeon, sur′jon, *n.* a doctor who treats injuries and diseases in which the body has to be cut.—*n.* **surgery** (sur′jer-i), act, or art, of treating diseases, injuries, by operation : doctor's, dentist's consulting room.—*adj.* **sur′gical.**

sur′ly, *adj.* gruff and cross in manner.—*n.* **sur′liness.**

surmise′, *v.* to suppose, to imagine.—*n.* **sur′mise**, something that is supposed.

surmount′, *v.* to overcome (e.g. a difficulty).

sur′name, *n.* a person's last name, i.e. his family name (e.g. Tom Brown's *surname* is Brown).—*adj.* **sur′named**, having the surname of (e.g. Brown).

surpass′, *v.* to go beyond, to be more than : to be better than.

surplice, sur′plis, *n.* a loose white gown worn by clergymen and by members of a choir.

sur′plus, *n.* the amount left over after using what is wanted.

surprise′, *v.* to come upon a person or an enemy when he is not expecting it : to cause a person to wonder.—*n.* an unexpected happening : a sudden attack.

surren′der, *v.* to give one's self up to another (e.g. Napoleon *surrendered* to the British) : to hand over.—Also *n.*

surreptitious, sur-rep-tish′us, *adj.* done in a secret, underhand way.

surround′, *v.* to go or be all round (e.g. The sea *surrounds* Britain).—*n.pl.* **surround′ings**, the country lying around a person or place : the people and places with which one has to do in one's daily life.

sur′tax, *n.* an extra tax.

surveillance, sur-vāl′ans, *n.* a close watch (e.g. The bridge was built under the engineer's *surveillance*).

survey, sur-vā′, *v.* to look over : to inspect : to measure out (e.g. a piece of land).—*ns.* **survey** (sur′vā), a wide view (e.g. over a country) : a talk or book dealing with a subject in a general way : a plan or map of a piece of land ; **survey′or**, one who makes plans or maps of land.

survive′, *v.* to remain alive : to live longer than.—*ns.* **survi′val** ; **survi′vor**, one who remains alive (e.g. after an accident).

susceptible, sus-sep′tibl, *adj.* liable to be affected by (e.g. He is *susceptible* to colds).—*n.* **susceptibil′ity.**

suspect, *v.* to think, without being certain (e.g. The car has stopped—I *suspect* that the petrol is finished) : to be doubtful about.—*ns.* **sus′pect**, a person who may be guilty : a person who may have a disease about him ; **suspicion** (sus-pish′on), a feeling of doubt about a person or matter (e.g. I have a *suspicion* that you took my pencil).—*adj.* **suspicious** (sus-pish′us), having a feeling of doubt about a person or matter : not deserving to be trusted.

suspend′, *v.* to hang up : to stop for a time (e.g. The shop *suspended* business for a week).—*ns.* **suspen′der**, an elastic garter to keep up socks or stockings ; **suspense′**, a time of anxious waiting (e.g. to hear how a sick friend is).—**suspension bridge**, a bridge which does not rest on a row of pillars or arches but is held up by steel ropes which stretch from one bank to the other.

suspicion, suspicious. See **suspect.**

sustain′, *v.* to hold up : to bear : to suffer : to give strength to (e.g. This food will *sustain* you).—*n.* **sus′tenance**, food.

sut′ler, *n.* one who follows an army and sells food, drink, etc.

suttee′, *n.* the Indian custom of burning the widow of a dead man along with his body.

suzerain, soo′ze-rān, *n.* a person or nation which has power over others.—*n.* **su′zerainty**, ruling power.

swab, *n.* a mop for cleaning a ship's deck : a piece of cotton-wool used for testing the throat.—*v.* to rub with a swab.

swaddle, swod′l, *v.* to wrap up a young baby tightly.—*n.pl.* **swad′-dling-clothes**, clothes used to wrap up a young baby.

swag'ger, *v.* to walk proudly, swinging the arms and body: to boast.—Also *n.*

swain, *n.* a lover: a country fellow.

swallow, swol'ō, *n.* a bird with pointed wings and forked tail; it flies to warmer lands for the winter.—*n.* **swal'low-tail**, a coat with a tail.

swal'low, *v.* to make food or drink pass over the throat into the stomach: to use up: to believe without doubting.

swamp, swomp, *n.* low ground made wet and soppy with water.—*v.* (of a boat) to fill with water: to be much too powerful for (e.g. The attacking army *swamped* the small force of the defenders).

swan, swon, *n.* a large, stately water-bird, usually white, with a long neck.—*n.* **swan'-song**, the last work of a poet or of a writer of music.

swank, *v.* to show off.—Also *n.*—*adj.* **swank'y.**

swap or **swop**, *v.* to give one thing for another.

sward, *n.* a patch of green turf.

swarm, *n.* a cluster of humming insects (e.g. bees): a thick crowd.—*v.* (of bees) to gather together in great numbers: to move in crowds.

swarm, *v.* (with *up*) to climb (a tree, wall, etc.).

swarth'y, *adj.* dark-skinned.

swas'tika, *n.* a sign shaped thus, ⤵, used as an emblem of the sun, and formerly of Nazi Germany.

swath, swath, or **swathe**, swāth, *n.* a line of corn or grass cut by a scythe.

swathe, swāth, *v.* to wrap round with clothes or bandages.

sway, *v.* to swing in a rocking manner: to try to make a person think or do as one wishes.—*n.* a rocking movement: rule, power (e.g. The Romans held *sway* in Britain for 400 years).

swear, *v.* to say (mentioning God's name or placing one's hand on the Bible) that one is telling the truth: to use bad language: to use holy names for no reason.

sweat, swet, *n.* the dampness from the skin when one becomes hot.
—*v.* to give out sweat: to work hard for very little pay.—*adj.* **sweat'y**, full of sweat.—*n.* **sweat'er**, a thick jersey.—**sweated labour**, hard work for which very little pay is given.

Swede, swēd, *n.* a native of Sweden.—*n.* **swede**, a large field turnip.—*adj.* **Swē'dish**, having to do with Sweden, its people, or their language.

sweep, *v.* to wipe or rub over with a brush or broom: to carry away with a long brushing movement: to travel over quickly (e.g. Fever *swept* the land): to move quickly in a proud manner.—*n.* a long, far-reaching movement: a stroke or blow: one who brushes the soot out of chimneys: (short for **sweep'stake**) a competition in which each person buys a ticket and the winner receives all (or most) of the money.—**a sweeping statement**, a very bold statement, sparing nobody; **to sweep the boards**, to beat everybody and win all.

sweet, *adj.* having the taste of sugar: pleasing to the taste: not sour or bitter: gentle, kind.—*n.* toffee, candy, chocolate, and such things: a dish such as a pudding, tart, jelly.—*v.* **sweet'en**, to make sweet.—*ns.* **sweet'ness**; **sweet'bread**, a part of the body lying near the stomach; **sweet'-bri'er**, a kind of wild rose; **sweet'heart**, a lover; **sweet-pea**, a climbing flower grown in gardens; **sweet-wil'liam**, a garden flower.—**to have a sweet tooth**, to like sweet-tasting things.

swell, *v.* to grow or make larger or louder: (of the sea) to become rough with waves.—*n.* a sea with large, heaving waves: a gradual rise in the height of the ground: a person wearing fine, showy clothes.

swel'ter, *v.* to be limp with the heat.—*adj.* **swel'tering**, very hot.

swerve, *v.* to turn quickly to one side.—Also *n.*

swift, *adj.* moving quickly: rapid.—*n.* a bird, something like the swallow.—*n.* **swift'ness**.

swig, *n.* a mouthful of liquid.

swill, *v.* to wash out : to drink a great deal.—*n.* a big drink : liquid food given to pigs.

swim, *v.* to float on or in water : to be dizzy.—*n.* a bathe in which one swims.—*ns.* **swim′mer,** one who swims ; **swim′ming-pond,** a pond specially made for swimmers.—*adv.* **swim′mingly,** smoothly and easily : with great success.

swin′dle, *v.* to cheat.—*n.* a fraud.—*n.* **swind′ler,** one who cheats : a rogue.

swine, *n.* a pig :—*pl.* **swine.**—*n.* **swine′herd,** a person who looks after pigs.

swing, *v.* to move to and fro (like the pendulum of a clock, or a **swing-door**) : to whirl round (e.g. a golf club) : (of ships at anchor) to sway to and fro with the tide : to walk quickly, moving the arms to and fro.—*n.* an act of swinging : a seat held up by two ropes.—*n.* **swing-bridge,** a bridge which swings open to let ships pass.—**in full swing,** going on without a stop ; **swing music,** jazz music.

swipe, *v.* to strike hard.—Also *n.*

swirl, *v.* to sweep along in a whirl.

swish, *v.* to cut the air with a whistling sound : to flog (e.g. with a cane).—Also *n.*

Swiss, *adj.* having to do with Switzerland or its people.

switch, *n.* a thin stick : a small brush : a small lever or handle for turning an electric current on and off : a piece of music in which several tunes are run on to each other.—*v.* to strike with a switch : to turn an electric current on or off : to turn quickly from one matter to another.—*n.* **switch′-back,** a railroad with steep ups and downs.

swiv′el, *n.* a joint that can turn round and round.—*v.* to turn round.

swoon, *v.* to faint.—*n.* a fainting fit.

swoop, *v.* to come down with a sweep (as a hawk does on its prey).—*n.* a sudden downward rush.

swop. See **swap.**

sword, sōrd, *n.* a weapon with a long blade for cutting or stab-

bing, used in fighting.—*ns.* **sword′-craft,** skill with the sword ; **sword′-dance,** a dance performed over swords lying crossed on the ground ; **sword′fish,** a large fish with a long pointed upper jaw like a sword ; **swords′man,** a man trained to use a sword skilfully ; **swords′manship,** clever use of the sword.

sworn, *adj.* (from *v.* **swear**) staying so for ever (e.g. *sworn* friends, *sworn* enemies).

sycamore, sik′a-mōr, *n.* a name given to several different trees—maple, plane, and a kind of fig-tree (the real sycamore).

sycophant, sik′ō-fant, *n.* a flatterer.

syl′lable, *n.* one of the sounds which make up a word (e.g. *cheese* has one sound or *syllable*, *but-ter* has two, *mar-gar-ine* has three).

syl′labus, *n.* a list of lectures, talks, debates, classes, etc., telling the subjects to be spoken about and the date of each talk.

sylph, silf, *n.* a spirit of the air : a fairy.

sym′bol, *n.* a sign (e.g. The dove is the *symbol* of peace) : a sign which is a short way of stating something (e.g. $+$ is the *symbol* for addition, $-$ for subtraction, $\times$ for multiplication, $\div$ for division).—*adjs.* **symbol′ic, symbol′-ical,** made up of signs : standing as the sign for.—*v.* **sym′bolise,** to be a sign of.

sym′metry, *n.* an equal balance in both sides of a picture, building, etc. : gracefulness of appearance.—*adj.* **symmet′rical,** not lop-sided in appearance : pleasing to look at.

sym′pathy, *n.* a feeling of pity or sorrow for a person who is in sorrow or trouble.—*adj.* **sympathet′ic,** feeling sympathy.—*v.* **sym′pathise,** to show one's sympathy (e.g. I *sympathise* with you in your trouble).

symphony, sim′fon-i, *n.* a piece of music for many different instruments.

symp′tom, *n.* a sign (e.g. A sore throat is often a *symptom* of fever).

synagogue, sin′a-gog, *n.* a Jewish church.

synchronise, sin′kron-īz, *v.* to happen at the same time: to fit a moving-picture film with suitable sounds.

syncopate, sing′kō-pāt, *v.* to change the beat a little in music: to play 'jazz' music.—*n.* **syncopā′tion.**

syncope, sin′kō-pē, *n.* a fainting-fit.

syn′dicate, *n.* a number of persons who join together to manage some piece of business.

syn′od, *n.* a meeting of clergymen.

syn′onym, *n.* a word which has the same (or nearly the same) meaning as another (e.g. 'ass' and 'donkey'; 'short' and 'brief'; 'to force' and 'to compel').—*adj.* **synonymous** (sin-on′i-mus), having the same meaning.

synop′sis, *n.* a short statement giving the main points of a book, speech, etc.

syn′tax, *n.* the correct putting together of words into sentences.

synthet′ic, *adj.* made by putting different substances together: (e.g. a *synthetic* dye, made from chemicals not from a plant): not natural.

syringe, sir-inj′, *n.* a tube-shaped instrument by means of which a liquid may be drawn in and squirted out.—*v.* to squirt with a syringe.

syr′up, *n.* a thick liquid containing much sugar: treacle made pure.

sys′tem, *n.* an arrangement of many parts which work together for a purpose (e.g. a *system* of taxation, education, spies): a regular way of doing something, a plan: the regular working of the parts of one's body.—*adj.* **systemat′ic,** following a regular plan: carefully thought-out, not put together by chance.

T

tab, *n.* a small tag or flap by which anything is gripped.

tab′ard, *n.* in olden times, a soldier's coat: a herald's coat.

tab′by, *n.* a female cat.

tab′ernacle, *n.* a place of worship.

tā′ble, *n.* a piece of furniture with a flat top and standing on legs: food: a statement of facts or figures set out in columns (e.g. multiplication *table*): a flat stone.—*v.* to put aside for the time being.—*ns.* **table-cloth; table-d′hôte** (tabl-dōt), a meal (in a hotel or restaurant) for which one pays a fixed price whether one eats all the courses stated on the menu or not; **ta′bleland,** a raised stretch of land with a level surface; **ta′blenap′kin,** a cloth used to wipe the hands and mouth while eating; **ta′ble-spoon,** a large spoon used at table.—**to turn the tables on someone,** to do to someone what he has been doing to you.

tableau, tab′lō, *n.* a picture: a striking group or scene:—*pl.* **tableaux** (tab′lō).—**tableau vivant**

(vē′vong), French for 'living picture,' i.e. a scene made up of living persons, imitating (without moving or speaking) some famous event or picture.

tab′let, *n.* a small flat plate on which to write, paint, etc.: a slab of soft toffee, chocolate, etc.

taboo′, tabu′, *adj.* holy, and not to be touched: forbidden.—*v.* to forbid having anything to do with.

tā′bor, *n.* a small drum.

tab′ulate, *v.* to set out in columns or rows.—*adj.* **tab′ular.**

tacit, tas′it, *adj.* meant but not said. —*adj.* **taciturn** (tas′it-urn), shy and quiet by nature.—*n.* **taciturn′ity.**

tack, *n.* a short sharp nail with a broad head: a side-to-side movement of a sailing-ship so that it may sail against the wind: a track (e.g. You are on the wrong *tack*).—*v.* to fasten or stitch lightly: (of sailing-ships) to move from side to side in face of the wind.

tack′le, *n.* the ropes, rigging, etc. of a ship: (in fishing) rod, line, hooks, etc.: ropes and pulleys for raising heavy weights: (in football, hockey, etc.) an attempt to stop, or take the ball from, another player.—*v.* to seize or come to grips with: (in football, etc.) to try to stop, or take the ball from, another player: to put questions to a person.—*n.* **tack′ling,** ropes, sails, etc. of a ship: the harness by which a carriage is drawn.

tact, *n.* careful dealing with a person, so that one does not hurt his feelings, or say or do anything which may cause trouble.—*adjs.* **tact′ful,** full of tact: very wisely said (e.g. a *tactful* remark); **tact′less.**

tac′tics, *n.* the plan used in arranging troops or warships during a battle: a plan to do something.—*adj.* **tact′ical,** having to do with a plan.—*n.* **tactician** (tak-tish′an), a clever planner.

tad′pole, *n.* a young frog or toad in its first stage after being hatched out.

taf′feta, *n.* a thin, glossy silk.

taf′frail, *n.* the rail round the stern, or back-end, of a ship.

tag, *n.* a metal point at the end of a shoe-lace: a luggage label: any saying that is often repeated: another spelling of the game tig.

tail, *n.* the part of an animal which sticks out behind the rest of its body: anything sticking out behind (e.g. *tail* of a coat, kite, aeroplane).—*ns.* **tail′-end,** the last part (e.g. of a story, procession); **tail′-light,** the light at the back of a motor-car, cycle, etc.; **tail′-spin,** (in aeroplanes) a steep, spinning, downward dive.—**to turn tail,** to run away.

tail′or, *n.* one who cuts out and makes clothes.—*v.* to make clothes.

taint, *v.* to make bad or rotten.—*n.* something bad or rotten: a mark of disgrace.

take, *v.* to lay hold of: to receive: to capture (e.g. a town from an enemy): to swallow (e.g. a meal, medicine).—*adj.* **tā′king,** pleasant (e.g. a *taking* manner).—*ns.* **tā′kings,** money taken (e.g. at a concert, fête); **take-off,** the set-

ting-off of an aeroplane: the place from which a swimmer dives.—**to take after,** to be like in appearance or manners; **to take heart,** to become brave; **to take heed,** to pay attention, to notice; **to take in,** to understand (e.g. a story): to deceive: to make (e.g. a dress) smaller; **to take in vain,** to use (e.g. God's name) without good reason; **to take leave,** to say good-bye; **to take off,** to make fun of: (in flying) to begin to move off; **to take place,** to happen; **to take to,** to get to like; **to take to heart,** to pay good heed to (e.g. a warning): to feel sorry over; **to take up,** to begin to learn about (e.g. Latin, motoring); **to be taken with,** to admire.

tale, *n.* story: number (e.g. '*tale* of bricks'—Exodus v. 18).—*n.* **tale′-bearer,** one who tells things about other people in order to do harm.

tal′ent, *n.* in olden times, a weight used as a measure of money: (*pl.*) great cleverness.—*adj.* **tal′ented,** very clever.

tal′isman, *n.* a charm, supposed to have magic powers.

talk, tawk, *v.* to speak.—*n.* speaking: gossip or chatter.—*adj.* **talkative** (tawk′a-tiv), fond of talking.—*n.* **talkie** (tawk′i), a moving-picture in which the persons speak.—**to talk shop.** See **shop.**

tall, tawl, *adj.* high: hard to believe.—*n.* **tall′ness.**

tal′low, *n.* the fat of animals, melted down.

tal′ly, *n.* a stick cut or notched to match another stick (once used in keeping accounts): an account.—*v.* to agree with (e.g. His story *tallies* with what we know).

tally-ho! a cry used by huntsmen.

tal′on, *n.* the claw of a bird such as the eagle or hawk.

tam′arind, *n.* a tree which grows in India and other hot countries.

tambourine, tam-boo-rēn′, *n.* a small one-sided drum, used in some dances; it has bells or jingles, and is hit with the hand, elbow, or knee.

tame, *adj.* not wild : used to living with human beings : not exciting or interesting.—*v.* to make tame.

tam′per, *v.* to open (a letter) dishonestly (e.g. My letters have been *tampered* with) : to meddle with, and break or spoil.

tan, *v.* to make an animal's skin into leather by treating it with **tan′nin,** a substance got from the bark of the oak and other trees : to have the skin burnt brown by the sun.—*adj.* **tanned** (tand).—*ns.* **tan′nery,** a place where leather is made ; **tan′ning,** a thrashing.

tan′dem, *n.* a bicycle with two seats one behind the other.—*adj.* (of horses) harnessed one behind the other instead of abreast.

tang, *n.* taste.

tan′gent, *n.* a straight line which touches a circle but does not cut into it.—**to go off at a tangent,** to go off suddenly in another direction.

tangerine, tan′jer-ēn, *n.* a small, sweet orange.

tangible, tan′jibl, *adj.* able to be touched : real : worth while.

tan′gle, *v.* to mix (e.g. threads) together in knots or in a confusing way.—*n.* a mix-up : a muddle.

tan′go, *n.* a S. American dance.

tank, *n.* a large metal holder for water, petrol, gas, etc. : a large steel-covered car armed with guns, used in war to break through the enemy's lines.—*n.* **tank′er,** a ship for carrying oil : a fuel aircraft.

tank′ard, *n.* a large metal drinking-mug.

tannin. See **tan.**

tan′sy, *n.* a plant with small yellow flowers.

tan′talise, *v.* to annoy by offering something and then taking it away.—*adj.* **tantali′sing,** raising hopes and then dashing them : annoying.

tant′amount, *adj.* equal (to).

tant′rum, *n.* a fit of bad temper : tiresome behaviour.

tap, *v.* to knock gently.—Also *n.*

tap, *n.* a hole or short pipe which, when opened, allows liquid to run through.—*v.* to fit with a tap and draw liquid away.—*ns.*

tap′root, a long-shaped root (e.g. the carrot) ; **tap′ster,** one who serves in a public-house.

tape, *n.* a narrow band or strip of strong cloth (used for tying).—*ns.* **tape′-measure,** a strong tape marked off in inches, feet, etc.; **tape′-recor′der,** an instrument for recording sound on magnetic tape.

tā′per, *n.* a thin candle (used for lighting fires, etc.).—*v.* to become smaller and smaller at one end.

tap′estry, *n.* a cloth with designs or figures worked in it (often hung on walls as a decoration).

tapioca, tap′i-ō′ka, *n.* a food substance got from the root of the cassava ; used for making puddings.

tā′pir, *n.* a wild animal something like a large pig.

tar, *n.* a thick, black, sticky liquid, got from pine-trees and from coal, and much used in road-making : a sailor.—*v.* to smear with tar.—*adj.* **tar′ry,** like tar: covered with tar.—**tarred with the same brush,** having the same (bad) habits.

tar′dy, *adj.* slow : late.—*adv.* **tar′dily.**—*n.* **tar′diness.**

tare, tār, *n.* a weed found growing among corn : the weight of a box, truck, etc. when empty.

tar′get, *n.* a mark to fire at : a small shield.

tar′iff, *n.* a list of prices : a list of the taxes to be paid on various articles when they are brought into a country.

tarn, *n.* a small lake among mountains.

tar′nish, *v.* to make or become dull or badly-coloured : to spoil (e.g. a person's good name).

tarpaul′in, *n.* strong cloth covered with tar to make it waterproof (used on boats, railway-trucks, etc.).

tarry, ta′ri, *v.* to stay behind : to be slow or late.

tarry. See **tar.**

tart, *n.* a small pie containing fruit or jam.

tart, *adj.* sour.

tar′tan, *n.* cloth with a square pattern of different colours—used for making Scottish kilts and plaids.

tar'tar, *n.* a kind of lime, left by wine in casks : a substance which gathers on the teeth : a bad-tempered person, who cannot be easily dealt with.—**cream of tartar**, a white powder used in baking.

task, *n.* a set piece of work to be done.—*n.* **task'master**, one who gives people hard work to do and sees that they do it.—**to take to task**, to scold.

tas'sel, *n.* a hanging bunch of threads, used as an ornament : anything like a tassel (e.g. the young leaves on a larch).—*adj.* **tas'selled**, having tassels.

tāste, *n.* the pleasant or unpleasant quality of something that is eaten (e.g. Sugar has a sweet *taste*, vinegar a sour *taste*) : a small amount : one's power to tell the difference between what is good and bad, polite and rude, ugly and beautiful (e.g. His remarks are not in good *taste*, i.e. are somewhat rude. His clothes show good *taste*, i.e. are well chosen and made).—*v.* to test by eating.—*adjs.* **taste'ful**, neat, of good appearance ; **taste'less**, having no taste ; **tās'ty**, good to eat.

tat'ters, *n.pl.* ragged clothes.—*n.* **tatterdemā'lion**, a ragged fellow. —*adj.* **tat'tered**, ragged.

tat'tle, *n.* gossiping talk about others.—*v.* to tell tales or secrets.

tattoo', *n.* a beat of drum and a bugle-call to call soldiers together : a soldiers' display, by torch-light or search-light.

tattoo', *v.* to prick the skin and mark it with coloured patterns, designs, etc. (often done by sailors).

taunt, *v.* to tease with unkind words : to make fun of unkindly.—*n.* an unkind, teasing remark.

taut, *adj.* pulled tight.—*v.* **taut'en**, to make tight.

tautology, taw-tol'o-ji, *n.* the repeating, without good reason, of the same thing in a different way (e.g. He *hit* and *struck* me).

tav'ern, *n.* a public-house, an inn.

tawdry, tawd'ri, *adj.* showy but not good.

tawn'y, *adj.* yellowish-brown.

tax, *n.* money paid by persons to the government of their country (to help to pay for parliament, army, navy, etc.) : heavy burden : difficult task.—*v.* to make persons pay a tax : to wear away (e.g. Your conduct *taxes* my patience).—*ns.* **taxā'tion**, the taxes which the people of a country have to pay ; **tax'payer**.

tax'i, *n.* (*pl.* **taxis**) a motor-car which may be hired, the fare being shown on the dial of a machine called a **tax'imĕter**.—*v.* **taxi**, to travel in a taxi : (of aeroplanes) to run along the ground.

tax'idermist, *n.* one who stuffs the skins of dead animals to make them look life-like.—*n.* **tax'idermy**, the work of a taxidermist.

tea, *n.* a drink made from the dried leaves of the *tea-plant*, which grows in India, China, and some other places in the East : a meal at which tea is drunk (esp. an afternoon or evening meal).— *ns.* **tea'-bread**, scones, buns, etc. ; **tea'-garden**, a garden where the tea-plant is grown : a wayside resting-place where tea may be drunk ; **tea'spoon**, a small spoon used for stirring tea.—**high tea**, a meal at which meat is taken with tea ; **Russian tea**, tea with lemon and no milk.

teach, *v.* to show : to help others to learn about a subject.—*n.* **teach'er**.

teak, *n.* a tree (found in Burma and Africa) whose wood is very hard.

teal, *n.* a small duck-like waterbird.

team, *n.* a number of animals moving together (e.g. a *team* of oxen drawing a plough) : (in games such as football, cricket) the members of a side.

tear, tēr, *n.* a drop of water coming from the eye (e.g. in weeping).— *adj.* **tear'ful**, weeping.

tear, tār, *v.* to pull (e.g. paper, cloth) apart by force. — *n.* a broken edge made by tearing.— **a tear'ing rage**, very great anger.

tease, *v.* to make fun of a person and annoy him : to pull out wool with a comb.—*n.* a person who makes fun of another.—*n.* **teas'er**, a very hard problem.

tea´sel, *n.* a plant with large prickly burs or heads.

teat, *n.* the part of an animal through which milk passes to its young.

technical, tek´nik-al, *adj.* having to do with some special branch of work, esp. with such things as engineering, machinery.—*n.* **technique** (tek-nēk´), the way in which a worker, artist, pianist, writer, etc. does his job.

te deum, tē dē´um, *n.* a hymn of praise.

tedious, tē´di-us, *adj.* long and tiresome.—*n.* **tē´dium,** wearisomeness.

tee, *n.* the square of levelled ground from which a golf-ball is driven: the peg or sand-heap on which the ball is placed for driving.

teem, *v.* to be very plentiful: to pour (rain).

teens, *n.pl.* the years of one's age from 13 to 19.—*n.* **teen´ager,** anyone of this age.

teeth, *n.* plural of tooth.—*v.* **teethe,** to grow one's first teeth.

teetō´tal, *adj.* drinking no strong drink.—*n.* **teeto´taller.**

tel´ecast, *v.* to send out a television programme.—Also *n.*

tel´egram, *n.* a message sent along wires by the use of electricity.—*ns.* **telegraph** (tel´e-graf), an instrument for sending messages in this way ; **teleg´raphist** ; **telephone** (tel´e-fōn), an instrument for speaking to a person at a distance, using an electric current which travels along wires.—*vs.* **tel´egraph** ; **tel´ephone.**—**radio teleg´raphy, radio teleph´ony,** the sending of telegraph and telephone messages by wireless.

telep´athy, *n.* the power by which persons, even when far apart, seem to be able to know each other's thoughts.

telephone. See under telegram.

telephotography, tel-e-fō-tog´ra-fi,*n.* the taking of photographs at a distance, using a special camera.

tel´eprinter, *n.* an electric machine that prints telegraph messages.

tel´escope, *n.* a tube (fitted with lenses or magnifying glasses) which, when looked through, makes far-off objects seem nearer. —*v.* to crush together, end to end (e.g. The carriages of the train were *telescoped* in the accident).

television, tel´e-vizh-on, *n.* the sending of pictures by wireless.—*v.* **tel´evise,** to send a picture by wireless.

tell, *v.* to say in words : to have an effect or result (e.g. The better training of our team will *tell* in the end) : to count.—*n.* **tell´er,** a bank-clerk who receives and pays out money : one who counts votes at an election ; **tell-tale,** one who, for spite, tells that another has done wrong.—*adj.* **tell´ing,** having great effect.

temer´ity, *n.* rashness, boldness.

tem´per, *n.* one's mood or state of mind (e.g. He is cross : he must be in a bad *temper*) : a state of anger : the amount of hardness in a metal.—*v.* to make (a metal) of the right hardness : to make less severe.

tem´perament, *n.* one's nature.—*adj.* **temperamen´tal,** changing one's moods quickly and without reason.

tem´perate, *adj.* keeping to the right amount, taking neither too much nor too little (e.g. of strong drink) : neither very hot nor very cold (e.g. Britain's climate is of the *temperate* kind).—*ns.* **tem´perance,** the habit of not drinking much strong drink ; **tem´peratūre,** the amount of heat or cold.

tem´pest, *n.* a storm, with great wind.—*adj.* **tempestuous** (tempes´tū-us), very stormy.

tem´ple, *n.* a place of worship : a church.

tem´ple, *n.* the part of the head above the cheek-bone.

tem´porary, *adj.* lasting only for a time : holding a position for a time only.—*adj.* **tem´poral,** belonging to the matters of this world, not to matters of religion. —*v.* **tem´porise,** to act in such a way as to put off time.

tempt, *v.* to try to persuade (a person to do something) : to put a person's temper to the test.—

n. **tempta′tion,** something which leads a person into evil.—*adj.* **temp′ting,** rousing the appetite (e.g. a *tempting* meal).

ten′able, *adj.* able to be held or defended.

tenacious, ten-ā′shus, *adj.* holding firmly: stubborn.—*n.* **tenacity** (ten-as′it-i).

ten′ant, *n.* one who lives in a house, farm, etc., and pays rent for it to another.—*v.* to hold and pay rent for.—*ns.* **ten′ancy,** the holding of a house, farm, etc. by paying rent; **ten′antry,** the people who live on an estate and pay rent for their houses, etc.

tench, tensh, *n.* a fresh-water fish.

tend, *v.* to take care of: to look after.

tend, *v.* to be likely or apt to (e.g. This well *tends* to go dry in summer): to move in a certain direction.—*n.* **ten′dency,** a leaning towards: a fondness for (e.g. There is an evil *tendency* in this class).

ten′der, *adj.* soft: easily hurt: loving: (of meat, etc.) easily chewed.—*ns.* **ten′derness**; **ten′derfoot,** a newcomer to a mining or timber camp: a Boy Scout who has passed the first test.

ten′der, *n.* a truck for coal and water forming the back part of a railway-engine: a small boat which carries supplies (of coal, food, etc.) for a large one.

ten′der, *v.* to make an offer (e.g. to do some work for a certain sum of money).—Also *n.*

ten′don, *n.* a tough cord-like substance joining a muscle and bone.

ten′dril, *n.* a curling shoot of a plant (such as the pea-plant) by which it hangs on to some support.

ten′ebrous, *adj.* dark: gloomy.

ten′ement, *n.* a block of houses in one building, with a different family in each house.

ten′et, *n.* a belief, opinion.

ten′nis, *n.* a game for two or four players, played with rackets and a bouncing ball.

ten′or, *n.* (in music) a man's voice of high pitch: meaning (e.g. The *tenor* of his speech was . . .).

tense, *adj.* showing that feelings are very strained (e.g. a *tense* silence, a *tense* situation).—*n.* **ten′sion,** the amount of strain (e.g. on a wire): strong feeling or excitement.

tense, *n.* a form of a verb which shows whether an action belongs to the present, past, or future (e.g. 'I *sing*' is present *tense*; 'I *sang*' is past *tense*; 'I shall *sing*' is future *tense*).

tent, *n.* a shelter made of canvas stretched by means of poles and ropes.

ten′tacles, *n. pl.* the thread-like 'feelers' of an insect: the 'arms' of the octopus and similar creatures, by which they grasp and move.

tentative, ten′ta-tiv, *adj.* done as a trial.

ten′ter-hooks, *n.* used in phrase **to be on tenter-hooks,** i.e. to be restless or worried because one is not sure what is going to happen.

tenuous, ten′ū-us, *adj.* thin.

ten′ure, *n.* the terms under which land, houses, etc. are held: the holding of an office (e.g. His *tenure* of the office of chairman was short).

tep′id, *adj.* slightly warm.

tercenten′ary, *n.* the 300th year since some event took place.

term, *n.* a length of time (e.g. a *term* of imprisonment): a division of a school year (e.g. the autumn *term*): a name (e.g. 'Tropics' is a *term* used for countries round the equator): (*pl.*) the rules of a bargain about money, or of a treaty.—*v.* **term,** to call, to name.—**on good terms,** friendly; **on bad terms,** unfriendly; **to come to terms,** to make a bargain.

ter′magant, *n.* a noisy, bad-tempered woman.

ter′minal, *n.* a screw to which the end of an electric wire is fixed: a terminus.

ter′minate, *v.* to put an end to.—*n.* **termina′tion,** an end.

terminol′ogy, *n.* words, language (e.g. scientific *terminology*).

ter′minus, *n.* the end of a line, route, or journey:—*pl.* **ter′mini.**

tern, *n.* a sea-bird like a small gull.

ter'race, *n.* a raised bank of land, like a big step : a row of houses. —*adj.* ter'raced, having rows of terraces, one above the other.

ter'ra-cot'ta, *n.* a mixture of clay and sand used for small statues, pottery, etc.: a brownish-red colour.

ter'rain, *n.* a stretch of land.

terrestrial, ter-es'tri-al, *adj.* having to do with the earth.

ter'rible, *adj.* causing great fear : very bad.—*adj.* terrif'ic, so great as to cause fear.—*v.* ter'rify, to frighten greatly.

ter'rier, *n.* a name given to many kinds of small dog (e.g. fox *terrier*, Scotch *terrier*).

ter'ritory, *n.* land, country (e.g. They were on enemy *territory*). —*adj.* territō'rial.—*n.pl.* ter-ritō'rials, citizens who, in peace time, train to help to defend their country.—territorial waters, seas close to, and under control of, a country.

ter'ror, *n.* very great fear : a person or thing which causes great fear. —*v.* ter'rorise, to frighten very greatly : to rule by making one's self greatly feared.—*n.* ter'rorist, one who tries to frighten people into doing what he wants.—*adj.* ter'ror-strick'en, struck by very great fear.

terse, *adj.* shortly and neatly said. —*n.* terse'ness.

tes'sellated, *adj.* having a pattern made up of many small different-coloured blocks.

test, *n.* a trial : a short examina-tion.—*v.* to try out (e.g. a new ship to see if the engines are in good order).—*n.* test-tūbe, a glass tube closed at one end.—test match, an important match (e.g. of cricket) between two countries.

tes'tament, *n.* a written statement (usually called a *will*) in which a person tells what he desires to be done with his money and goods after his death.—*n.* testā'tor, the person who writes a will :—*fem.* testā'trix.—Old Testa-ment, the first part of the Bible ; New Testament, the second part of the Bible (i.e. that which has to do with the life and example of Jesus).

tes'tifȳ, *v.* to tell what one knows and declare that it is true : to bear witness.—*ns.* tes'timony, the statement made by one who testifies : evidence ; testimō'nial, a statement (usually a written one) telling what one knows about a person's powers, char-acter, etc.

test'y, *adj.* easily made angry: bad-tempered.

tet'anus, *n.* a disease (lockjaw) which stiffens the muscles of the jaw.

tête-à-tête, tet-a-tet, *n.* a private talk between two people.

teth'er, *v.* to tie up (an animal) with a rope, rein, chain, etc.—*n.* a rope, etc. for tying up an animal.

tetrarch, tet'rark, *n.* an under-ruler.

text, *n.* the written part of a book (i.e. not the drawings, pictures, etc.): a verse (e.g. of the Bible) about which a sermon is preached. —*n.* text-book, a book telling the main points about a subject : a class-book.

tex'tile, *adj.* having to do with cloth-making.—*n.pl.* tex'tiles, cloths. —*n.* tex'tūre, the quality of a cloth.

thane, *n.* in old-time England, a noble of low rank.

thank, *v.* to show that one is pleased for having been treated kindly.—*n.pl.* thanks, a state-ment in which one thanks some-body.—*adjs.* thank'ful, full of thanks ; thank'less, showing no thanks : not likely to bring any thanks.—*n.* thanks'giving, a church service giving thanks to God (e.g. for a good harvest).

thatch, *n.* straw or rushes used to make the roof of a house.—*adj.* thatched, having a roof of thatch.

thaw, *v.* (of ice, snow, etc.) to melt. —*n.* the time of melting of ice and snow after a great frost.

theatre, thē'a-ter, *n.* a large hall on the stage of which plays are acted : a room in a hospital where sick persons are treated by cut-ting the body.—*adj.* theatrical (thē-at'ri-kal), having to do with plays : behaving as if in a play.

theft, *n.* act of stealing.

their, theirs, thār, thārz, *prons.* belonging to them (e.g. This is *their* house, and this car is *theirs*).

them, *pron.* persons already spoken about ; object of verb.

theme, thēm, *n.* subject : matter.

thence, *adv.* from that time or place : for that reason.—*adv.* **thencefor'ward,** from that time forward.

theodolite, thē-od'ō-līt, *n.* an instrument used in measuring off land.

theology, thē-ol'ō-ji, *n.* the branch of study which deals with God, and with man's duty to Him.— *n.* **theologian** (thē-ō-lō'ji-an), one who makes a deep study of theology.

theorem, thē'ō-rem, *n.* something which one proves to be true, by showing all the steps of one's reasoning.—*n.* **the'ory,** an explanation which one thinks is correct : the main ideas about some branch of knowledge.—*v.* **the'orise,** to make theories.

therapeutic, ther-a-pū'tik, *adj.* having to do with healing.

there, thār, *adv.* in that place : not here.—*advs.* **thereaft'er,** after that ; **thereby',** by that means ; **there'fore,** for that or this reason ; **therein',** in that or this place, time, or thing ; **thereof',** of that or this ; **thereon',** on that or this ; **thereupon',** because of that or this : immediately.

ther'mal, *adj.* hot.—*ns.* **therm,** a measure of heat ; **thermom'eter,** an instrument for measuring temperature.—**thermonuc'lear reaction,** the very high temperature reaction in the hydrogen bomb.

thē'sis, *n.* a long written composition :—*pl.* **thē'ses.**

thews, thūz, *n.pl.* muscles, sinews.

they, *pron.* persons already spoken about ; subject of verb.

thick, *adj.* fat : not easily seen through : stupid : crowded.—*v.* **thick'en,** to become thick. — *ns.* **thick'ness ; thick'et,** a bushy place, with few open spaces.— *adj.* **thick'-skinned,** not easily

hurt (e.g. by insults, mocking remarks).

thief, thēf, *n.* one who steals.—*v.* **thieve,** to steal.—*adj.* **thiev'ish,** fond of stealing : sly.—*n.* **theft.**

thigh, thī, *n.* the thick, fleshy part of the leg above the knee.

thim'ble, *n.* a metal cover for the finger, used in sewing.

thin, *adj.* having little thickness : not fat : not close or crowded : weak.—*v.* to make thin : to become less crowded.—*n.* **thin'ness.**—*adj.* **thin'-skinned,** easily hurt by people's remarks.

thing, *n.* an object which is not living : an event : (*pl.*) clothes.

think, thingk, *v.* to work out in the mind : to have an idea or opinion : to value (e.g. I *think* highly of him).—*n.* **thought,** that which one thinks.

thirst, therst, *n.* the dry feeling in the mouth caused by want of water, etc. : an eager desire for anything.—*v.* to feel thirsty : to wish greatly for.—*adj.* **thirst'y,** dry.

thistle, this'l, *n.* a prickly plant whose flower is the national flower of Scotland.—*n.* **this'tle-down,** the feathery seeds of the thistle.

thith'er, *adv.* to that place.

tho', short for **though.**

thole, *v.* to bear (e.g. pain) : to be patient.

thong, *n.* a piece or strap of leather to fasten anything : the lash of a whip.

thor'ax, *n.* the chest.

thorn, *n.* a sharp, woody prickle on the stem of a plant : a plant having prickles or thorns, esp. the hawthorn.—*adj.* **thorn'y,** full of thorns : prickly : causing arguments or quarrels (e.g. a *thorny* subject).— **thorn in the flesh,** a cause of worry.

thorough, thur'ō, *adj.* going through and through : complete. — *ns.* **thor'oughbred,** an animal (e.g. race-horse) whose father and mother are prize animals ; **thor'oughfare,** a public street.—*adj.* **thor'ough-gō'ing,** going right to the end, not leaving things half-done.—**no thoroughfare,** passing through not allowed.

thorp, thorpe, *n.* a small village.

though, thō, *conj.* even if.

thought, thawt, *n.* that which one thinks : an idea.—*adjs.* **thought'-ful,** full of thought : thinking of others ; **thought'less,** careless.

thou'sand, *adj.* ten hundred.

thrall, thrawl, *n.* a slave : slavery.—*n.* **thral'dom,** slavery.

thrash, *v.* to flog : to beat soundly.—*n.* **thrash'ing,** a flogging.—*vs.* **thrash or thresh** (thresh), to beat out grain from straw.—*ns.* **thrash'-ing- or thresh'ing-floor,** a floor where grain is beaten out ; **thrash'ing- or thresh'ing-mill,** a machine which beats out corn.

thread, thred, *n.* a very thin line of any substance (e.g. cotton, wool, silk) : the marking round a screw and inside a nut.—*v.* to put a thread through : to go through (e.g. He *threaded* his way between the trees).—*adj.* **thread'bare,** worn thin.

threat, thret, *n.* a promise to hurt a person if he does not do as one wants.—*v.* **threat'en,** to make a threat : (of the weather) to look as if it might rain, snow, be frosty, etc.—*adj.* **threat'ening,** looking evil or harmful.

thresh, thresh. See **thrash.**

threshold, thresh'ōld, *n.* a doorway of a house (really the piece of wood or stone under the door).

thrice, thrīs, *adv.* three times.

thrift, *n.* care about one's money or goods, in order that one may save.—*adjs.* **thrift'y,** careful about spending ; **thrift'less,** spending carelessly.

thrill, *n.* a wave of feeling (e.g. of joy, pain, pleasure) through the body.—*v.* to send a thrill through.—*adj.* **thrill'ing,** very exciting.

thrive, *v.* to grow strong : to get on well.

thro', throo, short for **through.**

throat, *n.* the back part of the mouth where the openings to the stomach, windpipe, and nose are.

throb, *n.* a beat (e.g. of the heart).—Also *v.*

throe, thrō, *n.* a pang of pain.—**in the throes of,** in the middle of doing (some hard job).

throne, *n.* the seat of a king or bishop.

throng, *n.* a crowd.—*v.* to go in crowds.

throstle, thros'l, *n.* a singing bird (the mavis).

throt'tle, *n.* the throat : (in engines) the part through which steam or petrol-gas can be turned on or off.—*v.* to choke by gripping the throat.

through, throo, *prep.* from end to end, or from side to side of : by means of : because of.—*adv.* from end to end.—*adj.* clear (e.g. a *through* road) : taking one all the way (e.g. a *through* train, *through* ticket) : finished with, tired of (e.g. I'm *through* with motoring).—*prep.* and *adv.* **throughout** (throo-owt'), in every part (of) : right through.

throw, thrō, *v.* to fling or hurl.—*n.* the act of throwing : the distance a thing is thrown.

thrush, *n.* a singing-bird (the mavis).

thrust, *v.* to push with force : to stab, pierce.—*n.* a sharp push forward (e.g. with a weapon).—*adj.* **thrust'ful,** eager, keen to get on.

thud, *n.* a dull, hollow sound.

thug, *n.* in India, a murdering robber.

thumb, thum, *n.* the short, thick finger of the hand.—*v.* to dirty with finger-marks.—*n.* **thumb'-screw** (-scroo), an old-time means of torture which worked by squashing the thumbs.

thump, *n.* a dull, heavy blow.—*v.* to beat heavily.—*adj.* **thump'ing** (*slang*), very big.

thun'der, *n.* the deep rumbling sound heard after a flash of lightning : any loud, rumbling noise (e.g. of guns).—*v.* to make thunder : to shout out angrily.—*adjs.* **thun'derous,** like thunder ; **thun'dery,** (of weather) close and stifling ; **thun'der-struck,** made silent by surprise, astonished.—*ns.* **thun'derbolt,** a flash of lightning followed by thunder : a very great and sudden surprise ; **thun'der-clap,** a sudden roar of thunder ; **thun'der-storm,** a rain-storm with thunder and lightning.

Thurs′day, *n.* the fifth day of the week.

thus, *adv.* in this manner : so.

thwack, *n.* a heavy blow.

thwart, thwort, *v.* to hinder a person from carrying out a plan.—*n.* a cross-seat for rowers in a rowing-boat.

thyme, tīm, *n.* a small sweet-smelling plant.

tiara, ti-a′ra, *n.* a kind of crown : a jewelled ornament for the head, worn by women.

tib′ia, *n.* the large bone of the shin.

tick, *n.* a small insect which bites dogs, sheep, etc.

tick or **tick′ing,** *n.* the cloth cover of a mattress or pillow.

tick, *n.* the sound made by a clock : a mark (√).—Also *v.*

tick′et, *n.* a marked card giving the owner a right to do something (e.g. travel by train, enter a picture-house) : a price-card : a queerly dressed person.—*v.* to place a ticket on.—**ticket-of-leave man,** a prisoner who, because of good behaviour, is allowed to leave prison before his sentence is up ; **season ticket,** a ticket (e.g. for a railway-train) which may be used over and over again during a certain time ; **that's the ticket!** that suits splendidly !

tick′le, *v.* to touch lightly and cause laughter : to please or amuse.—*adjs.* **tick′ly, tick′lish,** easily tickled : not easy to do (e.g. a *ticklish* job).

tide, *n.* the rise and fall of the sea which happens twice each day : time : season.—*adj.* tī′dal.—**tidal wave,** a great sea-wave (often caused by an earthquake under the sea) ; **to tide over,** to get over a difficulty for a time.

ti′dings, *n.pl.* news.

ti′dy, *adj.* neat : fairly big (e.g. a *tidy* sum of money).—*v.* to make neat.—*n.* ti′diness.

tie, tī, *v.* to fasten (e.g. with a cord) : (in games, etc.) to be equal.—*n.* a band worn with a collar and tied with a knot : an equal result (e.g. in an examination) : a game or match to be played.

tier, tēr, *n.* a row (e.g. of seats) with others above or below it.

tiff, *n.* a little quarrel.

tif′fin, *n.* (in India) luncheon.

tig, *n.* a game.

ti′ger, *n.* a fierce, cat-like animal with tawny coat striped with black : —*fem.* ti′gress.—*n.* ti′ger-lily, a lily with large spotted flowers.

tight, tīt, *adj.* packed or fitting closely : firmly stretched : short of money : (*slang*) drunk.—*n.pl.* **tights,** close-fitting trousers, usually of very thin stuff.—*v.* **tight′en,** to make tight.

tile, *n.* a piece of baked clay for covering floors, roofs, etc.

till, *n.* in a shop, a drawer for money.

till, *v.* to plough, sow, and reap.—*n.* till′age.

til′ler, *n.* the handle of a rudder.

tilt, *v.* to slope to one side : to attack on horseback, using a lance. —*n.* a slant : a thrust with a lance.

tilth, *n.* land for crops.

tim′ber, *n.* wood for building : woods of useful trees : the wooden beams of a house or ship.

timbre, tim′br, *n.* quality (e.g. of a sound, voice).

tim′brel, *n.* a kind of tambourine.

time, *n.* the hour of the day : the period at which, or during which, something happens : season of the year : (in music) the rate of movement.—*v.* to do just at the right moment : to measure the minutes, seconds, etc. taken in a race.—*adjs.* **time′ly,** in good time ; **timeous** (tī′mus), happening at the right time ; **time′-honoured,** thought much of because it has lasted so long ; **time′-worn,** worn out by old age : stale.—*ns.* **time′piece,** a small clock ; **time′-table,** a list showing the times of trains, buses, etc. : a list of classes, etc., with their hours ; **time′-sig′nal,** (in wireless) a number of 'pips' the last of which comes exactly at a certain time.—**the time being,** the present time.

tim′id, tim′orous, *adjs.* easily frightened : shy.—*n.* timid′ity.

tin, *n.* a silvery-white metal: a box or can made of thin iron covered with tin.—*v.* to cover with tin: to pack (fish, fruit, etc.) in tins.—*adj.* **tin′ny,** having a harsh sound (like a tin when it is struck).—*ns.* **tin′foil,** tin beaten thin (used for wrapping); **tin′-smith,** one who makes or sells tin cans, etc.

tincture, tink′tūr, *n.* a medicine mixed in a certain liquid.

tin′der, *n.* dry material set alight by a spark from flint (used before matches were invented).

tinge, tinj, *v.* to give a slight amount (e.g. of colour, feeling) to.—*n.* a slight amount (e.g. There was a *tinge* of sadness in his voice).

tingle, ting′gl, *v.* to have a sharp feeling (e.g. of cold, pain, joy).

tink′er, *n.* a mender of kettles, pans, etc.—*v.* to patch up clumsily: to meddle.

tinkle, ting′kl, *v.* to make a soft ringing sound.—Also *n.*

tin′sel, *n.* a sparkling or shining ornament (often used to make a Christmas-tree glitter): anything showy but of little value.

tint, *n.* a faint touch of colour.—*v.* to give a slight colour to.

ti′ny, *adj.* very small.

tip, *n.* the top or point of anything: a hint (e.g. about how to do a job, or who is likely to win a race): a small gift of money (e.g. to a waiter): a place for emptying out rubbish.—*v.* to cause to slant: to give a useful hint: to give a small gift of money: to empty rubbish.—*n.* **tip′ster,** one who gives hints about racing.

tip′ple, *v.* to be fond of taking strong drink.—*n.* **tip′pler.**—*adj.* **tip′sy,** rather drunk.

tiptoe, tip′tō, *v.* to stand, walk, or dance on the tips of one's toes: to go very quietly.—**on tiptoe(s),** walking on the tips of one's toes.

tirade, ti-rād′, *n.* a long, bitter, scolding speech.

tire. See **tyre.**

tire, *v.* to make or become weary.—*adjs.* **tired** (tīrd), weary; **tire′less,** never becoming weary, never rest-

ing; **tire′some,** making weary: annoying.

ti′ro, *n.* one who is new to a job: a recruit.

tissue, tis′ū, *n.* finely made cloth: substance of which flesh and sinews are made.—*n.* **tissue-paper,** thin, soft paper.—**tissue of lies,** set of lies.

tit, *n.* short for *titmouse*—name for several small birds (blue tit, coal tit, great tit).—*n.* **tit′lark,** hedge-sparrow.

tit for tat, blow for blow.

titan′ic, *adj.* huge.—*n.* **Ti′tan,** a giant.

tit′bit, *n.* a tasty little bit.

tithe, tīth, *n.* a tax paid to the church: a tenth part.

tit′ivate, *v.* to make neat and tidy.

title, tī′tl, *n.* the name of a book: a word in front of a name to show rank or honour (e.g. *Sir* Francis Drake; *Lord* Nelson): right, claim (e.g. He has no *title* to the money).—*adjs.* **titled** (tī′tld), having a title which shows rank; **tit′ular,** having the title without doing the duties.—*ns.* **ti′tle-deed,** a paper which shows that one is the real owner (of a house, farm, etc.); **ti′tle-page,** the page of a book on which are the title, author's name, etc.; **ti′tle-rôle,** the part in a play which is the same as the title of the play (e.g. the part played by Hamlet in Shakespeare's play *Hamlet*).

tit′mouse, *n.* a small bird.—See **tit.**

tit′ter, *v.* to giggle.—Also *n.*

tit′tle, a very small part.

tit′tle-tat′tle, *n* gossip, chatter.

toad, *n.* a creature like a large frog.—*n.* **toad′stool,** a poisonous growth, like a large mushroom.

toad′y, *v.* to give way to a person's wishes, or flatter him in a silly way, in order to gain his favour.

toast, *v.* to make bread brown at a fire: to warm (e.g. one's feet) at a fire: to take a drink and wish health to a person.—Also *n.*

tobac′co, *n.* a plant (grown in America, south-east Europe, and South Africa) whose dried leaves are used for smoking, chewing, or as snuff.—*n.* **tobac′conist,** one who sells tobacco, cigarettes, etc.

tobog'gan, n. a kind of sledge used for sliding down snow-covered slopes.—v. to go in a toboggan.

toc'sin, n. an alarm bell.

to-day' or today', n. this day: the present time.

tod'dle, v. to walk unsteadily, with short steps.—n. tod'dler, a young child just able to walk.

tod'dy, n. a mixture of whisky, sugar, and hot water.

toe, tō, n. a finger-like joint on the foot.—to toe the line, to do as others do.

tof'fee, n. a sweet made of sugar and butter.

tō'ga, n. the cloak worn by a citizen of old-time Rome.

togeth'er, adv. in the same place or time.

togs, n.pl. clothes.

toil, v. to work hard.—n. hard work.—n. toil'er.

toil'et, n. the act of washing one's face, doing one's hair, etc.: a room where one may do such things.—n. toil'et-soap, scented soap, done up in cakes.

toils, n.pl. nets: trouble (e.g. I am in the toils).

tō'ken, n. a mark or sign (e.g. Take this book as a token of my friendship): a piece of metal, vulcanite, etc. used as a coin for some purposes.

tol'erable, adj. able to be borne or suffered: fairly good.—v. tol'erate, to bear, put up with.—adj. tol'erant, willing to allow ideas different from one's own.—ns. tol'erance; tolerā'tion.

tōll, n. a tax (e.g. for crossing a bridge): loss, damage.—to take toll, to cause great damage.

tōll, v. to ring a bell sadly.

tom'ahawk, n. Red Indian war-axe.

toma'to, n. a fleshy, juicy fruit, usually red (sometimes yellow):—pl. toma'toes.

tomb, toom, n. a grave.—n. tomb'stone, a stone placed over a grave, with writing telling about the person buried beneath.

tom'boy, n. a wild, romping girl.

tom-cat, n. a male cat.

tome, n. a large book: a volume.

tomfool'ery. n. a silly show: nonsense.

to-morrow or tomorrow, too-mor'ō, n. the day after to-day.

tom'tit, n. a small bird (the titmouse).

tom-tom, n. an Indian or African drum.

ton, tun, n. a measure of weight (= 2240 lbs. or 20 cwt.).—n. ton'nage, a measure of space in a ship.

tone, n. a sound: the quality, height, or depth, of a voice or sound: colour.—v. (with in) to fit in with: (with up) to give strength to.—n. ton'ic, a medicine which gives one strength.

tongs, n.pl. an instrument for lifting coals, sugar-lumps: an instrument for curling the hair.

tongue, tung, n. a part of the body, inside the mouth, used in tasting, speaking, and swallowing: a leather flap in a shoe: a long, thin strip of land: a language.—adj. tongue-tied, not able to speak freely.—n. tongue-twister, a number of words which are not easy to say quickly (e.g. Shoes and socks shock Susan).—Hold your tongue ! Stop speaking !

to-night' or tonight', n. this night.

tonnage. See ton.

ton'sils, n.pl. two fleshy lumps at the back of the tongue.—n. tonsili'tis, a disease of the tonsils, causing a very sore throat.

tonsure, ton'shoor, n. the shaving of the top or front of the head (done by priests and monks).

tool, n. an instrument used by a workman (e.g. a spade, hammer): a person who acts for another, usually in the doing of evil.

toot, n. the sound of a horn.—Also v.

tooth (pl. teeth), n. the sharp bonelike points in the mouth used for breaking up food: the points of a saw, cog-wheel, comb, etc.—adjs. toothed, having teeth; tooth'some, pleasant to the taste.—ns. toothache (tooth'āk), pain in the root of a tooth; tooth'-paste, tooth-powder, paste and powder used for cleaning the teeth; tooth'pick, a sharp point for picking out anything (e.g. bits of food) from the teeth.—tooth and nail, with all one's strength.

top, *n.* the highest or upper part of anything : a spinning toy.—*adj.* placed at the top : highest (e.g. *top* price, *top* score).—*v.* to rise above : to do better than. —*adjs.* **top'-heavy,** heavier above than below ; **top'ping,** very good ; **top'most,** highest.—*ns.* **top'-boot,** a long-legged boot with a showy band of leather round the top ; **top'-coat,** an overcoat ; **top'-dog,** the winner in a fight ; **top'-dressing,** manure laid on the top of the ground, not dug in.

tō'paz, *n.* a precious stone.

tōpee', *n.* a sun-helmet used in hot countries.

tō'per, *n.* one who takes much strong drink.

top'ic, *n.* a subject spoken or written about : a piece of news.—*adj.* **top'ical,** telling about things which are happening to-day.

topography, top-og'ra-fi, *n.* the description of a place or district.—*adj.* **topograph'ical.**

top'ple, *v.* to be unsteady and fall.

top'sy-tur'vy, *adv.* and *adj.* turned upside down.

tor, *n.* a rocky hill.

torch, *n.* a light that can be carried in the hand.

toreador, tor-ē-a-dor', *n.* the man who fights the bull in bull-fights.

torment', *v.* to treat cruelly and cause great suffering : to tease.—*ns.* **tor'ment,** great pain or worry ; **tormen'tor.**

tornā'do, *n.* a hurricane, or great storm of wind, doing much damage :—*pl.* **tornā'does.**

torpē'do, *n.* a large cigar-shaped shell, fired by warships and aeroplanes ; it goes through the water and explodes when it hits its mark.—*v.* to hit or sink (a ship) with a torpedo.—*adj.* **torpē'doed.**—*ns.* **torpē'do-boat,** a small warship which fires torpedoes ; **torpe'do-boat destroyer** (usually called a **destroyer**), a small fast-moving warship, specially made for attacking submarines and torpedo-boats.

tor'pid, *adj.* having lost the power to move or feel : slow, dull, stupid.—*n.* **tor'por,** numbness : dullness.

tor'rent, *n.* a rushing stream : a heavy downpour of rain.—*adj.* **torrential** (tor-en'shal), coming in torrents.

tor'rid, *adj.* burning or parching : very hot.—**torrid zone,** the part of the earth on each side of the equator.

torsion, tor'shun, *n.* the act of twisting.

tor'so, *n.* the body, without head or limbs.

tortoise, tor'tis or tor'toiz, *n.* a four-footed creeping animal, covered with a hard shell.—*n.* **tor'toise-shell,** the shell of a kind of turtle (an animal like a tortoise) used for making combs, spectacle-rims, etc.—*adj.* yellow, red, and black in colour.

tortuous, tor'tū-us, *adj.* winding (e.g. a *tortuous* path) : deceiving.

tor'tūre, *v.* to treat a person cruelly or painfully, either as a punishment or in order to make him confess something : to annoy.—*n.* great pain, cruel treatment.

Tor'y, *n.* and *adj.* a name for one of the groups of members in Parliament.

toss, *v.* to throw up in the air : to move restlessly from side to side.—*n.* an upward throw : a fall.—**to toss up,** to throw up a coin and cry ' Heads or tails ? '

tot, *n.* a little child : a small amount of a liquid : an addition sum.—*v.* to add up.

tō'tal, *adj.* whole : complete.—*n.* all : the entire amount : the answer to an addition sum.—*v.* to add up.—*n.* **totalisā'tor** (for short, **tote**), a machine used on race-courses to work out the amount of money to be paid to those who bet on winning horses.

tō'tem, *n.* among American Indians and some other people, an animal or plant (or an image of it) used as the badge or sign of a tribe.—*n.* **tō'tem-pole,** a pole on which is a carved image of a totem.

tot'ter, *v.* to shake as if about to fall : to stagger.

toucan, too-kan', *n.* a South American bird with a very big beak.

touch, tutch, v. to feel (e.g. with the hand): to reach: to cause to feel pity (e.g. The story *touched* those who heard it).—n. the act of putting the hand on: (of artists, pianists) skill or style: (in football) the ground at the side of the field.—*prep.* **touch′ing**, about, concerning.—*adjs.* **touch′ing**, causing pity, sad; **touch′y**, having feelings that are easily hurt.—n. **touch′-hole**, in old guns, the hole where the match was put to the powder.—**to touch on**, to speak shortly about; **to touch up**, to do something to improve (e.g. a photograph, drawing); **touch-and-go**, a narrow escape, a ' near thing.'

tough, tuf, *adj.* not easily broken: hard to chew: stubborn: not easily beaten.—v. **tough′en**, to make or become tough.

tour, toor, n. a journey in which one visits various places and comes back to the starting-place: a pleasure trip.—v. to make a tour.—n. **tour′ist**, one who travels on a tour: a holiday-maker.

tournament, toor′na-ment, n. in olden times, a sport in which knights fought on horseback: a games competition.

tourniquet, toor′ni-ket, n. a bandage twisted tightly to stop the blood from flowing.

tousled, towz′ld, *adj.* out of order.—*adj.* **tous′y**, rough: shaggy.

tout, v. to go about asking favours.—n. one who does this: a racehorse tipster.

tow, tō, v. to pull (e.g. a ship, a motor-car) with a rope.—n. the rope used for towing: that which is towed: the coarse part of flax or hemp.

towards, **toward**, tō′ard(z), *prep.* in the direction of: near, about.

tow′el, n. a cloth for drying the body after washing.

tow′er, n. a high building, or a high part of another building (e.g. the *tower* of a castle): a fortress.—v. to rise high above. — *adj.* **tow′ering**, rising high above: very angry (e.g. a *towering* rage).

town, n. a large collection of houses, with shops, churches, etc.—ns. **town-council**, the persons (**town-councillors**) whom the people of a town appoint to look after the business of the town as a whole (e.g. its police, schools, libraries, lighting, etc.); **town′-hall**, the building where the business of the town-council is done.

tox′in, n. a poison.—*adj.* **tox′ic**.

toy, n. a child's plaything.—v. to play (with).

trace, n. a mark left: a footprint: a small amount.—v. to mark out: to copy a drawing on thin paper placed over it: to follow by marks or footsteps.—ns. **trā′cery**, the decorated stonework holding the glass in some church windows; **trā′cing**.

tra′ces, *n.pl.* the leather straps by which a horse draws a carriage.

track, n. a mark left (e.g. a footprint): a path: a race-course (e.g. for runners, cyclists): a railway-line: endless band on which wheels of tractor, etc. travel.—*adj.* **track′less**, (of e.g. desert) pathless.

tract, n. a stretch of land or country: a book of a few pages.—*adj.* **tract′able**, easily made to do what is wanted.

traction, trak′shn, n. the pulling of carriages, etc.—ns. **traction-engine**, a road steam-engine; **tract′or**, an engine for pulling loads, ploughs, etc.

trade, n. the buying and selling of goods: one's job (e.g. He is a carpenter by *trade*).—v. to buy and sell: to deal with.—ns. **trade′-mark**, a mark or name (e.g. *Vaseline*) put on goods to show that they are made by a certain maker; **trā′der**, one who buys and sells; **tradesman** (trādz′man), a shopkeeper; **trade-union**, a group of workers of the same trade who join together to obtain fair wages and good conditions of working; **trade-wind**, a wind which blows towards the equator (from the north-east and south-east).—**Board of Trade**, the branch of the government which sees to railways, shipping, factories.

tradition, tra-dish´on, *n.* any story, or fable, or custom which is passed on from father to son, and is so kept alive: the unwritten history of a nation.—*adj.* **tradi´tional**, passed on from father to son.

traduce´, *v.* to say evil about.

traf´fic, *n.* trade: the motor-cars, buses, cycles, etc. which use a public road: the goods and passengers carried by bus, train, or steamer.—*v.* to trade: to deal in.

tragedy, tra´jed-i, *n.* a sad event: a play with a sad ending.—*adj.* **tra´gic**, sad.—*n.* **trage´dian**, an actor in a tragedy play:—*fem.* **tragedienne** (tra-jē-di-en´).

trail, *v.* to pull along the ground: to drag one's self wearily along: to hunt (e.g. animals) by following footprints, scent, etc.—*n.* a track (e.g. of an animal): a pathway (e.g. through a jungle).—*n.* **trail´er**, a car or van pulled behind a motor-car: (in picture-houses) a short film telling about the main one which is to come later.—**to blaze a trail**, to mark out a path through unknown land.

train, *n.* a railway-engine with carriages or trucks: the part of a dress which trails behind the wearer: the attendants who follow an important person: a line (of thought): a line of animals carrying persons or baggage: a line of gunpowder which, when lighted, explodes a mine.—*v.* to make one's self or others ready (e.g. for some sport, for war, for a trade): to point a gun in a certain direction.—*ns.* **train´-band**, in olden times, a band of citizens who were trained to act as soldiers in time of war; **train´-bearer**, one who carries the train of a person's dress; **train´er**, one who prepares persons or animals for some sport; **train´ing-college**, a college where people are taught to be teachers; **train´ing-ship**, a ship on which boys are taught to be sailors.

trait, trā, *n.* a point that stands out in a person's character.

trait´or, *n.* one who goes over to the enemy's side, or gives away secrets to the enemy.—*adj.* **trait´orous**.—*n.* **trea´son**, the crime of being a traitor.

tram, tram´-car, *ns.* a car (running on rails and driven usually by electric power) for carrying passengers along streets.—*n.* **tram´way**, a town's tram-car system: the rails used by trams.

tram´mel, *v.* to keep back, to hinder.—*n.* a net for catching fish or birds.

tramp, *v.* to walk with heavy footsteps: to go on foot.—*n.* a journey made on foot: the sound of marching feet: a wandering beggar: a small cargo-boat going from port to port.—*v.* **tram´ple**, to walk over with heavy steps: to treat roughly.

trance, *n.* a deep sleep that is not natural: a dream.

tranquil, trank´wil, *adj.* quiet: peaceful.—*n.* **tranquil´lity**.

transact´, *v.* to do (a piece of business).—*n.* **transac´tion**, a piece of business: a written report.

transatlan´tic, *adj.* crossing the Atlantic Ocean.

transcend, tran-send´, *v.* to rise above: to be better than.—*adj.* **transcen´dent**.

transcribe´, *v.* to make a written copy. —*n.* **transcrip´tion**, a written copy.

tran´sept, *n.* the part of a church which lies across the main part.

transfer´, *v.* to remove to another place: to give to another person, especially legally.—*n.* the act of transferring: a kind of stamp bearing a picture which can be *transferred* on to a book, etc.—*adj.* **transfer´able**.—*n.* **trans´ference**.

transfig´ure, *v.* to change the form or appearance of.—*n.* **transfigura´tion**.

transfix´, *v.* to pierce through (e.g. with a sword).—*adj.* **transfixed´**, struck by wonder or fear.

transform´, *v.* to change the shape or appearance of.—*ns.* **transform´er**, an apparatus for changing electrical energy from one voltage to another; **transforma´tion**.

transfuse´, *v.* to pass (liquid) from one thing to another.—*n.* **trans-**

fū'sion, the passing of blood from one person into the veins of another (often necessary to save life).

transgress', v. to break a rule or law: to sin.—ns. transgression (transgresh'on), a sin; transgres'sor, one who breaks laws.

transient, tran'si-ent, adj. not lasting long.

trans'it, n. the carrying of goods, passengers, etc. from place to place (e.g. The letter was lost in transit, i.e. lost in the post): the passing of a planet between the sun and the earth.—adjs. transitive (trans'it-iv), in grammar, a name given to verbs which can have an object (e.g. to hit, to see); trans'itory, lasting only for a short time.—n. transi'tion, a change from one form or place to another.

translate', v. to turn what is said or written into some other language (e.g. to translate from French into English): to remove to another place.—ns. transla'tion; transla'tor.

transmigra'tion, n. the belief, held by some people, that the soul passes at death into some other body.

transmit', v. to send to another person or place: to send by wireless: to pass on (a message). —ns. transmis'sion, the act of sending or passing on: a wireless broadcast; transmitt'er, an instrument for sending messages (e.g. wireless transmitter).

transmūte', v. to change one substance into another.

transpā'rent, adj. able to be seen through (e.g. Clear water is transparent): easily seen to be true or false (e.g. transparent honesty, a transparent excuse).—n. transpā'rency.

transpire', v. (of secrets) to become known: to happen.

transplant', v. to lift and plant (a growing plant) in another place: to remove to another place.

transport', v. to carry from one place to another: to send a prisoner to some prison-station in a far-off land.—n. any means

of carrying persons or goods (e.g. rail transport, air transport): a ship for carrying soldiers or stores: strong feelings (either joy or sorrow).—n. transportā'tion, punishment of prisoners by sending them to a far-off land.—adj. transpor'ted, overcome (with joy or sorrow).

transpose', v. to cause two things to change places: to change music from one key to another.

transverse', adj. lying across.—adv. transverse'ly, in a cross direction.

trap, n. an instrument for catching animals: a plan or trick for catching a person unawares: a carriage with two wheels.—v. to catch in a trap, or in such a way that escape is not possible.—ns. trap'per, one who makes a living by catching animals (e.g. rabbits, beaver); trap'-door, a door in a floor.

trapeze', tra-pēz', n. a swing used in doing tricky gymnastic exercises. — n. trapē'zium, a figure with four unequal sides, two of which are parallel.

trap'pings, n.pl. gay clothes: ornaments put on horses.

trash, n. something of little worth, rubbish.—adj. trash'y.

trav'ail, n. hard work: pain suffered during the birth of a child. —Also v.

trav'el, v. to move: to go on a journey.—n. act of going from place to place, esp. in strange lands. —n. trav'eller, one who travels: a member of a business firm who goes from place to place and tries to persuade shopkeepers to buy his firm's goods.—adj. trav'el-stained, dirty and untidy after a journey.

traverse', v. to go across, pass through.

trav'esty, v. to make a copy of something in a mocking way.— n. a silly copy.

trawl, v. to fish by dragging a wide-mouthed net (called a trawl) along the bottom of the sea.—n. trawl'er, a small steamer which drags a trawl.

tray, *n.* a flat piece of wood, metal, etc., on which dishes can be carried.

treachery, tretch'er-i, *n.* the act of doing harm to those who have been one's friends : a breaking of one's faith.—*adj.* **treach'erous,** turning on one's friends : deceiving, dangerous (e.g. A *treacherous* pathway led along the edge of the cliff).

trea'cle, *n.* a thick, dark sugary syrup.

tread, tred, *v.* to walk : to crush under the foot : to dance.—*n.* a step : one's way of stepping : the part of a motor or cycle tyre which touches the ground.—*ns.* **tread'le,** (in a machine worked by the foot) the part which is moved by the foot ; **tread'-mill,** a mill turned by the weight of persons who are made to walk on steps fixed round a big wheel.

trea'son, *n.* the giving away of one's own country or its secrets to an enemy.—*adj.* **trea'sonable,** deserving punishment because of treason.—**high treason,** the doing or planning of harm to one's king or country.

treasure, trezh'oor, *n.* a store of money, gold, precious stones, etc. : anything of great value.—*v.* to value greatly.—*ns.* **treas'urer,** one who looks after the money (e.g. of a club, business firm) ; **treas'ury,** the part of a government which looks after the country's money ; **treas'ure-trove,** a valuable find the owner of which is unknown.

treat, *v.* to deal with in a certain way (e.g. He *treated* his horse kindly) : to try to cure a disease in a person (e.g. The doctor *treated* him for mumps) : to write or speak about a certain matter : to pay for a meal, drink, etc. for another person : to make terms of peace with an enemy.—*n.* something that gives much pleasure.—*ns.* **treatise** (trēt'iz), a long composition on some subject ; **treat'ment,** the way in which anything is dealt with (e.g. rough *treatment* ; a doctor's *treatment* for a disease) ; **treat'y,** the terms of peace made with an enemy.

treb'le, *adj.* threefold (e.g. wood of *treble* thickness).—*v.* to make three times as great.—*n.* the highest part in music.

tree, *n.* a large plant with a thick wooden stem and branches.—**fam'ily tree,** a drawing showing the different branches of a family.

trek, *n.* a journey, esp. by wagon.—Also *v.*

trel'lis, *n.* a network of strips of wood, wire, etc., used for holding up growing plants.

trem'ble, *v.* to shake (e.g. with cold, fear, weakness).

trēmen'dous, *adj.* very great or strong : immense.

trem'or, *n.* a quiver running through the body.—**earth tremor,** a slight earthquake.

trem'ūlous, *adj.* shaking with fear.

trench, trensh, *n.* a long narrow ditch dug in the ground (e.g. by soldiers as a protection against enemy bullets).—*v.* to dig a trench : to dig deeply with a spade.—*adj.* **trench'ant,** going deep, hurting (e.g. a *trenchant* remark).—*n.* **trench'er,** a wooden plate : a hat with a flat top worn in some schools and colleges.

trend, *n.* slope, direction (e.g. the *trend* of events, i.e. the way events are shaping).

trepidā'tion, *n.* fear : alarm.

tres'pass, *v.* to go where one has no right to go : to sin.—Also *n.*—*n.* **tres'passer.**

tress, *n.* a lock or curl of hair.

trestle, tres'l, *n.* a wooden support, with legs, used for holding up a table, platform, etc.

trews, trooz, *n.pl.* tartan trousers.

tri'al, *n.* the act of putting something to the test (e.g. I am giving the car a *trial*) : the judging of a prisoner in a law-court : trouble or suffering which wears one out : (in football, etc.) a practice match.

tri'angle, *n.* a three-cornered figure (e.g. △) : a three-cornered musical instrument, played by striking with a small rod.—*adj.* **trian'gūlar,** having three angles and three sides.

tribe, n. a group of families ruled by a chief.—adj. trī′bal.

tribūlā′tion, n. great grief or sorrow.

tribū′nal, n. a court set up to give judgment on certain matters.

trib′ūne, n. a high official in old-time Rome.

trib′ūte, n. money paid by a beaten nation to the winning nation after a war: praise (e.g. The master paid a warm *tribute* to the successful boy).

trice, n. used in the phrase **in a trice**, in a very short time.

trick, n. a clever action to puzzle, amuse, or deceive: one round of cards in a card-game: habit or manner.—v. to cheat by some quick or clever action.—adj. **trick′y**, not easy to do.—ns. **trick′-ery**, cheating, falseness; **trick′ster**, one who does tricks, esp. tricks which deceive.

trick′le, v. to flow in small amounts. —Also n.

tricolour, trī′kul-ur, n. the flag of France, which is made up of three stripes (red, white, blue).

tricycle, trī′si-kl, n. a cycle with three wheels.

trī′dent, n. a three-pronged spear (e.g. that on the back of a penny).

triennial, trī-en′yal, adj. lasting for three years: happening every third year.

trifle, trī′fl, n. anything of little value: a small amount: a pudding of whipped cream, sponge-cake, wine, etc.—v. to act or talk in a light, thoughtless manner: to amuse one's self in an idle way: to waste.—adj. trī′fling, very small in value or quantity.

trig′ger, n. a small lever on a gun which, when pulled with the finger, causes the bullet to be fired.

trigonom′etry, n. the branch of knowledge which has to do with the study of triangles.

trill, v. to sing with a quivering voice.

trim, v. to clip the edges of (e.g. a hedge, the hair): to shift the cargo of a boat so that the boat floats level: to arrange (sails)

for sailing.—adj. neat: in good order.—ns. **trim′mer**, a person who tries to please two sides; **trim′ming**, a fancy part added (e.g. to a dress, cake) as a decoration: a bit cut off while trimming (cloth, paper, etc.).—**in good trim**, in good order: in good temper.

Trin′ity, n. in Christian belief, the three Persons (Father, Son, and Holy Ghost) who together make one God.

trink′et, n. a small ornament of little value.

trio, trē′ō, n. a set of three persons: a piece of music for three persons.

trip, v. to move with short, dancing steps: to stumble, or cause to stumble, in walking or running.— n. a light, short step: a stumble: a voyage or journey: a picnic or outing.

tripe, n. part of the stomach of the cow or sheep used as food.

triple, trip′l, adj. made up of three: three times as large.—v. to make or become three times as large. —n.pl. **trip′lets**, three children born of the same mother at one time.

trī′pod, n. a three-legged stand (e.g. that used as a rest for a camera).

trite, adj. used so often that people are tired hearing it (e.g. ' A stitch in time saves nine ' is a *trite* saying).

triumph, trī′umf, n. a great success or victory: in old-time Rome, a procession through the streets in honour of a general who had won a great victory.—v. to win a great victory.—adj. **triumphant** (trī-um′fant).

triv′et, n. a small stand in front of a fire for holding a kettle or pot.

trivial, triv′yal, adj. of very little worth or importance.—n. **trivial′-ity**.

trŏll, n. (in old fables) a goblin.

trŏll, v. to sing a round: to fish by dragging a spinning hook through the water.—n. (in singing) a round.

trol'ley, *n.* a small truck (e.g. that used by porters at railway-stations): on electric street-cars or buses, the wheel on an overhead pole through which the electricity passes from the wire.—*ns.* **trolley-bus,** a bus which gets its power from overhead wires; **trolley-car,** a tram-car.

trom'bone, *n.* a trumpet with a sliding tube which changes the notes.

tron, *n.* in old-time Scotland, a great public weighing-balance.

troop, *n.* a crowd or collection of people or animals: (*pl.*) soldiers.—*v.* to gather in numbers: to march in a company.—*ns.* **troop'er,** a horse-soldier; **troop'-ship,** a ship for carrying soldiers. —**to troop the colours,** to carry a regiment's flag, with bands playing, past the lined-up soldiers of the regiment.

trophy, trō'fi, *n.* something taken from an enemy and kept in memory of the victory: a prize.

trop'ics, *n.pl.* a strip round the earth between the lines of latitude 23½° N. and 23½° S.: the hot countries in this region of the earth.—*adj.* **trop'ical,** having to do with the tropics: very hot.

trot, *v.* to run like a horse, with short, high steps.—Also *n.*—*n.pl.* **trot'ters,** the feet of pigs or sheep.

trōth, *n.* truth: faith.—**to plight one's troth,** to promise to marry.

troubadour, troo'ba-door, *n.* in old-time France, a wandering singer.

trouble, trub'l, *v.* to cause worry, unrest, grief, sorrow: to disturb. —*n.* worry: unrest: illness: care taken in doing something.—*adj.* **troub'lesome,** causing worry.

trough, trof, *n.* a long, hollow box or basin for holding animals' food or water: the dip between two sea-waves.

trounce, *v.* to punish or beat severely.

troupe, troop, *n.* a company (of actors, dancers, etc.).

trousers, trow'zerz, *n.pl.* clothing for the legs and lower part of a man's body.

trousseau, troo'sō, *n.* the set of clothes which a woman prepares for her wedding.

trout, *n.* a river-fish, good for eating.

trow, trō, *v.* used in phrase **I trow,** I think.

trow'el, *n.* a small spade used in spreading plaster and in gardening.

troy-weight, *n.* a system of weights for gold, silver, diamonds, etc.

truant, troo'ant, *n.* a school-pupil who stays away from school without permission.—**to play truant,** to stay away from school without permission.

truce, troos, *n.* a rest from fighting agreed to by both sides in a war. —**A truce to such remarks!** Stop saying such things!

truck, *n.* a wagon for carrying goods.—*n.* **truck'le-bed,** a low bed on wheels.

truck, *v.* to sell goods for other goods instead of for money.— Also *n.*

truck'le, *v.* to give way weakly to the demands of another person.

truc'ulent, *adj.* very fierce: warlike.—*n.* **truc'ulence.**

trudge, truj, *v.* to walk with heavy steps, as if tired.

true, troo, *adj.* agreeing with what really happened: not false: faithful: (in shooting) straight on the mark.—*adv.* **tru'ly.**—*ns.* **truth; tru'ism,** a statement which is so clearly true that it is not worth making.—**Yours truly,** a common ending for a letter about business matters.

truf'fle, *n.* a round growth of the mushroom kind, found underground and used in making certain foods.

trump, *n.* in some card-games, a card of more value than others: an action which will surprise and defeat one's rivals.—**to turn up trumps,** to play one's part nobly when things are difficult.

trumped-up, *adj.* made up to deceive (e.g. a *trumped-up* story).—*n.* **trump'ery,** showy rubbish.

trumpet, trump, *ns.* a musical instrument of the bugle kind.—*v.* **trum'pet,** to praise loudly.—*n.* **trump'eter,** one who plays on a trumpet or bugle.

trun'cāted, *adj.* cut off at the top.

truncheon, trun'shon, *n.* a short heavy staff or baton such as that used by policemen.

trundle, trun'dl, *v.* to wheel or roll along (e.g. a hoop).—*n.* **trun'dle-bed**, a low bed on wheels.

trunk, *n.* the main stem of a tree: the body (without head, arms, or legs) of a person or animal: the nose of an elephant: a large box or chest for clothes.—*ns.* **trunk'-call**, a telephone message to another town; **trunk'-line**, a main line (of railways, canals, telephones, etc.); **trunk'-road**, a main road.

truss, *n.* a bundle (e.g. of hay, straw): a bandage.—*v.* to draw together and tie.

trust, *n.* faith in another person's power to do something, or in his good character: a number of business firms worked together as if they were one.—*v.* to put one's faith in.—*adjs.* **trust'y**, **trust'worthy**, able to be depended on.—**a position of trust**, a high position given to a person because it is thought that he will be able to do what is wanted; **to take on trust**, to believe without testing.

truth, trooth, *n.* a statement which agrees with what really happened.—*adj.* **truth'ful**, not false.

try, *v.* to strive to do something: to test: to judge (a prisoner) in a court of law.—*n.* an effort, attempt: a test: one of the scores in rugby football.—*n.* **tri'al**.—*adj.* **try'ing**, hard to bear: worrying.—**to try on**, to put on (clothing) to test fit, neatness, etc.; **to try out**, to test by using.

tryst, *n.* a promise to meet someone at a certain place (*trysting-place*).

tsar, zar, *n.* the Russian word for emperor:—*fem.* **tsari'na**.—Also spelt **czar, tzar, czarina, tzarina**.

tset'se, *n.* a fly (found in Africa), whose bite is poisonous to horses and cattle.

tub, *n.* a round wooden bath used for washing clothes: a bath.—*adj.* **tub'by**, fat and round.

tuba, *n.* a large trumpet giving a low note.

tube, *n.* a pipe: an underground railway.—*n.* **tu'bing**, a length of tube (e.g. of rubber).—*adj.* **tu'bular**, hollow like a tube.

tuber, *n.* a swelling on the root or stem of a plant (a potato is a *tuber*).—*ns.* **tu'bercle**, a small tuber; **tubercu'losis**, a disease, usually called *consumption*.

tuck, *n.* a fold in a piece of cloth.—*v.* to gather cloth together into a fold.—**to tuck in**, to pack bedclothes round a person: to eat hungrily.

Tuesday, tūz'dā, *n.* the third day of the week.

tuft, *n.* a cluster or clump of grass, hair, etc.

tug, *v.* to pull hard: to drag along.—*n.* a strong pull: a small but strong steam-vessel which pulls large ships.—*n.* **tug-of-war**, a game in which two sides, holding a strong rope, pull against each other.

tuition, tū-ish'n, *n.* teaching.

tulip, *n.* a garden bulb-flower.

tulle, tūl, *n.* thin silk network.

tumble, *v.* to fall: to do jumping tricks.—*n.* a fall.—*n.* **tum'bler**, a large drinking-glass: a kind of pigeon.—*adj.* **tum'bledown**, falling to pieces.

tumbrel, tumbril, *n.* a kind of cart.

tumour, tū'mor, *n.* a swelling.

tumult, *n.* a great noise made by a crowd.—*adj.* **tumultuous** (tūmul'tū-us), noisy, excited.

tun, *n.* a large cask.

tundras, toon'dras, *n.pl.* the great level treeless plains of the far north of Europe, Asia, and Canada.

tune, *n.* notes put together in a pleasing order: the music of a song.—*v.* to tighten or loosen the strings of a piano, violin, etc. so that they may give the notes wanted: to move the dial of a wireless set until a certain station is heard.—**in tune**, making pleasant music: agreeing (with); **out of tune**, making harsh sounds: not agreeing (with).

tunic, tū'nic, *n.* a soldier's jacket.

tunnel, tun'nel, *n.* an underground passage (e.g. for a railway-train) cut through a hill or under a river.—*v.* to make a tunnel.

tunny, tun'ny, *n.* a large sea-fish.

tur'ban, *n.* a long piece of cloth wound round the head, worn as a head-dress by Indians and other Eastern people.

tur'bid, *adj.* muddy: thick.

tur'bine, *n.* a kind of wheel with blades; it is made to turn by means of steam or water, and is used in driving the machinery of ships, electric stations, etc.

tur'bot, *n.* a large flat sea-fish, used for food.

tur'bulent, *adj.* restless and noisy: angry.—*n.* tur'bulence.

tureen', *n.* a large dish for holding soup at table.

turf, *n.* short grass and the soil below it: a piece of land covered with short grass (e.g. on a golf-course or race-course).—**the turf,** the sport of horse-racing.

turgid, tur'jid, *adj.* swollen: sounding grand but meaning little.

Turk, *n.* a native of Turkey.—*adj.* Turkish.—*n.* turkey-red, a bright red dye.

tur'key, *n.* a large farm-yard bird, whose flesh is eaten mostly at Christmas-time.

tur'moil, *n.* din: disorder.

turn, *v.* to move or go round: to change direction: to face the other way: to shape (e.g. a piece of wood in a special machine): to change (e.g. The wizard *turned* the frog into a prince): (of milk) to become sour.—*n.* a change of direction: one round of a wheel, skipping-rope: a bend (e.g. in a road): a chance to do something (e.g. It is my *turn* next): a good or bad act towards a person (e.g. He did me a good *turn*): an attack of sickness (e.g. a fainting *turn*).—**in turn,** one following another in regular order; **out of turn,** out of one's order; **to a turn,** perfectly cooked; **to turn down,** to say no to (an offer); **to turn in,** to go to bed; **to turn off,** to screw the handle of a tap so that the water stops flowing; **to turn out,** to happen: to come as a result: to come to a meeting, parade, etc. (e.g. A large crowd *turned out*); **to turn up,** to arrive: to appear.—*ns.* turn'coat, one who leaves his friends and goes over to the other side; **turn'ing,** a bend (e.g. in a road); **turn'key,** one who keeps the keys of a prison; **turn'out,** a gathering of people (e.g. at church); **turn'over,** in a business firm, the total amount of money received and paid out during a certain time; **turn'pike,** a gate (across a main road) which is opened when the traveller pays a toll or fee: a main road on which there are turnpike-gates; **turn'stile,** a gate which turns round and allows only one person to pass at a time (used at football-grounds, etc.); **turn'-up,** an unexpected happening.

tur'nip, *n.* a vegetable, with a large round root, grown in gardens and fields.

tur'pentine, *n.* a sticky oily substance got from certain trees (used for mixing paints).

turquoise, ter'koiz, *n.* a precious stone, greenish-blue in colour.

tur'ret, *n.* a small tower on the top of a castle or other building: on warships, a tower in which are guns.

tur'tle, *n.* a large sea-tortoise, whose flesh is used in the making of soup: a beautiful, softly-cooing dove (also called tur'tle-dove).—**to turn turtle,** to capsize (e.g. The sinking ship *turned turtle*).

tusk, *n.* a large tooth sticking out from the mouth.—*n.* tusk'er, an elephant whose tusks are grown.

tussle, tus'l, *n.* a struggle.

tus'sock, *n.* a tuft of grass or twigs.

tutelage, tū'te-lāj, *n.* care or protection.—*adj.* tū'telary, protecting.

tū'tor, *n.* a private teacher.—*v.* to teach.

twad'dle, *n.* silly talk.

twain, *n.* two.—**in twain,** in two: asunder.

twang, *n.* a sharp quick sound like that of a harp-string: a tone of voice in which the words seem to come through the nose.

tweak, *v.* to pull sharply: to pinch. —Also *n.*

tweed, *n.* a stout woollen cloth, used chiefly for men's suits.

twee'zers, *n.* small pincers (for pulling out hairs, holding small things, etc.).

twelfth, *n.* one of twelve equal parts.—*n.* **twelvemonth**, a year.

twice, *adv.* two times.

twid′dle, *v.* to play with (the fingers, toes, hair).

twig, *n.* a small branch of a tree.

twilight, twī′līt, *n.* the time of half-darkness, between day and night.

twill, *n.* strong cloth with a ridged appearance.

twine, *n.* a strong kind of string.—*v.* to wind round : to twist together.

twins, *n.pl.* two children born of the same mother at the same birth.—*adj.* **twin**, born at the same birth : made up of two parts which look alike.

twinge, twinj, *n.* a sudden, sharp pain.

twink′le, *v.* to shine with sparkling light.—*ns.* **twink′le**, **twink′ling**, the blinking of an eye : an instant.

twirl, twerl, *v.* to turn round quickly.—Also *n.*

twist, *v.* to form a thread by winding two or three strands together : to turn from the true meaning : to hurt or break by turning round quickly.—*n.* a single thread : a hurt caused by a sudden turning.

twit, *v.* to remind a person of a fault and make fun of him for it.

twitch, *v.* to pull with a sudden jerk : to draw tight.—Also *n.*

twit′ter, *n.* the chirp of a bird : a slight trembling of the nerves.—*v.* to make a sound like that of a sparrow or swallow : to have a slight trembling of the nerves.—*n.* **twitt′ering**.

two, too, *adj.* and *n.* one and one.—*adjs.* **two′-edged**, having two edges ; **two′fōld**, double.—*n.* **two′-step**, a dance in which two steps are taken forwards then two backwards.

type, tīp, *n.* a letter (made usually of lead) used for printing : kind (e.g. All *types* of boys are in the class).—*ns.* **typewriter** (tīp′rī-ter), a machine with keys which, when struck, cause letters to be printed on a sheet of paper ; **ty′pist**, a person whose work it is to write letters, etc. on a typewriter.

typhoid, tī′foid, *adj.* and *n.* a fever causing pain in the bowels.

typhoon, tī-foon′, *n.* a violent storm of wind and rain in Eastern seas.

typhus, tī′fus, *n.* a fever which spreads easily in dirty places.

ty′rant, *n.* one who governs harshly.—*adjs.* **tyran′nical**, **tyr′annous**, cruel.—*n.* **tyranny** (tir′an-i), the rule of a tyrant.

tyre or **tire**, *n.* the thick rubber cover round a motor or cycle wheel.

tyro. Same as **tiro**.

tzar, tzarina. See **tsar**.

U

ubiquitous, ū-bik′wit-us, *adj.* being everywhere at once : found everywhere.—*n.* **ubiq′uity**.

ud′der, *n.* the milk-bag of a cow, sheep, etc.

ug′ly, *adj.* not pleasing to look at : angry ; dangerous.—*n.* **ug′liness**.

ūkulē′le, *n.* a small musical instrument played like a banjo.

ul′cer, *n.* a sore out of which matter comes.—*adj.* **ul′cerated**, having an ulcer or ulcers.

ul′ster, *n.* a long overcoat for men.

ultē′rior, *adj.* lying beyond : secret and evil (e.g. an *ulterior* motive, i.e. a secret, evil reason).—*adj.*

ult′imate, lying furthest : last, final.—*adv.* **ult′imately**, finally, in the end.—*n.* **ultimā′tum**, a statement sent by one nation to another saying that unless certain things are done within a fixed time, war will be declared.—*adv.* **ult′ra**, too, very.—*n.* **ultramarine** (-ma-reen′), a sky-blue colour.

um′ber, *n.* a brown colour.

um′bra, *n.* the shadow of the earth on the moon (seen during an eclipse of the moon).

umbrage, um′brāj, *n.* a hurt feeling (e.g. He took *umbrage* at my words).

umbrel′la, *n.* a folding shelter against rain, carried in the hand.

um′pire, *n.* a judge who is asked to settle a quarrel : (in cricket, hockey, etc.) a person who sees that the game is properly played, and decides doubtful points.— *v.* to act as a judge.

unaccount′able, *adj.* not able to be explained.

unanimous, ū-nan′imus, *adj.* all of one mind : having the same opinion.—*n.* **unanim′ity.**

unanswerable, un-an′ser-abl, *adj.* not able to be declared wrong.

unassū′ming, *adj.* modest, shy.

unaware, *adj.* not knowing.—*adv.* **unawares,** off one's guard.

unbal′anced, *adj.* not sensible : mad (e.g. an *unbalanced* mind).

unbeliever, un-be-lē′ver, *n.* one who does not believe what other people think is true : a heathen. —*n.* **unbelief′.**

unbend′, *v.* to remove a bend from : to behave in a natural way, without pride or stiffness.—*adj.* **unbend′ing,** not yielding : severe.

unblush′ing, *adj.* without shame.

unbosom, un-boo′zom, *v.* (with *one's self*) to tell freely one's troubles, secrets, etc.

unbrī′dled, *adj.* not held in check.

unbur′den, *v.* to take a load off : to tell one's story.

uncalled for, quite unnecessary : unwise (e.g. His remarks were *uncalled for*).

uncan′ny, *adj.* strange : full of mystery.

uncertain, un-ser′tān, *adj.* not certain, doubtful.—*n.* **uncer′tainty.**

uncle, ung′kl, *n.* the brother of one's father or mother.

unclean′, *adj.* dirty : having a terrible disease.

uncoil′, *v.* to unwind.

uncom′mon, *adj.* not common, strange.—*adv.* **uncomm′only,** very.

uncompromi′sing, *adj.* not willing to give in.

unconscionable, un-kon′shun-a-bl, *adj.* more than is reasonable.

unconscious, un-kon′shus, *adj.* not knowing : senseless, stunned (e.g. by an accident).

uncouth, un-kooth′, *adj.* clumsy, awkward : rude : odd in appearance.

undaunt′ed, *adj.* bold : fearless.

undeniable, un-dē-nī′a-bl, *adj.* not able to be denied : true.

underbid′, *v.* at a sale, to bid or offer less than another person.

undercharge′, *v.* to charge less than the proper sum.—Also *n.*

un′dercurrent, *n.* a flow or movement under the surface.

underdone, un-der-dun′, *adj.* not quite cooked.

underes′timate, *v.* to think too little of.

underfoot′, *adv.* under the feet.

undergo′, *v.* to pass through : to suffer or endure.

undergraduate, un-der-grad′ū-āt, *n.* a university student who has not yet passed his examination.

un′derground, *adj.* under the ground. —*n.* a railway which runs in a tunnel beneath the surface of the ground.

undergrowth, un′der-grōth, *n.* shrubs or low plants growing among trees.

underhand′, *adj.* done in a secret, deceitful manner.—Also *adv.*

underline′, *v.* to draw a line under.

un′derling, *n.* a person of lower rank : a person of little worth.

undermentioned, un-der-men′shond, *adj.* spoken about below.

undermine′, *v.* to do damage to (e.g. He *undermined* his health by too much study).

un′dermōst, *adj.* lowest in place.

underneath, un-der-nēth′, *adv.* and *prep.* beneath : below.

underpay′, *v.* to pay less than enough.

underrate′, *v.* to think too little of.

undersell′, *v.* to sell something cheaper than another person sells it.

undersigned (the), un′der-sīnd, *n.pl.* those whose names are written at the end of a letter or statement.

understand′, *v.* to see the meaning of : to know thoroughly : to take for granted.—*adj.* **under-**

' un-' at the beginning of many words means ' not.' Only the commonest of such words are given here.

stan'dable.—*n.* understan'ding, the power of seeing the full meaning : an agreement or condition.

understate', *v.* to state below the truth.

un'derstudy, *n.* an actor who learns the part of another actor so that, if that actor is unable to play at any time, he may act the part.—

undertake', *v.* to take upon one's self : to attempt : to have charge of.—*ns.* un'dertaker, one who sees to funerals : under-tā'king, something which is being attempted : a great job or task : a promise.

un'dertone, *n.* a low voice.

underval'ue, *v.* to value below the real worth.

underwear, un'der-wār, *n.* garments worn under others.

un'derwood, *n.* low wood or trees growing under large ones.

un'derworld, *n.* the place where evil-doers are punished after death : the law-breakers and evil-doers of a town.

un'derwriter, *n.* one who insures ships.

undisguised, un-dis-gīzd', *adj.* open, plain.

undo, un-doo', *v.* to unfasten (a coat, parcel, etc.) : to spoil what has been done.—*n.* undo'ing, ruin (e.g. His boldness will be his *undoing*, i.e. will ruin him).

undoubted, un-dowt'ed, *adj.* not to be doubted.—*adv.* undoubt'edly, without doubt.

undress', *v.* to take off one's clothes. —*n.* plain dress (not uniform).

undue, un-dū', *adj.*, undū'ly, *adv.*, too much, more than is necessary (e.g. *undue* expense, to worry *unduly*).

un'dūlāting, *adj.* having the appearance of waves (e.g. an *undulating* country, i.e. a country with many small hills and valleys).—*n.* undulā'tion, a rise in the ground, like a wave.

unearth, un-erth', *v.* to bring out from the earth, or from a place of hiding.—*adj.* unearth'ly, very odd, as if not belonging to this world.

uneasy, un-ē'zi, *adj.* uncomfortable : not at ease.—*n.* uneas'iness.

unemployed, un-em-ploid', *adj.* out of work.—Also *n.pl.*

unequivocal, un-ē-kwiv'ō-kal, *adj.* not doubtful : clear.

unerr'ing, *adj.* not missing the mark.

unē'ven, *adj.* not smooth or level : not all of the same goodness.

unexceptionable, un-ek-sep'shun-a-bl, *adj.* having no fault.

unexpec'ted, *adj.* not expected, sudden.

unfail'ing, *adj.* not failing or likely to fail.

unfair', *adj.* not just : dishonest.

unfasten, un-fas'n, *v.* to loosen (e.g. a tied horse, a buttoned coat).

unfeel'ing, *adj.* harsh: hard-hearted.

unfeigned, un-fānd', *adj.* real : sincere.

unflinching, un-flin'shing, *adj.* brave, fearless.

unfōld', *v.* to spread out : to tell (e.g. a story, plan).

unfor'tūnate, *adj.* unlucky.

unfound'ed, *adj.* not true.

unfrequented, un-frē-kwen'ted, *adj.* not often visited.

unfurl', *v.* to unfold (e.g. a flag).

ungain'ly, *adj.* clumsy in walk or manner.

ungrateful, un-grāt'fool, *adj.* not showing thanks for kindness.

ungrudging, un-gruj'ing, *adj.* giving freely.

unguarded, un-gar'ded, *adj.* without protection : careless.

unguent, ung'gwent, *n.* ointment.

unhand', *v.* to take the hands off : to let go.

unhinge, un-hinj', *v.* to take (a door) from the hinges : to upset a person's mind.

unhorse', *v.* to throw from a horse.

ū'nicorn, *n.* (in old stories) an animal with a body like a horse and one straight horn on the forehead.

ū'niform, *adj.* having the same form, size, goodness, etc. : not changing.—*n.* the dress worn by soldiers, sailors, etc.—*n.* uniform'ity, sameness : likeness.

ū'nify, *v.* to make into one.—*n.* unificā'tion.

' un-' at the beginning of many words means ' not.' Only the commonest of such words are given here.

unimpeach'able, *adj.* free from fault : blameless.

union, ŭn'yun, *n.* a joining together : marriage : a trade-union (see **trade**).—*n.* **Union-jack,** the flag of the United Kingdom.

unique, ū-nēk', *adj.* the only one of its kind : without like or equal.

ū'nison, *n.* (in singing) a tune in which all sing the same notes : agreement.

ū'nit, *n.* one : a single thing or person : a measure by which an amount is measured (e.g. The yard is our *unit* of length).—*n.* **ū'nity,** (in arithmetic) one : friendship, agreement.—*v.* **ūnite',** to join together : to become one : to act together.—*adj.* **uni'ted.**

ūniver'sal, *adj.* in general use : whole : total.—*ns.* **ū'niverse,** the sun, stars, and heavens : all created things : the world ; **ūniver'sity,** a place of learning where the higher branches of knowledge are taught, and which holds examinations and gives *degrees* to those who pass.

unkempt, un'kemt, *adj.* uncombed : rough.

unload, un-lōd', *v.* to take the load from.

unloose', *v.* to set free.

unman'ly, *adj.* mean, cowardly.

unmask', *v.* to take a mask or covering off : to show up (e.g. an evil plot).

unmatched, un-macht', *adj.* without an equal.

unmista'kable, *adj.* very clear.

unmit'igāted, *adj.* complete (e.g. an *unmitigated* disgrace, i.e. a disgrace for which nothing good can be said).

unmoved, un-moovd', *adj.* firm : calm.

unnecessary, un-nes'es-ar-i, *adj.* not needed.

unpack', *v.* to take out of a pack : to open.

unpal'atable, *adj.* not pleasing to the taste.

unparalleled, un-par'a-leld, *adj.* having no equal.

unpick', *v.* to take out (e.g. stitches) by picking.

unprēmed'itāted, *adj.* not thought out beforehand : done without thinking.

unrav'el, *v.* to unwind or take the knots out of : to solve a problem or mystery by looking into all the facts.

unremit'ting, *adj.* never ceasing.

unrequited, un-rē-kwī'ted, *adj.* not paid back.

unrest', *n.* want of rest : a state of trouble or discontent.

unruly, un-roo'li, *adj.* paying no heed to laws : badly behaved.

unsavoury, un-sā'vor-i, *adj.* having no taste, or a bad taste : filthy.

unset'tle, *v.* to disturb : to upset.—*adj.* **unset'tled,** (of the weather) not remaining the same for long : (of a country) not yet lived in by *settlers.*

unsheathe, un-shēth', *v.* to draw (a sword) from the sheath.

unship', *v.* to take out of a ship.

unshod', *adj.* without shoes.

unsightly, un-sīt'li, *adj.* ugly.

unsophisticated, un-sō-fis'ti-kā-ted, *adj.* simple : innocent.

unspā'ring, *adj.* giving freely.

unspeak'able, *adj.* too good or too bad to be put into words.

unstudied, un-stud'ēd, *adj.* natural.

unsuspec'ting, *adj.* not aware of coming danger.

unthink'able, *adj.* too bad to be thought of.

untimely, un-tīm'li, *adj.* happening before the proper time.

untōld', *adj.* not told : not able to be counted.

untoward, un-tō'ard, *adj.* happening at a bad time : unlucky.

untrue, un-troo', *adj.* not true : false : not faithful.—*n.* **untruth',** a lie.—*adj.* **untruth'ful.**

unveil, un-vāl', *v.* to remove a covering (e.g. The statue was *unveiled,* i.e. was first shown to the public) : to show up (e.g. unknown evils).

unwieldy, un-wēl'di, *adj.* not easily moved or handled : clumsy.

unwit'ting, *adj.* not knowing.

unwŏnt'ed, *adj.* unusual : more than usual.

' un-' at the beginning of many words means ' not.' Only the commonest of such words are given here.

up, *adv.* towards a higher place: on high: quite (e.g. He ate *up* the pie): at an end, over (e.g. Time is *up*).—**ups and downs,** rises and falls (e.g. the *ups and downs* of life, i.e. the times of good and bad).

upbraid', *v.* to scold.

up'bringing, *n.* the training (manners, schooling, etc.) which one has had from one's parents.

upheav'al, *n.* a violent shaking (e.g. an earthquake): great unrest or disturbance.

up'hill, *adj.* going upwards: hard to face.—Also *adv.*

uphōld', *v.* to support or defend (an opinion).

uphōl'ster, *v.* to fit chairs, sofas, motor-seats, etc. with springs, covers, and cushions.—*ns.* uphol'sterer; uphol'stery, covers, cushions, etc. for seats.

up'keep, *n.* the money needed to keep a house, car, etc.

up'land, *n.* high ground: mountain land.

up'per, *adj.* higher in position.—*adjs.* up'most, up'permost, highest in position; up'pish, rather proud.

upright, up'rīt, *adj.* standing up: just and honest.

up'roar, *n.* noise and shouting.—*adj.* uproar'ious, very noisy.

uproot', *v.* to tear up by the roots.

upset', *v.* to turn upside-down: to throw down: to ruin or make useless.—*adj.* worried, anxious: ill.—*n.* up'set, a fall: an unexpected happening.—**upset price,** the price at which the bidding starts at an auction sale.

up'shot, *n.* result: end of the matter.

up'side-down, *adj.* and *adv.* with the top part underneath: in confusion.

upstairs', *adv.* in or to the part of a house reached by stairs.—Also *n.*

up'start, *n.* one who has risen quickly from a humble to a high position: one who has suddenly become rich.

up'stream, *adv.* higher up the river, towards the source.

up-to-date, *adj.* new: not old-fashioned.

ūrā'nium, *n.* a hard metal from which *radium* is got.

ur'ban, *adj.* having to do with a town (oppos. of *rural*).—*adj.* urbane', polite, mannerly.—*n.* urban'ity, politeness.

ur'chin, *n.* a small boy: a dirty or ragged boy.

urge, urj, *v.* to drive on: to try to persuade.—*adj.* ur'gent, needing to be done or seen to at once.—*n.* ur'gency.

ū'rine, *n.* the water passed out of the body of animals.—*n.* ū'rinal, a place for passing such water.

urn, *n.* a vase for the ashes of the dead: a large metal can, with tap, used for making tea, etc

us, *pron.* the persons who are speaking—object of verb.

use, ūz, *v.* to put to some purpose: to treat: to spend or wear away: to be in the habit of (nearly always in past, e.g. I *used* (ūst) to go there).—*ns.* use (ūs), need (e.g. I have no *use* for it): fitness for a purpose (e.g. Hay is of *use* for feeding horses): a habit or custom; ū'sage, manner of using: treatment.—*adjs.* use'ful, suited for a purpose: helpful; use'less.

ush'er, *n.* one who meets people at the door of a hall and shows them to their seats.—*v.* to lead in.

usual, ū'zhū-al, *adj.* common: happening often.

usurp, ū-zurp', *v.* to take possession of (e.g. a throne) by force or without right.—*n.* usurp'er.

usury, ū'zhur-i, *n.* the lending of money in order to make more money: the asking of a very high price for money that is lent.—*n.* ū'surer.

ūten'sil, *n.* a useful instrument: a pot or pan for cooking.

ū'tilise, *v.* to use.—*n.* util'ity, usefulness: a useful service (e.g. tramways, waterworks).

ut'most, ut'termost, *adjs.* furthest: as much as possible.

ut'ter, *v.* to say: to make public.—*n.* ut'terance, way of speaking: something said.

ut'ter, *adj.* quite: complete.—*adv.* ut'terly.

ū'vūla, *n.* the small 'tongue' which hangs down in the back of the throat.

V

vā′cant, *adj.* empty : stupid, empty of thought.—*ns.* **vā′cancy,** a post or job not held by anybody ; **vaca′tion,** holiday.—*v.* **vacate′,** to leave empty : to give up.

vaccine, vak′sēn, *n.* poison which causes a slight attack of small-pox or other disease.—*v.* **vaccinate** (vak′sin-āt), to put vaccine in a person's blood. (The vaccine causes a slight attack of the disease, but this keeps away bad attacks.)—*n.* **vaccina′tion.**

vacillate, vas′il-āt, *v.* to move from one opinion to another : to hesitate.

vacuum, vak′ū-um, *n.* a space in which there is no air.— *ns.* **vacuum-cleaner,** a machine which cleans carpets, etc. by sucking up the dust ; **vacuum-flask,** a bottle with two walls, separated by a vacuum, for keeping liquids hot or cold.

vag′abond, *n.* a wanderer : an idle fellow : a rascal.

vagā′ry, *n.* a wandering of the thoughts : a queer fancy : a sudden change (of weather).

vā′grant, *adj.* having no settled home.—*n.* a wanderer or tramp. *n.* **vā′grancy,** wandering.

vague, vāg, *adj.* not clear.

vain, *adj.* full of showy pride : useless.—*n.* **van′ity,** silly pride. —**in vain,** without success.

vainglō′ry, *n.* empty pride : boast-fulness.—*adj.* **vainglō′rious,** boast-ful.

val′ance, *n.* hanging curtain above a window or round a bed.

vale, *n.* a valley.

valedic′tion, *n.* a farewell.—*adj.* **valedic′tory.**

val′entine, *n.* a lover chosen, or a love-letter sent, on St Valentine's Day (14th February).

val′et, *n.* a man-servant.

valetūdinā′rian, *n.* one who thinks a lot about his illnesses.

valiant, val′yant, *adj.* brave.

val′id, *adj.* sound, good (e.g. a *valid* reason) : able to be used, lawful (e.g. This ticket is not *valid*).—*n.* **valid′ity.**

valise, va-lēs′, *n.* a travelling-bag : a soldier's knapsack.

val′ley, *n.* low land between hills or mountains :—*pl.* **vall′eys.**

valour, val′ur, *n.* courage : bravery. —*adj.* **val′orous.**

value, val′ū, *n.* worth : price : im-portance : meaning.—*v.* to put a price on : to think highly of.— *adj.* **val′ūable,** of great worth.— *n.* **valua′tion,** value or price set upon a thing.

valve, *n.* a means for allowing air, steam, or a liquid to flow in one direction only (e.g. the *valve* on a cycle or motor-car tyre) : a lamp-like part in a wireless set.

vamp, *n.* the upper part of a boot or shoe : a flirting girl.—*v.* to play a quickly made-up tune on the piano.

vam′pire, *n.* in old-time tales, a ghost that sucked the blood of sleeping persons : a woman who lives upon men : a kind of bat (flying animal).

van, *n.* the front of an army or a fleet.

van, *n.* a large covered wagon or car for goods.

van′dal, *n.* one who wickedly de-stroys beautiful buildings, pic-tures, etc. (The *Vandals* were a race of fierce plunderers who lived in Europe about 1400 years ago.)

vane, *n.* a weathercock : the blade of a windmill, propeller, etc.

vanguard, van′gard, *n.* the guard in the front of an army or fleet.

vanil′la, *n.* a sweet-scented flavour-ing used in ices, puddings, etc.

van′ish, *v.* to go out of sight.

van′ity, *n.* showy, silly pride.

vanquish, vang′kwish, *v.* to beat (in battle).

vant′age, *n.* advantage.

vap′id, *adj.* dull : lacking interest.

vapour, vā′pur, *n.* moisture in the air (e.g. steam, mist) : the gas into which most liquids and solids can be turned by heat.

variable, vā′ri-a-bl, *adj.* changing easily or often : unsteady.—*n.* **variā′tion,** change : difference.

variance, vā′ri-ans. *n.* lack of agreement: a quarrel.—**.. va′riant**, a different form of spelling or reading (e.g. ' Color ' is the American *variant* of ' colour ').—*adj.* different.—**at variance**, not agreeing.

varicose veins, a disease causing badly swollen veins (usually of the legs).

variegate, vā′ri-e-gāt, *v.* to mark with different colours.—*n.* **variegā′tion.**

various, vā′ri-us, *adj.* different: several: of many kinds.—*n.*

variety (va-rī′e-ti), difference : a number of different things (e.g. I have a *variety* of books in my library): kind (e.g. What *variety* of cow is this ?): a theatre-show made up of a number of short acts (e.g. juggling, singing, dancing).

var′let, *n.* a footman : a rascal.

var′nish, *n.* a sticky liquid which gives a glossy, shiny appearance to paper, wood, etc. : a glossy appearance.—*v.* to cover with varnish : to cover up faults.

vā′ry, *v.* to make different : to change : to disagree.

vase, vahz, *n.* a jar of stone, metal, glass, etc. used as an ornament or for holding cut flowers.

vaseline, vas′e-lin, *n.* ointment made from petroleum. (See **trade-mark.**)

vas′sal, *n.* one who holds land from an overlord : a slave.

vast, *adj.* of very great size or amount.—*n.* **vast′ness.**

vat, *n.* a large tub.

Vat′ican, *n.* the Pope's palace in Rome.

vaudeville, vōd′vil, *n.* a play with dances and songs, usually comic.

vault, vawlt, *n.* an arched roof: a room (usually underground) with an arched roof: a cellar for storing wine, gold, etc. : the sky : a leap.—*v.* to leap, with the aid of a pole, or by resting the hands on something.

vaunt, vawnt′, *v.* to boast.

veal, *n.* the flesh of a calf.

veer, *v.* to change direction (e.g. The wind *veered* round to the west): to change the course of a ship.

vegetable, vej′e-ta-bl, *n.* a plant grown for food.—*adj.* of the plant kind.—*ns.* **vegetā′rian**, one who believes that vegetables are

the only proper food for man, and does not eat meat : **vegetā′tion**, plants in general : the plants of a place.—*v.* **veg′etate**, to grow by roots and leaves : to lead an idle care-free life.—**vegetable kingdom**, plant-life (not animals or lifeless matter).

vehement, vē′e-ment, *adj.* full of feeling : angry : violent.—*n.* **ve′hemence.**

vehicle, vē′i-kl, *n.* a carriage or motor-car: anything which travels on wheels.—*adj.* **vehic′ular.**

veil, vāl, *n.* a piece of thin cloth or netting worn by ladies to shade or hide the face : a curtain.—*v.* to cover with a veil : to hide.

vein, vān, *n.* one of the tubes which carry the blood to the heart: a small rib of a leaf : a crack in a rock filled with mineral : a mood (e.g. He was in happy *vein*).—*adj.* **veined**, marked with veins.

veld, felt, *n.* in South Africa, the name given to open grass-country, with few or no trees.

vell′um, *n.* a fine material for writing on, made from the skins of calves, kids, or lambs.

velocity, ve-los′i-ti, *n.* swiftness.

vel′vet, *n.* a cloth made from silk, with a thick, soft surface.—*ns.* **velours** (ve-loor′), **velveteen′**, kinds of velvet.—*adj.* **vel′vety**, soft like velvet.

vē′nal, *adj.* able to be bought or sold : willing to do evil if money is offered.

vend, *v.* to sell.—*n.* **ven′dor**, one who sells.

vendet′ta, *n.* a fight between families.

veneer′, *v.* to cover a piece of wood with another thin piece of finer quality : to give a good appearance to what is really bad.—*n.* a thin layer of wood: outward show.

ven′erable, *adj.* honourable : worthy of respect because of age.—*v.* **ven′erate**, to respect highly : to honour.—*n.* **venerā′tion.**

ven′ery, *n.* hunting.

venē′tian-blind, *n.* a blind for windows, formed of thin slips of wood hung on tapes.

vengeance, ven′jins, *n.* punishment on another in return for harm or wrong.—*adj.* **venge′ful**, seeking revenge.

venial, vē'ni-al, *adj.* able to be pardoned.

venison, ven'zn, *n.* the flesh of the deer.

ven'om, *n.* poison: spite.— *adj.* **ven'omous,** poisonous: spiteful.

vent, *n.* a small opening: a hole to allow air, smoke, etc. to pass through.— *v.* to pour forth (one's feelings, opinions, etc.).

vent'ilate, *v.* to allow fresh air to pass through: to talk about.— *ns.* **ventila'tion; vent'ilator,** a grating or other kind of hole for allowing fresh air into a room.

ventriloquist, ven-tril'o-kwist, *n.* one who can speak without showing that he is doing it; his voice seems to come from some other person or place.

ven'ture, *n.* chance, luck: a risky journey or piece of business.— *v.* to risk: to dare.— *adjs.* **ven'turous; ven'turesome.**

venue, ven'ū, *n.* meeting-place.

Ve'nus, *n.* among the Romans of old, the goddess of love: the brightest of the planets or stars which move round the sun.

veracious, ve-rā'shus, *adj.* truthful. — *n.* **vera'city,** truthfulness.

veran'da, veran'dah, *n.* a covered balcony beside a house.

verb, *n.* the word that tells what a thing does, or what is done to it (e.g. The match *burns*; the match *is struck*).— *adjs.* **ver'bal,** spoken (not *written*): word for word; **verbose',** containing more words than are necessary.— *n.* **verbos'ity,** love of talking.— *adv.* **verba'tim,** word for word.

ver'dant, *adj.* green: fresh (e.g. grass or leaves).— *n.* **ver'dūre,** greenness: freshness of growth.

ver'dict, *n.* the decision (' guilty ' or ' not guilty ') given by a judge or jury in a law court: a person's opinion on a matter.

verdigris, ver'di-grēs, *n.* the greenish rust of copper, brass, or bronze.

verge, verj, *n.* border: edge.— *v.* to lean: to be on the edge.— *n.* **ver'ger,** an attendant in church.

veriest. See **very.**

ver'ify, *v.* to prove to be true.— *n.* **verifica'tion.**

ver'ily, *adv.* in truth.

verisimilitude, ver-i-sim-il'i-tūd, *n.* likeness to life.

ver'ity, *n.* truth.— *adj.* **ver'itable,** true: according to fact: real.

vermicelli, ver-mi-chel'i, *n.* fine wheat-flour made into small worm-like rolls.

vermilion, ver-mil'yun, *n.* a bright-red colour.

ver'min, *n.* a name given to small destroying animals, such as mice, rats, etc., and to insects, such as bugs, fleas, and lice.— *adj.* **ver'minous,** full of vermin.

vernac'ular, *n.* the language spoken by the people who belong to a country.

ver'nal, *adj.* having to do with spring.

ver'satile, *adj.* turning easily from one subject or task to another. — *n.* **versatil'ity.**

verse, *n.* a line of poetry: a number of lines of poetry grouped according to a plan: a short division of a chapter of the Bible.— *n.* **ver'sion,** a translation from one language into another: a person's story of what has happened. — *v.* **ver'sify,** to write poetry.— *adj.* **versed** (verst), knowing much (e.g. He is well *versed* in arithmetic).

ver'sus, *prep.* against. Often shortened to **v.**

ver'tebræ, *n.pl.* the bones of the back-bone or spine.— *n.* **ver'tebrate,** an animal which has a back-bone.

vertex, *n.* the top corner or highest point :— *pl.* **vertices** (ver'tis-es). — *adj.* **ver'tical,** standing up on end, not lying flat: moving up and down.

ver'tigo, *n.* giddiness.

verve, *n.* lively spirit.

ver'y, *adv.* to a great extent (e.g. *very* good).— *adjs.* **very,** real, actual (e.g. in *very* truth); **veriest** (ver'i-est), used thus :—The *veriest* child would know that, i.e. even a child would know that.

ves'pers, *n.pl.* evening-service.

ves'sel, *n.* a ship: a hollow dish, barrel, etc. for holding anything: a vein for the blood.

vest, *n.* an undergarment worn next the skin: a waistcoat.

ves'tibule, n. the part of a house just inside the front door.

vestige, ves'tij, n. a track or footprint : a trace : (pl.) small remains.

vest'ment, n. a garment : a robe : (pl.) dress worn by clergymen during service.

ves'try, n. a room in a church in which the vestments are kept : a number of persons appointed to look after certain business of a parish.

vetch, n. a plant of the pea kind, grown for cattle food.

vet'eran, n. one who has had much service : an old soldier.

veterinary, vet'e-ri-na-ri, adj. having to do with the diseases of farm and house animals (horse, dog, etc.).—**veterinary surgeon,** an animal doctor.

vē'to, n. the power or right to cast aside.—v. to forbid.

vex, v. to make angry.—adj. **vexatious** (vex-ā'shus), causing trouble or worry.

via, vī'a, prep. by way of (e.g. via London, by way of London).

vi'aduct, n. a long bridge for carrying a road or railway over a valley, river, etc.

vi'al, n. a small bottle.

vi'and, n. food.

vi'brate, v. to shake, to tremble.—n. vibrā'tion.

vic'ar, n. a clergyman of the Church of England.—n. **vic'arage,** the house of a vicar.—adj. **vicā'rious,** filling the place of another person : done or suffered in place of another person.

vice, n. a bad habit (e.g. too much drinking, smoking).—adj. **vicious** (vish'us), evil : fierce : cruel.

vice or **vise,** n. an instrument (used by carpenters, smiths, etc.) with two strong jaws which can grip and hold tightly.

vice-, prefix, one who acts in place of another, or is second in rank to him, e.g. **vice-admiral, vice-chairman, vice-president.**—n. **viceroy** (vīs'roi), a high officer who takes the king's place.

vice ver'sa, vī'se —, adv the other way round (e.g. Tom hit James and vice versa, i.e. James hit Tom).

vicinity, vis-in'it-i, n. nearness : the place or places near by.

vicissitude, vis-is'it-ūd, n. a change from one thing to another : (pl.) ups and downs.

vic'tim, n. a person who suffers (death, harm, punishment, etc.). —v. **vic'timise,** to cause harm to : to take unfair revenge upon.

vic'tor, n. a winner.—adj. **victō'rious,** winning : unbeaten.—n. **vic'tory,** the defeat of an enemy : success in any struggle.

victō'ria, n. a four-wheeled carriage for two persons.—**Victoria Cross** (often shortened to **V.C.**), a bronze medal given in the British army, navy, and air force for very great bravery in battle.

victuals, vit'lz, n.pl. food.—v. **victual** (vit'l), to supply with food.—n. **victualler** (vit'l-er), one who supplies food.

vie, vī, v. to try to do better than (e.g. The boys vied with each other for the prize).

view, vū, n. a sight of anything : a scene : one's thoughts or opinions on a subject.—v. to look at : to consider.—n. **view'point,** a place from which a good view may be had : one's way of looking at a matter (also called **point of view**).

vigil, vij'il, n. a time of watching, esp. during the night.—adj. **vi'gilant,** watchful.—n. **vi'gilance.**

vignette, vin-yet', n. a picture or photograph shaded off round the edges, not closed in by a border.

vigour, vig'ur, n. strength of body or mind.—n. **vig'orous,** strong, full of life.

Vikings, vik'ingz or vī'kings, n.pl. pirates from the North of Europe who, about 1000 years ago, made raids on eastern England and northern France.

vile, adj. wicked : very bad.—v. **vil'ify,** to say wicked things about.

vil'la, n. a town-house with a garden.

vil'lage, n. a collection of houses, not big enough to be called a town.—n. **vil'lager,** one who lives in a village.

villain, vil′in, *n.* a wicked fellow, a scoundrel: in olden times, a peasant who was half-free, half-slave: the wicked character in a play.—*adj.* vill′ainous, wicked.—*n.* vill′ainy, wickedness.

vin′dicate, *v.* to defend: to prove (e.g. a claim) to be right or just.—*n.* vindica′tion.—*adj.* vindic′-tive, threatening revenge: spiteful.

vine, *n.* the plant on which grapes grow.—*ns.* vī′nery, a hot-house for growing vines; vineyard (vin′yard), a field filled with vines.

vin′egar, *n.* sour, acid liquid, used with some foods.

vint′age, *n.* the amount of grapes grown in a year: wine.—*n.* vint′ner, a wine-seller.

viola, vī-ō′la, *n.* a large violin.

viola, vī-ō′la, *n.* the family of plants to which violets, pansies, etc. belong.

violate, vī′ō-lāt, *v.* to do harm to: to break (e.g. a law, a treaty, etc.).—*ns.* viola′tion; vī′olātor.

violent, vī′ō-lent, *adj.* (of a storm) strong, doing great damage: (of a person's talk) excited and harmful: (of behaviour) using or showing great force, wild: (of an illness) sharp, severe.—*n.* vī′olence, force: harm.

vī′olet, *n.* a small bluish-purple flower.

vī′olin, *n.* a musical instrument with four strings, played with a bow.—*ns.* violoncello (-chel′o), a large violin held between the knees and resting on the floor; vī′olinist, a player on the violin.

vī′per, *n.* a poisonous snake, found in Britain.

virā′go, *n.* a bold, noisy woman.

virgin, ver′jin, *n.* an unmarried girl.—*adj.* pure.

virginal, ver′jin-al, *n.* an old kind of piano—sometimes used in *pl.*

vir′ile, *adj.* manly: strong.—*n.* viril′ity, manhood: manliness.

virtue, ver′tū, *n.* goodness of life: a good point (e.g. in a person's character): strength.—*adv.* vir′tually, really: actually (e.g. The victory was *virtually* a defeat because so many of the winning

army were killed).—*adj.* vir′tuous, living a good and honest life.—**by** (or in) **virtue of,** because of.

virtuo′so, *n.* one who knows much about music, painting, sculpture, old objects, etc.

vir′ulent, *adj.* full of poison: bitter: (disease) dangerous.—*n.* vir′ulence.

vī′rus, *n.* poison.

visa, vē′za, *n.* the mark put on a passport to show that it is correct.

visage, viz′āj, *n.* the face or look.

vis-à-vis, vēz′a-vē′, *adv.* facing one another.

viscera, vis′e-ra, *n.pl.* the inner parts of the body.

viscount, vī′kownt, *n.* a nobleman next in rank to an earl:—*fem.* vis′countess.

viscous, vis′kus, **viscid,** vis′id, *adjs.* sticky.

vise. See vice.

visible, viz′i-bl, *adj.* able to be seen.—*n.* visibil′ity, the state of the air (e.g. *Visibility* is bad to-day, i.e. the air is misty or foggy and one cannot see far.)

vision, vizh′n, *n.* the act of seeing: sight: a dream.—*adj.* vis′ionary, fond of dreaming dreams: not real.—*n.* a person who makes plans which could never be carried out.

visit, viz′it, *v.* to go to see: to call on: to punish.—*n.* a call on a person: a short stay.—*ns.* vis′itor, vis′itant, one who visits; visita′tion, a visit with great show: a punishment from God; vis′iting-card, a small card, with one's name and address, left in making calls or paying visits.

vī′sor, *n.* a part of a helmet covering the face: a mask.

vis′ta, *n.* a view (e.g. through an avenue of trees).

visual, viz′ū-al, *adj.* having to do with seeing.—*v.* vis′ualize, to have a clear picture in the mind.

vī′tal, *adj.* having to do with life: necessary to life: necessary.—*n.* vital′ity, life: liveliness of spirit: strength.—*n.pl.* vī′tals, parts of the body necessary for life.

vit′amins, *n.pl.* substances of different kinds found in very small quantities in various raw foods: they are necessary for health.

vitiate, vish´i-āt, *v.* to spoil : to make impure.

vit´riol, *n.* a name for sulphuric acid.

vitū´perate, *v.* to find fault with : to say evil about.—*n.* **vituperā´- tion.**

vivacious, vi-vā´shus, *adj.* lively : sprightly.—*n.* **viva´city,** liveliness of temper or behaviour.

viva voce, vī´va vō´sē (Latin words =by the living voice), spoken, not written.

viv´id, *adj.* lively or life-like : striking : bright.—*v.* **viv´ify,** to make lively.

vivisec´tion, *n.* the cutting up of living animals in order to examine the inner parts of their bodies.

vix´en, *n.* a she-fox : an ill-tem- pered woman.

viz., namely (e.g. Three games are played in this school, *viz.* foot- ball, hockey, and cricket).

vizier, vi-zēr´, *n.* a minister of state in some Eastern countries.

vocab´ulary, *n.* a list of the words used in a book, set out in alpha- betical order, with their mean- ings : the words a person uses.

vō´cal, *adj.* having to do with the voice : able to be heard.—*n.* **vo´calist,** a singer.

vocā´tion, *n.* one's work or trade (e.g. He is a carpenter by *voca- tion*).

vociferate, vō-sif´er-āt, *v.* to cry with a loud voice.—*adj.* **vocif´- erous,** loud in speech, noisy.

vod´ka, *n.* a Russian strong drink, made from rye.

vogue, vōg, *n.* the fashion of the moment (e.g. These hats are in *vogue*).

voice, *n.* the power of making one's self heard (by speaking or sing- ing) : in grammar, the form of a verb (*active voice, passive voice*). —*v.* to say : to give an opinion.

void, *adj.* empty : of no use : not to be taken into account.—*n.* an empty space.—*v.* to empty out.

vol´atile, *adj.* quickly turning into steam or gas : not steady in mood or behaviour.

volcā´no, *n.* a cone-shaped moun- tain with an opening through which melted rock, steam, etc.

rise up from the inner part of the earth :—*pl.* **volca´noes.**—*adj.* **volcan´ic.**

vole, *n.* the water-rat.

vol´ley, *n.* a firing of a number of rifles at the same time : an out- burst of words : (in tennis) a hard return of a ball before it reaches the ground :—*pl.* **vol´leys.**—*v.* to fire a volley : to return a ball before it reaches the ground.

vōlt, *n.* the unit used in measuring the force of electricity.

vol´uble, *adj.* speaking with a great flow of words.—*n.* **volubil´ity.**

vol´ume, *n.* a book : the amount of space taken up by anything : an amount of sound.—*adj.* **volū´min- ous,** bulky.

vol´untary, *adj.* acting of one's own accord, not forced by another : working without payment.—*n.* a piece of organ music played before or after a church service.

volunteer´, *n.* one who does some- thing (e.g. joins the army) of his own accord. —*v.* to offer to do something of one's own accord.

voluptuous, vo-lup´tū-us, *adj.* fond of the pleasures of life.—*n.* **volup´- tuary,** a voluptuous person.

vom´it, *v.* to throw up the contents of the stomach by the mouth.— *n.* matter thrown up by vomiting.

voracious, vo-rā´shus, *adj.* greedy : very hungry.—*n.* **vora´city.**

vor´tex, *n.* a whirlpool : a whirl- wind.

vō´tary, *n.* one who has made a vow to do some good service.

vote, *v.* to show which person one wishes to go to Parliament by putting a mark opposite his name on a paper : to show one's wish by raising one's hand : to de- cide to give money to (e.g. Parlia- ment *voted* the general £10,000). —*n.* a person's opinion (e.g. in an election).—*n.* **vō´ter.**

vō´tive, *adj.* given because one has made a solemn promise : holy.

vouch, *v.* to say that one is sure of (e.g. I can *vouch* for his courage). —*n.* **vouch´er,** a paper which says that money or goods will be given for it.—*v.* **vouchsafe´,** to be good enough to say, do, or give.

vow, *n.* a holy or solemn promise.—*v.* to make such a promise.

vow'els, *n.pl.* the letters *a, e, i, o, u,* and sometimes *y.*

voy'age, *n.* a journey by water or air.

vul'canite, *n.* rubber and sulphur mixed and hardened by heat.

vul'gar, *adj.* not polite, rude: having bad manners: having to do with common people.—*n.* **vul-gar'ity,** rudeness.—**vulgar fraction,** a fraction written thus:— $\frac{1}{2}$, $\frac{3}{4}$ (written as *decimal* fractions, these are ·5, ·75).

vul'nerable, *adj.* able to be wounded or harmed.

vul'ture, *n.* a large bird, which lives chiefly on the flesh of dead animals.

W

wad, wod, *n.* a mass or lump of loose stuff (e.g. wool, cloth, paper) pressed together : a bunch of bank-notes.—*n.* **wad'ding,** soft material (e.g. cotton-wool) used for packing, bandages, etc.

wad'dle, wod'l, *v.* to walk with short, unsteady steps.—Also *n.*

wade, *v.* to walk through water.—*n.pl.* **wā'ders,** waterproof coverings for the legs for use when wading.

wā'fer, *n.* a thin biscuit : an ice-cream sandwich.

waft, wahft, *v.* to carry along gently through the air or over water.

wag, *v.* to move from side to side or to and fro.—*n.* a person full of sport and fun, a joker.

wage, *v.* to carry on (a war).—*n.pl.* **wā'ges,** the money earned by a workman.—*n.* **wā'ger,** a bet.—*v.* to bet.

wag'gle, *v.* to move quickly from side to side.—Also *n.*

wag'gon or **wag'on,** *n.* a strong four-wheeled cart or truck.

wag'tail, *n.* a small black and white bird with a long tail; the name is given to it because of its habit of wagging its tail.

waif, *n.* a wanderer without a home.

wail, *v.* to cry or moan for sorrow.—Also *n.*

wain, *n.* an old word for a waggon.

wains'cot, *n.* the wooden covering sometimes found round the lower part of the walls of a room.

waist, *n.* the narrow part of one's body, between ribs and hips.—*n.* **waist'coat,** a short jacket, without sleeves, worn by men under the jacket.

wait, *v.* to remain in a place (e.g. I shall *wait* for you here): to be ready to serve a person (e.g. The maid *waits* on us at table).—*n.* time spent in remaining at a place.—*ns.* **wait'er** (*fem.* **wait'ress**), a servant who carries dishes to and from a dining-table; (*pl.*) **waits,** singers of Christmas carols. —**to lie in wait.** See lie.

waive, wāv, *v.* to give up a claim or right.

wake, *v.* to rouse from sleep or idleness: to remain without sleeping. —*n.* a night of watching beside a dead body : a feast or holiday. —*v.* **wā'ken,** to rouse a person from sleep.—*adj.* **wake'ful,** not sleeping: unable to sleep.

wake, *n.* the streak of foamy water left behind a moving ship.—**in his wake,** following behind him.

wale. See weal.

walk, wawk, *v.* to move along on foot.—*n.* one's manner of walking: an outing on foot, a ramble : a place for walking (e.g. a garden *walk,* i.e. path): a person's rank (e.g. persons from all *walks* of life).—*ns.* **walk'ie-talk'ie,** a wireless set for sending and receiving messages, carried on the person ; **walk'over,** a race in which only one person or horse runs; **walk'ing-stick,** a light stick carried when walking.

wall, wawl, *n.* a side of a house or room : a built-up fence of stones, bricks, etc.: the defending rampart of a town.—*v.* to shut in with a wall.—*ns.* **wall'-flower,** a sweet-smelling flower: (at a dance) a person who has no one to dance with, and sits at the wall ; **wall'-paper,** paper, usually with patterns, used for covering the walls of a room.

wallaby, wol′ab-i, *n.* a small kangaroo.

wallet, wol′et, *n.* a bag for carrying food on a journey : a pocketbook : a bag for tools or papers.

wallow, wol′ō, *v.* to roll about (e.g. in mud, water, etc.) : to live in a filthy manner.

walnut, wawl′nut, *n.* a tree whose wood is much used in the making of furniture : the nut of this tree.

walrus, wol′rus, *n.* a very large sea animal, like a seal, with two long tusks.

waltz, wawlts, *n.* a dance for two persons.—*v.* to dance a waltz.

wan, won, *adj.* faint : pale and sickly.

wand, wond, *n.* a long slender rod : a rod of a magician or fairy.

wander, won′der, *v.* to go from place to place for no real purpose : to lose one's way : to speak in a stupid manner (e.g. because of fever).—*n.* wan′derer.

wane, *v.* to become smaller or weaker (oppos. of **to wax**).—**on the wane**, becoming less.

want, wont, *v.* to need : to wish for : to be without food, warm clothes, money, etc.—*n.* the state of being poor and needy : something lacking.—*adj.* want′ing, lacking something : not good enough.

wanton, won′tun, *adj.* lively : playful : breaking all rules.

war, wawr, *n.* a quarrel beween nations in which fighting takes place.—*ns.* war′fare, any way of carrying on fighting (e.g. submarine *warfare*) ; war′head, the part of a missile that contains the explosive : war-horse, a horse for riding in battle ; warrior (waw′ri-or), a great fighter ; war′ship, a ship armed with guns.—*adj.* war′like, fond of fighting : ready for war.—**on the warpath**, ready to fight ; **war of nerves**, means used to frighten a people (e.g. threats of punishment).

war′ble, *v.* to sing like a bird.

ward, wawrd, *v.* to keep off (e.g. By gargling each day, one can *ward* off disease).—*n.* in a hospital, a large room containing a number of beds : one of the parts into which a town is divided for voting : a person who is in the care of another.—*ns.* ward′en, one who guards : a person in charge of a hostel or college : see **air-raid warden** ; ward′er, a jail guard ; ward′robe, a place where clothes are stored : a person's supply of clothes ; ward′room, a room for officers on a warship.

ware, *n.* a general name for goods made of any substance (e.g. iron-ware, glass-ware).—*n.pl.* wares, goods (e.g. a shopkeeper's *wares*). —*n.* ware′house, a building or room where goods are stored : a large shop.

warily. See **wary.**

warlock, wawr′lok, *n.* a wizard.

warm, wawrm, *adj.* fairly hot : earnest, sincere (e.g. He gave me a *warm* welcome).—*v.* to make warm.—*n.* warmth.—*adj.* warm′-hearted, kind.

warn, wawrn, *v.* to tell a person that he is in danger : to advise a person against doing wrong.— *n.* warn′ing, something (e.g. a notice) which tells that danger is near.

warp, wawrp, *v.* (of wood) to become twisted out of shape : to pull a ship by means of ropes wound round posts on the quay.—*n.* a strong rope : in a loom, the threads stretched lengthwise (the cross-threads form the *woof*).

warpath. See **war.**

warrant, wor′ant, *n.* something which gives a person the right to do a certain thing (e.g. I have a *warrant* to arrest you).—*v.* to be sure about something (e.g. He's a good lad, I'll *warrant*) : to deserve, to be worth (e.g. Such conduct *warrants* severe punishment).—*adj.* war′ranted, declared to be good : deserved.—*n.* war′rant-officer, in the Services, an officer holding a warrant.

warren, wor′en, *n.* a piece of waste ground full of rabbit burrows.

wart, wawrt, *n.* a small hard growth on the skin.—*n.* wart′-hog, a kind of wild pig found in Africa.

wā'ry, *adj.* careful, keeping a look-out for danger or cheating.—*adv.* **war'ily.**—*n.* **war'iness.**

wash, wosh, *v.* to clean with water: to flow over or against: to sweep away by water.—*n.* the act of cleaning with water: a number of dirty clothes ready for washing: the rough water left behind by a moving boat.—*ns.* **wash'er,** one who washes: a machine for washing: a flat ring of metal, rubber, etc. to keep bolts or nuts tight; **wash'erwoman,** a woman who is paid to wash clothes; **wash'-out,** a flood: (*slang*) something useless or worthless; **wash'stand,** a stand for basin, ewer, etc.—*adj.* **wash'y,** watery: thin.—**to wash one's hands of,** to have nothing further to do with.

wasp, wosp, *n.* a stinging insect, like a bee but more slender; it does not store honey.

wassail, wos'āl, *n.* a strong drink of olden times (made of ale, roasted apples, sugar, nutmeg, and toast): a drinking party.

wāste, *adj.* fit to be thrown away (e.g. *waste* paper): empty, bare (e.g. *waste* ground): in ruins (e.g. The enemy laid *waste* the country, i.e. destroyed the country).—*n.* a piece of bare, empty land: a desert: anything not fit to be used.—*v.* to spend carelessly: to destroy: to become thinner or weaker (e.g. through illness).—*ns.* **wās'ter, wās'trel,** an idle good-for-nothing fellow; **waste-paper-basket,** a basket for holding useless scraps of paper; **waste'-pipe,** a pipe for carrying away dirty water.—*adj.* **waste'-ful.**

watch, wotch, *v.* to look closely at: to keep guard: to look after, to mind (e.g. The boy *watches* the sheep): to keep awake.—*n.* the act of minding or keeping guard: one who keeps guard: (on ships) a division of time (4 hours—the *dog-watches* are 2 hours each): a small clock for the pocket or wrist.—*adj.* **watch'ful,** keeping a good lookout: careful.—*ns.* **watch'man,** a man who looks

after a shop, office, or factory at night; **watch'word,** a word which allows one to pass a sentry: a motto (e.g. Let courage be our *watchword* !).

water, waw'ter, *n.* the liquid of which rain is made: a stretch of lake or sea: liquid matter which gathers in some parts of the body (e.g. *water* on the knee).—*v.* to pour water on (e.g. flowers): to give drinking water to (e.g. horses): to mix with water: (of the eyes) to run with tears.—*adjs.* **wat'ery,** like water; **wat'er-logged,** soaked with water: (of wood, ships) filled with water and so not able to float; **wat'er-proof,** not allowing water to pass through (e.g. a *waterproof* coat); **wat'ertight,** not allowing water to pass in or out.—*ns.* **wat'er-biscuit,** a crackling biscuit, with no sugar in it; **wat'er-colour,** a paint used by mixing with water not with oil : a painting done with this paint; **wat'ercourse,** a channel for water : a river or canal; **wat'ercress,** a small plant, found beside streams, used for salads, etc.; **wat'erfall,** a place where a river falls over rocks; **wat'er-glass,** a kind of jelly in which eggs may be kept good for a long time; **wat'er-hen,** a dark-brown or dark-grey bird which lives about ponds or rivers; **wat'ering-place,** a place where people go to drink mineral waters, or to bathe : a seaside resort; **wat'er-lily,** a plant (with a beautiful floating flower) which grows in ponds; **wat'er-main,** a large pipe (under the street) from which houses, shops, etc. get their supply of water; **wat'er-man,** a boatman; **wat'ermark,** a faint pattern (usually showing the maker's crest or name) in a sheet of writing-paper; **wat'er-melon,** a large, very juicy fruit; **wat'ermill,** a mill driven by water; **wat'er-pōlō,** a game played by swimmers (seven on each side) with a floating ball; **wat'ershed,** a ridge of hills which separates the valleys of two rivers; **wat'erspout,** a moving column of water, often seen at sea (caused by a whirlwind); (pl.) wat′erworks, the place where the water of a town is made pure and stored.

watt, wot, n. the unit of electric power.

wattle, wot′l, n. a twig: a fence of woven twigs: an Australian tree.

wave, n. a moving ridge or ripple on the surface of water: a ridge in the hair: the sea: a sign made with the hand (e.g. in saying good-bye): a rush of anything (e.g. A wave of despair came over the army).—v. to make a sign with the hand: to move (e.g. a flag) to and fro: to curl the hair in waves.—adj. wā′vy, having waves. — sound waves, light waves, wireless waves, the ripples by which sound, light, and wireless messages travel through space (the distance between two such waves is called the wavelength); heat wave, a spell of very hot weather.

wā′ver, v. to be unsteady (e.g. in one's opinions): to look as if one is about to fall.

wax, n. the fat-like substance of which bees make their cells: any substance like it (e.g. wax of the ear, candle-wax): a quickly-hardening substance used for sealing letters, etc.—v. to rub with wax.—adj. wax′en, made of wax: like wax.—ns. wax′-cloth, cloth covered with wax (used for covering floors); (pl.) wax′works, a place where wax models of well-known people are shown.

wax, v. to grow (e.g. The moon is waxing, i.e. appears to grow larger each night).

way, n. road: distance: manner (e.g. Show me the way to do it).—adjs. way′ward, fond of doing one's own will; way′worn, tired by travel.—ns. way′fārer, a traveller; way′side, the side of the road.—v. way′lay, to hide, and come out upon a person as he passes (e.g. to rob him, or to speak to him).—to be under way, (of ships) to be sailing; to give way, to break: to yield; to get

(or have) one's way, to do what one wishes to do.

we, pron. the persons speaking; subject of verb.

weak, adj. not strong: feeble: in bad health: not able to rule well (e.g. a weak king).—ns. weak′ness, a bad point (in a person's character, in a plan); weak′ling, one who is weak in body or will.—v. weak′en, to make or become weak.—adjs. weak′ly, having little strength: not in good health; weak′-kneed (-nēd), not having a strong will; weak′-minded, having a weak will: not quite sound in the mind.

weal, n. good.—the public weal, the good of the country; weal and woe, good and bad times.

weal, **wale**, ns. a raised mark on the skin caused by a blow.

weald, n. a stretch of open country.

wealth, welth, n. riches: money.—adj. wealth′y, rich.

wean, v. to stop feeding a baby on its mother's milk and give it other food instead: to cure a person of a bad habit.

weapon, wep′on, n. any means used for fighting (e.g. a sword, gun).

wear, wār, v. to have on the body (e.g. He wears a hat; his face wore a smile): to waste away: to last a long time.—n. clothing (e.g. men's wear): wasting away (e.g. His car shows signs of wear): power of lasting a long time (e.g. There is good wear in these tyres).—adj. wear′ing, causing tiredness: annoying.—n. wear′er.—to wear on, to become later (e.g. The night wears on); to wear off, to become less; to wear out, to spend by using; wear and tear, the using up of a thing (e.g. A car owner must allow for ordinary wear and tear).

weary, wē′ri, adj. tired.—v. to make tired.—adj. wear′isome (-sum), causing tiredness: dull, not interesting.

wea′sel, n. a small wild animal, with a long and slender body reddish-brown in colour; it lives on mice, young rabbits, birds, eggs, etc.

weather, weth′er, n. the state of the air (hot, cold, wet, dry, cloudy, sunny, etc.).—v. to last out against (e.g. The ship has *weathered* many storms): to lose colour or freshness because of the weather.—*adjs.* **weath′er-beaten**, showing signs of having been out in all weathers; **weath′er-bound**, kept late by bad weather.—*ns.* **weath′ercock**, **weath′ervane**, a pointer (often in the shape of a cock) on the top of a building —it swings round with the wind and so shows the direction of it; **weath′er-glass**, a barometer.

weave, v. to plait threads and so make cloth: to plait cane, willow-sticks, etc.: to put together (a story, plan, etc.).—*ns.* **wea′ver**, one who weaves; **wea′ver-bird**, a small bird (found in Australia, Asia, and Africa) which weaves its nest very carefully, with the opening underneath.

web, n. the cloth made by weaving: the net made by a spider: the skin between the toes of ducks, swans, frogs, etc.—*adj.* **web′-footed**.

wed, v. to marry.—*ns.* **wed′ding**, a marriage; **wed′ding-ring**, a ring of plain metal (usually a gold) given by a husband to a bride at her wedding.—**silver wedding**, a party held to mark the 25th year of one's wedding; **a golden wedding** is the 50th year, and a **diamond wedding** the 60th.

wedge, wej, n. a piece of wood, metal, rubber, thick at one end but coming to a point at the other.—v. to make tight with a wedge: to squeeze in.

wed′lock, n. the state of being married.

Wednesday, wenz′dā, n. fourth day of the week.

wee, *adj.* tiny.

weed, n. any small useless plant growing in a garden or field: a worthless fellow.—v. to clear (e.g. a garden) of weeds.—*adj.* **weed′y**, full of weeds: worthless.

weeds, *n.pl.* a widow's mourning clothes.

week, n. the space of seven days, esp. from Sunday to Saturday:

the six working days of the week.—*ns.* **week′day**, any day of the week except Sunday; **week′-end**, the time from Saturday to Monday.—*adj.* **week′ly**, happening once a week.—*adv.* once a week.—n. a newspaper which comes out once a week.

ween, v. used in phrase **I ween**, I think.

weep, v. to shed tears: to cry.

wee′vil, n. a small beetle which destroys grain and flour.

weigh, wā, v. to find out how heavy a thing is (e.g. by putting it on a scale): to raise (a ship's anchor): to think over (a matter): to be a trouble or worry (e.g. His work *weighs* heavily on him).—n. **weight** (wāt), the heaviness of a thing (e.g. in tons, pounds, ounces, etc.): a stamped piece of metal of a certain heaviness used in weighing other articles: strength, importance (e.g. The *weight* of the evidence is against you): a load on the mind, worry.—v. to make heavy.—*adj.* **weight′y**, very heavy: important: serious.—n. **weigh′-bridge**, a large scale for weighing carts, trucks, etc.—**dead weight**, a very heavy, lifeless weight (as of a dead body); **to weigh in**, to test one's weight before or after a boxing-match or race; **to weigh up**, to think carefully over a matter.

weir, wēr, n. a dam across a stream.

weird, wērd, *adj.* very strange: ghostly: causing fear.—n. fate.

welcome, wel′kum, *adj.* causing gladness: free to make use of (e.g. You are *welcome* to my cricket-bat).—n. a greeting to a person on his arrival.—v. to greet a person.

weld, v. to join, esp. pieces of metal by heating them till soft and then hammering: to join closely.

welfare, wel′fār, n. comfort, good health, freedom from want: success.—**welfare state**, country with health service, insurance, etc.

wel′kin, n. the clouds: the sky.

well, n. a spring (e.g. of water, oil) gushing forth from the earth.—v. to pour out as from a well.

well, *adj.* in good health.—*adv.* in a good manner: completely.—*ns.* well'-being, comfort; well'-doing, kind actions; well'-wisher, a person who hopes for one's success.—*adjs.* well-advised, wise; well-born, born of a good family; well-bred, having good manners; well-disposed, favourable; well-informed, knowing about many matters; well-known, famous; well-off, well-to-do, rich; well-read (-red), having read many books; well-spoken, graceful in one's way of talking.—*adv.* well-nigh (-nī), very nearly.—**Well met!** I am glad we have met.

wel′lingtons, *n.pl.* high rubber boots covering the lower part of the legs.

Welsh, *adj.* having to do with Wales, its people, or their language.—*n.pl.* the people of Wales.—*n.* welsh′-rab′bit, a dish made of cheese melted on toast.

welt, *n.* a kind of hem or edging round a shoe.—*v.* to put on a welt: to flog.

wel′ter, *v.* to roll or tumble about in dirt.—*n.* a state of great disorder.—*n.* in boxing, a weight (10 stone 7 lb.) between *light* and *middle.*

wen, *n.* a small swelling on the body.

wench, wensh, *n.* a young woman.

wend, *v.* to go: to make one's way.

werewolf, werwolf, wēr′woolf, *n.* a person supposed to be able to change himself for a time into a wolf.

west, *n.* one of the four chief directions: that part of the sky where the sun sets.—Also *adj.*—*adjs.* v̇est′erly, coming from, or facing, t.he west; west′ern; west′ernmost; west′ward (also *adv.*).—**The West,** a general name for the countries of the west of Europe.

wet, *adj.* containing water: not dry: rainy.—*n.* water: rain.—*v.* to make wet.

whack, *n.* a loud slap or blow.—Also *v.*

whale, *n.* the largest sea-animal (a whale is not a fish).—*ns.* whale′-bone, a light, easily-bent, horny substance, got from the upper jaws of whales; whăl′er, a ship which carries on whale-fishing; whăl′ing, the catching of whales.

wharf, whorf, *n.* a platform (at the side of a harbour,or river) to which vessels may be tied when loading or unloading:—*pl.* wharfs or wharves.—*n.* wharfinger (whorf′-in-jer), one who looks after a wharf.

whatnot, whot′not, *n.* a piece of furniture with shelves for books, etc.: anything, no matter what.

wheat, *n.* a grain from which is made the flour used for making bread.—*adj.* wheat′en, made of wheat.—*n.* wheat′ear, a small bird, visiting Britain in summer.

wheed′le, *v.* to flatter a person in order to get something from him.

wheel, *n.* a round frame turning on an axle: in olden times, a method of torture.—*v.* to push on wheels: to turn round like a wheel: (in marching) to change direction.—*ns.* wheel′-barrow, a hand-cart, going on one wheel (used mostly in gardens); wheel′wright, one who makes wheels and carriages.—**Right (or Left) wheel!** a command (to marching soldiers) to turn to the right (or left).

wheeze, *v.* to breathe with a hissing sound.

whelk, *n.* a small shellfish.

whelp, *n.* a young lion: a puppy.—*v.* (of lions, dogs, etc.) to give birth to young ones.

when, *adv.* and *conj.* at what time.—*adv.* and *conj.* whence, from which place: because of which matter.

where, whār, *adv.* and *conj.* at, in, or to, which place.—*ns.* where′-abouts, the place where one is; wherewithal (-awl′), the means of doing something: money.—*conjs.* whereas (-az′), since: when in fact (e.g. He said he was in London, *whereas* he was in Paris); whereat (-at′), whereby′, wherein (-in′), whereof (-ov′), at, by, in, of which; where′fore, for which reason; whereupon (-up-on′), immediately after which.

wher′ry, *n.* a shallow, light boat.

whet, *v.* to sharpen (e.g. a knife) by rubbing : to make (e.g. one's appetite, one's desire to do something) keener.— *n.* whet′stone, a stone on which knives, chisels, etc. may be sharpened.

wheth′er, *conj.* if : which.

whiff, *n.* a sudden puff (e.g. of scent, smoke, gas).

while, whilst, *conjs.* during the time that.— *n.* while, a space of time. — *v.* to spend time pleasingly (e.g. I whiled away the afternoon reading a book).

whim, *n.* a strange passing thought : a queer idea.— *adj.* whim′sical, full of whims.

whim′per, *v.* to cry with a low, whining voice.—Also *n.*

whin. See furze.

whine, *v.* to utter a drawn-out cry : to complain in a cowardly way.— Also *n.*

whin′ny, *v.* (of horses) to make a quivering cry.—Also *n.*

whip, *n.* a lash, with a handle, for punishing or driving : a coachman : a member of a party whose duty it is to see that his fellow-members are there to give their vote when needed.— *v.* to hit with a lash : to beat (eggs, cream) with a beater or fork : to pull out (a gun or sword) quickly.— *ns.* whip′ping, a beating with a whip ; whip′-hand, the advantage in a fight or argument ; whip′per-snap′per, a fussy person of no importance.

whip′pet, *n.* a small greyhound : a small fast-moving army tank.

whir, *v.* to swing round with a noise.—Also *n.*

whirl, *v.* to turn round quickly : to wheel off quickly.— *n.* a quick round-and-round movement : great stir, confusion (e.g. We live in a whirl of excitement).— *ns.* whirl′igig, a merry-go-round, or a toy like one ; whirl′pool, a spot in a river or sea where the current goes round and round quickly ; whirl′wind, a great wind, with a quick-turning movement, which sweeps over some lands and often does great damage.

whisk, *v.* to move with a quick

motion : to stir or beat up (e.g. eggs, cream).— *n.* a small beater for eggs, cream, etc.

whisk′ers, *n.pl.* hairs growing on the side of the face.

whis′ky or **whis′key,** *n.* a strong drink usually made from barley.

whis′per, *v.* to speak very softly, under one's breath : to make a soft, rustling sound.—Also *n.*

whist, *n.* a card game for four players.

whistle, whis′l, *v.* to make a high, piercing sound (e.g. by blowing through nearly-closed lips, or through the fingers, or through a pipe).— *n.* the sound so made : any instrument for making a shrill sound (e.g. an engine *whistle*).

whit, *n.* a tiny bit.

white, *n.* the colour of pure snow : pale in the face.—Also *n.* and *v.*— *ns.* white′ness ; white′bait, young herring or sprats served as food ; whi′ting, a white powder made by grinding down chalk : a fish of the cod kind, but smaller.— *vs.* whi′ten, to make or become white ; white′wash, to cover a wall with *whitewash*—a mixture of water with lime or *whiting* (see above) : to try to show that a person is not so bad as people think.— *adj.* white-hot, hotter even than red-hot.—white elephant. See elephant ; white lie, an untruth for which there may be some excuse (e.g. one told to help a person out of a difficulty).

whith′er, *adv.* to which place ?

whitlow, whit′lō, *n.* a painful disease of the finger.

Whit′sun, Whit′sunday, *n.* the seventh Sunday after Easter : (in Scotland) May 28th.

whit′tle, *v.* to pare or cut (e.g. wood) with a knife.

whiz, whizz, *n.* a hissing sound (e.g. of a bullet flying through the air).—Also *v.*

whole, hōl, *adj.* complete : with no part missing : not broken : in good health.—Also *n.*— *adjs.* whole′-heart′ed, full of eagerness ; wholesome (hōl′sum), good for eating : healthy.— *n.* wholesale (hōl′sāl), the sale of goods in large quantities to a shop or merchant who is going to sell them in small quantities to ordinary buyers.—*adv.* **wholly** (hōl′li), completely, quite.—**whole number,** a number without any fraction ; **upon the whole,** when everything is taken into account.

whoop, *n.* a loud cry.—Also *v.*—*n.* **whoop′ing-cough, hoop′ing-cough,** a disease (mostly of children) in which there is a cough with a long-drawn-out sound.

whor′tleberry. See bilberry.

wick, *n.* the twisted threads (of cotton or wool) in a candle or lamp which draw up the oil or grease to the flame.

wick′ed, *adj.* sinful : bad : mischievous.—*n.* **wick′edness.**

wick′er, *n.* anything made of woven willow twigs (e.g. a basket, basket-chair). — *n.* **wick′erwork,** basketwork.

wick′et, *n.* a small gate : (in cricket) one of the stumps at which the ball is bowled : the ground on which the stumps are placed, and on which the batsmen run.

wide, *adj.* broad : stretching far.—*adv.* off the target (e.g. His shot went *wide*) : quite, completely (e.g. *wide*-awake, *wide*-open).—*n.* (in cricket) a ball which is bowled out of the batsman's reach and which counts one run for his side.—*ns.* **wideness, width.**

widgeon, wij′on, *n.* a kind of duck.

widow, wid′ō, *n.* a woman whose husband is dead.—*n.* **wid′ower,** a man whose wife is dead.

wield, wēld, *v.* to swing or handle (e.g. a cricket-bat, sword) : to use (e.g. one's power).

wife, *n.* a woman : a married woman :—*pl.* **wives.**

wig, *n.* a covering of imitation hair for the head.

wig′ging, *n.* a scolding.

wight, wīt, *n.* an old word meaning *person.*

wig′wam, *n.* an American Indian's tent.

wild, *adj.* fierce : angry : not tame : not grown in gardens.—*n.* a place (e.g. jungle or desert) far from the dwellings of men.—*ns.* **wilder-**

ness (wil′-), a desert ; **wild′-fire,** lightning in great broad sheets, without thunder ; **wild - boar, wild-cat,** etc., a boar, cat, etc. not tamed by man.—**wild-goose chase,** a troublesome and useless errand.

wile, *n.* a trick.—*v.* to pass away (time).—*adj.* **wi′ly.**

will, *n.* one's power of choosing or wishing : desire, command (e.g. ' Thy *will* be done ') : a written statement showing what one wishes to be done with one's money and goods after death.—*v.* to desire, to command : to leave money or goods by will.—*adjs.* **wil′ful,** fond of having one's own way : headstrong ; **will′ing,** ready to do what is asked.—*n.* **goodwill.** See good.—**with a will,** with all one's heart.

will-o′-the-wisp, *n.* a dancing light sometimes seen by night over marshy places.

willow, wil′ō, *n.* a tree (often found beside streams) with long slender branches : a cricket-bat.

wil′ly-nil′ly, *adv.* used thus :—He had to go to school *willy-nilly,* i.e. whether he wished to go or not.

wilt, *v.* to lose strength : to fade.

wi′ly, *adj.* cunning.—*n.* **wile,** a sly trick.

wim′ple, *n.* a hood or veil folded round the neck and face (e.g. of a nun).

win, *v.* to gain (e.g. a victory, a profit) : to bring to one's side (e.g. I *won* him over after much trying).—*n.* a victory.—*adj.* **winning,** pleasant in manners.—*n.pl.* **win′nings,** money made by gambling.

wince, *v.* to shrink or start back (e.g. after a painful blow).

winch, winsh, *n.* a handle : a hoisting-machine.

wind, *n.* air in motion : breath : a hint (e.g. The general got *wind* of the enemy's plan).—*v.* to hit in the stomach and so put out of breath : (wīnd) to blow a horn.—*adj.* wind′y.—*ns.* **wind′bag,** a chattering person ; **wind′-fall,** an unexpected gift of money ; **wind′-jammer,** a sailing-ship ; **wind′-gauge** (-gäj), an instrument for measuring the speed of the wind; **wind'mill,** a mill driven by sails which are made to move by the force of the wind; **wind'pipe,** the pipe leading from the mouth to the lungs; **wind'-screen,** a pane of glass in front of the driver of a motor-car to break the force of the wind.— *adv.* and *adj.* **wind'ward,** in the direction from which the wind is blowing.

wind, *v.* to turn or twist (e.g. the spring of a watch): to move in a curving or curling manner.— *n.* **wind'ing-sheet,** a piece of cloth wrapped round a dead body.— **to wind up,** to finish off (e.g. a speech, the working of a business company).

wind'lass, *n.* a means for hoisting heavy weights.

window, win'dō, *n.* an opening (in the wall or roof of a building) to let in light and air: the glass with which this opening is usually protected.— *ns.* **win'dow-pane, window-sash, window-sill.** See **pane, sash, sill.**

wine, *n.* a strong drink made from the juice of grapes.— *ns.* **wine'-bibber,** one who is fond of getting drunk; **wine'-glass,** a small glass, used for wine; **wine'-press,** a machine in which the juice is squeezed out of grapes.

wing, *n.* the part of a bird, bat, or insect by means of which it flies: the plane of an aeroplane: a side part of a house: the act of flying (e.g. The young birds took *wing,* i.e. began flying; The bird was shot on the *wing,* i.e. while flying).— *adj.* **winged** (wingd or wing'ed), having wings: swift.

wink, wingk, *v.* to move the eye-lids quickly: to give a hint by winking: to seem not to see (e.g. The boy's mother *winked* at his bad conduct).

winkle. Short for **periwinkle.**

winnow, win'ō, *v.* to separate the chaff from the grain by wind.

winsome, win'sum, *adj.* cheerful: pleasant: attractive.

win'ter, *n.* the cold season of the year.— *v.* to pass the winter: to feed (e.g. sheep) during the

winter.— *ns.* **winter-garden,** a garden covered in with glass, used for concerts, etc. during the winter; (*pl.*) **winter-quarters,** the place where an army lives during the winter; (*pl.*) **winter-sports,** snow-sports (e.g. ski-ing, tobogganing).— *adj.* **win'try,** stormy: cold.

wipe, *v.* to clean or dry by rubbing: to clear away.— *n.* the act of rubbing: a blow.— *n.* **wi'per,** a moving arm which wipes the screen of a motor-car.

wire, *n.* a thread of metal: a tele-gram.— *v.* to bind or fasten with wire: to send a telegram.— *adj.* **wi'ry,** like wire: thin but strong.— *ns.* **wire'-pull'er,** one who, in order to get something done, makes use of his friends who are in important jobs; **wire'-net'ting,** network (used for hen-runs, etc.) made of thin wire.

wire'less, *n.* the sending of messages, music, pictures, etc. through space (not along wires, as in ordinary *telegraphy*).— *v.* to send a message thus.— *n.* **wireless-station,** an important station for the sending or receiving of wireless messages.

wise, wīz, *adj.* able to know good from bad, what to do and what not to do (e.g. a *wise* king): likely to have good results (e.g. a *wise* act): full of learning: thoughtful.— *ns.* **wisdom** (wiz'-dom), the quality of being wise; **wis'dom-teeth,** large back teeth which do not appear in a person until he is grown up; **wiseacre** (wīz'ā-ker), one who pretends to be very wise.

wise, wīz, *n.* manner (e.g. He did it in this *wise*).

wish, *v.* to have a longing: to de-sire.— *n.* a longing: a thing de-sired.

wisp, *n.* a small bundle of straw or hay.

wistful, wist'fool, *adj.* sadly longing for something: thoughtful.

wit, *n.* power of understanding: the power of saying a thing cleverly, neatly, and funnily: a person who can do this.— *adjs.*

wit′ty, neat and clever: amusing; **wit′less**, foolish: stupid.—*n.* **wit′ticism** (-sizm), a neat and clever saying.—*adv.* **wit′tingly**, knowingly (e.g. I would not have done it *wittingly*, i.e. if I had known what I was doing).—**out of one's wits**, mad; **the five wits**, the powers of seeing, hearing, smelling, tasting, and touching; **to be at one's wits' end**, to be so worried that one does not know what to do; **to wit**, namely.

witch, *n.* a woman supposed to have magic power: an ugly old woman.—*ns.* **witch′craft**, the doing of magic; **witch′-doctor**, among savage peoples, a man who is supposed to work magic; **witch′-hāzel**, the rowan tree.

withal, with-awl′, *adv.* also, as well.

withdraw′, *v.* to go back or away: to take back (e.g. The general *withdrew* his army): I *withdrew* my money from the bank): to be sorry for (e.g. I *withdraw* my unkind remarks).—*n.* **withdraw′al**.

with′er, *v.* to become dry: to lose freshness: to waste away.—*adjs.* **with′ered**; **with′ering**, very hot.

withhōld′, *v.* to keep back.

within′, *prep.* inside.—*adv.* in the house.

without′, *prep.* outside or out of: not having: in the absence of.—*adv.* on the outside: out-of-doors.

withstand′, *v.* to stand against: to oppose or resist.

with′y, *n.* a tough twig, esp. of willow.

wit′ness, *n.* one who gives evidence that he has seen, or heard, or knows about a fact: one who looks on.—*v.* to give evidence.

wiz′ard, *n.* a man who is supposed to have the power of magic:—*fem.* **witch**.—*n.* **wiz′ardry**, magic.

wizened, wiz′nd, *adj.* dried up: thin.

woad, *n.* a blue dye got from the *woad-plant*.

wob′ble, *v.* to move unsteadily from side to side.—Also *n.*

woe, wō, *n.* grief: misery.—*adjs.* **woebegone** (wō′be-gon), sad-looking; **woe′ful**, sorrowful.—**Woe is me!** How great is my trouble!

wōld, *n.* an open stretch of country.

wolf, woolf, *n.* a wild animal of the dog kind, much feared because of its fierceness:—*pl.* **wolves**.—*adj.* **wolf′ish**, fierce: very hungry.—**to keep the wolf from the door**, to have only enough food or money to keep away hunger.

wol′fram, *n.* a metal used in electric light lamps and in the making of hard steel.

wol′verene, wol′verine, *n.* the name given in America to the animal called the **glutton**.

woman, woom′an, *n.* a female human being, when grown up: a female servant:—*pl.* **women** (wim′en).—*n.* **wom′anhood**, the state of being a grown woman.—*adjs.* **wom′anish**, not manly; **wom′anly**, like a woman: gentle and kind.

wom′bat, *n.* an Australian animal, like a small bear in appearance.

wonder, wun′der, *n.* surprise: anything which causes surprise: something very unusual.—*v.* to be struck with surprise: to wish to know.—*adjs.* **won′derful, wondrous** (wun′drus), strange: causing great surprise.—*n.* **won′derment**, surprise.

wont, wōnt, *adj.* accustomed (e.g. He was *wont* to go there).—*n.* habit.—*adj.* **wōnted**, usual (e.g. His *wonted* smile was absent).

woo, *v.* to make love to: to court.

wood, *n.* a collection of growing trees: the substance of which tree-trunks are made.—*adjs.* **wood′ed**, covered with trees; **wood′en**, made of wood: stupid; **wood′y**, like wood.—*ns.* **wood′-bine**, the honeysuckle; **wood′-cock**, a bird shot at for sport; **wood′craft**, knowledge about trees and forests; **wood′cut**, a picture cut on wood; **wood′-cutter**, a man who chops down trees; **wood′land**, land covered with trees; **wood′-louse**, an insect found in damp places, under stones, etc.; **wood′pecker**, a bird which taps the barks of trees with its beak, and pulls out insects with its long tongue; **wood′-pulp**, wood ground down and used for making paper;

wool 366 wrack

wood'work, the making of wooden articles: the wooden parts of a house, room, etc.

wool, n. the soft, curly hair of sheep and other animals: short, thick hair (e.g. that on a negro's head). —adjs. **wool'len,** made of wool; **wool'ly,** like wool: covered with wool.—ns. **wool'-gathering,** straying thoughts, day - dreaming; **Woolsack,** a great bag of wool in the House of Lords; it is the seat of the Lord Chancellor.

word, wurd, n. a written or spoken sign showing an idea: a message: one's promise (e.g. He broke his *word*).—adj. **word'y,** using too many words.—**word for word,** exactly (e.g. He wrote down the speech *word for word*); **to have words,** to quarrel; **to take a person's word,** to believe him; **the Word of God,** the Bible.

work, werk, n. task: that which is made by working: a job: a book or picture (e.g. the *works* of Shakespeare).—n.pl. **works,** a factory: springs, wheels, etc. of a clock: deeds.—v. to do a task: to make (e.g. a horse) to work: to have the result that was looked for (e.g. The inventor's machine *worked* at last): to shape or form (e.g. a pottery dish).—ns. **work'-bag,** a bag for holding tools, knitting, sewing, etc.; **work'house,** a house where very poor people are kept and fed; **work'er, work'man,** one who works, esp. with the hands; **work'manship,** skill in doing a piece of work; **work'shop,** a room where work is done.—adjs. **work'able,** able to be done (e.g. It is a *workable* plan); **work'man-like,** done as a clever workman would do it.—**the working class,** people who, to earn a living, work with their hands; **a work of art,** a fine piece of work, esp. a fine picture or sculpture; **to make short work of,** to get over a difficulty quickly.

world, wurld, n. the earth and all things on it: mankind: any planet or star: very much (e.g. There is a *world* of truth in what he says).—adjs. **world'ly,** belong-

ing to this world: thinking only of the things of this life (esp. of pleasures and the making of money); **world'-wide,** stretching all over the world.—**the New World,** N. and S. America; **the Old World,** Europe, Africa and Asia.

worm, wurm, n. any small creeping animal, without limbs or backbone: a miserable person of no importance: the thread of a screw.—v. to move like a worm: to draw a secret out of a person bit by bit.

wormwood, wurm'wood, n. a bitter plant.

worn-out, adj. rubbed away by much use: very tired.

worry, wur'i, v. to tear with the teeth: to vex: to be troubled and anxious.—n. trouble: anxiety.

worse, wurs, adj. more bad: more sick.—v. **wor'sen,** to make or become worse.

worship, wur'ship, n. respect paid to God: respect and honour shown to someone: a title of honour used in speaking to magistrates, etc.—v. to honour and respect: to take part in a church service.

worst, wurst, adj. most bad.—adv. most badly.—n. the greatest evil that could happen.—v. to defeat.

worsted, woost'ed, n. a strong woollen cloth.

worth, wurth, n. value: price: importance: merit.—adj. equal in value to: deserving of: having a certain amount of money (e.g. He is *worth* £1,000,000).—adjs. **worth'less,** of no merit or value; **worth'y,** deserving: of good character.—n. a highly respected person.

would-be, wood'bē, adj. trying or wishing to be (e.g. a *would-be* artist, i.e. a person who thinks he would make a good artist).

wound, woond, n. a hurt or bruise, caused by a bullet, sword-cut: a cut made by a doctor.—v. to make a wound in: to hurt (a person's pride).—n.pl. **wound'ed,** soldiers who have been hurt but not killed in battle.

wrack, rak, n. seaweed.

wraith, rāth, *n.* a person's ghost, seen before or soon after his death.

wrangle, rang′gl, *v.* to quarrel noisily.—*n.* **wrang′ler.**

wrap, rap, *v.* to cover by winding something round.—*n.* a covering or cloak.—*n.* **wrap′per,** a covering (e.g. of a book).

wrath, rawth, *n.* violent anger.—*adj.* **wrath′ful,** very angry.

wreak, rēk, *v.* to carry out (vengeance).

wreath, rēth, *n.* flowers or leaves fastened together into a band or ring : a garland : a bank of snow.—*v.* **wreathe,** to put a wreath on.

wreck, *n.* the destroying of a ship by the sea : the remains of anything destroyed (e.g. a ship, a car) : a person whose health or character is ruined.—*v.* to destroy.—**to be wrecked,** (of ships) to be destroyed by the sea.—*n.* **wreck′age,** the broken parts of a wrecked ship, car, etc.

wren, ren, *n.* a very small bird.

wrench, rensh, *v.* to twist : to pull with violence.—*n.* a violent twist ; a tool with strong jaws for gripping and turning a nut.

wrest, rest, *v.* to twist or take by force.

wrestling, res′ling, *n.* a sport in which one person tries to force another down flat on his back.—*v.* **wrestle** (res′l), to carry on this sport : to struggle (e.g. against a difficulty).—*n.* **wrest′ler.**

wretch, rech, *n.* a mean rogue : a worthless person : one who is to be pitied greatly. *adj.* **wretch′ed,** very bad : pitiful.—*n.* **wretchedness.**

wriggle, rig′l, *v.* to twist to and fro.

wright, rīt, *n.* a maker (e.g. a ship-*wright*).

wring, ring, *v.* to twist or squeeze (e.g. water out of wet clothes) : to cause pain to (e.g. The story *wrung* everybody's heart) : to force something from a person (e.g. I shall *wring* a promise from him).—*n.* **wring′er,** a machine for forcing water from wet clothes.

wrinkle, ring′kl, *n.* a valuable hint.

wrinkle, ring′kl, *n.* a small ridge : a small crease or fold on the skin.—*v.* to make wrinkles in.

wrist, rist, *n.* the joint by which the hand is joined to the arm.—*ns.* **wrist′let,** a bracelet ; **wrist′let-watch,** a watch worn on a band round the wrist.

writ, rit, *n.* a letter which orders one to do something (e.g. appear in a law-court).—**Holy Writ,** the Bible.

write, rīt, *v.* to form letters with a pen or pencil : to write a letter and post it : to put together (a book, poem, etc.).—*ns.* **wri′ter,** an author : (in Scotland) a lawyer ; (*pl.*) **wri′tings,** works or books written by an author.

writhe, rīth, *v.* to twist (the body, limbs, etc.) in pain.

wrong, rong, *adj.* not right : false : not according to rule or right or law : not fit or suitable.—*v.* to do evil to : to be unfair to : to hurt.—*n.* an injury or hurt to another.—*ns.* **wrong′-doer** (-doo′er), one who treats another badly or unfairly ; **wrong′-doing.**—*adj.* **wrong′ful,** unjust.

wroth, rōth, *adj.* angry.

wrought, rawt, *adj.* worked into shape.—*v.* (past tense) worked.

wry, rī, *adj.* twisted or turned to one side.—*adv.* **wry′ly.**

wynd, wīnd, *n.* (in Scotland) a narrow alley in a town.

X

X-rays, *n.pl.* electric rays which when passed through the hand or other part of the body show a shadow-picture of the bones on a photographic plate.

xebec, zē′bek, *n.* a small three-masted vessel much used in olden times by pirates.

Xmas, short for **Christmas.**

xylonite, zī′lo-nīt, *n.* a kind of celluloid.

xylophone, zī′lō-fōn, *n.* a musical instrument made up of a number of loose plates each of which gives a certain sound when struck ; the striking is done with two or more sticks like drumsticks.

Y

yacht, yot, *n.* a sailing or steam vessel, fitted up for pleasure or racing.—*ns.* **yacht'ing**, racing or sailing in such a boat; **yachts'-man.**

yak, *n.* the ox of Tibet, covered all over with a thick coat of long silky hair.

yam, *n.* a large root like the potato, growing in hot countries.

Yank'ee, *n.* a citizen of the United States of America.

yap, *v.* to bark.

yard, *n.* a measure of length (36 inches or 3 feet): a long beam on a mast for spreading square sails (each half is called a **yard-arm**): an enclosed space near a building.

yarn, *n.* wool or cotton spun into thread: one of the threads of a rope: a story (esp. a long or rather impossible one).—*v.* to tell a story.

yaw, *v.* (of ships) to go off the true course for a time.

yawl, *n.* a ship's small rowing-boat: a small fishing-boat.

yawn, *v.* to open the jaws wide from tiredness.—Also *n.*—*adj.* **yawn'-ing**, wide open (e.g. A *yawning* cleft in the rock opened before us).

ye, *pron.* you (meaning more than one, e.g. *Ye* are all knaves).—*adj.* the (only used along with the names of old inns).

yea, yā, *adv.* yes.

year, *n.* 365 days (e.g. 1st January to 31st December; 7th June 1901 to 6th June 1902). A leap-year has 366 days (29 in February) and comes every fourth year (e.g. 1936, 1940, 1944).—*adj.* **year'ly**, happening every year, or once a year.—Also *adv.*

yearn, yern, *v.* to long for.—*n.* **yearn'ing**, an eager longing.

yeast, *n.* a substance which is used in the making of beer and bread.

yell, *v.* to utter a loud, shrill cry: to scream.—Also *n.*

yellow, yel'ō, *n.* a bright colour like gold or butter.—Also *adj.*—*ns.* **yell'ow-fever, yell'ow-jack,** a dangerous fever causing yellowness of the eyes and skin; it attacks people in West Africa and South America; **yell'ow-hammer,** a small bird, yellow in colour, with a pleasing song.

yelp, *n.* the sharp bark of a dog.—Also *v.*

yen, *n.* a Japanese coin worth about one farthing.

yeoman, yō'man, *n.* a farmer; one who farms his own land.—*n.* **yeo'manry**, farmers: a troop of cavalrymen who serve of their own accord.—*adj.* **yeo'manly**, brave: sturdy.—**yeoman service**, splendid service.

yes'terday, *n.* and *adv.* the day before to-day: the past.

yet, *adv.* still, by now: however.

yew, ū, *n.* a tree (often found in churchyards) with dark green leaves and red berries. In olden times its wood was used for bows.

yield, yēld, *v.* to give in: to produce.—*n.* amount yielded or produced: a crop.—*adj.* **yield'ing**, giving way easily.

yō'del, *v.* to sing in a high voice, as the mountain people of Switzerland do.

yoke, *n.* wooden frame joining oxen when pulling a plough, cart, etc.: a pair (e.g. of oxen, horses): a frame fastened to the shoulders for carrying pails, etc.: a heavy load, a burden.—*v.* to harness: to join together.—**to bring under one's yoke**, to make to serve.

yō'kel, *n.* a country fellow.

yolk, yōk, *n.* the yellow of an egg.

yon, yon'der, *adjs.* at a distance within view.—Also *advs.*

yore, *n.* in old time: formerly.

you, *pron.* person(s) spoken to; *sing.* or *pl.*, subject or object of verb.

young, yung, *adj.* not long born: knowing little about life: fresh.—*n.pl.* animals not yet grown up.—*n.* **young'ster**, an active young person.

your, *adj.* belonging to you.

youth, yooth, *n.* the time of early life : a young man about 16 to 20 years old : young people.— *adj.* **youth'ful,** young : fresh.

yō-yō, *n.* a toy (a reel which spins up and down on a string).

Yule, yool, *n.* the season or feast of Christmas.—*n.* **Yule'tide,** Christmas time.—**Yule log,** a block of wood cut down in the forest, then dragged to the house, and set alight during Christmas rejoicings.

Z

zā'ny, *n.* a jester : fool.

zeal, *n.* great eagerness or keenness. —*adj.* **zealous** (zel'us), very eager or earnest.—*n.* **zealot** (zel'ot), one who is very keen (e.g. about matters of religion).

zē'bra, *n.* a wild animal of Africa, like a pony, but covered with stripes.

zē'bū, *n.* the humped ox of India.

zena'na, *n.* in an Indian house, the room where the women live.

zen'ith, *n.* the point of the heavens which is exactly overhead : the highest point.

zephyr, zef'ir, *n.* a soft, gentle breeze.

zep'pelin, *n.* a German airship (so called after its inventor, Count Zeppelin).

zē'ro, *n.* the figure 0: the 0-mark on a thermometer or other instrument.

zest, zest, *n.* relish : keen enjoyment.

zig'zag, *adj.* and *adv.* having short, sharp turns like the letter Z. —*v.* to move in a side-to-side manner.

zinc, zingk, *n.* a bluish-white metal.

Zion, zi'on, *n.* the Holy Hill in Jerusalem : the Christian Church : heaven.

zip-fastener, *n.* a sliding fastener.— Also called **zip'per.**

zith'er, *n.* a flat, stringed musical instrument, played with the fingers.

zodiac, zō'di-ak, *n.* an imaginary strip of the heavens, divided into twelve equal parts called *signs of the zodiac* ; the sun, moon, and planets all seem to move within this strip.

zone, *n.* a belt : a strip round the earth's surface : any division shaped like a belt.

zoo, *n.* short form of **zoological garden,** a large garden where a collection of wild animals is kept for show and in order that their habits may be studied.—*ns.* **zoology** (zō-ol'ō-ji), the branch of knowledge which has to do with the study of animals' bodies, habits, etc. ; **zool'ogist.**

zouaves, zoo'ahvs, *n.pl.* French footsoldiers who wear Arab dress.

zounds! a cry of anger and surprise.

Zulus, zoo'looz, *n.pl.* a South African people, once famed for their warlike nature.

LIST OF VERBS

The following list contains (a) verbs the parts of which do not follow the ordinary rules for past tenses; (b) some verbs the spelling of which sometimes gives difficulty. Parts given in *italics* are not often used.

PRESENT TENSE	PAST TENSE	PAST PARTICIPLE
I abide	I abode	(I have) *abode*
am	was	been
arise	arose	arisen
awake	awoke	awaked
awaken	awakened	awakened
bear	bore	borne
beat	beat	beaten
it befalls	it befell	(it has) befallen
I beget	I begot, *begat*	(I have) begotten
begin	began	begun
behold	beheld	beheld
bend	bent	bent
benefit	benefited	benefited
bereave	bereaved	bereaved, bereft
beseech	besought	besought
beset	beset	beset
bespeak	bespoke	bespoken
bet	bet, betted	bet, betted
bias	biased	biased
bid	bid, bade	bid, bidden
bind	bound	bound
bite	bit	bit, bitten
bleed	bled	bled
blow	blew	blown
break	broke	broken
breed	bred	bred
bring	brought	brought
broadcast	broadcast(ed)	broadcast(ed)
build	built	built
burn	burnt, burned	burnt, burned
burst	burst	burst
buy	bought	bought
can	could	—
cast	cast	cast
catch	caught	caught
chide	*chid*	*chid, chidden*
choose	chose	chosen

PRESENT TENSE	PAST TENSE	PAST PARTICIPLE
I cleave (=I split)	I cleft, clove	(I have) cleft, cloven
cleave (=I cling)	cleaved, *clave*	cleaved
cling	clung	clung
clothe	clothed, clad	clothed, clad
come	came	come
commit	committed	committed
cost	cost	cost
creep	crept	crept
crow	crew	crowed
cut	cut	cut
dare	dared, durst	dared
deal	dealt (delt)	dealt
develop	developed	developed
dig	dug	dug
do	did	done
draw	drew	drawn
dream	dreamed, dreamt (dremt)	dreamed, dreamt
drink	drank	drunk
drive	drove	driven
dwell	dwelt	dwelt
eat	ate	eaten
embarrass	embarrassed	embarrassed
envelop	enveloped	enveloped
fall	fell	fallen
feed	fed	fed
feel	felt	felt
fight	fought	fought
find	found	found
flee	fled	fled
fling	flung	flung
fly	flew	flown
focus	focused	focused
forbid	forbade	forbidden
forecast	forecast	forecast
forget	forgot	forgotten
forgive	forgave	forgiven
forsake	forsook	forsaken
freeze	froze	frozen
gallop	galloped	galloped
get	got	got, *gotten*
gild	gilt, gilded	gilt, gilded
gird	girt, girded	girt, girded

PRESENT TENSE	PAST TENSE	PAST PARTICIPLE
I give	I gave	(I have) given
go	went	gone
grind	ground	ground
grow	grew	grown
hang (e.g. a picture)	hung	hung
hang (a murderer)	hanged	hanged
harass	harassed	harassed
have	had	had
hear	heard (herd)	heard
hide	hid	hidden, hid
hit	hit	hit
hold	held	held
hurt	hurt	hurt
keep	kept	kept
kneel	knelt, kneeled	knelt, kneeled
knit	knitted, knit	knitted, knit
know	knew	known
lay	laid	laid
lead	led	led
lean	leaned, leant (lent)	leaned, leant
learn	learned, learnt	learned, learnt
leap	leaped, leapt (lept)	leaped, leapt
leave	left	left
lend	lent	lent
let	let	let
lie	lay	lain
light	lighted, lit	lighted, lit
lose	lost	lost
make	made	made
may	might	—
mean	meant (ment)	meant
meet	met	met
mislead	misled (mis-led')	misled
mistake	mistook	mistaken
mow	mowed	mown
must	must	—
occur	occurred	occurred
partake	partook	partaken
pass	passed	passed
pay	paid	paid

Present Tense	Past Tense	Past Participle
I picnic	I picnicked	(I have) picnicked
possess	possessed	possessed
prefer	preferred	preferred
profit	profited	profited
put	put	put
quarrel	quarrelled	quarrelled
read (rēd)	read (red)	read
rend	rent	rent
rid	rid	rid
ride	rode	ridden
ring	rang	rung
rise	rose	risen
saw	sawed	sawn
say	said	said
see	saw	seen
seek	sought	sought
sell	sold	sold
set	set	set
sew	sewed	sewn, sewed
shake	shook	shaken
shall	should	—
shear	sheared	shorn, sheared
shed	shed	shed
shine	shone (shon)	shone
shoe	shod	shod
shoot	shot	shot
show	showed	shown, *shown*
shrink	shrank	shrunk
shut	shut	shut
sing	sang, sung	sung
sink	sank, sunk	sunk
sit	sat	sat
slay	slew	slain
sleep	slept	slept
slide	slid	slid
sling	slung	slung
slit	slit	slit
smite	smote	smitten
speak	spoke	spoken
speed	sped	sped
spell	spelt, spelled	spelt, spelled
spin	spun	spun
spit	spat	spat
split	split	split

PRESENT TENSE	PAST TENSE	PAST PARTICIPLE
I spoil	I spoiled, spoilt	(I have) spoiled, spoilt
spread	spread	spread
spring	sprang, sprung	sprung
stand	stood	stood
steal	stole	stolen
stick	stuck	stuck
sting	stung	stung
stink	stank	stunk
strew	strewed	strewn, strewed
stride	strode	*stridden*
strike	struck	struck
string	strung	strung
strive	strove	striven
swear	swore	sworn
swell	swelled	swollen
swim	swam	swum
swing	swung	swung
take	took	taken
teach	taught	taught
tear	tore	torn
tell	told	told
think	thought	thought
thrive	throve, thrived	thriven
throw	threw	thrown
thrust	thrust	thrust
travel	travelled	travelled
tread	trod	trodden
wake	woke, waked	waked, *woke*
waken	wakened	wakened
wear	wore	worn
weave	wove	woven
wed	wed, wedded	wed, wedded
weep	wept	wept
wet	wet	wet
will	would	—
win	won (wun)	won
wind	wound	wound
work	worked, wrought	worked, wrought
write	wrote	written

COMMON PREFIXES AND SUFFIXES

A prefix is a part added at the beginning of a word ; a suffix is a part added at the end. The general meaning which a prefix or suffix gives to a word is shown in the middle column.

PREFIX	MEANING	EXAMPLE
a-	in, on	abed, ashore
a-, ab-, abs-	away from	avert, abrupt, absent
a-, ad-, al-, an-, at-	to, at	abase, admire, allure, annex, attract, etc.
ante-, anti-	before	antechamber, anticipate
anti-	against	antipodes, antagonist
arch-	chief	archbishop
auto-	self	autobiography
circum-	round about	circumference
com-, con-	together, with	compile, connect
contra-, counter-	against	contradict, counterattack
de-	away from	debar, detract
dis-	apart, away	dissect, dispel
e-, ex-	from, out of	emerge, exceed, exodus
en-, em-	in, into	enlist, embark
fore-	before	foretell
hemi-	half	hemisphere
il-, im-, in-, ir-	not	illegal, improper, infirm, irregular
in-, il-, im-, etc.	in, into	income, infuse, illumine, immerse
inter-	between	interval
intro-	into	introduce
mis-	wrong	misbehave, misdeed
mono-	one	monoplane
multi-	many	multiply
non-	not	nonsense
ob-, op-	against, in the way of	obstruct, oppose
pene-	almost	peninsula
per-	through	pervade
post-	after	postpone
pre-	before	predict
pro-	before, in front of	propose
re-	again	rebuild
semi-	half	semicircle
sub-	under	submarine
super-	over, beyond	superhuman

Prefix	Meaning	Example
tele-	at a distance	telephone
trans-	beyond, across	transport, transgress
un-	not	unhappy, untruth

Suffix	Meaning or Use	Example
-able	fit for, able (to be —)	eatable
-ance	used to make nouns	repentance
-dom	state, power	freedom, kingdom
-ee	one who is —	employee
-ence	used to make nouns	conference
-er	a doer	baker, writer
-er	to a greater extent	higher, harder
-ess	feminine form	countess, lioness
-est	to the greatest extent	highest, hardest
-fold	— times over	twofold, manifold
-ful	full of	delightful
-hood	state of	manhood, childhood
-ible	able (to be —)	edible
-ish	rather like	brownish, childish
-ist	a doer	typist
-less	free from, lacking	harmless, useless
-ly	used to make adverbs	sweetly, quietly
	and adjectives	manly, comely
-ness	state of being —	kindness, redness
-or	a doer	sailor, tailor
-ous	used to make adjectives	anxious, dangerous
-ry	a place of work;	laundry, bakery
	also used to make many	
	general nouns	slavery, poetry
-some	full of	gladsome, cumbersome
-stress	feminine form	songstress
-ty	a state of being —	honesty
-ward(s)	in a certain direction	eastward, homewards
-wise	in a certain way	lengthwise, endwise
-y	of a certain nature	dirty, easy

SOME COMMON ROOTS

Many words in our language have as their foundation a word which has been borrowed from another language. This borrowed word is called a 'root,' because our word has grown from it. The following list contains a few of the chief Latin and Greek roots.

(L. = Latin ; G. = Greek.)

ROOT	MEANING	EXAMPLE
annus	(L.) a year	annual, annuity
aqua	(L.) water	aquarium, aqueduct
arithmos	(G.) a number	arithmetic
astron	(G.) a star	astronomy
audio	(L.) I hear	audience, audible
capio	(L.) I take	captive, accept
caput	(L.) a head	captain, capital
centum	(L.) a hundred	century
curro	(L.) I run	course, excursion
decem	(L.) ten	decimal, decimate
demos	(G.) people	democracy
dens	(L.) a tooth	dentist, dental
dico	(L.) I say	edict, dictionary
dominus	(L.) a lord	dominion, dominate
duco	(L.) I lead	conduct, duke
duo	(L.) two	duel, duet
erro	(L.) I wander	error
facio	(L.) I do, make	factor, fact, effect
fortis	(L.) strong	fort, effort
frango	(L.) I break	fraction, fragile
ge	(G.) the earth	geography, geology
genus	(L.) kind	gender, general
gradus	(L.) a step	grade, gradual
grapho	(G.) I write	geography, graphic
gravis	(L.) heavy, serious	grave, aggravate
insula	(L.) an island	peninsula (= almost an island)
jaceo	(L.) I throw	eject, deject
jungo	(L.) I join	junction
juvenis	(L.) young	juvenile, junior
kuklos	(G.) a circle	cycle, cyclone
lego	(L.) I read	lecture, lesson
	I gather	collect, select
liber	(L.) free	liberate
liber	(L.) a book	library
locus	(L.) a place	local, dislocate
logos	(G.) a word	prologue, catalogue
magnus	(L.) great	magnify
metron	(G.) a measure	metre, geometry
mitto	(L.) I send	mission, submit

Root	Meaning	Example
navis	(L.) a ship	naval, navigate
novus	(L.) new	novel, renovate
pendo	(L.) I hang	suspend, pendant
pes	(L.) a foot	pedal, pedestrian
phone	(G.) a voice	telephone (=a voice from afar)
pono	(L.) I place	deposit, position
porto	(L.) I carry	porter, portable, export, report
primus	(L.) first	primitive, primer
quattuor	(L.) four	quadruped, quadrangle
rumpo	(L.) I break	interrupt
scribo	(L.) I write	describe, scripture
seco	(L.) I cut	section, dissect
senex	(L.) old	senior
skopos	(G.) a view	telescope (=a view from afar)
tendo	(L.) I stretch	extend, tent
traho	(L.) I drag, pull	tractor, attraction
unus	(L.) one	union, unite
video	(L.) I see	vision, revise
vinco	(L.) I conquer	victor, invincible
vivo	(L.) I live	vital, survive
volvo	(L.) I turn	revolve, revolver
zoon	(G.) an animal	zoology, zoo

COMMON ABBREVIATIONS AND CONTRACTIONS

A.B. Able-bodied seaman.

a/c. Account.

A.D., *anno Domini*=In the year of our Lord (e.g. A.D. 1900).

ad lib. At pleasure, as long as one likes.

a.m., *ante meridiem*=Before midday.

amp. Ampère.

Anon. Anonymous, by an unknown author.

Bart. Baronet.

B.C. Before Christ (e.g. In the year 55 B.C.).

Bros. Brothers.

C. Centigrade (thermometer).

c., ca., *circa*=about.

Capt. Captain.

c.c. Cubic centimetre(s).

cf. Compare. [partment.

C.I.D. Criminal Investigation Department.

circa. About.

cm. Centimetre(s).

C.O. Commanding Officer.

Co. Company.

c/o. Care of=at the address of.

Col. Colonel.

Coy. Company.

curt. This month.

cwt. Hundredweight.

d. Penny, pence (until 1971).

do., *ditto*=The same as above.

Dr. Doctor.

D.V., *Deo volente*=If God is willing.

E. East.

e.g., *exempli gratia*=For example.

Eng. English.

E.R. *Elizabeth Regina*, i.e. Queen Elizabeth.

Esq. Esquire (a title of respect).

etc. And so on, and other things of the same kind:—often written &c.

et seq. And the following.

Fahr. Fahrenheit (thermometer).

Fr. French. **ft.** Foot (feet).

G.B. Great Britain.

G.C., G.M. George Cross, Medal.

G.C.E. General Certificate of Education.

gm. Gram(me). [cation.

G.P.O. General Post Office.

H.C.F. Highest Common Factor.

H.H. His (or Her) Highness.

H.M. His (or Her) Majesty.

H.M.I.(S.). Her Majesty's Inspector (of Schools).

h.p. Horse-power (see horse in Dictionary).

H.M.S. Her Majesty's Ship (used for warships only).

H.R.H. His (or Her) Royal Highness.

ib., ibid. In the same place or book.

i.e., *id est* = That is, that means.

in. Inch(es).

inst. This month.

IOU. I owe you (see Dictionary).

K.C. King's Counsel (lawyer of high rank). **Q.C.** Queen's Counsel.

Kt. Knight.

l. or £, a money pound (e.g. £5).

L., Lat. Latin.

lb. The sign for pound weight.

L.C.M. Least common multiple.

Lieut. Lieutenant.

L.P. Long-playing.

L.S.D., £. s. d. Pounds, shillings, and pence—used to mean 'money'.

Ltd. Limited.

M. Monsieur (French for *Mr*).

M.C. Master of Ceremonies; (a holder of the) Military Cross.

M.C.C. Marylebone Cricket Club.

memo. memorandum.

Messrs, *Messieurs* (= Gentlemen), *pl.* of *Monsieur*.

Mlle. *Mademoiselle* (French for *Miss*).

Mme. *Madame* (French for *Mrs*).

M.O.H. Medical Officer of Health.

M.P. Member of Parliament; Military Police.

m.p.h. Miles per hour

Mr. Short for *Master*.

Mrs. Short for *Mistress*.

MS. Manuscript:—*pl.* **MSS.**

N. North.—**N.B.** North Britain.

N.B., *nota bene* = note well.

N.H.I. National Health Insurance.

N.I. Northern Ireland.

N.S.W. New South Wales.

N.Z. New Zealand.

Non.-com. Non-commissioned officer (e.g. sergeant, corporal).

No. Number:—*pl.* **Nos.**

ob., obit. Died.

O.B.E. Officer of (the Order of) the British Empire.

O.H.M.S. On Her Majesty's Service.

oz. Ounce(s).

p. Page (*pl.* pp.): new penny, pence.

P.A.Y.E. Pay As You Earn.

P.C. Privy Councillor (i.e. a member of the Queen's Privy Council); police constable.

p.c. Postcard; per cent.

per cent. Out of every hundred.

p.m., *post meridiem* = After midday.

P.O. Post Office; Postal Order.

pro tem. For the time being.

prox. Next month.

P.S., *post scriptum* = Written afterwards (see postscript).

P.T. Physical training.

P.T.O. Please turn over.

Q.C. See **K.C.**

q.v. 'See that word' (e.g. 'Xmas, short for Christmas, *q.v.*', means that the word *Christmas* should be looked up).

R.A. (Member of) the Royal Academy (a high title for artists).

R.A.F. Royal Air Force.

R.C. Roman Catholic.

Rev. Reverend (a clergyman's title).

R.I.P. May he (or she) rest in peace.

R.M.S. Royal Mail Steamer.

R.N. Royal Navy.

R.S.V.P. Please reply.

Rt. Hon. Right Honourable (a title given to certain statesmen, etc.).

S. Saint: South. **sc.** Namely.

Scot. Scottish.

SOS. Distress signal (not an abbreviation).

S.P.C.A. Society for the Prevention of Cruelty to Animals.

S.P.C.C. Society for the Prevention of Cruelty to Children.

S.S. Steamship.

St. Saint; street; stone (14 lbs.).

TV. Television.

U.K. United Kingdom (of Great Britain and Northern Ireland).

ult. Last month.

U.N.O. United Nations Organisation.

U.S.A. United States of America.

U.S.S.R. Union of Soviet Socialist Republics (i.e. Russia).

v. See

V.C. (A holder of the) Victoria Cross.

viz. Namely (see Dictionary).

W. West.

W.D. War Department.

Y.M.C.A. Young Men's Christian Association.

Y.W.C.A. Young Women's Christian Association.

380

SOME FOREIGN WORDS AND PHRASES

The commonest of such words and phrases are to be found in the main part of this Dictionary. Those in the following list, however, are often used in English.

au revoir, ōr-vwar′, till we meet again : good-bye. [Fr.]
bête noir, bet-nwar′, what one hates most. [Fr.]
com′pos men′tis, of a sound mind. [L.]
en route, ong-root′, on the way. [Fr.]
faux pas, fō pah, a false step, a mistake. [Fr.]
hors de combat, ord-kom′ba, out of action. [Fr.]
hors d'œuvre, or-dervr′, a small tasty course taken before a meal, to stir one's appetite. [Fr.]

in′ter alia, āl′ya, amongst other things. [L.]
merci, mār-sē′, thank you. [Fr.]
nom′-de-plume, a false name used by an author.
raison d'être, rez - ong - detr′, the reason for the existence of anything. [Fr.]
sang-froid, song-frwa′, coolness of behaviour, calmness. [Fr.]
sine qua non, sin′ā-kwa-non′, something very necessary. [L.]
ter′ra fir′ma, firm land. [L.]
via me′dia, a middle way between two extremes. [L.]

ROMAN NUMERALS

I	1	XI	11	XXI	21	C	100
II	2	XII	12	XXII	22	CC	200
III	3	XIII	13	XXIX	29	CCC	300
IV	4	XIV	14	XXX	30	CD	400
V	5	XV	15	XL	40	D	500
VI	6	XVI	16	L	50	DC	600
VII	7	XVII	17	LX	60	DCC	700
VIII	8	XVIII	18	LXX	70	DCCC	800
IX	9	XIX	19	LXXX	80	CM	900
X	10	XX	20	XC	90	M	1000

MM 2000. **VM** 5000. **XM** 10,000. **MCMXL** 1940.